Diane Ivocha

S0-BOK-450

# LIVING A LIFE

## OF *fire*

# REINHARD
# BONNKE

## AN AUTOBIOGRAPHY

**LIVING A LIFE OF FIRE**
**Autobiography**

Reinhard Bonnke
English

Copyright © E-R Productions LLC 2010
ISBN 978-1-933106-81-6

Edition 2, Printing 1

All rights reserved.
No part of this publication may be reproduced or transmitted
in any form or by any means, electronic or mechanical,
including photocopying, recording,
or any information storage
and retrieval system,
without permission in writing from the publisher.

Editor: Siegfried Tomazsewski
Cover Design: Brand Navigation, U.S.A.
Typeset & Layout: Roland Senkel
Photo Pages: Simon Wentland
Photographs: Oleksandr Volyk
Peter van den Berg
Roland Senkel
Rob Birkbeck
Karl-Heinz Schablowski
T. Thomas Henschke
Flower Pentecostal Heritage Center [pg. 147]

E-R Productions LLC
P.O. Box 593647
Orlando, Florida 32859
U.S.A.

www.e-r-productions.com

Printed in Singapore by PH Productions Pte Ltd

# Contents

## Dedication

For Hermann and Meta Bonnke,
true parents in life, and in the Lord.
And for Luis (Ludwig) Graf,
who obediently carried the gospel with the living fire
of the Holy Spirit to East Prussia,
and set the pattern for me to follow.

# Part 1

# A DIVINE APPOINTMENT

*Which thread should I choose, Lord? There are so many.*
*They hang before my eyes like strands of silk in a doorway.*
*Each promising that it will weave the finest tapestry of my life.*
*But it is not my tapestry. It is not my life.*
*So again I ask, which thread do I choose?*
*Which strand will pass through the very eye of the needle?*

# Chapter 1

I SIT QUIETLY with an explosion building inside of me. I lean forward to the edge of my seat. My hands explore the cover of my preaching Bible as my foot taps a nervous dance on the platform. Every molecule of my body anticipates what is about to happen. I think you would feel the same if you were in my shoes.

It is a tropical night in Northern Nigeria. We are in the heart of Africa. The air is warm and moist and full of sound. A local gospel group performs a melody of praise accompanied by a snakeskin drum. A chorus of birds, frogs and insects joins them from the surrounding trees. The vast crowd standing in front of me radiates heat and expectancy. Nearly 700,000 tribesmen have walked for many miles to this site. Many of them are Muslims. Their upturned faces draw me like a moth to a flame. 2,400,000 will attend in five nights of preaching. More than 1.4 million will accept Jesus as Savior at the invitations. Follow-up teams will disciple each one.

Anticipation makes my heart race. What about yours? As you begin to read my story, I wonder, are you like me? Does the prospect of seeing the Great Commission of Christ fulfilled drive you day and night? If not, then I pray that the story of my life will light a fire in you. A fire that will change everything. A holy fire that will convince you that nothing is impossible with God.

I see that some in the crowd tonight are crippled. Some lie sick on pallets. Others lean on crutches. Not all will be healed, but some of these crippled will walk. I must tell you, when they walk, I will dance with them across this platform! Wouldn't you? Some are blind, and some of those blind will see. I cannot explain why, but in Muslim areas I see more blind eyes open. I wish everyone could be with me to see it. Chronic pains leave bodies, cancerous growths disappear. These are but a few of the signs that follow the preaching of the good news.

I feel a low vibration. It is almost audible. Generators are purring inside their insulated containers nearby, feeding kilowatts of electricity to our thirsty sound towers and stage lights. We have imported our own power grid to this remote region. We are far beyond the reach of Marriott, Hyatt, Hilton or even Motel 6. Our team has installed a small village of trailer houses to shelter us for the duration. Cell phones are worthless. Satellites keep us connected. Few have even heard of this place. Yet more than a half-million are here tonight!

My throat constricts at the realization of it. Hot tears seek the corners of my eyes. This is joy beyond any I have known.

I smile and tilt my head up, looking into a sky of ancient constellations. I feel the Creator of the Universe smiling down on this corner of the world tonight. I breathe deeply. The smoke of cooking fires paints the breeze and brings me back to earth. I am a thousand miles from anywhere normal, and this is where I feel most at home. We have found another forgotten state where few have heard the way of salvation. I am Reinhard Bonnke, an evangelist. Welcome to my destiny.

Tonight, events will unfold like a well-rehearsed dream. I will be introduced. My eyes will sweep the crowd knowing that we have all come for the same Jesus. My heart will open to the Holy Spirit and in my mind an image will appear. I call it "the shape of the gospel." It is an outline that I will fill with an explosion of words that pour from my heart without rehearsal.

I must now make a confession. This has become an addiction for me. But it is an addiction I'd gladly share with you. Leading sinners to salvation en masse – or one by one – it is all the same. I eat it, I sleep it, I dream it, I speak it, I write it, I pray it, I weep it, I laugh it. It is my wish to die preaching this gospel. I am like a man starving until I can stand again with a microphone in my hand, looking across a sea of faces, shouting the words of His love into the darkness.

It is huge now. The results are huge. I am on my way to seeing 100 million respond to the gospel. More than 52 million have registered decisions since the year 2000. Without the decades of experience that brought my team to this harvest, we would be overwhelmed by these numbers. But we are not slowing down, we are erecting more platforms like this one in places you've never heard of. After reading my story I hope and pray that you will join me on each of those future platforms, sharing my excitement. If you are unable to be there in person, then I hope you will be there in prayer, in faith, in spirit.

In truth, I have done nothing alone. God has called me and has been my pilot. The Holy Spirit has been my comforter, my guide, and my power source. As you will read in these pages, He brought to me the perfect wife. He gave us our beautiful children and extended family. And He has provided a team that has grown with me through decades of working together. Beyond that, He has brought thousands to stand with us. They have supported us in prayer and in partnership. Our rewards in Heaven will be equal.

Oh! Excuse me. I have to go now. I have been introduced and there is a microphone in my hand. I stand to my feet and leap forward, ready to preach with the fire that I always feel in my bones. But just before I open my mouth I feel a holy hush descend over me. It washes over the crowd as well, and I drop to my knees in humility and reverence, raising my face to the sky. For in the air above me I sense an invisible crowd that dwarfs the almost 700,000 Nigerians straining to hear my next word. I am speaking of Heaven's cloud of witnesses, a numberless throng upon whose shoulders I am carried. And from that heavenly crowd steps a man, a German evangelist who has gone before me. I know him by reputation. He is in many ways like these Nigerians, overlooked, except by Heaven. His life was sown in weakness and some say in defeat. Yet tonight, every soul born into the Kingdom will also be fruit of his ministry. The very words that I speak first poured from his heart.

*Now I can begin.*

# Chapter 2

As I BEGIN the story of God's work in my life, I am flooded with wonderful possibilities. Too many to ignore. So, I narrow my search. I think specifically of origins. Not of His calling and His many directions to me along the way. Nor of the road that led to Africa and a harvest of souls beyond my wildest dreams. No, I first look back to Ostpreussen, to a time and place that is no more.

As I look there I feel a mysterious weight in a place near my heart. *What is this weight?* I ask. And then I know. I know that I know. It is the debt I owe to a man who died years before I was born.

*LUDWIG GRAF*

How easily I might forget him. He is unknown. His life and ministry uncelebrated. If I remain silent no one will think of his name in connection to mine. But I would know. And I must not fail to tell his story. Each time I step onto a platform and look across a sea of faces eager to hear the gospel, I feel his gaze upon me from heaven's cloud of witnesses. I could not stand ablaze with the Holy Spirit today if this forgotten brother had not carried the flame to the Bonnke family so long ago.

I examine the weight that I feel, and I think it must be like the debt a great oak tree owes to the acorn from which it sprang. Or the debt of a giant spruce to the seed that fluttered to the ground and died that it might one day stand tall as a watchtower above the German forest. Yes, this is the debt that I feel. It is the weight of a debt I owe to a man named Luis Graf.

ONE DAY, when I was still a very young man, I studied a chart of our German family tree. It was then I discovered the general ungodliness of our clan. I became amazed that my grandfather and my father stood out as men of faith in a spiritually barren landscape. I turned to my father, who was a Pentecostal preacher, and asked, "How did God break into the Bonnke family?"

My father's answer has marked my life and ministry to this day. He told me the story of Luis Graf coming to our village in 1922, 18 years before I was born. Luis was a German-born gunsmith who had immigrated to America as a young man. There, he had amassed a personal fortune through hard work and self-discipline. Following retirement, he returned to his homeland in the power of the Holy Spirit, after experiencing a life-changing baptism with speaking in tongues.

The longer I live the more I see the divine connections between myself and Luis, though I never met the man. So, as I prepare to repeat my father's story, will you please indulge me as I go beyond his words? I will share details that I have only recently learned about this servant of God.

The story of Luis Graf is more than a personal narrative. It is part of the history of an entire movement of which I am a second-generation preacher. The movement of which I speak is the Pentecostal Movement that began on the Day of Pentecost, blazed anew at the Azusa Street Mission in Los Angeles in 1906, and then exploded across the entire world. Today it is the greatest modern force in Christendom, with more than 600,000,000 adherents in our time. To understand the story of Luis Graf, for me, is to understand this great movement more perfectly, and to see my place within it.

For these reasons I have done more than research. I have let myself enter a time machine. I have gone to a bygone era where I have entered the skin of another evangelist, probing his feelings and thoughts during a time and a place that are not my own. And I have been rewarded. I have come away believing that surely his story passes through the very eye of the needle. It is the first thread in the tapestry of God's work in my life.

# Chapter 3

AN ARMY OF CLOUDS marched across the sky, dressed in shades of dismal gray. It was early spring in 1922, and the grip of a long winter was not ready to release the East Prussian landscape. A fine new Mercedes touring car eased along a carriage track through the forest. Its engine puttered like the cadence of a military drummer. Mud splattered its silver-white finish as it passed beneath the trees.

The car entered a large clearing. Across a field of deeply furrowed earth a farmer turned to stare. He leaned on his hoe beneath a cap of thick natural wool, his collar turned against the wind. The expression on his face was grim and hostile.

In this German enclave on the Baltic Sea an automobile was a rare sight after World War I. Russian armies had destroyed roads, factories, and cities before being driven back by the Prussian Army. The Great War and its subsequent inflation had depleted not only the bank accounts of the German people; it had gutted their very souls. More than 3,000,000 of Germany's best had perished in four years of fighting. The wounds of war were fresh and bleeding.

The Mercedes driver beneath his jaunty aviator's cap and goggles knew this full well. He was a German-born American recently returned to his homeland after the Great War. He understood that this poor farmer had nothing in common with someone who could afford to ride the countryside in a fancy touring car.

Still, the driver's heart remained tender toward the German people as he drove from one end of this war-torn land to the other. He gave a friendly wave to this farmer, hoping to at least spread some goodwill. Sadly, the man turned back to his hoeing as if he'd received an insult.

The driver turned his attention back to the road. It disappeared over a ridge ahead of him at the far end of the clearing. At that vanishing point, he saw great arms of sailcloth turning against the horizon. As his car topped the ridge, he could see that the flailing arms belonged to a large windmill working to extract power from the sky. At the base of the windmill sat a flour mill. Beside the flour mill, a large stucco bakery with white smoke rising from brick oven stacks.

The driver salivated. He had a kilometer to cover yet, but he could already taste the tortes, strudels, and hausbrot taken warm from the ovens. He might even stop to stock up on salted pretzels for the road. These, he recalled from childhood, were always folded carefully in a triad representing the Father, the Son, and the Holy Ghost. He chuckled to himself. *I'm not in America anymore. I'm in the land where religion has twisted Scripture into a pretzel.*

As he came closer he could see a small village of a dozen or so houses. They lined both sides of the road on the far side of the bakery where the forest bordered the clearing. He figured this small village would provide a welcome stop for a cold traveler who had lost his way. He imagined a warm fire. Perhaps he would pay for a bed for the night. The day was far spent.

He slowed the car and stopped near the bakery door, pulling the hand brake and cutting the engine. Immediately the aroma of fresh bread blessed his senses. He removed his driving gloves and opened the car door. Stepping out, he pulled off his goggles and leather cap. He stood for a while brushing flecks of mud from his cheeks and chin.

Globs of mire fell to the ground from the car's wooden spokes and pneumatic rubber tires. The stylized elegance of the Mercedes' fenders swept away from the main body of the vehicle like the wings of a swan in flight. But this swan had been grounded by the primitive roads of East Prussia.

A number of villagers stepped curiously from their houses to peek at the new arrival and his fancy automobile. The driver wore a fleece-lined leather coat with leather pants and boots. He was cleanly shaven, a distinguished-looking gentleman with wispy gray hair containing stubborn streaks of brown. A man perhaps in his fifties or sixties.

Meanwhile, a perfectly bald man with a full handlebar mustache emerged from the bakery wiping his hands on his apron. He watched the driver, who had now removed his neck scarf and was using it to wipe mud from the door panel. As he worked at it, a hand-painted sign on the metal surface could be seen emerging from beneath the mess. It read: *Jesus is coming soon. Are you ready?* The driver turned, noticing the baker for the first time.

"A good day to you, sir," he said, extending his hand with an energetic smile. "I am Luis Graf, a servant of God."

The baker slowly wiped his hands on his apron before taking Luis' hand. He spoke in a cautious tone.

"I am Gerhard, and we are all Lutherans here."

"Lutherans will do. Lutherans need Jesus. I was baptized Lutheran myself, but I have since met the Lord and received the second Pentecost. Have you received the second Pentecost?"

The man shook his head. He had no reason to know of such a thing.

"Well, I must tell you about that, because there is nothing more important to the times in which we live, my friend. But first … I was on my way to Königsberg, and it appears I have lost my way. Can you tell me what village I have found?"

"This is Trunz."

"Trunz. I'm not sure I've heard of it." He chuckled good-naturedly. "I'm more lost than I knew. But that's not a problem. I am sure the Lord has led me here to preach the gospel. Hallelujah!"

"I told you we are Lutherans," the man replied coldly.

In the meantime, a young man on a bicycle had ridden up and was now inspecting the Mercedes with awe and curiosity. Luis felt a trembling excitement in his chest. He often felt this vibration when the Holy Spirit spoke to his heart. A still small voice told him that bondages would soon be broken in this place. He nodded to the baker.

"I can see that my preaching here will have to wait until you have been made ready to hear it. These are the last days, Gerhard. Woe is me if I do not preach the gospel of Jesus Christ. Tell me, is anyone sick in this village?"

"Sick? Are you a doctor, too?"

"No, I am a preacher. But I represent the Great Physician. Let me ask you something, Gerhard. If I pray for someone who is sick and you see them healed, will you believe that I have been sent here to preach the gospel? Will you listen to me?"

Slowly, the baker began to smile and nod.

"Yes. Yes, I would listen." The baker knew something that Luis could not have known. Everyone in Trunz knew there was someone horribly sick there. And Gerhard was smiling because this naïve American was about to leave the village in utter defeat. He would never have to endure listening to his gospel sermon. "In fact there is someone sick here," he said. "Someone very sick. Listen." He pointed toward the village and then cupped his hands behind his ears.

Luis did the same. At first he could hear nothing but the sighing of the wind driving the arms of the windmill above him. Then, after a few moments he heard it.

"AaaaaaAAAAAAAArrgh!!"

He felt the hair rise at the back of his neck. The sound came from the far end of the village. It was something he might have imagined on a moonless night in the darkest wood. Perhaps a sound of demonic origin.

His first instinct was to leap into his car and accelerate toward another village. But he held his ground, rebuking the impulse of spiritual cowardice. The cry could be nothing if not the voice of a man. A sick man. Suffering as a man would suffer on a torturer's bench.

"Who is that?"

"His name is August Bonnke," Gerhard replied quietly. "He is the *Müller-meister* here. He owns this mill and bakery and is the leading man in Trunz. A great man who has been struck down by a terrible disease. Gout or rheumatism or some such thing. No one knows what it truly is. He has suffered for years, and the doctors can do nothing. He cries out in pain night and day."

"AaaaaaAAAAAAAArrgh!"

The terrible cry sounded again, but this time Luis heard it through ears of compassion. The elements of pain, desperation, and rage coming from the man in the house at the far end of the village were sounds translated in his heart by the Holy Spirit. Here was a soul trapped by Satan. A soul Christ had died to set free. Here was a desperate cry to God for deliverance. The kind of cry that would not be held back by pride or stoicism or German will power. This was the kind of cry God never refused. Luis immediately understood that God had arranged for him to become lost on his way to Königsberg for this divine appointment in Trunz.

"I would like very much to pray for Herr Bonnke," Luis said. "Do you think he would allow me to pray for him?"

The baker shrugged. He turned and called to the young man who was still enthralled with the automobile. "Hermann, come here."

The young man picked up his bicycle and walked it to where both men stood. "Yes, Gerhard."

"Hermann, tell your father that a preacher is here to pray for him."

Hermann looked in puzzlement from one man to the other, obviously surprised, not understanding what was going on. The baker turned again to Luis. "What kind of preacher should we say that you are, Reverend Graf? A Lutheran? A Catholic? Evangelical?"

Luis thought for a moment. "Have you heard of Azusa Street? The revival in America? In Los Angeles?"

Gerhard and the young man shook their heads. They had never heard of it.

"It does not matter. Tell Herr Bonnke that I am a man filled with the Holy Ghost. When I pray for him it will not be like when a priest prays for him. I will pray in the power of the Holy Spirit, and his body will be healed. Tell him that."

The baker turned to young Hermann and nodded that he should go and tell his father these things. The young man jumped on his bicycle and began to ride quickly toward the house at the far end of the village.

THAT YOUNG MAN on the bicycle was Hermann Bonnke, my father, just 17 years of age at the time. The sick man, August Bonnke, was my grandfather.

The Bonnke clan lived in an isolated area of Germany called *Ostpreussen*, or East Prussia. Our enclave had been created by international treaty at the end of World War I. It had been artificially cut off from the rest of Germany, and it faced the Baltic States and the Russian Empire to the east. Along our western border something called a "Polish Corridor" extended from modern Poland to the port city of Danzig on the Baltic Sea. Today, Ostpreussen no longer exists. Following World War II, all Germans were ethnically cleansed from this region.

In this isolated, cold, damp, and forested land in the spring of 1922, however, the flaming torch of the Holy Spirit would soon be passed. Luis Graf carried that fire, the fire of Pentecost that would eventually consume my life.

# Chapter 4

LUIS GRAF ENTERED August Bonnke's household like a blazing lantern in a dismal cavern. Cobwebs of religious doubt and stagnation were swept aside as he moved toward the bed where the *Müllermeister*, "the best man in Trunz," lay writhing in agony. He proclaimed liberty to the downtrodden, healing to the sick, and salvation to the poor needy sinner – Lutheran or otherwise.

He announced that the Holy Spirit had been sent for a demonstration of the power of God that could make all things new. Divine healings were signs and wonders to confirm the preaching of the gospel. He took the sick man by the hand and commanded that he rise and be made whole in the name of Jesus.

August felt a jolt of heaven's power surge through his body. He leapt from his sickbed and stood trembling like a criminal around whom the walls of a prison had just fallen. He looked at his arms and legs as if iron chains had just been struck from them. He felt his once swollen and inflamed joints, and they were renewed to a supple and youthful state. His wife, Marie, who had been at his bedside for years, began to weep.

He began to walk, then to run, then to leap, then to shout. He grabbed his wife and embraced her with tears running freely down his face. A moment ago he had been unable to endure the slightest touch on his skin. Now, he was a man set free of pain. He was free indeed. He could embrace life again. And embrace it he did! A new life of health and vigor had been given to a man condemned by an evil and tormenting disease. August Bonnke would never be the same and would never, until the day he died, fail to testify of what God had done for him that day in Trunz.

IN 1922, LUIS GRAF did not see the great harvest he had hoped to see after the dramatic healing of August Bonnke. Spiritually, Germany was hard and bitter soil. Just two accepted Christ as Savior that day; August and his grateful wife, Marie. Luis led them in the sinner's prayer. Then he laid his hands on them, and they received the gift of the Holy Ghost with speaking in tongues. The torch of Pentecost had been passed.

Two years later, Luis was invited to return for meetings at the local Pentecostal fellowship in nearby Königsberg. My grandparents traveled faithfully from Trunz to those meetings, which continued for four months. Attendance outgrew the church building. A city hall was hired, seating 800. Soon that was abandoned in favor of a stable at the fairgrounds holding 2,000. In all, 4,000 people were saved in the Königsberg meetings. This was an unusually large harvest in those days.

Hermann Dittert, a lifelong friend of our family and one who attended those meetings with my grandparents, later wrote, "Luis Graf was an evangelistic lawnmower."

I found this quote only recently, and it is fascinating to compare this "lawnmower" description to the one I began using as our crusades in Africa became too large for any stadium to hold. Meeting in the open air with standing room only, we began to see crowds with more than 100,000 in attendance. Within a few years we registered conversions in the millions of souls. I could feel an evangelistic paradigm shift taking place, and I said, "We have entered the age of the combine harvester."

I reflect now on the difference between a lawnmower and a combine harvester. It shows, I think, the difference between the era of Luis Graf and that of Reinhard Bonnke. In the 1920s the lawnmower was becoming a common tool. Through the following decades, the combine harvester was developed for the massive agricultural operations we see today. These two symbols also reflect a difference in faith horizons. In the 1920s, the Pentecostals of Germany were so marginalized from the mainstream of religious life that they only dared to see the harvest field as a lawn to be mowed. Today my team dares to envision an entire continent coming to Christ.

A great highway is built along the route of the pioneers who first blazed the trail. The spiritual trail blazed by Luis Graf in Trunz laid down a pattern for my life and ministry a generation later. Even more, that congregation of Pentecostal believers in Königsberg provided the rich soil of fellowship that nurtured the faith of my grandparents, and later, my parents, Hermann and Meta Bonnke.

Two years after the Königsberg meetings, at the age of 65, Luis sensed in his spirit that he should retire from all speaking engagements. The duration of his evangelistic effort was quite short. Merely four years.

This remains a mystery to me. Nor can I relate to it. I am celebrating 50 years in active ministry and am more passionate to preach the gospel than ever. I cannot imagine retirement. But in 1926, Luis Graf took that step and the evangelistic lawnmower fell silent.

Hermann & Meta engaged 1932

Nine years later, Adolf Hitler rose to power in the economic and political chaos that was Germany. As the world rushed toward the holocaust of World War II, Luis was called home to eternity at the age of 74.

# Part 2

# OUT OF GERMANY

*Now I lay me down to sleep.*
*I pray the Lord my soul to keep.*
*If I should die before I wake, I pray dear Lord;*
*keep Mommy and Daddy, my brothers,*
*and my little sister, Felicitas, safe.*
*And me, too. Amen.*

# Chapter 5

Peace and safety then sudden destruction. It was 1945 in Stablack, East Prussia. World War II was drawing to a close and Hitler's armies were beginning to collapse.

My comfortable childhood was shattered with the scream of artillery shells, explosions, and the drone of Russian planes. I had no idea what had changed. I ran to the window and looked out. The night sky flickered and glowed with the light of burning buildings. To my five-year-old mind, they seemed no more sinister than embers in a fireplace. No more dangerous than candles in a stained-glass window. Searchlights swept the clouds, and tracer bullets flew at the cross-winged silhouettes in the sky.

My mother, Meta, gathered all six of us children around her and began to pray. I snuggled together with Martin, the oldest at eleven years of age, with Gerhard, who was nine, and the twins – Jürgen and Peter – who were six. Mother held little Felicitas on her lap. She was not yet three years old.

Bonnke family 1941

Suddenly the door burst open. A soldier stood there. He was a foot soldier who had been sent by our father, Hermann Bonnke, an officer in the German *Wehrmacht*.

"Why are you still here, Meta?!" he shouted. "It may be too late. Hermann says you must take the children and run! Run now! Run for it!"

Mother sat on the stool of her beloved harmonium, her arms around us. She knew that she had waited too long. Day after day she had longed to see her husband again. She did not want to leave the secure nest they had made together in the military camp of Stablack. She simply did not want to accept that the end was so near for Germany. Hoping against hope, she had stayed in spite of the menace that grew each day. And now – this!

"Yes, tell Hermann we will go now," she said, nodding to the soldier.

He turned and disappeared into the night, leaving the door ajar.

"Dear Jesus, preserve us!" Mother whispered.

WEEKS EARLIER, quietly, out of earshot of the children, Hermann Bonnke had told his wife that the war was lost. "World War II will go down as horribly as World War I for Germany. The Allies are invading from the west. Here in the east, Stablack is surrounded. We will make a final stand, but Russia has built an overwhelming force, and they will prevail. We don't know when they will begin the attack but it could come at any moment."

He told her that he would have to stay with the troops. He might not be able to return home from the garrison to see her before the end. The army would make a final stand in an effort to allow refugees to flee. When all was lost he would be ordered to pull back to surrender to the British or French in the west, rather than fall into the hands of the hated Soviets.

He instructed her to sew backpacks for all of the children. We would use them to carry food and clothing. We would have to pack now and be prepared to flee at a moment's notice. It was early spring and we would have to endure temperatures below freezing, day and night.

"You must take the road toward Königsberg then turn south. The road to Danzig is cut off. You will have to cross the Haff. It is the only way."

The Haff was a frozen bay on the Baltic coast. Even though it was now February, desperate refugees were crossing the melting ice to reach Danzig.

Mother's parents, Ernst and Minna Scheffler, had moved to Danzig soon after the war began. It was a German stronghold in Poland, on the southwestern border of East Prussia. It had an ice-free port to the Baltic Sea.

Hermann knew that the German High Command had begun the rescue operation code-named *Hannibal*.[1] Key military personnel and civilians were being evacuated from Danzig. The newly built German passenger ship, *Wilhelm Gustloff*, was currently in port loading for a voyage to the German city of Kiel.

"This will be your very best escape," he said. "If you can make it to Danzig then your father can book passage for you."

Before leaving that morning, he took Meta's hands in his and together they prayed for our safety. Many times as they prayed my father could be heard speaking in other tongues, pouring his heart out to God in this desperate hour. Then they embraced and said a tearful goodbye. Mother knew this could be the last time any of us ever saw Father alive.

MOTHER HAD NOT ONLY SEWN PACKS for each of us boys, she had made them for each of the children of our neighbor. As the final Russian assault began, and after the warning by the soldier, she quickly called the neighbors to come join us. The time had come to bundle up for a long trip to Grandpa and Grandma's house in Danzig, she said.

Like most Germans, we owned no automobile. We would have to go to the road and try to find a ride on a farmer's wagon. There were eleven children and two mothers in our little refugee group. It was still the dark of night. We could not imagine the fears our mothers were dealing with on this journey. For us boys it sounded like a fun adventure. Something like a winter hayride.

Outside, we hurried toward the main road. In the distance we could see that the way was clogged with wagons, military lorries, and thousands of people on foot, all streaming west toward Königsberg. We joined ourselves to the stream.

Soon Felicitas grew tired. She began to cry. Mother bundled her in a blanket and carried her. In the darkness we did not manage to find a farmer's wagon that had room for our entire group. So we continued to walk until daylight.

We boys soon realized that this trip would be nothing like a hayride. All around people were talking of the atrocities. Russian tanks were coming along the road behind us, and they were running over people. Soldiers were shooting women and children.

"And those are the lucky ones," an old farmer said grimly, wagging his head as we quickened our pace. We heard the roar of an engine on the road behind us. Mother screamed at us to run into the ditch. All of the people scattered from the roadway.

But it was not a Russian tank. It was a military truck speeding past. A truck loaded with German soldiers from the battle front. They were fleeing for their lives, leaving us to fend for ourselves.

"Where are the Russians?!" screamed a refugee, as the truck rumbled on.

"They have taken Stablack!" shouted a soldier. "Run through the forest! Hide yourselves!"

"We cannot take these children through the forest," my mother said, as she looked at her frightened neighbor and friend. "A farmer's wagon is no match for the speed of a military tank. What are we to do?"

Another truck came by, and another. My mother was deeply distressed that she had not taken to the road much sooner. She now understood that she had made the danger greater for us by waiting until the last minute. Chaos was the order of the day. The possibility that we could be run over or gunned down by the Russian army was now her first concern.

"The next German troop truck will stop for our children," Mother said resolutely. "They will see that I am a German mother. They will have mercy."

The next time a truck sped toward us my mother stood on the side of the roadway hailing the driver. The truck swerved in order to go past. Mother leapt in front of it, and the truck slid to a stop in the mud. The driver cursed angrily.

"We have children! You must give us a ride!" she screamed.

"Frau, this truck is overloaded. I cannot stop."

With that, the driver put the truck in motion again, leaving us huddled beside the road.

"Someone will stop," Mother said with determination. "Dear Jesus, move the hearts of these men to take us to safety."

She attempted to stop the next truck and the next. They did not even slow down in their headlong rush to save their own lives. Mud splattered over us from their spinning tires as they sped past.

As we walked on, Mother hatched another plan. This time she would have our neighbor stand apart with us children. We would remain 15 feet or so behind Mother's position. If she managed to stop another truck and engage the driver, our neighbor would not wait for his answer. She would begin to toss children one by one into the back of the truck. We would land like eleven sacks of potatoes among the soldiers. Last of all, the women would beg the men to make room also for the children's mothers, expecting that they would not want to have to care for the children by themselves.

This plan worked. Once inside the troop carrier the soldiers made room for us where formerly there was none. It was standing room only, but they pushed against each other to make a small circle in their midst. Finally, they pulled our mothers into the truck and deposited them on the floor beside us.

The truck revved its engines and began to roll on toward the Haff. Mother sobbed and hugged us, thanking the soldiers again and again for their help. But they refused to look at her. The proud Prussian military had failed to protect its homeland. All had been lost, and now it was every man for himself. Their eyes darted left and right searching for any sign of Russian troops on the move.

Not long after, the men began to scream and pound their fists against the cab. Someone had spotted a plane approaching. The truck lurched to a stop, and the soldiers spilled out like scrambling ants. Hitting the ground, they raced for cover in a nearby grove of trees.

Mother grabbed her boys and Felicitas as a fighter plane swooped low over the truck and then pitched up into the sky to position itself for a bombing attack. We had no time to leap from the truck or catch up to the soldiers. We were a sitting target.

Mother took us like a mother hen hovering over her chicks. She put us under her body, spreading her coat over us and began to pray.

"Heavenly Father, protect these children. Give us Your angels for a shield. Let no weapon prosper. These are Your children, Lord. Keep them safe, in Jesus' name."

She continued to pray as the hum of ballistic shrapnel filled the air, arriving faster than the speed of sound. This was immediately followed by the roar of the fighter's cannons drowning all other sounds and thoughts.

The truck leapt and shook with the deep impact – *thump! thump! thump!* – of bombs pounding the earth in rapid succession. Explosions of soil burst over us as the plane banked toward the east from whence it had come. We could hear small-arms fire from the grove of trees where the soldiers were hiding. The sound of the plane's engine died in the distance. Nothing had hit the truck. Nothing at all.

We looked up. Mother shook soil from her cloak. "Thank You, Jesus," she whispered.

When the soldiers re-entered the truck they were deeply shamed. None had looked to our safety. As seasoned fighters they had been sure when they bolted for the trees that there would be nothing to come back to. No truck, no refugees. They went to great lengths after that incident to take extra care with us. We became their prized cargo.

Darkness fell again, and we continued on through the next night. In the pre-dawn darkness we stopped in a forested area near the Haff. Hundreds of other families huddled in the trees by bonfires. The soldiers carried us into the wood and told us to build a fire. With dawn breaking they would not cross the ice. The Russians were flying from their positions around Königsberg to bomb the refugees as they fled, they said.

I was happy for the chance to stretch my legs. The search for firewood in the forest was just what I needed. I began to hurry along, looking for scraps of deadwood that might burn. But the other families had done a good job. There were no scraps to be found. I went deeper into the woods, searching the ground diligently.

Suddenly I looked up and had no idea where I was. I ran to the nearest group of refugees. "Have you seen my Mother?"

"No."

I ran to the next group and the next. From bonfire to bonfire I hurried. No one knew me. No one knew my mother. All were strangers.

"Here is Meta," a voice called.

I rushed toward the sound of it. A man pointed to a woman I did not know. "Here is Meta."

"No!" I cried, and rushed away from them.

I had been suddenly wrenched from my sheltered life in Stablack. Now I was lost in a dangerous world full of nothing but strangers. All of the things that meant comfort and home to me had been snatched away in one frightful night. I began to cry like an air raid siren.

A kind lady came and asked if she could help me. Between sobs I told her that I had been looking for firewood and now I couldn't find my mother. She picked me up and carried me from group to group until, at last, I saw my mother with a worried look on her face, searching for me in the distance.

I leapt from that woman's arms and raced to Meta. I didn't even thank the kind lady. Mother embraced me tightly. My heart was beating so fast with the release from fear that I could hardly calm down. It was Mother's custom to hug her children once a year, only on their birthday. Her hugs were especially precious. On the brighter side, I had unexpectedly found a way to get an extra hug from Mother. It felt so good.

As morning grew in the sky, Mother and the neighbor lady lay their eleven children on packed bundles around a bonfire. We went to sleep hearing their prayers that God would provide safe passage for us across the ice.

Suddenly the soldiers were waking us up. They gathered us and loaded us quickly into the truck. We did not understand it yet, but God had performed an answer to our prayer. As we rumbled down the slope toward the Haff a thick bank of fog rolled in from the Baltic Sea. Soon we were engulfed in the most blessed whiteout conditions imaginable. This was the divine cover needed to hide us from the bombing and strafing Russian fighter planes.

As the truck ran across the Haff the driver had to slow down and use caution. It was late in the season and pools of water on top of the ice splashed around our tires. At times we would slide sideways, nearly out of control. Sometimes the ice would groan and crack beneath our wheels. February was normally too late to venture out here in a vehicle. But desperation and the provision of the life-saving fog drove us on.

Occasionally out of the ghostly mist we would encounter the dark circles of bomb holes. Bodies floated on the dark surface of the water. Thousands had lost their lives trying to cross before us. But we reached the other side in marvelous safety.

In Danzig we parted company with our neighbors. Soon Meta, with all six Bonnke children clustered around her, knocked at the door of Grandpa and Grandma Scheffler's second-story apartment. It was a tearful reunion. Mother's younger sister, Eva, was there, too. The first thing Mother wanted to know was if they had heard any news of Stablack, or any news of Father. No one could tell her anything. Communications had broken down.

Danzig had been under bombardment for days. As soon as the weather lifted, the bombardment resumed. We saw buildings burst into flames as planes and artillery hammered the city indiscriminately. Dozens of plumes of smoke could be seen around the apartment every day.

It was then that we heard the awful report that when the fog had lifted from the Haff the Russian air force had completely bombed out the ice crossing. That way of escape was gone for all the remaining Germans caught between Königsberg and Danzig.

"Oh, please God," Mother prayed, "show Hermann a way of escape. Don't let him be caught out there."

"And what about Grandpa August and Grandma Marie?" my brother Martin cried. "They are still in Trunz."

"We don't know where they are," Mother said. "But we will pray for their safety, too."

Grandpa Ernst seemed especially troubled. He wanted to get us out of the city as fast as he could to escape its fall into enemy hands. At the beginning of the war he had left his rural sheep farm near the Lithuanian border for a job with a woolen mill in Danzig. He was determined to stay until the end, but Danzig was no place for his wife, his daughters, or his grandchildren. Daily he would brave the bombardment and go to the harbor. There he would jostle through the crowds seeking passage for us on a ship.

"What about the *Wilhelm Gustloff*?" Mother asked. "Hermann said that we might find safe passage on that ship."

For a long time Grandpa did not answer. His face was a mask of seething anger. "She already sailed," he said hoarsely.

Mother assumed he was angry because they had sailed without us.

His wife, Minna, knew he was troubled for another reason, and she could no longer contain her grief. She burst into tears. "Tell them the rest of it, Ernst."

"Tell us what?" Mother asked.

"A Russian U-boat sank the *Wilhelm Gustloff.*"

Suddenly the gravity of the danger we were in became much more real. We had escaped from Stablack. But would we escape Danzig?

"Did anyone live?"

"There were 10,600 people on that ship. Almost 9,000 of them were refugees, the rest soldiers. Most of them perished."

Mother looked at her mother. "Then we must pray. We will pray that God will lead Papa to find the right ship for us."

"I will look for a ship that is not going to Germany," he said bitterly. "A ship that is not carrying soldiers."

Mother sat quietly for a while pondering. Might there have been a divine purpose in her delaying our departure from Stablack? Even under the threat of the

Russian invasion? What if we had arrived in Danzig in time to book passage on the *Wilhelm Gustloff*? We would all be at the bottom of the Baltic Sea.

On March 17 the city was still being bombarded. We had left our home more than a month ago, and the Russians had increased their positions throughout the country. Grandpa came home that day with good news. He had been at the port as an old coal freighter had docked. Visiting with the officers, he had obtained permission for us to ride along to Copenhagen the next morning. We would have to leave early.

He felt that this was an especially good vessel under the circumstances. It was not a military transport. He also thought that its destination bode well for an unmolested crossing. It was bound for Denmark, the country that had suffered less than others under German occupation. As the war ended, this seemed the best possible place for us.

That night Minna, Eva, and Meta fasted and prayed. Even though Grandpa Ernst had done his best for us, they were terrified. They wanted to hear from God about our journey on this ship.

After a while, Minna got up and took a small box from the mantle. She removed its lid. It contained hundreds of Bible memory verses printed on cards. She held it out to Meta and told her to take out a card. She believed that the card would contain a word from the Lord as to whether we should go on this ship or wait for another.

Mother reached out to the card box. She took a card and handed it to her mother.

"Isaiah 43:16," Minna began, "Thus saith the LORD, which maketh a way in the sea, and a path in the mighty waters …"

She could not read another word. Nor did Mother reply for a moment. The three women sat with tears streaming from their eyes. The Lord had spoken. He would be the captain of this voyage.

Now they burst out in praise to God. All of us came near to share the joy. We read the card again, and faith rose up in our hearts for the journey. Faith that God would see us through safely.

The next morning we packed our bundles for the trip. We walked down the hill to the shipyards. When we got there Grandpa was dismayed. Apparently others had seized upon the same idea. Thousands of people were packed onto the dock, ready to make the same trip. We were lost in the crowd. The ship could not possibly hold a fraction of those seeking passage. Our hearts sank.

Mother was determined she had heard from God. She took us children by the hand and pressed into the crowd. "Make way for children," she said, again and again, as we pushed our way forward.

Finally the press of the crowd became too great. We were within sight of the gangway to the ship but could go no further. Mother was fearful that one of us might be hurt. The people in the crowd were desperate.

Suddenly, someone began screaming and pointing to the sky in the east. A Russian fighter plane was sighted flying down the shipyard line, guns blazing, headed straight for where we stood.

People began to scream and run. Mother knew the children would be trampled, so she huddled us all together, telling us to get down and hide behind our luggage. Once more, as she had done on the military lorry, she shielded us with her body.

The air hummed again with the sound of ballistic shrapnel. Hungry bullets seeking flesh to destroy.

When the plane had passed over we were safe. Safe, but badly shaken. My oldest brother, Martin, to this day vividly remembers the terror of that moment. He said that he felt sure he would die from taking a bullet through his back. He was absolutely sure of it and found it hard to believe he was still alive afterward.

But we were not injured. Needless to say the crowd had thinned. My brother Gerhard remembers that Mother's sister, Eva, stood up at this point and began screaming at a ship's officer who stood near the gangway.

"Sir, look here! Here is a mother with six children! You must take them now!"

The officer turned his back to her, pretending not to hear. But she would not stop. She ran as close to the gangway as she could, repeating her demand.

More Russian planes were now circling above, seeking targets of opportunity. We grabbed our luggage and hurried after Mother toward the gangway. Eva continued to scream at the officer who seemed determined to ignore us.

Suddenly, without warning, he simply turned and opened the gangway gate to let us all in. In this way, God made room for us on that ship bound for Copenhagen. We turned and waved at Grandpa as we hurried up the gangway.

On board they hustled us beneath deck. Soon other refugees were crowded together with us. They filled the lower hold of the ship with as many passengers as seemed prudent. Then they withdrew the gangway. Many more people were left outside pleading for a place on board. But the great fog horn sounded, and the ship pulled slowly from the dock. Our voyage had begun.

Once on the open Baltic, the conditions below deck deteriorated fast. The sea was making considerable swells, and many were succumbing to motion sickness. The smell of vomit, feces, and urine began to reek in the air. In the middle of the night my bladder could hold no more.

"Please, Momma, I need to go on deck to pee."

Mother could not let me go alone. She sent Aunt Eva with me, who took great care, making sure I held tightly to her hand. We reached the main deck and entered the cold night air. I remember the salty fresh smell of it. It invigorated me after enduring the stench below decks. After using the latrine I looked up into the starry sky. As I gazed at Milky Way, slowly tilting with the roll of the ship I heard the faint drone of a plane.

Suddenly my heart nearly leaped from my chest. On deck of this civilian ship anti-aircraft guns had been mounted and hidden under tarps. The covers were suddenly removed and the guns began blasting into the heavens at the approaching fighter. Aunt Eva screamed and dragged me toward the open hatch, but I broke free, fascinated by the drama in the sky. Before she could grab me again and drag me down the rope ladder I saw the fighter plane burst into flames.

"Look! Look!" I shouted, pointing to it.

For a moment both of us watched transfixed as the plane fell like a burning meteor, splashing into the dark and icy waters off to one side. The passengers on deck began to cheer. It had been a Russian fighter that plummeted from the sky.

As Eva hurried me down below decks she was thanking God that at least we had escaped the strafing that had targeted us on the docks in Danzig. I also recalled the terror of the bullets and bombs that had rocked the military truck as we sat helpless on the road. Incident by incident, the realities of this war were becoming real to my five-year-old mind.

SOMETIME AFTER MIDNIGHT, we were awakened by an impact against the hull. Staring into the darkness, all we could hear was the constant churning of the ship's engine room continuing on course. All of the passengers had heard of the fate of the *Wilhelm Gustloff*. After some minutes, passengers began to panic as the ship listed hard to one side.

The crew rushed to the lower decks with gasoline-powered pumps. Either the ship had struck a mine or had been hit by a torpedo. Water was rushing in from a gaping hole in the hull. Soon the sounds of the pump engines could be heard below decks, removing the incoming water.

Mother called us to her side. Here was the supreme test of her promise from God. She began to pray, Minna and Eva joining her, reminding God that He was the God who had spoken, saying that He made a way in the sea, and a path in the mighty waters.

After some hours the ship began to right itself. The crew explained that the pumps had begun to work faster than the incoming water, and we were staying afloat. When the coast of Denmark appeared and we entered the harbor at last, everyone wept and cheered.

I looked at the distant shore without a clue as to what awaited us here. All I knew is that I wanted to stay close to the woman who had prayed us safely through the fall of East Prussia. Though I could not yet put it into words, in my heart I wanted to know the God she knew. And I wanted to know Him like she knew Him.

# Chapter 6

META BUNDLED FELICITAS in a blanket and carried her in her arms. She gathered all five blond-headed Bonnke boys around her, and together we stepped off the coal freighter into the freezing sleet of a Copenhagen spring. Eva held Grandmother Minna by the arm as they followed unsteadily down the gangway.

Other ships were unloading at the docks around us. Slowly we began to understand that we were but nine of a quarter million German refugees entering Denmark. 85 percent of them were like us – women with children.[2]

At first we were treated well. The Nazi-supervised Danish government did their best to feed and house us in empty schools, warehouses, and meeting houses. But in a matter of days, Hitler was dead, and Germany surrendered. The occupying German forces withdrew and everything changed.

The horrors of the Nazi death camps and crematoriums became headline news around the world, and we felt the hatred of the Danish people exploding in our faces. Some refugees were attacked by angry mobs who wanted to kill every German in sight. For our own safety we were removed to a military-patrolled detention center. It was ringed in barbed wire and hastily constructed guard towers, resembling those we'd seen at the prisoner-of-war camp in Stablack. The difference was that now we were the prisoners on the inside. This would be our home for the next four years as the world sorted out the terrible aftermath of World War II.

We shared a small bungalow with two and sometimes three other family groups. No one had money. We had a system of vouchers for rationed necessities like toilet paper, soap, toothbrushes, and clothing. We were fed en masse at a central kitchen. The food provided was unappetizing and barely nutritious. Many suffered from dysentery. In time, weaker adults and children began to die of malnutrition and dehydration.

For us boys, part of each day's routine involved helping to carry water and firewood to our cabin. Firewood remained in short supply, and getting warm and fed became the first goal of each and every day.

As the days and months passed, Mother nursed us through the normal fevers, colds, and bouts with flu, using home remedies and prayer. Doctors were not available. Only basic medicines and first aid could be found. During our first year in the camps, 13,000 died, mostly children under the age of five.[3]

Today, moss-covered stone slabs mark the resting places of these German children in nearly forgotten corners of Danish graveyards. In some cases one stone represents several children hastily buried in a single grave. I recall one I recently visited at the site of our internment. A single stone cross bears the names of George Kott, 3 months of age, Rosewitha Rogge, 3 months, and Erika Rauchbach, who died after four days of life. And the headstones go on and on like this, row after row, 7,000 in all. Even as the war ended, the tragic momentum of death it had spawned simply would not stop.

BUT OF COURSE, boys will be boys, even in a prison camp. My older brothers and I found ways to play our games as Mother, Eva, and Minna bore the full brunt of hardship. I vividly recall chasing a makeshift soccer ball through the camp. One day I chased it up to the barbed wire fence. Stooping to pick it up, I saw an armed guard in a tower. It reminded me that we were not free to run and play as we had been in Stablack.

It slowly dawned on me that we were not like the other children who sometimes stood on the other side of the fence staring. Sometimes their parents stood with them and pointed at us, and sometimes they cursed us for what we had done to the world.

I slowly became aware that the army my father had served belonged to an evil empire. The truth about Nazi atrocities and Hitler's insanity began to make their way even into the conversations of German boys and girls at play in the camps. Our father's military rank, which had once been a source of pride for the Bonnke boys, now became something we kept to ourselves. We were sobered and saddened. My brothers and I longed to see our father and to know that he was okay, and to learn from him the answers to these terrible accusations.

Mother had received no official word about Dad, but she reassured us that God would take care of him just as He had taken care of us on our perilous flight from East Prussia. But for many long months we were under a dark cloud, wondering if he had been crushed beneath the wheels of the advancing Russian tanks.

In response to our questions, Mother finally sat us down to tell us that we would never see our home in Stablack again. That part of the world had been taken over by the Soviet Union. She explained that the end of the war had caught us in Denmark and that in time we would be allowed to return to another part of Germany where we would build a new life. Until then, we would have to make the best of life in the refugee camp.

Carrying the full weight of parenting six children, Mother let the sternness of her Prussian upbringing come forth. No doubt her strictness was compounded by constant anxieties about our safety. We had to give account to her for our whereabouts at all times and get permission in advance to do anything or go anywhere with friends. She would tolerate no deviation from her every command. Nor would she allow other opinions to be expressed once she had spoken. To run afoul of her was to risk a *good hiding*, as she called it. The word had something to do with the tanning of an animal's hide, which meant the punishment would be sufficient to change the shade of one's skin, at the very least. She did not hesitate to spank or slap us with an open hand to make sure her authority was never taken lightly. And it seldom was. The threat was deterrent enough for everyone – that is, everyone but me.

Denmark refugee camp.
The background was a wallpaper.

Somehow I earned more than my share of hidings. I might run off to play with a friend and forget to ask permission. Or, I might express an opinion contrary to her rules, as if I had a perfect right to do so. I would become distracted while carrying firewood and end up playing soccer. On a sudden whim I might fashion a fort from the firewood I was carrying and engage in a furious chestnut fight with an opposing team of children. My clothes would become torn and filthy at the knees. At mealtime I might begin wrestling with a sibling and spill my food and drink. There seemed no end to the ways I could get into trouble. It got so that in the morning Mother would look at me and say, "You naughty boy! I might as well give you a good hiding right now and get it over with."

And she meant it.

As time wore on I began to feel that she was right; I was an especially naughty boy. No matter how often I was corrected it seemed I never learned my lesson. I wore my mother out. Often she would say, "I so wanted a little girl when you were born, but you were my *fifth* boy. Dear, Lord!" It began to dawn on me that I was a heavy burden to her, but I couldn't seem to rise above it.

Finally, it didn't seem to matter. Even when I managed to do everything right I still sensed an attitude of exasperation coming from her every time I was in the room. It was more than misbehavior that irritated her. I felt that it was me.

NOT FEELING WELL, my father Hermann Bonnke lay in his prison bunk staring at the wooden slats of the bed a few inches above his nose. He had been excused from work detail, which allowed him to spend some precious time alone in the British prison barracks. He thought of how many millions of prisoners had lain awake in claustrophobic quarters like this throughout the hellish war years. Victims of the Nazi regime. How many of them – millions of them – had died in horrible ways he wished he could erase from his mind.

He had only recently learned of Hitler's Final Solution. He was still in shock over it. The extermination of Jews appalled him beyond words. As a Pentecostal believer, he had regarded the Jews as the chosen people through whom God had revealed the Messiah, the Savior of all mankind. Knowing that he had served a government that had planned to exterminate all of them left him permanently shaken. It haunted his thoughts and even his dreams at night.

He wondered how the Stablack prisoners of war were faring. Those his men had guarded at the prison camp in East Prussia. They had been mostly Belgian and French soldiers. Some had returned to Europe with stories of even worse confinement after being liberated by the Russians.

How were his fellow German soldiers faring? How many had survived the final onslaught? He thought especially of those who had stayed behind in Königsberg so he could escape by sea. He recalled how they had sacrificed themselves.

"You are a father of six children," the officer in charge had said. "You must return to build a new Germany with them."

He had been given passage on the last mine sweeper to leave the harbor at Königsberg before the end. His fellow soldiers had held back the Soviets until his ship had made it safely into the open waters of the Baltic Sea. Rumors now had come that the men who had stayed behind had been marched away on the point of bayonets into the vast Siberian Gulag in Russia. They would never be seen again.

He raised his right hand and turned it over and over before his face. In the depths of his heart he wished he had never been the young boy who had raised a wooden sword in the village of Trunz, dreaming of glory in battle. Little had he known that the Prussian Cross he had so longed to wear would be hijacked from its godly heritage and twisted into Hitler's swastika. How the descendants of the Holy Roman Empire could be transformed into the Nazi regime, he still could not fathom. But he had seen it happen with his own eyes, day after day, with a helpless feeling in the pit of his stomach. It had taken only ten years for Hitler to seize absolute power over his beloved homeland. He would never live another day without regretting being German.

Hermann had been in this prison camp for 279 days and nights. Every minute of every day he felt the pang of longing for his wife, Meta, and his children. He saw each of their faces in his memory now, as he had seen them last in Stablack. He prayed for them by name, asking that they be preserved alive and well, and that they be reunited by God's grace in due time. He had inquired again and again through the Red Cross of their safety and whereabouts but had learned nothing. With each passing day the gnawing ache in his stomach grew stronger, whispering that they had not survived.

Still, in his confinement, he did not feel persecuted. It seemed small payment for the mega death and suffering dealt by the German army over the last few years. The trials for Nazi war crimes were even now beginning in the city of Nuremberg. He would not have to stand trial because as an officer in the Reichswehr, he had never joined the Nazi Party. But he had served their cause in a terrible killing machine. He thought that if he were given the death penalty as a prisoner of war now, it would not be too severe. But alas, it could not atone for so many sins. The war's sweep was too massive and its evils too many for any court to ever set right.

But there was One who kept perfect count. Not even a sparrow fell without His knowledge. The hairs of the heads of every war victim, not to mention of every perpetrator, had been perfectly numbered and recorded in His divine Book. One day the Book would be opened, and everyone would stand before the Great White Throne to give account for his deeds. God alone could balance the scales of justice.

And He had done so. In heaven there was a second Book. The Book of Life. The members of the human race would finally not stand or fall based upon their deeds – good or evil. They would be saved if their names had been written in the Book of Life. To accept Jesus as Savior placed their names in this Book. This was Hermann's hope and the hope of every Christian believer on both sides of the war.

As he lay there, in his imagination, he saw a pair of scales weighed down to the floor with an impossible debt. A tank, a bomber, a field helmet, a bayonet, an Iron Cross adorned with swastikas. Then, placed on the opposite side of the scale, the old rugged cross. Under the weight of that cross the scales were balanced. This alone was the equation of divine justice. God placed on Him the iniquity of us all.[4]

Tears ebbed from his eyes as his heart reached out to this infinite God in prayer. *My heavenly Father, I am Yours for the remaining years of my life. No more military service for me. It is my heart's desire to preach Your gospel and to serve You alone, until the day I see You face to face.*

Across the empty barracks he heard a door quietly open and close. Someone began walking softly across the floor. The flooring softwoods creaked beneath every step. Hermann thought perhaps it was a British guard coming to check on him. Or a doctor coming to see why he had reported feeling sick.

He rolled from the bunk and stood up to face him, and to his utter shock it was a man in white, wearing a seamless robe and Middle Eastern sandals. He was smiling as He moved toward him, hands extended as if to embrace him. His hair was long and His beard full, and when Hermann reached out to take His hand he saw that it was torn completely through from the force of a Roman nail.

"Hermann, I am so glad you are coming," the Master said, then vanished into thin air.

Hermann fell to his knees. He could do nothing but weep for the rest of the day and night. How could the Savior be made glad by one so guilty? Returning to his bunk, he lay down, his soul overflowing with the peace of God that passes understanding. Until this moment it had seemed inconceivable that an imprisoned soldier of the Third Reich could receive the smile of the Lamb of God, and that the Savior would express God's pleasure at his desire to serve Him as a minister of the gospel. The treasure of this encounter burned like a warming fire in his heart until the day he died.

What a day for us when the Red Cross delivered that wonderful letter! The first of many. Our father had found us at last! Mother's tears fell freely as she read his words again and again, stroking his handwriting with her fingers, knowing that her beloved Hermann had miraculously escaped the war's end. I jumped with joy as she gave us the news that he was alive in a British prisoner-of-war camp near Kiel, Germany. Kiel, she explained, was not far from Denmark, just across the narrow straights of the Baltic.

It would be years until we saw him, but just knowing he was alive and that he was that close to us in miles, was enough for now. Our entire family had been spared by the hand of God from the terrible end of the war. I watched the joy on Mother's face and I reflected her happiness. I spent my time in the refugee camp with a new measure of purpose thereafter.

DAYS LATER, while at play, I noticed a serious look on the face of my older brother Martin. He was speaking to Gerhard, Peter, and Jürgen near the compound fence, and he seemed deep in thought. I came near and heard some of what he was saying.

"… Why didn't God save the people on the *Wilhelm Gustloff*? They were Christians. What about the ones who fell through the ice on the Haff? Did God save the Bonnkes and not them? God didn't send the fog that covered us. That fog was just part of the weather patterns. We were the lucky ones, that's all. Some days the fog comes and some days it doesn't. God didn't do it."

These were big ideas. Too big for my now six-year-old mind. Hearing them from Martin made me feel terrible, like someone had stolen my most prized possession. I walked away quickly, deeply disturbed.

Later, I found Mother alone. "Mother, God kept us safe from the Russians, didn't He?"

"Oh, yes, Reinhard, He did." I could see her face glowing with thankfulness as she spoke.

"And did He keep Father, also?"

"Yes, and Father, too. God is so good. We must praise Him every day and be thankful for His protection over our family. So many perished, but we were spared."

My heart became peaceful again. Her faith was the solid rock that anchored my drifting soul. To this belief I would cling for comfort and joy. And in this way I began to walk a path separate and distinct from that of my older brothers. Our ways would eventually lead us to very different destinations.

AFTER NEARLY TWO YEARS in the camp, Grandpa Ernst Scheffler contacted Minna and Eva through the Red Cross. He had survived the fall of Danzig and had escaped to New Ulm, Germany. The old sheep farmer was working for a branch of the same woolen mill that had employed him in Danzig. He had secured a home and had found a way to free his wife and daughter from the camp.

We were sad, and at the same time so glad when we said our goodbyes. We wanted Grandma and Aunt Eva to be free, but we did not understand why we were not given our freedom at the same time. These were questions to which we could expect no answers. We were merely German war refugees who in the eyes of many deserved life in prison.

Meanwhile, we continued to receive letters from Father. These were the highlight of our remaining time in the camp. We would gather together and Mother would read them aloud to us, and we would feel connected again. We would dare to dream of a future in which we would be together with Father. It had happened for Grandpa Ernst, Minna, and Eva. It would surely happen for us.

I remember the day Father told us of his release from the prisoner-of-war camp. We shouted and celebrated and sang praise to God. He had been allowed to go to a city in northern Germany called Glückstadt. There he had found a room in a friend's house, and he had been offered a good paying job as a civil servant. He was preparing a place for us to come and live with him when we were released. We were ecstatic.

The name Glückstadt meant "Luck City." As Christians we did not believe in luck, but we certainly believed that it would be our very good fortune to live there with Father. Especially when we learned that he had found a little Pentecostal church in that town and had joined the fellowship. This would be our church home when we joined him. We were sure that our time of freedom was near. We began to dream of life in the house with Father in Glückstadt.

But as we waited, the days turned into weeks and into months, until finally we stopped asking, "Mother, when are we going to live with Father?" The question brought tears to her eyes.

Another letter arrived that threw everything into tension. More precisely, the letter threw Mother into turmoil. Now that I am an adult, I can better understand it. In this letter Father asked if she would support him in a decision to turn his back on the secure income he would receive in a civilian job. He wanted to become the pastor of a small group of Pentecostal refugees in the nearby village of Krempe. He explained that Krempe was only five miles from the house where he lived in Glückstadt. He could ride there on a bicycle and become their preacher. He had great compassion for these suffering people, he said, and it was the desire of his heart to serve the Lord by serving them, rather than receive another kind of paycheck.

He reminded her of his promise to God in the prison camp and of the visitation from Jesus he had received there. These things had been communicated in earlier letters. He also reminded her of his dedication to God before the war, when he had gone to a soldier's retreat at Reinbeck Castle. From that day on, he had wanted to respond to the calling of the Lord to full-time ministry, but he had been unable to obtain a discharge from the Reichswehr. Now, after the war, all of that had changed.

Mother prayed and sought God for her answer. This would not be easy. She was the struggling mother of six, living for years in a refugee camp hoping for a better future. It appeared that the Lord had provided that better tomorrow in Glückstadt with her husband. Meanwhile, millions of Germans were unemployed. To give up an income with post-war security was like letting go of a life preserver after the *Wilhelm Gustloff* had gone down.

In addition to her financial concerns, Mother could think of one other hurdle that stood in the way. Hermann had made a promise to her father, Ernst Scheffler, in order to obtain permission to marry her. She wrote a return letter to Father, reminding him of the solemn pledge he had made. Had he forgotten? Could any preacher be a true man of God if he broke such a promise?

# Chapter 7

MOTHER WROTE A LETTER, reminding Hermann of a pledge he had made to her father Ernst. In order to marry Meta, he had promised that he would never become a preacher of the gospel. It had been Ernst's one condition. What was to be done with that promise? Could it be simply discarded?

My father's reply was basically, yes, it could be discarded. He would approach Ernst to learn if he was still holding him to the promise. Surely he was not. But if so, he would have to inform him that he answered to a higher authority. Hermann remembered how he had signed away his life to the German Reichswehr while still a young man in his teens. Years later, after coming to the Lord, and coming of age, he had changed his mind. He wanted to leave the military and enter the full time ministry. But the government would not allow it. Bondage to a youthful vow had led him to serve the most horrific regime in history. Lesson learned. He would not be held to Ernst Scheffler's demand if it violated the call of the Man with the nail-scarred hands.

The question came back to the one between my father and mother. Would she support him if he followed this call? Once again she had to go to her knees in the prison camp, seeking assurance that God would supply for the family if Hermann made this change. At length, she received peace in her heart. She wrote Hermann back telling him that she would support him fully if he felt Krempe was the door God had opened for ministry. The promise he had made to her father could not compare to the visitation he had received from the Lord, confirming his calling. Besides, her mother, Minna, was a woman of biblical spirituality. She would help with any objections from Ernst.

Subsequently, our father was provided a bicycle by the pastor of the church in Glückstadt. He used it to ride the full five miles to and from church in Krempe each Sunday. Every letter from him from this time on was filled with stories of ministry. We learned of the extreme poverty among the refugees and how the town of Krempe had generously provided a hall for his meetings free of charge. Each letter contained information that made us feel a part of what he was doing.

Over time, Father's congregation grew to include 100 refugees. This growth forced them out of the free hall into a youth hostel that could accommodate the entire group. He told us of children in Krempe who would someday want to meet us when we came to join him in Glückstadt.

I tried to imagine what Glückstadt and Krempe looked like and what the other children in my father's church were like. All of the difficulty in the refugee camp seemed more endurable now that we had such a future before us.

Most of all I remember imagining my father in the pulpit. I was very proud to think that he was no longer a soldier but a preacher of the gospel.

MOTHER FOUND WAYS to be a blessing in spite of the challenges of camp life. She managed to get access to a sewing machine and kept us well outfitted for the Danish climate. She organized a camp choir, copying sheet music by hand.

When someone had a birthday in the camp she saw to it that they were properly celebrated in song. When anyone died she would conduct the choir as the chaplain said prayers and read Scripture. At Christmas our entire family celebrated with a concert of carols and strolling minstrels.

Grandma Minna was a woman of biblical spirituality.

As I grew older in the camp I continued to earn her anger and harsh discipline. Often my misbehavior would reduce her to outbursts even as she was engaged in leading the choir or sewing clothes. No one in those days thought anything wrong with a parent acting in this way. It was assumed that parents were responsible for the actions of their children. Under this kind of thinking, I was bringing shame to her.

Nearly three years passed in the camp. On her birthday, Mother was allowed to take us to attend a local Lutheran church. When we arrived she was thrilled to see that this particular edifice housed a fine pipe organ.

After the service ended she approached the preacher with a special birthday request. Would he allow her to play just one hymn on the great organ? He graciously allowed it. When she played, the preacher received a revelation. No one in his parish possessed mother's musical skills. He quickly realized that such a talent could make a marked improvement in the worship experience in his sanctuary. Now, he had a request for her.

"Would you please come back, Mrs. Bonnke, each Sunday and play for us?"

And of course, it was her great pleasure to do so and to bring all six of us to sit in the pews nearby. I remember how tall the vaulted ceilings were in that church, and how large the pipes on that organ. I recall the blasts of the various notes and instruments that seemed to explode from my mother's fingertips as she played – notes that echoed back like pelting rain from a vaulted heaven. It was for me a loud and intimidating form of worship. That mighty music in that cavernous church left me with a feeling that God was huge and far away and indifferent to the squirming behind of a young boy imprisoned in a hand-carved Danish pew. Until she finished playing, I was nearly beside myself to be free of that place so I could run and play soccer in the refugee camp field again.

My four years of internment from the age of five until nine marked on my psyche the wonderful difference faith can make. Especially faith in a loving and compassionate God. My mother, more than anyone else, etched that lasting impression upon me.

As spring follows winter, as those who mourn will be comforted, so Meta's music followed after the agonies of war. In my heart, and years later in my head, her performance on that great pipe organ became a magnificent anthem. Those great hymns like Luther's *A mighty Fortress is our God* have a way of imprinting themselves indelibly in the memory. Watching the example of my mother, as both a musician and a refugee, I began to know that the compassion of our Lord flows like a river toward those in prison. Whether victims or perpetrators, His blood was shed for the sins of all. No cause or effect of human failure is beyond His reach.

Years later, as I began to read and understand the Bible for myself, I came across the words of Jesus as He quoted from Isaiah 61: *The Spirit of the Lord God is upon me; because the LORD hath anointed me to preach good tidings unto the meek; he hath sent me to bind up the brokenhearted, to proclaim liberty to the captives, and the opening of the prison to them that are bound; To proclaim the acceptable year of the LORD.* My heart immediately recognized this good news as a message from the very heart of God. The God my mother knew. The God I longed to know, even though I was a very naughty boy.

# Chapter 8

*Pöppendorf! Pöppendorf! Pöppendorf!*

This word puffed from the stack of the steam engine that pulled our train along the shining rails – or, so it seemed to me. Pöppendorf was the name of the prison camp to which we were traveling. It was the place where we would meet Father again.

I could not sit down. For weeks after learning that we would be reunited, I had seen myself running faster than all of my brothers – and of course, my sister, too – and leaping first into Father's arms. While playing soccer in the camp in Denmark, I had secretly tested myself. I was sure that I could outrun them all. I was the swiftest Bonnke in the clan. By my own measure, at least.

As we rolled through the green farmland of northern Germany, I stood at an open window. I could smell and taste the sulfur-tinged exhaust from the coal-fired engine. The train took a long curve and I strained to see past the white trail of steam and cinder smoke. I was determined to shout, "Pöppendorf! I see Pöppendorf!" at the very first opportunity. My insides tickled like a balloon full of butterflies. I fairly bounced on my tiptoes with anticipation.

When last I had seen my father I had been 4. Now, I was almost 9. Mother told me that he would be very proud of how I had grown. I couldn't wait to show him how tall and how fast I was, and to make him proud. There would be time enough for him to learn what a naughty boy I really was.

"Pöppendorf! I see Pöppendorf!" I shouted, pointing to a large platform surrounded by barbed wire. I felt so proud that I had seen it first.

The other children joined me at the windows as the train began to slow its chugging pace. Martin was now 15, Gerhard 13, Peter and Jürgen 11; I was 9, and Felicitas 7. The wheels beneath us began to scream with brake friction as we rolled slowly to a stop.

Meta remained calmly in her seat. She knew that the time for happiness would be the actual moment of seeing her husband. There were many, many procedures to endure first. We were still refugees. For some reason we could not simply be released even after being detained for so long. The international community had to inflict one last indignity upon us, forcing Hermann to re-enter a prison camp for our reunification. It must have been hard for him after enjoying recent years of freedom.

Father had been a prisoner of war, a captured soldier. When his military service records had been produced and examined by the British, they saw that he had never joined the Nazi party and he had been released. The irony for us was that, as civilians running for our lives to Denmark, we had been incarcerated for almost three years longer than he had. Such are the iniquities of war.

Finally, we were being transferred from Denmark to British control at Pöppendorf. There we would have all of our release paperwork processed. The officials needed to confirm that we were indeed the family from Stablack who had been separated from Hermann during the fall of Ostpreussen and that we were registered properly with all of the new West German government agencies.

In Denmark we had been released from the camp, issued new papers, and shipped across the Baltic straights to the port of Kiel. There, we had boarded this train under British guard and now arrived at Pöppendorf. It was the most famous, or perhaps the most infamous, *displaced persons camp* run by the British army.

In Pöppendorf, before we arrived, the British had confined thousands of Jews who had survived the Bergen Belsen death camp. These desperate people had tried to immigrate illegally to Palestine aboard a ship they called *The Exodus*. The British navy had turned the ship around and forced the illegals to return to Germany, confining them in Pöppendorf. The firestorm of world opinion that followed embarrassed the British so badly that they had hastened to release the Jews. This embarrassment had also accelerated something quite unanticipated. An event that would forever change the world – the formation of the Jewish state of Israel in Palestine.

Mother and Father had corresponded with excitement about this great event. Out of the horrors of the Holocaust, God seemed to be orchestrating the fulfillment of Old and New Testament prophecy. In many passages it had been written that He would gather His chosen people from the ends of the earth and establish them again in the land He had promised to Abraham, Isaac, and Jacob. We were seeing these words fulfilled in our time. It created a sense that ours would be the final generation before the coming of the Lord. I heard the words of Jesus quoted often, as recorded in Matthew, Mark, and Luke: *Verily I say unto you, This generation shall not pass away, till all be fulfilled.*[5]

A year after the formation of Israel, it was our turn to pass through the gates of Pöppendorf. Once there, our papers were duly stamped and noted, our belongings searched. We were led to the section of barracks where they told us Hermann Bonnke would be waiting for us.

As the final barbed-wire gates to his compound were unlocked, I knew my time had come. I broke free of the others and sprinted across the common yard, searching among the other men who were waiting for their loved ones. Some of them were playing soccer and board games, others standing in groups taking in the sun. I ran as fast as my legs would carry me until I reached the wall of a Quonset hut on the far side of the field. There I turned, sides heaving as I gasped for oxygen. I had not seen my father. I had somehow missed him. I looked frantically right and left.

"Reinhard!" I heard Mother call, a familiar exasperation in her voice. "Reinhard, get back here now!"

When I turned to look back from whence I had run, there was my father near the gate on his knees, hugging all of his children – minus one – the fastest Bonnke in the clan. My disappointment was quickly overwhelmed by delight. I raced back and leaped on the pile, becoming the tipping point that threw the whole bunch of them to the ground.

Hermann lay for a while among his children, laughing and crying all at the same time. We each hugged an arm, a leg, his torso, whatever we could find for ourselves. We hugged and laughed and cried with him, unable to use real words to say just how we had missed him and how glad we were to see him again and how we loved him and a dozen other things we had been saving up to say for almost four long years.

He laughed and hugged us back because he could not help himself. And he cried, perhaps because he remembered that he was the man his buddies had put on the last mine sweeper to leave Königsberg so he could be here now, with his wife and children, just like this. And those men had paid with their lives.

He hugged each of us then, one by one, and told us how proud he was of us, remarking at how we had grown. In the joy and energy of this family reunion I did not find an opportunity to show him just how fast I could run.

"You see, Reinhard," Mother was saying, "you don't listen. You always have your own ideas. If I had not been here you would still be wandering around looking for your father in all the wrong places!"

"I know, Mother. I'm sorry. I'm sorry."

# Chapter 9

"MARTIN, YOU HAVE GROWN SO TALL and smart. And Gerhard, you are not far behind him. Nearly as tall. I can hardly believe it is you. Walk on your hands for me, Gerhard. Let me see that trick again."

Gerhard quickly tilted himself up and made his way from one wall of the room to the other, walking on his hands, his legs above his torso. At the far wall he turned and returned to the place from which he had started. It was something he had taught himself to do while in the camp in Denmark. Father laughed and clapped.

When I tried to do it, I fell awkwardly to one side. No matter how many times I tried to balance, I fell. But for Gerhard it seemed as easy as walking upright.

"Gerhard is the athlete of this family," Father said. "Martin, you will soon be old enough to join the military, but you are named Martin for good reason. You will preach the gospel like Martin Luther one day." Father went on joking with us and telling us what he felt we should become one day.

Night after night, eight Bonnkes were stuck in the single room Father had found after the war. We shared the house with several other families. Even worse, each night Father seemed stuck on the same topic. The happiness of our homecoming seemed to be sucked from the room as he talked about World War II.

"We fought for our country, which is a noble ideal, but our country had been taken over by Hitler and the Nazis. They took the greatest military the world has ever seen, and they wasted it for ego and insanity. They betrayed everything Germany stood for, and it is no wonder the world hates us. In the end, the Soviets overran us, and now an Iron Curtain divides Germany into East and West. It divides Berlin and most of Europe. This is what our war accomplished, boys. Your Grandfather August was killed by the Soviets when they crushed East Prussia."

"Now Herman," Mother cautioned, "do the children need to hear this?"

"My boys will soon be old enough to become soldiers. Boys naturally dream of glory like I did. They need to know the truth. When the Soviets overran Trunz they were filled with vengeance. Everyone ran in panic. Your Grandfather August was too old to keep up, and the soldiers kicked him and hit him again and again as he tried to take your grandmother to a train station. Grandmother Marie was beside herself. She could not make them stop. They did it just for sport, for vengeance. Still, Grandpa made it with her onto the train where there was hardly room to stand.

"As the train pulled from the station and reached full speed, he died from his injuries and fell to the floor. The passengers had no tolerance for a dead person on that train. Even our own Prussian people had become animals in the aftermath of the war. Some of them held Mother back as the others threw his body from the window of the train. This is how my dear father ended his days on earth. And now you can see what I mean when I tell you, war is hell!"

We were stunned to silence and deeply saddened. Felicitas was crying.

"Why didn't God protect Grandfather?" Martin asked somberly. "If He protected us, why didn't He protect him?"

It took a moment for Father to find his reply. "That is a very hard question, Son. I have wondered that myself. But for questions like this there will be no answers until we are on the other side and can ask God face to face."

For Martin, this answer was not satisfying. He remained deeply troubled. My other brothers seemed to follow his cue. As for me, I embraced my father's answer wholeheartedly. It became my own. One might say it was because I was merely ten years old and my mind was less aware of the full tragedy involved. Perhaps so, but I will add that a great blessing followed my childlike faith. A blessing that has returned dividends for the rest of my life.

Twelve members of our family had been marvelously preserved through the fall of East Prussia. But for a reason none can explain, the patriarch of the clan, my spiritual ancestor, August Bonnke was lost. To magnify one tragic loss above twelve miracles of preservation would seem to tarnish the joy and meaning of my relationship to God. By embracing my father's faithful answer I could remain open and trusting toward a God who I believed had our very best interests at heart in spite of the things we could not understand.

I have never improved on my father's answer. To this day, the unanswerable questions I leave in God's capable and loving hands.

EVERY EVENING IN GLÜCKSTADT we were jammed into that one room to sleep for the night. The Bonnke children shared blankets on the floor arranged around the one bed reserved for Mother and Father. We were crowded but happy to be together. At least we were out of the prison camp and breathing free air at last.

Glückstadt was a small port town near the mouth of the Elbe River. The river emptied northward from the tip of Germany into the North Sea. Its estuary was situated just west of the great penin-sula that connected Germany to the main land mass of Denmark.

Arrival in Glückstadt

In fact, our city, whose seal depicted "Lady Luck," had been founded in 1617 as the main trade center for the region. Fifty years before my family moved there, processed meat was shipped regularly from Glückstadt to America. This had kept the port viable for decades. But in the bigger picture the town had "run out of luck" in direct competition with a huge trading center upriver. The little burg now had an inferiority complex. Especially as it compared itself to Hamburg, the city of 1,500,000 that dominated the region. Ships from the port of Hamburg churned to and from the North Sea every day, passing the docks at Glückstadt without a pause. Only a few local fishing vessels were ever tied there.

Perhaps I was especially vulnerable to the inferiority of Glückstadt. I began to feel it within myself. Not just because of the small city in which I lived and the painful poverty of my refugee family, and the fact that I was a very naughty boy – but for other reasons, too.

OUR NEW LIFE IN GLÜCKSTADT held disappointments for me. First among them was my performance in school. As the Bonnke children entered the regular German school system, we discovered just how far behind we had fallen in the Denmark camps. Much of the energy I would rather have invested in playing childhood games now had to be focused on extra hours of study to make up for lost time.

Even so, I did not seem to overcome this setback as quickly and successfully as my older brothers did. They were energetic students. At the homework table they wrangled about the nuances of algebra, trigonometry, and calculus. They debated history and social sciences, biology and physics. And their improving grades reflected their efforts. Soon they won high praises from Mother and Father.

It was all endlessly Greek to me. My brothers seemed to soar academically while I plodded like an earthbound farmer sowing academic seeds that would not bear fruit for many seasons to come. Every class was hard work for me, but there was one class I detested above all others – English.

"Mother, Father, why should I have to learn English? I am German."

They tried to tell me that it wasn't for me to question why. It was a required course in all of Germany now. I had to do it, and I would be held accountable to do it well, like my older brothers.

Every day in school the teacher would dictate words in English. We obtained a standard workbook from the local bookstore and filled in the dictation on blank pages. When the book was filled we were given a final test. Words were placed on the blackboard that we were to translate and write on our final page.

On the day of the test I wrote my answers in anger. In truth, I knew that I was guessing. I simply did not know the rules of the English language. So I wrote out of frustration and turned in my test before any other student in the room had finished. I then made a show of handing in my booklet to the teacher before any of the others and being allowed to go out and play on the playground. What a shallow victory, doomed to backfire and make things worse.

The next day I was not surprised to see my workbook filled with red marks. The teacher's commentary on my work was not complimentary. Even though I knew it was coming, I was crushed.

As I placed that book in my bag and began to walk home, I knew that Mother and Father would see it and I would have to answer for my failure. The more I walked the heavier that bag became. Finally, the weight of it slowed me to stop in front of the Glückstadt bookstore. That's when a wonderful thought came to me. I could buy a new workbook using my lunch money. I could exchange it for the old one. I would not have to answer to Mom, Dad, and my brothers for my mistakes. I took the workbook filled with the accusing red marks and threw it into a trash barrel. In this way, I became foolish like Adam in the Garden of Eden, using a fig leaf to cover the awful truth.

Every thought in my head about school hurt. It weighed on me like a heavy yoke. I could not succeed and I could not escape. Now my sinful whitewash made the burden of it seem even heavier.

Adding to the load, I soon discovered the intense scorn that Lutheran school children had for Pentecostal children. On a typical Sunday, our father would be gone before sunup on his bicycle, traveling to minister in Krempe. We could not afford another bicycle, so none of us went with him. We attended the local Pentecostal congregation.

The Pentecostal believers in Glückstadt met in a small school room behind the Lutheran church. When we were seen leaving our humble meetings in the shadow of the great Lutheran steeple, the news quickly spread that the Bonnkes were tongues talkers. The teasing began. And it was more than teasing. Pentecostals were seen as primitive people, religious Neanderthals, a knuckle-dragging sect that only existed because of its ignorance. This gave the Lutheran children license to call us every name in the book.

As a boy I had no real argument to make in our favor. In fact, our faith did not spring from a seminary textbook, a baptism, a catechism, or a confirmation ceremony. Rather, both salvation and the baptism of the Holy Spirit came from a direct and powerful encounter with God. By that experience the Word of God became alive for us, and we were guided to the truth of Scripture through our spiritual relationship, rather than by the study of theology, or church history, or religious traditions.

Our kind of religion bypassed all that the Lutherans seemed to hold dear, and we were punished for it. We were considered unworthy of social standing. I remember how all of our women wore plain clothes and no jewelry and they never cut their hair, wearing it in an unstylish bun at the back of their heads. This was done as part of the holiness heritage that had been the cradle of Pentecostals worldwide. Holiness standards demanded that believers look and talk and act differently from the rest of the world as a testimony to the true nature of their faith. So, in the little town with an inferiority complex, we Pentecostals were below the bottom feeders. We were quite visible and gave the local residents something to look down upon.

My older brothers simply rose above it. They continued to excel in school winning praises from their teachers. Accusations of Pentecostal ignorance simply would not stick to them.

While they resented the teasing from their classmates, in their hearts they began to deal with even more difficult tensions. Pentecostal practice and the claims of education went to war in their souls. This meant that at church they might betray their academic beliefs under the influence of a guilt-inducing sermon. Then again, at school they might betray their Pentecostal faith when it seemed to fall short of the rational arguments of science.

This was a dilemma I came to understand much later in life because I did not share it at the time. Anything I encountered at school or from classmates or in textbooks that went contrary to my Pentecostal heritage was discarded without serious consideration. I felt the pain of rejection keenly, but in those days I never responded to it by considering that anything about Pentecostalism could be wrong at all.

FATHER'S CONGREGATION IN KREMPE began to grow, but they were still a group of poor refugee families who could leave little in an offering plate.

It seems the new chancellor of West Germany, Konrad Adenauer, had passed a law allowing soldiers of the Reichswehr to retire early and receive a pension for life. At the age of 44, my father had taken advantage of that law, believing that was the provision of God to fund his ministry in Krempe.

Mother thought it all sounded too good to be true. She did not trust the government to follow through on its promise to pay the pension. How would they raise enough taxes to support such a thing after the war?

On a day I shall never forget, the postman arrived with exceedingly good news. He handed her a government envelope containing the first pension check for 799 deutschmarks. She ripped it open, shouting praises to God. She danced around the room and insisted on giving the postman two deutschmarks as a tip. I had never seen such a display of generosity in my life.

Almost immediately, she sat down and wrote a postcard addressed to her parents, Ernst and Minna, now living in New Ulm. She was very eager to announce the good news. Tensions between the Bonnkes and the Schefflers over Father's choice to enter the full-time ministry had grown in recent months. Objections centered on the lack of a reliable income to support a family with six children. Now, that objection was gone. We would be able to move from the one room that we shared.

Mother reassured her parents that regardless of the amount of salary the little church in Krempe could pay their pastor; Hermann would be supported for the rest of his life because of his long-standing service in the Reichswehr. Something that had been a heavy burden for him had been transformed into a blessing. Mother gave all the glory for this benefit to God.

As a result, something was introduced into the Bonnke household with which I had little prior knowledge. Money! And soon, to my ten-year-old mind, money became nearly synonymous with chocolate.

This money-for-chocolate relationship began when I accompanied Mother to do her shopping one day. I saw her take a portion of Father's money from her purse to pay for meat, bread, vegetables, dish and laundry soap, and a small amount of chocolate candy. The money, it seemed to me, was like the ration coupons we had used in the camp in Denmark, except that the choices in Denmark had never included chocolate.

Mother brought all the groceries home and cooked them for supper. Then for dessert, with a glow on her face, she carefully rationed a portion of chocolate candy to each of her six children. This was like getting Christmas in July! Such luxuries had simply never been afforded since we had left our home in Stablack.

As I bit into the chocolate I experienced a revelation. What marvelous sensation was this? My taste buds had never been so turned on. The flavor went all over me with a sense of delicious well-being. Life seemed to consist of many things that were difficult and dull and tedious, like school and homework and chores. But now there was chocolate. I simply needed to have money to have more of it.

The solution became quite clear to me. Mother had plenty of money in her purse. Money was now readily available to our family. And it was free. She had given away two deutschmarks to the postman, hadn't she? A portion of chocolate would cost even less. She would not miss such a small portion of money from her purse.

Though I was merely an average student, I immediately became motivated to achieve at math. Well, at least the kind of math necessary to calculate the proper amount of deutschmarks necessary to buy an individual portion of candy. Once I had this figured out, all I had to do was wait until Mother had abandoned her purse in the bedroom and retrieve the exact amount from her change wallet. A little here, a little there.

Once, twice, three times over the next several weeks I managed to find the right amount of change. Just a few pennies. It resulted in a trip downtown to obtain the pure joy of a very intense and personal chocolate experience. Oh, how I savored it! And how I was filled with a sense of being wealthy. And finally, the day came when I took a full deutchmark from her purse.

In my heart I knew I was wrong. At the store, as I finished my chocolate pleasure, I began to feel a sense of guilt gnawing at my insides. I walked from that place, and I made a guilt-born vow: "One day I will repay Momma 100 deutschmarks to make up for the money I stole. That is what I will do."

How do mothers do it? How do they know? Where do they learn the exquisite art of timing? My hand was well into her purse when I heard her voice behind me in the gloom of the bedroom.

"Reinhard, what are you doing?"

I withdrew my hand as if a mousetrap had just snapped on my fingers. "Nothing, Mother. Nothing."

This was technically not a lie since I had emerged from her purse with nothing in my hand. Somehow, however, I knew that what I had been doing was much more than nothing, and it was very, very wrong, and I was about to get the hiding of my life. Which I positively deserved. I was hopelessly naughty.

Mother turned the light on in the room. She stood there thoughtfully for a long moment deciding how she would handle my transgression. Then slowly and deliberately, she came to sit on the bed. Every moment of this process was pure torture.

Opening her purse she looked inside. The change wallet was open.

"Reinhard, have you been stealing money from my wallet?"

"No, Momma. I don't know what the others have been doing with it." I wanted to pass the blame onto my brothers.

Patting the bed beside her, she indicated that she wanted me to sit down. I did.

"Look at me, Reinhard."

This was much worse than a hiding. I looked into the eyes of the woman I most loved and respected in the world and knew I had betrayed her. My pulse raced. It pounded in my temples, fueled by the foul vinegar of shame.

"Reinhard, you know that you have disappointed me again."

"Yes, Mother. I know."

"I have been missing money from my wallet before. Have you done this before?"

It took just a bit of mental reviewing to properly get this reply to come out of my mouth. I heaved a sigh. "Yes, Mother."

"I am so disappointed. But now, I am even more worried. It is one thing to misbehave, but it is another to be a sinner. Do you know that what you have done is a sin before God? It's called stealing."

Actually, I hadn't thought of it quite as stealing. I had seen it as a way of getting – well, sort of "sneaking" chocolate. But now that she mentioned it, there was no denying that what I had done should be called stealing. I had taken her money. Purely and simply. I nodded.

"Thou shalt not steal. It is one of the Ten Commandments."

I nodded again. I had memorized the Ten Commandments. I knew them by heart.

"When we break God's law, it is sin, Reinhard. You are a sinner, and I am worried about you because sinners go to hell for all eternity."

The pain of my transgression grew heavy indeed.

"Do you know this is why Christ died on the cross?"

I had never thought of His death as applying strictly to me. In church and in family devotions when we had heard about it, I had always thought of the sins of the whole world as causing the death of God's Son. Suddenly, my own sins were before me, slashing like a cat-o'-nine-tails into the flesh of the Lamb of God. The taste of stolen chocolate turned completely foul in my memory. It seemed to cost so much more than money now. I couldn't calculate the price. The death of God's Son. I began to cry.

"Jesus died to save sinners, Reinhard. He died so you would not have to go to hell for your sins. Would you like to receive Jesus as your Savior and be forgiven?"

"Oh yes, Momma, I would." In truth, I felt the awful reality of being lost. This was more than a life lesson. It was an eternal life lesson. One that marked me for the rest of my life and ministry. Only the Holy Spirit can accomplish this knowledge in the heart of a sinner. I did not want anything in my life ever again that cost God the death of His Son. Nothing! I wanted to please Him in every way. And I wanted to be forgiven.

I repeated a prayer after her, acknowledging that I was a sinner and accepting Jesus as my Savior. When we finished, she hugged me. It was a birthday hug and more. It was my new birthday. I felt as if a thousand pounds had been lifted from my shoulders. It was the last time in my life that I ever stole anything.

"There is something else, Reinhard. The Bible says that if you believe in your heart and confess the Lord Jesus with your mouth you will be saved. Do you believe that you have been saved?"

"Yes, Mother, I do."

"If you have believed it then you need to confess it. Sunday, when we are at church, I want you to stand up and confess to the other believers what happened here today. That will be *confessing with your mouth the Lord Jesus*. Will you do that?"

I was happy to say yes. And I did it. The people of the congregation welcomed me as a new member of the body of Christ that Sunday morning.

When I confessed the Lord Jesus, something further happened in me. I knew that I belonged to the Pentecostal Church. It was no longer just the church of my father and mother. It was now my church, too. They had welcomed me into the family of God. They were now my brothers and sisters. I felt affection for them. I began to love those who loved them and despise those who despised them. Needless to say, I had even less regard for the Lutherans in Glückstadt thereafter.

Soon we moved into post-war public housing. It was something called a Town Council Apartment. At last we had a space we did not have to share with other families. We had more than one bedroom, with a kitchen and bathroom of our own. Father's pension had made that possible and Mother was highly motivated to once again create a home that reflected her personality.

A harmonium was obtained. Musical instruments and lessons began for each of us. I learned to play the guitar and sing. I was told that I had a wonderful singing voice as a lad. We became the musical Bonnke household again, as we had once been in Stablack, singing and playing hymns of praise to the Lord.

I remember time after time, during this period, Mother would suspect money was missing from her purse again. The first place she came to inquire was to me.

"Reinhard, did you steal money from my purse again?"

"No, Mother, I swear I did not steal anything."

"There is money missing. You have been a thief. Do not lie to me. Did you steal money again from my purse?"

My eyes were flashing as I replied, "No, Mother. I did not steal money from your purse."

She looked deeply at me and lowered her tone of voice. "No, I can see by your eyes that you did not steal it."

Even so, the burden of my original sin haunted my innocence. I could never walk away from Mother feeling that she would not again suspect me of stealing. Sin had begotten the death of trust between us. How it pained me!

But even a sinful boy finds moments of reprieve. One Sunday, another boy my age at church invited me to explore the woods behind town. He said that he had seen a mother deer with twin fawns out there, and he might be able to find them again. We got permission from our parents and spent an hour following game trails without seeing anything more than tracks in the mud.

The bees were busy pollinating flowers, and the tall grass was buzzing with insects in the warm sun. As we walked and talked we forgot about the deer. We both decided that when we grew up we wanted to be preachers. The idea occurred to us to practice our preaching skills on the surrounding trees.

This became a regular Saturday activity for a number of weeks. We even took a Bible with us so that we could properly read our text before beginning a sermon. As time went by, however, I began to notice that my friend Hubert was a much better orator than me. His voice was stronger and his sermons more eloquent. Though I loved Jesus with all my heart, I found it difficult to express my heart in words that matched his.

This was a source of discomfort for me. After being born again I thought that I should be able to do better than this. Again, I felt inadequate. Deep inside I suspected that God knew what a troublemaker I was for my mother. In my immaturity I felt that somehow my salvation must not be as genuine as my friend's.

THOUGH SHE HAD MARRIED the Preaching Major, and attended a Pentecostal church, Mother too, felt inadequate. She had never received the baptism of the Holy Spirit with speaking in tongues. She had wanted to know God in this way but had not found it happening no matter how she prayed. Discussions about it between her and Father were a normal part of our family experience. Now that Father was a Pentecostal preacher, she felt the need for the experience even more.

I remember Mother reading Scripture on the subject. In the book of Acts it described that the people heard the sound of a rushing mighty wind, then tongues of fire descended on the heads of all those in the room and they began to speak with other tongues. Somehow this image of the tongues of fire jumped out at me.

I read the scripture with her, and I could almost see the flames in the Upper Room. God blessed His people with fire. I wanted my mother to have this experience.

"Mother, did the fire hurt the people? Did it burn on their heads?"

She heaved an exasperated sigh. "No, Reinhard. It was like the burning bush Moses saw. The fire of God did not burn up the bush. It's not like a normal fire."

"What kind of fire is it?"

"I think it was a signal fire. It was a sign to the Jewish people in Jerusalem to say that the Day of Pentecost had been finally fulfilled."

"Will you have a flame of fire on your head when you are baptized with the Holy Ghost?"

"No, Reinhard. I don't think so. The Bible says that we will receive power when the Holy Spirit comes upon us to be witnesses to the ends of the earth. With just human strength it is impossible to do what God commands. His Word says it is *not by might, nor by power, but by my spirit, saith the LORD.*[6] So when the Holy Spirit comes upon you, you will receive power to preach."

"I hope you will have the fire on your head, too," I said, "just like in the Bible."

In my heart I began to ponder the idea that what I needed, like my mother, was the baptism of the Holy Ghost. Perhaps this was the power that would make me able to express the gospel that so dominated my heart.

NOT LONG AFTER THIS CONVERSATION I attended a life-changing Sunday service. On this particular day, a husband and wife missionary team had been invited to speak. I do not remember much about them because as they were speaking the Spirit of God spoke to me in my heart. It was as if He said very clearly, "Reinhard, one day you will preach My gospel in Africa."

Until this moment I had been a boy born in Germany with very little exposure to the larger world. My mental picture of the continents was not well-schooled. But in my heart it was as if Africa had been suddenly written there.

When we are born again it is like this. Our names are written in heaven, and our eternal destiny is sealed there. But we can also receive an earthly destiny from our heavenly Father. That is what I received as a mere boy at ten years of age.

I have often wondered if the country of Africa had been suggested to my mind by those missionaries who spoke that morning. Germany had a historic presence in Africa during the colonial era. I had certainly heard of it, but nothing had been made personal to me concerning the Dark Continent. Perhaps this couple had been working in Africa and had shown pictures. I frankly do not remember. And little does it matter. What matters is that I heard God speak in my heart so clearly.

This was something I simply had to share with Father. I could hardly wait until he pedaled in from Krempe that day. I waited for him on the street. As I sat there, I knew he would understand the voice of God I had heard inside. He also had heard from God. I recalled that Jesus had even visited him while in the prison camp when he had decided to become a minister. Surely my father would become as excited as I was over my call to Africa, and he would confirm this great day in my life. When I saw him I raced to meet him.

"Father, Father, God spoke to me in church today and said I must preach the gospel in Africa!" I must have appeared to him like a bouncing puppy yapping out my excitement.

He did not seem to understand. He dismounted from his bicycle and asked me to repeat it. Then he looked at me with a puzzled and somber expression. "Your brother Martin will be my heir, Reinhard. He will be the preacher of the gospel in this family."

It was like a shower of cold water. "But Father, God has called me to preach in Africa."

He scowled. "How do you know that God has called you?"

Disappointment darkened my heart. His tone of voice spoke louder than his words. It told me he was in deep doubt about my claim. I thought he would understand how important it was that I had heard directly from God.

My mind searched for a way to explain to him the reality of it. What evidence did I have? Jesus had not visited me personally. Nor had I selected a scripture from a box of promises like Mother when she received a word from God about our crossing from Danzig to Copenhagen. Nor did I hear an audible voice. All I had was the evidence of my heart, and I was not eloquent enough to put it into words to please him.

On this day I began to understand that I had two fathers. An earthly father and a heavenly Father. Until that moment, I had assumed they spoke with one voice. After all, my father was a man of God. A minister of the gospel. Jesus had appeared to him in person. It was nearly crushing for me to realize that God might speak to me and my earthly father would not know it. But it happened that way.

In the months that followed I brought it up again and again. Each time, my father responded in the same way. He doubted me. He quizzed me about how I could know the voice of God. Each time I had to deal with my deep disappointment, and a gulf began to grow between us.

Though today I understand his caution, back then it was as if my father and I knew a different God. In reality we each had a relationship with the same God. A relationship that was as unique as our individual fingerprints. This is, of course, how God delights to relate to each of us. The very hairs of our head are numbered. He reads the thoughts and intentions of our hearts perfectly and designs our paths accordingly. Jesus pointed this out to Peter, who had asked, "What about John?" Jesus replied, ... *what is that to thee? Follow thou me.*[7] The steps my father took in his journey with the Savior would not be my steps. God does not make spiritual clones; He raises up sons and daughters.

Looking back, I now see what an important lesson this was for me. Above all, we are called to hear and obey the still small voice of our heavenly Father communicated to our hearts by the Holy Ghost. But if other voices are placed above that voice we may come to doubt the very voice of God Himself, even after we have heard Him clearly.

Jesus taught, *My sheep hear my voice, and I know them, and they follow me.*[8] At ten years of age, God was giving me voice-recognition lessons. More than I knew, God was testing to see if I would follow His voice above all others. In this case the voice of my own father seemed to contradict the voice in my heart. Jesus said, *He that loveth father or mother more than me is not worthy of me.*[9] Though I was too young to make that kind of choice consciously, I did make it in my heart. My father's doubts did not turn me away. The knowledge that God had called me to Africa at the tender age of ten has never left me.

THE PENTECOSTAL CHURCH IN GLÜCKSTADT announced that a special minister would visit the fellowship. He would hold a "seekers" meeting. This was a special meeting for those desiring to receive the baptism of the Holy Spirit.

Mother announced that she would go with Father. I wanted to go too, but they would rather that all the children stay at home. Mother already felt pressure enough. It was humbling and perhaps embarrassing for her to admit to the entire congregation that the wife of the Pentecostal preacher at Krempe had never known the experience for which the movement was named.

"I will pray that you receive the Holy Spirit with the flame of fire on your head," I said.

At the meeting the special speaker taught from the Scriptures about the baptism with speaking in tongues. Then he invited those who were seeking to come forward to have hands laid upon them. Mother went forward. She received their prayers. Nothing happened.

When she arrived home I ran to her.

"Mother, did you receive the gift and the flame of fire on your head?"

"No, Reinhard. I'm sorry. I prayed but I didn't seem to receive anything."

I could see that she felt very disappointed, and I felt that I had made it even worse by asking about the flame of fire. No one could console her, and we all went to bed.

Perhaps like the disciples in Gethsemane, I slept too soundly when I should have remained alert. So soundly did I sleep that I did not hear the sound of a rushing mighty wind as it hit the upstairs bedroom an hour later.

Once Mother had relaxed in bed, the false religious pressures she had felt at church melted away. Her self-consciousness and disappointment vanished. She reflected the words of Jesus; *If ye then, being evil, know how to give good gifts unto your children: how much more shall your heavenly Father give the Holy Spirit to them that ask him?* [10]

She had asked God for His Holy Spirit but had been so pressured and distraught by her concerns that she had not been able to see the gift she had been freely given. The baptism of the Holy Spirit was not an experience acquired by religious diligence. It was not so much about seeking as it was about receiving. It was a gift made available by a loving heavenly Father, and it was simply hers for the asking. Her faith to receive had been all mixed up with her own expectations, and those of Father, and those of the congregation.

Suddenly she felt herself falling into the loving arms of her Lord. Flooded with waves of divine love, another language began to pour from her mouth like a fountain. She wept and praised God and spoke in tongues for hours, completely exhilarated by the experience.

My brothers woke up and heard the commotion. I slept soundly through it all.

In the early morning hours, Mother was due to go to Hamburg on church business. She left before any of us children had awakened. On the breakfast table we found a note: *Dear children, last night Jesus baptized me with the Holy Spirit. Mother.*

When I read it I was dumbfounded. How had I missed it? All day I could hardly contain myself waiting to see her. I wondered again about the flame of fire.

When I saw Mother approaching on the street that evening I ran to meet her. The closer I got the more astonished I became. My mother was glowing. Her eyes sparkled. Her step was like the step of a young girl. She ran to me and swept me up in her arms, and it was not even my birthday. I could feel the love pouring from her like I had never felt it. It made me want to laugh and cry. Something had radically changed my mother. I no longer needed to see a flame of fire to believe she had received the real thing. Above all, I knew that I wanted to have what she had.

# Chapter 10

NEXT TO LAST. That was my place in the Bonnke lineup. Not last, which would have brought some measure of distinction, but *next* to last. I must have been easily overlooked in that dynamic mix of children.

Martin led the way – so talented, sensitive, bright, and the designated heir to The Preaching Elder. Gerhard followed close behind, adding his athletic prowess to the picture. Jürgen and Peter were highly remarkable because they were a set of twins. I was followed by Felicitas, the only daughter in the Bonnke family and the apple of her daddy's eye. Except for my reputation for getting into trouble, I think I must have fallen through the cracks.

"Oh yes, where is Reinhard? We also have a son named Reinhard. Is he here somewhere? Reinhard? Where are you?"

I would be presented to family guests as an afterthought.

As guests often do, they would ask, "Well, Reinhard, you seem like a fine young boy. What are you going to be when you grow up?"

"I'm going to be a missionary to Africa," I said without hesitation. In this, I distinguished myself. No other Bonnke child claimed to be called to Africa.

Father would hear this and chuckle, winking at his guests. "Children go through stages you know. They usually grow out of it."

This hurt me. I wanted my calling to be taken seriously. I took it very seriously. It was the only thing that gave purpose to my rather unremarkable life. Why would my father not help me move in that direction?

My older brothers took this signal from Father as permission to pile on with their own endless ridicule. They would snicker behind their hands and shake their heads at me as if I was an alien. *Reinhard the missionary.*

This was a difficult period for me. In German there is a word for how I felt: *null*. It is defined by the synonyms zero, naught, nil. In many ways I felt I was a zero, nonexistent, like I didn't really matter. Adding evidence to that feeling was that I was from a poor family, a social outcast, struggling in school, and the least child of the Bonnke clan. In the mirror of my own mind, Reinhard was not just a dull boy, he was *null*. Sometimes my own reflection simply disappeared.

I began to mention to my father how I needed the baptism of the Holy Spirit in order to have the power to preach the gospel in Africa. He did not deny that the Spirit baptism with speaking in tongues was for everyone. But he did not lead me to the experience. He considered me too young and immature. "Just because you are a boy with a mind of his own does not mean that you are ready to receive the Spirit baptism."

"Father," I asked one day, "since you do not believe that I have a real call from God, how do you know when you have a real one? How does it feel?"

I think he was surprised by my question. He thought for a while then he said, "Son, when you have a real call from God then you will know it. You will know it deep in your heart. You will know, and it cannot be shaken."

Every word that he said rang true in my heart, confirming my call from God. To me it did not seem to be just another example of having a mind of my own. "Father, I know that I know that I have a real call from God," I said.

The look on his face told me he was not comfortable to hear such confidence coming from the mouth of a child. Perhaps this was true because of his childhood. He had longed for military glory, and he deeply regretted the decision it had led him to make as a 17-year-old. In my case, however, the Spirit of God was leading me in the direction of divine service. My father had not known such a thing as a boy.

I am happy to add that many years later when he visited me in Africa, this conversation between us about my calling became one of his favorite stories to tell from the pulpit. His eyes would shine with tears as he confessed with great pride how wrong he had been in his judgment of me as a ten-year-old boy.

IN LATE 1950 and early 1951, I recall how Mother and Father shared stories of the weekly Pentecostal prayer meetings in Glückstadt. It seems the little group of believers were having visions, prophecies, words of knowledge, and other gifts of the Spirit manifested as they waited before the Lord. My heart thrilled as I overheard these stories, and I wanted to be among the people of God at every opportunity. But prayer meetings were considered inappropriate for children.

During my eleventh year, I began to ask Mother if I could go to the Friday night prayer meeting with her. Again and again, she denied my request.

In my heart I was sure I was being denied because I was unworthy. All the years of misbehavior and self-will had disqualified me to be in the presence of God's people. To make up for it I would do my chores all week and even do extra chores on Friday, trying to make her change her mind. Still she said no. Week after week it went on like this. I grew more disappointed, blaming myself for all of it. Finally, one day she said no, and I could not hide my pain. Tears spilled from my eyes.

Mother was taken aback. She sat down, astonished. She gazed at me as if she had not seen me before.

"What is this I am seeing?" she asked. "A boy of eleven who wants to attend prayer meetings so badly that he sheds tears? Your heart must be ready to be part of these things. I sense the Lord telling me I must change my answer to yes."

I leapt up and hugged her. "Thank you, Mother. I do want to go more than anything."

From that day, I began to attend every church service. Not just on Sunday but every service during the week. If the church was in session, I was there. In each service where there was singing, Mother saw to it that I had my guitar and could lend my voice to the songs of praise to God.

One weekday evening at the end of the prayer meeting, I was standing beside Mother and Father ready to be dismissed. The pastor made an announcement that Grandma Bauszuss, an elderly lady in the congregation, had experienced a vision. On his invitation, she stood and related her vision to the members of our little group.

"I saw a crowd of black people," she said. "A very large crowd. They were gathered in a semicircle around a little boy with a big loaf of bread. He was breaking the bread and giving it to the people, and as he did, the loaf of bread continued to increase." Then she turned to me and pointed. "The little boy that I saw was this one."

I cannot adequately tell you what happens inside a boy when something like this occurs. It was like pouring hot oil over my head, anointing me to see the vision from God confirmed and fulfilled in my life. Yet in that hour, neither I, nor Father nor Mother, could even faintly imagine just how powerfully this vision would eventually play out. We could only be thrilled with anticipation and wonder at this unexpected manifestation of a spiritual gift.

My father looked at me incredulously. I think for the first time he began to get a glimmer that perhaps I had actually heard from God. But I could tell that he still doubted. And as time went by it became quite clear that his hopes were still pinned on Martin to be the gospel preacher in our family. I'm sure that my continuing misbehavior helped move his thoughts in that direction.

ONE FINE SPRING DAY I accompanied Mother to the grocery store. As we entered, something in the window caught my eye. It was a colorful poster announcing the coming of a circus. I told Mother that I would remain outside as she shopped. When she had finished I would carry home the groceries she had bought. This gave me time to study the fascinating poster in the window more closely.

It featured a number of African lions jumping through hoops. There were trained stallions, bears, monkeys, and a wonderful circus elephant. A troop of acrobats, clowns, and a flying trapeze were also featured. At the bottom of the poster the dates for the circus were posted. I studied them. A circus train was shown in miniature, with an illustration of the trained elephant helping to erect the main pole of the tent. How I wanted to see that. It just fascinated me. The big top would be set up in a field at the edge of town. My blood raced at the thought of all of these wonders.

"Reinhard, what are you doing?" There was a familiar tone of disapproval in Mother's voice. I had lost track of time. She had finished shopping and was ready to head home with her bags of groceries.

"Look, Mother," I said excitedly, "a circus is coming. Can we go?"

"What? You are a boy who has been born again and you ask me that? Can't you see that this is a sinful activity? Absolutely not! Oh, Reinhard, when will I stop being disappointed with you?"

"Mother, the lions jump through the hoops and the stallions walk on their hind legs and the monkeys and elephants do tricks. Is that sinful?"

She walked over to look at the poster. Her face turned crimson. She turned to me with a look of near rage. "Have you been out here all this time looking at those nearly naked women on the trapeze?"

Honestly, I had hardly given them any notice. "No, Mother. No. It was the other things – the animals I was looking at."

Mother stuffed the grocery bags into my arms. "The circus is nothing but an excuse for women to flaunt their bodies and arouse sinful passions in men. Take these groceries and get your eyes off of that poster. I ought to give you a good hiding right here on the spot."

"I wasn't looking at the women, Mother. I was looking at the animals, I swear."

She gasped and stopped dead in her tracks. "You swear? You swear? Swearing is a sin. Do you see how one sin leads to another? My son is swearing."

"I didn't mean to swear, Mother, I'm sorry. But I wasn't looking at the women. I was looking at the animals. Are the circus animals sinful too? Are they?"

She sighed deeply. "There is nothing wrong with the animals, Reinhard. They are God's innocent creatures, except they have been made part of that god-less circus. That circus has spiritists, Gypsy fortune-tellers, palm readers, and all sorts of evil influences. No one from the Pentecostal church had better be caught dead there, I can tell you that for sure."

We walked on in silence for a while as she became calm and serious. "Rein-hard, how would you feel being at that circus when Jesus came? Do you think you would just rise to meet the Lord in the air while you are watching scantily clad women swinging through the air like that? Oh, dear Jesus, how could you go to an activity like that and think that you could be ready to meet our Lord? You can't live with one foot in the church and the other in the world, Son. Not if you want to be part of God's spotless bride. No you can't. The Bible says be hot or cold. *If you're lukewarm God will spit you out of His mouth.*[11] I had such high hopes when you gave your heart to the Lord, but now I worry that your heart is being led astray."

I walked the rest of the way without another word. All that she said raised new fears in my heart. I did not want to be led astray, but she had said that the animals were not sinful. That was the one bright spot in her exhortation. They were innocent creatures of God, she had said. I knew that was true in my heart, and I focused my mind on it. It made me feel better to think that I had not been attracted to the wrong thing, at least. I knew nothing about Gypsy acrobats and scantily clad fortune-tellers. They did sound evil, and I would cer-tainly avoid them. But the wonder of wild animals from Africa being trained to jump through hoops and perform at the circus seemed totally innocent and acceptable. My imagination ran wild as we continued to walk.

The day the circus train arrived in town I managed to get away to watch them. Tigers, lions, and bears paced in their railroad cages at the station. This was the closest I had ever been to an exotic wild animal. The sight of them at such close quarters filled me with wonder. I walked along the tracks looking at each of them.

The animal trainers used the stallions and the elephant to haul the big tent and its trappings out of a boxcar and into the field at the edge of town. I followed them, in awe at the process. The power of the elephant was amazing as he pushed the huge tent pole into place in the center of the field. Afterward, the crew stopped to eat a sandwich. The elephant trainer put a small cotton rope around the elephant's leg and tethered him to a tent stake. This amazed me. I knew the powerful elephant could pull that stake out of the ground without even trying. How could the trainer trust that he would not bolt for his freedom as soon as his back was turned?

I came close enough to engage him in conversation. He seemed to be a very nice man, and he explained how this particular elephant had come from the Hagenbeck Zoo in Hamburg. This was the most famous elephant training zoo in the world, he said, and it had been rebuilt by the Hagenbeck family after being bombed during the war. The new zoo, he said, was the best in the world. He recommended that I see it one day.

"Why doesn't the elephant pull the stake out of the ground?" I asked him.

The trainer smiled. "It starts when the elephant is a baby. We place a chain around its leg, and we stake it to a strong stake in the ground. The baby elephant pulls against it again and again with all his might, but he can't pull it out. Eventually, he is smart enough to stop trying. When he quits trying to break free, he is fully trained. You can put a thread around his leg, and when he feels the slightest tug he will think it is the chain and he will not go against it. His memory tells him that it's impossible. A full-grown elephant would be a very dangerous animal if he wasn't trained like this."

"It's a good thing he can't tell the difference between a chain and a thread."

"Exactly," said the trainer with a chuckle. "He's smart but not that smart."

All of this information just fascinated me. I stayed and watched the entire process of setting up the tent until it was done.

As I returned home, filled with vivid images from my experience, it suddenly came over me that something was terribly wrong. All my brothers and sisters were seated solemnly around the room. They were quiet and not looking at me. Mom emerged from the bedroom. I could see she had been crying. But on her face was not sorrow or pain. It was the rage I had seen earlier at the circus poster.

"Get in this bedroom. Now!" she ordered.

I knew better than to say anything at this point. I went obediently and silently into the bedroom. She shut the door firmly behind us.

"After I warned you, how could you go near that place of sin?"

"Momma, I just went to see the animals."

"You were seen by Sister Krüger. She said you were there all day watching the tent being put up. I told you the circus was a worldly pleasure. The Bible says we are to avoid the very appearance of evil. Did you do that?"

I couldn't deny it. "No, Mother."

"I am going to give you the hiding of your life!"

And she did. I will never forget it. I was literally black and blue in places. It was the most terrible punishment I ever received.

Perhaps the real effect of the hiding was much more than skin deep. I felt that something was truly wrong with me. I had failed to understand my own attraction to the circus. I had flirted with sinful activity when I should have fled from the very appearance of it. Mother had warned me. I had thought that after the chocolate incident I had really given my heart to the Lord. But now, I felt far from being a new creature in Christ. It was like I had to start all over again. Like I had to repent and be saved again.

Looking back, I can see that I was like the young circus elephant. A heavy chain had been placed around my ankle and tied to a stake too strong for me. It would one day be nothing more than a tiny thread, but my heart would tell me it was the heavy chain. The slightest tug on that thread would make me feel the weight of the immoveable stake in the ground, even though it was no longer there.

The good news was that I was not an elephant; I was a lamb in the flock of the Good Shepherd. He had spoken to me and I knew His voice. One day I would be able to grow in my relationship with Him enough to realize that He was not the author of this bondage.

But at the time I did not have enough life experience to see over this setback. When Mother left that bedroom I felt as if God Himself had left the bedroom. My mind knew better, but feelings can be very powerful persuaders. Her disapproval, and God's disapproval, seemed one and the same. It lay heavy on me.

As I lay in my bed I recalled the day Mother had come home from Hamburg after receiving the baptism of the Holy Spirit. I recalled how she had hugged me and how the fountain of love had poured from her very soul into mine. Until that bright day, I had felt that she would rather give me a good hiding than give me a hug. Suddenly, she had loved me without condition, and I felt that God must have loved me in the same way. I wept at the memory of it. Now, I had betrayed that outpouring of love. I no longer deserved it, from Mother or from God. How would I ever rise above my own sinfulness?

The first day of the rest of my life happened in 1951, the day I received the baptism of the Holy Spirit. I was still eleven years old. A special guest speaker came to Glückstadt from Finland. His name was Pastor Arthur Kukkula, and he was well known for leading people in receiving this gift. Rather than have a seekers meeting in the main hall, the local believers decided to have him come to a smaller gathering held in a home in the rural countryside. I had been to that house many times for Sunday dinner after church. It was one of my favorite places on earth.

This particular farmhouse was a bit of heaven because the family had rigged a rope swing with a spare tire on the end. Anchored on a giant oak limb, the arc of the swing would send the rider out over an embankment. You could feel your stomach come up in your throat as the ground dropped away beneath you. I had spent many hours on that swing. I couldn't get enough of it. In the back of my mind I thought that maybe I could go to the cottage prayer meeting and stay outside riding the best thrill ride in Glückstadt.

"Reinhard, you said you wanted the baptism like your mother. Why don't you go with me to this meeting?"

I was shocked. My father was asking me to go. Immediately, I felt condemned by my worldly thoughts. Instead of thinking of this meeting as my opportunity to receive the baptism of the Holy Spirit, I had been fantasizing about riding the swing. It was so typical of my naughtiness and my unholiness.

"No, Hermann," Mother quickly spoke up. "I hardly think Reinhard is ready for such an experience."

"Mother is right," I agreed. "I will stay home."

For some reason, Dad did not accept this answer. Maybe God was beginning to speak to him about me. I wonder.

"This does not sound like my Reinhard," he said. "He is always talking about needing the baptism for his calling to Africa. Reverend Arthur Kukula is here, Meta. We should not ignore this opportunity. Besides, the Lord Jesus Himself is the Baptizer with the Holy Ghost. If He desires to baptize Reinhard, who are we to stand in His way?"

And so I went with him. As we walked toward the farmhouse, I struggled with my feelings of unworthiness. How would God stoop to fill such a wayward boy like me with the Holy Spirit? I was surely not to be trusted with His priceless gift.

When we arrived at the house we could hear singing. Outside, the great swing in the oak tree swayed silently in the breeze, accusing me of my tendency toward worldly thoughts. I turned away from it, fervently asking God to forgive me, and followed my father into the house.

As soon as I entered the room with those saints, I felt something begin to tingle inside of me. Incredibly, it was a growing expectation that I would receive the gift of the baptism this evening. My heart trembled to think that God would do such a thing. Reinhard the *null* boy, the worldly boy, the naughty boy, would be visited by the power of the Holy Spirit! I began to be excited, and I felt broken inside. It was a good feeling because I felt broken before God, and I began to sense His love for me as a broken boy. Surely this gift would lift me above the string of failures I had wracked up.

As Arthur Kukula spoke, my faith leapt up and shouted "yes" within me. The words of Scripture seemed to come alive in my chest. Suddenly the entire experience was no longer about me. It was about God and His great love for His children. When Arthur invited those seeking the Holy Spirit to kneel and pray I did so immediately. No sooner had I reached my knees than I was overwhelmed with an incredible sensation. No one needed to lay hands on me to pray. I received the gift of speaking in tongues spontaneously and burst out in a heavenly language.

How can I describe it?

Let me say first of all that there are many who have experienced the Spirit baptism in a quieter and less dramatic fashion. What follows is not a "how to" receive. It is a description of how it happened to me at the age of eleven.

It seemed to come from beyond me and from within me at the same time. My mind began to receive a stream of pure light and love from the very throne of

God. It flowed over me and went straight through me at once. This was far more than a mere bolt of electricity. It was as if every cell in my body was being saved, healed, and invigorated by a surge of divine power.

The word love is inadequate to describe it because that word has been so abused and misused. Yet that is what the power and Spirit of God is – His pure, self-less agape love poured into us. It has nothing to do with transient human love. It reminds me of the prayer Jesus prayed at the Last Supper: ... *that the love wherewith thou hast loved me may be in them, and I in them.*[12] All of my disappointments, feelings of unworthiness, and condemnation were swept away and forgotten.

The heavenly tongue cascading from my lips was the outer expression of something flowing within me that was too wonderful for normal language. Between my spirit and God's Spirit great mysteries were being exchanged. Paul spoke of the peace of God that passes understanding.[13] Some blessings from God are beyond intellect. Spirit baptism is one of them. People who limit God to mere human rationality will never know this power and this ecstasy. As the Spirit flowed, I was being transformed from my human limitations to a place where all things were possible.

As children we had all heard the stories of how the Christian martyrs of the first century died. Some were burned alive to light Nero's garden parties. In the natural they should have been screaming in pain, but ancient history books tell us they died singing praises to God. Before experiencing my Spirit baptism, such stories made me feel small and inadequate. Reinhard, the worldly boy, could never live up to them. I could never be that brave. But now I understood instinctively that the first-century martyrs were not brave. Rather, they were believers like me who had been swept from the natural to the supernatural on a flowing fountain of the Spirit. During my baptism, I could have easily sung in the flames with the martyrs; *Not by might, nor by power, but by my spirit, saith the LORD of hosts.*[14]

As my experience continued, it was as if I received a "mind transfusion." My thoughts were being replaced by an infusion of pure and heavenly thoughts that were simply not my own. Under their influence, I held nothing against anyone who had ever wronged me. No persecution or insult or act of spite or misunderstanding could find a place of bitterness in my overflowing heart. Forgiveness was as easy as breathing, and it flowed from me on a tide of tears. Believe me, this was a mind-expanding experience for a boy of eleven. Every form of fear, self-consciousness, and natural self-centeredness was blown away like chaff as God poured His love through me. Once I experienced it, nothing else compared.

I immediately recognized the source of this blessing. It could only come from God. This was because the Spirit of Christ, which already lived inside of me, was programmed to recognize Him. Abba, Father! [15] God is love.[16] The Scripture informs us that if the Spirit of Christ does not live in us then we have not been born again.[17] I had already entered a relationship with Him by accepting Jesus as my Savior. Under the influence of the baptism all doubt was erased about the validity of my salvation. I had been truly born again when I prayed with Mother after stealing money from her purse to buy chocolate. Spirit Baptism was not the same as the new birth that had happened then.

The Bible tells us that after new birth, the Spirit of Christ comes to live within us. Yet we may not feel its effect, and we cannot see its essence. Still, we are told that one day this same Spirit will raise our dead bodies from the grave.[18] Yet, day in and day out after my new birth I had not been able to see evidence that this powerful Spirit was living in me. Nor did I readily see it in other believers. I needed a Helper.

Under the experience of Holy Spirit baptism the Helper became fully alive to me. The reality of the Spirit's presence sprang up in me like a fountain that became almost unbearably wonderful. Suddenly love made it easy to believe. Neither life, nor death, nor angels, nor principalities – nor even my mother leaving the room in strong disapproval – could separate me from the source of this love. I was lost in loving God and being loved by Him. This was life eternal. By the Spirit I instantly knew that we are all *null*, we are all zero, until we leave our reality and enter His.

At the age of eleven, the Spirit baptism began to lead me on an adventure of faith that has not ended. I literally took off like a rocket ship, and no one could stop me. I continue to be empowered by it to this very day.

WHEN FATHER AND I ARRIVED HOME after the meeting with Reverend Kukula, Mother was sitting in her big rocking chair knitting a woolen shawl. Dad announced that the Lord had filled me with His Spirit, and I had spoken in tongues.

Mother froze in mid-stitch. The chair stopped rocking.

"No!" she said in disbelief, a stunned look on her face. It was plain to see that in her mind, I was hardly a candidate for such a gift from God.

Her response did not offend me. I was still aglow with the experience, overflowing with love just like she had been the day after receiving her baptism. In my heart I had begun to understand that the baptism was a free gift, not a salary earned, or a reward for diligence and good behavior. If we could make ourselves worthy to receive the Holy Spirit, then we would no longer need the Holy Spirit.

The first step toward being filled was to be empty of self. I had walked in that farmhouse door a zero, feeling totally unworthy, with absolutely no confidence in my own righteousness. That turned out to be the perfect attitude in which to receive. I wanted to shout praises to God who loved me so much. To think that He would fill me with His Spirit, simply by my asking. I ran to my mother and hugged her.

EVERY DAY THAT FOLLOWED, I begged my parents to allow me to follow the Lord in water baptism. I was so eager to identify completely with Jesus after being filled with the Spirit. Mother's response was, "If the Lord was willing to baptize him in the Holy Spirit at such a young age, how can we deny him water baptism?" And so I was baptized in a special service held in Hamburg, Bachstrasse 7a, in 1951.

Soon after, I became a nuisance to my young friends at church. "We must preach the gospel," I urged them. "Let's go preach. We must preach to the lost."

They did not quite share my level of enthusiasm. They still saw me as the boy who had barely outlived his dismal attempt to preach to trees.

One day I took my guitar and headed to a street corner in downtown Glückstadt. I had quite a nice singing voice as a boy, thanks to the training from Mother. I began to sing until a small crowd gathered. Then I put down my guitar, reached for my Bible, and preached the simple invitation to receive Jesus. To my amazement one man knelt and prayed the sinner's prayer with me right there on the street!

I raced home as fast as my legs would carry me, bursting into the living room completely out of breath. Mother and Father must have thought that the city was burning down.

"Father, Father!" I cried. "It works! It works! A man came to hear me preach today, and he accepted Jesus! The Holy Spirit really gives us the power to preach!"

The look on their faces was something that I began to see quite often. It was a look as if they were wondering if they had been given the wrong baby at the hospital.

I know many people – yes, even Pentecostal believers – who have encountered the power of the Holy Spirit, yet have returned to lead lives of quiet desperation.[19] Reinhard Bonnke is not one of them. My life is filled with challenges, yet it is also full of passion, meaning, joy, enthusiasm, peace, and blessing. I did not produce these wonderful things. These are fruits that flow from an intimate relationship with my heavenly Father. They can be yours as easily as they are mine. You do not have to become worthy. If you are spiritually lukewarm, and neither hot nor cold, it is not a curse but an opportunity. According to Scripture He stands at the door of your heart, knocking.[20]

*"I am the bread of Life,"*[21] Jesus said, to a crowd of religious doubters. Doubt is transformed into faith by the power of the Spirit.

I like that so much. I am still the boy in Grandma Bauszuss's vision. I break now a piece of the loaf of living bread He has given me and I offer it to you. Would you accept a piece of His pure goodness? Turn to Him now. Begin your journey of faith and fruitfulness. It is that simple. ... *if any man hear my voice, and open the door, I will come in to him, and will sup with him, and he with me.*[22]

# PART 3

# SCHOOL OF THE SPIRIT

*Heavenly Father,*
*unbelievers send ships from Hamburg every day.*
*I see them come and I see them go.*
*You have called me to Africa.*
*How long must I wait for a ship to take me there?*

# Chapter 11

I STOOD ON THE FAMILIAR PIER in Glückstadt watching ships in the Elbe River. High tide from the North Sea had filled the estuary to capacity, enriching the air with the salty scent of the ocean. The river was more than two miles wide at this point. The lonely call of gulls and the sound of water lapping at the pilings inspired me. On a brisk and sunny day, these sounds would carry my thoughts away to Africa.

As a boy, I loved to get away from school, away from my teasing brothers, away from chores and every mundane thing, and come to the waterfront to dream. Every hour of the day, huge seagoing freighters would ply silently up and down the channel. All that could be heard was a deep vibration from their engine rooms as diesel furnaces drove propellers powerfully through the water.

As the ships left Hamburg again, and headed downriver to the ocean, I longed to be aboard, sailing away to the Dark Continent. Thinking of the years ahead, waiting to fulfill my calling, left an ache in my chest. I felt as if I would never get there, no matter how I longed to go.

On this particular day something unusual had taken place. A large ship had tied up at the Glückstadt pier. It was the only one I had ever recalled seeing at our little port. Perhaps it had been a temporary mooring, awaiting an open berth in Hamburg. For whatever the reason, it sat now blocking my upriver view, its large side towering over the docks.

I was reminded of the day in Danzig, now Gdansk, when Mother had led us across the crowded dock on our desperate voyage to Copenhagen. It seemed long ago, but I glanced nervously at a low-flying seagull, recalling the strafing we had received from Russian fighter planes. God had marvelously delivered us from their blazing cannons. He had also preserved the ship after it had struck a submerged mine. Mother had prayed and the ship had righted itself. The captain had been quoted later as saying, "I left Danzig an unbeliever; I arrived in Copenhagen a believer." I smiled to recall that the God I served was Lord of the wind and the sea.

I approached the great ship tied so close to the dock. Huge hemp ropes descended from the bow and stern, anchoring the vessel weighing thousands of tons close enough to the dock to touch. I could not resist. A boy of twelve, I reached out from the dock and placed my hand against its great bulk. Even though the air was brisk, the metal was warm from the rays of the sun.

As boys are prone to do, I placed both hands on the steel and pushed against it with all my might. To my utter astonishment, the ship moved a few inches away from the pier. My eyes lit up with delight and revelation. I could hardly believe that I could move that mountain of steel.

Of course, I knew that on land it would be impossible for me and a thousand others to move it a fraction of an inch. But on the water it had been placed within the realm of the possible, even for a preteen boy. What a wonder. And I felt God speak in my heart. He told me that when He asked me to do the impossible, I should obey and not question how to see it done. His ways are limitless.

As TIME PASSED, I fell into a degree of anxiety in my Pentecostal beliefs. I was not aware of it as such. It is something I can see looking back from the perspective of years and experience.

This anxiety arose from hearing repeated teaching at church about a difference between the "baptism" of the Holy Spirit and other subsequent "fillings" with the Spirit. This teaching was an attempt to deal with the way such a powerful encounter with the Lord could fade and perhaps be renewed again. We grew anxious to keep our Holy Spirit baptism "topped up," as we called it.

Ironically, this teaching tended to downplay the element of faith. Rather than trust in the gift that had been given, the insecure believer would storm heaven to obtain a "refilling" of the Holy Spirit. Nevertheless, this was our heritage. A great deal of responsibility for seeing the power of God at work in our lives rested squarely on our own shoulders. Thus, a degree of anxiety was present in our worship.

Unscriptural ideas crept into our language, into our prayers, and into our singing. *Oh, for a new anointing* … But I thought, the gifts and calling of God were without repentance. *Give us another Pentecost* … I did not find it in Scripture that the first-century church ever returned to the upper room once they had received the initial experience. *Lord, be with us* … He had said that He would never leave us nor forsake us. *Fill my cup, Lord* … How could a mere cup contain the rivers of living water He promised to pour through us? As I grew up with these contradictions, I began to know that errors were present in our fellowship. Still, none of these errors seemed fatal to me. Rather than turn my back on the Pentecostal movement, I sought God to clarify these issues for me.

Our Pentecostal prayer meetings sometimes became times of deep introspection. The influence of the holiness movement was seen here.[23] There was much preaching about "keeping short accounts with God." That meant that we must confess any and every sin to God in prayer, not to mention our sinful thoughts, so that all of it was "under the blood" and not "hindering" our relationship to God. Going back to Azusa Street, I have read that there was teaching like this at the very beginning. Some had held that total sanctification enabled and preceded the baptism of the Holy Spirit. It became something someone had to earn, or deserve, through holy living.

This part of the Pentecostal tradition explains why some seekers "tarried" for so long, as in the case of my mother. She felt great pressure about having not spoken in tongues as the wife of a Pentecostal preacher. The longer she tarried, the more it seemed to indicate that she had some "unconfessed sin" in her life that was holding her back. This kind of peer pressure actually kept her from receiving the gift until she was at home alone in her bed. In this, I can see that she, too, was a circus elephant with a thread around her ankle that felt like a chain.

Another emphasis at Azusa Street can be found printed repeatedly in the *Apostolic Faith*, the official publication of the revival. This emphasis was on power more than purity.[24] The leader of the Azusa revival, William J. Seymour, had emphasized that the baptism of the Holy Spirit was for the empowerment of the Great Commission in the last days before the coming of the Lord.[25]

This emphasis comes from Acts 1:8, where Jesus told His disciples to tarry in Jerusalem until they received power, not holiness. *But ye shall receive power, after that the Holy Ghost is come upon you: and ye shall be witnesses unto me both in Jerusalem, and in all Judaea, and in Samaria, and unto the uttermost part of the earth.* This missionary and evangelistic emphasis of Pentecost, of course, has had the greatest effect worldwide. It has permeated the Charismatic movement that followed the Pentecostal revival. The result is the greatest harvest of souls in the history of mankind.

Need I mention that this is the emphasis that I also embraced? Even as a boy. I am so blessed and thankful that it came from Azusa Street, it passed through Luis Graf to August Bonnke, and to his son Hermann. Praise God, it stuck to me!

But, in Glückstadt and Krempe, all of these elements were so entangled in our weekly worship that it was impossible to separate one from the other. We were caught up in it. The good and the bad, the truth and the error, the clear and the contradictory – all in one big bundle. None of us in those days had the perspective to step back and separate the issues so that they could be better understood.

As the years have gone by, I have interacted with other Christian denominations and traditions. I see that they also have dealt with this problem. Our dilemma was not a particularly Pentecostal dilemma. It was, in fact, a human dilemma. The Christian faith has been handed forward in imperfect earthen vessels through every movement of history, through every denomination, every organization, and revival from the first century onward.

In fact, I now see that this is part of God's design. It is part of the mystery of His church, and part of the mystery of *Christ in us, the hope of glory.*[26] Jesus said, *He that receiveth you receiveth me, and he that receiveth me receiveth him that sent me.*[27] Receive or reject. The one who receives the imperfect Christian receives Christ; the one who rejects the imperfect Christian rejects Christ. And the one who rejects Christ rejects God the Father, too. This important relationship between God and His Son and His children was not stated with qualifications. How an individual responds to this relationship leads to very different ends. It can lead to heaven or hell.

To rebel and chafe against the imperfections of the church, and of God's people, is to fail to see the imperfections in your own mirror. The rebel suffers great loss over time. The unrepentant rebel suffers ultimate loss in eternity.

In the Gospels, Jesus spoke a parable about the nature of His kingdom. *The kingdom of heaven is like unto leaven, which a woman took, and hid in three measures of meal, till the whole was leavened.*[28] This seems to indicate that God is well aware that His kingdom will make an imperfect appearance in our fallen world. It will be hidden inside a church body, or inside a believer's body, for a period of time. "Hidden" means it will not reflect the full glory of His kingdom in its early stages. In time, however, it will go through a transformation till the whole is leavened. It is always a mistake to discard three measures of meal before the leaven has had time to finish its work. More importantly, it is vital to grasp by faith that the leaven of His kingdom is at work even when our eyes cannot see it.

*Faith is … the evidence of things not seen.*[29]

My father's pension allowed us to abandon his bicycle and ride by train together to and from Krempe. I delighted in this opportunity to be with him for his Sunday assignment. His church had shrunk in attendance as refugee families became settled elsewhere in Germany. By now it had become possibly the smallest congregation in all of Germany with perhaps 25 in attendance.

I recall one prayer meeting in my father's church in Krempe where we were "tarrying" all night. Admittedly, our prayers contained a tone of anxiety as if we were trying to twist God's arm to show up in response to our tenacity. I think it is so wonderful that God did not require that we always "get Him right," but rather that our hearts were "right with Him." That's what counted. The leaven of His kingdom works by grace and mercy. At some point in the prayer meeting, dear Sister Eliese Köhler received a vision. She stood and said that she had seen clothes on an ironing board. Some of the people in the room laughed aloud when they heard this homey illustration. She went on to say that the clothes had come from the laundry. They were clean garments, she said, but full of wrinkles. These wrinkles were being ironed out.

Her vision had been inspired by the words of the apostle Paul in Ephesians: *That he might present it to himself a glorious church, not having spot, or wrinkle, or any such thing; but that it should be holy and without blemish.*[30] Sensing that all was not right in our little fellowship, her application of this vision was to say that we had been washed in the blood and had been made clean, but we still found ourselves full of wrinkles. In our times of prayer and fellowship together, we were in the process of having the wrinkles ironed out of our Christian lives.

Now, I found this priceless! A picture from the Spirit that applied gently to our situation. We were clean but needed work. Who would have thought of such a thing? I have submitted myself to have more and more wrinkles ironed from my robes from that day until this.

But this same illustration drew ridicule from some believers, like my older brothers. To them it was proof that the gifts of the Spirit were not valid. In their view, people simply used so-called visions, and words of prophecy, knowledge, and wisdom, to present their own home-spun opinions with God's name attached. God, they said, would not stoop to such an illustration of divine truth. My brothers, and in fact many others in Pentecostalism, reacted so strongly against imperfections in God's *three measures of flour* that they threw the spiritual baby out with the bathwater.

I could not do that. My new birth and Spirit baptism were absolutely real to me and beyond compare. I already knew that God had favored me to hear His voice. Reinhard, the *null* boy, the zero, had been graced with His calling, and a confirming vision of a boy with a loaf of divine bread had been given to seal it. This indicated to me that He hadn't chosen the brightest and best for His service. But He had chosen one who would value the right things.

The baby was worth so much more to me than the bathwater that it became my birthright. Though my father never gave up his hope of seeing Martin preach the gospel, as the Bonnke firstborn, Martin rejected and came to despise his Pentecostal heritage. His calling skipped over the pecking order and landed on me.

This is a recurring theme in Scripture. We see it in the selection of Gideon and his army, and in the selection of Joseph over his brothers, and David over his brothers. Finally, the apostle Paul distilled the idea in his great passage found in 1 Corinthians 1:26-29: *For ye see your calling, brethren, how that not many wise men after the flesh, not many mighty, not many noble, are called: But God hath chosen the foolish things of the world to confound the wise; and God hath chosen the weak things of the world to confound the things which are mighty; And base things of the world, and things which are despised, hath God chosen, yea, and things which are not, to bring to naught things that are: That no flesh should glory in his presence.*

How could it be said better than that?

ONE PARTICULAR MANIFESTATION of a spiritual gift in Krempe took me by surprise. I went to an evening prayer meeting with my father. It was held at a local residence. It was what we called a "cottage" prayer meeting, held in a home rather than in the meeting hall. All of the members began to share their prayer needs, as usual. Some requested prayer for healing from illnesses and injuries, others for the salvation of unsaved loved ones, and others for God's provision for financial

Photo-Session? I ran into the house to pick up my Bible (1953).

needs. Then we all began to pray at once, some in German, others in tongues. And yes, some with perhaps an element of faithless anxiety.

As the meeting progressed, the Holy Spirit came upon me in a way like never before or since. At first I wasn't sure it was the Holy Spirit at all. I thought I might be dying. It was like an electrical charge had penetrated my body and surged from my hands up to my shoulders. As I continued to pray, the Lord fastened my eyes on a woman across the room who had requested prayer for an illness. No one was praying with her.

I instantly knew that this visitation of the Holy Spirit was not for me but for her. No one had to tell me that if I laid my hands on her she would be healed. That is the kind of knowledge one automatically knows under the influence of the Spirit.

Now, my problem was in the natural. My father would not allow me to lay hands on that woman. He saw me as the son who always had a mind of his own. This kind of action would be presumptuous – one step short of rebellion – in his mind. I knew that. If I stepped out of line and did what the Holy Spirit seemed to be telling me to do, I ran the risk of incurring my father's wrath, which could be greater and of more consequence than my mother's.

So a debate raged in my mind. But not for long. I remembered how I had moved the ship in the Glückstadt harbor. On this night, the Holy Spirit was giving me orders, and my job was to obey, simply obey, leaving the outcome to God.

But I was still afraid of my father. I ducked behind furniture and began to work my way around the room on my hands and knees. With each movement of my arms the super charge running through my hands made me buck and tremble like a man with palsy. As I reached the place behind the woman, I rose up and placed both hands on her shoulders. She screamed and was jettisoned from the chair to the floor. Peeking over the back of her chair, my eyes met the eyes of my father.

"Reinhard, what did you do to her!?"

"Father, the Spirit told me to lay my hands on her."

Before he could recover from his surprise she leaped from the floor. "Brother Bonnke, Reinhard laid his hands on me, and it was like a bolt of electricity shot through me from top to bottom. I am healed! I am healed! Praise God, I am healed!" She leaped and praised God, dancing around the room with joy.

I looked now at my father and rose from my knees. I could see that there would be no punishment for what I had done. But he seemed stunned and somewhat undone. Now that I am older, I think perhaps he wondered why the Holy Spirit would overlook the faithful pastor of the Pentecostal church in Krempe and move with a dramatic spiritual gift through the least of his children. Indeed, I think the apostle Paul might have given him the best answer: *... and things which are despised, hath God chosen, yea, and things which are not, to bring to naught things that are ...*[31] The world's rejects are God's elects.

DURING THESE GROWING UP YEARS I had a vision of Africa. It happened during another of those prayer meetings; I don't remember if in Krempe or Glückstadt. It bore a peculiar mark of authenticity to prove it was not from my own imagination.

In the vision I saw a map. I recognized it as the continent of Africa. In the vision the name of the city of Johannesburg was illuminated as if God was indicating that my assignment to Africa would be there. Perhaps this was where I would break the bread of life and see it multiply, as seen in the vision by Grandma Bauszuss. In my mind this map vision of Johannesburg puzzled me because earlier I had seen an actual map of Africa and from memory had placed Johannesburg at another location. I kept the vision to myself and puzzled over it as I went home that night.

The next day in school I went to the library and looked up the Atlas of the World. Finding South Africa, I located the city of Johannesburg. It was not where my memory had recalled it. In fact, it was where the vision had shown it to me. God's Spirit is more than accurate. His directions come from the very mind of omniscience, and I should not be surprised to learn that God knows His geography better than I. After all, He was the One who spoke and divided the continents from the seas. So, my heart became set not only on Africa, but specifically on Johannesburg, South Africa.

MY BROTHERS WERE GROWING WORLDLIER by the day. As I entered my teens they were far ahead of me in every way. They had begun to notice girls and were saying things about them out of earshot from Mother and Father. Things that made me blush, though I confess, I did not understand the half of it. Seeing my awkwardness, they enjoyed ridiculing me, calling me "the missionary boy," "the holy boy," and "naïve." I didn't even know what the word *naïve* meant. I guess they were right.

But it was more than naïveté. I had the Spirit of Christ in me that informed me of the way I ought to think about girls and women. They were automatically precious to me because they were precious to God. I took offense at disrespectful language and images. Eve had been created especially for Adam. I had read in Genesis that in the Garden of Eden they had been naked and unashamed. This was God's idea, not some lewd boy's description. I wondered what the full difference was.

One day as I walked along the Glückstadt waterfront past city hall, I looked up and noticed the flag of our city flying below the West German flag. The symbol for our city was Lady Luck, and she was naked. Why had I never noticed before? As the flag undulated slowly in the breeze, I also noticed that a banner bearing her title had been conveniently painted across her midsection. Still, her breasts were bare and open for all to see. I felt a stirring in myself that made me uncomfortable. I suddenly worried about what my mother had meant when she had spoken of women who would "flaunt their bodies and arouse sinful passions in men." Is that what I was feeling? Was it sinful passion?

Something had to be done about this right away. I would go to my dad. He was a man of God. Surely he understood these things. God would not create this kind of beauty and this kind of desire and not have a wonderful plan to deal with it.

So, I took up the conversation with him as we rode the train toward a prayer meeting in Krempe.

"Father, have you noticed the city flag of Glückstadt?"

"I never let my eyes go there. And neither should you. It's disgusting."

This confused me a bit. I wouldn't have called it disgusting. Wrong, yes, but not disgusting. "What is the right way a man and a woman are naked, Father?

Like when they were in the Garden of Eden in Genesis, it says they were naked and unashamed."

"Reinhard, we're on our way to church. You should be thinking of the things of God."

"We are His creatures. I am thinking that one day I will marry someone, and I know that marriage is not sinful. You and Mother are married. You have children. I know that is not something sinful. I want to know how that works. How do a man and a woman who love God get married and have children and not be sinful?"

"Well, marriage is the only way. Otherwise, it is something that will send you to hell."

So, his answer was marriage. Period. This was obviously right, but it seemed like such an incomplete answer to my question.

We traveled in silence for a time then began to talk again. He talked of several seekers in the congregation he thought were close to receiving the gift of the Holy Spirit. One of them had stopped smoking; the other had given up a nightcap of Peppermint Schnapps. A woman had stopped braiding her hair in accordance with the instructions in the book of 1 Timothy.[32] Another brother had confessed that he had slipped and cursed during the week. He felt that if he fasted and prayed he would be ready at the next invitation to receive the gift of the Holy Spirit. And on and on.

I needed my father to step up to his role. Sexuality was such a big discovery for me, and I was lost in the woods. I didn't want to learn any more details from my brothers, or friends at school, or from the city flag, or from another circus poster with scantily clad trapeze artists flying through the air. But he had changed the subject and without saying so, had forbidden me to bring it up again.

That day my father stepped down from his high position in my eyes. To find my answers I would seek my Father in heaven for guidance. I would look for clues in the Bible and wherever else I could find them. And I would never do this to my own son when I became a father. In the meantime, nearing the age of 14, I would remain naïve for a while longer.

MY FATHER APPROACHED ME not long afterward saying, "Reinhard, if you want to become a missionary to Africa you must learn a trade. Our Pentecostal denomination requires it. In poor countries, most of our missionaries have to support themselves with a local profession. The support of church offerings is seldom enough. I have found a carpentry school here in Krempe. Carpentry is a basic trade throughout the world. Wherever you go you can find work. I want you to attend this apprenticeship and begin the training that will support your calling."

I did not feel good about this idea. But I was an obedient son, and I went to the school. The master carpenter was a very rough man. He screamed at me for the smallest mistake. And I made many. So much about carpentry simply escaped my understanding. It was almost as bad as trying to learn English. I was totally intimidated.

Week after week, I attended the workshop, and the master tormented me with his angry outbursts. Finally, one day he just chased me off, screaming, "You will never be a carpenter. Get out! Get out!"

I remember that it was an eight-kilometer ride to my home on my bicycle. All the way home I cried, thinking, *I cannot be a missionary because I am not suited to be a carpenter.* There could be no greater defeat for me.

At home I told Dad what had happened. He felt very sorry for me. He returned to the carpenter school and spoke with the headmaster. He explained to him that I had to find a trade that I could practice as a missionary one day. "Please try Reinhard one more time."

He did. After a few weeks he came to me again. He was not shouting anymore. In sympathy he said, "Reinhard, you had better look for another trade to support your African ministry. You will never be a carpenter."

A heavy burden lifted from my shoulders. I understood. He was right. I could now tell my father that I had simply tried the wrong trade. Something else would be the right trade for me. I rode my bicycle home this time with joy in my heart. *I'm free. I don't have to be a carpenter,* I thought.

Father accepted this verdict, realizing that I had been obedient. I had tried and had given it my best. I was even willing to try a second time. Now we could move on.

I was now 15 and as most boys my age, I found an internship in Glückstadt. In this case it was a job that fit my abilities. It was at a local *EDEKA Wholesale and Export* with the goal that I would eventually become a professional merchant. It involved three days of the week in internship and two days in vocational school. At the end of each month, my boss would count into my hand the pay I had earned. I felt so good. I had accomplished something, and I had earned this money. At the end of each week, I took my money home and put it into a jar that I kept in my bedroom. It began to build in volume.

I was working at EDEKA.

10, 20, 50 deutschmarks and more. I watched it grow and began to dream of ways to spend it.

The second Sunday in May in 1955 our church prepared to celebrate Mother's Day. We were instructed as sons and daughters to find some way to honor our godly mothers.

At home I decided I would give Mother a very nice card from the bookstore. I went to remove money from my growing jar of money. Suddenly, the vow I had made at the age of nine returned to me. Counting the money, I found I had accumulated somewhat more than 100 marks. I knew what I must do.

I went to the store and bought a fine card and signed it. Inside I tucked 100 deutschmarks in cash. When Mother opened it she could not believe her eyes.

"Reinhard!" she gasped. "Why did you do this? It's so much money!"

"No, Mother. It is not so much. Remember when I stole money from your purse to buy chocolate?"

Her jaw dropped. She replied slowly, "Yes."

"I had a debt to pay. I vowed that one day I will give my mom 100 marks. Now I have done it."

From the look on her face I knew that I had completely dumbfounded her. Never in a million years had she expected it. But I was so happy that I had not forgotten. I was even more happy that I had remembered on Mother's Day.

How should I properly describe the operation of the gifts of the Spirit during those Pentecostal prayer meetings in Germany? They were fantastic. Indeed, things took place there that I still cannot classify. At times we experienced common visions. One, two, or three people would report seeing the same scene like on a movie screen. The others would interpret its meaning. This kind of thing does not happen in all times and places. But it happened then and there.

One day when I was 16, I attended an all-night prayer meeting in Krempe. I was lost in prayer for hours when I received a word from the Lord. This idea entered my consciousness from the realms above. It sliced across my mind and sent all other thoughts out of my head. *You and Manfred Fischer are to go preach in Tostedt.* Now I knew where Tostedt was. It lay 50 miles beyond Hamburg and across the Elbe River. We had enjoyed fellowship with another Pentecostal congregation from there when coming together at special joint meetings. But the idea of Manfred and I preaching there seemed impossible.

My own father did not invite me to preach in his church. How could I expect a pastor from a distant town to allow a 16-year-old, or even Manfred, who was 17, preach from his pulpit? The idea was preposterous.

But as I prayed, a scripture came to mind in connection to the original out-pouring of Pentecost. The apostle Peter had stood in Jerusalem and explained the manifestation of the Spirit to the curious crowd. He had quoted from the prophet Joel. Part of that quotation came back to me now: ... *I will pour out of my Spirit upon all flesh: and your sons and your daughters shall prophesy* ...[33] I knew that the word prophesy was our word for preach. Scripture seemed to back up the idea that under the influence of the Spirit one did not need the maturity of years, or the education of a seminary, to be enabled to preach. Still, I felt reluctant. How could I presume to do this thing?

I felt a tap on my shoulder. Raising my head from prayer I looked into the eyes of Manfred Fischer.

"Reinhard," he said, "The Spirit of God has spoken to me. We are to go to Tostedt to preach."

Youth camp Ratzeburg 1956

I felt the hair rise on the back of my neck. More than that, I felt faith leap up in my heart. I was totally energized by the voice of the Spirit speaking to both of us about the same thing.

How could we do this? We decided that we would invite others and go as a group of young people from our church to the church in Tostedt. If the pastor there would have us, we would come and conduct a service for him. Sons and daughters prophesying.

After putting the idea before my father and receiving his approval to pursue it, we put our heads together and wrote a letter to the pastor in Tostedt. His name was Pastor Rudolph Winter. We told him how the Spirit had spoken to us during a prayer meeting. We also quoted the scripture from the day of Pentecost where Peter had spoken to the crowd. "If you agree that this is something from the Lord then we would be pleased to respond to your invitation," we wrote.

A few days later an invitation arrived in the mail from Pastor Rudolph Winter. Manfred and I were ecstatic. I showed the invitation to my father, and he gave the approval for the dates. Then we were filled with dread. What would we say?

I had never preached from a pulpit before.

Bolstered by a group of three other young men who accompanied us, we took the train from Glückstadt to Tostedt. When we arrived the pastor introduced us to his congregation by saying, "The Holy Spirit sent them." I had my guitar, and we led singing and praise and then began to offer exhortations as the Spirit gave us utterance. One after another the young people spoke. The crowd received us well.

Then I took my Bible to preach. This was not an evangelistic sermon. I was not yet an evangelist, though I had led one man to Christ while preaching on the street. This was something else that I spoke to the believers in such a way that I still do not understand. It was as if the Holy Spirit began to fall on that crowd like a gentle rain. They began weeping all across the room. There was such sweetness in the atmosphere that you could almost smell it, like the perfume of lilac blossoms. We worshipped and took a long bath in the refreshing flow of the Spirit. Gifts of the Spirit manifested, and the service was out of my hands.

When we returned home, Pastor Winter told my father what had happened. He especially noted the response of the congregation when I had spoken. Father listened and took it all in, but we were not asked to repeat our ministry in his pulpit. It would be another three years before he opened his pulpit to me. In the meantime he continued to say, "Martin shall be my successor," though his voice had lost its normal tone of absolute certainty. Martin had begun his higher education in a secular university.

Just recently I was preaching in Germany. After the sermon an old Pentecostal saint approached me. She was still clothed and groomed in the way of the old-time holiness believers. Her hair was long and straight and fixed in a bun. Her clothes were drab, and not a sign of a ring or a jewel could be seen on her anywhere. Not even a brooch. With eyes shining, she took my hand. "Do you remember when you were just a boy and you came to Tostedt and preached?"

"Yes, of course I do."

"I was there."

She took my hand in both of hers and tears welled in her eyes. "It is something I shall never forget."

The tremble of her voice, and the tone of it, suggested to me that the memory had somewhat different meanings for the two of us. For me, Tostedt had been a confirmation that I was moving in the right direction as a young man. It showed me that obeying the voice of the Spirit would produce remarkable and unexpected results, and I should continue to walk in faith and obedience.

For her, the experience had become nostalgic; something that took her back with longing to a time that was no more. I sensed that she felt something had been lost in Pentecost since then.

For me, nothing could be further from the truth. So much had been gained! Tostedt was merely a launching pad, a beginning; not an end in itself.

I have not been able to recall the disagreement to this day. It was one of those issues that make no real impact. Has no lasting value. Yet the kind that drives people apart and leaves them raw and angry. It was one of the *little foxes, that spoil the vines*,[34] as Solomon called them. The thing I remember most was that I was right about the issue, and my father would not accept new information that would help him see my point of view. That was the general character of the disagreement.

We were riding the train together to a prayer meeting in Krempe when it happened. As we discussed it, my father reacted far more forcefully than the issue required. He concluded by berating me severely and summarily imposing his will over mine. I suppose the roots of the conflict were in the impression that I was a boy with a mind of my own, and I had the temerity to express myself. That is just a guess at this point in time, and my father is not here to clarify it. At the time, I knew his action was unfair, and it hurt me deeply. I could do nothing but submit to his authority and fall silent. We rode the last mile to Krempe in that stony kind of silence that says more than the argument itself.

Out of the smoldering atmosphere of our train ride we walked into the meeting room. There we put on our smiles, greeted everyone, and turned our minds toward worship. I played my guitar and led singing as usual. Then we received the list of prayer requests from those assembled. Finally, we began to pray.

As the saints entered their prayer zone, Sister Eliese Köhler spoke up. "I see a vision," she said, her voice rising with a quiver of anguish above the others. "I see a shepherd with his sheep on a meadow, but there is something wrong with the shepherd. He has his shepherd's crook upside down in his hand. The crooked end is on the ground instead of upright. The crook, which is meant to protect the sheep, has injured one of the lambs."

A deep and thoughtful silence followed.

Then I heard my father sob across the room. I looked up and saw that his head was in his hands. From where he sat he cried out, "Forgive me, Reinhard. I am sorry, son. Please, forgive me."

I went to him and we embraced. Our tears flowed freely. Everyone saw it. Together in Krempe, by the gifts of the Spirit, God was ironing wrinkles from our robes.

# Chapter 12

Father invited a Pentecostal "elder statesman" from England to preach in Krempe. His name was Reverend Morris and Father greatly respected him.

When Morris came, he was very impressed with the spiritual fervor he found among our Pentecostal youth in the greater Hamburg area. He proposed to organize a friendship bus tour to England. He would arrange for 50 German Pentecostal youth to travel there. We would visit two churches, Peniel Chapel in North Kensington and People's Church in Liverpool. Both of these churches were vibrant fellowships with strong evangelistic outreaches.

Morris wanted us to take our musical instruments and sing and preach in German. None of us spoke English, so he would travel with us and be our interpreter. He was excited to share the Spirit-led ministry of German youth with English youth. He felt such a gesture would be good for both parties. 14 years after these two nations had stopped bombing each other in the war, the time was right. Father agreed.

This opportunity fired my imagination. I had been reading for years about John Wesley's revival, and later, the Welsh Revival. These movements of God had more than filled the churches in England; they had changed the entire culture. As a result, it seemed to me that the British Isles had a better spiritual heritage than our homeland, even though we were the birthplace of Protestantism. Lutheranism seemed dark and oppressive to me. German Pentecostalism seemed to labor under the inferiority complex of *The Berlin Declaration*. I was eager to visit my brothers and sisters in England.

After I spoke at People's Church in Liverpool, the pastor there, Reverend Richard Kayes, took me aside. I was nervous, hoping I had not said something in German that had hit a wrong key. Using Reverend Morris as an interpreter, he asked me about my plans for the future. I told him that I had been called to Africa.

"Reinhard," he said, "you should consider enrolling in a Bible college that suits your calling. Not just any Bible college. You need a school with an evangelistic and missionary heart. What Bible college opportunities do you have in Germany?"

"There is a German Pentecostal school," I said.

"I do not know about that school, but I do know a first-rate missionary school. It is the Bible College in Swansea, Wales."

Reverend Morris agreed. "I will talk to your father when we get back," he said. "I think you should consider the school in Wales."

My heart nearly skipped a beat. I knew this was the school founded by Rees Howells. He had been a coal miner in 1909 when the Welsh Revival exploded. Totally transformed, he had gone in the fervor of that revival to southern Africa as a missionary. After seeing great results, he returned to start the Bible college of Wales as an act of tremendous faith. There were absolutely no funds. He prayed in every pound and over the decades had sent hundreds of missionaries around the world. His faith was celebrated like that of George Müller, his predecessor in the faith from nearby Bristol.

I had read about Müller, too. I had even more in common with this man. He had been a German from Prussia and a vile sinner even as a Lutheran seminarian. After he met the Lord, he became famous throughout the world as a man of great faith. He moved permanently to England and learned to speak English. Eventually, he preached in crusades around the world, including a tour from one end of America to the other during the days of the Holiness Revival.

Starting in Bristol with only pocket change, he and his wife had prayed in secret and had seen the Lord provide millions of pounds miraculously, providing for the great orphanages they built there that housed and fed more than 2,000. It was a story that resonated strongly with me because of our common heritage. It had been part of my longing to follow his path. Now it seemed that it might be possible by attending school in Wales, not in Germany.

A dozen years after Müller's death, Rees Howells had emerged from the Welsh Revival. The school he built was not primarily about academic achievement. It was a two-year school of practical ministry. It emphasized relationship with God over theology, prayer over good works, and faith above all. Howells had died in 1950, and his son Samuel had taken over. Samuel faithfully followed his father's ways. Everything about this school seemed to shout my name. I immediately sensed this was God's leading.

Upon my return, my parents were not pleased with this news. They wanted me to attend our own German Bible school. But I had felt a strong connection to the descriptions of the school in Wales. It was a direction I felt compelled to go in. I immediately filled out an application and sent it.

In the meantime, God did not wait for Bible College. My life of ministry began on May 1, 1959. It was a Friday, and I was in prayer because I had received an invitation to preach for the summer in Berlin. My father had not allowed me to preach in his pulpit but this invitation came from one of my former Sunday School teachers, Marion Franz. She and her husband Eduard had been led by the Spirit to work with East German refugees in Berlin. The Berlin wall had not yet been constructed and 2 million fellow Germans had fled the Soviet lifestyle, seeking a better life in the west. Their conditions were horrible.

When Eduard and Marion described their work with the Berlin Refugee Mission, all of the oppression of my years in the Danish prison camp came flooding back to me. These memories were transformed into a godly compassion for these lost refugees. I went before the Lord in prayer and God spoke clearly to me, calling me then and there to full-time service. I was 19 years of age. To this day, I mark this date as "year one" in my life of ministry.

I immediately began to raise support for the mission, which would last for the summer months. But for some reason my efforts seemed to stumble. The funds necessary for me to make this trip were simply not coming together. I presented myself to various Pentecostal groups in the region, requesting their help. The help I received was meager. It seemed I could more readily raise train fare to preach in Tostedt than to arouse compassion for lost refugees in West Berlin.

This reality began to settle upon me in a way that tested my faith. The way I responded to this difficulty would lay down a pattern that I would follow again and again, decades later raising funds to preach the gospel in Africa. The world found it easy to overlook refugees and blacks, dismissing them as inconsequential to the best efforts of world evangelization. When first dealing with this in connection to my summer ministry in Berlin, I was tempted to depend on resources other than those supplied by the Holy Spirit. That temptation nearly proved disastrous.

In a neighboring village, a young Swedish pastor had established a Pentecostal work. I will not use his name here for reasons that will become clear. While presenting my mission to his congregation, he took me aside.

"Reinhard," he said. "You need to learn how to raise funds. You don't really seem to know how it's done. I can teach you."

After the service he took me for a ride in his brand new Volvo 544 sedan. I was more than impressed. Here was a minister of the gospel who lived in true abundance. I was completely intimidated. My father had never been able to own even a primitive car. This was a fiery red speedster with sleek lines and a high-performance engine. It was something completely unheard of in Pentecostal ministry.

When we got inside, he switched on the Stromberg-Carlson AM radio and dialed in a powerful station from Hamburg. The fine upholstered interior of that car was suddenly filled with the pulsing sound of Elvis Presley, singing "… blue, blue, blue suede shoes!" He was all the rage in Germany.

Starting the 4-cylinder engine, the minister revved it several times before roaring off down the street. Shifting the four-on-the-floor manual transmission like a road-race veteran, he quickly covered the winding back roads to Glückstadt. My body was used to traveling at the speed of a bicycle, or of a diesel-powered commuter train. This trip sent me into sensory overload.

When we arrived at my house I was literally trembling. Before dropping me off, he made a stunning proposition. "Reinhard, I am going to make a fund-raising tour through Sweden in a few weeks. I will be raising money to fund a ministry at an orphanage. Why don't you come with me? You can play your guitar and sing, and I will teach you the secrets of fundraising. We will be gone for six weeks."

This seemed like a gift from God. I was swept completely off my feet. "Thank you so much," I replied. "I really need to learn, and I would really like to do this. I will give you a tentative yes, but I need to talk to my father. I will also pray about it. I must hear from God before I do anything like this."

"Fine," he said. "I will need your answer in one week so we can make plans."

"I will give you my answer."

Mother and Father were at the window watching as I entered the house. Their jaws had dropped in amazement. I told them of the proposition and asked what they thought about it.

"It seems like a wonderful opportunity," Mother said. "We will all pray with you about it."

"But I have never seen a preacher driving a car like that," my father said with a disapproving frown. "I'm not sure what to think about it. If he is raising money for orphans, how much of it is going to make payments on that automobile?"

"I would not judge him at first sight," I said. "I know that he is helping a lot of orphans as well as pastoring a thriving congregation."

"What about Berlin?" Dad asked. "I thought God had called you to minister in Berlin to the refugees."

"He has, and I will. Maybe I will be better equipped to do it after I have learned how to raise funds. I would like to go to Sweden first, then to Berlin."

As I prayed that night I felt no peace. This indicated to my heart that God was saying no. I didn't understand why. In prayer I continued to argue in favor of the trip. My discouragement with sluggish fund raising was driving the desires of my heart.

A FEW DAYS LATER, my brother Peter came home from the university. He was determined to become a medical doctor. By this time all of my older brothers had graduated from high school and were pursuing higher education. Martin had his sights set a doctorate in the natural sciences. Gerhard was a mathematics whiz and was following that path toward an accounting degree. Jürgen had entered the military.

Peter and I took a walk through Glückstadt together, visiting old haunts.

"I hear that you are going to be a preacher."

"Yes, God has called me to full-time service."

"None of us – Martin, Gerhard, Jürgen, me – none of us understand you, Reinhard. Why would you choose something like our father has chosen? What future is there in it? Look at his church. It is the smallest in all of Germany. And the Pentecostals are embarrassing. Why would you choose to follow Dad in this profession?"

"It is not a profession. It is a calling. The greatest thing in the world is to serve God."

He snorted in derision. "Reinhard, where is God? Do you see Him anywhere? Look around you. Did He build these buildings? Did He invent the railroad? Did He win the war? Look at the world; it is changing. Exciting things are happening in science and education, and you could make yourself a part of it. Be a doctor, a lawyer, a musician, a politician, a professor. Be something that counts. Anything but a preacher. You've got to learn that God has no real leverage in this world, little brother. Don't you see that?"

I became angry. "God has more than leverage. He is the very lever itself. Nothing that exists in this world exists without Him. You do not take one breath without His permission. I am choosing to serve the very highest calling."

"I breathe my own air. God gets nothing done. Why doesn't God stop the bad things, if He is so powerful? He has no leverage. Look at Mom and Dad. Without Dad's pension from the government his ministry would fall apart. Do you think for one moment he could have given us a roof over our heads with what he gets from Krempe? Hah! What a joke. Show me God's leverage. Where is it?"

"I'll show you. I just met a Pentecostal preacher who drives a Volvo 544," I said, driving the name of the car home like a spike.

He stopped in his tracks. "No!"

"Yes. He gave me a ride in it. He wants me to go to Sweden with him a few weeks from now. How's that for leverage?"

"You're lying."

"I'm not lying. I spoke in his church, and he is going to teach me about fund-raising. I will show you that God has leverage in this world. All preachers don't have to be poor like Father."

He shook his head and began to walk again. "I've never heard of a preacher driving a 544."

"That's just the beginning," I promised.

We had reached the waterfront, and to my surprise I saw that another large tanker ship moored at the town pier. It gave me an inspiration.

"Come with me," I said. "I will show you something."

We walked onto the pier and up to the huge side of the ship tied to the pilings. I put my hand on it and pushed with all my might. Nothing happened. It did not move one inch. It was as if I didn't exist. I felt a bit taken down.

Looking down, I began to understand why. The tide was out. The harbor was shallow, and the full weight of the tanker had responded to the pull of gravity. It was now settled in the mud.

"When I was twelve years old I came here when the tide was in," I explained. "I put my hand on the side of a ship, and I could move the whole thing because it was lifted by the water. Now the tide is out. I can do nothing. God is like the tide, Peter. With Him nothing is impossible. He has leverage."

Peter smiled a superior smile and shook his head. "I feel sorry for you, Reinhard. This is the time of your life when you should choose a career wisely. You will never have these days of your youth back again once they are gone. Put your energy into something real, not something you simply wish to be true."

He made me feel sad. I felt like our family was coming apart at the seams. Mother and Father would not tolerate this kind of talk coming from him. Nor would he say it in front of them. He spouted such nonsense behind their backs. After seeing the hand of God in our family, how could he not embrace the Lord above all? We made our way home again.

As the day for the decision about the trip to Sweden approached I grew agitated. No matter how I prayed I could not feel peace about it. The agitation came from how much I wanted to go and could find no reason not to – except for my lack of peace. It was as close to arguing with God as I had ever come.

I accompanied Dad to Krempe again. On the way he suggested that I seek out the help of Sister Eliese Köhler in making this decision. She was known as a woman of prayer and a woman who received gifts of the Spirit. She also knew nothing about the decision facing me.

"I will do it," I said.

I found her as soon as we entered the building and asked her to go with me into a small prayer room adjacent to the meeting hall. She agreed to do that.

"Sister Köhler," I said, "I have a problem. I don't know what to do. I've come to pray with you about it. Maybe the Lord will show you what I must do."

"Certainly," she replied. I could feel her eagerness to perform this act of support and kindness. She took my hand, and we knelt together immediately.

We had been praying for perhaps ten or 15 minutes when suddenly she spoke up. "I see a vision. I see a fast car going along a straight road," she said. "Suddenly, I see an angel of the Lord step into the middle of the road and the car stops. That's it." She looked up at me. "I do not know what the vision means."

I smiled at her and replied "but I *have* the interpretation of this vision ..." and I felt the warmth of the peace of God that passes understanding flood my heart. The peace did not come from her vision. It came from submitting my own ambitious desires to the voice of the Spirit. God had already spoken in my heart. I had wanted a different answer. Her vision was a marvelous and gentle confirmation of His will for me. I needed no other prompting.

I went home and wrote a quick letter to that Swedish pastor. *I am not coming with you to Sweden,* I wrote. *I am going to Berlin to minister for the summer.* He was very angry with me.

Only a few years later I found that the decision was the right one since there where some stories around this minister that could have taken me off the very road I was going. The voice of the Spirit had disapproved from the very start. Oh, how I needed to learn to obey and not to question Him.

I MANAGED TO RAISE the necessary support for my Berlin summer mission on my own. This was another lesson in itself. The slow start to fund raising did not demand a new strategy after all. It only required faithfulness to the call.

Soon I had packed my bags and had purchased a train ticket. Mother accompanied me to the station. Father had business at the church. This was the first time I would be gone so long from home. Mother fretted and worried over little details of my packing, asking again and again if I had packed my comb and toothbrush and extra underwear. I reassured her that all was well and I was ready to leave.

We arrived on the Krempe-Holstein train platform early. Suddenly we were alone with nothing to occupy our time. Our ability to carry on a conversation was polite at best. Usually, we had related to one another with Martin, Gerhard, Jürgen, Peter and Felicitas in the mix. Now the boys had gone to various colleges. Felicitas had gone to piano lessons. The silences between us grew awkward.

After ten minutes, at last we saw the puff of the steam engine rounding the corner down the long shimmering track. My heart raced. Long before the train arrived I picked up my luggage and stood with both hands full, eager to board. The smoke from the stack seemed like the smoke of my altar of service to the Lord. My destiny was approaching, approaching, approaching – ever nearer. My life of ministry was about to begin. I wanted to run to meet it.

As the train pulled to a stop, releasing a cloud of steam across the platform I suddenly became aware of another sound. A sound of anguish. Turning to my left I saw my mother doubled over in pain. She was sobbing uncontrollably. In shock I dropped my luggage and ran to her, taking her in my arm.

"What is wrong, Momma? What's wrong?"

She could not speak. She could only shake her head and sob into her handkerchief even more. I had never seen such pain. At first I assumed that she had become sick with some life threatening illness. But as she carried on I realized that she was not in physical pain, but emotional pain. It slowly dawned on me that she was mourning my leaving. But her emotions made no sense. I had thought she would be glad to see me go. I had been the boy she wished had been a girl. All those years I had felt myself a burden to her. I had been the naughty one that she might as well give a good hiding to at first sight. The boy who stole money for chocolate and could not be trusted. The one who lusted after the sinful circus. How was she now in such anguish to see me go to Berlin for the summer? I could hardly take it in.

I embraced her again and again. "Don't cry, Momma."

The conductor called out, "All aboard!"

My train was preparing to leave and still she sobbed. Not one word of explanation had yet come from her lips. I began to struggle with a feeling that I should not leave her. If I stayed, her emotional turmoil would surely end. How could I go and willingly cause such suffering for my own dear mother?

The conductor swung himself from the platform onto the doorstep of the passenger car. I wondered if some terrible thing would happen to me if I went through with my plans. Would I die in Berlin? No, no, these were not my plans. God had called me to Berlin. I had been invited. Suffering refugees were in need of the gospel. Jesus said, *He that loveth father or mother more than me is not worthy of me ...* Perhaps this was the very kind of dilemma He had anticipated for His servants.

The engine chugged once and a wrenching shudder ran the length of the train. It chugged again and began to move and I knew that my destiny lay in the direction of Berlin. Kissing her once more on the cheek I grabbed my two suitcases and leaped past the conductor into the doorway of the moving train. My choice was clear. I followed the Lord. I turned and waved but Mother could not wave back. She was still weeping uncontrollably into her handkerchief.

As the chugging engine gained speed and increased the distance between us I felt a deep root being ripped slowly from my chest. The pain of it was terrible and wonderful at the same time. This was the way a boy became a man. He left his mother and followed God. Still, as the train platform faded in the distance, I felt such sadness. I did not understand my mother's outburst.

Only years later when I had children of my own would I gain that perspective. The grief that she had felt on the platform that day was the grief of revelation and regret. The revelation was that I had been the child she had overlooked. She had seen me through attitudes and assumptions, and had never truly stopped to see me for who I was until that train came into view. Then it was too late. Suddenly, her eyes were opened and she knew how much she loved me. She had her revelation just as I was leaving the nest.

I smile now. All was forgiven. She had been God's good gift to me, and she had given me so much more than she knew. Nothing would ever diminish that fact. In time, God worked it all for the good of our relationship.

I SERVED THE BERLIN MISSION in every way possible for the next three months. They had me involved in feeding, clothing, helping obtain government papers and citizenships for the refugees. I was also able to preach the gospel there, several times each day. A few received the Lord as Savior as a result. It was a difficult environment.

Furthermore, as I continued there, Mother and Father telephoned me with bad news. The reply from the Bible College in Wales had arrived. I had been rejected. The reason was the school instructed only in English. I spoke only German. I was devastated.

"Do you remember how you resisted learning English?" Mother reminded me. I heard that familiar scolding edge in her voice. "You always said, 'Why do I have to learn this subject?' Now it has stopped you from being able to go to Wales."

Even in this conversation I could hear her old attitudes toward me. She could not help herself.

"This cannot stop me," I said. "This *will not* stop me. I know God wants me to go to that school. I know it."

"Why to *that* school?" My father said. "What's wrong with our Pentecostal school? Maybe now you will listen to me."

"Father, I will always listen to you. I will not always agree with you. I will learn English. I am not the little boy who could not do his English homework. I have grown. My mind has grown, and I know God will enable me to learn fast."

"But it is too late. They have rejected you, son. You need to face it and go on."

I did not reply for a long time. I felt hot tears well up in my eyes. "I just don't understand it. I was sure this was God's direction for me."

I hung up the telephone. Nothing could be done so I continued in the mission and prayed for God to intervene.

He intervened so beautifully. Reverend Morris returned to Krempe to follow up on our youth trip to England. My parents informed him of my Bible school rejection.

"Why?"

"Because he does not speak English."

"No, no!" cried Morris. "That is no obstacle. Not for Reinhard. Let me write a letter to Sam Howells. He knows me well. I have interpreted for Reinhard, and I know that he is not far from grasping the language. He is bright. He can do it."

My parents could hardly say no. Morris wrote the letter and sent it.

When I arrived home from Berlin Mom and Dad presented me with the letter from the Bible school in Wales. The school had reversed its decision and opened the doors for me to come. After Morris' intervention, they had agreed to tutor me in English even as I undertook my two years of studies. I was ecstatic! I ran around the room with that letter in my hands, praising God for His goodness.

My parents' objections were overwhelmed. Nothing could hold me back. I hugged them both. My mother was once again sobbing. They both realized that my life was taking a completely new direction. Not one of their choosing, but certainly one that God was blessing.

As THE TIME of my departure neared I could see a change in my father. He was beginning to accept that Martin would never be his successor. Martin was studying for a career in medicine. Hermann had invested so much of his hope in his eldest son, but it would be his youngest who took up the torch of ministry. He also realized he had done very little to prepare me in his stead. In an awkward sort of gesture, he invited me at last to speak to his little church in Krempe.

It was my last Sunday in Germany before leaving for Wales. I stood and opened my Bible. As I began to speak, it was a repeat of Tostedt. The people were deeply touched and responded with tears and a time of worship.

As I shook the hands of all 25 or so members at the door, my father stood beside me. He heard them say to me again and again, "Reinhard, you are called of God. You are truly called."

Afterward, as my father and I rode the train toward home, he asked, "Reinhard, where did you get that sermon?"

"From the Bible, Father."

"But you've never been to Bible school. Where did you get those ideas about it?"

"When I read the Bible, Father, things pop out of the page at me."

He rode some time in silence. "I've read those same passages, and I've never seen those things that you spoke of today."

At home I prepared to catch my train to England. One day I noticed a large, leather-bound volume on a bookshelf. It was a genealogy Martin had compiled of the Bonnke family history. It represented a great deal of research. Only someone with my brother's intellect and tenacity would have compiled it. To me it seemed impressive in a dark sort of way. And as I browsed through it, it disturbed me.

I sensed that I was part of the Bonnke family history and breaking away from it at the same time. Two opposite clans were reaching out to define me – the historic family and the spiritual family. Like Abram leaving Ur of the Chaldees, I was departing Germany, but I could not completely shake its dust from my feet.

"Father," I said, "as I look at our family heritage, I am amazed that any of us serve the Lord today. Who in our family serves the Lord besides you?"

"Very few," Father said, as he sat down opposite me.

"How did God break into the Bonnke family? How did He do it?"

This was the defining question I wrote about in chapter 2. For the first time, I heard the story of Luis Graf coming to Trunz. Of Grandfather August's healing and conversion. And it was the first time I heard the story of Father's tuberculosis, his healing, and his subsequent surrender to God.

In these stories, as I prepared to leave for another nation and another culture that I admired, I began to gain a sense of my roots, both natural and spiritual. God's call on my life could not be totally separated from my East Prussian origin. This had been part of His mysterious design. Whatever He chose to do with me in life would grow out of this dark soil. It would be something similar to Isaiah's words concerning the coming of the Messiah. He would come forth as ... *a root out of a dry ground.*[35] My life would follow an unlikely path.

But I had already learned that God seemed to specialize in such triumphs. As I looked at the genealogy and the impressive list of godless Bonnke heroes, I saw my brilliant older brothers choosing to follow in those pagan footsteps rather than Father's. The words of Paul returned to me, *For ye see your calling, brethren, how that not many wise men after the flesh, not many mighty, not many noble, are called ...*[36]

# Chapter 13

I TRAVELED BY TRAIN from Germany to Calais, France. Taking a ferry, I crossed the English Channel at its narrowest point to Dover. From there I caught a train through London, switching to a final connection that took me across the island to Wales. Greeted at the train station by a fellow student, I was escorted to Swansea by bus. Near the coast we entered a walled compound through a small green door that the students affectionately called "the narrow gate."

Inside were a group of houses, student dormitories, classrooms, and lovely gardens on a slope that overlooked the sea. Always in that compound I can remember the chatter of songbirds and the cooing of homing pigeons housed in a keeper's hutch. To me, this lovely place promised to become a spiritual Garden of Eden where I would feast on biblical and practical lessons pertaining to my calling. I was brimming with excitement for what God had in store for me here.

Soon, however, "the narrow gate" took on an added meaning. I was surprised to learn that there were only two Pentecostal students in the entire student body. This I learned from my roommate, Bryn Jones. Shortly after being introduced to him he informed me that he was the other Pentecostal student at Swansea. He instructed me that we were not to speak in tongues. It was forbidden.

I looked at Bryn with amazement. "But Paul said in 1 Corinthians ... *forbid not to speak with tongues.*[37] How can a Bible school take a position that is unbiblical?"

"You should not press that issue here, Reinhard. Look at it this way; they know we are Pentecostal. That's why they have housed us together. They obviously want us here. Let's just abide by the rules and get all the Lord has for us."

"Of course, you are right. At least they have not signed a document like *The Berlin Declaration* saying we are of the devil. That is truly something to be thankful for."

Still, to me this was a shock. I had not imagined that people of such vibrant faith might not speak in tongues. Pentecostals were the only Christians in Germany I knew who had any faith at all. Well, any with an ounce of life that might be detected. During my youth group visit during the summer I had only visited Pentecostal churches. The pastor of *The People's Church* had recommended this school to me. He was Charismatic. I had just assumed he would not recommend me to a school that did not approve of speaking in tongues. But in fact, he had not recommended the school for its Pentecostal beliefs. Rather, he had recommended it for its evangelistic and missionary reputation.

After a while, I began to learn more about the Great Welsh Revival that had given this school its identity. It had happened during the era called the Holiness revival, a couple of years before Azusa Street in America. It had changed Wales from bitter to sweet but had not featured speaking in tongues. Those who did not agree with tongues often looked to the Welsh Revival as their example of a true revival – their Azusa Street, if you will. In that sense they wanted to preserve what was pure and true about their own tradition. The discussion of tongues always seemed divisive to them, and they wished simply to avoid it, concentrating instead on the things that united them.

As I spent two years among them, I met Methodists, Anglicans, Presbyterians, and Baptists who obviously loved Jesus and were serious about living fully for Him. The ministry of the Holy Spirit was alive and well among them. I could sense the reality of the Christian brotherhood we shared in spite of our denominational differences, and this exposure became important to me later in Africa. It was on the Dark Continent that I expanded into mega-evangelistic crusades, and they included the sponsorship of many denominations.

"Well," I said to Bryn on that first day, "perhaps they have housed us together to contain the tongues issue in one room. We will try not to let the cat out of the bag."

As I BEGAN to attend classes, I had my hands too full to even think about theological and denominational differences. In the beginning, I took notes in a kind of English-German phonetic shorthand that only I could read. This primitive stage of learning preceded my mastery of writing in English. Though my spoken English was awkward and halting, I was reasonably well understood. Because of my calling, I was highly motivated to learn to speak the language fast, and I did. The lectures about the Bible and the work of the gospel taught in English made much better sense to me than the dull and lifeless language lessons I had suffered in German schools.

As the first weeks passed, I learned that the word sea in Swansea stands for its place by the ocean. The school was perched where the Bristol Channel enters the Celtic Sea. There are a few sunny days in this part of the world, but mostly rain, rain, rain. All the necessary ingredients to maintain the beautiful gardens. But in this region, when the sun does shine, people take full advantage of it. In our case, we took our classes from the classrooms to the beautifully landscaped lawns and fairways. These are some of the most blessed memories I have of this place.

Ian Jones was my favorite instructor. He was the senior member of the faculty and had been a contemporary of Rees Howells. I felt I was rubbing shoulders with history being near him. When I was introduced to his Bible courses, I only thought I knew my Bible. Hearing him was like drinking from a fresh flowing fountain as he expounded the Word as I had never heard it before. I could hardly endure the time between his classes, feeling something like a palpable hunger for more of the Word. He could see my eagerness, and I felt a special bond with him.

He also taught the required course in homiletics, which is the art and craft of preaching. Before coming to school, I had never thought of pulpit delivery as an art form, or a craft. To me, preaching was simply opening my Bible and speaking as the Spirit gave utterance. With this approach, the audiences in Tostedt and Krempe had been deeply moved. I had also been effective in Berlin. Plus, I had seen a man come to Jesus in my first street sermon as a boy. I knew nothing of homiletics.

Within two months of my arrival, Ian asked me to deliver my first sermon in front of the homiletics class. I would speak, and the class would critique the delivery. Actually, the assignment was called an exposition, and the specific topic was the book of 2 Timothy. I had a personal grasp of 2 Timothy, Paul's final address to his young protégé. I could hardly wait to let loose on the subject. But "letting loose" on the subject was not exactly the assignment. An exposition is a disciplined delivery, something a teacher, or even a college professor might present.

As expositions go, I would say that I delivered more of an exhortation. Ian was not impressed. My halting English was not the problem. He and the entire class, in fact, began to take my exposition apart, criticizing its lack of structure, forethought, and organization.

Bible College Class

For them, my sermon was purely an academic exercise. They focused their criticism not so much on what I said but how I said it. The art and craft of pulpit delivery had apparently escaped me. I thought Ian Jones would understand the heart of my presentation and that he would stand up for me. But he did not. Perhaps I had totally misread what I thought was the special bond between us. I was devastated. For me this was not academic. It was an acid test of my ability to preach the gospel. I had delivered my soul and had fallen short of connecting to my audience.

In deep pain, I escaped into the far reaches of the Italian garden to a stone tool shed. It was secluded and hopefully soundproof. I crept inside and broke down in tears. "My Father, I am not a preacher or an expositor or a teacher or an evangelist – *But I have called you to be an evangelist!*" In mid-cry the Spirit stopped me dead in my tracks and dried up my tears with these words. Everything else became meaningless.

I heard it and saw it and accepted it. My sermons might never be homiletical masterpieces. They might never be printed in books and reproduced as examples of form and content. They were meant for the ear and the heart of the sinner, not for professors, or grade books, or classrooms. Before God, the only critic that counted was the man or woman who raised their hand and came forward to receive Jesus. All else counted as dung.

"Yes!" I shouted. "I am an evangelist! You have called me to be an evangelist."

From that day to this there has never been any doubt about my calling. God confirmed it to me in that little stone shed after flunking my first homiletics test. God's true lessons are never academic.

The glory of the Swansea bible college was that it forced us to live by faith. We prayed for everything. For the huge supply of winter coal necessary to heat our buildings, to the bus fare to take us street preaching on the weekends. The school supplied only food and lodging for us. All the extras we were instructed to "pray in." And always, we were required to pray in secret without publicly mentioning our needs. This had been George Müller's legacy and the legacy of Rees Howells as well. Now Rees's son Samuel followed the faith path. I learned to embrace it.

Whenever a student or staff member saw their need met by the Lord they would testify about it. These stories were meant to encourage the other students to live in complete dependence upon God. The phrase that was used when God met a need was, "I've been delivered."

Samuel Howells joined us in a student prayer meeting one morning not long after I arrived. Winter was knocking at the door. Nighttime temperatures were plunging toward the freezing mark. He asked that we pray for several hundred pounds to buy coal to heat the classrooms and dormitories. This amount was needed by the end of the week. To me this seemed like a huge sum. I had never faced a need so large. Nor had I been forced to come up with such an amount so quickly. I joined my prayers with the others and waited to see what God would do.

At the end of the week Samuel returned to our prayer meeting. His eyes were bright and his face beaming.

"Praise God! We've been delivered," he said.

Right then, I prayed in my heart, *Lord, I also want to be a man of faith. I want to see Your way of providing for needs.*

Soon thereafter, a missionary visited the college. As he spoke, I heard the Lord speak in my heart to give all the money I had received from home. My parents and the church in Krempe and Glückstadt sent packages containing gifts and money to help me with expenses beyond room and board. This was all I had. I agreed to give it, but then I decided to hold back one pound for emergencies. Just one pound, I reasoned. As I prepared to make the gift, I knew God had asked for all of my spending money. How would I know what He would do if I continued to hold back? I gave it all.

Time passed, and I had nearly forgotten about it. One Saturday, an invitation came asking me to minister on Sunshine Corner Beach near Swansea. This was a popular weekend gathering place for families. A local church had established a regular outreach to children there. I invited Teun de Ruiter, a fellow student from Holland, to accompany me. As we searched our pockets, we found that I had exactly enough bus fare to get us both there but no money to bring us back. We prayed and decided that we would put our faith to the test. We would go and believe God for the return fare.

We went. The ministry was fine. As we finished and returned to the bus stop, the pastor of the church came walking along the street. He recognized us and knew we had been ministering on the beach. I felt immediately that I was witnessing the deliverance God had planned for us.

"Hey boys, would you join me for a cup of tea?"

"We would love to," I said.

He took us to a local cafe near the beach, and we had several cups of tea and passed the time in pleasant conversation. When we finished, he called for the bill and opened his wallet to pay. I looked inside and saw more money than I could imagine. I began talking to God about it. I felt sure He had brought this man to us as our provision for the return trip. Surely God would move on him in his abundance to donate our return bus fare now. We would say nothing about it.

"Well, thank you for the tea," I said. "We must be going now. We have to catch a bus back to school."

This broad hint fell on deaf ears. He paid the bill, closed his wallet, and did not offer to pay for anything more. We smiled grimly at one another as he walked away, leaving us at the bus stop.

The bus would soon arrive, and we had no fare. How would we make it? In my heart I prayed, "Lord, where is the fare? How will You provide?"

Just then, a woman who was leaving the beach area saw us at the stop. As the bus approached, she came running.

"Boys, here is a little something for you. Thank you so much for ministering on the beach today. I so appreciate it."

She grabbed my hand and pressed money into it, then walked away leaving us standing there. When I looked down and counted it, it was exactly enough for bus fare for both of us to return to school.

"Praise God, Teun! We've been delivered!"

I felt that day like I was walking in the footsteps of George Müller and Rees Howells. More than that, I was learning something important about my relationship to my heavenly Father. It is never my job to second-guess His provision. He might use a preacher, a woman, a layman, a criminal, a saint, a natural disaster, a beggar – or He might tell me to take my fishing pole and go look in the mouth of a fish for my bus fare. He is unlimited, and it is His delight to surprise us.

Most of all, I was beginning to learn that faith in God would take me places I would not otherwise go. It would produce results I would not otherwise see. Jesus said that with faith we could speak to a mountain and see it removed into the sea. I was not moving mountains yet, but with faith, my relationship to God had come alive. It was dynamic, making a difference in the world around me.

As the first year of school came to an end, I was praying one day and felt strongly that I should return home for the summer break. This feeling came in spite of the fact that I had no money to purchase the train fare. After praying more about it, I decided I would trust God to supply the money. I would not tell anyone of my need, but I would act as if the need was already met. That day I went to a travel agent in Swansea and booked a reservation in advance. No deposit required.

As the day of my departure approached, I received a packet from home. My heart rejoiced. I thought, *this is it*. I opened it thinking that the money I needed would be inside. It was not there.

The day of my booking arrived. I packed my bags. Still no money. I found my friend Teun and asked him to agree with me in prayer for the supply. We went into one of the empty classrooms and began praying. I did not feel our prayers were effective. As we continued, the words of a song came to mind.

"Teun, we've prayed enough. God has heard us. Let's sing together."

I led him in a song we often sang in Swansea. *There is nothing too hard for Thee ... I am trusting alone in Thee ... It is never too late for Thee, dear Lord.*

Suddenly I received the answer in my spirit. "The money is there, Teun."

"Where?"

Somehow I had received in my spirit the evidence of things not seen. "It is there. I don't know where. But it is there. Let's go get my bags."

We ran from the classroom and across the garden area. As we headed toward the narrow gate, a fellow student named Jim approached me. He was an upper classman, graduating that year. I did not know him well.

"You need money to travel home," he said. "I'd like to help. How much do you need?"

"God knows how much. I will not say."

He also was a student of faith. He reached in his pocket and pulled out a wad of money, placing it in my hands. Then he abruptly turned and walked away. It was the last time I saw him as a Bible college student.

As Teun and I hurried to the travel agent's office, I counted it. Teun recounted it. "Praise God, Reinhard! We've been delivered!" It was just the amount needed for the fare.

The Sunshine Beach story and the train ticket story may seem small compared to other faith stories that come later in my life. But they may be the most important stories of all. In our life of faith we must begin small and graduate to greater challenges. In that respect, we are like the boy David. He first killed a lion and bear while protecting sheep, and then he was ready to kill Goliath, delivering his people from the Philistines.

And what was true for David is true for all. You have faith stories, too. No matter how small, remember them, recite them, count them, and celebrate them. They build your faith for what is coming next in your life.

As THE FIRST YEAR at Swansea became the second year, the cat got out of the bag. My Pentecostal beliefs became fully known. For one thing, I could not keep totally quiet about it. For another, most everyone at the school was curious. Some were more than curious. Many times Bryn and I were invited into polite discussions of the baptism of the Holy Spirit at odd times and places.

When someone asked, I answered. In fact, the official rule of the evangelical school was that we were not allowed to talk about it. But discreetly, even instructors would come after hours and ask Bryn and me to tell them about our experience. Most of them compared their own experiences and could see that we had something they didn't. In general, they tended to lose the enthusiasm of their experiences with God, while ours burned endlessly in our hearts. This attracted rather than repelled them. Though, I suppose for some, there was a kind of spiritual jealousy. For the most part, we developed great respect for one another, even though there remained an official divide.

Finally, all arguments for the baptism of the Holy Spirit fall short. It is seldom good biblical positions that win the day. Rather, it is the example of the Spirit's overflow.

One day, after hours, my Dutch friend, Teun de Ruiter, came to me. "Reinhard," he said, "I want what you have. I want the baptism in the Holy Spirit. Let's go to one of the empty classrooms, and you pray for me to receive it."

"Of course," I said. And off we went.

Once there, he said, "I want you to know that I want the baptism, but I do not want the speaking in new tongues."

He said it like I had the power to hold back that part of the blessing. For a moment I was stumped. I thought, *how can anyone receive the Holy Spirit without speaking in tongues? Should I pray, Lord, baptize Teun with Your Holy Spirit, but hold back on the speaking in tongues, amen?* But then I thought, *Jesus is the Baptizer. Let's see what He does.*

"Very well, Teun," I said. "I will pray for you to receive just the baptism of the Holy Spirit. Nothing more."

We prayed for about ten minutes. Then lightning struck. He fell from his chair and began rolling on the floor. He was not just speaking in tongues, he was trumpeting in tongues. On and on he went until finally, after several minutes, he calmed down.

"You got it, Teun," I said. "You got it. You even spoke in new tongues."

"No! I didn't." His face was flushed with embarrassment.

"You did."

"I did not."

"Well, then, what did you speak when you spoke what you spoke? What did I hear? It was loud enough that I feared you might draw the attention of the school authorities."

A puzzled look came over his face. He thought long and hard about it before replying. "I just spoke unspeakable words," he said at last.

I burst out laughing. What a fine euphemism!

We are friends to this day. Teun went on to be a respected lecturer at a Bible college in the Netherlands and even worked in the administration. Today he pastors a Pentecostal congregation in the Netherlands.

I GRADUATED IN 1961. I was 21 years old. As I neared the end of my time, I wrote my father, asking if I could perform a practicum under his leadership in Krempe. In the meantime our family had moved there. The church had built an apartment in the second story of the meeting house. Mother and Father were both living there and the train commute was a thing of the past. Serving with Father would allow me to be exposed to the realities of actual church ministry before I assumed such duties for myself. It was a required period of testing before ordination and licensing within the German Pentecostal church, the *Arbeitsgemeinschaft der Christengemeinden in Deutschland*, or *ACD*, as we

called it (in 1982 it became the *Bund Freikirchlicher Pfingstgemeinden KdöR /
BFP*). Father was delighted by my request and immediately agreed to it.

Furthermore, he informed me that the *VM*, Velberter missions board, which
was the mission works of the ACD, would require that I follow the practicum
with two years of pastoring a church before they would consider a missions
appointment to South Africa. He told me that he would welcome me to do this
pastoring also at his church. This sounded like my best opportunity to follow
my calling, so the plan was set.

After finishing school in Swansea, I said my goodbyes. Lifelong relationships
were begun there at the school in Wales. So many memories. The fellowship,
the tests of faith, and the wonderful Bible classes – these had now become
forever a part of me and would follow me wherever I went. Furthermore, my
English had become passable.

I TRAVELED BY TRAIN to London. Having some money to spare, I decided I
would simply take an unguided sightseeing tour of the great city. Big Ben, the
famous Parliament building, Trafalgar Square, the Tower of London. I hopped
from bus to bus, crisscrossing the city as if on a holiday. Which, in fact, I was.
My first holiday.

At length, I arrived at a place called Clapham Commons, a large park in a
lovely residential section of the city. With no specific destination in mind, I
decided to stretch my legs. I began walking through the surrounding neighborhood totally at random. All of a sudden I stopped because I saw a blue
nameplate in front of a house. On that nameplate I read, "George Jeffreys."

I thought to myself, *could this be the great George Jeffreys who had founded the
Elim Pentecostal Churches in Ireland and England?* I had read much about him.
He had been a great firebrand evangelist who had traveled across the world
preaching to overflow crowds in some of the largest venues. Miraculous signs
and wonders had accompanied his preaching. I recalled that 10,000 had been
converted in his historic Birmingham crusade. 14,000 had responded during
a crusade in Switzerland. He was known to many as the greatest evangelist

Britain had produced after George Whitfield and
John Wesley. My heart pounded with anticipation to think that of all the residences in London
I might have stumbled upon, I had stumbled
upon his.

George Jeffreys

I paused at the gate. Should I go in and introduce
myself? I felt almost compelled to do it. But who
was I to do such a thing?

I felt a spiritual and natural link with this man. As
with so many other British revival leaders, Jeffreys
had been born in Wales to a miner's family. He
had been a teenager during the great Welsh Revival of 1904 and 1905, and for
him, the fire had never gone out. What especially linked him to me was that
he had also ridden the tide of the Pentecostal revival that followed from Azusa
Street and onward. He had embraced both revivals.

You only live once, I decided. I walked through the front garden gate and climbed
the porch, pausing at the door. There I rang the bell. A lady opened the door.

"Pardon my intrusion, ma'am. Does the George Jeffreys live here who was that
famous firebrand evangelist I have heard so much about?"

"Yes, he does."

"May I please see him?"

"No. Under no circumstances."

She had hardly said no when I heard a deep voice from within the house say,
"Let the young man come in."

I squeezed past that lady in a heartbeat and into the house. As my eyes
adjusted to the dim light, I saw him coming slowly down a staircase, holding it

unsteadily as he made his way toward me. As he reached the landing, I stepped forward, took his hand, and introduced myself. I told him I had a call of God on my life to be an evangelist and to preach the gospel in Africa. That I had been to college in Swansea and was now returning home to Germany.

WHAT HAPPENED NEXT was extraordinary. All of a sudden, he took me by the shoulders and fell to his knees, pulling me to the floor with him. He placed his hands on my head and began to bless me as a father blesses a son, as Abraham blessed Isaac, who blessed Jacob, and on and on. The room seemed to light up with the glory of God as he poured out his prayer over me. I was dazed by that glory. I do not remember the words with which he blessed me, but I do remember their effect. My body felt electrified, tingling with divine energy.

After about a half hour he finished. I stood up and helped him to his feet. He seemed very frail. We said goodbye. The lady came and escorted him away. He could hardly stand. Nor could I, for different reasons. I stumbled from his house and staggered back toward Clapham Commons like a drunken man. There, with my head spinning, I waited for a bus to carry me on my way to the railway station.

What were the odds that this had happened to me? Even more, what did it mean that it had happened to me? It seemed like a dream. I had to convince myself, again and again, that it had actually happened. Why would God grant me this unexpected and unplanned meeting as a 21-year-old Bible college graduate in London on his way home to serve a practicum at the smallest church in all of Germany?

I did not know. I kept it to myself.

I arrived at home and began the process of serving with my father in Krempe. I had been home for just a few months when one day Father said to me, "Son, did you hear the sad news?"

"No, what news?"

"George Jeffreys died in London."

"George Jeffreys! That's impossible, Father. I just saw him. I met him." And then I told him the story of my meeting with him in London.

In fact, he died on January 26, 1962. I was still 21, three months short of my 22nd birthday. As I absorbed the news, I realized something wonderful had happened in London. I had caught Elijah's mantel that day. God had connected me with former generations of evangelists – George Whitfield, John Wesley, Evan Roberts, George Müller, Rees Howells, George Jeffreys. The gospel is like a baton in a relay race. That day I got the baton into my hands. The fire I had already within me. The fire is always fresh. The baton of the gospel is always old, and it is passed on. I now understood that on that day in London, the baton and the flame had met.

I could not yet dream of what it would mean.

# Chapter 14

Upon returning to Krempe I became something of a novelty within German Pentecostal circles. To some I was considered a prodigal, having left the fold for an evangelical school in Great Britain. Others thought I had snubbed our denomination's Bible school, as if I had thought I was too good for it. Still others regarded me with curiosity, wondering how my Swansea education might change me. Had I lost my German Pentecostal identity?

In fact, some things had changed. Soon after arriving, I departed even further from the norm by acquiring a new Volkswagen Beetle. The Beetle was a great choice, the most inexpensive and reliable car in Germany. It was just beginning to become popular in America and elsewhere. Designed by Ferdinand Porsche in the 1930s, the ugly little rear-engine car had been mocked by western auto makers. But after the war, the Volkswagen began to write automobile history, making affordable transportation available to people like me.

My humble little Beetle was hardly a prestigious Volvo 544, nor did it resemble the elegance of Luis Graf's Mercedes, but it was a huge departure from the way my father had always operated. The Volkswagen's transmission required a skilled double pump of the accelerator when gearing up or gearing down. It was a source of pride for me not to brush the teeth of the transmission when shifting gears. In America they call it grinding the gears. I enjoyed driving the little car with real expertise. No grinding the gears.

Not long after arriving at home, a leader from the Pentecostal Fellowship ACD (Arbeitsgemeinschaft der Christengemeinden in Deutschland) came to visit and inspect our practicum arrangement. After having dinner at our house, he said to me, "Reinhard, the ACD does not recognize that college in Wales. It is not Pentecostal. The academic credits you earned there will not count with our organization. You will have to start over in our Bible school if you are serious about your missionary appointment."

I was stunned to silence. When at last I found my voice, all I could say in reply was, "No sir, I will not go to Bible school again."

He left our house with an appreciation for something Mother and Father often said of me: "He has a mind of his own."

In fact, having my own mind was not the issue. It was God who had led me to Swansea. I would not think of it as something less than what it truly was – a great preparation for the mission field.

PETER CAME HOME from the university. Among other things, he wanted to see if I had stuck with my calling, or if my experience in Wales had changed my mind about becoming a minister.

"You are serving a practicum with Father in Krempe?"

"Yes."

"So you are going to take Martin's place, eh? Like Jacob and Esau."

"No, I will not take Martin's place. I will not be Father's successor. I am going to be an evangelist and a missionary in Africa."

"You still haven't let go of that idea?" he chuckled. "You have always been a little slow to catch on to things."

"I would rather be slow on the right track than fast on the highway to hell."

"You do sound like Father. Do you plan to get married like him?"

"Yes."

"Then I think you are going to be one of the most irresponsible people on earth."

"What do you mean?"

"You are going to have children and not be able to pay for their education. Education is the only thing that stands between your children and poverty. Without Father's pension, the church in Krempe could not have allowed any of us to go to college. Think of that."

"God's work pays in more than money. And education is overrated. There are a lot of college-educated fools."

He sighed like he was dealing with a dimwit. "Well, maybe I will make enough money to keep you from starving," he said. "I am going to be a doctor. I want to be where the money is. It's money that gets things done and being a minister of the gospel just doesn't seem to have any financial leverage in this world."

"God has plenty of leverage. More than enough." It was the same old argument.

After the conversation I felt deeply pained. I went to my room and placed my Bible on the bed in front of me. "Lord, I need to hear from You. You have called me to Africa. How will You take care of me? Will I be in poverty like Peter says? Or will You see to it that I am not a poor beggar? Speak to me, I pray."

I opened my Bible at random and read the first verse that came before my eyes. I did this in the same way Mother had done it when asking whether or not He would protect us crossing the Baltic Sea to Copenhagen.

The verse that I read was Nehemiah 9:15. *And gavest them bread from heaven for their hunger, and broughtest forth water for them out of the rock for their thirst, and promisedst them that they should go in to possess the land which thou hadst sworn to give them.*

I made a deal with God right then. Perhaps the reward for serving Him was not luxury food and drink. His provision might be simply bread and water. The basics necessary to sustain life. "OK, Lord," I said. "If You provide bread and water that is good enough for me. I accept it, and it will be like a gourmet meal to me. I would rather serve You and eat Your bread and drink Your water than feast with wealthy men who do not know or care about You."

Of course, as the years passed, I found that the bread He provided has been the finest cake with frosting. And the water has been the most exquisite tea. His supply has always been more than I asked for, as the next story will illustrate. At the moment, I had concentrated on the "bread and water" part of the scripture, but the full promise involved possessing a land that flowed with milk and honey.

After a few weeks of serving the practicum, Father and I climbed into the Volkswagen and traveled north to the town of Rendsburg for a regional pastor's conference. It was near the Pöppendorf prison camp where we had first been reunited as a family after the war. Along the way we visited the old camp and recalled the difficulties of those times. Father did not want to spend much time there. The first thing I noticed was the absence of that ugly barbed wire. Vegetation grew where once fear and misery ruled.

Then, on to Rendsburg. During the pastor's meeting, the host, Reverend Franz Wegner approached me with some startling news.

"Every year in summer," he said, "we have a tent revival here. I have been praying about it, and the Holy Spirit tells me that you, Reinhard, are to be our tent evangelist this year."

Father and I were both amazed. Pastor Wegner was one of the senior clergymen in the ACD. He was well respected.

"I have just come from Bible College and don't have any experience," I said. "I am merely doing my practicum at this time."

"I know that. I have also heard that you are called of God. In fact, it is known that your calling is the call to be an evangelist. This is what we need here in Rendsburg. An evangelist."

"How long do the tent meetings last?"

"As long as you need to get the message out. We will not put a limit on your sermons."

"No, I mean, how many days will the meetings continue?"

"Three weeks. Sunday morning services included."

I didn't say anything, but my math skills had improved so that I could quickly calculate the number of sermons I would have to preach. 24 in all. In my Bible college files I might be able to find a dozen sermons ready to go. My preaching disaster in Ian Jones' homiletics class also came to mind. I had barely begun my practicum. I hardly felt ready for this. It seemed impossible. "So, the Holy Spirit has spoken to you?" I asked.

"He has."

"Well, I am confident that if He has spoken to you He will also speak to me. I will pray about it."

"OK. You pray, Reinhard, and then call me," he said cheerily.

I honestly thought I had shaken him off my trail with that answer.

Back in Krempe I knelt at my bedside. "Father, should I accept this invitation?" Expecting to hear nothing, I imagined that I would simply say to Pastor Wegner, "God has not spoken, therefore I cannot accept."

The opposite happened. Suddenly, these words were burned into my heart. *Go, and twelve baskets **full** shall remain!*

I immediately knew this answer had not come from my own mind. It was not the answer I sought. Furthermore, it was a profound statement, the kind that had the familiar imprint of the Holy Spirit on it. God was stirring up the vision

Grandma Bauszuss had seen when I was ten. She had seen me distributing a loaf of bread to a large crowd. The loaf continued to grow. This scene had been inspired by the gospel accounts of the feeding of the 5,000.

In that story, found in Matthew, Mark, Luke, and John, a little boy had provided five loaves and two fish to Jesus in the face of a hungry multitude. Jesus had used the boy's lunch to feed them all. Afterward, twelve baskets full of bread fragments had been gathered in order to show that the Lord had not only met the need, but had supernaturally provided more than enough. *Go, and twelve baskets shall remain!* This word from God could not have hit the mark more perfectly.

Without hesitation, I called Pastor Wegner. "The Lord has spoken to me," I said. "I will come and preach in your tent meetings."

I began to prepare in prayer and Bible study. I reviewed the dozen sermon outlines I had made in Bible school. That's when I noticed that I did not have a dozen sermons. I really had just one. One sermon presented in a dozen disguises. Seeing this for the first time made me feel even more inadequate.

But today, I understand it. I still have only one sermon. I am an evangelist. I preach the simple ABCs of the gospel. When I preach I am not trying to sound like a professor, or a Bible scholar, or a homiletics expert. I am helping people who are outside of the kingdom of God enter it by the blood of the Lamb. So I repeat the ABCs over and over again, each in perhaps a new disguise, or with a new illustration, or applied to a new culture or occasion, but always the same good news of God's invitation to join His family.

I was soon to be 22 years old. When the day of the meeting in Rendsburg arrived, I drove my Volkswagen northward from Krempe. It was a lovely spring day, and the trees were blossoming. The fragrance of apple and cherry blooms filled the air.

I arrived in Rendsburg early. The tent had been set up at the huge Viehmarkt Square, and a woman was seated in a chair at the main entrance. The flaps were open. I parked my Beetle and approached her, smiling, looking inside. Feeling a bit shy, I did not introduce myself. I looked at the rows of chairs set up beneath the canvas and felt a nervous knot in my stomach.

"If I may ask a question. How many seats are in the tent?"

"There are 250 chairs."

"How many people do you think will show up?"

The woman sighed wearily and shook her head. Her attitude struck a familiar chord with me. For a moment I thought she might say, *I ought to give you a good hiding right now, young man, and get it over with,* as my mother had said to me so often in my younger years. But then, I quieted my thoughts, realizing that my mind was taunting me with old memories. I was not a naughty boy anymore. I was called to be the evangelist here in Rendsburg. There were 250 seats in that tent for the hearing of the gospel.

"Well," the woman continued, lowering her voice in a confidential tone, "I'll tell you the truth. Our pastor has put us on a limb. He went against the board of elders and invited some young evangelist who isn't even dry behind the ears to be our preacher this year. I won't be surprised if we don't fold the tent and go home early."

"I see," I said. "Thank you."

I returned quickly to my car, feeling suddenly anxious and unbalanced. That woman had no idea the power of her words to turn my confidence into mush. Satan himself could not have put a greater scare into me. Looking back, however, I suppose it was a test arranged by my Father in heaven.

I drove out of town to a secluded spot on the Nord Ostsee Kanal, a man-made waterway that crossed the peninsula between the Baltic and North Seas. I stopped the car, fixing the hand brake. "Oh, Lord," I prayed. "Help me, help me, help me. How can I possibly go on if You do not rescue me now?"

As I prayed and talked to God about it, I began to feel peace. It is the kind of peace that only comes from Him. My thoughts returned to the truth. I had not come to Rendsburg because I was barely out of Bible college and hardly dry behind the ears. I was here because the Holy Spirit had spoken to Pastor Wegner. He had also spoken clearly to me. As the voices of doubt and fear were slowly replaced by the voice of the truth, peace again flooded my heart. I praised His holy name in English and in other tongues.

From the outspoken lady I had learned that Pastor Wegner had obeyed the Spirit even above the voice of his board of elders. She may have seen it as a bad sign, but to me it was a sign that I was God's choice. *If God be for me who can be against me?* I thought. I stayed in this place of faith and peace and prayed until the time for the start of the first service.

When I arrived at the tent it was full. Perhaps the people had come out of curiosity to see how the young preacher would fail. Maybe they thought it would be entertaining.

Pastor Wegner met me outside. He was very excited and led me to the platform. The music was beginning. I sat down and looked out over the crowd. Pastor Wegner stood and announced that evangelist Reinhard Bonnke had arrived and would be our crusade evangelist tonight.

In the front row of the audience my eyes met the eyes of Mrs. Meyer who had spoken to me earlier outside the tent. She gasped and her hands flew to her cheeks. Her face turned red and she bowed her head low in shame and embarrassment. But it was totally unnecessary. I was already seeing the humor in it. Later, this became a good story for both of us to repeat.

When I stood to preach, I opened my Bible to a redemption scripture. As I read, I saw in my mind what I might describe as the shape of the gospel. My preaching did not depend upon notes. My brain visualized the path for my words to follow. God put an outline there, and I simply filled in the outline with words and ideas and scriptures as they flowed into my mind. It was the ABCs of the gospel that came out of my mouth. It was the gift of the evangelist at work. In the hearts of the people, the Holy Spirit did His work. Many raised their hands for salvation in that service and in every service that followed. My heart overflowed with gratitude.

As the meetings continued I began to notice a pretty girl in the audience. She seemed very engaged in the meetings, and I sensed she was a godly person. This drew me to her even more and my interest became strong. I found myself making excuses to be near her and to have conversation with her after the meetings. Others were attracted to her as well because she had a very pleasant personality. I could not help but wonder if such an attractive girl might be a lifelong match for me.

One day we were speaking of spiritual things. I asked her the question that was most on my mind. "If God called you to Africa, would you go?"

"No," she replied immediately. "Never. I would never leave Germany."

My interest in her died on the spot. No longer did I seek to be near her or to have conversation with her. This incident revealed to me that I was seriously seeking a wife who would share my calling. I had no interest in dating as a pastime. My heart was set on Africa, and I had no time for anything that would distract from that purpose.

In the second week of the meetings, the local newspaper sent a reporter and a photographer to do a front-page story for the Rendsburg newspaper. Word of the meeting had begun to circulate in the town. The reporter came to Pastor Wegner, who introduced him to me.

"You have misunderstood," the reporter said, "I want to speak to the main speaker, not to his apprentice. I need a statement from the evangelist."

"But this is the evangelist. This is Reinhard Bonnke."

He laughed and shook his head. Licking his pencil lead, he began to write on his notepad. "Have you saved your first soul, young man?"

"Oh, I have. I saw a man come to Jesus when I was just a boy of eleven."

"Just a boy of eleven, huh? You don't appear yet to have had your first shave. Am I right about that?"

"Yes, sir."

"How old are you?"

"21."

In fact, I had not yet shaved in my life. My hair was a boyish shade of blond and my beard so light that it didn't show. The photographer took my picture, and the story about the boy evangelist hit the front page. The tent would not hold the crowds.

What a wonderful evangelistic crusade it was! My first tent meeting. I preached every day for three weeks, and twice each Sunday. In terms of numbers it certainly does not compare to the crowds that were to follow. But God is not only a God of the big numbers; He is God of the smallest of numbers, too. Some of the people who were saved in that meeting in Rendsburg are still among my ministry partners. They support me as I reach out to crowds of millions with the ABCs of the gospel today.

God kept His promise. I did not run dry. When the meetings ended I could have extended for another three weeks. *Twelve baskets remained!*

FOLLOWING THE MEETINGS, Pastor Wegner brought a number of the converts from the meetings to Krempe. Father invited his church members in Krempe to join us in a special joint service. The new converts stood in front of the people and, with tears and praises to God, told of their conversions in the Rendsburg tent meetings. One woman had been bound by demonic forces, and she told how she had been set free. The fruit of the meetings was bountiful, and my father, Hermann, was moved to tears to hear these testimonies.

Little did I know that the meeting in Rendsburg would begin a small landslide of offers to preach. Word spread quickly through the ACD that if you want new people in your church, call Reinhard Bonnke. Offers came from all over Germany. Some from as far away as Switzerland and England.

Not long after that, I was approached by Pastor Ludwig Eisenlöffel, the ACD official who had declared my Wales Bible college education invalid. He extended his hand to me and shook it warmly. He then assured me that the ACD recognized the anointing of God upon my ministry. They would not hold my Swansea education against me.

As my father saw this happen, it pleased him, but it also strained our relationship. In his military mind, rules were rules. They should not be bent for anyone. He did not bend the rules, and rules were not bent for him, nor would he want them to be. He was a straightforward man, a faithful servant. Also, he did not receive offers to preach like I did. His preaching style was faithful, steady, yet a bit bland in its delivery. At this stage in his life, the pattern was well set for him.

By contrast, I was his youngest son, barely out of Bible school, not yet ordained, still serving a vicariate – and I was breaking the mold. Already I received invitations to preach from far and wide. Of course, when reason prevailed, he understood that my calling was different to his. He was a pastor. I had the calling of an evangelist. Still, whether consciously or sub-consciously, he began to put pressure on me not to accept these preaching invitations. In fact, I never bowed to his pressure, one way or the other. I did decline many offers after praying and not feeling God's peace about it, but never because of my father's pressure.

After a while, Father could not seem to help himself. If I went to the right, he leaned to the left. If I said I would go, he found reasons for me to stay. If I spoke of my call to Africa, he insisted that I stay in Germany. More and more, we did not see eye to eye on important matters.

I CELEBRATED MY 22ND BIRTHDAY on April 19, 1962. Father and I began to discuss the necessity of my taking the pulpit in Krempe for two years. The ACD required that the church I served be affiliated with the denomination. Afterward, they would appoint me to a mission station within the fellowship.

"They simply must appoint me to Africa, Father," I said, one day.

"Well, the board determines appointments. They may have a missionary need in India, or Indonesia, and not in South Africa in the beginning. Are you saying that you would refuse it?"

"I would have to refuse it. Are you saying that the missions board would not consider my call to South Africa?"

"Oh, yes they will consider it, but it may not be available."

"Available? How could it not be available? Would they appoint me to some place God has not called me?"

"It has happened to others. Perhaps you should prepare yourself that it might happen to you."

"I do not want to prepare myself that way. I will pray that God will move on their hearts to appoint me to the place He has appointed me. If they do not acknowledge that, I am not sure what I will do."

"Reinhard, I must say that I do not feel your call to Africa should come before the needs of the place where you live. You were born in Germany. This is your home, and we need revival. How can you go off to preach in Africa when the needs are so desperate around you here? It seems hypocritical. Let revival begin here first. Jesus said that after the Holy Spirit came on the disciples at Pentecost, they were to go to Jerusalem *first*, then to Samaria, then to the uttermost part of the earth.[38] You seem to be jumping to the last of the list before serving the first. Many of us have done the hard work of sowing in this hard German soil for decades. Still, we have not seen much harvest. The Lord said, one sows, another reaps.[39] How will we reap if our reapers go off to Africa?"

I had to think this argument through before replying. My own heart and calling was on the line. In fact, it was in that very place of my calling that I found my answer. I said to him, "The Lord said to pray that the Lord of the harvest will send workers into His harvest field.[40] It is not for me to decide where I will serve, Father. If God sends to me Germany, I will go to Germany. If He sends me to Africa, then I must go to Africa. The other issues are in His hands."

This difference was never settled between us until I actually went to Africa. In the meantime, Father continued to make this "Jerusalem first" argument. It was a great test of my calling. If I had not been so sure of my direction, I might have found it compelling. I might have changed my course and missed so much of what God had planned to accomplish through me.

I BEGAN TO RECEIVE OFFERS to serve my two-year vicariate beyond Krempe. In fact, some of the largest churches in the denomination called me. For a young

Plenty of open-air meetings

man my age, this was unheard of. Father was again taken aback at this early success. It placed more strain on our relationship, and forced me to think more deeply about how and where I would pastor for the required two years. The more I thought about it, the more I began to consider that I should accept none of these fine offers. Nor would I serve in Krempe. Not only did I not want Father to feel slighted, but I did not want my brothers to think that I was trying to take Martin's place as Father's successor.

Instead of a choice between Krempe and one of the larger churches, I began to see a third way. I felt I should make a completely new mark. Since evangelism was my calling, I could go where no church existed. I could see people converted and after two years leave a brand-new church behind when I left for Africa. I began to make a mental checklist of possible cities where I could accomplish this kind of plan.

Also, as I thought about being a pastor for two years, I thought about the extra challenge it would create being unmarried. When preaching in other churches, I found myself receiving too much attention from women who wanted to introduce me to their eligible daughters. This could distract me from a full focus on evangelism. I did not want this complication to continue when I began my work as a pastor. Being married to a woman who shared my calling would be a great blessing and a great relief of mind.

AT THAT TIME, Father and I escorted some of our young people to a musical youth rally held in Neumünster. All of the church youth from the region sent musical groups to represent them at this rally in a kind of talent contest.

While there, a beautiful mandolin player caught my eye. She never once looked my way, but I had a feeling she saw my every move. How could I know that? Well, actually, I didn't know that. I just wanted it to be true so badly that I imagined it was so. I certainly saw *her* every move, even though I pretended not to. I watched her all evening from the corner of my eye, not wanting to be obvious. If I was so smitten by her, oh how I wanted her to be smitten by me, too! But as the night wore on, I began to doubt that she knew I existed. Not once did I have the satisfaction of receiving even a sideways glance. The challenge of gaining her attention grew to the sky.

During the service she occasionally shared secrets with another girl from Marne. Boys never did things like that. She cupped her hand and whispered into her friend's ear. Suddenly, I wanted to be the subject of that secret she shared. I wanted to be special to her in that way. Every move this beautiful young musician made ignited my imagination with a greater desire to know her.

Other groups stood on the platform to perform their musical numbers. As they did, I noticed how she cradled her mandolin like a child, stroking its teardrop-shaped soundboard with her fingers. As a member of the musical Bonnkes and a guitar strummer myself, I appreciated that she had chosen an unusual stringed instrument. This Italian dual-stringed guitar produced delicate tones. It was a descendent of the romantic lute, and of David's harp. In Germany, we were used to music played with pomp and bombast. The mandolin was a rare choice here, and I liked that about her.

At last, it was announced that the musical group from Marne would perform. She stood with her friend and walked to the platform. Now, I knew where to find her. The city of Marne was some 50 miles to the north of Krempe on the North Sea coast. Already the scheming began. Perhaps, I thought, I will be invited to preach there one day.

From the platform she plucked the mandolin strings and they began to vibrate, creating a lovely melody. The girls began to harmonize. Soon I saw a look of consternation cross their features. Something was wrong. As in most musical performances, the musicians should never betray that anything is wrong. Part of the challenge of performing is to make sure the audience is at ease. But the problem they faced was insurmountable. The limits of their vocal range would not allow them to reach the song's climax. They stopped.

"I am sorry," the mandolin player said. "I set the key too high. We will have to start again."

She began to strum the introduction again, playing in the adjusted key, and the song was performed beautifully. Any hope of placing in the contest, however, was lost.

I was so impressed with her grace. She had spoken with great poise and dignity in an embarrassing situation. The entire contest was at stake, but she had handled it as if nothing was lost. It made her natural beauty twice as appealing to me. I began a conversation with God. Might such a girl be His choice for me? Certainly, to follow His calling to Africa I would need a wife and mother with her kind of character.

Afterward, I was too shy to approach her. I asked others, "Who is that girl from Marne who sang and played the mandolin?"

"That is Anni Sülzle," I was told.

I loved her name from the moment I heard it. I forgot the names of others but never that one. I prayed, *Lord, how can I connect with that girl? I so much want to talk to her.*

I cannot say that I waited for an answer. In fact, I took matters into my own hands that night and did something totally manipulative. Perhaps later, I suffered uncertainty because of it. I went to her pastor from Marne with a suggestion. I told him I was doing a practicum at my father's church in Krempe, and I offered to swap pulpits with him. He liked the idea, and that is how I got to Marne and finally met Anni.

When I preached there, I was introduced to her, and we had a good conversation after the meeting. I learned that she had been born in Romania into a family of eight children. Her family had moved to Marne after suffering terribly during the war. They lived a farm life and always had plenty of food on the table. Friends and guests were made welcome. She had accepted Jesus as her savior in Sunday school.

I told her that I would like to see her again. She said she might be able to come visit me in Krempe on her way to the ACD Bible College. I was very pleased to learn that she was planning to attend the German Pentecostal School.

When she came to visit, she told me she had been called to be a missionary.

"Do you mean God has called you to preach?"

"Well, no. It is just that since becoming a Christian I have always wanted to become a nurse so that I could serve the Lord on the mission field."

I was relieved. I did not want to marry another preacher. What I sought was a wife, a helper, and a mother for my children. But of course, a mother with a missionary's heart would be essential to my calling. Africa lay ahead. I placed it before the Lord again, reminding Him that the wrong wife could put all of it at risk. I asked Him to make it clear to me if Anni was the one He would choose for me to marry.

I am not outlining a prescription for finding a mate here. I am simply relating my own story. I know of many others who have taken different paths just as successfully.

Over the next year, Anni and I found it hard to be together. We wrote letters to one another. She was busy at school, and I was working with Father in Krempe, or else traveling in various churches and crusades. It just didn't work out for us to spend much time together after our first meeting. This began to allow doubts to creep into my mind about our relationship.

Meanwhile, my father campaigned against it. He said that Anni was no match for me. She was not well educated enough. In this, perhaps he thought *too highly* of the education I had received in Wales. But his objections did not really impact my thinking about her. I had to deal with my own doubts. Perhaps I had been presumptuous to act on my feelings in our first meeting, not waiting for a clear signal from God.

I wrote to Anni and suggested that we put our relationship on ice for a time. She graciously understood and agreed. She was busy with school and with preparation for a life in missions work.

After that, I began to look seriously for another candidate. As I traveled around in preaching engagements, there were lovely girls everywhere. But to connect meaningfully with just one proper candidate was not so easy. Along the way I met another young preacher who told me about his beautiful sister. He said that his family lived in southern Germany and would welcome a visit from me if I would like to get to know her.

The visit was arranged. His sister was indeed beautiful.

We were all at dinner with the family at their house. I hoped that I was making a good impression. I thought she would make a prize for any man. Suddenly she turned to me and said, "I understand that you are the son of a poor preacher."

It was as much the disapproving tone of her voice as the words themselves. Nothing more needed to be said. I thought, *she should marry one of my brothers. They are of the same mind.* My attraction for this lovely girl vanished. My interest could not have been resurrected with a deep-channel dredge. I would have departed immediately except I had to stay and endure the rest of the planned visit. In the end, I said my polite thank-you for the hospitality and said goodbye. I could not wait to return home and renew my correspondence with Anni.

As I continued to pray about it, I felt the Lord saying to me, "Anni is My choice for you."

IN FEBRUARY OF 1964, I wrote a letter to break the ice I had placed between us. The ice didn't break; it melted in a heat wave. Our letters were filled with much more than casual affection. Suddenly, our romance was off to the races.

I arranged to come see her at the Bible College. However, they had a rule that no boy could meet a girl on campus. We met outside the campus near a grove of trees. Taking a picnic lunch, we walked together. As we walked, I took her hand. So much is communicated in a touch. I began to know in my heart that Anni was the one for me. We were bonding, and I could sense that my passion for her could be lifelong.

I told her that I was almost finished with my practicum. The ACD president, Pastor Erwin Lorenz, was coming soon to conduct my ordination ceremony. Immediately afterward, I explained, I would be required to serve as a pastor for two years in order to receive a missionary appointment. Furthermore, I told her that I would not serve as a pastor in Krempe, nor in another church within the ACD. Rather, I would seek a new city that had no Pentecostal church, and establish a congregation there for the required two years.

She did not show a trace of fear or uncertainty about how this would be done. She had no questions about the difficulties of such a pioneering effort. Her eyes sparkled as she talked with me about it, and I could see that she loved the very idea. Yes, she was the adventurous girl who had chosen to play the mandolin and had the wisdom to stop and change the key when she had started wrong. This Anni Sülzle was someone special.

I visited her again and again. In the meantime, I found an engagement ring and bought it. My ordination was completed in March. In May, we walked beneath the blossoming apple and plum trees in our favorite grove. I dared to take her in my arms and kiss her for the very first time. I suppose the feeling was second only to the charge of the Holy Spirit that had surged through my hands when I had prayed for the woman in Father's prayer meeting as a boy.

"Anni, will you marry me?"

"Yes."

I have never seen her face so radiant. I placed the ring on her finger and kissed her again. I could have swung through the trees, or pounded my chest. My days of waiting and dreaming of Africa were over. The reality of following my calling with the love of my life was about to begin.

Immediately, I felt the controlling bonds to Hermann and Meta Bonnke slip from my shoulders. In their place, a new bond with my life partner took hold. Anni and I were together now, as one before the Lord. I could hardly wait to marry her and make a place to call our own.

# Chapter 15

THE PLACE WE BEGAN our married life was Flensburg. The name of this city came to me as a strong impression during a time of prayer. It was the northernmost city in Germany, near the Danish border. It had the reputation of being the best city between Hamburg and Copenhagen. Situated at the end of a rocky fjord from the Baltic Sea, it was a unique maritime community surrounded by dairies and rich farmland. I knew not one soul there, which made the choice just about perfect.

As usual, my father took issue with the decision. More and more, the way I conducted my life left Father scratching his head.

"There are so many better choices," he said. "It is freezing cold in Flensburg. You have given yourself a handicap by going to a city where there is no Pentecostal church. Why? It is unnecessary."

"Father, I've heard from God," I replied. "I am going to Flensburg."

"But you are going to be married in November. Where will you live with your new bride?"

"We will live in the place God provides for us."

"But you don't even have a church. I have worked all these years in Krempe, and it still doesn't pay the bills. How will you make a living?"

"Bread and water," Father. "God has promised bread and water. We will not starve."

My plan began to take shape. It was late summer and I would go pitch a tent and let it stand for six weeks. Every night I would preach the ABCs of the gospel. When the meetings were finished, I would take the harvest of souls God had given me and find a permanent place of worship. In the process of seeing all of this take place Anni and I would be married. Father would conduct the ceremony.

*What a great way for Anni and I to start our life together*, I thought.

In Krempe, Glückstadt, Hamburg, Tostedt, Rendsburg, and across the whole of Germany, I knew enough talented young musicians to schedule special performances throughout the meetings. The groups would take turns so that none were obligated beyond reason. I also had found a preaching companion named Evangelist Erich Theis. He agreed to share the preaching schedule with me so I could remain fresh. Everything was set.

When we had organized the crusade, Erich and I went to Flensburg with the tent. We obtained permits from the city to pitch it on a large field at the edge of town called the Exe. Everyone knew where it was. To advertise that we were set up at the Exe would be immediately understood by anyone in the region. That seemed perfect.

Erich Theiss and I

We placed our advertising around the town and waited for the first crowd. It was modest in size. I preached and one old gentleman came forward to accept Christ. He was a German farmer in his seventies. This truly inspired me. Night after night the momentum began to pick up. About midway through the meetings, I was exhilarated. I had seen 50 people come to the Lord. Already, I had doubled the size of Father's church in Krempe.

Then, the devil moved in next door to us – literally. A large circus came to town and pitched its big top right next to our tent. It towered above us, dwarfing us. We were being eclipsed by a monster of sinful entertainment. As I watched them put up that massive canvas, I remembered the elephant, the lions, and the other wonderful animals from the circus of my childhood. But I also remembered Mother's description, "The circus is an excuse for women to flaunt their bodies and arouse sinful passions in men." I felt as if the Enemy had thrown a wet blanket over my meetings in an attempt to smother our little revival fire.

One day as I tidied up the interior of our crusade tent, a man came through the opening. He walked up to me and introduced himself. "I am the circus director," he said. "I would like to speak with the man who is preaching in this tent."

"That is me. I am Reinhard Bonnke."

"I would like you to preach in my tent."

I was stunned. "Preach to the circus crowd?"

"Yes. I will advertise a special meeting to be held here on Sunday morning before the circus begins. I would like you to preach. Would you do that?"

What better place to preach the gospel than in a tent full of sinners! How could an evangelist refuse? "Yes, I will be there," I said. "I'll be there."

I shook his hand like a water pump. My vision of his sinful circus took on new meaning. The circus had not come to take away from the harvest, but to add to it. I felt as if the Lord had broken a restraining thread around my ankle that had once been a heavy chain.

On Sunday morning I arrived early and walked through the tent. High above me, the great tent poles held the canvas taut against the elements. Strong supporting ropes were rigged inside and out, making a comfortable space for people to gather.

"Father," I prayed, "someday I want a circus tent as big as this one just for preaching the gospel. And I want to see it full of people who have come – not to see a circus – but expecting to meet Jesus."

A few workers were making last-minute adjustments to the trapeze gear and the main performance ring. I introduced myself. A clown in all his makeup brought his performance props into the main ring. Seeing me, he quickly took them to one side and sat on them to wait until I had finished delivering my sermon. People from Flensburg were already gathering, finding seats in the bleachers.

When the time came for the sermon, I preached the ABCs of the gospel. I had an altar call, and a few people responded. As I prayed with them, I heard the sound of weeping. It was coming from behind me. Turning, I saw something I have never seen before or since. That circus clown had come all undone. Trembling from head to toe, he came to where I stood and knelt in the center ring, his tears falling into the dust.

"I want to receive Jesus as my Savior," he said.

I led him in the prayer for salvation. When the circus finished its run of performances, he left his old life behind, quit the circus and joined my congregation in Husum.

MERELY TWO WEEKS REMAINED in the tent crusade. I went to my next point of business. Where would I find a building for the 50 converts? I took my Volkswagen for a drive into the heart of downtown. The city was charming and picturesque, perched at the end of the natural waterway. As I made my way along one of the main streets, a large shuttered building caught my eye. Looking closer I noticed that all of the shutters on the ground floor were closed tight while all those on the second floor were open. I heard the Holy Spirit say to me, *The ground floor is your church building.*

I parked the car and climbed to the second floor. People were working there in a group of offices. One of the door signs read "Hansen Rum." This company was quite famous in the region. It imported fermented sugar cane and molasses from a distillery on the island of Aruba. Here at this factory it was further distilled and blended for bottling and sale in Scandinavia and northern Germany. Many a sailor and many a farmer had ruined his soul with this infamous stuff.

I almost turned around and left, feeling as if I had made a mistake. What good could come from this place?

*Lord,* I asked, *would You really use a rum company to provide my church building?*

In some corner of my head I heard the words of Nathanael when he heard that the Messiah was supposedly from Nazareth, "Can there any good thing come out of Nazareth?" [41] Nazareth was a despised place, a ghetto in the biblical world.

Once again, like a detective dusting a crime scene, before my very eyes, God's fingerprints began to emerge on the door with the Hansen Rum sign on it. I was ever learning that He enjoys using unlikely sources.

I knocked on the door. A man rose from his desk and approached me.

"Excuse me," I said. "I am wondering if the ground floor of this building can be rented."

"No. This building is scheduled to be demolished. We have built a new plant across town."

*So it is impossible,* I thought. *Nothing can be done with a building to be demolished.*

But again, I was thinking too small. A new thought came into my head. In response, I asked, "When will the demolition begin?"

"Oh, they say in two or three years. Another company plans to build a shopping market on this site."

Immediately I saw the new possibility. "Would you mind showing me the first floor? I have an idea about using it in the meantime."

He gave me a tour. It had a large, empty main room. I could envision 75 people fitting easily into the space. I also saw two small anterooms along one wall. One was empty; the other contained a small, workers' kitchen. What a bonus! Anni and I could use this for an apartment. Everything would work. They told me the agent in charge of the space was located in the nearby town of Kappeln.

I drove there and met him. He was a cripple in a wheelchair. Soon, I could see that the Holy Spirit had gone before me. I sensed that I had great favor with this man. I told him who I was and what I wanted to do with the first floor of the building. He seemed to emanate warmth toward every word I said.

"Do you know that the building is going to be demolished?" he asked.

"Yes. But it can provide us with a good space in the meantime. We will look for a more permanent home when we are better established. I would like to rent it."

"I will rent it to you."

"I don't have much money. We are a new congregation and still small. How much would you need?"

"Oh, about 1,200 deutschmarks per month."

I cleared my throat and my eyes grew wide. He could see that I was out of my financial depth. The bottom dropped out of my enthusiasm. This was a price far too high for my little congregation to pay.

"What can you pay?" he continued.

"250," I said, somewhat sheepishly, realizing that we were world's apart on price.

"It's yours," he said smiling. He leaned forward in his wheelchair, his hand extended.

I could not believe it! As we shook hands, something occurred to me. "There is something else," I said. "It is very cold here in the winter, and I will need to heat the place. How much will that cost?"

"Oh, don't worry about that. We have to heat the building anyway. I will just say that it's included in the rent."

This provision had the mark of a loving heavenly Father all over it. God wanted to provide our church building through the generosity of a rum company. Why not? He had supplied converts through a summer circus. Both unlikely sources.

In this series of events, I began to see how I might miss God's provision if I limited Him to my preconceived standards. My walk with Him was becoming more and more of an adventure of faith. I should not predict where it would lead.

Before leaving town I found a chair supply store and priced 75 chairs for our gatherings. I believed that we would need chairs enough to grow beyond our present numbers.

I returned to the tent that night to make the announcement that we had a church home in the Hansen Rum building. More than that, I shared the incredibly reduced rent as a sign of God's favor. I was so excited. The people shared my enthusiasm. "Now, we will seek God to supply the chairs we will need for seating."

That night, the old German gentleman who had been my first convert asked me to come visit him on a dairy farm in the neighboring village of Handewitt. The following day, I drove across the farmland in my Volkswagen, recalling the tears in this man's eyes as he had raised his hand and come forward in our little tent meeting.

In the barn, I found him sitting on a milking stool. That was his job. He was a milker. Not the owner of the dairy, merely the hired hand. I sat on a stool opposite him. He showed me the technique for milking a cow, and of course, amused himself by insisting that I give it a try. That cow thought about as much of my attempt to milk her as the master of the carpentry school in Krempe had thought of my efforts to be a carpenter. She wanted to kick me right out of the barn.

"There's a reason why I am a preacher and you are a milker," I said, releasing the udder.

He laughed. After pleasant words, I asked him why he had asked me to come see him. He said he wanted to make a donation for the chairs. He reached inside his shirt and pulled out a folded piece of newspaper, handing it to me.

I thanked him and looked inside. His gift was enough to buy all of the chairs. He was such an unlikely candidate to make this donation. Simply a hired farm hand. Just the kind of person that I would overlook in the natural. And just the kind of person God delights in using for His glory.

That night I stood before the tent crowd. "Praise the Lord, people, we've been delivered!" I shouted. "We have received a donation, and I have purchased all the chairs for the new sanctuary."

My faith was rising like a tide to believe God for even greater things.

"Do you, Reinhard Bonnke, take Anni Sülzle to be your lawful wedded wife, to live in the holy estate of matrimony? Will you love, honor, comfort, and cherish her from this day forward, forsaking all others, keeping only unto her for as long as you both shall live?"

My father's voice filled the first story of the Hansen Rum building with the words I had been waiting five months to hear. My first 50 converts filled their share of the chairs we had recently bought. Another 50 members from both sides of our family, and dozens of well-wishers, sat in rented chairs that crowded the extremities of the room.

"I do," I said, looking at Anni's smiling face. She never looked more beautiful to me than on that day, dressed in white, her oval face framed in lovely flowers. In my imagination I could hear the most delicate tones of a mandolin playing. Whatever the tune – it was from heaven, and it was our song.

In our invitations to the wedding guests, Anni and I had stated our goal to go to Africa after two years of service in Flensburg. We asked them to give us only gifts that we could carry with us. We suggested that they make gifts of money to a missions fund that would help us on our way.

After bringing the traditional wedding ceremony to its final moment, my father delivered a short homily to the gathered guests. Had I been preaching, of course, it would have been the ABCs of the gospel. But Dad was a pastor not an evangelist. He opened his Bible and read a scripture that he knew would have great significance for our marriage. He also wanted the audience to appreciate it. "Whatsoever he saith unto you, do it." [42]

Hermann Bonnke had not agreed with me on many things through the years. He had not agreed on my calling to Africa. Nor on my timing. Nor on my choice to marry Anni. On this day, he had changed his mind. He was more than agreeing with me. He was as much as admitting that his judgment of my choice of Anni, and of many other of his opinions, had been wrong. And it was not just that we had a difference of opinion. Nor was it that I simply had a mind of my own. In this sermon text taken from John 2:5, he explained that I had heard from God, and this had made all the difference. Father in his wedding sermon wanted to bow to that higher voice in my life. Whatsoever he saith unto you, do it. This was a most priceless gift from him to Anni and me.

Our wedding in 1964

"When God speaks," he said, "nothing else matters."

As I thought about it, the scripture had even more layers of meaning for both Anni and I, especially on this, our wedding day. The words of Scripture Father had chosen were the words spoken by Mary, the mother of Jesus, at the famous wedding feast in Cana of Galilee. It seems that the host of the wedding had run out of wine. The crisis was potentially embarrassing and would have tainted the celebration for the bride and groom. Grabbing her son by the sleeve and advising Him of the shortage, Mary had turned to the servants of the host standing by, saying, "Whatsover he saith unto you, do it." That was the context for my father's text.

As father enlarged on his topic, I glanced around the room, smiling. *Water into wine, I thought, and a rum factory into a place of worship. God, You are so gracious!*

"You may now kiss your bride," Father said.

My thoughts returned to the present. I needed no further encouragement. It was a kiss like the finest wine from the Savior's water pots. We broke the bread of communion together and then dismissed our guests. Our honeymoon began in that small anteroom in Flensburg. I had purchased a used hide-a-bed. During the day it would double as a sofa and at night we would make it down into our bed. Quite the efficient solution, I thought. We retired to our two-room living quarters and had everything we needed. We had the Lord of the wedding feast, and we had each other.

In spite of my father's failure to teach me the way of a man with a woman at the age of 14, we needed no instructions on that day. The flame of our kiss guided us through the night, and ignited our relationship across the years. Our love will continue as long as we both shall live.

# Chapter 16

OH, WHAT REVELATIONS await the newly married man. My Anni began to look at everything in our small apartment with new eyes. Things that seemed perfectly okay before we were married were suddenly no longer adequate. Windows could no longer be covered with bed sheets. They needed real curtains with something called valances. The sofa arms needed lace doilies with matching crochet patterns. Perfectly adequate floors suddenly needed throw rugs. The bathroom needed matching towels and wash cloths. We needed wicker wastebaskets instead of discarded metal mop buckets.

How would I have ever known?

I am convinced that part of God's plan in creating romantic love is that the man should not hesitate to make these changes for his beloved. Anni's wishes became my commands. But lo, barely had one wish been granted than a new one appeared. In my simple male mind I thought each wish was an end in itself. But, no, what I did not suspect was the other part of God's plan in creating romance. It is that the woman should have these urges because she is by nature a nest builder. And the nest she is building is not a love nest for two – rather, it is the kind of place in which to nurture children.

Ah! The revelations were coming fast. One day I came into the apartment to see Anni staring at the bare wall above our sofa. Her arms were crossed and one of her mandolin playing fingers was tapping thoughtfully upon her lips. By now I knew what this meant.

"What is missing, my love?"

"We do not have much space here. I think we should take advantage of that big bare wall."

"What do you have in mind? A mirror? A picture?" I had yet to learn never to answer for her.

"I don't know," she said. "I'm not sure it exists, but something that would hold things, like shelves for books and pictures, plants, knick knacks, our phono. Can you see it? It would cover the entire wall and straddle the sofa. It would be the showcase for this room. If we had guests sitting on the sofa there would be a sense that we are people of substance. What do you think?"

In fact, I began to picture it in my mind. "Let's sit down and draw it," I suggested. "This will need to be custom made and I know just the person to do it."

In our congregation was a man who made smaller shelves and pieces of furniture. His name was Mr. Hornig. I had seen his shop and his finish work was exquisite. This would be a big job for him but he would pour his energies into it with abandon. He would want to make the finest piece of furniture for the preacher and his wife. All of our guests who admired it would learn that he had done it and new business would come to him. Perfect.

I took Anni's drawing of the wall unit to him. He made an estimate and the cost was high. But I knew his work. It was second to none, so his price should not underestimate the outcome. Anni and I dipped into the precious monetary gifts people had made to us on our wedding day. We barely had enough. But this would be the crown jewel in our living space for the two years we would spend in Flensburg. I agreed to the price and paid some money down so that he could begin work immediately.

As we anticipated the outcome I began to feel that I had outdone myself. I had really provided something that was symbolic of my love for Anni and something that would slow down the pace of what men call the "honey do" list – "Honey, do this … Honey, do that …"

One Sunday at church Mr. Hornig announced that he would have our wall unit delivered the next day. He was glowing with pride and I knew that he had something that was far beyond his normal scope of work. We were filled with excitement and high expectations. He made a time in the morning for us to meet him in the square outside the main entrance.

The next morning we both stood on the doorstep watching the cobble stoned square in front of the Hansen Rum building. To our left the street descended from a hill and entered the intersection. The main thoroughfare handled two way traffic traveling in the other direction.

Suddenly, a feeling of dread hit the pit of my stomach. Looking to the left I saw Mr. Hornig, our woodworking brother, driving his car down the incline toward the intersection. He had strapped our prized wall unit on top of his Volkswagen sedan. It protruded from the front and back and over both sides. Ropes and pads were holding it like Gulliver strapped down by the Lilliputians. I could hear his brakes squealing as he struggled to keep his speed down on the steep descent.

How could he have jeopardized all of his weeks of craftsmanship this way? He did not want to spend a portion of his profit margin to obtain two men with a truck to haul this prize properly. I was furious to see it. Had I known what he had planned, I would have put up the extra money to have it delivered myself.

At the bottom of the hill the worst that I could imagine happened. He suddenly encountered traffic. Fearing a collision as he entered the square he engaged his emergency brake. The wall unit ejected from his roof and flew forward into the intersection, sliding across the cobblestones and smashing into the steps of a neighboring building where it broke into pieces.

He leaped from his car holding his head in his hands. "I'm ruined! I'm ruined!" he cried. "I have lost everything!"

I had to disagree. He had not lost his life, which was something I felt like taking from him at the moment. I could almost see myself strangling the man.

He ran to the wall unit and fell to his knees. "I'm ruined! All is lost!" He carried on like one of his children had been struck by a car.

I looked at Anni. We were both speechless and horrified. The crown jewel of our humble parsonage lay shattered in the street.

I went to where the man was kneeling in anguish. "What about insurance?" I asked. "Surely you have insurance to cover such a thing."

"Yes, but if I collect it my rates will be too high to maintain. My insurance was not made for claims of this size."

At this point I began to pray inside myself. *Lord, what should I do?* The answer came immediately with a sense of complete calm. *You must spare your brother.*

Though I had every right to demand that he use his insurance to make us a new wall unit, I would not do that. I knew that he would not be ruined by it, but in his mind he believed that he would be. All of the hopes and expectations Anni and I had built up for this day were let go. Plan B became God's plan A. It was more important to save my brother from his own perceived disaster than to impose my standards on him.

"Here is what I propose," I said. "Let's get these pieces into the house and you bring your tools to put them back together. I want you to patch it up and see if you can make it look like new. We will take delivery of this wall unit."

That is what we did. As we recovered from our shock and disappointment, he was actually able to repair that unit until only one part of it appeared damaged. Nothing could be done to repair the left side base where the cobblestones had removed significant portions of the wood. When he had finished his repair, Anni took a large floor plant and placed it in front of the damage.

"There," she said, "smiling grimly. Who will know?"

I learned a great lesson. When dealing with human beings anything that can go wrong, probably will, sooner or later. We should hold our expectations in check with this truth. We take precautions whenever we can to avoid disaster. But sometimes we cannot cover all the bases. We are at the mercy of the people God has placed in our circle.

The Apostle Paul put it this way, "We then that are strong ought to bear the infirmities of the weak, and not to please ourselves. Let every one of us please his neighbor for his good to edification." [43]

As our two years in Flensburg passed that wall unit became a symbol of something far more than we had first expected. It reminded Anni and me every time we saw it that we were our brother's keeper. Our pleasure at owning something fine and elegant was replaced by the Lord's eternal pleasure at having spared our brother.

"I AM WITH CHILD," Anni said softly. She stood looking down at her midsection, one hand resting lightly there.

It still amazes me how these words could slam the brakes on every activity in my brain. Since our wedding day I had been in constant motion. We were both so excited and blessed to be serving God together in Flensburg. Time had flown like a train at top speed, and we had hardly been able to stop to catch our breath. Each night we converted our sofa into a sleeper and back again into a sofa at the break of dawn. There were more activities on our list of things to do than we could possibly check off in a week.

There were worship services to conduct, Bible studies, prayer meetings, board meetings, organizational meetings, paperwork, counseling, preaching, paying the bills, celebrating weddings, and conducting funerals. In between, we did odd jobs to keep house and home together, and we constantly put money away for Africa. But when Anni said she was pregnant, the treadmill stopped instantly.

I didn't know what to say at first. "Hallelujah!" I finally shouted when I could find my voice. I hugged her and then stupidly asked, "I wonder, is it a boy or a girl? Of course, how could you know?"

The words had just slipped from my mouth, and I immediately sensed a bit of trouble. How often had I said it? During our courtship, in the months leading up to our marriage, in the weeks that followed. I had said again and again in my youthful enthusiasm, "Anni, give me a houseful of boys. I want six boys. Yes, six. I love boys, and I so want to be a good father to them."

Why had I been so thoughtless? What if this child was a girl? It began to dawn on me that with an actual pregnancy I now had to consider realities, not fantasies. And the consequences of my exuberant words were suddenly serious. It was then I began to know the root of my problem.

How often had my mother spoken of her disappointment at my birth? Too many times to count. It was like a broken record. Though she loved me, she often recited the fact that she had wanted to have a girl in the worst way, and I had been her *fifth* son. My birth seemed to have weighed her down like an extra burden. It never occurred to her that her words would have a lasting effect on me.

Of course, if I had any choice in the matter I would have chosen not to disappoint my mother. In so many subtle ways I had tried to make up for it. But my efforts had only backfired. I had been the naughty boy, the troublesome one, the disappointment. This was a load a child should not have to carry.

Now I could see why I had become so overly zealous in my wish for a houseful of boys. I didn't want just one boy, or two, or three – I had stated my ridiculous wish for six boys. Why? Because I did not want a son – especially not my *fifth* son – to feel unwelcome the way I had felt. Not even for a moment.

How often does it happen that a childhood vow ends up producing the curse it seeks to cure? After speaking so thoughtlessly to Anni, a daughter born of this pregnancy might now produce disappointment in her. She so wanted to give me one of those six boys just to please me. *Oh wretched man that I am! Who shall deliver me?*[44]

I began a campaign of reassurances. "Anni, you know this child you are carrying is from God, our heavenly Father. He has sent the perfect baby to us. If it is a girl, I will be as happy as if it were a boy. Do you know that? Do you?"

She smiled and nodded, but there was a veil deep in her eyes. I could see it. My words could not be retracted. I had intended no harm, but the harm had been done. Anni carried a burden with this child growing in her womb. In spite of her better judgment, in some part of her soul she surely felt she *must* produce a boy.

In the meantime, there was nothing the doctor could do to solve the question. These were the days before ultrasound, by which parents can learn the sex of the child after only 20 weeks. We would have to wait nine months to know the outcome.

These were also the days before birthing rooms. Fathers were not considered worthy to be present at the advent of their children. For better or worse, it was an event reserved for the doctor, the nurse, and the mother.

As Anni went into labor and entered the hospital, I remained in our apartment, pacing and praying. I prayed God's full protection over her and His blessing on the doctor, and nurse, and on everything involved with the birthing process.

These are the waiting hours when the Enemy likes to sow fear, doubt, and torment. Fear that somehow the child would disappoint Anni. Doubt that God is good, and suggestions that He would want to exact some kind of punishment upon this child for our shortcomings. Torment that the child would carry a curse, a birth defect, or a fatal illness. All first-time parents want their babies to be normal. All the fingers and toes in the right order. And we know that sometimes children are born tragically flawed. We are not in control. We are vulnerable to the Enemy's lies.

But I resisted the devil and all of his suggestions, and they fled away from me. My prayer laid hold upon the truth and the promises of God's Word. He is good. No matter what comes, He has borne our grief and carried our sorrows. We are saved from the Devourer. In Him we have rest. The phone rang. "Reverend Bonnke, you are the father of a fine son."

My jaw dropped. A *son!* Anni had been spared the effects of my words. I felt so exceedingly blessed and unworthy. "Is Anni safe? Is she OK?"

"She is just fine. Mother and baby are doing fine."

"Hallelujah!" I shouted. The entire Hansen Rum building could hear me now, but it wasn't enough. I needed a huge celebration and I knew just the ticket.

On Anni's wall unit we had placed the phono. I found a long play record album of Handel's *Messiah* and set the turntable to the *Hallelujah Chorus.* Turning the volume as high as the speakers would bear, I raced to the windows and threw them open. Leaning out, I shouted to the cars and the pedestrian traffic crossing the square, "Hallelujah!

Evangelist Harold Herman dedicated our son Kai-Uwe to the Lord (1966).

I have a son from God!" The Hallelujah Chorus backed me up. It was a fitting symphony to match the joy in my heart.

I decided that this would become a traditional way for us to welcome each new child into our family. I would announce them with the Hallelujah Chorus at full volume on the phono. Two girls were to follow our son in the years ahead, and I can testify that the celebration for each was as joyful and fresh as the first one.

He was a beautiful baby. We named him Kai-Uwe, pronounced *Kye-Uva*, a traditional German and Scandinavian name. His full name was Kai-Uwe Friedrich Bonnke. His name has many shades of meaning, but I was pleased to learn that in certain cultures, *Kai* had the meaning of "fire," and *Uwe* came from the word for "blade." And so, my son would be "a sword of fire" in the hands of the Lord. Amen, and amen. God is so good. Our family was off to a rich start.

"We do not send missionaries to South Africa."

The words echoed in the cold hall like plaster falling from the ceiling in an empty room. It was one of those rooms where the scent of mothballs waged a battle against the omnipresent smell of mildew. Anni and I huddled together. A half dozen members of the Velberter Missions Board looked at us from across a long table. They were the official missions arm of the ACD in Germany. They worked under the auspices of the Apostolic Faith Mission in South Africa. The AFM provided training and guidance and the ACD provided the financial support to our German workers who worked there. That was the arrangement. As we waited in the room bare light fixtures dangled from electrical cords high above us providing illumination. I suppose the white light in the white room was a fitting atmosphere for an interrogation. To us, it seemed a bit like an inquisition.

"You say you were called to Africa when you were just ten years old?"

"That is correct."

"Africa is a huge continent with many nations."

I nodded.

"So why do you insist that you cannot go to Zambia?" one of the members asked. "The AFM can provide a position for you in Zambia."

"It is very simple," I answered, "A few years after God called me to Africa He called me to South Africa, very specifically. In a prayer meeting I received a vision of the city of Johannesburg on a map. I did not know where the city actually belonged on the map. When I later checked a world atlas, I found that the vision had been correct. God knows His geography. He called me to the country of South Africa."

"But the AFM has no openings in South Africa."

"I do not need an opening. I will gladly pioneer a new work from the converts God gives me, as I did in Flensburg."

"That would be wonderful, but we have no way to provide oversight if you do not go to Zambia."

"Then, what am I to do with my calling?"

"We can offer you Zambia. It is south of the equator, as close to South Africa as we can get. Besides, it is a beautiful country. The great Victoria Falls are there on the Zambezi River. You could start there and later move to South Africa, if that is still your heart's desire."

"Oh, no, South Africa is not my heart's desire," I said. "It is the place God has called me. That is an important difference."

It was a long interview. I stuck to my guns about my call to South Africa. Eventually, they agreed to a compromise. I would serve a South African apprenticeship for a year under an AFM minister named Reverend Stephanus Spies. His work was anchored in Ermelo in the Eastern Transvaal. His sphere of ministry covered the Transvaal region, and extended into Swaziland. When the ACD, the AFM, and Reverend Spies all agreed to the plan, I felt that God had given me great favor. Most of all, I was so very pleased that we had honored His call given to me in the childhood vision. We would be working on the edge of Johannesburg.

IT WAS 1967. Anni and I prepared to leave in earnest, but another surprise waited in the wings.

"Reinhard," she said, "I am with child again."

Kai-Uwe was not a year old and another child was on the way! Once again, my thoughts were arrested. Our departure for Africa would be made the more challenging, especially for Anni. But as we discussed it, she assured me that she had trusted God from the beginning. She was called to the life of a missionary and such challenges went with the territory. We would continue packing, uninterrupted. The only difference was I refused to allow her to lift things.

It also helped that we were packing light. The wall unit went to Anni's mother. The sofa bed was sold. All of our belongings that remained made a very small package. We kept nothing that would tie us down.

The Volkswagen Beetle was traded for a Volkswagen Type 2 campervan. In America, this rear-engine vehicle was becoming popular as a hippie van. Its boxy looks made it appealing to the growing counterculture. But for Anni and me, it would provide a shipping container for our belongings, and reliable transportation once we arrived. Not to forget it would covert easily into temporary living quarters. We felt this would prove ideal when ministering in primitive areas of Africa. It also provided low-cost travel expenses as we made our way southward on the German autobahn.

We crossed the Swiss Alps and the Italian Alps to Trieste, racing to meet a departure date on a ship bound for Durban, South Africa.

This VW Camper was bought from Willard Cantelon and went with us to Africa.

As the sky blue water of the Adriatic Sea came into view, I flashed back to my boyhood when I used to stand on the Glückstadt pier, feeling like this day would never come. How time had passed. It did not seem like such a long time ago. We would not be departing from Hamburg but from Trieste, Italy. It would be a long-awaited epic voyage for us, nonetheless.

Saying goodbye to our friends, family, and church in Germany had not been difficult. Our eyes had been set on this day since we first met, and we had been saying goodbye, in effect, to everyone for years. We were so excited to finally be going. When you pull up roots in order to fulfill a divine destiny, there is not a sense of pain or loss. Rather, there is a great expectation for things to come.

From Trieste our cruise ship went to Venice, however, the Lord slowed us down for our own good. In fact, a dock worker's strike played to our great advantage. It delayed our departure in Venice for ten days, which provided us with an unexpected honeymoon in one of the most romantic cities on earth. Those were days we have never forgotten.

Three other missionary families were traveling on the same ship. Each day Anni and the wives took turns babysitting the children so the others could spend the day exploring Venice. That gave Anni and me two days out of every three to be together, just the two of us. What an abundant blessing! We thoroughly enjoyed our honeymoon in Venice, expenses paid!

AT LAST, WE SAILED for Africa. Our route took us through the Adriatic passing by Italy's "toe of the boot" and into the open Mediterranean. These were the waters sailed so often by the apostle Paul. We continued southeast past the Greek Islands to Egypt and to the entrance of the Suez Canal. The canal would take us into the Red Sea, which in turn led us into the great Indian Ocean. Sailing south along the east coast of Africa we would eventually reach the port of Durban.

As we entered the Suez Canal I remained on deck, watching the process. The strip of water was a man-made wonder that allowed ocean-going vessels to sail 100 miles through desert sands between the Mediterranean and the Red Sea. It had no locks because the sea level on both ends was virtually the same, and no elevation changes were needed, such as were found on the Panama Canal.

As we sailed through the sands of Egypt, we passed an airfield. I noticed that it was filled with hundreds of brand-new, white Russian Mig 21 fighter jets. In recent days the saber-rattling between Israel and her Arab neighbors had increased. I had been keeping my eyes on the news.

"Anni," I said, "Look at those Migs. I feel that war is near. Very near."

In fact, our ship was one of the last to pass through the canal before Egypt ordered United Nations peacekeepers out, and took control of the canal. Soon after, Israel launched a surprise attack, beginning what is now called the "Six Day War." Israel virtually destroyed Egypt's air force on the ground, including all of the shiny new Russian Migs I had seen on the bank of the Suez. The loss of military hardware was far more than Egypt could afford. Even though greatly outnumbered by the armies of Egypt, Syria, and Jordan, in a matter of six days, Israel had gained control of the entire Sinai Peninsula, the Gaza Strip, the Golan Heights, the West Bank, and Eastern Jerusalem. It stands as one of the most miraculous military victories in modern warfare and called to mind Bible prophecies that God would once again fight for Israel.

As the Middle East fell into turmoil, the passengers on our ship discussed our near miss. If the dock workers strike in Venice had gone on for one more day, and we had enjoyed more sightseeing, we might have found ourselves in the middle of the conflict. Our ship would have been held up in the Suez Canal until the mess was resolved. In fact, 14 ships that followed us remained trapped for the next eight years. Once again, we saw the blessing and confirming hand of God upon the choice we had made to follow Him. *Whatsoever he saith unto you, do it.* [45]

WE NEEDED THAT CONFIRMATION because an immediate trial came to test our faith. As soon as we left the canal and entered the Red Sea, Anni became very sensitive to the motion of the ship. We joked about Moses and the children of Israel crossing the Red Sea on dry land. She would have gladly walked rather than endure more of the sensation. We were not sure if it was motion sickness, or morning sickness, or a combination of the two, but her condition became worse. Her complexion became like green cheese and she got so sick that – forget the dry land – she would gladly have allowed herself to drown with Pharaoh's army rather than go on like this. We called the ship's doctor, and she was kept under medical supervision as we continued toward the Gulf of Aden and our entrance into the Indian Ocean. We had a long voyage ahead, and I so wanted her well enough to enjoy it. My hopes were dashed. In fact, she was miserable for the rest of the trip.

For several days we continued down the eastern coast of Africa, sailing through the Mozambique Channel between the African mainland and Madagascar. The voyage grew long, and I had brought along an accordion. I began to sit in a deck chair and teach myself to play it as Anni lay in the infirmary and the hours wore on. As I think back on it, my fellow passengers may not have appreciated my diligence in this matter. By the time we arrived at our destination I had become quite accomplished.

We emerged again into the waters of the Indian Ocean near the southern tip of Africa and cruised toward our berth in the harbor of Durban. At last, Anni was able to get out of bed and walk. Perhaps she was inspired by anticipation of soon being able to place her feet on solid ground. The worst of her ordeal was over.

I had received scant instructions from Reverend Spies that we would be met in Durban by a man named du Toit, a French name. That is all I knew – du Toit. As we approached the docks I could see more than a thousand people waiting to greet passengers. Out of that great crowd, how would I ever find du Toit?

Coming down the gangway I had an inspiration. My eyes swept the crowd, and I shouted to the top of my lungs, "Hallelujah!" Sure enough, out of the crowd one voice shouted back, "Hallelujah!" He was a white man, which disappointed me. I had come expecting to be met by an African. Very few black people were in the crowd waiting to greet our ship.

I held Anni's arm as we left the gangway and felt the dock beneath our feet. She held little Kai-Uwe in her arms and began to gain new strength with each step on solid footing.

When we approached the man who had returned my "Hallelujah," I extended my hand. "du Toit, I presume?"

He laughed heartily, recognizing the famous line from the meeting in Africa between Stanley and Livingston. He took my hand.

Yes, he was du Toit. After he gave us directions we took off, heading to Ermelo and to the home of Pastor Spies. And that is how we took our first steps onto the soil of Africa, our land of destiny.

Part 4

# PREPARATION YEARS

*Father,*
*may everything I do prepare me*
*for everything You will do.*

# Chapter 17

IN MANY WAYS my first year in South Africa was the most difficult. I was filled with great expectations, high aspirations, and a sense of divine calling. But I ran smack into apartheid, the ugly policy of racial separation. And right where I did not expect to find it – entrenched within the Pentecostal church.

White South Africa was a prosperous land dominated by European society. The people who ruled were Dutch, German, French, and British. They enjoyed life with every modern convenience while most black South Africans suffered in deep poverty. My call from God was to the black people. I had preached to enough white faces in Germany. Why should I be required to do more of it before launching my ministry? But if I was to continue under authority, I would have to submit to the program the Velberter Mission (VM) and the AFM had created for me.

We took up an extended temporary residence with Reverend Stephanus Spies and his wife Cecilia in Ermelo. They were very kind and provided well for us until we were able to move out on our own, where our second child Gabriele was born and I could raise my voice with the great *Hallelujah Chorus*.

They lived in the designated white part of the city. Ermelo also had a town for blacks. The Apostolic Faith Mission had church buildings in both the white and black areas. The congregations worshipped separately.

Reverend Spies also told me that he conducted preaching missions to the blacks in outlying areas. He said he would take me with him on his next assignment. I was delighted. "Bring your guitar," he said.

When the time for the mission outreach came, he drove his pickup truck. He and I sat in the front with my guitar. Three black pastors rode in the back. He explained to me that this riding arrangement was proper apartheid policy. He believed in the wisdom of the racial system. It had been developed over many decades by trial and error as the best way to keep good order in the country.

The location we were to use for the meeting was a schoolhouse in an outlying village. When we arrived, the gates had been chained and padlocked.

"These people seldom show up and do what they are supposed to do when they are supposed to do it," Spies said disgustedly. "The gates have not been unlocked so we will have to make do." He smiled and climbed over the fence. "Follow me for the next one or two years and you'll know just how to minister in South Africa."

I handed my guitar over the fence, and we all climbed over after him. Later someone showed up to unlock the gates. We were eventually joined by three people from the local area who had shown up to hear Spies' sermon. Three people! There was no electricity. He lit a candle. I could not believe it. Five preachers and three listeners. We could have done better on any street corner.

I listened to his sermon, waiting for some sign of life. It never came. I knew I would not last long with this man, given my burning desire to see black Africans come to Jesus. In the meantime, he informed me, I would not be allowed to preach in white Apostolic Faith Mission churches.

"That is no great loss to me," I said. "I came to preach to black Africans."

"You will not be allowed to preach to blacks either."

"Excuse me?"

"You will not preach at all until we have taught you the South African way," he said. "And, of course, we have to examine you to be sure you are not a Communist. After that, you may get your own district."

At first I thought he was joking. He was serious. The Communist Party had gained traction in South Africa because of apartheid. There was a lot of fear that a revolution might break out.

I began to feel as if I had been bound and gagged in the basement of the Grand Inquisitor's hall. I could not imagine that Jesus Christ would obey the laws of this unjust system if it kept Him from saving one soul. But in opposing apartheid, Jesus Himself might be suspected of Communist sympathies. I requested a meeting with Dr. F. P. Möller, president of the Apostolic Faith Mission Board in Johannesburg. Spies graciously allowed it.

With Möller, I found an understanding ear. He agreed to order Spies to loosen his grip and allow me to preach. He encouraged me to remain in the program for one year. Then he would recommend to the missions board that I be assigned to a black African part of South Africa. I thanked him profusely and returned to the mentorship of Reverend Spies, feeling that I might be able to endure it.

Soon after, he gave me a preaching assignment in the black church in Ermelo as well as in his whole district. I was so happy for this opportunity. I spent much time in prayer, asking God to give me just the right words for this group of believers. Spies drove me to the church and introduced me.

This was so special. My first sermon to a black audience in Africa. In my mind I saw the shape of the gospel and preached the words that filled the outline. I felt a great anointing. It was a message from the throne of God. And I could tell that the Lord had answered my prayer. The faces of those beautiful people lit up with delight as I delivered the ABCs of the gospel in a way that made them know they were the apple of God's eye, not second-class citizens in the kingdom of heaven.

After the meeting Spies took me aside. "You committed grave errors," he said.

"What errors are you speaking of?"

"First, you shook hands with black people. That is not to be done. Then, in your sermon you called them 'brother' and 'sister'."

For a moment I could not believe my ears. "What should I call them?"

"Call them 'mense'."

"What is mense?"

"It is a word that means people. They understand it. It is apartheid."

I looked at him for a long moment before answering. Then I shook my head. "Reverend Spies, if the blood of Jesus does not make us brothers and sisters, then I will never again preach the gospel."

It was as if I had hit him with my fist. He turned red at the collar and pale around the eyes. He could not reply. We were two preachers from two different planets. I was beginning to wonder if we preached two different gospels. I could not imagine how this apprenticeship arrangement would last a full year.

In the meantime, Anni and I found a house we could afford to rent at 8 Ennis Street, and we moved into it. Our first challenge was to find furniture. We looked at beds and found the prices far too high. Off to one side in the store, we saw some metal bed frames that were well within our budget. They would work just fine.

A white sales lady took the order from me and shouted to the back of the store, "Moses, bring up two servants' beds."

At first I wondered how she knew that we were servants of God. Then it hit me that black people slept on metal beds in South Africa. This was what she meant by "servants' beds." I immediately embraced the idea with delight. Jesus had said, "... *he that is greatest among you shall be your servant.*"[46] I was happy to accept those beds in the name of Christ and identify myself with the black people of South Africa. Over the years, I had many a fruitful night's sleep on those beds, and many a divine dream. They live warmly in my memory to this day.

One day there was a knock at our door. To our surprise, a lady from the Ermelo City Council stood there.

"I understand that you have hired a black housemaid."

"Yes, my wife needs some extra help. It allows her to travel with me."

"I am here to inspect your kitchen."

"Oh," I said, "you are a building inspector." I thought I understood the purpose of her visit.

"No, not the whole building," she said, "just the kitchen. You see, we know that you are new to South Africa. That's why I have been sent to see that you are in compliance."

"Compliance? What will make us in compliance?"

"You must have separate dishes and serving ware for your housemaid. These are to be handled separately, and kept separately. That is apartheid."

I felt sick. I began to wonder why God had called me to this particular place, knowing about its racial problems. If I had known the suffocating system I would labor under with the AFM, I would have chosen Zambia. At least there, I could preach freely to black people, I could shake their hands; I could call them 'brother' or 'sister.' But in my memory I had not seen the name of Zambia in a vision. I could still see the name of Johannesburg gleaming before my spiritual eyes. Since God had called me here, surely He knew how to make a way for ministry under the yoke of apartheid. I prayed for guidance.

As we talked it over, Anni and I decided we could not dismantle apartheid on our own. We would not be able to preach the gospel if we made that our aim. But we could preach the true gospel, which brings liberty not bondage. And we could resist the system in as many ways as possible.

One day Reverend and Mrs. Spies came to visit. Anni had just announced that she was pregnant again. I had continued to receive the missionary magazine put out by the Velberter Mission of the ACD in Germany. One issue featured

South Africa. It cited a statistical study of whites and blacks, comparing income, life expectancy, infant mortality, and other quality-of-life issues. It vividly demonstrated that the standard of living for blacks was far below that of whites. The differences were disturbing. I showed the study to Mrs. Spies and asked her opinion. She scowled and studied it but made no comment.

Days later, Reverend Spies asked me to come see him at his office. As I took a seat, he placed the copy of the Velberter Mission magazine on the desktop between us. Apparently his wife had given it to him for his opinion.

"Are you making a habit of distributing offensive material?"

"A habit? No, sir. In fact, I have better things on my mind."

"Was this the only copy in your possession?"

"Yes. Why do you ask?"

"You didn't order extra copies?"

"No."

"You didn't distribute this material here?"

"No. I am, of course, still on the ACD mailing list. And I am here with the cooperation of the Velberter Mission. It is only natural that I would continue to get their magazine. I don't write it. I don't edit it. They decided to do the feature on South Africa on their own initiative."

He pushed the magazine toward me with disgust. "Well, Reinhard Bonnke, your traffic light in South Africa has turned from green to yellow. One more incident like this and it will turn red."

With this, I am afraid I hit my limit. "Reverend Spies, my traffic light is worked by heaven. If heaven turns my light red, only then will I go."

I must make it clear that even though Reverend Spies and I stood squarely opposed, we did become lifelong friends. This was especially true after I was no longer under his supervision. But our confrontations during those days built a kind of bridge of personal respect between us. Because of my father, Hermann's, struggle with the rise of the Nazi regime in Germany, I had a certain sympathy for how a system like apartheid can sneak up and capture good people. They become caught up in a system until they can no longer look at it with clear eyes. All of South Africa was headed for a tremendous upheaval in the years ahead. These events would force the ruling regime to enter the modern era. Spies represented the old way that was passing. By following my calling, God had automatically aligned me with the future.

I SUFFERED THROUGH the first year under Spies' scrutiny. I had not accommodated smoothly to apartheid, but he had at least become convinced that I was no Communist agitator. Dr. Möller made good on his promise to recommend me for reassignment.

After deliberation, the AFM board gave me a choice of four positions they would make available to me. One of them was with one of the largest white churches in South Africa. This amazed me. After being allowed to preach in both black and white churches, I suppose I had established a reputation that opened up this possibility. It was a very lucrative and attractive position, and it gave real political power to the one who filled the pulpit. If I had wavered in my call from the Lord I might have considered this position as a place from which I could wield a stronger influence against apartheid and make progress in favor of white support for missions and outreaches to the blacks. As it was, I rejected it without serious consideration. Reverend Spies was astonished, much as my father might have been back in Krempe.

Another of the four positions, the least attractive of all, was the Kingdom of Lesotho. It was a small landlocked nation of native Africans south of Johannesburg. The AFM did respect Lesotho as an independent nation; however their administration came from South Africa. It was a district that no one else wanted to handle. If I chose Lesotho, they would make me the AFM overseer of three small churches that they had managed to establish there over the years. I felt the Lord leading me to take this assignment, and I gave them my decision.

In 1968, I moved my family to Ladybrand, a small settlement on the very border of the kingdom. Shortly after moving there, Anni delivered our third child, our second daughter, Susanne Herta Bonnke. With another resounding *Hallelujah Chorus*, our family looked forward to serving in Lesotho as a true missionary family.

I began to travel in my Volkswagen to see the country for myself. It is no bigger than the state of Maryland, but because of its natural beauty, it is called the Switzerland of South Africa. This is where the Drakensberg Mountains rise 11,000 feet above the Zulu plain. The headwaters of the Orange River, the longest river south of the equator, tumble from glacial snow banks in the highlands.

Nearly all of Lesotho's 1,200 miles of road were unpaved. The high country had rocky, narrow trails that ate missionary vehicles for breakfast. Often I would drive as far as my van would go and be forced to walk or ride a horse or mule to reach a particular village. An average Basuto village sheltered no more than 250 souls.

On horseback
in mountainous Lesotho

The 1,348,000 Basuto tribesmen I found living in this high-altitude kingdom were an independent breed. They were Africa's cowboys, highly skilled wranglers who pastured herds of grass-fed cattle in rich, natural meadows. When a man married in Lesotho, he would give 15 head of cattle to the bride's family, a proof that he was an adequate provider. Often, when a man was sentenced in court, he was required to pay his fine in cattle. Families lived where they tended their herds. Their huts consisted of mud and handmade brick with thatched roofs. They were scattered at unpredictable intervals across this high and lonesome land.

On my first journey through the mountains I saw a group of shepherd boys tending goats and sheep in the pouring rain. I got out and approached them. They were nearly naked, shivering in the cold, but they were not seeking shelter. I gave my coat to one of the boys as a gesture of goodwill. When I returned on the next trip I brought an ample supply of clothing for them. They seemed to receive it with joy. But when I returned two weeks later I found the same boys in the same condition, nearly naked, tending their flocks in cold weather. It was such a discouragement for me. But I pressed on, seeking God for the key to this land.

It was surprising to learn that nearly half of these African cowboys and herdsmen were literate. They were largely bilingual, speaking English and Sesotho. Two-thirds had received formal education. This had come through missionary schools that had been active in Lesotho for more than a century.

Even with a Christian background, however, I found half of the tribesmen remaining true to ancestor worship. The other half came from families that had converted to Christ generations ago but had become hardened to the gospel over the years. Few of the Basuto had a living faith. The churches I found were dry and empty.

During this time Anni and I attended a national AFM conference in Johannesburg. We spoke with others about our choice of assignment. They described Lesotho as a hard place. They called it the bone yard for failed missionaries. I was beginning to understand the spirit in which the missions board had recommended this land. Perhaps it was a kind of test. If I chose Lesotho over the other choices they would know that I was truly called by God, or was perhaps crazy.

At the same conference I was delighted to meet a black Zulu preacher who was highly celebrated in the AFM. He was holding great tent meetings all over South Africa, and his name was making headlines because of salvations and miraculous healings. His name was Richard Ngidi, and he told me that if I went to Lesotho he would be glad to come and hold meetings to help me get started. This greatly encouraged me.

Soon afterward, the missionary bone yard almost claimed me for its own. While traveling in a remote area, I exhausted my canteen and felt myself nearing dehydration. In those days we did not carry large quantities of bottled water as we do today. I was so driven by thirst that I ignored the wisdom to always boil water before drinking. I knew better than to do that. In my travels I had already encountered the graves of many missionaries who had died from deadly black water fevers. I drank straight from a well. When I arrived home that night the awful stomach cramps began. I knew I was in a fight for my life.

I began to hallucinate and drift in and out of consciousness. My appetite was gone, and Anni had to work to get fluids into my body. After three terrible days of delirium, I began to see a kind of vision. I saw something like a black blanket, a dark shroud floating down over me. It seemed that I would be smothered by it. Death was very near for me, I knew. Then, somehow I could see through the blanket. On the other side, I saw the face of Jesus, and a wonderful peace flooded my heart in the midst of my delirium. In the next moment I heard the voice of dear Sister Eliese Köhler praying for me. I knew that voice from the many prayer meetings I had attended in Krempe. I heard her crying out to God to spare my life. In that moment the fever broke and I began a slow and steady recovery.

As I gained strength, I wrote a letter to my father asking him to go to Sister Köhler and ask her what happened that day. The story I got back truly touched my heart. Early in the morning before the break of dawn, the Spirit of God awoke her, saying, "Pray for Reinhard. Intercede for his life, because he is dying in Africa." She prayed for most of the day until she felt a breakthrough, a release by the Spirit from the prayer assignment she had received from the Lord. That is when the fever broke and I began my recovery. Once again my spiritual connection with the German Pentecostals proved to be a divine appointment.

At last the missions board made my appointment to Lesotho official. They assigned me to supervise in and around Maseru, the capital city. This was the largest town in Lesotho, yet it had a population of merely 38,000. It was not far from Ladybrand, just a short drive across the border. We moved there and left apartheid behind, finding a home in this black town. Our house was small with a corrugated metal roof. We moved our metal-framed servants' beds into the bedrooms. Kai-Uwe was three years old, Gabriele two, and Susanne merely an infant.

I found an office in town that seemed suitable for my church management duties. Only after moving in did I discover that I had established the AFM church offices next door to the offices of the local Communist Party! We could hear them cursing through the walls. They could hear us praying. *Dear Lord,* I thought, *what will Reverend Spies think?* Not only that, everywhere I went in Lesotho, in my heavy German accent I announced myself as a German who had no allegiance to apartheid. That might have endeared me to some of the locals, but to Communists, the history of bloodshed between the Soviets and the great German enclave of East Prussia rendered all Germans anathema in their eyes, even those like me who might want to reject the South African way. Every day when I approached my office I expected to see it burned to the ground, or perhaps vandalized with anti-German slogans.

I chuckled to myself and considered that God's mysterious guidance was somehow at work here. He had given me converts at a sinful circus in Flensburg. He had housed my first congregation in the Hansen Rum building. Now I was rubbing shoulders with Communists. What next?

I found that the city of Maseru had a different quality of life than in the rural areas. The men living here were no longer proud wranglers herding cattle in the high country. These former cowboys now worked far away from home in the gold and diamond mines of South Africa. Mining only allowed them to visit their wives and children for a few weeks of the year. Family life had broken down. The men sent money home, and this flow of South African currency propped up Lesotho's frail economy. It was a devil's bargain.

In the exchange, the independent Basuto tribesmen lost an idealized way of life. The mining jobs were demeaning, and the wages made them forever dependent on apartheid South Africa. They were not happy campers. Most men remained unemployed. The Communist Party had moved into this climate of misery. They preached their godless doctrine everywhere, promising a brave new world for the people of Lesotho. Of course, Communism is a pipe dream on which they could never deliver.

As soon as possible, I traveled to visit each of the three churches I was to oversee. The first was about 30 miles northeast in the village of Fobane. Not a dozen people were in attendance, plus the local elder. I took bread and wine to conduct a communion service. In Germany we had always used red wine for our observance. As I poured the first glass, the elder took it up and drank it in one gulp. I thought, *Oh my! This man must be hungry for God.* I poured another cup for him to share, but he did not share it. He drank this one down also. *Thank God I have another bottle in the van.* As I prepared to pour another cup, one of the parishioners whispered, "Pastor, he can't help himself. He is a drunkard. I don't think he's ever tasted such a fine wine."

I turned to the man. He did not deny it.

"A drunkard shall not serve as elder in this church," I said to him. "You, sir, are dismissed. You need to repent and prove yourself worthy of this assignment. Do not call yourself an elder."

The next Sunday I visited the second AFM church in another outlying village. In this one the elder began telling me the wonderful things God was doing through ancestral spirits. These Christians were actually continuing the idea that their dead ancestors were still present with them and would intercede for them with God.

I told them, "This is evil. It is not from God but from Satan. You must repent from this."

They were greatly offended at me. I realized that since they had been exposed to the gospel and had turned to this pagan practice instead of continuing their relationship with God through the Holy Spirit, I would be wasting my time and energy trying to straighten them out week after week. This was not my calling. There were others not in church that would receive the true gospel and not have this compromise. Those were the ones I had been commissioned to call to repentance.

Finally, I visited the church in Kolonyama. Rev. Pitso with the main congregation did not even understand why I wanted to see people saved. He did not understand that there was a difference between being born again and being lost. There were a total of five people sitting in his pews. I thought it was five too many.

For me, there is a mystery here. Africa is a place where Christian missionaries invested more than a century of effort before my coming. I must say that I respect the work they have done. I am constantly reminded that the harvest of souls I see today is a harvest I did not plant. Others sacrificed their lives to scatter the gospel seed to these regions long before the invention of the tools we use to harvest massive crowds today. Those who have gone before us have labored in obscurity, laying the foundations of faith among these tribes. I must never forget that.

However, the mystery to me is how the life-giving message of Jesus can become dead, how a fresh move of God can grow stale. It happens. The first step, I think, is when methods that worked in the past are enshrined, and any new wind of the Spirit is resisted. Old ways are repeated without inspiration by many who labor as professionals. Perhaps they do it for money. They become what Jesus called a hireling for the Lord.[47] If one comes who dares to break the accepted patterns, he is persecuted. They have forgotten that the Lord seeks a living and growing relationship. He resists being entombed in a method, or a building, or an organization – no matter how successful it might once have been.

Jesus spoke of the problem of putting new wine into old wine bottles.[48] The old bottles will burst, He said. This helped me to see my way forward in Lesotho. I told Anni that I was not going to invest myself in those dead churches. I did concede to preach at the local church on Sunday, but the rest of the week I began to seek out new converts on the streets and in the villages of Lesotho. I am happy to report that my approach of going to the people with the gospel eventually brought revival to those dead churches as well. But that happened many years after this small and very discouraging beginning.

I began to take my accordion to the streets and play and sing to gather a crowd. I would take up a spot near the market and at bus stops, any place where people were likely to be passing. Eventually people would gather to hear the nice-singing German boy with the blond hair and blue eyes. Then I would take up my Bible and launch into the ABCs of the gospel very quickly, before they could get away. It was just like my first street meeting as a boy in Glückstadt. In both cases I saw someone come to Jesus.

At the end of my very first sermon at a bus stop in Maseru, a tall, thoughtful young man stepped forward. I'll never forget him; his name was Michael Kolisang. He wore a colorful blanket wrapped around his shoulders. It was

the popular fashion for Basuto tribesmen, those who still worked cattle. He spoke to me through my interpreter. "I want this Jesus you have just preached. I want Him."

Michael Kolisang and I

What better response could I ever want to a sermon? "I want this Jesus you have just preached." I thought, maybe it will be this way every day in Maseru! Little did I know it was beginner's luck, pardon the expression. After that day I preached many sermons and saw no response.

I took him into the front seat of my Volkswagen microbus. With the interpreter helping from the backseat, I led him through the salvation scriptures. Then I prayed with him to accept Jesus as his Savior. Michael Kolisang has been at my side ever since. He is today a bishop in Lesotho, pastoring a thriving congregation of thousands, overseeing several other churches and running a nationwide Christian Radio Station called *Jesu Ke Karabo*.

In some ways Lesotho reminded me of Germany. It was a gospel-hardened land. Everyone was religious and believed they already knew what Christianity was all about. They had a "been there, done that" attitude. Responses like Michael Kolisang's were few. Dolphin Monese's was more typical ...

DOLPHIN MONESE was a bright, young student in Maseru. He had a big, happy smile and flashing brown eyes. But when he argued, his brows would knit together and his jaw would clench. He took his arguments seriously.

Dolphin studied the teachings of the Jehovah's Witnesses. He liked the way they attacked the Christian church. The church in the Kingdom of Lesotho had become weak and ineffective. Rather than follow a dead Christian religion, Dolphin attacked it. That was his way. In Maseru, he had become a Jehovah's Witness champion.

He walked to school each day with a group of friends. They would discuss the great issues of life, and he would impress them with his knowledge. One day, as they walked along, they saw a blind man at a bus stop playing a piano-accordion for money. Dolphin wanted to take a closer look, especially since the blind beggar was a white man. But as he came close, Dolphin could see that the man was not blind and was not a beggar. He was singing happy songs of praise to Jesus in the local Sesotho dialect.

*The man is a simpleton,* he thought. Suddenly, the man put down his piano-accordion, picked up his Bible and began to preach. One of the men in the crowd began to interpret for him. It was a trick. The man had used his music to attract people out of sympathy. The simpleton was clever, at least, Dolphin thought. He knew that it was not easy to gather a crowd in Maseru to hear preaching.

No problem. Dolphin had read many books about the Bible. He knew that Christians considered Jesus to be equal with God, a part of what they called the Holy Trinity. Since he could easily defeat these silly doctrines, he would listen to the preacher's message, and then argue to set him straight. It would provide amusement and another way to impress his friends.

As you might have guessed, I was the blind beggar on the street corner that day, preaching my heart out. As soon as I finished my sermon, Dolphin stepped forward, not to accept Jesus, but to argue with me. Since he spoke English, he was able to argue without an interpreter.

My interpreter George Masoka, was happy for the break. He often said that he had never worked so hard for a preacher in his life. I wore him out with four street sermons per day, and he wanted a raise in pay.

Dolphin jumped into his Jehovah's Witness arguments headlong. I just smiled and listened. I knew that I could not change the young man's mind by meeting him on some battlefield of the mind. I invited him to sit down with me on the curb. He did, but he never let up.

I knew that deep inside, Dolphin was worn out by the demands of his own arguments. But I didn't know if he was tired enough to let go of them. He seemed to like arguing so much. He went on and on with his attack on Christianity until the entire crowd that had gathered that day had gone away. Even his friends had departed. It was the two of us sitting on that street curb, and only one was talking – Dolphin.

"May I say something?" I interjected.

He was in the middle of a thought and had to finish it before he could stop himself. At last he paused. "Yes. What is it?"

"I want to say how much God loves you. You and I and everyone in the world were born in sin. We were bound for eternal hell, yet He loved us enough to – "

"– There is no hell," he interrupted. "Punishment in hell is an idea the popes made up. They did it to make people afraid so they could control them. I'm not falling for any of that."

"You will have to argue with the Scripture, Dolphin. Eternal torment is clearly in the Bible. The popes did not make it up. But that's not the good news. The good news is that God loved the world, even in its sin, and gave His only Son as a sacrifice for us. Salvation is a free gift, paid for by someone else. We cannot earn it by being smart, or by learning all the right things, or by doing all the right things. When we accept God's great gift, He fills us with love and peace, and we are promised eternal life with Him in heaven. Have you accepted Jesus as your Savior?" I gave him the ABCs.

Dolphin went away promising he would come back to complete the correction of my bad theology. I welcomed him to return, but I must say, inwardly, I hesitated. I knew he would take advantage of my open door.

And he did. He returned every day after that. His school breaks were timed so that he could come hear me at the bus stop. Then his after-school walk brought him by my market location for another sermon. He would start more arguments. This pattern continued day after day.

In time I found the opportunity to counter most of his arguments from Scripture. But still, this was not enough to convert him. He came again and again to argue, and perhaps for other reasons he would not admit to me. He was a tough nut to crack.

One day as I preached, I sensed a powerful anointing and presence of the Holy Spirit. After my sermon that day Dolphin stepped forward.

"I am ready to accept Jesus Christ as my Savior," he said.

Amazement, almost disbelief, leapt up in my heart. This was an incredible moment. Suddenly, this young man who had come to argue had no arguments.

In that moment the Holy Spirit whispered inside of me, telling me what to do. I sensed in my inner conversation with the Lord that Dolphin must not just make a decision for Christ; he must make a clean break with the Jehovah's Witnesses at the same time. This was a source of bondage that still remained for him.

"Let's get into my car," I said.

He did. When we were inside, I said to him, "We will drive to your house and burn all your Jehovah's Witnesses books. Are you ready to do that?"

Immediately, Dolphin had an inner struggle. So much of his knowledge was bound up in those books. They had given him pride and a place in the world.

They had made him feel superior. I thought that if I did not place a clear choice before him, he would go into a time of struggle that would last for a long time before he would finally be free. Years of unfruitfulness could follow.

"Choose Jesus or Jehovah's Witnesses," I said. "This is the choice you make. Not two ways, just one."

At last he nodded. "Yes, you are right. Let's get the books."

This was a sign to me that the Spirit of Jesus had entered his heart. He was opening himself up to its cleansing power. By burning these books he was burning bridges to his past. Bridges that the devil would have loved to have kept under constant traffic, back and forth, back and forth, between Jesus and Jehovah's Witnesses for unnumbered days ahead. Religious bondage is the worst kind.

I drove to his house. He went inside and brought out an armload of books, depositing them in my Volkswagen microbus.

"Are these all of them?"

"I have another shelf of books at my grandma's house in the village."

"We will go there and get them. Get in, I'll drive."

"But I don't own those books. They're borrowed."

"I will pay for the books you borrowed. But we will burn them all today, borrowed or not."

Dolphin agreed. He gathered all the books from the village together and put them in the car. I purchased a gallon container of gasoline. We drove to his brother's house where he knew he could find a barrel for burning. I had him place the books inside. We doused them with the fuel.

I handed him the match. When he lit it and dropped it into the barrel an explosion of flame leapt into the air. I felt a great sense of relief. As the books burned, I could see a new Dolphin Monese emerge. The burden of carrying a heavy religious yoke was exchanged for the easy yoke and the light burden of life in Jesus Christ. Joy, peace, gentleness, meekness – all the fruit of the Spirit came pouring forth.

In the years that followed, Dolphin grew in his faith. I asked him to be my interpreter on many occasions, and he learned much about preaching and ministering through this process. He went on to Bible school. Today he is the pastor of a wonderful church in Lesotho. His intellect and personality are submitted to the will of the Lord, and his winning smile and pleasant face is a joy and comfort to many thousands.

Both Dolphin Monese and Michael Kolisang were young men with me in Lesotho. Today we are growing old, and when we get together we share so many fond memories of those early years. It is one of the great blessings that come from a life of serving God.

Dolphin Monese and I

STILL, THAT FIRST HUMBLING YEAR in Maseru was a challenge. I remember my Volkswagen van took such a beating on the roads that I stopped having the body repaired from the minor – and not so minor accidents.

Eventually, the solenoid switch went out on the starter. We could not find a replacement. Therefore, the starter would not engage, even though the battery had enough electrical charge to turn the engine over. So we developed a method of always parking on a downward slope with clearance in front of the car so that with a little push we could gain some momentum and pop the clutch, starting the engine. However, at our house, which had no slope, Anni usually had to drive while I pushed the car. It didn't take long, but soon we had enough momentum for her to pop the clutch and start the engine.

Then she would take the other seat, and I would take over and drive us wherever we needed to go.

One night we awakened, and she was hemorrhaging badly. We realized that she was having a miscarriage. I needed to get her to the hospital across the border in Ladybrand as quickly as possible. I bundled Kai-Uwe, Gabriele, and Susanne into the van as quickly as I could, but in Anni's condition, she could not sit behind the wheel and pop the clutch. So I opened the door and began pushing until a little momentum had been achieved. Then I jumped into the driver's seat, put in the clutch, engaged a gear, and popped it out. By that time the little momentum I had achieved was lost, and I had to begin the process all over again. Praying under my breath, after several tries, I managed to get the car to cough and turn over and away we went, speeding to the hospital over those bouncing, rugged roads.

After Anni's second miscarriage and a similar trip to the hospital, I wrote a letter to my father describing the ordeal and asking for his and mother's prayers. Not long afterward, a new Mercedes Benz was delivered to our home. I thought surely my father had shared the letter with Pentecostal believers in Krempe and someone had responded. I wrote to him, thanking him. But then I discovered the truth. He had nothing to do with it. This car had come from a friend of ours in Herrenberg, a town in Southern Germany. This friend had been supernaturally moved upon by the Spirit to provide this reliable transportation, not knowing how desperately it was needed.

So there we were in the middle of poverty stricken Maseru, with a car that only the blessed rich could afford to own. We had no choice but to park it in the driveway outside our missionary house with its corrugated tin roof. Thank God, we never again had to rush Anni to the hospital. After consultation with the doctors, we realized that the Lord had already blessed us with the son and two daughters He intended for us to raise for His glory. There would not be six Bonnke boys after all. Our divine parenting roster was full. I sang the "Hallelujah Chorus" many times over as I drove to various meetings in the van. My joy was in knowing that Anni and the children had reliable and comfortable transportation back home.

# Chapter 18

AFTER MANY MONTHS, my main congregation in Maseru grew to 50 members. Word began to circulate that I was an effective preacher. Many white South African churches began to extend invitations to me as a guest speaker. At first, I turned these invitations down. 50 new converts was hardly a drop in the bucket to the kind of move of God I desired to see. I had much work to do.

I continued my street evangelism efforts, but the daily schedule of preaching was physically exhausting, and the results were pitifully few. My original interpreter had quit. Worn out. Dolphin Monese had taken over and now served with the true heart of an evangelist. But the hardened religious soil of Maseru was taking its toll. It was then that Anni and I came up with a new strategy.

On Fridays, we began to hold a youth service in our home. Dolphin and Michael Kolisang helped me gather interested young people from the streets of Maseru into our home. There we would serve refreshments and I would teach them from the Scriptures, always ending with an invitation to accept Jesus. I had found a small, round coffee table at a secondhand store. Those who wanted to be saved I invited to kneel at that table in our living room. These were the most effective outreaches I saw in those early years. As the young people knelt, I led them in the prayer of salvation. I really felt the presence of God in those invitations.

Perhaps they were more ready because they were young. It also might have been that their hearts were opened by being welcomed into a white person's home. All I know is that many of the future members of my evangelistic team were born again right there around that coffee table.

After that very first Friday youth meeting, Anni and I cleaned up the house. Suddenly Anni called to me. "Reinhard, come here and see this."

I came into the living room. She was kneeling at the little coffee table with a wet cloth poised in her hand. But she was not using it. With her other hand she pointed to the surface of the table. When I came near, I saw that the table was covered with tears.

How the gospel touches a soul so deeply is due to the work of the Holy Spirit. We were honored to see this evidence of hearts opened to the Lord of the universe. And it had happened in our living room. As the weeks passed, more and more tears stained that coffee table, corroding its lacquer finish.

To our family it was no longer merely a coffee table. It became a treasure, a monument, a reminder. We called it our table of tears.

ANNI AND I LOVED living among the black people in Maseru. But soon this led to an important question. Kai-Uwe had grown old enough to attend his first grade in school. Where would we educate him?

"I heard such sad stories about this," Anni said to me. "When I was in Bible school in Wales, many of those students were children of missionaries. They had been sent away from home to white boarding schools because there was no education possible for them on the mission field. In every case, these children were hurt and embittered against their parents. I do not want that for our children."

She got no argument from me. I did not want to send our children away from home under any circumstance. However, I did know that there was no education possible in this place. It had caused years of struggle for me. I gave my fear to the Lord and committed with her that we would have our children educated in the

Kai-Uwe's 2nd birthday in Africa

local black schools with their friends and neighbors. As best we could, we would supplement their schooling with books and educational materials that would broaden their experience at home. That's what we did.

After only a few days in school, however, Kai-Uwe came home in tears. I took him aside. "You are so sad. What is wrong?"

"The other boys make fun of my name."

"Bonnke?"

"No, Kai-Uwe. They say it all sorts of funny ways, and it makes me feel bad."

It had never occurred to me that this name choice would cause ridicule for my son. Something had to be done about it. In the modern era we often hear of parents filing discrimination lawsuits to get better treatment for their children. Such solutions only add to the problem. In Maseru, it would have been totally ridiculous.

It is interesting to note, however, that discrimination is a human problem. It has nothing at all to do with being black or white. Here my son, the only white boy in a school of blacks, suffered discrimination for his funny-sounding name. If the only black boy in a white school had a funny-sounding name, it would have been exactly the same. People are people. This was not a problem for the authorities to handle. It was a classic problem for a parent to solve. And I was determined to solve it.

"Well, son," I said, "you have a middle name. We'll use that. Friedrich." As soon as I said it I knew that it was not going to be an improvement. "Ah, no, I have a better idea. How about Freddie? There's a name that comes from your middle name but sounds like everyone else's name. We'll call you Freddie."

"Freddie? Yeah." He liked the sound of it. "Yeah, Dad, they could call me Freddie."

"Well, then, Freddie you are from now on!"

The next day I accompanied him to school and announced that my son, Freddie, was not going to be called Kai-Uwe anymore. He was going to be called by his middle name. It took a few more days for the original name to be forgotten, but Freddie he became, and the problem ceased.

AFTER MUCH HARD LABOR in Maseru I saw that if I didn't change my ways I would never reach the far-flung villages of Lesotho. I had started a Bible school in my church to provide training for Dolphin, Michael, and three other young converts. Five students in all were taking so much of my time and energy that there was little left over for expansion. Then it came to me that I could design a Bible correspondence course that would go far beyond me. It could be distributed to the many literate Basuto tribesmen by regular mail. Using the pattern of teaching I had used with my five students in the Bible school, I wrote a course of five basic lessons in following Christ. I was able to raise enough money to buy a small offset-press and learn to print myself. This developed into huge dimensions. At that very time, a missionary from the Velberter Mission, Bernd Wenzel, felt called of the Lord to join our team. He was a professional printer from Germany.

Preaching, praying … and writing

Soon hundreds and then thousands were enrolled. With the increasing printing press costs, I suddenly realized that I should take the speaking invitations that were coming to me from white South African churches. I would go to them and challenge them to support these efforts.

That is what I did, and soon the funds were available to continue growing the enrollment. I also expanded the printing operation to include an evangelistic magazine. The magazine followed the correspondence course and began to find wider and wider distribution. I traveled and told the story of what God was doing, and the white churches very graciously responded, sending more money.

It was at this time that I began to hear of resentment from other missionaries. Perhaps they were not experiencing the same breakthroughs. Or maybe they were unable to raise the funds I was raising in the prosperous South African churches. Then again, it might have purely been jealousy. Whatever the cause, some of my fellow missionaries began to talk about me in negative ways. This became one of the most difficult challenges I have ever faced.

Some suggested that my ego was leading the way, that I thought I was special. My new methods and ideas were described as somehow arrogant. When I heard of it I vigorously defended myself. I wanted to make sure everyone knew that I was led by a burning desire to see souls saved. But no matter how I wanted to make that clear, people continued to say and believe what they wanted to say and believe. It hurt me deeply and truly distracted me. I am by nature a fighter.

At AFM conferences I found times in which I would confront my accusers, argue with them, and defend my actions. But this, too, was a mistake. Nothing seemed harder to ignore than the critical words of my brothers in Christ. Some made no effort to hide their criticisms. I was forced to learn to bless those who cursed me. Anni alone knew how hard my struggle was.

One day I emerged from my office to be confronted by a horde of cursing Communists. They cursed God and blasphemed the name of Jesus to my face. Here were enemies I could understand. We served different masters.

Suddenly I felt the power of the Spirit surge within me. I said, "In the name of the One whom you are cursing, I say to you that within a year your feet will no more walk the streets of Maseru!" I knew as I spoke that I prophesied. The Spirit had spoken through me with these words. They were not from my own mind. Neither did I know that a few months later, Lesotho's prime minister, Leabua Jonathan, would declare a state of emergency, and all Communists would be rounded up and sent to jail.

It happened exactly that way, and the story of my prophecy raced around Maseru like lightning. Some people began to fear me. Rumors ran about that God talked to Reinhard Bonnke and that He would even tell Reinhard what people were thinking. Of course, this was superstitious nonsense.

In this situation, however, my brethren worked to discredit me. It was even suggested that I had lied or exaggerated what had really happened. Some thought I was motivated by ambition, not by the Spirit of God, and that I was trying to make a great name for myself. In desperate prayer and in counsel with my wife, I began to let go of these things. Until I let go of them they would not let go of me. It is said that resentment is like drinking poison and waiting for your enemy to die. There is no room for such a waste of energy in the service of God. I began to learn that it is not my place to defend the work of God. But I must confess there were times when it took all of my German willpower to hold myself back.

IN MY CONGREGATION, as in all of Maseru, there were many unemployed young men. One day it came to me that I could give them employment while furthering the gospel in Lesotho at the same time. The plan was to give each young man a bicycle equipped with a weatherproof box. I would send them from house to house, village to village, offering our ministry magazine for free and selling a hymnal and a Bible to those who wanted them. In this way I could

Some of the 100 "bicycle-evangelists" in Soweto

train witnesses to reach Lesotho and provide employment for these young men at the same time. In the land of the African cowboy, these young witnesses became a version of circuit-riding preachers. It was a method of spreading the gospel that had been used effectively in history. As I traveled in white churches, I presented this vision and found sponsors willing to provide the specially designed bicycles.

I started with five, then ten, and then finally I had 30 riding the rough trails of Lesotho's high country. It was so successful, they soon earned more than twice the average wage of other young men in Maseru. Some of them went beyond sales and became true soul winners, and eventually, pastors. Within two years, this group of hardy travelers had visited every village in the Kingdom of Lesotho, exposing 1,348,000 to the gospel message. Hallelujah!

The idea of combining soul winning and salesmanship did not set well with some of my fellow missionaries. Soon, a lot of talk emphasized the money side of things, as if this was the only reason I had conceived the venture. It seemed futile to respond. But the negative talk reached the ears of my missions board in Germany. A showdown loomed. I felt the pain of this more than any other opposition I faced.

Staff and students in my Maseru Bible School

Eventually the correspondence course enrolled 50,000 students. This was success beyond my wildest dreams. No one could ignore the effectiveness of this outreach, especially in a hard land where missionaries were expected to fail. In the meantime, the Bible College I had founded in Maseru that had begun with an enrollment of five students, now had grown to 40. In a missionary bone yard, we had seen dead bones live again. With no allegiance to the methods of the past we were forging a new future by following the voice of God. It happened not because we were special, but because we obeyed. I offered the loaf of living bread. He multiplied it in my hand.

MY PHONE RANG. Brother Harold Horn, someone I had known since my arrival in Lesotho, said, "Reinhard, come to Kimberley and preach to us."

I said, "I will come."

I knew that Kimberley was a town of about 100,000 residents, located about 160 miles to the west. Like Maseru, Kimberley was an isolated community. For a century it had been famous for its diamond mines. The world's largest diamonds had come from there. The entire area was steeped in the lore of fortunes mined from the earth. Mining continued to be the backbone of the economy.

The Kimberley mines were owned and operated by the descendants of white settlers. However, the backbreaking toil in the mines was performed by black men, many of them from my own country of Lesotho. The church that I would visit in Kimberley, however, was a "whites-only" congregation.

When I arrived, I remember, it was a cold evening. The skies were patchy with clouds, and a chilly wind gusted from the peaks around us. Harold drove me to the church where I was to preach. We had agreed to a Friday, Saturday, and Sunday series of meetings.

That first Friday night as I sat on the platform I looked across a gathering of 200 people. Not one young person did I see in the room. Not one.

I leaned over to Harold, who was near to me, and asked, "Where are the young people?"

He nodded sadly, acknowledging that I had correctly seen the problem. Every head in the room was gray.

I preached. The service was closed, and the people filtered out to their cars to go home. When they had gone, Harold came to me.

"Reinhard, would you like to see the answer to your question? Would you like to know where all the young people in Kimberley are?"

"Yes, I would," I replied.

"I will show you. Get into my car, and I will take you there."

"Where are you taking me?"

"It's a surprise," he said. He remained mysterious about it.

He drove through the streets, turning this way and that until he came to a large building at the edge of a warehouse district. The building was ablaze with gaudy neon signs. One large sign blinked out the word, *disco, disco, disco.*

The parking lot was jam-packed to overflowing with vehicles. We parked on the street a block away. As he turned off the key I could hear the boom, boom, boom, of the heavy bass beat coming through the walls of that building. The so-called music seemed to shake the very ground beneath us with an ungodly spirit.

"This is a den of iniquity," I said sadly. "How awful. This is where the young people have gone?"

He nodded. "This is the latest thing, Reinhard. It is called a discotheque, a dance club. It is a craze that is sweeping the whole world right now, and young people everywhere are very attracted to it."

I felt a shiver go down my spine. How could the church compete for the attention of their youth against such temptation? The quiet little church building we had just come from, and this pulsing, giant warehouse could not seem more opposite. The disco was so large, so energetic, so loud, and so overwhelming.

Again, I could see the faces of the old people I had preached to just an hour ago. They had all come to hear Reinhard Bonnke preach to a room with no young people in it. Now they were, no doubt, sitting at home in houses with no young people in them. The young people were here, indulging in all sorts of sensual pleasures. At least they could feel confident that their parents and grandparents would not disturb them here. The older generation would not dare to enter this jarring and frightening atmosphere.

Harold got out and stood for a while, leaning against the hood of his car, listening. I got out too and stood next to him.

We could hear the music now, above the booming bass. It was terrible, terrible music. I couldn't really call it music. I thought of how gently I played my piano-accordion, singing happy songs about Jesus to attract crowds on the streets of Lesotho. The sound of my little accordion here would have been totally drowned out. No one could have taken any notice at all. I began to feel small and insignificant.

"What do the young people see in this disco, Harold?" I asked.

He shook his head, mystified. "I don't know. I truly don't know."

After a while, he said, "Let's go inside."

Bonnke family 1972

"Oh, no," I said. "Let's go home. I have never gone to such a place. It would be an abomination to me. I would not know how to act. And what would people think of me as a preacher? It's unthinkable."

To this moment, I had gone along with Harold simply out of curiosity. *Where were the young people?* I had asked. Now I knew. It was a sad reality of modern life, but I could do nothing to fix the gulf between young and old in neither Kimberley, nor anywhere else in the world. Only a revival of faith in Jesus could do that.

I would go back and preach my heart out to the old people again on Saturday and Sunday. Perhaps God would move on their hearts, and they would begin to make a difference in the lives of their own young people. That seemed the best I could hope for.

But as I turned to get into the car I felt bad inside. I stopped in my tracks. This is when the Holy Spirit began to speak to me. Since I had come this far, something seemed wrong if I now turned away. But I had no idea what the Spirit wanted me to do. I just couldn't leave.

"Let's take a look inside," Harold suggested.

Suddenly, this seemed exactly right. Everything in my spirit said yes. I nodded. "OK, Harold. Let's just take a look at this disco."

We began to walk toward the building. What would I do? I had no idea. It was against everything in my body and my mind, but not against my spirit. I simply obeyed the gentle urging inside. We came to the door and stood there. I felt the Spirit say to me very clearly, *Look inside. I will show you something you do not know.*

I took a deep breath then opened the door. The blast of music must have knocked the hair back from my forehead. I have never heard such volume in my life. It was deafening. But it was in that instant that I received a spiritual vision of the reality of the disco. In the flash of the strobe lights, I did not see young people dancing with joy. I saw frozen images of boredom, fear, loneliness, and insecurity, one after the other, captured on the faces of those young people. The split-second flashes of light revealed these images, over and over and over again, like stop-action. Each of those haunted faces spoke to me of emptiness. Pure emptiness.

Now I knew what the Spirit had wanted me to see. It was not what I had expected. These young people were coming to the disco seeking something they did not find. No matter how they threw themselves into the beat of the music, it always came out the same – empty.

I understood in that moment that I had what they were looking for. I could show them the way to a relationship with God through Jesus Christ. I could show them the power to live a life of joy in spite of the world's many disappointments. But all of the blessings of life in Jesus would never come to them in a disco, no matter how many dances they pounded out. And how would they hear the truth without a preacher? No preacher would be caught dead in this place.

Curiosity and revulsion was gone. In its place I felt the undeniable compassion of Jesus surging within me. I wanted to weep for the precious searching young people of Kimberley. They lived in a city that was diamond crazy. They did not know that they were the precious jewels God sought for His own crown. They were more precious than all these mountains of wealth. He cared enough to die for them.

Suddenly, I could not care less what anyone thought of me. I knew that I would preach in this disco. Nothing could deny the love of Jesus that I felt.

I shut the door and looked at Harold. I heard the Holy Spirit say in my heart, *Find the owner of this place.* And so, I said to Harold, "Help me to find the owner of this disco."

"What good will that do?"

"I must talk to him. Let's find him now."

"But what will you say to him?"

"I will ask him to let me preach in his disco."

Harold laughed. "You won't do that, Reinhard."

"I will. I absolutely will."

Harold followed me now. I inquired inside the disco, and we were led to an office at the rear of the building. The owner was a middle-aged businessman who looked to be very much a part of the rock-and-roll culture. He had long hair, gold chains around his neck, an open-collared shirt, and blue jeans.

I said to him, "Sir, I've come all the way from Germany. I am asking you for permission to allow me to address the young people in your disco for just five minutes."

He looked at me from top to toe. "You're a preacher," he said.

I was still dressed in my suit and tie. I nodded.

He said, "If you want to preach you should preach in a church."

"There are no young people in the church," I said. "They don't come to the church, so the preacher must come to the young people. Now give me five minutes, only five minutes, I ask of you."

"You've got to be kidding." He shook his head in disbelief, then turned around and walked away. "There is no way, man." He had no sympathy for my plea at all.

As he was walking, suddenly the Holy Spirit touched me. He said to me, *Tell him what you saw when you looked into his dance hall.* I went after the man and took him by the arm. He turned to face me again.

"One question, sir," I said, looking deep into his eyes. "Do you think the young people find what they need for life in your disco?"

Slowly the face of that man changed. He looked down thoughtfully. When he looked up again he said, "It is very strange that you would say that. I have children of my own. I've thought many times that the disco will not give the young people what they need for life."

"I beg you, sir, give me five minutes with them."

He was thoughtful for a moment. "OK, but not tonight. Saturday night, tomorrow night at midnight, I will give you the microphone for five minutes."

I grabbed his hand and shook it. "It's a deal, and thank you, sir. I will be here."

I was so happy I could have kissed him. I could feel the Holy Spirit in the whole thing that was happening. It was something I would never have thought of on my own.

As Harold drove me to my room, I began to beat myself up a little bit. I had only asked for five minutes. How could I be so stupid?

I started to pray. I said, "Lord, I foolishly asked for only five minutes. Now I am stuck with five minutes because I put that number in his head. Why did I say that?" After riding some more in silence, I prayed again, a bit better this time. "Lord," I said, "nothing is too hard for You. You created the world in six days; You can save the disco in five minutes. Please do not let my foolishness be a problem. Amen." All that night I tossed and turned, and prayed. I prayed and prayed.

The next night I preached to the old people at the church. I remember nothing. I think I must have preached badly because my heart was pounding with anticipation for preaching to the lost in the disco that night. When the congregation had gone home to their houses, I asked Harold to drive me back to my room. I undressed from my suit and dressed in casual clothes. I did not want to look like a preacher just coming from church. I needed disco camouflage. Harold went home and quickly changed his clothes, too.

As we got in his car he paused to look at me. "Reinhard Bonnke, what do you think the people of the church would think if they knew where you were going tonight?"

"I think they would never come to hear me again," I said. "You won't tell them, will you?"

He smiled and shook his head. "No, of course not."

"Nor will I."

Breakfast in South Africa. Left: Rev. Peter van den Berg

We drove to the disco, arriving at 11:30 p.m. I had a half hour to wait. The parking lot was even more crowded on Saturday than it had been on Friday. I guess in Kimberley they had what you call "Saturday night fever." I took my Bible under my arm and my piano-accordion. I don't know why I took the piano-accordion, but there it was. I took it with me into that disco like a security blanket.

Inside, it was insanely crowded. Shoulder to shoulder, we had to push our way between the people to get past them to find a place to sit. Finally we came to a bar with a stool. I sat on the stool and waited for midnight.

When at last the clock struck twelve, the music stopped. I jumped up and onto the stage where the records were being spun. I took the microphone from the disk jockey and shouted, "Sit down, sit down, sit down. I've come all the way from Germany, and I've got something very important to tell you."

Suddenly the young people began sitting down everywhere. It was then I realized I was not in church but in a dance hall. There were no pews. Only a few bar stools at the perimeter. Most of the young people plopped right down on the floor. There they sat, smoking cigarettes and chewing gum, waiting for me to tell them something very important that I had brought with me all the way from Germany.

I started to preach one minute, two minutes; suddenly the Holy Spirit was there; I mean the wind of God blew into that disco. Suddenly I heard sobbing. I saw young people getting out their handkerchiefs and starting to wipe their eyes, crying everywhere. The disco dance floor was quickly becoming another table of tears. And I had preached enough to know that when people start shedding tears, it's time for an altar call. I said, "How many of you want to receive Jesus Christ as your Savior? How many want to find forgiveness for your sins and enter God's plan for your life, as of tonight?"

Every hand that I could see in that place went straight up. I said, "Alright, repeat after me." We prayed the prayer of salvation together. My five minutes were up. My work was done. I left walking on cloud number nine, rejoicing, absolutely rejoicing that I had been privileged to help these young people find what they would never find in a disco.

A year later I returned to Kimberley. Harold met me at the airport. He said, "Get in my car. I have a surprise for you."

I got in his car. He did not say anything about it; he just drove through the winding streets until he came to the warehouse district. The car stopped. I looked out of the window. I could not believe my eyes. I wiped them and looked again. Instead of seeing the big disco sign, there was a huge white cross on the front of that building.

"This is not the surprise," Harold said. "Come inside."

We walked up to that door where we had stood one year ago, the door the Spirit had told me to open. I remembered the pounding beat of the music that had assaulted my ears as we stood there that Saturday night. Now I heard another sound coming from inside. It was a kind of chant, growing in volume.

"Are you ready for this, Reinhard?" Harold swung the door open, and I looked into a packed house full of young people. They were chanting, "Bonnke, Bonnke, Bonnke."

I cried out with joy. They rushed to me, hugging me and shaking my hands, bringing me inside. One young man said, "Remember me? I was the disk jockey that night that you came."

Another grabbed my hand. "I was operating the light show." Another said, "We were dancing the night away. Now we are serving Jesus."

The Bonnkes in South Africa. Left: Hermann Bonnke

"After you left town, the disco went bankrupt," Harold shouted to me. "This disco is a church!" He was beaming from ear to ear.

A fine-looking gentleman came up to me. "We heard about what happened to the young people here. My church has sponsored me to be a pastor to these kids."

I stood again on that disco stage looking at those faces, so different from the ones I had seen in the strobe lights a year ago. The lights were up full now. Even more, the light of the Lord's favor was shining on every face.

I pointed my finger to the heavens and shouted, "Jesus!" – "Jesus!" they shouted back to me as one, making the walls to tremble.

"Praise Jesus!" – "Praise Jesus!"

"He is Lord!" – "He is Lord!"

"Hallelujah!" – "Hallelujah!"

Now that disco was rocking the right way. Kimberley's true diamonds were shining in their Father's eyes.

# Chapter 19

I HAD A DREAM that changed everything. I saw a map of Africa. Not South Africa, not Lesotho, not Johannesburg, but the entire continent. In my dream the map began to be splashed and covered with blood. I became alarmed. I thought surely this meant some kind of apocalyptic violence was coming – perhaps a bloody Communist revolution. But the Spirit whispered to me that this was the blood of Jesus that I saw. The terrible violence that spilled His blood happened 2,000 years ago on a cross. Then I heard the words, *Africa shall be saved.*

When I woke up I had a problem. My mind filled with new thoughts that made me uncomfortable. Before going to sleep I had been happy to see 50,000 people enrolled in our correspondence course in Lesotho and further afield. After this dream I could not be happy with that number. I am a German who had struggled with math as a boy. But even I could do these calculations. I had learned that the continent was home to 478,000,000 souls. If it had taken me five years to reach 50 people in Maseru, plus another 50,000 beyond the walls of my church through correspondence, that pace would average 10,010 souls per year. There is nothing wrong with that number but I would have to live to be at least 47,752 years old to see a blood-washed Africa! I thought I had done well. In light of this dream I could see that I was far behind God's agenda.

In my mind I began to discount the dream. Perhaps I had simply eaten bad bananas. The next night the same dream returned. And the next night. And the next. There were not that many bad bananas in all of Maseru. After this fourth night I said to my wife: "Anni, I think that God is trying to tell me something". He now had my full attention. Would I take seriously what He was saying to me? Or would I deny Him? Would I choose to believe God's math? Or would I believe my own?

God had brought me to another crossroad that would define the future. Never mind that I could not compute it. Never mind that my progress so far was a mere drop in the ocean. God had said, *Africa shall be saved.* Would I repeat

His words? Would I begin to speak in faith what I had seen in my dream? Or would I retreat into silence like another corpse in the missionary bone yard?

I knew one thing that would keep me silent. It was the fear of what others would say or think. I could hear my critics: "Who are you to say, *Africa shall be saved?*" they would say. This is the cutting question Satan throws at God's servants in order to silence them – "Who do you think you are?"

I wondered, will some people say again that I am ego-driven if I speak this dream? Yes, they will. Will my words make some people uncomfortable? Absolutely. I sensed that these words would mark me as surely as Joseph's coat of many colors marked him in the eyes of his jealous brothers. It would be like painting a target on my chest. But then I asked myself, is that a reason to be quiet when God has spoken? No. A thousand times no.

It was not about me. It was about God and His call. Since I was a boy I had obeyed His voice. I was one of His sheep. The Bible tells us that all of His sheep know His voice. But some teach themselves to ignore it. He calls, and they conclude it is bad bananas. This we must not do.

Whenever God spoke to me, even as a child, I made my mind fit His words, not the other way around. God had given me the dream of the blood-washed Africa. Then I would begin to speak it because of who God is, not because of who I am. All that I am, I am by the grace of God. So I have nothing to lose by obeying Him. Rather, I have everything to gain.

I decided that I would begin to say, *Africa shall be saved,* at every opportunity. More than anything else to date, these words began to separate me from my fellow missionaries. Going back to that small tool shed in the garden at the Bible school in Wales, when I had failed at homiletics, it was then I had received from the Lord the calling of an evangelist. Perhaps being directed by the dictates of a missionary board had clouded the full scope of my calling for the past five years. I was not a missionary in the way they had conceived it. As I began to speak His vision everywhere – "Africa shall be saved" – my role was redefined, both in my own eyes and in the eyes of my colleagues. I was no longer a missionary but a missionary-evangelist.

Thrilled to be on radio in Lesotho

I BELIEVE SO STRONGLY that God is the worker of miracles for his people. I believe the signs that followed Jesus as He walked the earth could – and should – be true in our lives today. Jesus said to His disciples, *He that believeth on me, the works that I do shall he do also; and greater works than these shall he do; because I go unto my Father.*[49] But I was not seeing miracles in Maseru and it distressed me. In fact, I often confessed to Anni in those days, "My church is a miracle-free zone. What is wrong?"

No matter what I tried, or how I prayed and fasted, the situation did not improve. As time went by, in my heart, I began to blame the people for their lack of faith. If only they had faith, I thought, they would experience wonderful miracles like those seen in the Book of Acts. God had some work to do in my heart. First, He used Richard Ngidi to open my eyes.

Richard was a Zulu evangelist well known in AFM churches throughout South Africa. After preaching he would minister to the people in individual prayer and the miraculous power of God would always manifest. The lame walked, the blind saw, cancers disappeared. If you longed to see the miraculous power of God on display – or so the prevailing wisdom went – book meetings with Richard Ngidi. And so, I did. I had come to know him from attending AFM conferences in South Africa. One day I invited him to minister at my church in Maseru. He accepted and I secretly felt sorry for him. I imagined that the faithless people of my "miracle-free" congregation would ruin his reputation.

In fact the opposite was true. When he ministered in Maseru I saw the power of God as never before. The blind saw, the lame walked, and diseases disappeared. Richard Ngidi trusted the Lord no matter what he faced. He was bold in the face of great problems and he had what I called a reckless faith. In his very loud, deep voice and confident manner he commanded disease and sickness to go from God's people. It was as if blindfolds dropped from my eyes watching him. I was almost in a state of shock.

I said to Anni, "When God speaks it is not for us to ask questions but to obey the prompting of His voice. His word is above all else. I can see it now! I can see it now! Anni, God's word is not a question mark, it is an exclamation point! I have been too timid."

Richard Ngidi and I

My eyes were now open but the truth did not fully possess my heart. After seeing a breakthrough in Maseru with Richard Ngidi I was still timid. Perhaps, I thought, I did not have a gift of faith, or a gift of the working of miracles as described in the writings of the Apostle Paul. I decided to invite another notable evangelist who had that reputation. I invited a man named John Bosman to come. He was a remarkable Dutch Reformed minister from Pretoria and he was seeing miracles everywhere he preached. Perhaps having another exposure to the miraculous power of God would push me into the place of believing. I ordered our team to begin advertising.

Meanwhile, our printing press in Maseru had become quite busy. Sponsors had stepped forward and helped us build the structure that housed it. In effect, we had our own little publishing company. After getting into trouble for naming it the AFM Press, I asked God what He would have me call it. He dropped the name into my heart that would define the rest of my ministry: Christ for all Nations. Our printing press became CfaN Press. Bernd Wenzel, our professional printer who had joined us earlier, cranked up the CfaN Press to fill all of Maseru with the announcement of John Bosman's meeting at our church. We were able to coordinate local radio promotion for the meeting as well. We announced to the people that they should come expecting to see the miraculous power of God to heal the sick. Excitement was building.

When the weekend finally arrived our church building was packed out. People were crowded around the outside of the building. Many sick, lame, and blind had been brought because of John's reputation for healing miracles. We had never seen this level of excitement for the work of the Lord in Maseru. I sensed that it would be the start of something big. A breakthrough. Bosman's ministry would burst the bonds of religious stagnation and satanic power that seemed to grip the region.

With great pride and pleasure, I introduced John to the crowd. He came to the pulpit and preached. I was not especially impressed with his preaching. Like most of the people there I had come expecting to see him demonstrate his gift of healing. But then something happened that shook me to my toes. After preaching only a modest sermon he turned to me and said, "Close the service."

I gasped. "But not now. All these people have come expecting you to pray for the sick. I cannot possibly close the service."

"Close it."

I was absolutely flattened. "John, how can we do this? I will dismiss the people, but you must promise to return tomorrow and pray for them. Will you let me make that promise?"

"Tell them the sick will be prayed for tomorrow."

With a great deal of confusion I did as he asked me to do. I closed the service, announcing that John would return in the morning to pray for the sick. When I turned, he had already gone to his hotel room.

I slept hardly a wink that night, praying and seeking God in confusion about what John had done. The next morning I got up early and went to pick him up for the meeting. Passing by the church I could not believe my eyes. The house was packed to capacity. Even more people were lined up outside, hoping to get in. The word had gone out that John would pray for the sick. Many more sick had been brought to the meeting site.

I went to the hotel. When I arrived, John was loading his suitcases into a waiting car.

"What is going on?" I asked in total confusion. "Where are you going?"

"Home," he said.

He could not have done more damage if he had taken a baseball bat and swung it to my midsection. I could hardly breathe. "What do you mean you are going home? I just went by the church. It is already packed with people who have come. You promised to pray for the sick. That is why they have come."

"I promised that the sick would be prayed for. You promised that I would do the praying."

"Stay, John. I'll do the preaching. That's what I do best. You pray for the sick. That is what you do best. We'll do this together."

"Reinhard, the Holy Spirit told me I must go."

African Messenger in print

With that he got into the car. The driver put it in motion and drove away down the street and then out of my sight. I stood there hoping that this was some kind of joke. I felt like my best friend had just deserted me. I had so looked forward to sharing ministry with him. But when he said the Holy Spirit had told him to go, I had no comeback. That was the entire point of everything. We were to do what the Holy Spirit commanded no matter how it went against our natural senses. I got into my car and drove toward that packed out church of people who had come expecting miracles.

Suddenly faith rose up inside of me, along with what I would call a "holy wrath." Behind that steering wheel I cried out to the God, "Lord, I am not a big-time evangelist, but I am Your servant also. Now I will go and do the preaching and praying for the sick and You will do the miracles."

Peace filled my heart immediately. It is the peace that only comes through our relationship with God when we abandon the world of the ordinary and enter His realm of the impossible. Hallelujah! As I drove on, I remembered the time when I was only ten years old and I had laid my hands on the woman in Father's church in Krempe. In very dramatic fashion she had been healed. How I prayed that something similar would happen to me now.

I walked into the church and told all my pastors that John had gone home. The Holy Spirit had ordered him to leave. I could tell by the way the light went out of their faces that they did not see me in the same category as the great South African evangelist. To them, even though I had led them to the knowledge of the Savior, I had become the prophet without honor in his own country.[50]

Without tolerating another doubt I began to take charge of that meeting with my words. "I will preach," I said to my men, "and God will do miracles today."

With that, I went to the pulpit. "The evangelist John Bosman has gone home," I announced. "But I have great news for you today. Jesus showed up. I will preach, and I will pray for everyone who has come for healing, and we will see miracles."

As soon as I said it a man and woman seated on the front row got up shaking their heads and headed for the exit. This was disheartening, but no sooner had they done it than two other people from outside the building rushed in to fill their seats. I wasn't sure these new additions had heard my announcement so I took small comfort. My only hope was in the power of God showing up.

I stood to preach. I saw the shape of the gospel. It was different this Sunday morning. I had never sensed the message quite like this. When I opened my mouth all timidity was gone. I spoke with an authority I had never known before. Suddenly, the room became charged. The Holy Spirit was confirming the word in the minds and hearts of the people. About midway through my sermon, Dolphin Monese, who was interpreting for me was overcome by the power of the Spirit and fell to the floor.

Everything stopped, except the listening crowd. They waited breathlessly for the next word. I waited for Dolphin to recover. As I waited I was taken away from that place in my mind. It was as if all sounds and sights became muted, and I heard words of the kind that I could never conceive – *My word in your mouth is as powerful as My word in My mouth.*

I could only take it in by the Spirit. My senses would not go there. There was no question that I was now entering new territory in my relationship with God. This thought would never have occurred to me. It came on the heels of watching Dolphin crumple to the floor as he tried to repeat the words that had just come from my mouth. Something was happening here that only the Spirit could give sense to. My authority in Him was far greater than I had ever imagined. As long as I was in harmony with God's will, I was to speak things as God spoke them, and to expect to see God's own results.

*Call those who are totally blind, and speak the word of authority,* the Spirit said to me. This rang a bell of memory in my heart. Luis Graf had treated the healing of the sick and the saving of souls as two sides of the same calling when he came to the Bonnke household with the flame of the Spirit in 1922.

"There are blind people here this morning," I said. "I ask all of you who are totally blind to stand to your feet. Stand at once. I will pray for you." Around the room several people rose. They stood swaying slightly, straining their other four senses to compensate for their loss of sight.

"I am going to speak in the authority God has given me, and when I do, you blind will see a white man standing before you. Do you hear me? Your eyes will be opened!" With that I took a deep breath and shouted. "In the name of Jesus, blind eyes open!"

A woman began screaming. She rushed from the back of the crowd grabbing people as she went, looking at them, crying, "I see! I see! I see!"

The room broke into pandemonium. Shouts of praise to God filled the morning, and no one was left seated. They were leaping and praising God.

The entire room and many outside crowded in so that no one could even pass between the bodies crushed against the platform.

When the woman reached the front I invited her up on the platform. I asked her what had happened. She said that she had been blind for four years. Now she could see. I took my Bible and placed it before her. I asked her to read. She read, *The Spirit of the Lord is upon me, because he hath anointed me to preach the gospel to the poor; he hath sent me to heal the brokenhearted, to preach deliverance to the captives, and recovering of sight to the blind.*[51]

It was all she could read before recognizing that Jesus had healed her. She was leaping and crying and praising God all over the platform area. The people were with her, filling that room with a surge of praise that threatened to raise the building off its foundation.

I looked across the raised hands and the sea of heads before me and saw a sight the likes of which I have never seen again. A young child was being passed forward from the back of the room, from hand to hand. At last the child arrived at the front and was deposited in my arms. I looked down at a boy of perhaps three or four; his twisted little limbs were not what they should be. As I just looked at that boy, seeing his twisted legs – I forgot to pray! Suddenly his little body began to vibrate in my arms. He slipped out of my arms and landed on his feet – running around.

That day I learned that the Holy Spirit is a Healing Spirit. When He moves, people don't just speak in new tongues but all things are possible. In the heart of the missionary bone yard a dead church had become alive and overflowing with the power and love of God. The meeting did not stop all day long, until out of exhaustion I had prayed for all of the sick. We had seen many more healings and miracles, and everyone knew that a new day had dawned in Lesotho. As the people left, I watched them and tears were running down my face. I began to pray, *Precious Holy Spirit, I want to apologize. I now believe you send John Bosman away because today you launched my ship!*

As I finally made my way home in the waning afternoon, I saw the pattern for the future. *This is how all Africa shall be saved,* I thought. *Not by might, nor by power, but by my Spirit, saith the lord of hosts.*[52] It was not a natural calling. It was not a natural enabling. It was supernatural.

NOTHING WAS THE SAME in the days ahead. It was as if I was catapulted from one level to another. From one place to another. We acquired a secondhand tent and began to set it up at various locations and hold meetings. Soon a storm ripped the tent to shreds. Its rotten canvas was no match for the winds. We began to seek another.

Some of the new expenses had depleted our cash on hand. Rent was due, and I didn't have it. I had walked to the office, which was not far from our home. While walking back home I began to talk to my Heavenly Father. "Lord, we need 30 rand today, where will I find it to pay rent on time?"

Suddenly the voice of the Lord spoke in my heart. *You've asked for 30 rand. Why don't you ask Me for a million?*

I felt a chill run down my spine. Once again, God was challenging my small thinking. What if He gave me a million? What would I do with it? I began to calculate the improvements I could make. The fine tent I would purchase. The trucks and vehicles I would buy to carry all of our literature and people to the next campaign.

Suddenly all the fantasies stopped and I became choked with tears. I realized that once again I was thinking too small. With people passing me as they walked along the road I stopped and cried out from the very depths of my soul, "No, Lord! I am not asking for one million rand. I am asking for a million souls! One million souls less in hell and more in heaven, that shall be the purpose of my life and ministry."

The Holy Spirit replied, "You will plunder hell and populate heaven for Calvary's sake." It became the motto of my life.

I felt my Father's full pleasure. I had no doubt that it would take far more than a million dollars to see a million souls saved. But I knew that I valued the souls above money. It was now God's challenge to supply the money necessary to reach a million souls. It was simply my challenge to obey His voice, day by day. To me it seemed that I had crossed a threshold in my relationship with Him, and I was very happy. But several years later I realized that even in this answer, I had been thinking way too small. It is good that God takes us forward one step at a time.

Shortly afterward, I was told that I would be visited by a member of the Velberter Mission, the missionary outreach of the ACD (Arbeitgemeinschaft der Christengemeinden in Deutschland), the association of Pentecostal Churches in Germany. The missions' board had heard reports of the correspondence course I had begun, of my purchase of a printing press, for which they had sent the expert printer Bernd Wenzel. They had also heard of my fundraising for the bicycle circuit riders, and more recently of the purchase of a tent, and of its demise in a thunderstorm. It was known that I sometimes had trouble making rent, let alone managing all these extra activities. Other VM (Velberter Mission) missionaries had reported these things, complaining that Reinhard Bonnke was able to exercise more freedom in his mission than they were. The board had decided to send someone to investigate. The man they chose was the director of the missions board himself, Pastor Gottfried Starr.

When Gottfried arrived I was sure that I would be able to show my German brother the extent of what God was doing in Lesotho. And I believed that once he saw the obvious blessing of the Lord he would place his stamp of approval on it. In each of my methods, I assured him that I took full responsibility financially and otherwise. But he did not receive this explanation from me. He corrected me, assuring me that in any disputes about property or liability, the VM would be taken to court, not I.

"Legally, no one will sue you to recover damages," he said. "They will sue the organization behind you. We have considerable assets at risk. Your assets are meager. So in a sense you are putting us out on a limb. You are putting our neck on the block. Do you see that?"

I saw his point, but I couldn't agree completely. If he stuck to this reasoning then all of my success here was actually a liability to the VM.

"My dear brother," I said. "Do you not agree that there are certain risks worth taking? Especially when you are in the business of saving souls?"

He did not answer. When the investigation was complete, Pastor Gottfried Starr stood firm. "The VM cannot allow you to expand any further, Reinhard. The risks are too great." A few weeks later the full board in Germany agreed with this assessment in writing.

My soul was smitten within me, as if I had been disowned by my own family. I had to leave Anni and go off by myself in desperation. I needed to talk with God and even more, I needed Him to talk to me. As I prayed, I perhaps slipped into some self-pity. I told the Lord that I was sick of always being the naughty boy, always accused of having a mind of my own. "Why am I always getting in trouble when I obey You? I want to be at peace with my brothers," I pled. "Shouldn't we be, as Paul says, ... *forbearing one another in love; Endeavouring to keep the unity of the Spirit in the bond of peace?* [53]" I want to submit to the VM and stop being driven by the burning vision You've given me of a blood-washed Africa."

Well, sometimes we say things, even in prayer, that we do not mean. God is gracious not to break off the conversation. The Lord spoke back to me sharply. *Yes, you can do this. But if you drop My call, I will have to drop you and I will have to look for someone else.*

Just like that, my whining to the Lord was over. I went home and told Anni, "Today I am resigning from the Velberter Mission."

Taking that action also meant that I would have to sever my relationship with the Apostolic Faith Mission in South Africa. AFM churches had become my main source of funding. After I wrote and sent the letter to the VM, I called Dr. Möller at the AFM headquarters and told him what I had done and why. He was deeply grieved. He asked me to withdraw my resignation until he could intervene with the German organization, pleading my case before them. I agreed to this.

Möller flew the German General Superintendant of the ACP, Pastor Reinhold Ulonska, to South Africa to discuss my ministry. With Möller's explanation he agreed to release me from the restrictions of missionary work to do the work of an evangelist. In the end this wrenching exercise worked to our benefit. I remained a member of the Velberter Mission and continued my work with their blessing. But I was not happy that it had required my resignation to move this impasse forward. How many missionaries in the missionary bone yard were there because they did not have the stamina to break free and follow the Lord?

None of this was easy for me. I was forced by these circumstances out of my comfort zone. It was God's time for me to enter into one of the most difficult transitions of my life. As I look back I realize that sometimes that is the only way He can get us to move in His direction. It is never easy, but it is always for His glory, and ultimately for our good. Later I heard the chairman of the Velberter Mission, Pastor Alfred Koschorreck say in meetings," we have one Reinhard Bonnke and stand with him, but we don't want a second one". I could hardly believe my ears and said to myself *wie schade!* (what pity). Reflecting today I would say that the Velberter Mission was the baking-oven in which God put me. The heat was atrocious, but the cake came out delicious.

I recall that during this time my son had broken his leg. He had been doing acrobatic stunts on his bicycle and had taken a bad fall. By this time his cast had been removed and his crutches put away, but he was still limping. He came home from school one day and said, "Dad, today we did long-distance running, and I won the race."

I broke into a great grin. "I am so proud of you, Freddie. I guess you are just like me; we are both limping to victory."

Not only was I forced to redefine my role with my church, I also heard the voice of the Lord leading me to leave Lesotho. This was difficult in other ways. Whenever challenges like those that we faced in Lesotho are met and overcome, the heart grows fond of the hard places in life. I should say, *especially* fond of the hard places in life. In this way, Anni and I had grown firmly bonded to Maseru, in the Kingdom of Lesotho. We would have lived happily there for the rest of our lives but God had other plans.

Still, it is never easy to leave the land where your dreams come true. Success blinds us even more than failure. When you have gone to a corpse and breathed new life into it, you have seen more than most people see in a lifetime. Why move on? But I have found that God's thinking is never so limited. Unless we leave the land of our dreams we may never see the land of His destiny.

As I pondered the future, I remembered my boyhood vision from the Lord. The city of Johannesburg glowed like a beacon on the spiritual map. It was calling me now. I saw that I must go there, and I founded my own ministry organization to accommodate the vision for a blood-washed Africa. I called it Christ for all Nations, or CfaN, using the name we had given the little printing press in Maseru.

The Lord led me to locate the headquarters near the international airport, because in evangelism I would be traveling heavily. I spoke to Anni about this. She knew that she would not always be able to travel with me. It was a sacrifice she had to be willing to make if the blood-washed Africa vision was to be realized. Her heart for the lost overruled her homebound instincts. She agreed. For this, I praised God for her. I remembered the process of asking God if she was the right choice for me. He knew. What a blessed choice she has been through these years.

And so, on December 6, 1974, I moved my family to a place called Witfield, near the Johannesburg airport. After we loaded all the boxes into the new house, Anni and the children seemed to be making the transition just fine. They were meeting new people, looking into new schooling, and settling into the new neighborhood, which had much more to offer them by way of nice things.

But I experienced what might be called a depression. I felt totally exhausted and drained and just sat around. This was not like me. I could not get up and get going. I felt like an uprooted plant. I had not found new soil yet. What made it worse is that it seemed God had stopped talking to me. For four weeks I continued in this condition.

Finally, Anni made an appointment for me with a doctor we had met through the AFM. He saw me and diagnosed me with ulcers. This was apparently from the stress of making the break with the Velberter Mission and Lesotho at the same time.

When people decide not to take risks, this is why. They fear they might suffer unexpected consequences. And, as my ulcers and depression proved, the risk is real. But is that reason to hang onto the past? To cling to mediocrity? No. Doing that is the first step along the path of seeing a living faith become a dead one. The old place, the old building, the old method, the old success, is comforting. The new step is frightening. We must place our trust completely in God to move beyond these comfort zones in life.

That night as I lay sleepless in bed, the voice of the Lord spoke to me: *Go to the city of Gaborone in Botswana.* This word came out of the blue. But rather than lay in my depression until I died of bleeding ulcers, the next morning I telephoned a pastor I knew in that city, Pastor Scheffers. I told him I wanted to come see him today. He agreed. Then I asked Anni to take me to the airport. I purchased a ticket on the next flight to Gaborone. Obeying God's voice was life itself to me.

When I got off the plane I realized that I had not even prepared for the trip. I had not brought enough money for food or taxi fare. No problem. God had called me here. This was an adventure of faith. So I walked into the city.

Sometimes an anonymous walk through an unknown land will quiet the mind and instill the heart of the Lord in a man. I walked like Jonah through Nineveh and opened my senses to the city God had called me to. I encountered the sights and sounds of the children playing, chickens seeking insects on a swept dirt floor, laundry being beaten against a rock, tripe stew boiling on a bed of charcoal, a mother steadying a jerry can of water on the head of her barefoot daughter. It was a place of desperate poverty and need. Like Lesotho, I thought only someone called by God should venture here in Gaborone. I walked through the markets and neighborhoods sensing the presence and compassion of the Lord reaching out to this community.

*Turn right,* God said. I turned right, and there before me was the Botswana National Sports Stadium. *You will preach My name there.*

My entire being broke into a full smile. The transition was complete. I was hearing my Father's voice again. And my ulcers were gone.

# Chapter 20

LATER THAT MORNING I arrived at Pastor Scheffers' home in Gaborone. I told him that I wanted to meet the city officials and book the National Sports Stadium for a meeting in four weeks time. He looked at me as if I had lost my mind.

"I am a pastor who has 40 people in church on a good Sunday. How do you expect to fill a stadium that holds 10,000?"

"I don't know about your 40 people. But I know that I just heard the voice of the Holy Spirit, and I want to obey Him."

"But 10,000 seats to fill, Reinhard. You have to build up to that."

"Alright, we'll build up to it. What is the largest hall in town? I want to book it. I will start there and then end up in the stadium."

Bless him. He was humble enough to drive me to the authorities. I created a contract between Gaborone and CfaN, hiring a hall seating 800 for the first week, then the stadium for the final nights of the campaign. However, as I put my signature on the line I began to perspire. Somehow, I already saw that vast stadium with only 40 people inside. I had to find a way to fill it.

As soon as I had finished I called Anni and told her I was extending my stay in Gaborone. I would take some time to organize the local churches. I got a list of all the local pastors, and one by one I visited them all.

"Hello, I'm Reinhard Bonnke. In four weeks time I will have a gospel campaign in your city. I have hired the National Stadium, but we will start off with the smaller sports hall. Please, let's all work together."

In sub-Saharan Africa we have a very large vulture-like bird called the Marabou Stork. It is a scavenger that waits for animals to die in order to eat them. That's why it is called the "undertaker bird." These Gaborone pastors looked at me like a Marabou Stork contemplating road kill.

"That all sounds very good," they said, "but who are you?"

I said, "I am a nobody, but God has spoken to me, and I believe it's going to happen as He said."

They said, "Anyone can say that."

I said, "But He really has spoken to me."

"Sorry, but we've got something else on our calendar for those dates."

Indeed, I felt like road kill. I was tempted to berate myself for poor planning. What an amateur mistake to plan a campaign before securing the cooperation of the local churches. One after another the pastors turned me down until all of them had said no.

It was then that I woke up, spiritually speaking. "Lord, You spoke to me and told me that I would preach Your name in that stadium. This is Your campaign. I will do the preaching, but You must fill the stadium."

Peace came into my heart, and I took the next plane back to Johannesburg. Anni and I prayed and fasted and cranked up the printing press. We had one thing going for us; Pastor Scheffers had promised that his congregation would support the meetings and would plaster campaign posters all over Gaborone.

In the meantime I attended an AFM conference that had long been scheduled in KwaThema near Johannesburg. I wanted two things. First, I wanted to maintain my good relationship with Dr. Möller and our many supporters in that denomination. Second, I desperately wanted to ask the great Zulu evangelist, Richard Ngidi to come join me in the CfaN organization. He was a man who was known for the many healing miracles that accompanied his ministry. I would preach; he would pray for the sick. We would be like salt and pepper, white and black together on the platform. This would be a testimony against apartheid. But I promised myself that I would not ask him to join CfaN. I would not want to seem to be stealing a prize minister from the AFM fold.

When I arrived for the conference Richard saw me and came running up to me. "Pastor Bonnke!" he shouted. "I hear you are starting your own evangelistic organization. You must let me help you. We must minister together."

All the people in the lobby of that convention hall heard him say this. Well, the Lord had solved my problem. I was being pursued by Richard. I was not stealing talent from the AFM. As we spoke further, Richard said that he felt he would serve with me for two years, and then he would return to his regular schedule with the AFM. I was happy. Two years seemed like a long time at the moment, and the Gaborone meeting was sitting on my shoulder like a hungry Marabou Stork. I quickly added Richard Ngidi's name to my publicity material.

WE BEGAN TO EXPLORE the area of Johannesburg where we lived. One day as I drove past a large abandoned farmhouse, I heard the Spirit say, *That is your new headquarters building.* It had been overgrown with grass, and its hedges were untrimmed. I went to the owners and made an offer even though I had no money to back it up at the time. Soon I had received enough money to follow through with the contract, and this became the new CfaN headquarters.

As this was happening I felt another urge to travel south of Johannesburg and take a good look at the black township of Soweto. I did not want to close my eyes to this difficult place. So many whites were able to ignore it by separating their cities into black and white.

Sprawled along the southern outskirts of Johannesburg, Soweto was a ghetto created by the South African gold rush. Rural blacks had been lured here for a century by the promise of good money to be made in the gold fields. As usual, the good money was made by the owners. The mine workers did the dirty and dangerous work and barely made enough to survive. Furthermore, apartheid required that they not live in the white portion of town, so Soweto had grown as the city for colored people south of the city limits. It lay beyond the great slag and tailings piles made by the processed gold ore.

I arranged to be driven through Soweto in a local taxicab, so as not to draw attention to myself. It was a city with no electricity. It had no sewer system, pavement, flood control, zoning, or building codes. It was a shanty town with a million inhabitants and up to 15 people living in a single room. Witchdoctors dominated the spiritual life of the neighborhoods. People who were able to find jobs traveled to the surrounding white territory to work during the day, returning to Soweto at night. Unemployment remained high and crime rampant. At night the police would not venture here. The streets were controlled by rapists, murderers, drug dealers, addicts, and thieves who would kill for the change in your pocket or the jewelry on your hand.

As I drove through the dirt and dust of that place, the Lord spoke to me: *Soweto is like the poor man Lazarus lying at the door of the rich man, Johannesburg.*[54] *You must do something for him.*

After seeing the place, I did not think it wise to gather a crowd there. The atmosphere seemed poisoned with bitterness and unrest. Another strategy occurred to me. One that I had tried successfully in Lesotho. We would raise a force of 100 colporteur evangelists with bicycle containers full of Bibles, gospel literature, and hymnals. We would train these men as witnesses and send them from house to house during daylight hours until all of Soweto had heard the gospel. Again, this plan came to me before the funds came. But I began to present the vision in the white churches where I preached, and soon money began to come in to support it.

One little grandmother handed me enough money to sponsor one bicycle evangelist. "I will be thinking of that young man every day and praying for his safety and his success," she said.

I knew immediately that this was from the Lord. I instructed my co-workers to be sure to match each witness with a prayer team that would hold him up in prayer each day as he went about his route. My growing team attached a giant map of Soweto to the wall. They divided the city into 100 districts and began seeking young men to train and assign to the various sections. The timetable for completing the entire plan was eight months.

At this stage, the Gaborone meetings were scheduled to begin, and I flew with Richard to Botswana. I had decided to conduct the campaign according to the words of Jesus recorded in His Great Commission: *Go ye into all the world, and preach the gospel to every creature. He that believeth and is baptized shall be saved; but he that believeth not shall be damned. And these signs shall follow them that believe; In my name shall they cast out devils; they shall speak with new tongues; they shall take up serpents; and if they drink any deadly thing, it shall not hurt them; they shall lay hands on the sick, and they shall recover.*[55] In my mind, I saw myself preaching the gospel sermons and Richard Ngidi conducting the healing ministry. Again, I thought we would be like ebony and ivory. Our presence together would send a message to the entire region that we were brothers in Christ, of equal value before God, and together, we would cover at least two points in Christ's Great Commission – salvation and the signs that follow, specifically healing.

As we entered the meeting hall I could feel the emptiness; I could hear it, I could smell it. I looked about and immediately realized all of our advance publicity had failed. When I counted heads there were exactly 100 present, myself included. The room was designed for 800. I counted from right to left and left to right. Recounting did not make it better. 100 is 100 from every angle. I was quite disappointed.

I sensed that Richard was also uncomfortable. Not even his name had helped build the crowd in Gaborone. Perhaps that was because he was a Zulu, and we were now in the land of the Bushmen of the Kalahari. Pastor Scheffers then leaned over to me and told me proudly that all 40 members of his flock were in attendance. That deflated me even more. It meant that we had drawn no more than 60 souls beyond the members of his congregation. Pastor Scheffers had every right to say, "I told you so." I remembered the day a few weeks ago when I had arrived at his house with the wild idea of filling the National Sports Stadium. Now, this!

After preliminaries, I stood and opened my Bible to preach the ABCs of the gospel. I had preached perhaps 10 to 20 minutes when a woman on the left side of the group of 100 stood up and shouted, "I've just been healed."

I stopped speaking to hear her. Soon another and another stood and did the same. Four or five people in all stood and made this claim of being spontaneously healed. I thought, *This is strange, I am preaching the gospel of salvation, yet people are being healed. We have not even laid hands on them according to Scripture.*

At the conclusion of my sermon I called for anyone else who was sick to come forward. I told them that I would lay hands on them and pray. Something very strange began to happen. Each person I laid my hands on collapsed to the floor, and there they lay, row after row of unconscious people. I looked at Richard since I was not familiar with this manifestation.

A man came running from the back of the room to me. "I demand an explanation!" he said. "What have you done to make these people faint and fall to the floor?"

"I can't explain it. I need an explanation myself. Are you a doctor? Do you know what has happened to them?"

"No, I don't know."

"All I can tell you is I didn't ask these people to do this. What I have done is to lay hands on them according to the words of Jesus in Mark 16:18. So I suppose what has happened to them, Jesus is responsible for."

At that moment one woman got up from the floor. "I can see! I can see! I can see!" She had fallen down blind, but she got up seeing. This woman was well known to all the people. Another prostrate man who I had prayed for went down with a pair of crutches. He got up walking and running without any need for them.

Immediately, the man who had been demanding an explanation no longer seemed angry. He was amazed and began to praise God. All 100 people began shouting and dancing and screaming. They filled that nearly empty hall with a tremendous volume of sound that was heard in the surrounding neighborhoods. Some people came running to see what had happened. It was a repeat of the service in Maseru.

Within two nights that hall was packed to capacity. God performed His own publicity. People sat on other people's laps. Others sat in windowsills. There were 2,000 people crowding outside, wanting to get in. We placed a loudspeaker outside for them. For the first time in my life I saw crowds of people running to the front to receive Jesus at my invitation. They were crying tears of repentance as they came. I thought heaven had come down to earth. "Africa shall be saved," I repeated under my breath again and again.

Each night I asked Richard to pray for the sick after I had given the invitation for salvation. His great healing gift was evident, as well as his deep compassion for those he ministered to. Many other healings manifested as "signs following" the believing of the gospel of Jesus Christ.

Finally, we moved into the great stadium, normally filled for national soccer matches. By the second night we had filled it to capacity for the hearing of the gospel. I will never forget seeing in the crowd the faces of many of those pastors who had denied cooperation with these meetings. How things had changed. The Marabou Stork look was gone. And I had never felt less like road kill.

One night near the end of the campaign, nearly half of the population of Gaborone had packed into the stadium. The entire soccer field, as well as the stands were both filled. The Lord spoke to me, *I want you to pray for the people to receive the baptism of the Holy Spirit.*

This startled me. I had never heard of such a thing. This was a stadium meeting. Back home in Germany we had not sought for the baptism in our regular meetings where unbelievers might be present. We did it in private meetings restricted to believers only. I said, *Lord this is a stadium. Many people looking on might be confused by this display. They will misunderstand.* Still, I felt the urging of the Lord to do this thing.

I recalled how my mother had prayed and tarried for so many years for the experience. My own experience had been spontaneous, but it had nothing to do with a group experience. How was it that God would fill an entire group at once in a public meeting? But on the Day of Pentecost it had happened to the 120 assembled in the upper room. Those outside the meeting hall certainly heard them speaking in tongues. Many had mocked and misunderstood but that had not mattered. Empowered by the Holy Spirit, Peter preached a sermon he had not prepared for, and 361,000 souls were added to the Jerusalem church. Maybe now I would see something similar. I invited those who wanted to receive the baptism to come forward. Nearly 1,000 gathered at the front.

Since he had a better grip of the language, I asked Richard Ngidi to explain how to receive the gift. As he explained it, he left out a fundamental part – speaking in tongues. I stood to correct him, but the Holy Spirit checked me. I felt that I should say nothing. So, with no further explanation, I told the people that in response to God's voice, I would now pray for them to receive God's gift.

As I finished the prayer I instructed them to lift their hands to heaven and close their eyes. I did not close my eyes. I wanted to see what God would do. When they lifted their hands I saw a transparent wave coming from the right to the left, sweeping over that stadium. As it hit those people it was as if a mighty rushing wind blew them to the ground en masse. All of them were speaking in tongues and prophesying as the Spirit gave utterance. I had not said one word about speaking in tongues. This confirmed to me that I had indeed heard the voice of the Spirit in my heart. I had heard Him true. It also demonstrated the reality of speaking in tongues without any hint of suggestion or manipulation.

I am not a weepy man, but tears began to flow down my face. I was greatly moved and changed inside to witness this divine moment. The scripture came to mind, *And it shall come to pass in the last days, saith God, I will pour out of my Spirit upon all flesh.*[56] I became convinced that the vision of a blood-washed Africa will only be realized by a mighty outpouring of God's Holy Spirit. A deluge that will sweep great throngs of people into His kingdom, leaving hell empty and heaven full.

As the meetings closed we held a public baptismal service. 500 converts followed the Lord in water baptism that day. This was the end of the first CfaN campaign.

I CALLED MY CO-WORKERS together back in Johannesburg. *What we have seen is God's pattern to fulfill His vision for a blood-washed Africa. We will take this gospel from Cape Town to Cairo.*

*Cape Town to Cairo* became our motto.

We rented an old circus tent that we were told would shelter a crowd of 800 people. I thought this was a good size since our first facility in Gaborone had housed as many. If the crowds outgrew the tent, we would do as we had done then, and try to find larger accommodations. But we had to start somewhere. I began to tell anyone who would listen that we really needed a tent that would seat 5,000 people. No one seemed to take up this idea and offer support. With that, I dispatched team members immediately to arrange a campaign in Cape Town.

News of the Gaborone meeting began to create a stir in the white churches where I spoke. During a speaking engagement in a local white church a wealthy man approached me after I told of our colporteur plan for Soweto. "How many bicycles have not yet been sponsored?" he asked.

"85," I replied.

"I will sponsor those 85."

My heart leapt with joy. I hugged him and went straight to the bicycle manufacturer and signed a contract for the full order. Well, the money did not come. I reminded God that He was my source of supply, not any man, and especially not this rich man. As events unfolded, I would simply trust God to lead me to the right source of funding for this project.

As I departed for the Cape Town meetings my mind was full of these thoughts. Suddenly I heard the Spirit say, *Next year you will preach in America.* This seemed to come out of nowhere. My mind was on South Africa, not America. I knew not one person there. Besides, I was merely 35 years old; CfaN was an infant, not even one year old. My reputation would certainly not carry me very far in America.

During the Gugulethu meeting I asked Richard Ngidi to pray for the sick. There were many notable miracles, including a crippled man in a wheelchair who got up and walked. A local TV news camera happened to be on hand, and the miracle made headlines. The crowds grew and we saw wonderful results.

Back in Johannesburg, I attended the annual AFM conference at Maranatha Park. While there, a man approached and introduced himself. His name was Paul Schoch. By his very name I could tell that we shared a German heritage. He said he was the pastor of an Assemblies of God church in Oakland, California. He had heard of my Gaborone meeting. "When are you coming to America?" he asked.

"Next year," I replied, smiling to myself. I recalled the words of the Holy Spirit as I had flown to Cape Town, *Next year you will preach in America.*

Paul was delighted with my answer. He made arrangements for me to preach at his church when I came. He also booked me on a preaching circuit to other churches. We became lifelong friends, and over the years he introduced me to many other churches in America, for which I am eternally grateful.

After the AFM convention, I made a special trip to Germany. I visited with Father and Mother. Father had retired from preaching. I spoke in Karlsruhe, Hamburg, Krempe, and other places friendly to our cause. On that trip the German believers became the primary sponsors of the remaining bicycles needed for our Soweto campaign. That made me so happy. I was received as a son in churches of Erwin Müller, Paula Gassner and many ACD churches.

As our first year with CfaN came to a close, we had already made plans for the following year. Port Elizabeth, Windhoek, Namibia, and two Swaziland campaigns at Manzini and Mbabane. I was soon to be hit by another challenge from the Holy Spirit that would take us to another level.

# Chapter 21

THE CAMPAIGNS OF '76 proved that the available rental tents in South Africa were too small. We tried several different sizes seating crowds from 800 to 3,000. Still, our crowds were greater outside the tents than inside. I continued to seek support for purchasing a super tent that would seat 5,000 but nothing seemed to come of it. It was one of those visions that wouldn't fly. It seemed rooted in cement like my early attempts to raise support for the Berlin ministry to refugees.

But the need was growing with our growing crowds. Richard Ngidi suggested that my name had become an unexpected draw for the meetings. Especially those we held in the rural Zulu regions. In the Zulu tongue, "Bonnke" had the meaning of "everyone together." What a delightful coincidence! I believe my heavenly Father is ultimately in charge of all such good gifts. Thank You, Lord.

In Port Elizabeth we hired the 4,000-seat Centenary Hall, a local boxing arena. I will never forget the night my sermon was interrupted by people streaming forward to confess their sins and to make restitution. I had not asked them to do any such thing. But out of the crowd things began to fly onto the platform. Witchcraft fetishes, cigarettes, booze, stolen articles, and even switchblade knives, nunchakus, and other gang-related weapons. One young man whose face was a network of knife scars came forward and offered a wicked-looking homemade blade. "I have decided to give my life to Jesus," he said with tears in his eyes.

I looked at the fierce countenance of this Xhosa criminal and marveled, *The Holy Spirit has just done what no policeman could ever do.*

In the next campaign in Namibia, Richard Ngidi had to leave early. I felt that Michael Kolisang had matured to the place where he could take over the prayers for the sick. As I watched him minister my heart was stirred by the memory of our first meeting with him. He had responded to my very first street sermon at a bus stop in Maseru. "I want this Jesus you have just preached," he had said.

Today, he was ministering to the sick, laying his hands on them according to Scripture, and many were receiving healing. He was a spiritual son to me, and I would rather see him used of God and receiving recognition than me. This kind of reward is greater than all others to me.

A man sought me out in the meeting. He asked me to pray for his ears. He had cancer in one ear and no eardrum in the other. I prayed, commanding the cancer to be gone and the ear to hear. Suddenly he began to jump up and down. He said he could hear in the ear with no eardrum. We tested it and it was true. All I could think was that the Creator must have had spare parts He could use in this case, because there was nothing there to heal.

Our reputation for miracles began to grow throughout South Africa. I was not comfortable with that. Michael and I wrote a pamphlet addressing the issue, and I recorded it as a tape for distribution. "I am not a healing evangelist," I insisted. "I am a salvation evangelist, who also prays for the sick. God told me Africa shall be saved, not Africa shall be healed. Sickness is not the ultimate evil; therefore healing is not the ultimate good. Sin is the ultimate evil, and salvation is the ultimate good. I have seen evangelists who come and set up a tent and do not open their Bibles. They begin to perform healings. That is not evangelism; that is a signs-and-sensations show. I do not want to be on such a platform. We conduct evangelistic campaigns, not healing campaigns. The healings are signs that follow the preaching of the gospel. They open the door for salvation on a large scale." Then I related several notable miracles we had seen.

I thought of Luis Graf in this regard. In 1922, in the power of the Holy Spirit he had prayed for Grandpa August's healing in order to preach the gospel in Trunz. That torch had been passed to me, as well as the pattern for ministry.

Not long after releasing the teaching tape and pamphlet I was asked to come to the Johannesburg hospital to pray for a man dying of leukemia. I heard the words of Psalm 118:17 in my head. *I shall not die, but live, and declare the works of the Lord.* This seemed like a very strong confirmation that I was to go pray for the man. I asked Anni to go with me. When we got to the hospital the parking lot was absolutely full. I could not find one parking spot. I told Anni, "Let me out and circle the hospital. I won't be long."

She did. I went into the cancer ward and found a man named Mr. Kruger lying with all kinds of needles and mechanical things attached to his body. He seemed to struggle for breath. As soon as he saw me he asked, "Do you have a word from God for me?"

"Yes, I do." I read the scripture to him that God had given me: *I shall not die, but live, and declare the works of the Lord.* He seemed to relax. I prayed for him and then apologized that I had to leave in a hurry, explaining that my wife, Anni, was circling the hospital until I came out. I said goodbye and left.

A few months later at an AFM conference a gentleman passed a note asking me to come to Pretoria to pray for a woman with terminal cancer. She had been sent home to die. At first I was not inclined to do so. Then I heard the voice of the Spirit whisper in my heart, saying, "I am sending you." Upon hearing that, I made no argument. I immediately agreed that I would come. The man gave me directions, and I made an appointment for the next day.

Michael Kolisang was in the offices the next morning and I took him with me, hoping we could pray together in agreement. I wanted him to be used in the healing ministry.

When we met the gentleman at a junction on the Johannesburg-Pretoria Highway, he became distressed. "My friend is from the Dutch Reformed Church," he said. "I have no problem with black people, but they might not want to have Michael come into their home."

*Dear Lord! How long must we put up with this nonsense?* I asked in my heart. "OK," I said. "Michael understands South Africa. He can stay in the car."

Michael drove, and I tried to prepare myself in prayer for this assignment. As we went along the Lord dropped an Old Testament scripture into my mind. It was not a passage I would have chosen. It made absolutely no sense in this situation. *Although the fig tree shall not blossom, neither shall fruit be in the vines; the labour of the olive shall fail, and the fields shall yield no meat; the flock shall be cut off from the fold, and there shall be no herd in the stalls: Yet I will rejoice in the Lord, I will joy in the God of my salvation.*[60]

*Lord,* I prayed, *I can't give a dying woman this verse of Scripture. Everything described here is going wrong. It sounds as if she is going to die.*

But as we traveled along, I reread the scripture and felt the confirmation of the Spirit again. *OK, Lord. I will be obedient even though I can't understand it.*

We entered one of the suburbs in Pretoria. Here lived the white ruling class of South Africa in isolated splendor. Wide streets, nice homes, fine gardens. We parked outside a house. Michael remained in the car, and the gentleman escorted me inside. He took me into the woman's bedroom. I saw a mask of death on her countenance. As I walked in, however, she lit up like a Christmas tree. He introduced me to her. Her name was Dinnie Viljoen.

"I've just been listening to your cassette about healing," she said. "I have so wanted to meet you and Michael Kolisang."

Now it was my turn to light up like a Christmas tree. "I have good news for you, Mrs. Viljoen. He is waiting in the car. I will go get him right now."

And so I did. I was so happy to bring Michael into this house, not as a serving boy, but as an honored guest. Even though they were Dutch Reformed, we sensed no racial prejudice in the home. What a blessing.

As I began to minister, I told her the Holy Spirit had impressed a scripture upon me that I would now read to her. I read her the passage from Habakkuk. As I did, the words touched some deep place in her soul and she began to weep. I didn't understand her reaction.

"Pastor Bonnke," she said, "read the next verse."

I looked down at my Bible. The next verse was the very last verse in the book of Habakkuk. *The Lord God is my strength, and he will make my feet like hinds' feet, and he will make me to walk upon mine high places.*[57]

"Yes," she said, "I believe the Lord has spoken to you about me. I have been reading, *Hind's Feet on High Places.* It is a book based on that very scripture in Habakkuk."

She handed the book to me. In the style of *Pilgrim's Progress*, it is the story of a young woman named Much-Afraid. She leaves her Fearing family and learns to enjoy the High Places of the Shepherd, guided by two companions, Sorrow and Suffering. I could see that nearly every line in the book had been underlined. It had obviously meant very much to Dinnie Viljoen.

"Well," I said, "I am convinced that God wants to do a miracle today. Let's pray."

Michael and I came near and laid our hands on her. As we prayed a prayer of agreement for her healing she said, "I see a vision. I see myself standing under a great waterfall."

I sensed that God had healed her, and as we said goodbye, she did look stronger to me. Less than a week later she entered the Cancer Research Institute for a complete battery of tests. All the tests were negative for cancer. The doctors were unable to explain it. Dinnie explained it to them, but such explanations have no place in medical textbooks.

Through this woman I became more known in the Dutch Reformed Church throughout South Africa. Dinnie traveled in many high places and told her story. The ranks of my supporters swelled with many of their number. I could not have made such a thing happen. It was a divine appointment.

One day Dinnie walked into my Witfield offices. She asked to see me.

"Reinhard," she said, "the Lord has spoken to me about your future. He showed me how much money He's going to give you. It is a number I have seen in a vision. Let me write it down for you."

I got her a pad and a pencil. She wrote down a number: $650,000,000.

"This amount is in dollars," she said, "not rand. That may mean that this money will come from America."

Of course, the value of the dollar was higher than the rand, so this pleased me very much. But I still had very little connection to America, and this staggering amount of money seemed beyond comprehension. We still struggled to make payroll and pay rent. It seemed to me this word was meant to open my mind further to the realm of God's provision.

"Dinnie, I accept this amount in the name of Jesus," I said. "I accept it and thank you for being obedient to the voice of the Lord."

Soon after, Anni and I were invited to the home of an heiress. When we arrived we knew that we had crossed the threshold to a level of society that we could hardly comprehend. We discovered that this woman had inherited the untold wealth of one of South Africa's legendary diamond mines, and she had many other holdings in natural resources that could produce more wealth. As we spoke together she asked what kind of support I needed to continue the work I was doing. I managed to give her some ballpark numbers. She said that she would like to underwrite my entire ministry financially. Anni and I were stunned. This was beyond our ability to ask or think. Her plan was to form a trust fund of all her wealth and dedicate half of it to CfaN. She indicated that I would never have to rely on other donations. She seemed to be a very sweet and sincere woman. I told her that I would seek the Lord to know what to do.

Some time later I had a frightening dream. In the dream I came to a strange river. It looked shallow but I could not see a bridge or a regular place of crossing. A small man appeared. He offered to guide me across. Assuming that he was a local native who knew the way, I followed him. When we got to the middle of the river suddenly a hippopotamus arose from the water directly in front of us, his huge jaws open, baring his tusks. I knew that in Africa the hippo kills far more people than lions, elephants, Cape buffalo, or any other animal. I knew I was in great danger. As I turned to escape, another hippo arose out of the mud behind me to block my escape. Then others popped up on all sides. I awoke in a sweat.

"Lord, what does this mean?" I asked. I sensed that the dream had come for a definite reason.

Later that morning the heiress called. She wanted to take Anni and me on a tour of one of her vast properties. We joined her and enjoyed seeing some of South Africa's most beautiful landscape. As we neared her property line, however the land rover stopped. We had come to a natural barrier. A river. Suddenly it dawned on me that I was looking at the river of my nightmare right in front of us. I needed no further discussion or deliberation. When we returned to her mansion, I turned her offer down as graciously as I knew how. The Lord had spoken in a dream.

My relationship with the Lord has much to do with trusting Him as my financial source. I also had the sense that as sweet as her offer seemed to be, it had a bitter core. This great wealth had unseen dangers in the depths of it. Unseen strings were attached to the use of this money. The priorities and purposes of the ministry could have become compromised simply by reaching for financial security from a source other than the Lord. I could not allow such a thing to happen to CfaN.

IN EARLY JUNE OF 1976 the last bicycle evangelist completed his route canvassing the township of Soweto. For eight months, 100 men had worked long hours in difficult circumstances to accomplish this mission. Every home had been visited with a gospel presentation. As a result many people accepted Jesus as Savior, others were healed, and Christian literature made available to all.

No sooner had our workers completed their routes, than on June 16, 1976 a peaceful demonstration of students erupted into the worst racial violence in

South Africa's history. Hundreds of young black students in Soweto were shot down. The headlines of newspapers worldwide screamed the death toll, and the pictures of the dead and wounded had more impact than words. The tide of world opinion began to build against apartheid.

Now I understood the urgency that I had felt in my spirit a year ago. I thanked God every day that He had given me the idea to canvas the city. That He had given me the number of bicycles needed – 100. Without all of them working in precise order we would not have finished the job before the violence broke out, and the long night descended in which no man could work. After the riots Soweto was not a place to venture for many months to come. In the back of my mind, however, I knew we were going back. And when God opened the door, CfaN would not have a bad name in the township. Quite the opposite. What we had done there before the riots would be remembered, and we would see a great harvest. I knew it in my spirit.

AT OUR FINAL CAMPAIGN in Swaziland that year, something happened that made me wish to return to the diamond heiress and reconsider her offer. We set up a rented small tent in Mbabane, and as usual, found it much too small. We pitched it in a kind of land depression that gave the crowd amphitheatre seating on three sides outside of the tent. The crowds spilled out on all sides, and we were forced to mount extra loudspeakers to reach them all with the message. It was the best we could do.

By this time I had gained enough experience to know that I must never be without a flashlight. Each of my co-workers was instructed to do the same. We powered our speakers and lights with a Briggs and Stratton gasoline generator. During the meetings the generator would develop problems and quit on the average of twice during each of my sermons. The lights and sound would suddenly vanish, and I would rush from the platform in the dark, using my flashlight to troubleshoot the generator and get it started again. In Africa, this was taken as a matter of course.

Suddenly, during the meeting it began to rain. Then the generator went out. I rushed from the platform too quickly and slipped head over heels into the mud. I got up, prepared to preach the rest of the sermon with my backside plastered in thick goo. But I never got the chance. The heavens opened and the rain came down in such torrents that the three-sided amphitheatre became a funnel of rushing floodwaters. They poured right through the tent. In the regenerated lights I saw that everyone was running for high ground. Everyone, that is, but the cripples and sick who had come for prayer. They were being swept away in the mucky water. Some were crawling for safety. Others were being helped to higher ground. The sight of it struck me like a hammer blow.

"Lord, where is the 5,000-seat tent?" I cried in anguish. "When are we going to have a roof over our heads in these campaigns?!"

In the pouring rain I heard the voice of the Spirit speak so clearly, *Trust Me for a tent to seat 10,000 people.*

Amazing. The Holy Spirit's idea was twice the size of my own. Not 5,000 but 10,000. "But Lord, my pockets are empty," I cried out in the rain.

The answer came without hesitation. *Do not plan with what is in your pockets. Plan with what is in mine.*

If this was the true heritage of my calling, I was to not worry about the supply. Dinnie had seen $650,000,000 given to this work. I became angry at myself for my persistent small thinking. These people had come to the meeting with high expectations only to be swept away on a senseless flood. "Lord," I said, "from now on I'm going to plan like a millionaire!"

I ended our second season back at headquarters searching for anyone in South Africa who had a tent that would seat 10,000. No one did. Not only that, such a tent could not be manufactured in all of South Africa. I had no idea how improbable a 10,000-seat tent would be. Finally, I located a company in Milan, Italy, that could manufacture one that large. This was the only way to go. I flew there and sketched the huge tent with their designers. They put their pencils to the finished design and told me it would cost 100,000 rand to construct. For me, this was a staggering sum. I told You I was going to plan like a millionaire, I reminded the Lord. *You said for me to plan with what was in Your pockets, not mine. You own the cattle on a thousand hills.*[58] *The silver and gold are Yours.*[59] *We need 100,000 rand, Lord.*

I soon learned that we would need much more than that. The manufacturer explained to me that to travel with such a tent required a large professional crew. We would need a project engineer plus capable young men to handle the large apparatus.

"Perhaps we can purchase an African elephant," I joked. "I saw a circus tent go up in Glückstadt with the help of an elephant when I was a boy."

"No elephant can handle this job," I was told. "You will need to haul special equipment to the location in a truck in order to erect the main masts of this structure."

In fact, we would need to buy a fleet of trucks. The masts and cables that held up the canvas would weigh seven tons. The canvas weighed even more. Larger generators would be needed to power larger light systems and sound systems. Trailer houses would have to travel to each site to house the crew. Other trailers would be needed as kitchens and others for food, refrigeration, and pure water storage. The big tent would change everything, and our operational costs would skyrocket. In faith, I told the Milan firm to begin the fabrication and construction immediately. We would pay as they went, and we would plan for delivery in nine months to a year.

As I waited to board my plane to return home a scene flashed across my memory and I had to chuckle. I saw myself standing at the bus stop with Teun de Ruiter in Swansea, Wales. We had just finished a student ministry project and had no bus fare to return. The pastor had come along and bought us tea and crumpets, flashing his fat purse full of money. I thought surely God would use him to supply our need. But no. He had not used him. Then we were met by that unexpected lady who had seen us minister on the beach that day. In gratitude she had rushed up and pressed money into my hand as we waited for the bus with no fare in our pockets. It was exactly what we needed to return to campus. "We've been delivered, Teun!" I had shouted. What a lesson! What a lesson!

*We've come a long way from that bus stop, Lord,* I said, as I boarded the plane and settled back in my seat. *I am not planning with what is in my pockets but with what is in Yours. And I have no idea how or who You will use to fill this need. If the past is any indication, it will be through thousands of unknown people like that little lady in Swansea, not necessarily those major players with the full wallets.*

It would be a year before the tent and the new equipment would be ready for use. In that year of 1977 I had scheduled seven campaigns in the rural and tribal areas of South Africa. When possible we would hire stadiums or larger halls to house the crowds. Between campaigns I would travel to white churches in South Africa, Germany, and the United States presenting my vision for using the 10,000-seat tent. The Lord would move on those He chose to support it.

Our first campaign was to be held in Bushbuckridge, South Africa, on the border of the great Kruger National Park. I was so excited. At last I was living my boyhood vision of ministering in Africa. This was the primitive tribal region. Bushbuckridge was in the Northern Transvaal region. The people would come from their mud-and-thatch huts, most of them walking for many miles, to attend our crusade. I could hardly wait to present the gospel of Jesus Christ to them. And Richard had agreed to pray for the sick. We had sent out his picture with mine on all the advance posters.

I went personally to pick Richard up in my car. He would meet me at the train station in Springs. When the scheduled train arrived I was waiting. All of the passengers walked past me on the landing, but no Richard. I had the same feeling that had come over me when John Bosman told me to close the Maseru meeting. And when, the next day, he had packed his bags and left. I felt deserted.

But then, I thought Richard must have surely missed his train. So I waited for the next train. And the next. When he did not step off the final train the Lord spoke to me, *Ngidi will not come. You must go on without him.*

I recalled that Richard had first committed to two years of ministry. Only the period of one year had just passed. But he had not resigned. He had not mentioned that this was the end. Rather, he had specifically promised to meet me at this train station. However, he had broken his promise. "Lord," I asked, "how will the crusade be without him?"

*I am with you.*

These words burned into my heart and mind, and I left at once for the meetings. In one sense, I traveled with a lonely sensation, a feeling of pain in my heart. I had so wanted to share the podium with Richard. Richard never came back. Now I was alone, but hardly alone. As a human being I wished it could be otherwise, but if God had said He was with me, what else really mattered?

The first meeting was well attended; the event Israel Malele, a young student from the University of the North had organized. Many had come expecting Richard to be there. I announced, as I had done in Maseru, that Pastor Ngidi had failed to turn up but that Jesus did turn up. Some left. After preaching the gospel I felt urged of the Lord to pray for the sick in a particular manner. I first called all of the totally blind people to come forward. When they had assembled I told them to keep their eyes closed until they heard my command. Then I laid my hands on each of them, praying for their dead eyes to be opened. Finally, I stood on the platform and commanded, "Blind eyes, open!"

A young man in his twenties began to scream, "I can see! I can see! I can see!"

No one had to tell me what would happen next. Such news travels far and wide. Crowds overflowed the small borrowed tent. In fact, we might have overflowed the 10,000-seat tent if we had been ready with it. It was a super crusade, and I knew the Holy Spirit had indeed spoken truly to my heart. Jesus was with me.

The next crusade at Giyani astonished me beyond words. It began in the 400-seat auditorium of a Christian school. The local postmaster came forward in the first meeting to receive Jesus. He testified that he had had a dream in which two men in white robes appeared to him. One of them said, "Go to the school. There you will learn the way of life." He came to the meeting, not drawn by publicity posters but by an angelic visitation, and he was gloriously born again.

He had been a notorious man who abused his wife. This encounter with Jesus totally changed his life and ignited the imaginations of the people.

Healings! "These signs shall follow ..."

Miracles of healing also happened. Within three nights the seating capacity of the auditorium was overwhelmed. The school principal suggested we move to a fairground some five miles away. It was a difficult decision but necessary. Nearly all of our people were walking to the school site. It meant that they would have to walk five miles farther to reach our new place of meeting. But they did.

As I prayed for the sick many people who had arrived walking on crutches left their crutches behind like litter on the ground. They walked home without them. There were so many crutches that I instructed our team to pick them up and assemble them in a pile. As the pile grew to the final night, we posed for a picture beside it. I sent it to all the people who were supporting our campaigns.

As we left the area I paid a visit to the school principal who had given us our starting place. I thanked him. The man paid me what may be the greatest compliment I have ever received: "Pastor Bonnke," he said. "How do you do what you do? I have been traveling this area for many years. I know these people, but everything has changed since this campaign. The whole area is different. My church has had a school, a hospital, and a mission in the district for 20 years, and you have accomplished in seven days what we have been unable to do in all that time. We have had other evangelists. When they leave, the people are talking about what wonderful preachers they are. But I am not hearing from the people about Reinhard Bonnke. I am hearing about Jesus."

I tell you, that blessed me beyond description. His words warm my heart to this day as I recall that moment. I thanked him and shook his hand warmly. We have met as friends many times since then.

I brought the crutches back to our headquarters. There was a tree on the property, and I thought we could decorate it like a Christmas tree, using the crutches as ornaments. Some people were offended by it, but we had a lot of fun. As we stood back to admire our work, Michael Kolisang stood beside me. He turned and said, "Richard Ngidi was wrong."

"Wrong to leave? Yes, I think he was."

"No. I mean, he was wrong about you."

"About me?"

"He said, 'When I leave, Bonnke is finished.'"

I could not believe my ears. "He said what? What do you suppose he meant by that?"

"I think he meant that you could not go on without him."

This felt like a hard punch to the stomach. It also told me what he thought of the work of God. He must not have been impressed with what he had seen in one year. Even if I had been unimpressive, the blessings of God we had seen had spoken for themselves. How could he say such a thing? I could tell that it disturbed Michael as well, and he was trying to move past it in his heart. I wanted to help him.

"The success of the work of God does not depend on any of us, Michael. It is all accomplished through dependence on Him. I cannot imagine a circumstance in which Richard might say such a thing about a brother. I just cannot go there. I am a zero that God is able to use only because I value His voice above other voices. It has nothing to do with special abilities that I have. I feel very bad for our Brother Ngidi."

And perhaps I took his words too personally. I promptly became vulnerable in my body and went to bed with a case of the flu.

ON THE HEELS of our glorious meeting in Giyani, the devil began to oppose our next meeting in Sibasa. It was a city further north in Vendaland, near the borders of Zimbabwe and Mozambique. Our reputation had gone before us, and we knew there would be far greater crowds than a rented tent could hold. The city had a large soccer stadium, but my team members could not obtain permission to use it. Every request met with a resounding "no." My people had given up in frustration.

While suffering with the flu I awoke in the night. In the dark I saw the name Sibasa as if illuminated in floodlights. I knew that this was confirmation that we were to go there regardless of closed doors. As soon as I had recovered I went to Sibasa by car to personally see the person who had blocked our request. I was surprised to find out that he was a Christian man. Something changed in his attitude toward our request when I delivered it in person. He gave us a permit to hold meetings in the soccer stadium for ten days in August.

This part of the country is usually cool and dry that time of year. I thought the timing was perfect. I drove my Volkswagen van and parked it beside the stadium. The local government gave me a little hut for accommodation during the whole period. I entered the stadium and saw that its great amphitheatre seating was at least three times larger than the National Sports Stadium in Gaborone. *Dear Lord,* I prayed, *You must do it again. You must fill this stadium with people eager to hear Your gospel.*

As the time for the first meeting approached it was as if the devil unleashed his hordes. The sky grew dark beneath an army of marching clouds. It was not a passing rain storm. It was a deluge, and it had come to stay. The roads turned to mud. The soccer field turned into a bog. People were seeking shelter.

One of the audience stands was covered with a leaky roof. We huddled under it at one end of the stadium with a crowd of only 200 on opening night. My generator powered merely three floodlights along with the speaker system. Not only did it rain but a cold wind blew. My teeth were chattering as I preached. As usual we had to deal with the generator failures during the meeting.

At the invitation, a man named Elijah Mulawudzi came forward. He was in obvious pain. He said that he suffered from a chronic stomach disorder. When I prayed for him he was instantly relieved. He received Jesus as his Savior and left that night a new creature in Christ. He seemed totally oblivious to the weather and promised that he would return the next night, bringing his friends and neighbors.

The next day the cold, rain, and wind continued without letup. Much to my surprise, however, the crowd doubled to 400 that night. Elijah was back, and true to his word, he had brought a score of others. He was absolutely ecstatic. His stomach pains were gone, and his new life in Christ was better than anything he had ever known. More people were saved and healed that night. By the third day the rain stopped, and on the seventh night we looked out on the reason the devil had so opposed us here in Sibasa – the crowd had swelled to 30,000 souls! I was staggered. This was the largest crowd I had ever seen so far.

The next day as I was praying in my shack I felt a strong impression that I should buy a gift for the "President" of Vendaland, Mphephu, the man who ruled the region during apartheid South Africa. He had surely heard of the sensation our meetings had created. It would be a fine gesture to ask to meet him and present him with a token of our appreciation for the use of the stadium. If nothing else, this would be good public relations for CfaN. I knew that Sibasa did not have much to offer in the way of fine gifts, so I drove to Pietersburg, a town 50 miles to the south, and purchased a beautiful vase and had it gift wrapped. Then I returned.

No sooner had I returned than Michael Kolisang rushed up to me. "We are invited to visit the president at his house. We must be there by 4 p.m."

When I told Michael how the Spirit had urged me to buy a suitable gift for the president, and that I had it under my arm, he was delighted. We put on our best suits and away we went. I had someone carry my accordion, in case we should be asked to hold an impromptu service. It was the very instrument that had first drawn Michael to my gospel sermon on the streets of Maseru.

At the president's mansion we were ushered into a large sitting room. The president and all his cabinet members and all of their wives were assembled, waiting for us. The president stood and made a welcome speech.

"Pastor Bonnke, I am sorry to hear of the difficulties you have had in holding this meeting in Sibasa. I have heard that God has blessed my nation through you, and I have called you because I would like to hear what God has to say to us."

I could not imagine a more open door for an evangelist. What would I preach? The ABCs of the gospel, of course! And I did. It was one of those sermons that would never have passed muster in Ian Jones' homiletics class back in Wales, but I felt the power of the Spirit in the room. But as I drew to the end of the sermon I began to wonder, should I give an altar call? How will that be received in the president's house? What is the proper protocol?

The voice of the Spirit spoke immediately in my heart, *Altar call – not protocol!*

I proceeded to make an appeal for these leaders to receive Jesus. To my surprise, the first hand raised was the hand of President Mphephu himself. His cabinet members soon followed, whether from protocol or altar call, I could not be sure. It was not my place to ask questions. It was my place to lead that group in reciting the sinner's prayer. It is a wonder to lead the entire executive branch of a government to faith in Jesus Christ. I was as happy as a ten-year-old boy in a chocolate factory. I will never forget it.

The final night of that crusade, my new brother in Christ, President Mphephu, sat beside me on the platform. Every member of his cabinet joined him. As I took the podium to preach my final sermon, tears filled my eyes. I could not help it, and for a time I could not speak. I looked from one end of that vast stadium to the other. 40,000 had gathered to hear the ABCs of the gospel in Sibasa! For a moment I was back in Glückstadt, hearing the voice of Grandma Bauszuss ... "I saw a crowd of black people," she said. "A very large crowd. They were gathered in a semicircle around a little boy with a big loaf of bread ..." Then she had turned to me and pointed. "The little boy that I saw was this one."

Oh, how I wished she could have stood here beside me on this night. Her vision was now a total physical reality.

Campaigns followed that year in Phalaborwa, Tzaneen, Messina, and Louis Trichard. I had never imagined that a man could live such a fulfilling year of life as a minister of the gospel. I knew big things were ahead with the 10,000-seat tent, but without it, we were seeing a blood-washed Africa everywhere we went. As reports of our meeting went out to our partners, income for the new projects poured in. God's pockets were certainly full. It was hard to imagine that CfaN was merely three years old. What a mighty God we serve!

MY TELEPHONE RANG. It was Dinnie Viljoen. As usual, she was overflowing with the Holy Spirit and with an infectious enthusiasm for life. We had become an unusual pair of friends since the day she had been healed of cancer. She, from the high Dutch Reformed tradition, and me, a fiery evangelist from what they would consider a low Pentecostal background. We were the religious odd couple, for certain.

"Reinhard, it has been a year since the Lord healed me of cancer."

"Yes, it has! Isn't that wonderful! You sound so healthy and full of life. You are an inspiration to so many."

"I want to celebrate the anniversary of my healing. I went to the dominee of my Dutch Reformed congregation. You know, he lives just down the street, and I asked for the use of the chapel because my home won't hold the group. I have invited 50 Dutch Reformed women to attend. This will be a celebration for women, if you don't mind. Just an intimate little gathering to give praise to God for His wonderful gift. Would you come and preach to us?"

"Dinnie, Anni and I will both come and be part of your celebration, and I will be so happy to preach."

And so the date was set. It so happened that Anni and I were scheduled to fly to Germany on that date and make another tour of churches there. I was able to move my schedule back one more day and accommodate Dinnie's celebration. As the time grew near, Dinnie called again.

"Reinhard, I just need to tell you that more women have contacted me about coming to my little celebration. It appears there will be 200 rather than 50. Is that alright?"

"Of course. It means that your testimony has gone far and wide. I understand why so many would want to come."

On the day we arrived, the church was packed with over 500. People were standing inside and out. Dinnie had written and published a book of her testimony. It had traveled far in the Dutch Reformed circles and had opened many hearts and minds to the Charismatic renewal as a result. Many of these people had come to celebrate Dinnie's first year of total health.

It was a wonderful celebration. Dinnie stood and gave her testimony. We gave thanksgiving and praise to God in song. Then I preached, and we had a nice little reception. Anni and I went straight to the airport.

When we returned from Germany and stepped off our plane in Johannesburg, we were met with the news that Dinnie Viljoen had died soon after the one-year celebration we had shared together. She did not die of cancer. She dropped dead from another cause no one had suspected.

Immediately, I quoted for Anni the scripture the Lord had given me for Dinnie before I had even met her. *Although the fig tree shall not blossom, neither shall fruit be in the vines; the labour of the olive shall fail, and the fields shall yield no meat; the flock shall be cut off from the fold, and there shall be no herd in the stalls: Yet I will rejoice in the Lord, I will joy in the God of my salvation.*[60]

"Anni, I was so concerned that day that the Lord had given me the wrong scripture. It did not sound good. I asked the Lord, 'Is this the right scripture? It sounds as if she will die.' The Spirit spoke to me again. *This is the right scripture.* It turned out that she was studying the classic story, *Hinds Feet on High Places.*

These very scriptures had inspired that story of Much-Afraid and her journey to God. When I read those scriptures it very much touched her and ignited her faith to believe for her healing. And now, so suddenly, she is gone."

Scripture tells us that it is appointed unto man once to die.[61] For some, Dinnie's appointed time snatched away the joy of her healing the previous year. For many others, there grew a sense of wonder that God had intervened in her life so beautifully, knowing what was ahead.

In all things there is a perspective of cursing and a perspective of blessing. I choose the way of blessing. Removing the cancer from her body gave her another year of vibrant life. That year, in many ways, exceeded all the previous years she had lived. That is what she told us in her final celebration. Looking back now, that service became a fitting memorial for her.

And I know it is much more than that. God used her in ways that only heaven will reveal. She did not live on this earth to see the fulfillment of the vision God gave her for the future of CfaN. But I know she is present with the Lord now, and the things that she sees makes all earthly glories fade to a mere shadow. *The Lord God is my strength, and he will make my feet like hinds' feet, and he will make me to walk upon mine high places.*[62] For Dinnie now – the highest places of all!

I SWITCHED OFF the generator. The gasoline powered Briggs and Stratton engine sputtered and fell silent. The lights strung between poles around the green canvas tent winked out. I was plunged into total darkness.

It was near the end of our campaign season in 1977. Another African grassland crusade had come to an end. The singing of a million crickets seemed to fill the night around me, reminding me of where I stood. I was in a large, open field in the northern Transvaal Basin of South Africa. We had no tent, but an open air meeting in a place where the rolling plains bear the occasional thorn tree. After my preaching and praying for the sick, the African crowd of several thousand had slowly wandered away to their mud-and-thatch huts. They had gone in every direction of the compass. As members of the Suto tribe, these

people lived in scattered villages
surrounded by kraals, which were
enclosures made of rough pickets.

Meanwhile, the local pastor had
driven his wife home in their car.
They lived in a modest western-style
house a few miles away, where they
had provided a guest bedroom for

Michael Kolisang, myself and Pastor Adam Mtsweni

me. Michael Kolisang and my interpreter had retired to their quarters. I had
remained behind to shut down the lights at the open air field. On this final
night, I wanted to spend some time alone with God before I followed.

I looked up. There were no stars in the sky. Not the faintest glow penetrated
the clouds. I looked right and left into nothing but blackness. Moving my
hand in front of my face, I could detect no movement. It still amazed me to be
reminded of how dark a night can be in Africa. Electricity is a rare treasure.

How I loved this moment alone in the wild. I drank it up, inhaling the fresh
air, feeling a cooling breeze on my face. The Lord was standing with me. He
had brought me to this place. I had come in response to His dream of a blood-
washed Africa, and the promise, *Africa shall be saved*. The dream had finally
become a waking vision being played out before my eyes. Thousands were
responding to the gospel. What a privilege it was to follow and obey the vision
from God. I thanked Him for so honoring me.

"Africa shall be saved," I whispered into the darkness. "Africa shall be saved."

Putting my hands out protectively, I slowly turned and walked toward the
place where I had remembered parking my car. At last, I could detect its faint
outline. I reached for the door handle and opened it, flooding the immediate
area with light again. I got in and started the engine, switching on the headlights. Then I drove across the open field toward the place where a dirt lane
would guide me to the pastor's house. I had traveled this route each night for
the past week. I followed my tire tracks through the tall grass.

As I neared the edge of the field, suddenly a slight boy, just a teenager, ran into the path of my headlights. He waved his arms to flag me down. I stopped and rolled down my window.

"Is something wrong?" I asked.

He would not come close to the window. I could see that he wanted to be polite. It was part of his tribal heritage.

"Please, Moruti Bonnke," he said, using the title of respect reserved for pastors, "I want you to lay hands on me and pray for me."

A physical weariness was on me. I had finished a vigorous sermon under a strong anointing. Many had come to the Lord. I had prayed for the sick. The natural letdown that follows such effort had set in.

"How old are you, son?"

"17," he said.

"Why do you want me to pray for you?"

"I got saved in your crusade. Jesus has forgiven me of all my sins. But I knew you would pass here, and I wanted to ask you to pray that I would receive the Holy Spirit before I return to my village. It is far away."

This request went to the heart of my call to Africa. My weariness lifted at once.

"I will pray for you," I said, and got out of the car. I left the car running with the headlights on so I could see what I was doing.

"What is your name, son?" I asked.

"David."

"I will pray for you, David." Then I began, "Lord, according to the promise of Your Word, I ask that You fill David with Your Holy Spirit." I laid my hands on his head. "Receive the gift of the Holy Spirit, in Jesus' name."

He undulated like a bolt of lightning had run down his spine. Then he began to cry and praise God. This was a familiar sight to my eyes. I had prayed for many people in the course of many meetings who had reacted in exactly the same way. I seldom understood what God had accomplished. I just had to leave it in God's hands and move on, trusting that the power of God would bear fruit in His own time.

After a few moments, I said goodbye to David, and wished him a safe walk back to his village. I climbed into my car and drove on toward my sleeping quarters. As my headlights panned away from him, David's slight barefoot form was swallowed up in that ink black night. I never expected to see him again. He was one of many I had prayed for in the past week, and God alone knew each of their paths. As I followed my tire tracks in the grass, I felt wearier than ever, my body craving sleep.

Months later in Johannesburg I began to hear reports of a revival that had broken out in the northern tribal region. When I asked who the preacher was, I was told that he was no preacher at all. Just a boy God was using greatly. It never entered my mind that David was that boy. I would learn the truth in due time.

# Chapter 22

A MAN WALKED INTO our Witfield offices like he owned them. He was a robust figure, beaming with energy and enthusiasm. He politely asked the receptionist if he could speak briefly to me. Well, our offices were still fairly small, and I heard his voice as he entered. But I had absolutely no recognition of him.

When I came out of my office he rushed to me and shook my hand vigorously. "Do you remember me?"

"I'm afraid I do not."

"Well, I looked quite different when last we met. I was in the cancer ward at the hospital in Johannesburg."

You could have knocked me down with a feather. "You are Mr. Kruger?"

"I am." He began to weep with joy.

"What happened?"

"As soon as you left my room I called the nurse. I told her I wanted to go home. They did everything in their power to keep me there but I would have none of it. If God had told me that I would live and not die, then I was healed and nothing else mattered. They made me sign a disclaimer holding the cancer ward blameless regarding any result of my leaving the hospital. Then they loaded me down with pills and prescriptions of every sort. As soon as I left the hospital I threw them in the trash. Every day I got better, and when I went back for tests they found no leukemia. I'm healed, praise God!"

What a day in the offices of CfaN! We took pictures together and celebrated for hours! I am always amazed and humbled by God's healing power. The entire building seemed to hum with divine energy for the rest of the morning. And then Mr. Kruger went his way.

If anyone would be tempted to say they fully understand healing, it would not be me. At the time of this dramatic miracle, my own mother had fallen seriously ill back in Germany. All of our prayers did not result in seeing improvement. Such trials test our faith. For some, this could be the end of their praying for the sick. If God does not heal your own mother, how can you pray for complete strangers? But I pray in obedience to the Word of God, not because I have perfect understanding. I do not have all the answers, and some questions are too big for me. I leave them in God's hands.

My friend, healing evangelist Richard Ngidi, in his reckless brand of faith preached against doctors and medicine. He preached that God alone was the Great Physician, and submitting to any form of medicine was a betrayal of our inheritance in Christ. I did not share his conviction. I believed that God granted medical knowledge to the world to help us. In some cases, truly amazing cures are brought about by doctors, surgeons, and medicines. Since God is for our health and not against it, I encouraged my mother to seek the best in medical help.

She was diagnosed with diabetes, and after some time her kidneys began to fail. Surgeons considered her for a transplant until they discovered her circulation had become so poor it was not possible. My dear mother, who had seen us through the awful escape from East Prussia and the difficult years in the refugee camp, now faced her final storm. She began to live every day as if it could be her last.

Our entire family was affected. Some for the better, some for the worse. Knowing that to be absent from the body is to be present with the Lord,[63] the believing Bonnkes approached Mom's test with the blessed hope of eternal life with God. We were heartened to see her making a round of visits with all of her children while she was still able. Other Bonnkes who had not invested their faith in Christ found the failure of her body to be more evidence that God made no difference. She had given her life to Bible study and prayer. She had served Him faithfully as a mother and minister's wife; why had she not been healed as we had prayed for her? Once again, it became plain to see that these two perspectives lead to opposite destinations – bitterness or blessing.

Neither side receives a clear answer in this life. Therefore, I think it always makes better sense to choose life and blessing over bitterness and cursing. And I continued to pray for her healing, as well as for the healing of others.

WITH THE DRAMATIC INCREASE in my speaking schedule, my home life was also changing drastically. I had to be away not only for crusades but for fund-raising and ministry meetings in churches all over the world. Seldom could my family travel with me. The schedule made my home time very precious to me.

How can I say it? When I was home I was home. My mind was at home. When Susanne, or Gabriele, or Freddie crawled onto my lap, nothing else mattered in the world. If there was a Final Cup match, or a Super Bowl on TV, or a sermon to prepare, or some correspondence, or some other business demanding my attention – none of it could turn my head from my children. This was my family time, and I treasured every minute of it.

Anni was the one who made all of this possible. She made my coming and going seamless for the kids. Travel was just part of the ministry calling we had each embraced as young people. She did not depict it as a special burden. She saw it as a special privilege in serving the King of Kings. The children picked up on her attitude and reflected it.

Whenever I returned from a trip, I recall how we would get out of bed and not get out of our pajamas until noon. We loved sitting at the kitchen table and talking together. Each one had something to contribute – a story to tell, a question to ask, a problem to solve – and it filled the space in our household with joy to let them each speak in turn. As much as I loved to speak, I must say that I enjoyed listening to my children even more. Every child's voice was respected at our table. I can truly say that none of my children felt that their father or mother was disappointed in them. In fact, some might accuse me of being too indulgent. I told Anni, "As long as they ask me for water and not beer I will get it for them." Surely they knew they were the apple of my eye. And somehow, that made the long absences more tolerable for each of us.

One day, Freddie came home and talked about a special friend he had met in school. He was excited, wanting to go over to his house to play. Immediately, I was concerned to know who this boy was and what kind of family he came from. So I said, "Let's have your friend come to our house and we'll throw him a party. I would like to know him too."

We did that, and it soon led to a time of getting to know his parents as well. When I was sure that he was a good boy from a good home, then I gave permission for Freddie to go to their house and play. That is how I watched over my children as they grew up. I automatically wanted to trust my son's or daughters' judgment in choosing friends, but I could not do that. I had to verify that they had chosen well. That is what I considered my duty as their father.

People ask me sometimes, "Your children are well behaved. Aren't you the disciplinarian?" Well, yes, both Anni and I disciplined the children, but how that discipline is done is very important.

For example, one day I came home to Witfield. I wanted to do something nice for Anni. We did not have an electric dryer yet. She used a rotating clothesline in the back yard. Of course, we loved it because it gave our clothes a fresh air smell. But the metal on the clothes rack had become rusted. I saw that and decided I would repaint it a nice silver color. So I added silver paint to my list of errands that I would do in town that day.

As I left I offered to take Freddie with me. Anni was happy for the break. He was at an energetic, curious, and mischievous age. So, father and son got into the Mercedes for some hours of running errands in Germiston.

Along the way we came to the paint store. It was a fascination for Freddie. He loved the smell and pigments and the mixers they used to create the right tint for our purpose. They mixed up a tin and gave it to me. We took it back out to the car and placed it on a paper blotter on the back seat. At the next stop on my list I told Freddie I would not be gone long, and he could stay in the car. Then I laid down the law: "Freddie, whatever you do, do not open the paint can. Do not even touch it."

The errand took longer than I had anticipated. When I returned to the car I did not see Freddie sitting there. My heart panicked. It was every parent's nightmare. Had he been kidnapped? Had my reputation become large enough that my children had become targets? Crazy thoughts ran through my mind. I looked frantically up and down the street. I saw nothing. Finally I ran over to the car and wrenched open the back door, and there he was curled up on the floor in a near fetal position, his head buried beneath his arms.

And then I saw why. He had gone directly against my instructions. He had not only touched the can of silver paint, he had opened it, and it had tipped over, spilling badly on the seat covers and the floor. But that was not the worst of it. In his childish thinking, he thought he could clean it up and get it back in the can. His hands and arms were covered with paint from his desperate efforts. Now he tried to hide himself on the floor in total despair. He was sobbing his heart out.

I picked him up. I could see that he was badly traumatized, and it really frightened me. He did not need punishment. His punishment was already more than he could bear. "Freddie, Freddie," I said. "It's OK, it's OK, it's OK. Daddy will clean it up."

I sat him on the seat. "Don't touch anything because you have wet paint on your hands. You will make it worse. But I will drive back to the paint store now and get something that can clean you up and make the car like new again. OK? It's going to be alright. Just settle down."

At the paint store I bought some containers of turpentine. I also got rolls of paper towels and trash bags to put everything in. Then I returned to the car and began the long task of cleanup. I was determined that he would not remain in a hopeless state over his disobedience. The seat cover I removed and discarded. "We will buy new seat covers today, Freddie," I said. "We will put them on and tell your mother that we bought her some new seat covers in town today. She will not even need to know about the paint."

As we continued our tedious task, my mind flew back to when I was his age. Mother had caught me stealing money from her purse to buy chocolate. I had expected a good *hiding* for my sin. But I had been introduced to God's grace instead. The shock of God's love toward me at that time has never left me.

"Freddie," I said, "do you see how what you've done is like sin? You went against my strict orders and something bad happened. It is that way when we disobey God's law. We make a mess of things, just like this paint. When we try to clean it up it gets even worse. The only thing that will remove the paint is turpentine. Not wiping it with a rag, not even water will clean it. In the same way, the only thing that will remove the stain of sin from our lives is the blood of Jesus."

I suppose as disciplinarians go, I'm more of an evangelist. But I will tell you that it has been my great privilege to lead each of my three children to the knowledge of Jesus Christ as their Savior. They each insisted that I baptize them in water, and of course, I did so. I was there when they were baptized with the Holy Spirit and fire and spoke in other tongues. Our children are still in close fellowship with us today, along with our grandchildren. All of them serve Jesus. I do not say these things with an ounce of human pride. I could not write a book on fathering that would be worth much. But our heavenly Father does all things well. He has made this one of the benefits of following His call for my life, and I am blessed beyond measure.

WE BEGAN THE 1978 SEASON with a campaign in Seshego near Pieterburg in the north, a city renamed Polokwane in the new South Africa. This was our first outing for the new tent. At delivery time we had paid not 100,000 rand for the tent, but 200,000. Costs had ballooned in the construction process. In addition, we had hired a full time tent master and had purchased a fleet of trucks for transporting our equipment. We also had cars that hauled trailer homes for living quarters for me and all of our team. A new large speaker system had been purchased to hang inside the tent, plus we had booster speaker systems for the outside. After drawing the crowd in Sibasa, we knew that in many crusades the tent would not hold the crowd. We made quite a show on the road with our caravan rolling northward, advertising our presence in South Africa. It was an even greater show when that big yellow tent went up on the meeting site. People came to watch in fascination.

Before leaving Witfield for any campaign in those days, it was Anni's duty to go to the nearest grocery store and buy food for the team. On this occasion she took along a young black preacher named Kenneth Meshoe. Kenneth and his wife Lydia had joined our team in 1976 after graduating from college. All of the young black men who worked with us called Anni "Mama." It was a term of endearment and respect among Africans.

At the store they both gathered a great quantity of food at the checkout counter, making several trips. They were carefully following a checklist. Suddenly Kenneth saw on the list an item they had missed.

"Mama," he said, "we forgot the paper towels."

He suddenly realized that they were near the checkout counter. He had felt so natural with Anni he had forgotten himself. He could see that the white cashier had overheard. She grew red-faced, obviously offended.

"Do you call this lady 'Mama'?" she asked, her eyes flashing at him with racial hatred. "Do you? Do you dare call this lady 'Mama'?"

Anni quickly came to his side, putting her arm around his shoulder. "Yes, of course he calls me 'Mama.' He is my son."

Kenneth never forgot that moment. He eventually became an associate evangelist with CfaN, and then went on to found a church of 10,000 at Vosloorus. After the end of apartheid, he founded the African Christian Democratic Party in South Africa and now serves in the National Parliament, where he raises his voice for Jesus and loves to repeat this story from the old days. I am so proud of him.

I remember several times in those days when I would be on the road with both black and white team members in my car. We would stop for drive-in food at a roadside restaurant. When the food was served they would often place the food of the white occupants on plates and bring the food for the blacks wrapped in newspaper. I would refuse it, asking the attendant to bring plates for all members of my party.

"I'm sorry, sir, but the owner will not allow that."

"Then take all of your food back. Tell the owner that we are not going to eat here."

I felt that was the least I could do against apartheid. I had to be careful not to do too much, however, or they would revoke my visa. Today, in the new South Africa, we are remembered kindly for such small gestures.

DURING THE MEETING WITH THE BIG TENT in Seshego, I ordered seating for 10,000 set up under the canvas. When the team had finished, using simple plank benches, I ordered a count of the seating capacity. It was less than 10,000. This was unacceptable. The tent master measured the aisles and went over the legal requirements for setup once more, just to be sure. Still, we could not fit all of the seating that I had dreamed and planned for under the tent.

I was stunned. I had flown to Milan and sat with the designers. My first order was clear – to design a tent to hold 10,000 people. "What happened? Had the tent shrunk?"

"The tent has been under-designed," the tent master answered.

I was greatly distressed to hear this. When I got to the bottom of it I discovered a lack of faith on my own management committee. I had been specific from the beginning that the tent was to follow the word of the Lord to me. It was to seat 10,000. But my own tent experts had encountered problems after manufacturing had begun. Without informing me, they had made design alterations that deviated from the vision. One thing led to another and the compromise became irreversible. Perhaps out of fear – which amounted to a lack of faith in the vision – they had failed to tell me of it until now. I suddenly wished that I had never delegated the task. I actually said to my board-members "If you cannot trust God, trust me – and I will trust HIM."

But I quickly put my disappointment into perspective. The new tent attracted a full house, and for the first time they were sheltered in real comfort. A few scattered thundershowers passed over us during the meetings and we were high and dry. The tent was all I had dreamed of except for being slightly undersized.

Our second outing of the year was scheduled for a location in Vendaland again. Instead of holding the meeting in the soccer stadium in Sibasa, however, I had targeted a remote area called Njelele. I had contacted President Mphephu of the Venda Homeland and invited him to attend our final night at the crusade. He said he would come if at all possible.

We scouted the location for setting up the tent. I chose a site that seemed good. It sat at the very base of Njelele Mountain, a large stony outcrop that loomed above the plain. A local pastor approached us and advised that we move our location. "Years ago, another evangelist set up a tent on this very spot. Before he could begin the meetings, a violent storm came down from Njelele Mountain and ripped his tent to shreds. He packed his tent and equipment and left as fast as he could go."

He told us that the local legends said the ancestral spirits that lived in the mountain ruled this area. They would not tolerate a challenge to their power. Our yellow tent would be like a red flag in front of an enraged bull.

"Well," I replied confidently, "we won't be run off. We saw bad weather in Sibasa, too. Look at the result. We are going to put our tent up right here."

Because of what happened next, some have suggested that I threw down the gauntlet to the Enemy with this statement. Perhaps I did. Some have even suggested that I should watch my words because Satan is listening and responding to them. But I will not allow the words of my mouth to be governed by a fear of Satan. Not fear, but faith should govern my speaking. And so, my faith and experience had made me confident that greater is He that is in us than he that is in the world.[64] And I spoke boldly that day.

In Africa, I had seen how the spirit world is taken very seriously. Witchdoctors ply their trade making bargains with evil spirits. They create fetishes and charms to ward off the torment that people suffer. Witchdoctors are everywhere. They can place curses on people, and the people can grow sick or die. This strengthens the power of the demon spirits over the people under their influence. In Africa, when you preach the gospel, often you are flying in the face of centuries of superstition, fear, and witchcraft. Satan loves to make the confrontation dramatic so that weak-minded people become more fearful of the devil than of God. Anyone who operates in fear can be manipulated and placed in spiritual bondage. I have learned not to let the devil make a dramatic scene. This is one of the lessons I learned through our experience at Njelele Mountain.

The fleet of trucks arrived, and the team set up for a stay of several weeks. As soon as the massive seven-ton tent masts were erected, strange people came out of the bush. They wandered around the tent site moaning, groaning, and mumbling. These people were obviously demonized, trying to intimidate. At night they became bolder. They would utter blood-curdling screams that sounded as if multiple voices were rippling through their throats. The tent master called me and reported what was going on. I told him not to lose his nerve but to go on with the work as if nothing was out of the ordinary.

When they finished the erection process it was as if the demon spirits of Njelele Mountain had seen enough. Fierce gusts of wind began to blow down from the mountain. Some of our trailers were almost knocked over by the force of it. Sleep became impossible for the men. I arrived for the first meeting and realized that we were under a full-scale attack. The clouds opened a torrent of rain that transformed the meeting site into a quagmire.

That night I pressed on with our opening rally, determined not to let the Enemy stop us. A few hundred people had braved the elements like the first crowd we had seen in Sibasa the last year. However, the wind became so fierce that I could look up and see the great masts swaying beneath the force of it. Water was cascading from the sides of the tent like waterfalls. Some of it was running into the tent, creating mud pools inside. I pressed on and began to preach. As I finished the sermon and gave the invitation Eugen Würslin, my tent master burst into the tent. He came running up the ramp to the platform, his hair plastered to his head with mud and water. "Close the meeting!" he shouted at me. "The pegs cannot hold any longer. Some are beginning to pull out of the ground. When they go, seven tons of steel will come down on this audience."

I closed the meeting and evacuated the tent, but I could see that my tent master was already defeated. He had ordered his men to begin taking down some of the tent to relieve stress on the masts and the cables. I reversed that order. "We are not going to run. In the name of Jesus we will continue the meetings."

That night word came to us not to venture onto the roads. Bridges and roads had been washed out and the streams so swollen that cars were being swept away. The next morning I awoke to a horrible sight. One of our main mast beams was bent. Worst of all, the rain had created a 20-ton reservoir in the sunken canvas. This weight now threatened to topple the other mast and rip the remaining pegs from the ground. The only alternative was to slash the tent fabric and allow the water to rush into the tent. This would at least save the full structure. I allowed the tent master to do it immediately. As 20 tons of water poured through the opening, chairs were swept away like toothpicks. A cavern appeared in the ground in the middle of the audience section, and the rip in the tent fabric grew to a massive size.

With the first break in the weather that day I ordered the repair work to begin. That night I looked at our great 10,000-seat tent, and it looked like a battered ship on a stormy sea. Its sails were ripped and flapping uselessly in the wind. For a moment a demonic voice began to mock me. I was taken back to the flood of our tent in Mbabane. After I had cried out to the Lord for a roof over

our head, I had heard the Spirit say, *Trust Me for a tent to seat 10,000 people.*
I heard those words now as the sing-song mocking of a demonic spirit, as if to
say, do you trust the Lord's promise now? And I have found that this is where
the devil always overplays his hand. If there was one thing I knew in this situation it was that the only thing I could trust was the word of the Lord. Nothing
else mattered. But I was also a steward of the Lord's good promise. It was my
place to provide a safe place for the people to hear the gospel. The Lord would
honor no less. At this point, the tent was too unstable to do the job. My tent
master advised that we strike the tent and return to fight another day.

I stood in the rain contemplating my decision when I felt the presence of
someone beside me. Turning to look, I saw the face of Elijah Mulaudzi gazing
up at the ruined tent beside me.

"You are not thinking of leaving are you?"

I had to chuckle out loud. If there is one thing dear to me it is the faith of a
new convert. I knew that God had sent him to me. "Actually, we have to make
a decision about safety here. I am thinking about leaving."

"Pastor, when you prayed for my stomach to be healed in Sibasa last year, did
you not say, 'all things are possible to him that believes?'"[65]

"Yes, Elijah. I did say that. I was quoting the words of Jesus found in Mark's
gospel." I knew what I must do. I turned to my tent master and said, "Assemble
the team here, right now."

As we waited I hugged Elijah. "All things are possible to him that believes,"
I repeated.

With the team assembled before me in the rain, I said, "Men, I take full
responsibility for everything that happens here. I relieve you of all responsibility because I am giving orders for you to follow. This tent is not going to be
taken down. We are going to stay and preach the gospel until the last day of
this campaign."

That afternoon the sun broke through and the ground began to dry as the team resumed work, strengthening the tent and repairing the damage. That night lines of people could be seen coming down the trails from the slopes of Njelele Mountain. They were coming to hear the gospel. In the next few days the crowds overflowed the tent. Finally, there were more people standing outside than inside.

On the final night President Mphephu joined me on the platform. I heard the voice of the Spirit tell me to call the people forward to receive the baptism of the Holy Spirit. As I prayed for them we saw a repeat of what happened in Gaborone. 1,500 of them were swept to the ground en masse speaking in other tongues.

The president leapt from his chair behind me and came to my side. "Pastor, what power is this? I have never seen such a thing!"

"Your Excellency, it is the power of the Holy Spirit."

"You must come back and have another crusade in Vendaland." He obviously recognized that the power of the Holy Spirit was much better for his people than the spirits they had been heeding for centuries.

ONE NIGHT AFTER PREACHING, I heard a knock at my trailer house door. I opened it, and there stood a young man. His face was beaming with joy. There was something so familiar about him.

"Moruti Bonnke," he said, "it is me, David."

Then I remembered him. I had prayed for him to receive the Holy Spirit after a campaign a year ago. "I remember you," I said. "I prayed for you to receive the Holy Spirit in the field after the service that night."

"Yes. May I come in and tell you what has happened?"

"Of course. Please, do come in."

He came in, and I invited him to sit down. Anni made some hot tea, and we began to talk. "Tell me, David. What happened after I prayed for you?"

"Well," he said, "it was very far to my village that night. After you prayed, I walked home. It was like walking on air. I did not feel the journey. It was not until dawn that I arrived. As I first saw my village in the morning light, I noticed a woman leaving the kraal. She was carrying a bundle in her arms, and I thought that I could hear her crying. I knew this woman. She was well known in the village. The week before I came to the Christ for all Nations meeting, she had lost a child to black fever. I called to her, 'Mother, where are you going?'"

In South African tribal culture, "Mother" is a title of respect for any woman who has borne children. This is especially true if the person addressing her is a boy like David, not yet a man.

"She did not reply," David said, "but she came to me. She knew me. She was not weeping as I had thought, but she held out the bundle in her arms, and I could see that she carried her second child, a young boy. He was taken by a violent fever and was making a very strange cry. This is the cry that I had heard. I could see that this child, too, soon would die. This woman would lose both of her children to the fever.

Just hours ago, Moruti Bonnke, you had prayed that I would receive the Holy Spirit. I could still feel Him within me. When I saw this woman I felt love come from me like I had never known. I could not contain it. The Jesus that you preached about surely cared for this child, and this woman."

"It was against tribal rules," David said, "but I felt so much love that I decided to risk it. I asked her if I could pray for the sick child the way you had prayed for sick people in the tent meeting. I said, 'Mother, can I pray for your child?'

She said, 'Yes, yes, anything, please.'

I laid my hands on the child, and I could feel the fire of the fever burning in his head. I asked God to take the fever from the child. Suddenly he stopped crying. The child sat up and said, 'Mommy, I'm hungry. I'm thirsty.' The mother was amazed. She felt the child's head, and the fever was gone.

That woman's eyes grew so large! She ran with the child to the village ahead of me. She went straight to the chief's house. She told him, 'David prayed for my child and healed him. Look, the fever is gone.' She fed the child and gave him water, and he seemed to recover his strength immediately. He went outside and began to play with the other children.

I went to my hut. I began telling my family about your prayer for me, and about what had happened that morning. Suddenly, a runner came. He summoned me to an audience with the chief.

I was afraid because the chief was so high above my family. I had never been to his house. He is our respected king, our royal leader. He is rich enough to support many wives and children. I came and bowed to him. The woman whose son had been healed was there with the boy.

The chief said to me, 'David, I heard what you did for this mother. I have a daughter that no doctor can help. She is crippled. She was born with twisted limbs.' He said, 'I have taken her to the finest doctors in Cape Town and they can do nothing. I have taken her to witchdoctors. Nothing has been able to help. Please go to her hut and pray for her as you prayed for this child today.'

I told him that I would do as he commanded.

The woman whose child had been healed went with me. When we entered the hut, at first I could see nothing. But as my eyes adjusted I saw a crippled girl lying there. She was on a pallet. Her legs were terribly twisted beneath her. Again, I felt that powerful love of Jesus coming from me toward her.

I told her about Jesus. I told her how you had prayed for me to receive the Holy Spirit. Then I told her that I could not do a miracle, but Jesus Christ could do what is impossible for us. So then I laid my hands on her and started to pray. As I began to pray we heard a popping and cracking sound. I did not know what it was at first, but then I saw that the girl's legs were straightening out before our eyes. That's when I realized that it was the sound of her bones popping and cracking.

The woman who was with me screamed and ran from the hut to tell the whole village. They came running together. In the meantime, I helped the girl to her feet. She was crying. She stood for the first time in her life and walked with me from that hut. The chief was there to see her as she came out. The whole village had assembled. Even my family had come.

You cannot imagine the shouting, the screaming, and the dancing that started then. At last the chief quieted them down and had me speak to the people. I told them how you had prayed for me to receive the Holy Spirit, and now I was able to see people healed in Jesus' name.

At that moment the chief announced that he would host a week of meetings in the village kraal. He sent runners to all the tribal villages, commanding them to come and hear the gospel. I have been preaching and praying for the sick every day since then."

"You are the one," I said. "David, I had no idea you were the boy they have been telling me about. Reports are running all over South Africa that God has been using a boy to bring revival among the tribes. This is glorious."

"Yes," David replied. "People are accepting Jesus everywhere I go."

"But David," I asked, "what do you preach? You told me that you only accepted Jesus as your Savior in my tent meeting that night. You have not been to Bible school. Where do you get your sermons?" I feared that he might have begun to preach a mixture of Christianity and animism. It is a common heresy in Africa.

He smiled. "I preach everything that I heard you preach."

I said, "If you preach what I preached, then thank God, you have preached the gospel. What are you doing with the new converts?"

"Pastors are coming to baptize them after I preach. Their churches are growing with new people. They are happy. I want to thank you, Moruti Bonnke, for laying your hands on me, and praying for me to receive the Holy Spirit."

"You are most welcome. Praying for you in the field that night was obviously a divine appointment."

After he had gone, Anni and I reflected on his story. I felt an odd kinship with him. I was reminded that, like him, I had been just a boy in Germany when I received the baptism of the Holy Spirit in my father's Pentecostal church. At the age of ten, I had received a call to preach in Africa. For many years, my father and mother did not take that call seriously. I was so young. But just as David had broken with his tribal traditions in order to pray for the woman's child, I had also gone against my father's authority when I had prayed for the woman at the prayer meeting in Krempe.

I wondered what had pushed him past the strong tribal taboos that he had respected. What had caused him to ask to pray for the woman's sick child? He had said it himself – it was an overwhelming feeling of love. This too, had been the force that had moved me past all the expectations others had placed on me. I called it Spirit baptism, compassion, the love of Christ, the call of God. It was so much more than sympathy, or empathy, or affection. It came from the indwelling person of the Holy Spirit. David's description of God's irresistible love seemed to fit my experience of it as well. In these things, I identified much with the Venda boy from the Transvaal.

OUR 1978 CAMPAIGNS CONTINUED, and the team prepared to set up the big tent in a place called Acornhoek in Green Valley. Our tent crew was becoming more sophisticated with each location. The tent master in particular learned that the soil in one region of the country is very different from the soil in another region. Soil has different holding properties and that affects the security of the tent. A sandy loam, for instance, will not hold a tent peg as securely as good solid clay or a black earth type of soil.

My tent master Eugen Würslin called from Acornhoek. I'm sure he was remembering the near disaster in at Njelele Mountain. He said the Green Valley soil would hold well until it rained. "If it rains," he said, "moisture changes the entire makeup of this soil. We will see a major catastrophe. I am warning you as a professional; the entire tent might collapse."

Somehow I felt this was more than advice I was hearing. These were words intended to strike fear in my heart. Fear was the territory of my Enemy. My spirit remained calm at the center of this storm of information. "Pitch the tent," I said. "In the name of Jesus, I tell you as an evangelist; it is not going to rain."

"For 17 days? You can say that?"

"I just said it. It is not going to rain. Pitch the tent."

When I arrived the tent was in the middle of a large plain. This was not the big city but the Northern Transvaal. A place I loved. As the sun began to go down people began to arrive from every direction of the compass. I stood out near the tent, listening to their voices as they talked and laughed on their way to the meeting. They were walking the trails they had made while grazing livestock over centuries. Now they were headed for the pastures of heaven with a spiritual hunger only Jesus could satisfy. I loved to watch and hear them come. Nearly 8,000 gathered under the tent that night. A wonderful start to any campaign. I preached the ABCs of the gospel again with an interpreter. Michael prayed for the sick.

On the next night I listened to the people coming again. This time, however, I could hear them singing gospel songs as they walked. There is perhaps no sound more wonderful than 8,000 Sothos singing praises to God as they come from every direction of the compass to hear the preaching of His Word.

On the eighth day of the crusade I was sitting in my trailer, reading my Bible when a gust of wind hit us. Then another, and another. My mind flashed back to the battle at Njelele Mountain. A member of the team came running to my door with fear in his eyes.

"Come look," he said.

The sky had turned pale with dust in the air. He pointed to the north and my eyes followed. There on the horizon above a stretch of mountains, a huge band of thunderheads were rising. Already the wind from their thermals whipped at us on the plain. In short order we could see that we were right in the storm's path.

I heard the whisper of the Spirit in my heart, *Rebuke the devil. Resist him and he will flee from you.*[66]

I pointed my finger at the clouds and began to walk toward them. Suddenly the words that came from me were not planned, they were prophetic: "Satan, in the name of Jesus, I am talking to you. If you destroy this tent I am going to trust God for another one three times the size of this one!"

My words drifted across the open field and then something happened that nearly made me gasp. The huge line of thunderstorms split in the middle and began to move to the north and the south. In the course of the next hour the storms rolled past on either side of us without touching the tent. I heard the Holy Spirit say, *Faith frightens Satan.*

As I stood there watching this happen I felt uneasy about what I had done. I recalled the warning Jesus gave to His disciples, *… rejoice not, that the spirits are subject unto you; but rather rejoice, because your names are written in heaven.*[67] I knew that the witchcraft of this region was completely taken up with making deals with Satan. Somehow, I had just done the same, only in the name of Jesus. Jesus had said this is nothing to rejoice about. Then I knew that I was not through. I had not made a deal with Satan. I had made a deal with heaven. I had spoken prophetically. "Satan!" I shouted, as the clouds continued to march past us on the north and the south, "I speak to you once more in the name of Jesus. Although you have withdrawn the wind and the rain that does not mean that I have made an agreement with you. I will build a bigger tent anyway!"

Already in the back of my mind a plan had begun for building the biggest tent ever seen on the face of the earth. From this day forward I began to dream it, to talk it, to pray it, and to think it. It would be a tent several times the size of the one we now had and would require more faith in the design and construction than had been present ever before. I would not delegate this task but would oversee the details myself. In my mind I could already see the crowds filling it and, with sides lifted up, I could see them standing outside looking in from every direction of the compass. This adventure of faith was becoming a high speed autobahn with no rest stop.

# AFRICA SHALL BE SAVED

In the beginning the
"crowds" were countable.

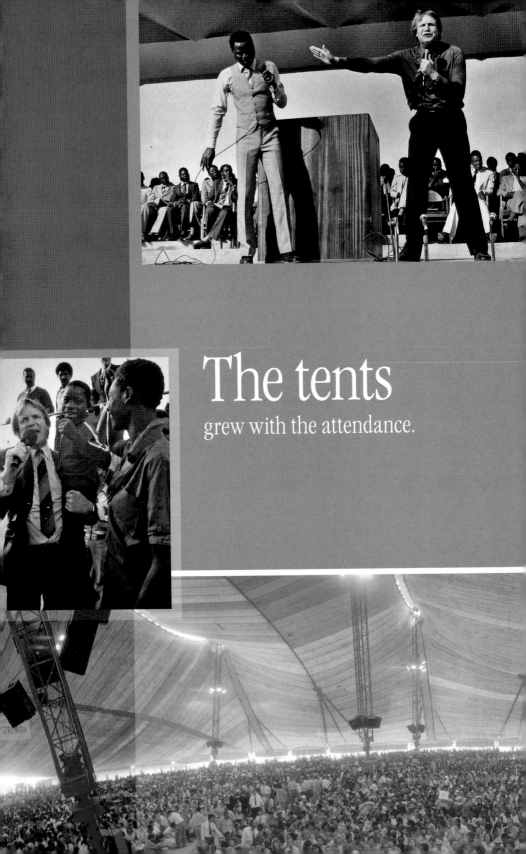

# The tents

grew with the attendance.

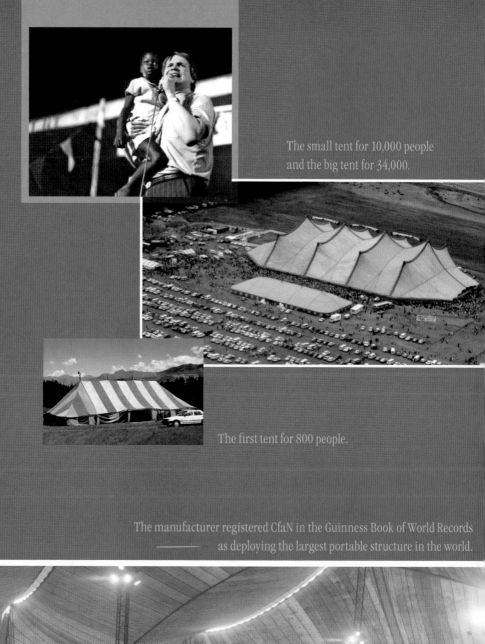

The small tent for 10,000 people and the big tent for 34,000.

The first tent for 800 people.

The manufacturer registered CfaN in the Guinness Book of World Records ——— as deploying the largest portable structure in the world.

# Kaduna, Nigeria

The meetings concluded in Kaduna with a total attendance of 1,670,000! CfaN had never seen a greater crusade in history up to that time.

Chief Olusegun Obasanjo was elected
for president of Nigeria in 1999.
It was the first time in 16 years that
Nigeria had seen a civilian head of state.

An endless stream of people move in one direction to the crusade ground.

# Freetown, Sierra Leone

# Mbuji Mayi

The diamond mining center of
THE DEMOCRATIC REPUBLIC OF CONGO,
where 360,000 gathered to hear the gospel
in one meeting.

# Kumasi, Ghana

Bakili Muluzi, former president of Malawi.

*Now that you are saved* is the follow-up booklet
in every crusade. 86 million copies printed and
published in more than 50 languages.

Top-picture: Sierra Leone's President, Dr. Ahmed Tejan Kabba, visited the Gospel Campaign.

KODAK EL-2  23    24  KODAK EL-2

23A    24    24A

Totally blind for the last 6 month, now he can see!

People were touched when Reinhard taught
at the Fire Conference in Lagos, Nigeria.

Ogbomosho, Nigeria

Benin City, Nigeria

Ibadan, Nigeria

Ado Ekiti, Nigeria

Lagos, Nigeria

Khartoum, Sudan,

Ibadan, Nigeria

Nairobi, Kenya

Freetown, Sierra Leone

Full attention in the meeting.
My PA Andrew Colby and I.

Monrovia, Liberia

Dr. Ron and my sister
Felicitas Shaw 1989

Revival happens
wherever
the gospel
is preached
in power.

Peter van den Berg
has been 30 years
on my side as
vice-president.
His sermons and his
technical knowledge
are inimitable.
He is leading
all CfaN offices
world-wide.

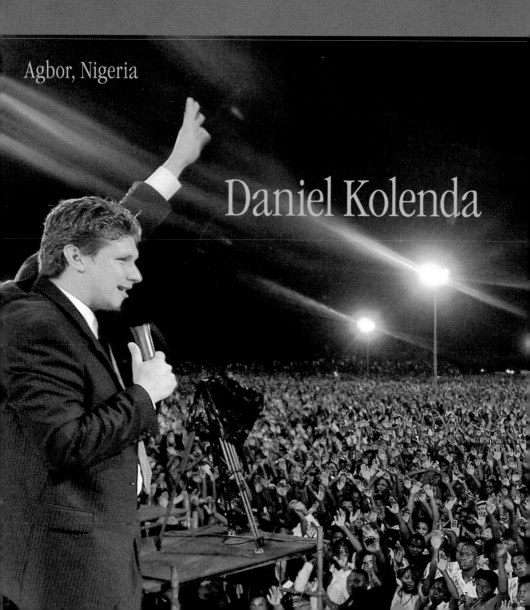

 I have shared the platform with a young evangelist who shares my passion for the lost. 99

Reinhard Bonnke

Agbor, Nigeria

Daniel Kolenda

Reinhard and his family

The CfaN Planning Team in 2009

CfaN
CHRIST
FOR ALL NATIONS

# Part 5

# THE WORLD'S LARGEST TENT

# Chapter 23

SHE LAY IN HER BED in her usual depression. Life had become unbearable. The divorce was days away. Maybe legally breaking the marriage vows would end the anguish and she could find a new life. She and her husband never spoke anymore. She slept in her bedroom, he in his. When they passed in the hallway of the house they never made eye contact. He despised her, and it reeked from every fiber of his being when she was in his presence. She was beginning to despise herself. Oh, that it might just end.

Sleep was an escape, and she desperately needed it. But on this day it was impossible to find. She jammed the pillow over her head to smother the sound that intruded into her bedroom.

I did not know of her struggle. I had come with CfaN to the black suburb of Rocklands in Bloemfontein, South Africa. Our team had set up a huge tent with monstrous speakers, and no one in the general area could escape the sound of my voice. The singing had gone on for an hour. My preaching could continue for another hour. I preached in English and my interpreter repeated everything in Suto. Later, this suffering woman, who spoke English, told me that it was like having to hear my sermon twice. I praise God that she heard it at all.

Finally, unable to find sleep, she pulled the pillow from her head and began to listen. What she heard was the ABCs of the gospel. The simple words seemed to drop onto a blank page in her soul and make a picture there. In a black and white part of her, a full-color word picture emerged. She saw a man on a cross and His blood spilling down. His death made all the difference in the world. It was a picture that could make sense of her tragedy and loss. A picture that said God loved her in spite of her failure. That He cared for her even as she lay on her bed, steeped in depression. The shape of the gospel fitted perfectly into the vacuum of her soul.

Still listening near the window, she hurried to dress herself. Before the invitation was given to receive Jesus as Savior, she had walked from her house several blocks to the field where the huge tent was pitched. She came inside and stood near the back where she listened with her arms folded.

I made the altar call as I usually do, asking those who would like to receive Christ to raise their hand. She did, along with hundreds of others. Then I asked those who had raised their hands to come forward. The people began moving toward the platform from every aisle in the tent. She came among them. As she neared the platform, however, she suddenly stopped. She grabbed the back of a nearby chair as if she might fall. Then she covered her mouth with one hand, stifling a guttural cry. Turning in desperation, she raced quickly from the tent sobbing uncontrollably.

The next morning she woke up slowly. Her head ached fiercely. The sleeping pill and the alcohol had helped to numb her racing thoughts, allowing her to manage a few hours of priceless sleep. Now their residue assaulted her nerves. It was another day to go to work. At least she could do that. She feared she would be late. Stumbling into the kitchen she was surprised to see her husband making coffee. He looked at her and smiled.

Her heart nearly stopped. A smile? From him? He looked at her again, more tenderly this time. He spoke her name. "Can you ever forgive me?"

She found no way to stop the tears. He came to her and embraced her, and now her tears flowed in a full torrent.

"Darling, something wonderful happened to me last night," he said. "I went to the big tent and received Jesus into my heart. I do not feel the same about anything this morning. I am a new creation in Christ, and I have no wish to divorce you. Can you ever forgive me for what I have put you through?"

His words pierced every defense that pain and mistrust had erected. It was the sight of him at the platform last night that had stopped her in her tracks. How could God accept a man like him, she had wondered? A man who so despised his wife and was determined to divorce her? With her hopes dashed at the very sight of him, she had run from the place of salvation to hide in her bedroom again.

"I can forgive you," she whispered. "I can, and I will forgive you. Will you do something for me?"

"Yes, anything, darling. What is it?"

"Will you go with me to the tent tonight? There is something I must do."

Anni Bonnke ministers

Today, these two people are dear friends of mine. They serve the Lord together in a wonderful congregation in Rocklands, Bloemfontein, South Africa. I am so aware that in this life hearts grow hardened. But I am even more aware that no one is truly heartless. Beneath the disappointment and cynicism beats a heart of flesh that longs to love and be loved. And I know one thing more: there is no story like the story of God's love for us in Jesus Christ to reach beneath the hurt and pain and hardness, to revive the true heart of a man or woman. When I see those hands raised at an invitation I know that it is the work of the Holy Spirit, not my eloquence that has done this. I must never forget it.

ONE OF MY FAVORITE STORIES in the New Testament is the story of Zacchaeus. I often tell of his meeting with Jesus and the change it made in his life.

When I explain it, amazing things happen. People want to do what Zacchaeus did. They want to give to the poor and restore things they have stolen. It is a universal response to the gospel, but in South Africa it has seemed especially dramatic.

I think it is because of the history of domination of whites over blacks. The decades of apartheid. Under the bitterness and despair of that unfair system, which in recent years has been abandoned, many blacks justified stealing from the white man. But sin is never justified by the hypocrisy or tyranny of another. With the story of Jesus meeting Zacchaeus, somehow a powerful impact is made in this area. People come forward confessing. Many times, the night after I have preached the sermon, I will find stolen items placed on the platform from one end to another. We have received stolen cars, refrigerators, air conditioners, jewelry, dishes, and serving ware. The list is endless. Often my team is forced to hire a truck to take all of the stolen items to the local police station. It is a wonderful testimony to the transforming power of the gospel.

In Arusha, Tanzania, a man came forward leading a cow on a tether. A small calf trotted beside it, nursing from its mother. At the end of the service the man came to me. "Moruti Bonnke," he said, "I stole this cow and I must return it to its rightful owner. But while it was in my care my bull mounted it, and it later gave birth to this calf. Will I be able to keep the calf?"

What an unusual dilemma. Here was a precious story to share with Anni and the children at our next family meal. I could not help but be amused even as I knew what the answer must be. "No, you will return the calf as well. You would have nothing if you had not stolen the cow."

We found the owner and he presented him with the cow and calf. The owner was so moved that he gave the man the calf back. The presence of Jesus makes people want to restore what they have stolen. In the same spirit, it can make the person who has been wronged understand that mercy triumphs over judgment.[68]

After preaching on Zacchaeus one night in a city location, a fine-looking couple came to me. They were well dressed and well spoken. Speaking in confidential tones the husband said, "Pastor Bonnke, I need you to help me. I have done something terrible and I need to make it right. I am a furniture salesman, and I have managed to steal all the furniture in our home from my employer. But if you do not go with me to restore it, I am afraid that I will be sent to jail and not be allowed to repay the debt."

I said, "I will go with you tomorrow to your employer. But I want you to do something for me. I want you to go home tonight and make a complete list of the furniture you have stolen. Your employer will have to tally the cost."

Then his wife began to weep and wipe her tears. She said, "I, too, have stolen. I was a mortgage company employee. I learned how I could cook the books and put money in my pocket. I have been able to pay the mortgage on our home with this money. When our home was paid for I quit because I was afraid I would be found out. I want to make it right now. Will you go with me when I do this?"

After preaching on restitution, how could I refuse? This was an amazing confession. The wife stole the entire house; the husband stole all the furnishings. "I will go with you, but you also must come with proof of your crime. Find the financial papers that will show what you have done."

The next morning I woke up and spent time in prayer seeking the Lord for His wisdom in handling this matter. I accompanied the husband to the furniture store. It was a very fine store indeed. We went inside, and he introduced me to the owner. The owner was a typical white South African businessman. But he seemed delighted to let me know that the man who had brought me into his store was his number one salesman. He beamed with pride, saying that this man's sales numbers consistently exceeded every other employee in the store.

Oh! I immediately saw how the stakes grew higher. What he was about to learn about his number one salesman would be devastating.

"I wonder if we could find a place where the three of us can speak in confidence."

The man graciously invited us into his private office.

"I am Reinhard Bonnke, an evangelist. I hold campaigns, and we preach salvation through Jesus Christ."

"Yes, I have heard of you."

"I also preach that salvation requires a change of life. I preach that we should take steps to make restitution for the sins of our past. This is great evidence that Jesus has entered a person's heart. Last evening, your number one salesman came forward to receive Jesus as his Savior. He came to me with a confession of sin, and now, he has something to say to you."

He spoke in the way that black employees were schooled to speak to their white employers, with a title of utmost respect. "Boss, I have stolen much furniture from this shop."

There was a stunned silence. "That's impossible. This must be a joke. You are my best salesman. The furniture that leaves this shop is paid for. This is some kind of practical joke. Am I right?"

The man pulled the list from his pocket and placed it before his employer. "This is the list of things I have stolen, Boss. And I want to make it right." He looked at the man who had for years made his standard of living much more than it would have been otherwise. Meeting Jesus had caused him to know that he owed his former employer honesty and integrity, but that he had dealt treacherously instead. Tears began rolling down his cheeks.

The owner frowned and pulled his reading glasses from his pocket. Then he bent to examine the list. He read it from top to bottom. When he had finished he removed his glasses and sat back. He could not look at either of us. His expression had grown very grave. "This conversation is over. I will call the police, and you will need to hire a lawyer, I assure you of that."

*Help me, Lord. What do I say to this?* I find in moments like this that I do not try to reason what to say next. I go to the Lord in the Holy Spirit. It is like there is a tongue of fire on my head which then connects with my tongue of flesh and my thoughts enter into it, and what comes next out of my mouth is not from me.

"Sir," I said. "Before you call the police I feel that I am here to remind you of something. First of all, we would not be here now, and you would know nothing of this crime, if Jesus had not come into this man's life and convicted him of his sin. His confession is a result of that. Nothing else. And that places this entire matter not only before the police and the imperfect courts of South Africa, but we are three men who will stand one day before the perfect throne of God and answer for what we do here today."

That was it. The Spirit had spoken through me. I let the silence work the words into this man's mind and heart.

He fidgeted in his seat, obviously thinking it through. I don't know, maybe he gained a picture of himself standing before God answering for far more than the confession of this wrong. Slowly he worked himself around and looked at his best salesman who was still shedding tears in his chair. Then he looked at me. "OK. I give him one more chance, one more chance, because he is my best salesman, and the rest – " he took the list and wadded it up, throwing it into the trash can – "the rest of this is forgiven and forgotten as far as I'm concerned. This conversation will not leave this room. Is that understood?"

"That is understood." And that is why no names or places are used in the telling of this story.

I next had to deal with a crime of even greater magnitude. I went with his wife to the mortgage company where she used to work. She instructed me to drive to a high-rise office building downtown.

We went inside and she introduced me to her former employer. I introduced myself to him in the same way I had with her husband, and this employer had also heard of our CfaN crusades. I asked for a meeting in his private office.

"Boss," the woman said, weeping. "When I worked for you I stole money. I used that money to buy my house. I want to make it right."

The employer exploded with rage. He was up and pacing the room. His reaction was so strong that he forgot I was there, and the whole context of the matter. I have found that some people react like brute beasts. There is no thinking or reflection on a matter, there is only reaction. I sensed that this encounter was not going to end as well as the other. All he wanted to do was call the police and have her arrested immediately.

"Sir," I said, "may I remind you that you did not catch this woman in her crime. She has come here today with tears of regret to confess. Please, I am asking you to find a way to help her. Can you do that?"

"No. No, it's impossible. I can't do anything to help her."

"Is there someone else? Someone with more authority than you who I could present this to? Someone who could make an executive decision?"

"As a matter of fact, this matter will have to go to the very top. You must see the president of this company. His office is in the penthouse suite."

I looked over at the woman and she began to tremble. Apparently this man had the reputation of a pit bull.

We entered the elevator and took the ride to the top. Large mahogany doors, mirrored glass and fine furnishing distinguished this office as that of the top executive. We were invited into a sitting area and introductions were made once again. This time when I presented myself, the man smiled broadly at me and replied, "Praise God for you, Brother Bonnke. I have accepted Jesus as my Savior, and I rejoice at what God is doing in our country through your ministry."

The pit bull knew Jesus! I knew immediately that things would work out much better in the penthouse than in the middle management office below. This time as the woman confessed her crime, weeping, the big boss behind his desk wept with her. My heart was so moved. Here was a man who understood the power of Jesus to change a life. Sin could be covered through the blood of Jesus. And so could a crime.

"Because you have come forward to confess, I forgive you. Your debt is forgotten."

"But Boss, I do not truly own the home. It belongs to you."

"As of today I give it back to you. You own your home, and you owe me nothing."

I think heaven sings at a time like this. Angelic choirs gather around and give each other high fives. They so long to see things done on earth as they are in heaven. When it actually happens, I believe they throw a party.

That is how we felt as we returned to the big tent that day. *Blessed is the man unto whom the Lord imputeth not iniquity,*[69] King David wrote in his book of songs. That blessed man or woman is anyone who will accept the sacrifice of Jesus and allow Him to be their lawyer before the throne of God.

We will all stand there one day. When we do, the Accuser will have his say. His evidence will be overwhelming. When he screams into our face, "Guilty or innocent?" we will all be guilty. But before we have a chance to reply, our Lawyer will raise a holy objection. He will step forward and say, "Oh Judge of the Universe, there is a special provision in Your law, and I believe My client will enter a third plea."

"You have been accused," the voice thunders from the throne. "Guilty or innocent? How do you plead?"

"Oh Lord, Maker of heaven and earth, I humbly plead the blood of Jesus."

Oh, what a party heaven will throw on that day! The marriage supper of the Lamb. He is the Lamb of God who takes away the sins of the world. It is the passion of my life to lead millions to this saving knowledge of Jesus Christ until hell is left empty and heaven full!

I am Reinhard Bonnke. A zero. I give this message away again and again in a loaf of bread. As I give it away it grows because it is the Bread of Life.

Do I have a great job or what?

SHE WENT TO SLEEP and never woke up. My mother, Meta, had been ailing for nearly two years. On January 22, 1979, she slipped into a coma. When she arrived at the hospital the doctors performed a number of tests. They traced her problem to a break in her small intestine. It appeared to have happened a couple days earlier. The toxins that invaded her bloodstream put her to sleep. The doctors did what they could to help her body recover as she lingered in the hospital for 20 days. On February 10, mercifully, she died in her sleep at the age of 66.

The family gathered in Itzehoe to lay her body to rest: Martin, who now employed his brilliance as a doctor of natural sciences; Gerhard, who served the world of money as a bank auditor; Peter, who had become a medical doctor; Jürgen, who served in Germany's Secret Service; and Felicitas, who had married Rev. Ron Shaw from India and become a surgical nurse in Mark Buntain's Calcutta Mission. All of us were together again to honor the woman who had brought us through the fall of East Prussia, four years in the prison camp and our upbringing in Germany. Certainly the pain and discomfort she had known was now over. We mourned our loss and her gain.

I could see that the one who was most lost without her, however, was Hermann. Dad's life as a young officer of the Wehrmacht had been forever changed after hearing Meta play the church organ. They had produced six "musical Bonnkes" and had served the Lord in ministry together all of their lives. Now the music had gone out of his house. He was 75 years old. I sensed that, if he was to thrive again without her, he should move beyond the boundaries he had accepted for himself all these years. I invited him to return with me to South Africa.

The next year he made the move. Anni and I prepared an annex to our house in Witfield where he could be close to us. He began to travel with me on occasion, as he was physically able. His eyes were opened as never before to the great harvest God was bringing through CfaN. At times he described his heart as "burning within him" with excitement and blessing at the flood of salvations.

The strain and the differences of opinion between us were long over. Though he had once opposed my marriage to Anni, he now took pains to compliment her at every opportunity. These became the very best years of our lives together.

I WILL CALL HIM NATHAN but he could be Natasha or Johann or Kersten. He is one of so many who have come forward to receive the Lord at an altar call. When the numbers become so large they lose their meaning, sometimes I think we must find a way to speak of just one; one person, one soul out of millions. And so, I speak of Nathan.

He wanted a supervisor's job in Johannesburg. His late father had held the position before him. He had idolized his father. He knew that if he filled his shoes, he could afford to marry his childhood sweetheart. He wanted the position so much that he cheated on a qualifying test and was caught. The disgrace was made known, his reputation ruined, his job lost. The engagement to the love of his life fell apart.

Nathan looked for new ways to succeed after his fall, but everyone knew his shame. No one seemed ready to give him a second chance. His life had become stuck in the muck of iniquity, and he had no one to blame but himself. This is the all-too-common story of sin.

But I did not know any of this, so how could I care about Nathan? What moves me is to know that the Holy Spirit is not limited the way that I am. He knew every detail of Nathan's failure, and He cared for him perfectly. He cares about all the "Nathans" in our world. No one is left out. We must believe this with all of our heart if we are to be true evangelists.

As this story begins, the big tent campaigns were in full swing. Crowds grew in every location. 10,000 pressed in under the canvas, and many thousands more crowded around the outside to hear the gospel. Already, I had met with a Christian engineer and designer named J. J. Swanepoel, to design the largest tent ever built. It would replace the one we now used. It was a structure that would seat 34,000. But a restless feeling was nagging on the inside of me. What could it mean?

One night I went to sleep and began to dream. In this dream I wore a sea captain's uniform. I stood on the bridge of a great ship. I gripped the helm. I could feel the powerful engine room vibrations through the wheel in my hands. The deck moved beneath my feet as tons of water was displaced by this moving giant. The ship was a floating city. It seemed as large as the infamous German Bismarck battleship of World War II.

I noticed, however, that the ship was not on the open seas where I would expect it to be. In my dream, I was guiding the ship upstream along the twisting course of an African river in the night. Peering ahead in the gloom I could see a bend. Looking to each side, I saw that the banks were growing narrower as I passed upstream. I slowly realized that my great ship was doomed. It would never make it around that bend. We were in dangerous waters.

I looked to see if I could turn around to avoid disaster, but the channel had no room. There was no going back. The hair rose on the back of my neck as I realized that there was no going forward, either. Such a dilemma!

In my dream, I broke into a terrible sweat. Everything was at stake, and all so suddenly. My hands trembled on the wheel as I watched the huge ship move closer and closer to unavoidable disaster. In desperation, I cut the power to the engines. They fell silent, but I had acted too late. Our massive momentum carried us forward.

Suddenly, I heard the horrible sound of steel groaning and screeching against the rocks. Gaping holes were torn in the hull. The huge Bismarck-sized battleship lurched to a stop as the narrow banks caught and held it fast in the African night. I stood riveted to the spot, swallowed up by the sound of the rippling current and the chatter of bush insects in the darkness.

I awoke to find my bed sheets soaked with sweat. No one had to tell me that I had just had a dream from God. But what did it mean?

"Lord," I cried, "what is it?"

*The ship,* the Lord said, *is a picture of your organization, Christ for all Nations.*

"Lord, will we get stuck?" I asked.

*No.*

I felt great relief to hear this. Still, I knew we were in dangerous waters. I must carefully listen to what the Lord would say about how to avoid shipwreck.

*A great battleship needs more than firepower,* I heard Him say in my spirit. *It needs maneuverability.*

"Yes, yes," I agreed. I could still recall the terrible moment when I realized that I could not turn the ship around to avoid getting stuck. The entire ship, with all of its marvelous firepower, had become locked in an immovable position by two ordinary riverbanks.

*Your foundation is too narrow and too small,* the Lord said to me. *The battleship is fine, but I will widen the river for you so you can pass. I will add prayer partners to Christ for all Nations. Every prayer partner will widen the river by one inch.*

Now I understood the restless feeling in my spirit. God had been warning me of trouble that I didn't know was there. In His great love and wisdom, He had given me His plan for avoiding disaster. All of my energies became focused now. In obedience, I would find ways to gather new prayer partners to widen the river.

I did not know, as I began this new direction, that Nathan's life had run aground in a much different way. His dreams of being a supervisor and a respected family man had been torn apart. His efforts to rise above his own shame continued to fail on every side. His family and friends had deserted him. His reasons for living had gone.

I did not see him as he took a butcher knife from the kitchen drawer. Day after day, he had been thinking of ways to make the pain of his life end. He had read a book that described how others had slashed the veins in their wrists and had gone to sleep forever. This sounded like heaven to him. Just to escape his ruined life.

I could not hear Nathan as he began to sob all alone in his bedroom, holding that knife to his wrist. My ears were filled with the sounds of an engine room on a great battleship. I was hearing myself repeat the words, "Africa shall be saved." I was thrilled to feel the ship moving again on that continental river. My job was to guide Christ for all Nations to see a blood-washed Africa. I did not hear Nathan's cries – but the Holy Spirit did. And He cared for him in his agony as much as He cared to widen my river.

Someone told me to go to a breakfast. It was a meal sponsored by another evangelist. I went. What I saw opened my eyes. I saw that this man of God had invited people to a special meal at which he presented his vision and invited his guests to become prayer partners. The Holy Spirit spoke to me that I should do the same thing.

The finest hotel I could think of in Johannesburg was The Carleton. I wanted nothing but the best for my partners. We hired it for a breakfast. I sent out invitations to the finest Christian leaders in all of Southern Africa. I wanted them to come to a Christ for all Nations meal where God would widen my river.

And how they came! As I sat at the head table, my heart swelled with gratitude at the response. I remembered my early years in Lesotho. My how the tide had turned! There was not an empty chair at any of the tables in that large ballroom. I looked across the faces of wonderful Christian leaders from all denominations and ministry organizations in the region. Some of my former critics were there – people who had said bad things about me, but now wanted to support our ministry. I saw Christian business leaders, politicians, pastors, friends, and ministry executives. *Christ for all Nations has certainly become a great ship of evangelism,* I thought, *especially if it enjoys the favor of this blessed crowd.*

The breakfast was served to the guests, and a time of warm fellowship followed. I can still hear the wonderful hum of conversation in that room, mingled with the tinkle of glasses and silverware on plates. It moved me to know that all of this activity was leading to the presentation of a vision of seeing perhaps millions of souls saved through Christ for all Nations in the years ahead.

Then came the time for me to present the vision. I stood and walked to the podium. Again, my heart overflowed. I thanked my guests for coming. I let them know that it was an honor to know they cared enough to respond to our invitation to this breakfast. Then I presented God's plan for increasing the maneuverability of our organization. The time had come to ask them to consider joining us as prayer partners.

Suddenly, the Spirit whispered in my heart, *Give an altar call.*

I stopped talking at the podium. Surely I had heard wrong. This was not a crowd of sinners. These were Christian leaders. They might be insulted if I gave an altar call for salvation. Or, if one in the room who had a great reputation was somehow still unsaved, that person would be exposed for his or her hypocrisy by responding in this public meeting. It reminded me of the time in President Mphephu's sitting room when the Spirit had said, *altar call – not protocol!*

I heard the message clearly this time. No mistake about it.

"My friends," I said, "I have heard from the Holy Spirit that I should give an altar call. In a crowd like this, I must say, I did not plan to do this, but I will simply obey. Will you please bow your heads just now?"

There was a lot of clearing of throats in the room. There were coughs. You could hear the scraping of chairs and rustling of garments as the crowd of believers slowly bowed their heads. Now they waited in silence.

"I would like to ask everyone to examine themselves honestly this morning. If your life should end today, do you know where you would spend eternity?

Do you have that certainty? If you have received Jesus as your Savior, of course, to be absent from the body is to be present with the Lord. But if you have not accepted Jesus as your Savior, then you have ignored the one gift of salvation that God Himself has provided for you. How can you escape if you reject so great a gift? I would like to ask those in this room who would like to accept Jesus as their Savior, to raise their hands."

In every altar call there is a moment of recognition for the audience. It comes when they have bowed their heads in prayer and then hear the pastor or evangelist say, "Yes, I see that hand." These words mean that in the assembled group, someone is not saved, and that person has acknowledged it by raising his hand. He has made his private lost condition a matter of public knowledge. It would be fair to say that among these Christian leaders, each was highly curious to know if any of their number would respond. No doubt, they would be shocked if one hand was raised. And, frankly, so would I. You could hear a pin drop in that room as I asked for a show of hands.

"Yes, I see that hand," I said. "And you, and you, and you, and you, and another, and yet another. Yes, yes, yes, yes, yes ... I see that hand." And still, there were more.

You could feel something like electricity ripple through the atmosphere. But what none of my Christian friends knew was that I was receiving a great revelation of God's love and grace. It was coming to me in a way I would never have imagined.

Each member of that crowd was, no doubt, asking him or herself, how could so many wonderful Christian leaders not know Christ as their Savior? Some in the audience even began to break from their positions of prayer to see who had raised a hand.

"This is a solemn moment," I said. "I ask that we remain in an attitude of prayer. The Spirit is speaking to many hearts here this morning. We do not want to miss what He is doing."

After another moment, I said, "I would now like to ask those who raised their hands to come forward and stand here in front of me. Do not delay. If you need to receive Jesus this morning, come now."

I will never forget it. 17 people came forward, some of them running. They quickly assembled in a line in front of that speaker's platform, some weeping aloud, others trembling, all moved by the Spirit to accept Jesus as their Savior.

Then I said to the crowd, "You may lift your eyes now, and see what God has done."

That crowd of Christian leaders raised their heads. Now they received the same revelation that had already come to me. Each of the 17 persons standing in front of me wore a Carleton Hotel uniform. These were the people we had overlooked in our search for prayer partners. These were the black servants, the waiters we had not counted in our minds as we had enjoyed our breakfast. 17 waiters who had walked that morning from Soweto to the white part of the city to work – these people wanted to know Jesus.

I looked at this crowd of Christian friends, and said, "Is this not why we came here? We should all go home today with the greatest of joy. By coming to this Christ for all Nations breakfast, we have helped to make these 17 divine appointments possible."

A holy silence had fallen across that room. Nothing I could have said or done better illustrated the nature of our calling to be witnesses and evangelists of the good news. My fine white guests began wiping their eyes.

Pastor Ray McCauley

My dear friend and colleague Ray McCauley was totally changed that morning. He vowed from that day forward that he would never address any group, anywhere, for any reason, and not give an altar call. Such evangelistic faithfulness will always bear fruit. In his case, his church eventually grew to encompass a congregation of 40,000 members in that city.

I went on to lead those 17 waiters in the sinner's prayer. Then I greeted them, one by one, shaking their hands and letting them know that this was not the end of their relationship with the Lord – just the beginning.

I reached the last waiter in line – a young man. I took his hand. As I did I could not help but notice that his wrists were mutilated. Jagged scars of an attempted suicide.

"And what is your name?" I asked.

"Nathan."

"Nathan," I said, "welcome to the family of God."

He nodded and smiled at me with tears streaming down his face. He held my hand in both of his, and for a long time he just kept shaking it. He would not let it go. I could tell he was deeply moved. I didn't have time to ask, but I knew that a very long and important story lay behind this moment of decision in his life.

There is a story like Nathan's behind each of the decisions for Christ that we register. Today those stories number in the many millions. Won't heaven be wonderful? We will be given more than enough time to hear them all, from beginning to glorious end.

# Chapter 24

IT IS ALWAYS TRUE that a vision is vulnerable to the people who gather around it. Many want to be part of something that is big and growing bigger – something that is breaking new ground, making headlines, forging a new paradigm. There is a kind of excitement that goes with this kind of work that gives meaning to even the tasks of the janitor, the secretary, or the warehouseman. They are not just doing a job; they are part of the overall mission and harvest.

With slogans such as, "Africa shall be saved," "From Cape Town to Cairo," and "We are building the world's largest tent," the people who worked for me in 1980 knew a great sense of purpose. All of them were attracted to it. Some were addicted to it. But not all of them were called.

As the vision for a blood-washed Africa unfolded over time, it went through changes. Some of the coworkers had grown attached to the way we did things when we rented tents and other facilities. Designing and owning our own 10,000-seat tent caused them to lose their sense of belonging, and they had to adjust to the new level. Some moved on. Then, as the huge undertaking of building and employing the 34,000-seat tent got under way, even more coworkers were thrown off-balance. Growth creates discomfort.

In 1980 our team had grown to 130 individuals. In addition to the normal management and office and warehouse team, we had added 60 riggers, welders, drivers, engineers, draftsmen, and technicians. These were necessary to handle the logistics of setting up the 10,000-seat tent with its staging and sound system, plus handling the fabrication of the world's largest tent. By 1980, our crusades had expanded northward into Zimbabwe, and for the following year, we were scouting and planning five campaigns even farther north into Zambia. We owned a fleet of trucks and cars to handle the various tasks of running the ministry.

I had added people with backgrounds in chemical engineering, structural engineering, welding, fabricating, and construction for the newer tent. These folks were actually building it on our property. After the under-designed delivery of the big yellow tent, I had decided that I would no longer entrust those details into the hands of the designers, engineers, and manufacturers. We would do the construction ourselves so we could insure that corners would not be cut.

The new tent was actually not a tent in the traditional sense. It was a tension-fabric structure, something new in those days. Today, the roof of Denver International Airport and other tension structures have made this type of architecture world famous. But at the time, we were among the first to experiment with it. Everything about the huge tent had to be extremely precise. It placed a lot of stress on the structure itself, as well as on our people.

As the leader of the ministry, I became very concerned to see that the right people got into the right positions to move the ministry forward. But I was not a personnel expert. I had to rely on the Holy Spirit to lead me to the right people and to lead the right people to me.

IN 1979 OUR TEAM had been traveling to Zimbabwe to organize an extensive five-month campaign, scheduled for 1980. As the time arrived, we set up the 10,000-seat tent in the capital city of Harare. My father traveled with me to these meetings and sat beside me on the platform. I cannot tell you how his presence added to my joy.

On the opening night the tent was almost full. I gave my father the microphone and allowed him to greet the largest crowd he had ever addressed in his life. He told the story of how he had not taken my call to Africa seriously when I was a ten-year-old boy. Then he told of Grandma Gerda Bauszuss' vision of me as a boy sharing bread with a large crowd in Africa. When I gave the invitation that night I saw the greatest response to the gospel of my entire ministry. 3,000 souls crowded the front. I turned and saw my father's eyes full of tears. So were mine.

Within three nights the tent overflowed. We had more people outside than inside. That night my father had a disturbing dream. The next morning he told me he dreamt that the tent was empty. He was worried that something was wrong.

"No, Father," I said, "nothing is wrong. Your dream is correct. Tonight the tent will be empty. We will move to the Rufaro Sports Stadium where we can accommodate 30,000 people."

On the final night the crowd tripled. My father was astonished. I handed him the microphone again. He told his story again, this time choking back emotion as he spoke. 5,000 new converts pressed forward to receive the baptism of the Holy Spirit. A wave of power prostrated many of them as they raised their hands to receive. They were speaking in tongues by the thousands. My father had never seen such a thing in the hardened spiritual soil of Germany. He was overwhelmed.

In the following meetings in Bulawayo, our campaign attracted the attention of the national television media. My father watched as interviews and clips from the meetings were broadcast on national television. He never dreamed he would live to see such a thing. It was beyond his wildest dreams, and it was another unexpected reward for me to share it with him.

IN 1981 WE PUT UP the 10,000-seat tent in Soweto, the poor Lazarus lying at the rich man's gate. After the violence of '76 we had gained confidence that we could hold meetings in the city with relative safety. In those meetings, to everyone's surprise, we saw a number of white people in attendance. This spoke of the changes that were underway in the apartheid regime of South Africa. It seemed that the normal after-dark crime wave also subsided in the vicinity of the tent. I thought often that we were reaping the harvest of those 100 CfaN bicycle evangelists who had canvassed this so-called location in '75 and '76. Surely they had been casting the seed of goodwill that we were reaping in these meetings.

A great breakthrough happened when witchdoctor Pauline Mbatha, who had ruled Soweto for more than a decade, raised her hand to receive Jesus as Savior. She shocked everyone as she came to the front in all of her fetishes, beads, bracelets, and regalia and asked that they all be cut off and burned. Local journalists took pictures of the resulting bonfire, and our yellow tent could not hold the crowds that followed the press coverage. We were forced to move into a soccer stadium. Hallelujah!

The next crusade that year, held in Lusaka, Zambia, required that my men roll our convoy of trucks 1,200 miles to the north across the great Zambezi River. While there, we continued with a total of five campaigns, ending at Livingstone near Victoria Falls. The crowds were overflowing, and the press added to our cause.

As the meeting began there, I realized that at last I was ministering in the land that the Velberter Missions Board had first asked me to accept instead of South Africa. We counted 11,000 decisions for Christ in these meetings. At the end of the campaign, I was invited to minister to President Kaunda at the State House. This was obviously the Lord's time for me to come to Zambia. I wished that the Velberter Missions Board could have been with me on this trip. Surely they would have appreciated the difference between man's timing, and God's.

I RECEIVED AN INVITATION from a group of churches in Birmingham, England, to come preach a crusade in their city hall. It held 2,000 or 3,000 people. That was a sizeable audience for me to draw in Europe in those days. We agreed on a schedule near the end of 1980. I took Michael Kolisang with me. Coming from South Africa, we would testify in England against apartheid by ministering side by side again, like salt and pepper, as full brothers in the Lord.

When we arrived we saw that the meeting was being run by a group called Rufaro. The name was a native Zimbabwean word, meaning "exuberance" or "joy." They were a contemporary gospel trio led by Peter van den Berg, a former resident of Zimbabwe. Peter's wife, Evangeline, and brother-in-law, Oliver Raper, finished out the group. I noticed that Peter was a very good organizer and master of ceremonies. He handled the many details of the Birmingham meeting well.

The name of his group, "Rufaro," resonated with me because just the year before, we had held a meeting in the 30,000-seat Rufaro Sports Stadium in Harare. That same year, Prince Charles of England had come to the stadium to celebrate Zimbabwe's independence. At that event, reggae star Bob Marley had made one of his final appearances. Among the youth of the British Isles, the name Rufaro resonated on many social and political levels.

Musically, Rufaro was experimental. They had modern instruments, hair styles, and coordinated costumes intended to attract young people. In fact, they had become quite successful throughout the British Commonwealth.

I liked them especially because they were evangelists. They used music as I had used my accordion on street corners in Lesotho. The music drew a crowd so they could deliver the gospel. We also shared the experience of receiving sharp criticisms for daring to update the methods of a former religious age.

Oliver Raper, Peter and Vangi van den Berg
– the very day we first met.

For the duration of the Birmingham meetings, I stayed as a guest in a private home. On the last Sunday of the meetings a knock came on my door. I opened it and there stood Peter van den Berg. He told me that the Holy Spirit had spoken to him that he was to join my CfaN team.

I felt slightly bad for him. I couldn't imagine one job in my organization that would fit his abilities.

"Peter, if the Holy Spirit has spoken to you, He will need also to speak to me. I do not want to be responsible for breaking up the success of Rufaro, for one thing. Number two, I do not need another preacher. You are a well-qualified minister and evangelist, but I don't need a dozen evangelists on the platform. Nor do I need another singer. I have musicians who travel with me, and I am happy with them. So, what could you do?"

"All I know is that I was doing some repair work at a home here in Birmingham before you arrived. I saw your magazine. It showed all the trucks and high-tech gear that you take on the road, and I heard the Holy Spirit say to me, 'You have a role to play in this ministry.' I did not hear what the role would be."

"Well," I said, "if you saw the trucks, I can tell you one thing that I need desperately. I need a mechanic."

"Wow! I could do that," Peter said, his eyes lighting up.

"No, Peter. You are a preacher, and a fine singer, not a mechanic."

"No, you don't understand. My father owned a car dealership back in Zimbabwe. He required that I take mechanic's schooling, and I have a degree in motor and aviation mechanics. I am well qualified to service your needs."

"You would be willing to come and be my mechanic?"

"Absolutely."

I couldn't believe my ears. After hearing this, I began to suspect that this man had really heard from the Holy Spirit. He did not see CfaN as a preaching platform. We were not a stepping stone for his music career. Because the Spirit had spoken, he was willing to come and work as a mechanic. That spoke to me deeply.

A few months later he showed up in Johannesburg. He had his coveralls on and a large supply of tools. We prayed together about his assignment. Then I took him to the workshop and showed him the fleet of cars and trucks. There was much work to be done, and he began immediately.

Soon after he arrived I began to notice improvements. Every vehicle was given a regular maintenance schedule. The buying of tires, fuel, and supplies was streamlined and made more efficient. He power-washed and painted the floor of the garage. Vehicles were given assigned parking spaces. He organized meticulous charts for their use. Someone was made responsible for their every movement.

For example, I did not know that the ministry had been paying the traffic and parking fines for our drivers. Under Peter, that stopped. The guilty party was identified and required to pay his own fine. The violations greatly decreased. The stewardship of the transportation department improved greatly.

One day I remember telling Anni, "I think God has placed a goldfish in our pond."

Within a matter of months my general manager left. I could think of no better candidate to replace him than Peter van den Berg. Suddenly, all of his past engineering training, people skills, and ministry skills were all needed at once. The design of the big tent, the materials, the construction methods, the costs – everything about the 34,000-seat structure was increasing in difficulty. Managing this area alone required all of Peter's skills in abundance.

Before Peter joined our team it seemed that every minor problem was brought directly to me for a decision. After Peter came, the buck stopped with him for almost everything. He had the skills to see the big picture and keep his eye on the prize. But he also had enough technical and engineering background to make decisions in those areas. With good leadership we began to see teamwork and camaraderie among the 60 or so co-workers who worked on the world's largest tent. They all became focused on seeing this great dream become a reality. God had truly placed a goldfish in our pond.

The tent was a staggering undertaking. It was eight times larger than the largest circus big top. Twelve masts supported the fabric. They were big enough that a man could climb up the inside of each of them. Each mast was seven stories tall – that's 27 meters, or 88 feet. They had to be put in place by a crane and held in place by a network of supporting cables. The masts were planted on underground cement bases. They jutted into the sky at precise angles that would offset the force of gravity as the high-tension fabric pulled between them. Finally, the fabric itself, under high tension, stabilized the masts so that a man could walk on it like walking on solid ground.

Sections of fabric would be fitted to huge rings that would rise up around each mast on a pulley system. The rings alone weighed nine tons. Each section of fabric weighed 6 tons. There were 80 shackles to tie the fabric to the rings. Each shackle weighed 500 pounds. 17,000 square meters of fabric had to be laid out on the ground and then hauled up the masts and locked into place by hydraulic jacks placed under the base of each mast. A steel mesh cable went around the perimeter tying all of the fabric down. This main cable alone weighed 28 tons. Valley cables crossed the top of the tent in parallel, each weighing two tons. All of the pieces of the tent were so heavy they had to be manipulated into place by a crane or some other form of heavy equipment.

Big tent

To install the tent at any particular location, the team first needed to do soil tests. The composition of the soil would dictate how deep to drill into the ground in order to install cement anchors that served as tent stakes. These anchors would tie the fabric down to the ground around the perimeter of the tent, keeping it from becoming a huge sail in the wind. The anchors were made by injecting cement into the drilled holes. This fast-setting cement would bind to the soil and give the anchors their holding power. Each anchor needed to withstand 15 to 20 tons of pressure.

Once the holding formula was calculated, the team would bring in a large drilling machine and make a hole for each anchor, injecting the cement. This awesome machine made people wonder if we had come to drill for oil. The problems of engineering this monstrosity grew more challenging each day. Some of my team members despaired that they would ever see the huge tent erected.

A few of them quit, overcome by discouragement. The job seemed unending, and the challenges grew each day. It would be another year and a half before the team could be given a green light for the first test installation of the world's largest mobile structure.

In the meantime, my team was planning the South African, Zambian, and UK campaigns of 1981, plus a full dozen campaigns scheduled for 1982. The '82 meetings were being coordinated in South Africa, Swaziland, and Nairobi, Kenya. This was more activity that we had ever seen in six full years of running

CfaN. Peter van den Berg was the right man to pull these challenges together. God had brought him to me. I must admit, however, this was quite an acid test for a mechanic in his first year with the ministry.

THIS WAS ALSO THE YEAR for me to help Freddie take a big step toward manhood. He had reached that age where hormones were beginning to change his body. His voice was becoming deeper, and his boyishness was vanishing before our eyes. Unlike my experience with my own father, I was determined to help him understand the way of a man with a woman. I remembered my own frustration 30 years ago in Glückstadt, trying to put such impulses in a proper perspective.

I decided to take my son on a car trip to Johannesburg and open up the topic for discussion. This, I believed, would provide a good opportunity for me to make an uninterrupted explanation of sexual intimacy between a husband and wife.

We got in the Mercedes and I drove the scenic route. In the course of our trip, I began to explain the anatomical differences between Adam and Eve, Dad and Mom, and between his sisters, Gabriele and Suzanne, and him. I then urged the conversation on toward the fact that God had designed the differences for a wonderful fulfillment in marriage. I explained that the sexual act was not just for having children, but God had also intended it for the pleasure of a man and wife.

After opening the topic in what I believed was an appropriate way for someone his age, I then used my fatherly wisdom to leave the door open for further discussion. I said to him, "If you have any questions about this subject whatsoever, in the future, then I want you to know I am here for you. I will answer truthfully and fully any questions you have, Son. Whatever it might be."

"OK, Dad."

He never asked anything. The next day I took him for another trip in the car. On this trip, apparently the information had worked on him overnight.

"Dad?"

"Yes, Son."

"Do you remember yesterday when you said I could ask anything and you would answer me?"

"Yes, I do. I meant that." I was thinking, *Now here comes the real questions. This will set my relationship with my son completely apart from the relationship I had with my own father 30 years ago. Here, I bury the family curse.*

"Well, Dad, what I'd really like to know is, how does grass grow?"

I didn't know whether to laugh or cry. These are the moments that humble a man's soul. He had asked the question that most concerned him. Perhaps it had come from his frustration over having to mow the lawn every week. Why wouldn't the green stuff just stay mowed? For whatever the reason, my lifelong quest for a meaningful father-son talk about the birds and bees had just been reduced to a question about photosynthesis.

"Son," I said, "grass begins as a seed. A blade of grass grows from a seed, but how that happens, I do not really know." I had some thoughts about the biblical term for seed and its larger meaning, but decided that would definitely be too much information at this point. "When we get home we'll get out the encyclopedia and look up how grass grows together. How's that?"

That was pretty much it for my long-awaited fatherly role.

God was good to me, however. He provided a wonderful counterpoint to this episode. We had gathered as a family at the supper table. My father, Hermann, had joined us. Gabriele came home from high school that evening just glowing. At supper she told us why.

"Daddy, I was so proud of you at school today."

Whoa! My ears perked up. "You were? Why?"

"My teacher went to the Soweto meetings. She got up in front of the class today and she said, 'Do you know who my favorite preacher is? It's Gabriele's father, Pastor Reinhard Bonnke.' And Daddy, that made me so proud. I was proud to be your daughter."

Now here was an unexpected reversal of my own childhood experience. I looked at my father and did not need to say anything. We both recalled how in Glückstadt we had been called every foul name in the book. No one in that Lutheran society respected the Pentecostal preacher at all. Now, here my daughter came home with this wonderful story. It blessed me so deeply because it was more than a daughter being proud of her father. It was a daughter being proud of her father as a man of God. That was the greatest blessing of all. Sharing it with my own father added an extra measure of depth to my joy.

WE PAID ALL MINISTRY EXPENSES plus the fabrication costs for the new tent as the funds came in. As the costs grew larger, the last-minute rescues became more difficult to endure. But the faith lessons I had learned in Swansea, Wales, continued to guide me, and it didn't seem to matter to God whether the amount was large or small. The principle was the same. It was putting trust in Him that counted, and I was planning the ministry growth with what was in His pockets, not mine. I made the commitment not to use bank loans. Still, there were times when the lack of money brought us to a standstill. I remember with great pain when many members of my team skipped a paycheck because the need was so critical.

Yet, I received the largest gift of my life that year. I had returned to do some preaching in Germany. I presented pictures and reports about our ongoing campaigns. I also briefed the audience on the big tent project. But I did not ask for money. I told the people, "When I make these presentations, I do not ask for money – *I pray for it.*"

They all laughed, but I said it in all seriousness. I must not manipulate for funds. God must be the source of supply. But often, God would move on some of those in the audience to be part of the answer to my prayer. That was between them and God. The amount I needed, and the amount I received, was between me and God. The money came in, one small gift at a time. But in those days, it was beginning to add up to millions per year.

After the last meeting of the campaign in Germany, a woman came up to me. She said, "God has told me to give you some money for your new tent. But I have been sick at home and have not come to the meetings. Last night I had a dream. I saw you stand and wave. I jumped out of bed, got into my car, and here I am." She handed me a check for $12,500. This was the largest amount I had received to date for CfaN.

Later that season, after appearing on David Mainse's *100 Huntley Street* broadcast in Canada, the viewers there collected $30,000 for the tent. As the project became larger it seemed that larger gifts were attracted. However, the bulk of the giving came in smaller donations from thousands of wonderful people around the world.

One day in 1982, I approached a serious financial deadline. A particular supplier needed a check for $37,500. If they did not receive this amount by a particular date then they would cancel the contract, and we would lose the initial $87,500 that we had already paid to them. This was unthinkable to me. I prayed. I left it in God's hands and waited.

Two days before the deadline, it still had not come. We were sitting down to breakfast when the phone rang. It was long distance from Germany. I heard a man's voice on the other end of the line. The man introduced himself. He said he was a Roman Catholic who had heard of our work through some source in Germany. "Pastor Bonnke, I cannot sleep at night."

"What is the problem?" I thought he was calling to ask for prayer.

"When I close my eyes at night, all I can see in front of me is your face. And I hear a voice saying, 'Pastor Bonnke needs money.' Is that true? Do you need money?"

"In fact, it is true."

"How much do you need?"

"Well, I should not tell you that. If I tell you the amount you might think I am too bold. I will rob you of the joy of hearing the amount from God."

"No, please. I really need to know how much you need. This is what my dream is about. I must know the amount."

"Well, alright. I am looking at a deadline in two days to pay $37,500. If I don't have it, my construction of the tent will have to stop. Also, I will lose the money we have already paid to this supplier."

"Thank you, Pastor Bonnke. I will transfer that amount to your account today. And now, maybe I can get some sleep."

Praise God. While I was sleeping I left the deadline in God's hands and He turned it into a lifeline. This man was not allowed a restful sleep because he had the money God wanted to use to supply our need. I said to my family, as I often said to anyone who would listen in those days, "God pays for the things He orders, and the big tent is His, not mine."

"WHAT'S IN A NAME?" This famous question was posed in William Shakespeare's play, *Romeo and Juliet*.[70] I knew a man in South Africa with a very strange name, indeed. He was named, Naude van Zyl (pronounced Noddie van Zill). Naude played an unusual role in the life of the Apostolic Faith Mission in South Africa. He was a prophet.

Some people don't believe in New Testament prophets, but the book of Acts records that they were a vital part of the early church. Those of us who believe that the book of Acts is still a present reality, find it easy to accept all of God's gifts to the church. Prophets included. This does not mean, however, that all prophets and all prophecies are automatically to be accepted. All of God's servants can have their gifts distorted by the flesh. In Acts 21 I recall how the prophet Agabus warned Paul that he would suffer persecution in Jerusalem. While the prophecy was true, the apostle Paul disagreed entirely with the way Agabus and the other disciples interpreted the prophecy. It was not a warning that he should stay away from Jerusalem. In this case we see that the prophecy of Agabus had to be applied with the apostle's greater gift of discernment.

I can still see Naude coming toward me outside my ministry headquarters. He wore a black sloop hat and a long, dark cloak that billowed in the wind. He cared little for convention. Over the years, I had seen him at conferences in South Africa. He was a true prophet. I had seen his words come to pass.

"I have a word for you, Brother Bonnke."

"A word from the Lord, I trust."

"Yes. You are taking the gospel from Cape Town to Cairo, but I have seen a vision. This vision, I believe, shows that there is a problem in your way. I saw your trucks going northward, and they got stuck in the Zambezi River, of all things. Then, from the other side of the river I saw people – white people – throwing money at you. These were not local currencies, they were American dollars. With that money a bridge was built, and you were able to continue your journey northward into the heart of Africa."

"That is quite a picture, Naude. Thank you. I will keep it in mind."

I was immediately encouraged by this prophecy. It did not guide me as much as it encouraged me. It encouraged me to know that God was talking to Naude van Zyl about my situation. In fact, the trucks that I had were insufficient to transport the new tent under design. I knew that the African roads they would travel as we continued to push northward were too rough for them. They would fall apart from the beating. I also knew that the expense involved in buying adequate trucks was beyond the level of giving of my current network. This vision from Naude made sense, and it caused me to look in a new direction.

God was already stirring in my heart to seek help from partners beyond South Africa and Germany. America seemed to be the missing piece in the network. The time had come for me to present my vision to those who would hear it across the USA.

THE NEED is not the call. This piece of wisdom has saved the lives of many a missionary, especially in Africa, where the needs are so great that they can pull you to pieces. A missionary can put out so many fires trying to meet needs around him that he suffers burnout. I have known missionary friends who said, "I hear the cry of lost souls calling me into the mission field." These workers are headed for the missionary bone yard. They have responded to the call of the need rather than the call of God.

We must go where God sends us, speak what He gives us to speak, hear His voice and obey it – this is our best protection from burnout. It will also guide us to the very best strategy for accomplishing His mission. For everything a man does to follow the call of God, there are ten things he does not do. We cannot do everything. We must focus on the call and not simply the needs.

Following the call of God to Africa, and the promise that *Africa shall be saved*, many things had changed in my life and ministry. I began to feel that the time had come for a more accurate strategy. The press was beginning to send news of the big tent around the world. Before I dared to use my newfound notoriety to chart a course, I felt that I needed good advice. I began to seek out others who had spent their lives doing what I was doing.

I met with missionary evangelist T. L. Osborn in Tulsa, Oklahoma. He had used huge open-air meetings evangelism in Africa and in 90 other nations to great effect. I also visited Freda Lindsay's Christ for the Nations Institute in Dallas, Texas. In 1983, I attended Billy Graham's Amsterdam Conference for Itinerant Evangelists. I was able to meet him and was surprised to learn that he knew of my ministry. In fact, he asked about reports of a miraculous Gospel Crusade I had just conducted in Finland. I was impressed with the way that Billy Graham had conducted his conference.

For years I had been sensing that I should sponsor a conference for evangelists as well. I especially wanted to ignite a passion in the hearts of other evangelists for the Holy Ghost-powered evangelism that I knew. I was not drawn to pastors in this effort. Like Billy Graham, I was drawn to fellow evangelists. Especially to those in Africa. I felt that we could locate 1,000 of these men, pay their way to our conference, and send them back to their homes charged with the Holy Ghost fire for seeing the lost come to Jesus. I called it a Fire Conference and I felt we could schedule such an event in the big yellow tent even as we held our main campaign in the world's largest tent next door.

We targeted the year of 1986 for our first Fire Conference. We would hold it in conjunction with our crusade in the city of Harare, Zimbabwe. It was a city large enough with facilities to handle all the evangelists we would bring to the event plus those who would attend on their own initiative. I liked Harare since we had already attracted so much positive media attention there. Harare had spread the news of our gospel campaigns across central Africa. I knew that the big tent would be complete and field tested by 1986. This Harare campaign and Fire Conference would send CfaN to another level. It would enlarge our strategy.

IN THE MEANTIME I had received an invitation to hold a crusade in the city of Perth, on the sunny west coast of Australia. My friend Pastor Ray McCauley of Johannesburg had contacted Brian Baker, a pastor friend of his in Perth. They had managed to acquire the use of an 8,000-seat Entertainment Centre. After praying and feeling a green light from the Lord, I agreed to a date early in 1983.

The first night the hall was packed. The local Channel 4 news team arrived to make a story for their late edition. As I sat on the stage looking over the crowd, I began a conversation with the Lord. "What will you do here tonight, Lord?" My eyes were drawn to the far right side of the auditorium where a lady in a blue dress sat in a wheelchair. The Lord said to me, *Tonight I will heal that woman in the blue dress.* I accepted it.

Early in the meeting, I got up to greet the people. I took the microphone and announced, with great excitement, "Today a great miracle is going to happen here in Perth, Australia. Right in this entertainment center." I pointed to the woman in the blue dress, "That woman over there is going to be healed, and she is coming out of her wheelchair." The Channel 4 news team took eager notice of it, for better or worse.

When I made this announcement, I had hoped to stir an expectation in the crowd. I had learned that this can help build an atmosphere of faith. Until this day in Perth, I had found that unless faith was present, miracles did not happen. I based this on my own experience, as well as on Scripture.

In the Gospels of Matthew and Mark we read that Jesus' miracle-working power was limited by the unbelief of the people in Nazareth.[71] Certainly if a lack of faith can limit Jesus' power to do miracles, it can limit mine. Other times we find Jesus saying to people who were healed, *Your faith has made you whole.*[72] If Jesus credited miracles of healing to the faith of the sick person, so must I. This was my theology of faith in a nutshell. In this case, I learned that God likes to crack theological nutshells.

As I made my bold announcement about God healing the woman, it did not seem to build an atmosphere of faith in the room. In fact, the opposite happened. The woman did not receive my announcement as good news. She ducked her head in her hands and tried to hide herself. I must have sounded to those people like an insensitive South African preacher who had presumed upon a poor woman's illness. It appeared that she wanted to drop through a hole in the floor. For a moment, so did I. The crowd did not respond positively. The atmosphere grew cool, and I sat down.

What I did not know was that this woman had merely come as an invited guest. She was not religious at all. She had no knowledge or expectation of healing. Of course, neither did I know her condition. I was relying only on what I had heard from the Lord in my spirit. It turns out the woman had a degenerative disease called "brittle bone" disease. To stand up would cause her bones to crack. The doctors had said she would never walk again.

As I waited for the time for preaching, I said within myself, *Oh Lord, she doesn't have faith. How's this going to work?*

In a moment the Holy Spirit spoke back to me, *Today it's not her faith, it's your faith. You are going to see a great miracle.*

This idea was too big for my theology-in-a-nutshell. She didn't have faith, but my faith was enough for her miracle? Immediately my mind raced through the Scriptures. Could I find an example in the New Testament that would demonstrate that Jesus healed someone based on the faith of another?

Suddenly it came to me: the story of the paralyzed man who was let down through the roof to Jesus. In the story, the man shows no faith of his own. His friends take him to Jesus. They cannot get into the house where He is teaching, but they are so sure of Jesus' power to heal, they remove the roofing material and let the man down next to the Lord inside the house. The Bible says that when Jesus saw their faith, He forgave the man's sins and healed his body. This was clearly a gift of faith from the man's friends to him through Jesus. The story is found in the second chapter of Mark.[73] Who was I to say it couldn't be done that way in Perth, Australia in 1983?

Now I had my text for the evening. When I got up to preach, I preached to myself as much as to anyone else. I built up my own faith by this Bible story so that when the time came to pray for the woman, I would not expect her faith to be present.

At the end of the sermon I announced that I would now pray for the woman in the wheelchair, as I had promised. On the platform behind me was Pastor Ray McCauley. He whispered, "Reinhard, you're on your own now." By this he meant that he had seen the woman's lack of faith and was not going to share in my embarrassment.

I went with the voice of the Spirit. I came down from the platform and walked to the wheelchair. The TV crew got in position to record the event.

"What is your name?" I asked.

"I am Mrs. McKelt."

"Mrs. McKelt, God has told me you are going to be healed today."

As I prepared to lay my hands on her, I felt a tap on my shoulder. It was Ray. "One shall chase a thousand," he whispered, "but two can chase ten thousand." He was speaking now of joining his faith with mine in this prayer. I would have prayed without him, but I was glad to have him there.

I laid my hands on her head and commanded, "In the name of Jesus, get up and walk!"

Slowly, unsteadily, she stood to her feet. The people seemed to be holding their breath. Channel 4 was filming away.

"Now walk," I said.

She began to walk like Frankenstein – *clump, clump, clump*, across the floor. She moved like she was wearing lead boots.

"Run in Jesus' name!" I shouted. "Run!"

Suddenly, she took off like a shot. She began running and screaming and laughing and jumping. She acted like a person who has just received an extreme makeover from the Creator of the Universe, pain free, in ten seconds flat.

News 4 ran the story. The next day they did a follow-up, taking their camera to her house. When she answered the door the camera revealed her wheelchair folded up in a corner of the entryway. Needless to say, our meetings in Perth were standing room only from that point on.

Years later, Mrs. McKelt attended a Christ for all Nations partners' banquet in Perth. She came to show me that she was completely healed. No more broken bones. She was a child of God set free. For me she was another example of God's love and amazing grace. I just praise Him.

Through Mrs. McKelt I learned to be careful about putting God in a theological box. But even when I do, I know that I can be made free by listening to and obeying the voice of His Spirit. Today, when I pray for someone and that person is not healed, I do not blame it on a lack of faith. The longer I live the less I pretend to know about the mind of God. I do not know why some are healed and others are not. I only know that sometimes it is the faith of a sick person that makes them whole, and sometimes it is the faith of others.

# Chapter 25

WE SECURED A PIECE OF LAND in KwaThema near our headquarters where the team could do a test run of the great tent apparatus. A full erection involved twelve masts. Our test run would use only six. We positioned it near the freeway where passing traffic could not miss it. Peter van den Berg scheduled the erection of the masts as I left on a preaching trip to Uganda.

It was 1983. The notorious regime of Idi Amin had been deposed three years before. Milton Obote had come to power in Uganda and was involved in a long civil war that would eventually lead to his ouster in 1985. But in '83 the scene in the city of Kampala was calm, and local pastors were calling me to hold a public crusade there. The Lord seemed to smile upon the timing.

Under Amin more than a million had been slaughtered. Pentecostals and Evangelicals had often been the targets of his evil paranoia and rage. Their homes had been raided and lives lost. In the emerging climate of tolerance I believed we could see souls saved. As a bonus, we could give visibility to the idea of religious freedom in this troubled country. But in the back of my mind, something nagged at me.

As my plane made its approach to Entebbe, where the famous Israeli raid had first broken the grip of Amin on this nation, I was reminded of a prophetic warning. It had come recently during a prayer session between some of our team: "… a time will come when some of us will lay down our lives … The path we are treading is red with the blood of martyrs who have gone before us … but the blood of the martyrs is the seed of the church … no matter the cost, this prophecy will find fulfillment." I prayed that the increasing dangers we faced would be met by an even greater force of divine protection and preservation. I do not want to see one life lost, Father, in Jesus' name.

As we drove from Entebbe to Kampala, I commented on the absence of posters in the markets and public transportation terminals where I normally saw them. That is the primary way we have to advertise our meetings. I was told that the locals had not seen such posters in many years. As a result, people were stealing them and using them to decorate their homes. I sincerely hoped that these well-intentioned thieves would come to the meetings and repent. Perhaps they would come with their households, and perhaps even their neighborhoods. Otherwise, we were in trouble.

Our meeting site was located on the city square, just a stone's throw from the Supreme Court building. I was happy to see that a good crowd of several thousand showed up the first day. Many responded to the invitation. God's power was displayed. Healings were manifested. In fact, that first day we made so much noise praising God that the court had to adjourn. We were asked to cancel the afternoon meeting scheduled for the next day so the Supreme Court could conduct important business.

Crowds grew, and the final meeting of the campaign was held on a Sunday afternoon. As we gathered I could see giant storm clouds building to the south over Lake Victoria. They were headed our way. I preached a hurried sermon. No sooner had I concluded than large raindrops began to fall. Then the sky opened up as only it can on the equator. I quickly got into a car that had been parked for me nearby. As I watched, I expected the crowd to leave. The opposite happened. I saw a spiritual hunger so real that a full tropical downpour would not dampen it.

That really touched my heart. I got out of that car and grabbed the microphone again. If they would endure the rain, so would I. Someone tried to follow me with an umbrella, but I got drenched anyway. I ministered and prayed for the sick until we had finished our course. This turned out to be an important dress rehearsal for the future when I would preach in many rainstorms as a matter of course.

As we flew out of the city I sat near a window, searching for a possible tent site in the landscape below. Given Uganda's spiritual hunger, I felt sure that we would return here one day for a crusade with the 34,000-seat tent.

After landing in South Africa, Anni met me and drove us toward Witfield. She asked a dozen questions about the Uganda meetings as we traveled. I gave her my stories, one after another. Then I noticed a new construction project against the skyline. Six large cranes were installing a huge steel superstructure beside the freeway. Suddenly, I realized what I was seeing. I looked at Anni, and she was smiling to herself. I couldn't speak anymore. Tears came to my eyes.

Anni pulled off the highway and into the field so I could savor the sight. This was the test installation of the big tent. It was so big I had not recognized it at first. After so many setbacks, seeing those six masts rising so high was almost more than I could absorb. What a mark it made on the skyline. What a milestone for CfaN.

I still did not have the kind of heavy trucks necessary to haul this tent on the rough roads of Africa, however. After doing some shopping, I estimated they would cost somewhere in the neighborhood of 1.5 million rand. I did not ask for the money, but I prayed for it. And I planned a trip to America. The words of Naude van Zyl continued to encourage me in that respect.

Once installation was complete, we held a series of meetings right there on the test site. In the half-tent, we registered 8,000 decisions for Christ. I left for America bursting with a new excitement. And I had a story to share.

To this day I have many American supporters who tell me that this is the time when they first became aware of me. News about the world's largest tent put CfaN and Reinhard Bonnke on their minds. I was a guest on Pat Robertson's *700 Club* and on David Mainse's *100 Huntley Street* program in Canada. Both men took up generous offerings to help with the purchase of our needed trucks.

On my return trip I planned some speaking engagements in Germany. While there, I came across an unexpected blessing. A fleet of six-wheel-drive heavy-duty trucks were available for purchase. These had been custom manufactured especially for military duty in Africa. Originally, they had been ordered by Muammar Gaddafi of Libya, but he had cut the order back, and now they were useless surplus items that no one seemed to want. The manufacturer was ready to negotiate liberally. This divine appointment allowed me to purchase the trucks at half price.

I was ecstatic over God's provision. He had provided my first church through a rum factory. Now he had provided transportation for a blood-washed Africa from the man Ronald Reagan called, "the mad dog of the Middle East." I had Mr. Gaddafi's trucks repainted. Slogans were emblazoned on their sides, turning them into rolling billboards: "Jesus Christ heals broken hearts," "Jesus lives and loves you," "Christ for all Nations," and "Jesus Christ is King." Then they were shipped to South Africa where they could transport the tent and all its apparatus to Soweto for our first full use of this evangelistic tool. The trucks had only one drawback. Each cabin was equipped with a machine gun hatch which had been designed for Mr. Gaddafi's troops. The hatches could not be removed and our crew had many a good laugh over that little design flaw.

ON SATURDAY, FEBRUARY 18, 1984, we prepared for the dedication service for the world's largest tent. As I waited with Anni and my father in a nearby trailer a knock came at my door. My friend Ray McCauley stood there with Kenneth and Gloria Copeland from Ft. Worth, Texas. I asked them to come in. They had been drawn to the reports of our work and had come to see it for themselves. "I want to support CfaN," Kenneth said. "I preach to the saved, you preach to the unsaved. We should be partners."

I thanked him for that. But honestly, I had no idea how incredibly powerful his words would prove to be over the decades to come.

"I am being instructed in the Spirit to prophesy to you," he continued. "I declare that you have seen nothing yet. You will see a day in which one million souls will respond to the gospel in a single meeting. Thus saith the Lord."

Gloria & Kenneth Copeland and I:
True partners in the gospel

How can I describe this moment? It was as if a bucket of ice had been tossed into my face. This idea had never entered my head. One million souls in a day. Nothing like it had ever been done in the history of evangelism. I could not even visualize a crowd that large, let alone that many hands raised to heaven in response to an invitation. The very thought of it sent shivers down my spine and flushed my eyes with stinging tears.

Until now, one million souls had been a lifetime goal for me. Not the work of a single meeting on a single day. In fact, I had asked God for one million souls in Lesotho. This had happened when I had first asked God for 30 rand to make rent. He had responded by challenging me to ask Him for one million rand. "I do not ask for a million rand or even a million dollars," I had prayed. "But I do ask You now for a million souls." This word from Kenneth Copeland made me feel as if I stood on the nose of a rocket about to launch. Everything I had done had prepared me for everything that would now come.

"God is saying more to me," Kenneth went on. "You have come from Germany, and the Pentecostal experience in Germany has been difficult and dark. But I tell you by the power of the Holy Spirit that change is coming to your homeland. Doors will be thrown open, minds will be renewed, and the wall that divides Berlin, and divides Germany into east and west will come down and be ground to powder. I declare this in the name of Jesus Christ, the King of Kings, before whom every knee will bow. Consider it done."

My mind was reeling. I could not take it all in. *For the word of God is quick, and powerful, and sharper than any twoedged sword, piercing even to the dividing asunder of soul and spirit, and of the joints and marrow, and is a discerner of the thoughts and intents of the heart.*[74] I sensed that I had heard a living word from the mouth of this brother in Christ, and it was shaking me up from the inside out.

Later, my father, my sister Felicitas and Anni sat beside me on the dedication platform. We looked across the faces of 50,000 guests packing the tent and the surrounding field in Soweto. For the first time this great crowd did not seem large to me. My mind had been expanded and I saw everything in a different

The Big Tent packed with people.

light since receiving Kenneth Copeland's prophecy. It was a sunny day and the side flaps had been pulled up for visibility. A cool breeze whispered through the air.

I smiled at Anni. She had recently cut her hair and styled it for this event. That may seem like a small thing, but I knew it was like an amputation for her. We had come from the German Pentecostal tradition in which women never cut their hair but wound it behind their head in a very conservative style. It had long been a burden to Anni in Africa. Shorter hair took less time to maintain and was cooler and did not weigh as much. In the African climate, cutting her hair would have made life more comfortable and convenient. But she had been hesitant to do it for all of these years. With the dedication ceremony of the big tent pending, she had taken the plunge. She had her hair cut for the first time, and styled in an attractive way. I thought she looked marvelous. I could tell she was pleased with her new look, even though she was still self-conscious about it.

I looked at my father. I knew that he was amazed to see so many other religious denominations and organizations represented on the platform. This impressed him even more than the size of the crowd. Representatives from the Dutch Reformed Church were here, as well as many others. Dad was dumbfounded. Even governmental officials were present. How could he be sure they were all believers? In fact, they were not all believers. Certainly not all believers of the Pentecostal variety. He had never seen such an example of unity in all his years of ministry, and I could tell he was uncomfortable with it.

He and all Pentecostals shared a deep fear of achieving false unity through compromise. They often cited the example of the Ecumenical Movement and the World Council of Churches. These liberal organizations had achieved unity by compromising the essence of the gospel in favor of social action programs. To this point, I agreed. But the Pentecostal fear of compromise was so great that they tended to accuse any evidence of unity as a sure sign of compromise. At this diverse gathering, I knew that I was in danger of that accusation from my critics.

I will add here that I know this fear of compromise is not unique to Pentecostal believers. It is human nature to cling to core values. This is true of all denominations. All human organizations, for that matter. Over the years, as I examined the compromises that were so feared, I often found that they were superficial. They were seldom compromises of essential doctrines. In some instances the religious group had developed a series of litmus tests such as hairstyle, or a speaking style, or a style of dress, or a translation of the Bible, or a Bible school, or marginal theological position. Even earning an advanced degree could be considered suspect by one group, and essential to another. Preaching in a disco could be considered anathema, or holding church in a former rum factory.

Beneath all these surface issues, the Pentecostals were trying to protect their central doctrine and experience of the baptism of the Holy Ghost and speaking in tongues. This made them distinct from other groups. On these issues, they were right to fear compromise. I preached the baptism of the Holy Spirit as the power for reaching the world with the gospel, but I had also engaged in Christian fellowship with those who did not believe these spiritual gifts were active. For this, I was vulnerable to accusations of compromise by some of my brothers in Christ.

Sweeping the crowd with my eyes I recalled my Bible college years in Wales, where I had first learned to appreciate believers who did not share my Pentecostal heritage. This had prepared me to be able to enlarge my tent to include them now. Above all, it did my heart good to know the reason we stood together under the largest tent on the planet was to see Africa saved. I knew my father would appreciate that central fact. And he would appreciate that the evangelist who had brought these groups together was his own son – a Pentecostal preacher. In recent months, he had traveled with me to various campaigns. He had seen first hand that the power of the Holy Ghost was not a compromised issue with me. It was the driving force behind the harvest. Hermann Bonnke knew that everything happening in this tent today owed itself in some measure to Azusa Street, to Maria Woodworth-Etter, and to Luis Graf.

Next to the big tent we had pitched our 10,000-seat tent. Our co-workers and trained volunteers would use it to counsel and pray for those who came forward for healing and salvation. Seeing the two tents side by side was a revelation. I recalled the day when the Lord had challenged me to use a 10,000-seat tent. No such tent existed in South Africa at the time. How daunting that task had seemed. How far beyond my reach. My pockets had been empty. Now the two visions stood side by side, promising that the vision of a blood-washed Africa was not beyond imagining. The 10,000-seat tent had been the seed for the 34,000-seat tent. At this point, I had no idea that the large tent was but a seed for something beyond my wildest dreams.

Television camera crews moved in and around the tent during our dedication meeting. An American Christian television network had been with us for weeks preparing a full documentary. BBC News crews quickly shot headline news features for airing in the UK, Australia, Zimbabwe, and other countries. The big tent had succeeded in attracting media attention to the work of the gospel simply by its size. It was a dream come true for me.

I hoped that some of this news would eventually reach my brother Peter in Germany. I remembered his challenge to me when I had just returned from Wales. He had so despised my calling to the ministry. All he could visualize for me was Father's struggling work in Krempe.

"I am going to be a doctor," he had said. "I want to be successful, and God just doesn't seem to have any leverage in this world."

"God has plenty of leverage," I had replied. "More than enough."

At the time there had been no evidence to back up my claim. But if Peter could see what God had done here in Soweto, I was sure he would agree with me. The bigger irony was that I had not allowed a bank to be involved in this great undertaking. I looked up at 100 flood lights hung from the superstructure inside the tent. They had been purchased at $1,200 each. The sound system and speaker towers had cost even more than that. No lending institution could lay claim to any of these assets. The tent had been built as donations had come in from the people who shared our vision.

At the invitation that day, 5,000 people raised their hands and came forward. During the meetings that followed, we saw more than 25,000 decisions for Christ in Soweto. What a demonstration of God's leverage! Plenty of it! More than enough!

As SOON AS WE HAD FINISHED the Soweto meetings we disassembled the big tent and trucked it southward to the Valhalla Sports Field in Cape Town. Setting up the big tent there would symbolically begin our push from Cape Town to Cairo.

The location was a notorious crime zone. Locals called the area "Kill me quick" because of its reputation for murder. My crews were instructed to hire security during the months of setup. We could not afford to lose anything to theft or vandalism, and certainly, we wanted no loss of life.

The sheer size of our caravan, and the raising of the huge masts in Valhalla, ignited a surge of excitement and expectation in the churches of Cape Town. They began praying for a great revival in the city. 5,000 volunteers came to be trained as counselors to those responding to the invitations. 1,500 more came to be trained as ushers and stewards.

Meanwhile, I had accepted an invitation to speak at the Full Gospel Businessmen's Fellowship International Conference in Singapore. Anni, with her smart new hairstyle, agreed to make the trip with me. We would also visit my sister Felicitas and her family in India on our return.

Before leaving, I met with Peter van den Berg. He had concerns over the composition of the fabric that covered our big tent. It had ripped and torn in several places. Repairs were in motion, but he feared that something was fundamentally wrong with the entire fabrication process. He had scheduled a meeting with Dow Corning in the USA to discuss it. They were working on the cutting edge of this type of tension fabric construction and would look at samples of our tent top. And so we flew our separate ways as the erection process continued in Cape Town.

The meeting in Singapore was held at the Grand Hyatt Hotel. It had a ballroom seating 5,000 or more. We had a blessed time of fellowship with these believers. After the meeting local pastors nearly mobbed me. They had heard good reports about CfaN. They were so blessed by the preaching, they begged me to return to Singapore for a crusade in a large stadium that would hold 80,000. They were sure we could fill it. This surprised me. I promised them that we would return as soon as possible.

The conference meetings at the Mandarin Hotel had been attended by the Anglican bishop of Singapore. His official name and title was The Right Reverend Dr. Moses Tay Leng Kong. He invited me to call him Bishop Tay, and I was relieved to do so. He was among the group of pastors who had officially invited me to return for a stadium crusade. Privately, he asked if I would come speak at his cathedral before leaving town.

This invitation surprised me. It is one thing to preach in a secular stadium. It is another to preach in the official edifice of the Church of England. I had come a long way from the nondescript meeting rooms I had known as a Pentecostal child. I was certain that no Lutheran bishop in Germany would have extended Bishop Tay's offer to me. He asked me to pray for the sick after preaching. After seeing that kind of ministry in the Full Gospel Businessmen's meeting he wanted the same for his congregation.

I accepted his invitation. On Sunday morning the people gathered in a large and beautiful stone cathedral. I had never preached with such a tower of stained glass looming behind me. At the end of my sermon I invited the sick to come forward and told them that, according to Scripture, I would lay my hands on them and pray for healing. As I began to do so, people began to fall to the floor. It reminded me of the scene in Gaborone. Then I noticed that Bishop Tay was following my example. He also was laying his hands on the sick and they, too, were falling to the floor. This was another surprise for me.

*Lord,* I asked, *can this be? He is a highly religious Anglican. Do You mind?*

The Lord said to me, *I don't mind. The anointing breaks the yoke.*[75] *I don't mind.*

This was a great lesson for me, and it changed my outlook. I opened my mind more to God's surprising ways. I saw that labels mean nothing with Him. It is the content of the bottle that counts.

Anni and I flew on to Calcutta. My sister, Felicitas, worked there as a surgical nurse in Mark Buntain's hospital. She and her husband, Dr. Ron Shaw had set up a hall for a series of meetings.

Upon our arrival she warned me that Calcutta is known as the graveyard for great evangelists. I replied, "No worry, Sis. It doesn't apply to me, I'm not a great evangelist."

She laughed and told me that mass evangelism simply did not work here the way it did in Africa. All of that may have been true, but the Holy Spirit works the same in every culture. We were delighted to see nearly 4,000 decisions for Christ in those meetings. What a precious harvest. I encouraged the new believers to depend upon the Holy Spirit and to rid themselves of idolatry. They responded by cutting off occultist bracelets and charms from their necklaces, arms, legs, and waistbands. We made a great bonfire and burned them. We were told that no other evangelist in Calcutta had challenged the people to do such a thing. We saw miraculous healings of the blind and lame. Hallelujah!

As I ministered on May 5, the Lord spoke to me: *The tent is destroyed.* It was stated as a matter of fact. Pure and simple. That night I told Anni what the Lord had said.

"What do you think has happened?"

"I do not know, but I am worried."

"Of course you are worried."

"No, I am not worried about the tent. That's what worries me. I should be worried about it, but I'm not. I feel nothing but peace."

Two days later the news arrived from Cape Town. On Saturday, May 5, the tent erection was complete. That afternoon a storm of wind and rain descended. A few rips appeared in the fabric. They had been quickly repaired.

As evening fell the wind increased. Gerhard Ganske, who was in charge of the tent's anchor system, circled the tent checking the security of the cement reinforced anchors. Everything held securely.

Milton Kasselman, the chief electrician, went inside the tent. It held the wind at bay. Overhead the twelve masts swayed slightly, as they should. He checked the mounted flood lamps and the speaker towers. All was well.

Tent master, Kobus de Lange, and his assistant, Horst Kosanke, checked the miles of cables that counterbalanced all the forces of wind and gravity. They were doing their job. He ordered the crew back to their quarters to sleep and wait out the storm.

Suddenly, at 4 a.m., they were awakened by the sound of ripping fabric. As they rushed outside, winds were ripping the tent to shreds. It was not a hurricane. It was not even a wind strong enough to cause normal alarm. The damage they were seeing seemed supernatural, as if evil demonic forces in the wind were violently attacking the structure. They watched helplessly as pieces came loose and flew across the surrounding city of Cape Town. By 9:30 a.m. only a few strands of fabric remained. All of the steel and cable structure remained unhurt. It looked like a huge skeleton with no skin or meat remaining on the bones.

Some of the crew were reduced to uncontrolled weeping. Five years of focused labor was destroyed in five hours. The atmosphere became like being at a funeral. That Sunday morning churches across Cape Town mourned the loss. Their hopes had been raised so high only to be dashed to pieces by the demonic wind. Shreds of the world's largest tent became collectors items for the residents of Cape Town. They were found scattered for miles downwind of the tent site.

Curiosity seekers came to the sports field to see the destruction. Some laughed at the calamity. They stood in the high-rise balconies and on bridges and other vantage points from which to view it. Christians gathered on the grounds, weeping, falling to their knees beneath the steel structure, praying. News media made the story front page all that day and the next.

I told my crew chief that God had given me a great peace about this event. He was to encourage the crew and to clean up the site and wait for my return.

My peace remained as we boarded a flight that took us to Australia before returning to South Africa. In peace, I went to sleep in my window seat. It must have been around midnight that I awakened. As I looked out the window all I could see was the lights of a great city. A vast, huge city stretching like a galaxy of stars to the horizon. The Lord spoke in my heart: *I want you to preach the gospel there.*

My pulse quickened. A city this size would certainly produce a lot of listeners hungry for the gospel. *Yes, Lord,* I thought. *But my geography is not so good. What city is it?*

As if to answer my question, the captain came on the speaker system: "Ladies and gentleman, we are now flying over the city of Jakarta, Indonesia."

I grabbed a notebook and wrote the name down. Then I heard the Lord speak again in my spirit: *I want you to tithe a portion of your campaigns beyond the borders of Africa.* This became a new policy for CfaN. When we landed in South Africa I immediately sent John Fergusson to Jakarta to inquire with pastors about organizing a crusade there.

Meanwhile, the crusade committee from Cape Town had already decided that we should go ahead with the meetings. While meeting in emergency session immediately after the event, they had received a prophecy from one of their members, the wife of Pastor Dave Onions. "My glory shall be the canopy that covers the people, and the praises of My people shall be the pillars."

Bolstered by the words of this prophecy the committee immediately voted to proceed with the campaign. This decision would require a weather miracle. May weather in Cape Town is notoriously wet. The churches banded together in a vast network of prayer for good weather. We would seat people under the stars, using the floodlights and speakers as designed for the tent.

As I returned to my office I found telephone calls, telegrams, cards, and letters from around the world waiting for me. The news of the disaster had gone as far as the news of the big tent. Most of the response was overwhelmingly encouraging. But a large minority of naysayers had their day.

From the beginning I had dealt with the normal array of critics. Many people criticized the size of the tent. They said it wasn't practical. It was too risky. The project ate money like a gambling machine. It was not good stewardship. The entire endeavor was ego driven.

With this disaster, those people had much more to say. "This is God's judgment on you." "You're out of the will of God." "You've moved out from under the umbrella of divine protection." "There is sin in your camp." The one that hit the lowest came from a dear Pentecostal sister back in Germany. This lady had supported our work faithfully and substantially over the years. She wrote to tell me that she had seen pictures of the tent dedication in Soweto. The pictures showed that Anni had cut her hair. This sin, she said, had led to this disaster. She pledged that she would no longer send money to CfaN. She would only pray for our repentance. I must confess, that fiery dart of the Enemy got through my armor for a few days.

Even some of my co-workers lost heart. They felt that we'd been overcome by the Enemy. This was one of our darkest days. A rumor circulated that Muslims from Valhalla had marched around our tent site and had called down a curse on it. No one could offer me proof, and I gave no credence to this report. I find that when people believe an urban legend like this, it is because they desperately want to believe it. They have lost sight of their God and Savior and His unlimited power and have looked at the wind and the waves. Like Peter, who started out so well in his walk on water, he began to sink. Some of our people sank right here.

But here is the greater story of the Cape Town disaster. It was not a disaster at all! It was our greatest triumph! First, God held the weather at bay for a full three weeks. Local weathercasters described it as an "Indian summer." Furthermore, the destruction of our canopy had made us a household word in Cape Town. The media had trumpeted our story to everyone. Incredible stories of believers taking pieces of our canopy and laying it on sick people and seeing them healed were told. Believers and sinners came by the droves to our meetings.

Our first meeting drew a crowd of 25,000. By the third night the crowd reached 40,000. By the second Sunday we saw 60,000 in attendance. On the final night, 75,000 filled the field. At this point everyone began to see that the tent had never been big enough to hold the crowd God intended to attract in Cape Town.

During this crusade the notorious district of Valhalla did not record a single crime. The police came to see what had hit their city. They saw criminals tossing guns and knives onto the platform in repentance. We turned truckloads

The tent-roof blown off by a hurricane did not hinder us to continue.

of stolen material over to them for restitution. Miracles happened every day. At times the platform was littered with empty wheelchairs, discarded crutches, and canes. White citizens of Cape Town, who had never set foot in Valhalla out of fear, came to see it transformed by the gospel.

A Muslim couple came to the meeting. They wanted me to bless them on their pilgrimage to Mecca. After hearing the gospel, they responded to the invitation to meet Jesus. The encounter changed them so drastically that they testified that they were not going to Mecca but Jerusalem. Many Muslims were among those who made decisions for Christ in these meetings.

By the final night we had counted 29,000 conversions to Christ. Several churches were pioneered during the campaign follow-up. In other local congregations, pastors were kept busy for weeks baptizing new believers. Hallelujah! Cape Town was impacted as never before.

WE FINISHED OUR CAMPAIGN SEASON of 1984 in Harare, Zimbabwe. Without the big tent we were forced to hold open-air meetings again in Rufaro Stadium. 38 denominations cooperated in this meeting. As I met with the local pastors I was confronted with my South African organization. Apartheid was on the minds of everyone. How could I tie the message of the gospel with such an evil system, they wanted to know.

I emphasized that I was a German who had been called by God as a young man to Johannesburg. I had not chosen apartheid. It had been an unwelcome surprise to me, a system that I resisted in every way possible. My platform and my campaigns were integrated. In securing Harare's Rufaro Stadium, where the liberation of Zimbabwe from its former white Rhodesian Government had been celebrated, government officials grilled me on CfaN's South African connection. CfaN was being painted with a wrong brush. More and more my South African address was putting me on the defensive.

Behind the scenes, I began to discuss the problem with Peter van den Berg. In our scouting trips across Africa, I had been forced to use my German passport, and Peter, his Zimbabwean passport. To make matters worse, in each of these countries we began to see the signs that we would attract much larger crowds than any we had yet seen. Knowing this made the South African handicap almost unbearable for me.

I asked the Lord if He was indicating that our time in South Africa was over. I knew one thing for sure. If I pulled CfaN out of South Africa I would lose my largest financial partner. This meeting in Rufaro Stadium was underwritten primarily by white South African money. If I made that fact public knowledge, however, I might be looking at a very empty stadium the next day.

In one of our early meetings in Rufaro Stadium, an elderly lady came forward for prayer. She was blind and walked with great difficulty. When hands were laid on her she felt sudden warmth and then blinked her eyes. She thought she saw stars in the distance. Suddenly they grew into our stadium lights. She could see clearly! I could not keep that lady from rushing me on the platform and demanding to tell the people what had happened to her. It electrified the crowd.

On the final weekend a fine drizzle began that turned into a downpour. Some of the people scrambled for cover, including me. When I looked to the field, however, most of the people had remained in their places.

The campaign committee huddled under umbrellas and suggested that we close the meeting. They would announce one more meeting to be held in the afternoon tomorrow, hoping for better weather. But out of the rain a chant began to come to my ears: "We want the gospel." Over and over they repeated it.

This sound in my ears could not be ignored. The lesson of Uganda came to mind. If these people were that hungry to hear another sermon, I was going to deliver it. I preached a message on the baptism of the Holy Spirit. Many received the gift that night and spoke in tongues in the pouring rain. It was a sound like I have never heard. Pouring rain that could not drown the fire of the Holy Spirit. The words of the Cape Town prophecy returned to my mind, "My glory shall be the canopy that covers the people, and the praises of My people shall be the pillars."

We saw a total of 31,000 decisions for Christ in Harare. An even bigger harvest than in Cape Town! I called the former Rhodesian, Peter van den Berg, and told him about our results.

"Do you realize that those figures make this the greatest year of harvest CfaN has ever known?" he said. "150,000 souls have come into the kingdom this year!"

"Hallelujah!" I shouted.

I told him that I felt sure the time had come for us to concentrate our campaigns further to the north in Africa. We had given South Africa more than its share of campaigns. Launching the Fire Conference next year in Harare seemed an idea ordained of God. We discussed the possibility of taking CfaN out of South Africa. Where would we go? There were two places in my mind – Kenya because it was still in Africa, yet centrally located, and Germany, because it was where I began and where our second-largest body of support came from. We left the discussion at that point.

Tommy Saaiden – our Soloist

Peter told me he had located another company that would manufacture a tent top for us that would not blow apart in a storm. It was a deal he could broker through a company in England. However, our insurance settlement was becoming locked up in court. He told me with a worried look in his eye that it appeared it could take many years to settle.

At this time I found that our team was in a general state of unbelief. I wanted to encourage them.

"I don't know what to do," I said. "I simply know that I'm not worried about the tent."

From the looks on their faces they must have thought I had lost touch with reality. But the opposite was true. Looking back in time, I was amazed to see how God had brought us through many financial trials. Sometimes it felt as if a mouse carried an elephant. That was no problem with God. I wished the elephant a happy ride. As I said goodbye to my weary team, I said, "If you can't trust God today, trust me, and I will trust Him."

With that, I caught a flight to America. On the long trip I had a new surge of excitement in my soul. I reflected again on Kenneth Copeland's prophecy that I would see a million souls won in a day. A million? It still seemed unthinkable. But if we were to see a million decisions in one crowd, the entire crowd would have to exceed that number considerably. Not everyone responded in a meeting. To accomplish it, many things about the way we ran a campaign would have to change. I began to feel sure that one of those changes involved moving CfaN from South Africa. The vision of the blood-washed Africa was coming closer to reality. Unfortunately, with so many powerful thoughts running through my head, I was too excited to sleep on the intercontinental flight.

I had no sooner landed at the Dallas-Ft. Worth Airport than I was whisked away to a pastors' conference hosted by Kenneth Copeland, already in progress. They seated me on the front row, and Kenneth greeted me. The TV cameras turned my way, and I was on the spot. This was not good. As he preached I was so hammered by jet lag that I pinched myself black and blue to keep my eyes open. It was sheer torment.

After the meeting Kenneth and Gloria invited me to join them at a nice restaurant for dinner. I was too far gone to say no. Somehow I managed to keep moving and not fall prostrate. At dinner Kenneth told me he had heard about the tent. He asked me to tell him what happened. I told him how the fabric had failed in the wind. We had discovered that it had a design flaw. An insurance settlement was tied up in court. It would be years before we saw the verdict. In the meantime, Peter van den Berg had found a new fabric through a company in England that would hold in a hurricane.

"How much will it cost?"

"$800,000."

"The Lord has told me to give you what you need. I am giving you $800,000. Go buy a new top for the tent."

I was too stunned and too jet lagged to reply at first. "When God tells me to give, I get excited. He's telling me to plant a seed in good soil with CfaN. My faith puts the seed in the ground where God directs. The harvest belongs to the Lord. And let me tell you, His harvest will sweep my little financial troubles away like so much chaff on the wind. Hallelujah! Praise God."

It did my heart good to hear this man of faith. "I believe that too," I said.

When I finally closed my eyes that night my happiness and exhaustion were complete and total. I felt like a body surfer picked up by a tsunami. As I drifted into fitful sleep, I heard my own voice speaking to Anni when we were in Singapore, "I am not worried about the tent. That's what worries me. I should be worried about it, but I'm not. I feel nothing but peace."

# Chapter 26

THE SCHEDULE FOR COMPLETING our new tent was set, thanks to the generous check from Kenneth Copeland. It allowed us to plan beyond 1985. The new canopy would be delivered and tested in time to erect both tents side by side in Harare. The big tent for the main meetings; the smaller yellow tent for counseling and follow-up. The Harare Sheraton and Conference Center would house our Fire Conference for evangelists with an auditorium seating 4,500.

In the meantime, we entered the new year of 1985 without the big tent. Our campaigns for that year were scheduled with a new emphasis in mind. We were deliberately heading north from South Africa, targeting the rest of the continent. Meetings were scheduled for Zambia, Democratic Republic of Congo, Ghana, and our first "tithed" campaign in Singapore, Malaysia.

As these events were in motion, planning for the Fire Conference continued to require time and energy from our co-workers. It was a challenge to select the right 1,000 evangelists to attend. There was transportation, parking, food, lodging, and other details to be arranged. Special speakers were to be booked. There was crowd control, seating, shelter, emergency facilities, toilet facilities, and ministry product placement. We formed a special task force at CfaN that began full-time preparation for Harare under the leadership of Chris Lodewyk. Their work would continue for more than a year and extend right through the conference itself. In this gathering of evangelists at the Sheraton, I sensed a great momentum would be achieved. The gospel would move from addition to multiplication. I sensed that my effort would be multiplied through the lives of many others, and they would catch fire with the unlimited power of the Holy Ghost.

"Number one on the invitation list," I said to the task force, "is a young man named David. He would be around 25 now. He was a 17-year-old Venda boy who ran into my headlights in a field in the Transvaal eight years ago. He wanted to receive the Holy Spirit. And did he ever receive! He went home, and God performed miracles of healing through him. Whole villages were brought to Christ. Find him. I want to sponsor him to this first Fire Conference. We'll put him up first class in the Sheraton and pay all of his expenses. I believe we'll see great things from him in the future."

This idea of helping evangelists enlarge their vision was overflowing in my heart. We eventually completed our list of 1,000 sponsored candidates. Following that milestone, I had to find sponsors who would share my vision and take up the cost of these 1,000 evangelists. The Lord knew who they were. All the funds were in His pockets.

A few weeks later my co-workers approached me sadly. They had located David. It was not what I had hoped for. He had become embittered by disappointments, they said. There had been conflicts with other ministers, betrayals, hypocrisies. He had been unable to adjust to these hard realities and had left his life of ministry. He had lost himself in drink, and now hid in the chaotic slums of Soweto. Those who had seen him last, said he had cursed God and wanted nothing to do with the gospel of Jesus Christ.

I was crushed to hear this news. Lord, I prayed, *did I wait too long to reach out to that boy? Was there something more I could have done?*

With an ache in my heart, I took a personal warning from David's fall. No matter how the power of God has been demonstrated in our lives, we can choose to walk away. Let him who thinks he stands take heed that he does not fall,[76] the Scripture says.

A fall like this is, no doubt, a process. It must be like a frog in a kettle of water heated slowly to the boiling point. We are slowly desensitized to the very thing that is killing us. Many things can insulate us from God's love. The cares of life can choke the Word and make it unfruitful.[77] Jesus warned of this in a parable. For someone like David there must have been failures, disappointments, setbacks, trials, tests, temptations, discouragements – these come to all of us in ministry. But we must choose, by faith, every day to take up our cross and follow Him. If not, one day any of us could find ourselves like the Prodigal Son,[78] spiritually bankrupt, living in our own pigpen, wondering how we got there.

I got in my car and drove across the finely manicured suburbs of Witfield, on through the high-rise glory of Johannesburg, and into the filthy backstreets of Soweto. I was just driving. Looking for David. Not that I expected to find him. That would be like finding the proverbial needle in the haystack. Still I drove, and as I drove, night fell.

Around me hundreds of shebeens – illegal liquor stores – opened for business. The raucous sounds of drunken laughter and arguing filled the air. The pounding bass beat of rock music blared across the darkness.

I thought to myself, *What would I say if David suddenly appeared in the beams of my headlights again? Staggering, drunk. Would I even know him? How would I respond?*

My answer came from a surge of divine compassion in my heart. I knew that I would leap from the car and run to him, putting my arms around him. I would assure him that the love of God is the same today as it was on that dark night in 1977 when he had run into my headlights in the Transvaal. He could begin again. Jesus stood at his heart's door, knocking. All he had to do was open the door again, and He would come in and have a fine supper with him.[79] I would tell him that Jesus' way of dealing with failed preachers is to invite them to a meal.

If he gave me enough time, I would encourage him with the story of Peter who had returned to the Sea of Galilee to take up fishing after denying three times that he knew the Lord on the night of His crucifixion. Even Jesus' resurrection from the grave and appearances to His disciples had not erased his shame. For this failure, Jesus didn't scold Peter, didn't condemn him – He went and found him.

He came along the shore and filled Peter's nets with fish so he would remember the Lord's original call, *Follow Me, and I will make you fishers of men.*[80] Then He cooked him a meal and broke bread with him. As they were eating, Jesus asked him three times if he loved Him. Three questions for the man who had made three denials. Peter got the point. The breaking of Peter's heart was a good and necessary thing. It helped him to finally admit the truth; his love for the Lord was not worthy to be compared to the love Christ had shown him. That was the beginning and end of it. That confession qualified the Big Fisherman to return to the ministry.

"Feed My sheep," Jesus said.

I'm so glad He did not say, "Your character is too weak for the ministry, Peter." I'm so glad He did not say, "Since you chose to go back to fishing instead of fishing for men, now I can no longer use you." No, He did not say that.

Some would use the words of Jesus in Luke 9:62 to condemn David, or Peter, for his failure: *No man, having put his hand to the plough, and looking back, is fit for the kingdom of God.*[81] They would tell him that he must now take a back seat on the bus to heaven and never again preach the word of the gospel. But that is not what Jesus taught. For the honest listener He was demonstrating that no human being is ever fit for the kingdom of God. No one has ever taken up his cross without having second thoughts, without faltering, wavering, looking back. There was only One who fulfilled the requirements perfectly, and it is in Him that we overcome.

"Come back and feed His sheep," I'd say to David. "By the way, would you let me sponsor you to the Harare Fire Conference next year?"

Sadly, I never got the chance to say that. I have never seen David again.

I BEGAN SPEAKING IN CHURCHES and conferences across South Africa, telling about the coming Fire Conference. David's story became a story I would tell in those meetings, explaining to the people the urgency I felt to serve my fellow evangelists. People began applying to come to the conference. Others began recommending those who should attend. And partners began to sponsor the 1,000 evangelists we had targeted for this wonderful service.

In the town of Pietermaritzburg in Natal Province, I preached one Sunday. As I was speaking, a man entered the building late and sat on the back row. I recognized him immediately. It was Richard Ngidi.

My heart leapt at the thought that he might want to come to the Fire Conference. I would, of course, sponsor him. But that is not why he had come. After the service closed he approached me hesitantly. I could see that he was uneasy. We had unfinished business from the time he had failed to show up for the Bushbuckridge meetings. In the eight years that followed, he had offered neither explanation nor apology. No matter. I was ready to forgive him and see our relationship restored.

I hugged him and we greeted each other as old friends. Then he said to me, "Is it true that you spoke to 80,000 in Cape Town in one service?"

"No," I replied, "I'm sure it was only 75,000."

"Oh," he said, nodding. "Now I know what a mistake I have made."

"What mistake, Richard?"

"Oh, no," he said, looking away. "This is between God and me."

He bowed his head and walked away.

I knew what he meant. He had told Michael Kolisang, "When I leave, Bonnke is finished." From the evidence of the crowd in Cape Town, obviously God was not finished with me. Therefore, Bonnke was not finished.

I watched him move slowly toward the door, unsteady on his feet. I felt such sadness. I wanted to find some way to go back to the purity of our first meeting, our first embrace, and our early meetings when we had ministered together. I remembered the power of his example to me at the beginning. I had so looked up to him in the healing ministry. But something had entered his mind that had driven us apart. He had seen me as dependant on him, when in truth, I was dependent on God.

I took it as another warning to myself. Never should I see myself above another servant of God. What God had done through me, He could do through anyone, ten times over. I didn't ever want to forget that.

Weeks later, I stood at Richard's casket, looking down at the quiet flesh that had once glowed with a reckless faith. He had died at age 66 of complications from diabetes, refusing to see a doctor to the very end. He was a giant in the kingdom of God. Yet there were mysteries about him that I will not understand this side of heaven. I greatly mourned my Zulu friend and fellow servant, and comforted myself knowing that his pain was over, and he was now with the Lord.

BENSON IDAHOSA OF NIGERIA asked me to meet with him. This was a man with a tremendous international reputation for evangelism. Peter van den Berg joined me, and we flew from Witfield to Benin City. On the trip we discussed this historic meeting. Benson represented a huge untapped mission field in Africa. In our push from Cape Town to Cairo, CfaN would surely have to make a major investment in his homeland of Nigeria. 120 million souls lived there. One in four persons on the African continent was Nigerian. Half of their population was Muslim. The other half was split between ancestor wor-

Archbishop Idahosa and I in a combined crusade

ship and Christianity if the statistics are correct. Already, I had been seeking the Lord for an approach to this great nation. I was eager to hear what Benson had to say.

He had been born to a pagan family in Benin City in 1938. Abandoned by his family he had converted to Christ as a young man. Immediately, miracles of healing had happened as he prayed for the sick. Some had been raised from the dead. He had educated himself extensively and had risen to become bishop of 2,000 churches that he planted across Nigeria. He had conducted crusades in 123 nations under the motto: "Evangelism, our supreme task." I was excited to meet a fellow evangelist who had accomplished so much.

When we arrived Benson wasted no time getting to his point. "In four weeks from today I have scheduled a one-week crusade to be held in Ibadan. It is the third largest city in Nigeria, behind Lagos and Kano. I have secured Olubadan

Stadium, which will hold a very large crowd. It is located in the heart of the city surrounded by neighborhoods with over 4 million people. All of this is good. But, I have never done well in this city. The population is a Muslim majority. I am afraid if I go there alone I may meet violence. I could suffer from the truth of that old proverb, *A prophet is not without honor except in his own country.*[82] As I was praying about this the Lord put your name before me. Would you join me in this crusade?"

In my heart I asked the Lord for the answer. Benson was an evangelist like me, but I knew enough about him to know that I disagreed with his general approach. I preached the gospel of salvation first. Miracles of healing followed that preaching. Benson conducted healing ministry first, then preached the message of the gospel. For all of my years in ministry I had been critical of this approach. *Lord, would You smile on this joint effort?*

To my mind came the lesson I had learned in Perth, Australia. My theology of healing had been too small for God's miracle for Mrs. McKelt. Likewise, my methodology might be too small to accommodate a great blessing awaiting us in this campaign. Though our methods differed, Benson and I were brothers in wanting to see Africa won for Christ. I felt the Holy Spirit rising up in my heart to say yes. That was enough. Without further debate, I agreed to join him.

Peter began to immediately consult with Benson's co-workers concerning how we would accomplish such a gigantic effort with only four weeks of preparation. Of course, I left those details to Peter. My "mechanic" had more than proven himself by this time.

On the flight back to Witfield I asked him what our costs would be. "100,000 dollars," he said. I rocked back in my seat. "We don't have that much."

"I know."

"But I felt the Spirit urging me to do this. So let's go full speed ahead and plan with what is in God's pockets, not our own."

A few days later back at Witfield, I received a phone call from a California businessman, Mr. Barry Hon. Later we became the best of friends and close partners in the harvest of souls. I had met him on one of my earlier trips to America. He said that the Lord had told him I needed money. He was sending me a check for $40,000. I thanked him for listening to the Lord. To me, this was confirmation that I had heard the Spirit correctly about Ibadan and the joint meetings with Benson Idahosa.

Four weeks later our plane touched down at the Ibadan Airport. When I emerged with my team to the tarmac I was not prepared for the welcome. A fleet of Nigerian military vehicles and police motorcycles waited beside a Mercedes automobile, ready to escort us across town. As we traveled through the primitive streets of this major city, the poverty was amazing. I was told that only a third of the houses had running water. Only half had electricity.

In spite of their bitter poverty, the people were still very friendly. They smiled and waved as our motorcade passed. This was in sharp contrast to what I had observed in Soweto. Under apartheid, people in poverty were constantly reminded that their lack was due to the oppression of the white minority. Bitterness showed in their countenances. In Nigeria, poverty seemed to be taken as a matter of course, and the contrast between rich and poor did not seem to ignite the same resentments.

At the hotel, Benson met us as we prepared for the first meeting. He asked that I observe local custom and wear a full-length Nigerian robe. This would help identify me with the local people. For the first time in my ministry, I did so. It was quite colorful. "I will call it my 'garment of praise,'" I said.

Benson's organization had publicized well. When I walked onto the platform that night I was stunned. The size of the crowd exceeded anything I had ever seen. I had no way of estimating how many had come. All of the stadium stands were filled but so was much of the main soccer field. No one on the field was sitting. They were standing and crowding forward toward the stage. All the normal indicators of crowd size were not present here. It was exhilarating to know that they had come for one reason – to hear the gospel.

When I preached, occasionally a roar would erupt in a section of the crowd. Someone in that section had been healed. The noise of their excitement over-powered the speaker system at times. A paralytic started walking. He leaped to the platform, and I gave him the microphone to tell what had happened. Another man, blind for 25 years, regained his sight. A man deaf for seven years heard and was able to repeat a few words into the microphone.

Night after night, Benson and I alternated preaching. Each night the crowds grew. In the hotel I purchased a local paper. "Never in the history of the Nigerian Federation have people gathered in such large numbers ... Not even the visit of Queen Elizabeth of Great Britain ... or the historic Independence Day, or any political rally ..." I praised God out loud as I read this account. Crowds had been so large; traffic cops were unable to control the congestion. Pedestrians and cars blocked every intersection for two miles around the stadium.

One local newsman estimated the largest crowd to be a half million. I had Peter do his own method of counting. He said that the best calculation he could make was 250,000. It was more than I could wrap my mind around. I was deeply moved by CfaN's first Nigerian experience, and I knew that it would not be the last. In my heart the Holy Spirit whispered these words; *The day of reaping with a sickle is past. The time for the combine harvester has come.*

OUR NEXT CRUSADE was a return to Lusaka, Zambia. Without the big tent we still had a convoy of equipment to transport, plus the yellow tent. My crew rolled out with seven semi-trucks and three passenger vehicles. They set up at the Matero Soccer stadium.

Upon our arrival I was interviewed by a local television reporter. After the interview he confided that he had been saved in the yellow 10,000-seat tent in 1981. His wife had been healed of a plague of abscesses, which no doctor had been able to cure. In the same crusade, his boss had received the Lord. Beyond that, this television reporter and his boss had the effect of providing a public relations firm to CfaN at no additional cost! Our evangelistic story was being trumpeted as legitimate news across equatorial Africa.

It did my heart good to see that the fruit of our first campaign had remained and flourished. Hundreds of others came to us during the meetings to testify that they were continuing with the life in Christ they had begun in 1981. The conversions were lasting.

Our crowds during the week grew to 20,000. On weekends we saw 40,000 in the stadium. In the yellow tent we registered 18,000 decisions for Christ in Lusaka. Many healings manifested among the people.

Zambian National Television sent a crew to produce a documentary of our success. The head of the documentary crew was a young man named Frederick Chiluba. He was a believer, and our counselors led him into the experience of the baptism of the Holy Spirit. Little did we know that we were ministering to the future president of this country. Five years later, when he came to power in a landslide election, he declared Zambia a Christian nation. Hallelujah! As political correctness drives Christian morality from the public square in the west, Zambia is moving in the opposite direction. What a blessing to have been a part of it!

From Zambia our trucks rolled for the first time across the border to Zaire, which had been known as the Belgian Congo until 1960. 40 million souls lived there in the tropical heart of the continent. This is the nation that had been called "darkest Africa" for its endless primitive jungles stretching across the equator. Famous missionaries had come here: Livingstone, Stanley, C. T. Studd, and many others.

Since its independence from Belgium, it had been a troubled land, red with the blood of martyrs. When self-rule began, chaos descended. 31 missionaries were slaughtered, along with hundreds of native pastors, and thousands of precious believers. As our trucks entered the city of Lubumbashi, they saw bullet-riddled buildings burned to the ground. The scars of the old civil conflict were still visible.

As the trucks rolled on, the convoy was mobbed by hordes of children. A population boom was in process in Zaire, and these children were everywhere – and unsupervised. The situation was dangerous and annoying. At the Mobutu Soccer Stadium the team had to guard every piece of equipment night and day to keep it from being vandalized or stolen by the wild children. They constantly heckled and harassed the team. Dirt and dust were constantly kicked up, and occasionally a rock was thrown.

With these reports coming to me, I didn't know what to expect. But on the first night I looked out at a crowd of 70,000, most of them standing in front of the platform on the soccer field. But I also saw that this crowd was peppered with groups of young boys playing soccer. They screamed, shouted, fought, and ran back and forth paying no attention whatsoever to the meeting. No matter how I appealed to them and to the crowd to bring them to order, it couldn't be done.

I think I preached the shortest sermon in the history of CfaN. First, I asked for a show of hands for those who wanted to receive Jesus as Savior. 10,000 hands were raised. I did not have enough counselors to deal with them. Rather than invite them forward, I sent the counselors out to meet them in the crowd and register their decisions.

Then I asked for a show of hands for those who were sick and in need of prayer. I prayed a general prayer for healing and invited those who had been healed to come forward. This was a mistake. People surged forward in a rush. Many of the soccer boys came with them.

I remembered that Pope John Paul II had spoken in this stadium the week before we arrived. To me it seemed that the children were coming for a "blessing" from another "Holy Father." I doubted that they had received healing from my prayer. Some of them reached the platform and leaped onto it; they danced around, showing off for their friends, distracting from what we were doing.

Adults too, seemed out of control. The mob began to crush against the platform so violently that I saw people who were in danger of being trampled to death. We began to rescue the weakest victims, pulling them onto the platform. For a while the platform was chaos and in danger of collapse.

With a lot of effort we were able to restore order. I managed to locate a few who had been healed. I allowed them to give their testimonies, and then I closed the meeting. I was amazed that 10,000 hands were raised to receive Jesus. It was a mixed blessing. One I would never want to miss. But it was also a near disaster that I did not want to repeat.

In meetings with local authorities the next day I reluctantly allowed a row of policemen to establish a safety zone in front of the stage. They instilled some order in the stadium thereafter, and kept the people from injury as we continued.

A national television truck came to the stadium and broadcast three of our meetings live to millions across Zaire. Michael Kolisang and I both prayed for the sick. Two crippled children, a ten-year-old boy, and a nine-year-old girl were healed. The boy jumped up and down on the platform while his sister raced around demonstrating her joy at being able to run for the first time in her life. These images became indelible in the minds of those who attended, as well as those who watched via television.

In a land of great trouble, God brought forth an even greater grace. Each night we saw another 10,000 hands raised to receive Jesus. It hurt me deeply to know our counselors were not able to reach them all. We needed to retool ourselves to become the combine harvester the Lord was speaking to me about.

We learned much from this outing. There were crowd control issues, security issues, staging issues, counseling issues. Mistakes in judgment had been made because we had not properly studied the differences that awaited us in the Zairian city. The idea of training certain members of our team to be scouts came from this experience. In the future we would send them on the road to places where we were scheduled to hold meetings. They would carry a checklist of all the issues we had discovered, in order to make us better stewards, and to make us safer and more efficient.

As we packed to leave, my people seemed a bit rattled by their experience in Lubumbashi. We had become aware that the forces of evil were not neutral. They were out to destroy us before we could bring the light of the good news to regions steeped in darkness. At a team meeting, Peter van den Berg broke down emotionally during his delivery of a devotional. That was not like him. His voice choked up, and he asked, "We have been tested here, brothers and sisters. I ask you, are we – am I – prepared to sacrifice even my life in this cause?"

Before driving the convoy from the stadium, the crew held hands in a circle and prayed for wisdom, guidance, and safety. It was 9 a.m. on September 3, 1985. Within four hours, two of CfaN's best, Horst Kosanke and Milton Kasselman were dead.

I WAS SEARCHING FOR WORDS amid the scent of burned flesh and fuel. Their charred bodies lay beside me in two plastic bags in the back of the charter plane, mostly ashes and very little bone. They had been practically cremated in the accident. I would not return to Witfield without them, so I sat on the floor next to these two fine men who had paid the ultimate price to see a blood-washed Africa.

What would I say to their wives, Lydia and Jane? Or to their children, Rüdiger, Ingmar, Linda, and Riaan? In my mind I could see their faces as they waited for me back at Witfield. They would not be able to look me in the eyes. Not for very long, at least. Some part of them would want to blame me. Blame the vision that drove me. Blame the God who had given the vision, or to blindly blame themselves, blame the devil, blame anything that would allow their pain and their anger to find an adequate target.

What would I say to my co-workers? No matter what they had proclaimed publicly, I knew that deep in their hearts they wanted to believe that working for CfaN would provide perfect protection from such tragedies. That is a human desire. Something we all share. Now, that idea had been horribly shattered. How helpless death renders us when it comes for someone we love. How desperately we want to strike back. Death is the final enemy to be overcome by the Lamb of God. Until that day, preachers will always be asked to find words at a time like this.

"Horst, Milton, you served Him well," I said to their bodies. "Now you are face to face with Him. It looks like I still have a ways to go before I join you. But you have reminded me that I have no guarantee."

The drone of the plane's twin engines reminded me that with every revolution of the propellers I was being flung closer to the rendezvous I most dreaded in Witfield. I could speak to these corpses – but to the living? What could I say?

The accident had been a head-on collision with a fuel tanker. On the narrow and terribly maintained road in north Zambia, a fuel tanker had run onto the shoulder as it passed our group, stirring up a fog of horrible dust that obscured the next fuel truck coming behind it. In the temporary blindness, Horst, who was driving the third truck in our convoy, hit the trailing truck head-on. Both he and his cab mate, Milton Kasselman, were killed, and their bodies incinerated in the fiery explosion that followed.

Worse yet, Horst's son Rüdiger was in the truck following his dad. He had been seen running up the road toward the blazing inferno screaming, "Where's my dad?! Where's my dad?!" Later, he was seen crumpled beside a burning lake of spilled gasoline, tearing his shirt from his body, ripping it to shreds, wailing like an animal between spasms of grief and rage.

How much comfort would he receive if I told him the truth? "Your dad is with the Lord, Rüdiger." Like most statements of pure truth, we don't get it in the moment. Later, much later, when enough time has passed, it becomes something we can see as if through a darkened glass. It brings a measure of comfort. But nothing, nothing, nothing would ever bring Rüdiger's father back.

To be comforted requires more than a doctrinal statement. It is to see the Lord with Horst and Milton in those flames. It is to be with the Lord Himself in some mysterious way. In His presence, where all such questions no longer have meaning. Horst and Milton were there now. The rest of us were not. So, Lord, where are my words for these grieving families? All I heard in reply was the drone of the engines as they suddenly changed pitch and we began our descent to the airfield. I have never felt so bleak and alone.

Milton Kasselman and Horst Kosanke

To the families I brought home the bodies. I brought my tears, my embraces, my grief. And as I faced them I knew the answer to my question. There are no words of adequate comfort for the living. There is only one true Comforter. He is the Holy Spirit. His work is beyond mine and reaches like a surgeon to the inner workings of the human heart. Though, as a preacher, I always want to find just the right words. At such a time as this, the less said the better. I am instructed to weep with those who weep.[83]

But as the funeral service came to an end the Lord spoke a special word to my heart. There is a gap in the team. It needs to be filled. I opened my mouth and repeated what I had heard. "Who will step forward to fill this gap," I asked. "Is there someone the Lord has spoken to about this today?"

Immediately Horst's son Rüdiger leaped to his feet, both hands raised, tears streaming from his eyes. "I will," he said.

The gap was filled and the CfaN team moved forward to see a blood-washed Africa. Only our Lord is worthy of such a response.

ONE MONTH LATER I ENTERED ACCRA, the capital city of Ghana. We had scheduled a five-day campaign there. This was new territory for CfaN. Ghana lay beyond Nigeria on the western bulge of the continent. It boasted a mild climate and Atlantic beaches of fine white sand. A city drawing on an area of three and a half million people, Accra was among the more prosperous places in all of Africa.

Fresh from the fantastic response in Ibadan, Nigeria, I was hopeful to see something similar here. The culture of this region seemed more ready for the preaching of the gospel. But at the last minute we had been forced to switch our venue from a stadium to a racetrack. All of our advertising had been for the stadium. I feared disaster.

On the first night I looked at a crowd of only 20,000. But as usual, God drew His own crowd His own way. Several miracles of healing caught the attention of the city. By the final night, the crowd had swelled to 120,000. But I was completely blown away by the number of responses to the invitation. An incredible 70,000 decisions for Christ! My eyes were being lifted from the southern tip of Africa where I had spent so much time to an untold harvest waiting in other countries to the north.

Once again, in Ghana, I faced the barrage of questions about apartheid from the crusade organizers and local government. As I flew back to Witfield the Holy Spirit spoke clearly to me. Given the other difficulties of the year, the last thing I wanted to be for my co-workers was a bearer of bad news. I sought the Lord repeatedly, but His word was clear. I could do nothing but obey. I have learned that dealing with a difficult truth early on is better than delaying the inevitable and creating false expectations. False expectations can create a fountain of explosive pain if not dealt with in their infancy. I called my co-workers together as soon as I arrived to tell them about it. They would need some time to prepare, but as for me, I had no more time to delay this difficult announcement: "In one year CfaN will no longer be based in Witfield. Begin planning your decisions now. I will announce our new home when the Lord reveals it to me, but I have heard the Lord clearly say that South Africa is no longer our home. After the Fire Conference in Harare, we will not return here."

The reaction from my people was deep and wide. I do not think they were more devastated when the big tent blew apart. Some of them were sure that I had missed God's voice. The move was unthinkable for them. Insiders knew that 55 percent of our support came from South Africa. Apartheid was iso-lating South Africa in the international scene. If I left at this time, our loyal South African supporters would feel deserted in their hour of need. We would likely lose all of their offerings. Furthermore, many of my co-workers would not be able to make the move with us, no matter where we went. It was a challenge to manage these undercurrents of opinion and emotion in the days ahead. If I had not been sure that I had heard from God, I would not have held to my decision.

In my mind I could only contemplate two possible destinations for our new headquarters. Nairobi, Kenya or Frankfurt, Germany. Both places had good international airports. In my heart I wanted to move to Nairobi.

There were many reasons I did not want to base our ministry outside of Africa. It was the place of my evangelistic calling. Africa was the place in which I had overcome many obstacles and had seen breakthroughs. I loved it. It was the place where I would primarily minister in the future. Kenya was centrally located on the continent. However, it was subject to local African politics, and I must remember that in Africa things could change quickly. I consoled myself that if anything ever made Kenya too difficult I could always make the final move to Germany.

Germany was the only other place I could call home. I was a citizen there. A German identity would hold advantages for international travel, and the Frankfurt airport was unequalled in its flight choices to all of Africa and to the rest of the world.

Kenya or Germany, Lord? Kenya or Germany? While contemplating this question, I received a phone call from Johnnie Bosman, a minister friend from Bloemfontein, South Africa. He said that he felt God had given him a word for me. I asked him what it was. I will never forget his answer.

"You cannot jump a donga in two jumps. You must do it on one. I don't know what this means, Reinhard, but that's it."

I laughed out loud. "Oh, but I do know what it means. It means we go to Frankfurt!"

A donga is a deep chasm formed by soil-erosion through sudden heavy downpours during the rainy season. When hiking in the South African desert, a donga can present a real challenge. Its sides are too steep to climb. It is too deep to climb out of. The only solid option is to look to the other side, make a flying leap with all your strength, and try not to consider the consequences of falling short.

Having leapt across a few dongas in my day, I knew that I must not take halfway measures in my move from South Africa. We would not land in Kenya. We would leap all the way to Germany. The Lord had spoken.

I ENDED THE CAMPAIGN SEASON OF 1985 with meetings in the Singapore National Stadium. Among the local pastors was my new friend, Anglican Bishop Tay. We saw 50,000 people filled the stands with another 25,000 seated on the field. The response to the gospel was absolutely fantastic. This was my first "tithed" CfaN campaign outside of Africa, and the number of conversions told me that I had truly heard from the Lord concerning the tithing policy.

With the CfaN team working on future meetings I could take time to remain at home for a season. I enjoyed spending this time with my wife and children. We took time to do the things we had promised ourselves to do as a family, knowing that we would be leaving South Africa in less than a year. We visited amusement parks, water parks, and the Great Kruger National Park, where we could enjoy seeing the great variety of African wildlife in their natural setting. This was a time for remembering our trials and triumphs in this land, and for making final memories

# Chapter 27

THE FOOTBRIDGE HAD NO STABILIZERS, no supports to keep it from swaying. It stretched dangerously above a deep, rocky chasm. The walkway had been constructed of two cables with wooden slats strung between them, nothing more. There were not even handrails. To my way of thinking, this bridge was not a proper crossing. It was a deathtrap. I would not think of stepping onto it.

It was then I noticed a foolish soul attempting to cross. Like a high-wire amateur, the man held out his arms for balance. He crept, inch by inch, toward the other side, staring down at his trembling legs and feet. The wooden walkway tipped and swayed beneath him.

I rushed to the edge of the cliff and looked over. The bottom of the gorge could not be seen below. It was covered in morning mist. The fog moved like a river through this great gash in the earth.

I looked back at the man. He had made surprising progress, bringing himself nearly halfway to the other side. In my heart I wished him well, but suddenly, the cloud of fog rose on an updraft from the canyon. It engulfed the walkway just in front of the man. He was unaware of it. His eyes were trained on his own feet, and I knew as surely as I breathed that if that man stepped into the fog he would lose his balance. He would plunge to his death.

I rushed to the base of the bridge to see if I could rescue him. Arriving there, I could see that if I placed one foot on that rickety walkway it would totally destroy the man's equilibrium. I could only warn him.

"Sir, stop!" I shouted. "You must stop! The fog is in front of you."

The man turned and glanced back at me. In that moment, a shaft of pain stabbed through my soul. The man was my own brother, Jürgen. Ignoring my warning, he turned quickly and disappeared into the fog.

"Jürgen! Jürgen!" I cried.

In a moment, I heard a cry and then a terrible scream. It faded and echoed below as he fell. "Reinhaaaaard!"

I awoke. My sheets were drenched in sweat. My heart pounded in my chest. A thousand buried feelings rose up in my heart and washed over me. I wanted to weep aloud for Jürgen. I knew that he had wandered far from Jesus.

*Lord, what is this I have seen?*

The answer was clear and specific: *Jürgen is on the bridge to eternity. If you don't warn the godless I will require his blood at your hand.*

I objected. *Lord, this makes no sense. I know Jürgen is far from You, but how should I warn him when he knows the way of salvation as well as I do?*

*If you don't warn the godless I will require his blood at your hand.*

Why did I question God? I don't know. Perhaps I reacted like the Virgin Mary when the angel Gabriel announced that she would have a baby. It made no sense to her natural mind. She said, *Lord, how will this happen since I have never known a man?* [84] This is not a question of unbelief, but a question of how to obey.

Jürgen and his twin, Peter, were close in years and experience to me. We remember many things alike. They were nearly six and I was five when we were forced to flee for our lives at the end of World War II. Mother had prayed and read her Bible every day for guidance and protection. We had survived internment camp together.

When released from military duty our father became a Pentecostal pastor and soon we were joined. However, as the years moved on, all of my older brothers – Martin, Gerhard, Peter, and Jürgen – began to question the family faith. Even the stories of deliverance in the fall of East Prussia came into question.

They found other natural ways to explain our escape at war's end. It was not the hand of God, they said, it was chance, luck, coincidence, fate – anything but God. Even our father's healing from tuberculosis could be explained in terms of psychology and psychosomatic symptoms, they decided.

I know this is a familiar story. It happens in many families. Some children remain true to the faith while others go astray. The Bible repeats a sad phrase from the history of God's people: ... *and they forsook the Lord God of their fathers, which brought them out of the land of Egypt.*[85] This scripture came true before my eyes as Jürgen and I grew up. He and my older brothers forsook the way of the Lord. It was hurtful for me.

My younger sister, Felicitas, and I were part of that same family, and we held to the faith of our parents until it became completely real to us. What made the difference? There are probably as many explanations as there are families.

I know that in Germany after the war there was much blaming. Everything from the older generation came under criticism. Our father's claims to God's miraculous favor were placed in the same basket with death camp discoveries and other wartime Nazi horrors.

"Where was God?" my brothers asked. "Do we think the Bonnkes were His favorites? We were allowed to escape, while thousands of others died around us! What kind of God would do that?"

With questions like these, my brothers rejected faith and began to worship intellect and science. They were determined never to make the same mistakes as the older generation in Germany. They saw belief in the Lord as something easily manipulated, and they wrongly thought that by using their minds they would rise above it. They invested themselves in schooling as I began to invest myself in our father's church activities. Our paths went east and west.

In recent years while building CfaN, I had returned to Germany a number of times. My heart would hurt as I saw so many decisions for Christ around the world, yet my own brothers were still completely hardened to the gospel.

Jürgen's house was the place I least enjoyed to visit. He had married a woman who thought of herself as highly intelligent. To her way of thinking, Christian faith was a superstition to be ridiculed and attacked. She remained completely hostile to the gospel. When I visited, she would become aggressive, constantly challenging me to answer questions about the failure of the church. She attacked me with so much vigor that Jürgen was put to shame. I could tell that he loved me as a brother, even if he had chosen a different path. He could gently oppose me, but did not want the conflict to become as mean spirited as this. But she was so adamant he knew he would risk his marriage to oppose her. He suffered in silence.

When visiting each of my brothers' homes, I took *the soft answer turneth away wrath* [86] approach. I stopped talking of things that I knew would rile their emotions. Instead, I spoke in more general terms, and I spent more time and effort listening. Since we all shared the same gospel-filled childhood, I believed that I should win them with sugar, not confrontation. This approach had borne some fruit.

My brothers and I, including Jürgen and his wife, had been together for a family reunion two years earlier. During our stay, we sat each day at mealtime around a long table and shared conversation. On one occasion, Martin, the oldest and most respected brother, told a story. He said that the name Bonnke was all over the newspapers in Germany thanks to me. Reporters, he said, flew to my crusades around the world to take pictures of the vast crowds and report on what was happening. Their stories included some fantastic accounts of miraculous healings. This, he said, had created a problem for him. The name Bonnke was unusual in Germany, and people were now calling him on the telephone, mistaking him for me. He told this story to illustrate his point:

"As you know," he said, "my name is in the phone book in the Frankfurt area. Recently my phone rang."

"Dr. Bonnke?" It was a woman's voice.

"Yes, I am Dr. Bonnke."

"Dr. Bonnke, I am sick with cancer. Heal me! Would you please heal me?"

"Lady, I can't heal anyone, I'm not a medical doctor. I'm a chemist."

"Your name is Bonnke? B-o-n-n-k-e?"

"Yes, Bonnke."

She said, "You are Bonnke. I read about you in the newspaper. Heal me! Please!"

"The lady was desperate," he said. "No one has ever come to me like that. 'Lady,' I said, 'you want my brother Reinhard. Not me. But let me tell you something; he doesn't heal anybody either. Jesus does.'"

I could not contain my laughter. "Oh, Martin," I replied, "Jesus is the healer. You solved your problem by preaching the gospel. How unique is that?"

Everyone had a good-natured laugh. It was a moment to be treasured. My brother's story had broken through a lot of the old tension between us. It was good to know that my oldest brother was finding a way to acknowledge me in front of the others. Even if in a backhanded way.

Later, when I was alone with my brother Gerhard, he told me that the brothers had taken an informal vote. They had evaluated the lives of all the Bonnke offspring based on their impact on the world and they had agreed that Reinhard was the best horse in the family stable. What a generous thing for Gerhard to share this story with me.

I had not been prepared for such warmth and acceptance coming from my brothers. It meant so much to me. I had grown to expect that in their eyes I was still the *null* boy, the zero, the troublemaker – a usurper of sorts. For as long as I could remember, Martin, Gerhard, Jürgen, and Peter had ridiculed the things that now made me, in their own words, "the best horse in the family stable." I thanked Gerhard for sharing this information with me, and I must confess I had to wipe some moisture from my eyes. By this gesture I could see that the animosity between us had been replaced by real affection, even though we did not share the same living faith.

Family members can deal us the deepest wounds in this life. But they can also be instruments of great healing. It gave me hope that one day my brothers might take the next step and acknowledge that my life had impact because of Jesus Christ alone. I prayed that they once again would accept His Lordship.

After waking up from my dream about Jürgen, I presented my case to the Lord. *Lord, see the progress we have made with sugar, not with sermons? Why do You now tell me, "If you don't warn the godless I will require his blood at your hand?" What do You mean? Am I to preach him the sermon he has heard a thousand times? Will he learn anything new if I tell him again he is a sinner and bound for hell? He knows that You sent Jesus to die for his sins. I don't understand.*

The Lord whispered to my heart, *Write him a letter and tell him what you have seen in this dream.*

Yes! This sounded like God speaking to me. It was not an idea that would have occurred to my natural mind. *I will do it, Lord,* I said. I turned over and went back to sleep.

The next morning I woke up and started another day with the family. In all of the normal excitement of preparing to move to Germany, I forgot about my dream. Suddenly, in the middle of the day, I heard the Spirit speak clearly to me. *You did not write the letter. I will require his blood at your hands.*

I stopped everything. Excusing myself for a few minutes, I sat down and wrote that letter, telling Jürgen what I had seen in the dream. Then I sent it via airmail.

In the weeks to come I did not hear a reply. I left it in God's hands. I had obeyed. Now I went on with my life and eventually it left my mind.

WE STARTED THE 1986 CAMPAIGN SEASON with two meetings in Ghana, in the western bulge of Northern Africa. Again we saw record crowds and conversions as we had seen in our first visit. I wanted to do so much more. But frankly, my plate was too full with necessary activities. Preparations for the move to Germany continued at full speed, and the scope of the Harare Fire Conference and Campaign grew beyond expectations.

When I announced that we would hold the Fire Conference I was driven by a mighty passion. I wanted to fan the spark of evangelism in the hearts of the delegates into a roaring flame by the power of the Holy Spirit. I believed these men and women would return to their places in Africa and set entire nations alight with the name of Jesus. But my co-workers had never organized such a large and complicated event. They were getting a huge dose of "on-the-job training."

Plus, as always, there was the "Africa factor." Things do not work in Africa the way they work in the rest of the world. Contracts can become meaningless as circumstances suddenly change. Corruption and power maneuvers can take you by surprise. Each government asserts itself in unique ways that need to be understood and addressed. Wealth and poverty operate by different rules, and both sides must be brought to the table. Telephone, mail, package services, and roads are not reliable. CfaN was becoming quite good at dealing with these challenges but not in this context. Not with the full cost of moving to Germany, plus continuing our regular crusade schedule, plus planning the very first Fire Conference.

In mid-January I called my team together because I was told finances for the Fire Conference were alarmingly low. My director said I needed $400,000 within a week or we would have to cancel essential contracts. 22 hotels and a host of other suppliers needed promised down payments to move forward. Our big tent team needed to start immediately drilling the ground anchors for the installation, which would take six months. We simply didn't have the money. Word of our move to Germany had already sent our South African support into a free fall. New funds were not coming in to make up for the losses.

This is the mantle of leadership. Those who lead must be able to hear things like this without reacting and allowing fear to cloud their vision. We must remain in faith. Self-doubt and second thoughts can paralyze the work of the Lord, and this is one of Satan's greatest strategies. Yet, it is also true that faith does not wear rose-tinted glasses. It is realistic. So I listened to my co-workers as they painted one gloomy picture after another, each situation building like a dark cloud in a gathering storm. All of it added up to a mound of evidence that I had committed the ministry to the wrong challenge at the wrong time.

Was this true? I searched myself before God. The real question was, had I heard Him clearly or not? Perhaps I should postpone the Fire Conference until we had become established in Germany. But as I mulled these thoughts, the Spirit of God came over me in a flood of peace. This did not come from any change in circumstances. It came from an impression that I should not look at the impossibilities, but at the Savior Himself. Once again, I was to plan with what was in God's pockets, not my own. I looked at my director, and with absolutely no idea how it would happen, I said, "You will have your $400,000 on time." These words were prophetic.

Within days the money poured in, over and above operational costs. At the time of the crisis God had already moved on the hearts of those He would use to supply our need. If I had cancelled those contracts using natural forecasting, we would have missed this blessing.

Plans for the conference went ahead at full speed. We finalized our purchase of the tent top and began pouring the gigantic earth anchors to hold the tension cables. Our plan was to conduct the Fire Conference by day, but each night we would see the practical outworking of our sessions in an actual evangelistic campaign in the world's biggest tent. When we took delivery of the new tent the manufacturer registered CfaN in the Guinness Book of World Records as deploying the largest portable structure in the world. As we prepared for the conference we were again making news around the world with the big tent.

We booked guest speakers. Loren Cunningham of *Youth with a Mission*, Kenneth and Gloria Copeland from Texas, Ralph Mahoney of *World Mission*

*Assistance Plan*, Dr. Robert Schuller of *Crystal Cathedral*, Benson Idahosa of Benin City, and other notable men with a passion for evangelism all said yes to our call.

I was so pleased to hear that among the delegates, 41 of the 44 nations of Africa would be represented at that first Fire Conference. In this great success, I saw the evidence that the vision for the Fire Conference was His alone. Other evangelists registered from America, Great Britain, West Germany, Norway, Sweden, Denmark, France, Singapore, and Australia. My heart overflowed to think that so many nations and denominations would be united at the Fire Conference in the cause of preaching the gospel to the ends of the earth.

The meetings ran for six days in April of 1986. The speakers were inspiring and powerful. I challenged the delegates with a message of urgency. I told them preaching the gospel is not a passive ministry. "An unpreached gospel is no gospel at all," I shouted. I let them know that there has never been a revival without aggressive evangelism. Each generation has only their lifetime to reach their generation, and time is running out. Then I urged them to step out and see the miracles that would confirm the preaching of the Good News.

First Fire Conference ever: Harare, Zimbabwe.
It became our key to Africa.

During one session a mighty move of the Holy Spirit descended. David Newberry, an American evangelist came to where I stood and laid his hands on me. I felt the power of God hit me like a cloudburst and I went to my knees. He began to prophesy. The content of his utterance was not something I would have wanted to hear about myself. But in this context, and at this time, I simply wanted to be like any other delegate – I wanted to be available for all that God had for me, and to say as the prophet of old, *Here am I; send me.*[87]

This man said that I would stand before kings and rulers and entire nations would receive Christ. What a mind-expanding word! He said that God was no longer restricting me but was giving me the key to the supply of the harvest. "The harvest has come," he said. This word raced through the whole building, igniting new possibilities in the minds of those delegates who heard it. Furthermore, he declared that God was calling many servants from that conference that would have the anointing of a thousand men. This made me feel even more deeply moved. It went to the very purpose for the conference. It was not about Bonnke; it was about them.

Kenneth Copeland blesses me and Ray McCauley

I felt again like a surfer on an ocean tsunami. This wave was big enough to baptize an entire continent. *Africa shall be saved!* I began to enter the spiritual reality of that statement. Others felt the same exhilaration. Many people in that room were called into full-time evangelism. The prophecy galvanized the core of the team that would remain with me through the move from South Africa to Germany. Replacements were called out to fill the void left by those who would remain behind.

For many of my team the success of the Fire Conference was a double-edged sword. On the flip side of every fantastic moment of triumph there was the pain of knowing this would be the last time we served together. In the power of these sessions they clearly saw that CfaN had not reached its pinnacle, it was just beginning. The work we had accomplished together would soon become a scrapbook of memories compared to the new chapters about to be written.

Michael Kolisang, my very first convert in Lesotho, informed me that he would be leaving my team after the Malawi crusade which would take place in August that year. He would return to Maseru and become a shepherd to the new congregations that had sprung up in that area. I was sad to see him go but so happy to see him listening to the Lord. Over the years I had seen him grow to be a man of God with the confidence and maturity to make such a decision. I supported him with all of my heart. What a graduation day!

Each one of my co-workers who was a South African citizen and wished to come with us to Germany was forced to renounce their citizenship and leave their homeland. Apartheid had become anathema worldwide. Their visas were no longer honored. Those who decided to remain felt like they were watching a bullet train leaving the station at the Fire Conference. It is natural to feel abandoned and unappreciated in a circumstance like that. It is natural – but it is utterly false.

I am reminded of a Nigerian who came up to me at the end of the conference. He unknowingly expressed the correct attitude:

"Pastor Bonnke, sir," he said. "What you are doing is not so special. Any man can do these things."

I nearly leapt from my skin with joy. Here was a brother who got it! He had captured the essence of the Fire Conference. In normal circumstances, however, his words might have sounded brash, arrogant, and insulting. If I had listened with my natural ears, or with my ego, or with my heart on my sleeve, I might have been tempted to "put him in his place." I might have said, "Oh, young man, you have no idea. Talk to me after you have tried to do what I am doing." But the opposite was true. I heard someone who was perhaps a "zero" saying, "Here am I, send me." He may have been naïve, he may have been a bit presumptuous, he may even have been ignorant of the hidden challenges in everything he saw – but so was I when I began. This Nigerian correctly saw that it is not about Bonnke; it is about the Lord who leads ordinary people to do extraordinary things. If Bonnke could do it, he could do it too. Amen!

As he walked away, I was reminded of another friend who had walked away. Not with a confident step, but a defeated one. I was thinking of the last time I saw Richard Ngidi. "When I leave, Bonnke is finished," he had said to Michael Kolisang. No, no, a thousand times no. When God leaves, Bonnke is finished, and not one day sooner. It is so important for God's servants to keep the correct thinking about these matters.

I did not return to Witfield. I flew to Frankfurt and began the next chapter of Christ for all Nations. The young Nigerian delegate returned to his homeland and began to do what Bonnke did. He preached the gospel and prayed for the sick. He depended on the power of the Spirit to provide results. Today, he is a fruitful evangelist with a ministry I am happy to support financially.

My former South African co-workers went home and endured the next eight difficult years as their homeland transitioned from apartheid to its new form of democracy. In time, I trust they all learned that no one needs the CfaN bullet train to take them anywhere in Christ. Our vehicle is Christ Jesus alone.

WE SETTLED IN OUR NEW HEADQUARTERS in Frankfurt. Immediately, things began to improve on every side. We found that our German passports and visas were universally accepted. Money transfers were seamless. Airline ticketing unquestioned. All of the sanctions that were leveled against South Africa disappeared from our operation as soon as we changed our address. This confirmed the wisdom of the decision.

Finances also improved. While our South African support fell to just 5 percent of its former level, German and UK supporters increased in even greater numbers. It was as if they suddenly thought of us as one of their own with our headquarters now located in Europe. We did not anticipate that. The benefits of relocating continued to pile up.

When Anni and I returned from Harare, waiting for us at home was a huge stack of mail. We gathered the children – Freddy, Susanne, and Gabriele – to sort it out. The children were anxious to hear from the friends they had left behind in Witfield, and so were we. After spending some time sifting through it, Anni came to me and dropped a hand-addressed envelope in my lap.

"You had better read this one right away," she said.

I took the envelope and examined the address. It was from Jürgen Bonnke. Suddenly I remembered how I had written him from South Africa weeks ago. I had heard nothing back, and in all the excitement of the Harare Fire Conference I had forgotten about it completely. Now, here in Germany came this letter.

Anni and the children knew how important family communication was to me. They gathered around, eager to see what "Uncle Jürgen" had to say.

I ripped open the envelope and unfolded the document inside.

*Dear Reinhard, my wife has left me. My best friend recently died of cancer. I have been so frustrated I felt that life was no longer worth living. I wanted to kill myself. But in the night I had a dream. I was walking on a bridge. It was unstable and had no handrails and I slipped and screamed as I fell. I woke up, sweating with fear ...*

At this point my voice began get husky with emotion. Anni and the kids did not understand this. They did not know that Jürgen was describing my dream. I had said nothing to them about it. I continued reading ...

*I jumped out of bed and said, 'Almighty God, You know that I don't even believe in You, but I have a brother who serves You. If You have spoken to me through this dream, speak to me through Reinhard.' Sometime later your letter came. Your dream was my dream. I have given my life to Jesus. He has forgiven me of my sins ...*

At this point I was weeping and could not even talk. I could not help myself, and it took quite an effort to bring Anni and the kids up to date on the details behind Jürgen's story. Once they understood, however, they too shared my tears and my joy. This kind of thing prostrates my soul before the King of kings and Lord of lords. How it reveals His great heart of love for us.

The ties that bind a family together must surely mean more in the Spirit than we can know in the flesh. God had linked us together, though we were 5,000 miles apart, causing us to dream the same dream. This is so much more than coincidence. God spoke to me, telling me to share the dream in a letter. I almost neglected His still small voice.

Today, my brother Jürgen is saved, yet he is also a broken man. His health is gone, his mental abilities nearly wiped out. He lives in a nursing home.

WITHIN DAYS OF MY RETURN to Germany I received a letter from the government of Malawi inviting me to conduct a crusade in their country. I had been trying to clear the red tape in Malawi for years. Suddenly we were given a green light to come in August.

My team was ready. The big tent had been dismantled in Harare and packed into 58 shipping containers, ready for the road. We trucked the containers across the narrow strip of Mozambique. After crossing the beautiful Zambezi River, they entered the southern tip of Malawi at Blantyre, a city of 300,000 residents.

We found a piece of land suitable for erecting the big tent. It was in a large, natural amphitheatre. We set up our trailer village for the team, and our engineers set about testing the soil for its anchor-holding properties.

Meanwhile, the local pastors, who had come to Harare and had seen the big tent in action, began to tell us that the tent would not be big enough for the crowd. They said interest in our campaign in Blantyre was beyond anything we could imagine. Peter van den Berg flew to the site. He found that the fire restrictions in Malawi were not nearly so severe as in South Africa, so he devised a way to fit many more people under the big top. He had special benches built so people could squeeze together rather than occupy individual chairs. The aisles were made narrower so more seating was available. At last, he calculated that we could squeeze 50,000 into the tent.

Soon the information came that seating for 50,000 would not be enough to handle the crowd. The decision was made. The big tent would remain in the containers. We would hold the meeting on the open field.

At this point I flew from Frankfurt to see for myself. I toured the field and stood on the platform looking across the benches set up for the crowd. We had created a banner that stretched the full length of our tent. We normally strung it between the first and the twelfth masts. It was huge. It read, "Jesus Christ is King." I told them that if we would not set the tent up then I wanted that banner strung at the far perimeter of the field in a line of eucalyptus trees. It was agreed.

When I arrived for the meetings I stood on the platform and read the great sign across the field. It gave me a sense of continuity to see our banner even though the big tent was not present.

Before the meetings started, I was first asked to attend a special dinner set up by my crusade director. It was a way for local leaders to meet with us and hear my vision for the campaign. The man who sat beside me was the Minister of Transport of the Malawian government, the Hon Bwanali. During the dinner he leaned close to speak to me in confidence.

"Do you know why we invited you here?"

"No, I do not know. For a long time I was not allowed to come to Malawi. Something has changed."

"Yes. Something has changed. It is because at the Fire Conference in Harare you put the evangelists from Malawi in the finest hotels. White and black ministers were treated equally. When we saw that, we decided that you were a friend of Malawi, and we changed our policy for you."

I was so grateful. This was an unintended consequence of our decisions. We had not dreamed that housing those men in first-class style would open doors beyond Harare. I had simply done it to demonstrate my heart for the work of the African evangelists, no matter black or white, or what country they were from, large or small. I wanted them to know that I highly esteemed their calling. Now this open door had resulted. God is so good.

The opening night of the crusade we were too big for the tent. I saw 60,000 people in front of our platform. Peter had trained 2,000 local counselors from local churches. These people he had positioned behind the stage in a roped-off area. When I gave the altar call, we planned for the people to come forward into that area, passing through a bottleneck between the container trucks and the apron of the stage. From our experience we expected to see up to 6,000 responses on this first night. Each of the 2,000 counselors was instructed to take two or three people, give them literature, and register their names and addresses for follow-up.

When I asked to see the hands of those who wanted to accept Jesus as Savior, many more hands were raised than I expected. When I gave the invitation, 15,000 surged forward. As the crowd poured through the opening, pushed from behind by the greater mass of people, a stampede resulted. I turned to see our counselors running for their lives.

"Slow down! Slow down!" I cried into the microphone. "Counselors come back! It will be alright. The people will slow down once they are through the opening."

Eventually we managed to avert disaster. We estimated that 15,000 decisions for Christ were made that first night. The Malawi Miracle was off to a phenomenal start.

Malawi Gospel Crusade:
4.5 times more people than the big tent-capacity

After the first night I met with Peter and the team. "I can no longer give an altar call as I normally would do," I explained. "We cannot call these people forward and risk disaster again. We will have to counsel them in the crowd where they are. That is the only way."

"But that's impossible," Peter said. "You cannot expect the counselors to maneuver down the long rows of benches to reach the people where they sit."

That is when the light went on for me. "Remove the benches and chairs," I said. "Tomorrow the people will stand. I have seen crowds stand in Nigeria and Ghana. They can stand here, too. Using benches for seating is a technique that belongs to the past. We must grow with this harvest and change our ways to move into the future of the combine harvester."

And that is the last time we placed benches or chairs for seating in our open-air meetings. The crowds grew every night. As I stood to preach on the final night, 150,000 had gathered. Half the population of that city stood before me to hear the gospel. There would never be a tent large enough to shelter them. From the platform we looked across that sea of humanity and saw our great banner hanging from the eucalyptus trees: "Jesus Christ is King." It was dwarfed by the size of the crowd. It vividly demonstrated to our team how inadequate our tent was to shelter such a crowd. We took a picture and sent it to our supporters to help them understand what was happening. We called it "The Malawi Miracle."

After the final meeting I met with the team. They were speechless, totally in awe of the crowd. These men had labored for many years to make the world's largest tent a reality, yet the tent had been overwhelmed by the crowds in Blantyre. I found the reverent silence of the team in stark contrast to their reaction in Cape Town when the first tent had been shredded in the storm. Then, they had been devastated, weeping, moaning, suffering depression. This time, they could only bow to the greater purposes of God, who had drawn a crowd large enough to fill our tent more than three times over.

"Are we finished with the tent?" Peter asked.

I shook my head no. "We'll know when the time is right. Move the tent to Nairobi, Kenya. If the crowds are too large there, we'll take it to Rwanda, then to Tanzania. I have said that we will use the tent until it no longer holds the crowds. I am not ready to say that we have arrived. But we will be there soon."

At the conclusion of our campaign in Blantyre the president of Malawi, Dr. Hastings Kamuzu Banda sent a special invitation for us to return to the capital city of Lilongwe and hold a second crusade in two months time. He was in poor health but he wanted to open the meetings with an official word of welcome to the people. I did not automatically accept. Before giving a reply, I sought the Lord in prayer.

As CfaN had grown from a Mom and Pop organization in Johannesburg into a multi-national corporation, my stewardship had begun to change. I realized that I needed to be more careful of the public image God had given us. I was just beginning to see the implications of political damage since leaving

Audience with Malawian President Bakili Muluzi

South Africa. It now occurred to me that any political leader seated on my platform would bring baggage to the event. Some would be offended by his presence, others delighted. We could not calculate all the possible results. So I went to the only reliable source of wisdom. I asked the Lord for guidance. In the end my stewardship was not determined by careful political analysis, but simply by the voice of the Lord. In the case of our return to Malawi He gave us peace. I ordered our team to do a u-turn with the equipment, moving 150 miles north to the capital city of Lilongwe. In this city of 500,000 we would hold another meeting without the big tent.

I arrived in the capital city at the end of October. Just before the meetings began I was told that The Honorable Bwanali, Minister of Transport was coming to the hotel to take me for a ride in his car. I knew the minister from our previous visit. He had informed me at the welcoming banquet in Blantyre that our Fire Conference had opened the doors for us to preach in Malawi. At that time I learned that the president was ailing and would be unable to attend the crusade.

I dressed, and as usual, took my Bible with me. I also took Peter van den Berg along. It occurred to me that I should take precautions and never go anywhere alone anymore. I needed a witness and a backup. There could be a thousand ways a man of God could be compromised and manipulated when he least expects it. I instructed Peter to keep me company and watch my back. As we were driving, the minister suddenly said to me, "The president would like you to speak to the House of Parliament."

"Of course. When would he like me to do this?"

"We are on our way there now."

"Of course," I said calmly, glancing at Peter. I spoke as if this was the sort of thing I expected to hear, but in fact a storm went through my mind. *Oh, Lord, I silently prayed, what am I to preach?*

*Preach on the blood of Jesus,* came the immediate reply.

I was happy to hear this. I felt that the "Blood of Jesus" was my very best sermon. I did not know how to properly conduct myself in a purely political gathering. The best possible solution was for me to preach. They had invited me knowing that I was an evangelist. An evangelist is what they would get.

When we arrived at the House of Parliament I found it packed. Not just the parliamentarians but top secretaries, government ministers, and their wives had assembled. I learned that President Banda had adjourned Parliament for one hour and requested that I speak to them. He was feeling too ill to come himself. They were my captive audience.

The words of the prophecy given at the Harare Fire Conference came back to me. It had been said that I would stand before kings and rulers and that entire nations would receive Christ. Could it be that I was beginning to see it?

The speaker of the house stood up, and introduced me. I stood up. I said, "Mr. Speaker, I want you to know that I am also a speaker but I am a mouth piece of the living God and I've come to bring His word to you and to this House." With that, I launched into my sermon on the "Blood of Jesus." At first the crowd seemed formal and stiff. No doubt they had expected something other than a sermon. But then, at some point in my delivery, I heard a "hallelujah" off to one side. Then I heard an "amen," then another and another. After 20 minutes or so it was like being at a soccer match. The place exploded at times with shouts of praise to God. When I came to end of my message, I heard the Spirit say, *Make an altar call.*

"Everybody, bow your heads," I said. "Who wants to receive Jesus and be washed from all his sins by the precious blood of Christ? I would like to pray with those, please raise your hands."

More than half of that crowd raised their hands. I prayed with them the prayer of salvation, and then sat down.

The Speaker stood up. "There have been many important things said here today. Some of you still have questions. I hereby make my office available to Reverend Bonnke," he said. "He can use it today to counsel those who have responded to this sermon."

He took me to his office. Peter came with me. A long queue began to form outside that office. People scrambled to get in line to speak privately with me.

The first man through the door closed it behind him and fell on his face, confessing his sins. I had not asked him to do this and I was not sure what to expect in this situation. The people came from many different religious backgrounds including Catholic and pagan. This man and hundreds more unburdened their guilt at the foot of the cross and left that office smiling. Others came with sicknesses. I prayed and saw miracles. Again and again I had to remind myself that I was doing this ministry in the office of the Parliament of Malawi. How I praised God that He had taught me to always abandon protocol in favor of an altar call.

THE SMELL OF BURNING CANDLES and fresh cut flowers filled the air. The funeral parlor was cold and quiet. Once again, it was up to me to find words of comfort in a time of grief. After returning to Germany, my father, Hermann Bonnke, at last lay down his earthly temple to be with the Lord. I looked down at his body in the casket and suddenly felt his absence. I began to realize more than ever that life is a relay race. The baton of the gospel, now in my hand, I had taken from him.

I smiled to myself remembering that I had indeed, *taken* it. It had not been in his mind to *give* it to me. In his mind, it had always belonged to Martin. But in the end, all was forgiven. My father and I had shared these recent years of ministry together, and his heart had overflowed to see blessings on a scale he had never imagined. Time after time I had assured him that everything he saw had arisen from a chain of events put in motion by the Holy Spirit. First, sending Luis Graf to heal August Bonnke in 1922. The chain had continued through Dad's healing and conversion and his shepherding that little flock in Krempe. Surely Dad had run his leg of the relay well. Now, he had finished. And what a race it had been.

Father had carried the flame of the Spirit through quite an obstacle course. Struggling as an idealistic young officer in the Wehrmacht, he had watched the terrible rise of Hitler and the unleashed horror of World War II. In prison camp, he had committed the remainder of his life to preaching the glorious gospel of salvation. Then Jesus had appeared to him, confirming that calling.

Suddenly, in my mind's eye, I could see myself running again. Running so hard as a boy of ten to see him at the Pöppendorf prison camp, passing through the crowd of soldiers in the yard. My heart had been filled with a desire to show him how I had grown and how fast I could run. I was the fastest Bonnke of them all. But I had run right past him in my enthusiasm. Mother called me back to where Father was hugging the other children. In my effort to be first, I had become last.

As it was in the natural, so it is in the spiritual. I had not kept exact count, but I estimated conservatively that more than one million souls had made decisions for Christ under my ministry so far. When my father had retired he may have seen 200 converts. Looking down at his body, I knew afresh that the books of heaven record things differently than on earth. *But many that are first shall be last; and the last first,*[88] Jesus had promised.

All of the rewards of my ministry I shared with this man whose spirit had now departed his body. When God ultimately rewards His servants, many who served in the background will receive the full reward of the man on stage. Father, like Luis Graf, was one of those. And there will be many, many more than I can imagine. God does not reward by cutting each of us a piece of the heavenly pie. If He did, then every reward taken would diminish the size of the next reward given. If God's blessing is a pie, what happens when the pie runs out? No, God has a full pie for each one of us. As He said to Abraham, *I **am** thy ... exceeding great reward.*[89] (The bold-italics are mine.)

That says it perfectly. Dad finished his race, running as fast as his legs would carry him into the arms of his heavenly Father. Perhaps in heaven he recognized Him right away, having seen him once before in the prison camp. The words, "Well done, good and faithful servant," would fill his heart for all eternity. God Himself was now his "exceeding great reward."

"See you later, Dad," I said.

I wondered if God might have allowed a very special angel named Meta to sit at the grand pipe organ in heaven and play Dad's entrance there. If not, knowing His goodness, it was something far better than that. Pastor Rolf Cilwik led the

The Bonnke "children" in full life

funeral service. Looking at Dad's familiar features, so cold and still in that coffin, I sensed the profound absence of his spirit. I felt the sting of tears in my eyes. Tears of my loss and his great gain.

A few hours later I stood before the Bonnke clan. They had gathered in an attitude of respect and quietness. I had first noted them in the family genealogy as a young preacher, so long ago. "How did God break into the Bonnke family?" I had asked in bewilderment. Now many of those names on the page had gathered in person before me, waiting to hear what I would say. Looking across their faces I saw a few who now shared with me a priceless bond of faith. Just a few. The Lord had given me this day and this occasion to address them all, believers and unbelievers.

As always, I was an evangelist. In my mind I began to see the shape of the gospel. *Precious in the sight of the Lord is the death of his saints,*[90] I began … and before I finished, each of them would have the opportunity to meet their Savior over the open casket of Hermann Bonnke.

Part 6

# THE COMBINE HARVESTER

# Chapter 28

UNTIL 1987 I DID NOT KEEP AN OFFICIAL RECORD of conversions in my meetings. All of the statistics had been informally collected and were based on estimates, and whatever hard data we might have been able to gather. In the meantime I had met Dr. Vinson Synan, the leading historian and statistician of the Pentecostal and Charismatic movements. Starting with the Fire Conference in Harare, we had become friends, and that friendship began to influence my thinking about a system for keeping meticulous records.

We were polar opposites in our personalities and our approach to life. He was a thinker, and I was a doer. I did not take time to analyze my life and ministry. I listened, and when I heard the voice of the Spirit, I obeyed. That approach kept me too busy and too excited for academic research. As a result, I didn't see myself in the larger context of the Pentecostal and Charismatic outpouring of the 20th century. That was the gift Vinson gave me.

He opened my eyes to the bigger picture. From him I learned that I was participating in what was called the "third wave" of the latter day outpouring of the Holy Spirit. He showed me that there was only one outpouring of the Holy Spirit in our age, but it was being seen in the Azusa era, in the neo-Pentecostalism of the Charismatic movement, as well as in the Catholic Charismatic movement. These three streams were now flowing together by the Holy Spirit. All of it was resulting in the greatest harvest of souls in the history of the planet. He urged me to keep meticulous records of the attendance and conversions at my meetings. I decided that record keeping was indeed good stewardship.

Sitting down with Peter van den Berg, I instructed him to begin a process of crowd counting as well as an official registration of decisions for Christ. We studied Billy Graham's organization and others to guide us in this process. In most cases, our numbers were rounded to the nearest thousand. This new method began with our first crusade that year in Tamale, Ghana.

80,000 decisions for Christ were officially registered. The crowds grew to 55,000, with 240,000 attending over six days. What a great first entry in our book of CfaN statistics! Hallelujah!

We scheduled nine more campaigns in Africa that year. Four in Ghana, one in Nigeria, one in Cameroon, one in Malawi, and two in Tanzania. In Tanzania we ran into difficulties. Our campaign scheduled for Arusha was cancelled by the government, and the campaign in Dar es Salaam was shut down after only four days. Even so, we registered 510,000 decisions that year, with a total attendance of 1,425,000. The Harare Fire Conference prophecy about being given the keys to the harvest seemed to be coming true before our eyes in spite of all opposition.

We had planned to use the big tent in Nairobi but abandoned the plan when it became clear that it would not hold the crowds. The same happened in Douala, Cameroon, with crowds of 70,000. We did not use the tent in Dar es Salaam because the soil was too sandy to hold the anchors. It turned out that the crowds grew to 40,000. I told the team that next year we would try one more time to erect the big tent in Nairobi. If the crowds there exceeded the tent's capacity, I would give it away to another ministry that could make use of it.

I WAS INVITED to speak at the Catholic Charismatic Leadership Conference in New Orleans. The invitation came through my friend, Dr. Vinson Synan, who was well received as a Pentecostal historian in Catholic circles. The conference had a theme, which I do not recall, and I was asked to contribute about 20 minutes of remarks concerning this theme. I was one of several speakers they had lined up for that particular night.

When I arrived in New Orleans the Holy Spirit spoke to my heart. I was not to address the theme of the conference, but I was to be an evangelist. This was not according to the invitation I had received. I went to my friend, Vinson. He was thoroughly familiar with the leadership of that organization.

"Vinson, this is not my meeting. Can I preach what the Holy Spirit has laid on my heart? Yes or no?"

"Yes, of course," he said.

"OK. Thank you."

As I waited on the platform, many other speakers went before me. I spoke to the Lord in my heart. *Lord, I only had five minutes to preach at the disco in Kimberley. I saw what your Holy Spirit accomplished there. I ask for the same anointing here in New Orleans. I have only 20 minutes.*

When I got up to speak, I delivered the ABCs of a salvation message. As I spoke I sensed the Holy Spirit descending across that crowd. These were leaders of the Catholic Charismatic movement, yet I was preaching the basics of accepting Jesus as Savior. On the surface it seemed absurd. Theologically, it offended some. The baptism of the Holy Spirit, which these people had supposedly received, was held to be an experience that followed the new birth. Therefore, I would normally have assumed that everyone in the room was saved. But the Holy Spirit knew better. He had urged me to preach salvation.

I gave an invitation. I did not believe my eyes. Nearly 10,000 people stood to receive Jesus. Somehow I must have misspoken.

"No, no, no," I said. "Sit down. I will try again. I am asking for those who have never in their life accepted Jesus as their Savior to stand. Only those who have never asked Jesus to be their Savior."

Preaching in the Super Dome of New Orleans

It was stunning. Even more people stood this time. God was doing a mighty work. I prayed a mass salvation prayer with that crowd. Then I asked for those who were sick to raise their hands. As I began to pray for them people leapt from wheelchairs, blind eyes opened, others began to claim healings all over that crowd. New Orleans did not respond differently to the preaching of the gospel than Blantyre, Malawi! Except, my sermon was somewhat shorter.

When I finished, I had ten minutes left. I invited those who had stood to accept Jesus to come forward to the front of the platform. Then I encouraged those who knew Jesus as Savior to counsel them. When I concluded my time, I had obeyed the voice of the Lord. A mighty move of signs and wonders had followed the preaching of the gospel. But I had thoroughly offended the organizers of the event. They had been embarrassed to see a clear demonstration that many of their number had never met Jesus. They have never invited me back.

On a plane returning from New Orleans, Oliver Raper, one of my team members overheard two nuns talking in the next seat.

"Did you receive Jesus as your Savior at the conference?"

"Yes, but secretly. I didn't want Mother Superior to know."

God only knows the full scope of the harvest at that New Orleans meeting. No one had been officially interested in recording the numbers.

WE CALLED IT *Euro Fire Germany*. It was the first Fire Conference of a new strategy. We would begin to conduct conferences in Europe that would stand alone. Meaning, they would not be held in conjunction with an ongoing crusade. Our intention was to ignite a passion for the lost among European Christians, as well as to raise the consciousness of European audiences to the presence of the Charismatic and Pentecostal streams in their midst.

We held this first event in our new home city of Frankfurt. Until now, the German press had followed me to Africa to report on my meetings. At last, I had brought CfaN back home. Now, my fellow Germans could have a good look at us up close and personal, so to speak.

14,000 attended. The entire German religious establishment – Pentecostal, Evangelical, and Lutheran – expressed great skepticism that the kind of results we had seen in Africa would be seen in Frankfurt. German public television came and placed their cameras in the conference hall to broadcast it to the nation. There were no Christian television stations in Germany in those days.

Euro Fire in Frankfurt am Main, Germany

This was a landmark event. It succeeded beyond my wildest dreams.

I invited my friend, Benny Hinn, to join me. He asked why I would invite him to a place where he was unknown. His reputation would not help draw a crowd in Frankfurt, he said. But I knew Benny's ministry in those early days and had seen the dramatic way the Holy Spirit manifested as he prayed for people. I said that I wanted to see that same manifestation in Germany. In my heart I wanted to see some of my arrogant, stiff, fellow Germans flat on their backs, blown down by the power of God.

May God forgive my indulgence. Or perhaps He inspired it. I had been raised in this oppressive culture. My father and his generation of Pentecostals, living under the shame of The Berlin Declaration, had labored in vain to see the power of the Holy Ghost break into the mainstream. Living on the despised margins of German society, my older brothers had grown weary of the load and had pursued higher education in order to obtain "respectable" professions. I had held to the truth of Scripture, refusing to throw out the baby with the bathwater.

Now I had the opportunity to stage a Fire Conference in my homeland, and I did not want to "make nice" with the religious establishment. I would not bow to kiss the ring of dead religious powers. I did not want to leave Germany to its comfort zone. So Benny came, and Benny ministered as he does everywhere, with dramatic manifestations of the Holy Spirit. This time, it was witnessed across the entire nation on public television.

The press overreacted. The denominations raged. Their discomfort backfired. A buzz was created all across Germany, and Benny has since become a household word there. Hallelujah!

Dr. Loren Cunningham   Rev. Ray McCauley   Rev. Bob Weiner   Rev. Paul Schoch   Dr. Vinson Synan   Rev. Roger Forster   Rev. Everett Fullam

Rev. Benny Hinn   Pastor Wolfgang Wegert   Missionarin Suzette Hattingh   Rev. Peter Vandenberg   Rev. Wayne Myers   Rev. John Shelbourne

I had also invited Loren Cunningham of *Youth with a Mission*. As he spoke, he prophesied that the Berlin Wall would fall. In fact, this was the third time I had heard this prophecy since Kenneth Copeland first gave it privately in Soweto in 1984. Now, all of Germany heard it on public television. What controversy! My fellow Germans attacked his words. They said that he was speaking as an American. His prophecy was rooted in the politics of wishful thinking. I replied that he was speaking by the power of the Holy Spirit. Two years later as the wall came down, his words found new respect.

This Euro Fire Conference was sensational, and everywhere I go in Germany today I hear echoes of its impact. Lives were changed, ministries ignited, and the demonstration of the power of God made the difference. Oh, that Luis Graf, August Bonnke, and my father had lived to see this day! The seeds they planted in faith and obscurity so long ago were bearing abundant fruit.

IN 1988 THERE WERE 750,000 REGISTERED DECISIONS for Christ through CfaN. We held seven campaigns in Africa and one in Manila, Philippines, with a total attendance for the year of 3,935,000. The largest single crowd was 200,000 people. They gathered in Uhuru Park that year, in Nairobi, Kenya.

Nairobi had always presented a challenge to CfaN. In order to go through all of the intricacies of the proper insurance and permits in order to erect the big tent, we were required to register a CfaN office inside the country. This had not been possible no matter how we tried. The government seemed to create obstacles for us at every turn. Our team concluded that a doorkeeper placed high in the government had taken a dislike to our organization and was working behind the scenes against us. This is how it seemed. This puzzled me because I knew that Daniel Arap Moi, the president of Kenya, was a true Christian brother. This condition seemed hopeless until we were assisted by a man of great influence and integrity, a minister in Nairobi named Dr. Wellington Mutiso.

At the time he was working with World Vision. He was a Baptist minister and a representative of the Evangelical Alliance of Germany. He had been a respected delegate at Billy Graham's Amsterdam '83 Conference, the International Conference for Itinerant Evangelists that had inspired me to do the first Fire Conference in Harare. In fact, Dr. Mutiso had attended our Harare Fire Conference.

When he learned of our dilemma, he offered his own ministry organization as an umbrella for CfaN in Kenya. Using his protection, we soon were able to schedule our meeting for eight days in June of 1988. Today, Dr. Mutiso is chairman of the Evangelical Alliance of Kenya. His opinion and help is sought by top leaders concerning all issues affecting religion and government in the region.

As we went forward with our Nairobi plans under the protection of Dr. Mutiso's organization, it soon became apparent that the big tent was a dinosaur. The anticipated crowds were so large that we never even installed the ground anchors for the structure. As I had promised, I called Peter Pretorius in South Africa and offered him the tent as a gift.

"Peter, I have a gift for you. The world's largest tent. I give it to you with all the technical gear and the fleet of trucks to transport it."

He said that he would not travel with the tent but would make it a permanent installation for a medical clinic. On the spot he donated the trucks back to me. I was grateful and thanked him for that because I still needed those specially built trucks to transport equipment to our crusades. Besides, Gaddafi's machine gun turrets were still a source of endless amusement for my team.

At this time, I had a visit from some of my German Pentecostal overseers, among them Pastor Reinhold Ulonska. As many men in his position might do, he found it entertaining to needle me in one way or another. After all, the denomination had never found a way to equal CfaN's success.

"So, the big tent was used once, eh?" he said.

"Yes, just once, at the Harare crusade."

"What a shame."

"No, why would you say that?"

"Well, it was a huge investment for nothing."

"Oh, no, not really. I am not in business to demonstrate the latest tent technology. I am in the business of saving souls. The tent helped us do that."

"Well, the world's largest tent had to be the most expensive billboard in the history of evangelism, don't you think?"

I could see that his comment was a double-edged sword. I would not tolerate the implications of it. "I think you chose the wrong analogy in this case," I replied, remembering something Peter van den Berg had said to me. "The world's largest tent was a Saturn 5 booster rocket. The rocket has served its purpose and has fallen into the sea, but it was not an expensive billboard. It was the vehicle that launched CfaN into high orbit. Praise God!"

WHEN I ARRIVED for the Nairobi meeting I was put up in the Serena Hotel near Uhuru Park. From my room I could see where the platform had been erected. The opening meeting saw a crowd of more than 100,000. The preaching of the gospel was accompanied by signs following, and the crowds began to grow nearer to the 200,000 mark. We were making a big stir in the capital city.

On the fifth day of meetings my telephone rang in the hotel. I was told that His Excellency, President Daniel Arap Moi, would like to attend my meeting that day. I looked at the clock and saw that the meeting was only two hours away.

"That is wonderful," I replied, looking out the window at my barren platform. "I have just one problem. I do not have any chairs for the president."

"Do not worry," the official replied. "His Excellency will bring his own chairs."

Indeed, when I arrived on the platform I saw an entire section of government chairs set up in the front row of the crowd. Let's be honest. These were great, gilded, golden chairs fit for a king. They were thrones. I was introduced to the president and several of his high ministers, and then I took my seat to await the preaching of the Word. As I sat there I asked the Lord what I was to preach. The Lord spoke very clearly to me: *Preach as if the President was not here.*

President Arab Moi and I

Here was another opportunity to put the altar call before protocol. I would certainly welcome the president in my opening remarks, but after that I would ignore him and preach the gospel. That is exactly what I did. There was a great response for salvation and for prayer for the sick at the end of the sermon. When I finished ministering and turned around, the president and all his fancy chairs had gone.

The next day my phone rang again in the morning. "The president would like to visit with you at the State House."

They sent a car for me. I took Peter van den Berg and Stephen Mutua, our East Africa Director, with me. At the State House we were invited into a nice garden courtyard and served chai tea. It was my first chai tea and a drink that I began to enjoy on a regular basis thereafter. The president arrived and joined us.

"I go to many different churches in Nairobi," he said. "I visit one church each Sunday. Yesterday was the first time a preacher did not change his sermon for me. I don't know if you noticed but some of my staff accepted Jesus at your invitation. I would like to have your follow-up materials. I myself will counsel with the new converts about following Jesus."

I was so thrilled and happy. "I am so glad to know that we both serve the same Lord," I said. "We will be glad to supply you with materials."

For an hour he asked questions. The meeting was a very pleasant one. Then I asked him for a favor. I told him of the trouble CfaN had encountered over the years trying to register as an official organization in Kenya. "In fact," I said. "We are not even here under our own auspices. Dr. Wellington Mutiso has offered us his organization as an umbrella. Otherwise we would not even have a permit to preach the gospel in Uhuru Park."

He motioned with his hand, and all of his aides in the room came close to hear what he had to say. "I herewith cut all red tape for the registration of Christ for all Nations in Kenya."

And so it was done.

After the meetings had concluded, Dr. Mutiso received a communication from his Evangelical Alliance overseers in Germany. He was told that he would have to choose his alliance with them or with Reinhard Bonnke. One or the other, but not both. It was up to him. He told me later that he weighed the 140,000 souls he saw saved in Uhuru Park with the absence of conversions he saw through the efforts of his overseers, and made his choice. He is a blessed friend of CfaN to this day.

Our campaign in Nairobi saw a total of 850,000 people attend over a period of eight days. The miracles and size of the crowd made headlines every day in the news media. We attracted both admirers and enemies. As we left the city, an editorial writer submitted an open challenge to CfaN in the newspaper. He accused us of conducting our meetings on the comfortable side of town.

Real Christianity, he said, would not avoid the real poverty and violence of Nairobi's notorious slums.

I took this challenge and told my team to prepare a return campaign in Nairobi. We would set up our equipment in the heart of the very worst part of the city. I had seen it during our visit, a slum built around the city's garbage pit. It was a place called Mathare Valley, a dense collection of 180,000 souls living in mud houses, beneath corrugated metal roofs. Their dwellings were built on stilts over a seeping river of raw sewage. This mission field would represent the worst conditions in which we ever attempted to hold meetings. The schedule was set for three years later.

SHE STOOD WEEPING at the far edge of the crowd, beyond my field of vision. 200,000 gathered in Uhuru Park that day. The president and members of his cabinet sat on the platform behind me. I preached, and we saw thousands come to the Lord. Healings manifested among the people. I was thrilled with another day of obeying the Lord and seeing His power to save sinners. But Teresia Wairimu was not a sinner, and she did not come forward. I never knew she was there.

She had soaked her pillow for countless days before I came to Nairobi in 1988. In recent months, her dream of serving God through serving her family had been shattered. The grief of this loss tore at her soul like a raging windstorm.

From childhood, Teresia had longed to serve the Lord. Attending church had filled her imagination with wonderful desires to marry a minister. When she finally came of age she met a charming European missionary. With this man, everything fell into place in her mind. The desire to serve God and the desire to serve this missionary merged into one. She could see nothing but happy days ahead.

Her parents had red flags about it. They did not approve of the union. To them, a racially mixed marriage was a recipe for disaster in Kenya. Besides, they were a respected business family and were ashamed to think that their daughter would marry outside traditional African values. But in the thrall of love, and in her intense desire to serve the Lord, Teresia felt sure that God had provided the answer to her prayers in this wonderful Christian man. She became willing to go against her parents' wishes to marry him.

It was a decision that haunted her a dozen years later when her missionary husband turned against her. No amount of appealing to his Christian faith made any difference. He took cruel advantage of a male-dominated court system to divorce her and leave her and their daughter with no support.

How this story touches my heart. Like Teresia, I knew the longing to serve God as a child. When I was just ten years old in Germany I had heard the voice of the Lord calling me to Africa. I also knew the desire to be married to one who shared that calling. I could not imagine where I would be today, or how I would carry out God's call, if my precious Anni had ever turned against me. The very thought of it produces enough pain in my heart to silence all of my sermons. I have been deeply touched to learn of Teresia's agony.

As she stood weeping in Uhuru Park that hot and steamy day, she could sense the great gulf between the two of us. It was more than physical. I preached with a confidence she did not feel. She had been cruelly discarded by the one man she had most wanted to please. As she stood there, she blamed herself for choosing so badly in her desire for a ministry mate. She further blamed herself for not being able to make the marriage work in spite of her husband's problems. Perhaps her husband's problems were actually her fault, she thought. She had not been good enough, not enough like Jesus to change his heart. Round and round her thoughts spun like the arms of a ceaseless windmill, beating her down, down, down.

She had no place to go. Her family would now reject her. They would tell her that she had only gotten what she deserved. She couldn't bring herself to even tell them of the divorce. The church was no better. Divorce was a terrible shame among Kenyan Christians; the kiss of death to anyone with a desire for ministry.

The only refuge Teresia found was in God. Though she felt rejected, Teresia somehow knew in the core of her soul that God had not rejected her. She was cast aside by a bad husband, not abandoned by a good God. She clung to the hope that someday, somehow, God would give her feet a solid place to stand again. A place no devil of hell could ever take from her.

This is why she wept as she stood at the far perimeter of the crowd in Uhuru Park. As she later described it, she heard my voice preaching the Word of God with positive power and authority. The very sound of this kind of preaching caused hope to leap up in her heart. She had not heard the gospel preached that way. The ministers she had known had been trained in seminaries. They had been taught not to raise their audiences' hopes by their words or their tone of voice, lest someone be disappointed and blame God in their despair. Even the hope of the Good News had been watered down so that unbelievers might not be offended.

But the Reinhard Bonnke that she saw that day preached the uncompromised gospel. Even in the presence of the president on stage, she had heard Bonnke let the chips fall where they may. He shouted the Good News into his microphone with gusto. The way he spoke and the way he moved on stage told everyone that here was a man who believed his message and would stake his life on it. He acted like he really knew the God he preached about.

*If Reinhard Bonnke can be that way,* Teresia thought, *then I can too.* And tears of longing spilled from her eyes.

When I called for the sick to come forward, Teresia watched as I laid hands on them. Blind eyes opened, lame people began to walk. People who were deaf could suddenly repeat my whispers, word for word. It was like another page being written in the book of Acts.

Teresia saw that I possessed a living "fire" that was beyond the cold religious embers of her own experience. This was the gift she sought with tears that day. She would settle for nothing less. From the very depths of her soul she cried out, *God, oh please God, if you can give Bonnke 100,000 souls, give me 100, just 100, Lord, and I'll be a happy woman!*

Once Teresia said this, she knew something else, deep down in her heart. She knew that to receive her answer from God, Reinhard Bonnke would have to lay his hands on her head and pray for her.

What is this? I don't know. It is something I cannot explain except to say she had faith like the woman who touched the hem of Jesus' cloak[91] and was healed. A story recorded in the gospels of Matthew and Mark. It was not Jesus' idea that the woman touch him. It was the woman's idea. In fact, Jesus was on His way to heal someone else when she chased Him down and touched the hem of His cloak. When she did, she was healed. Jesus turned to her and said, "Daughter, your faith has made you well."

Teresia's faith was like this woman's faith. Somehow she knew that I must lay my hands on her and pray for her, and then she could step into her full blessing from God.

This is not a formula for getting anything from God. I tell you there is no special power in my hands or my prayer, any more than there was special virtue in the hem of Jesus' robe. It was the faith of the woman in the Bible that mattered. And it was Teresia's faith that gave this idea of my laying hands on her its peculiar power.

Teresia left Uhuru Park that day without a chance for prayer. The crowds were pressing around the platform with many needs, and God was directing me to the ones He was healing. I never knew she was there.

Six years would pass before our paths would cross again. In that future meeting I would lay my hands on Teresia and all heaven would break loose.

IN 1988, I HEARD THE VOICE OF THE LORD calling me to preach the gospel in Hamburg, Germany. I was excited for many reasons. First of all, growing up in Glückstadt, my family had lived in the shadow of Hamburg. Our little town had been built on the Elbe River to service ships sailing to and from the North Sea. But upriver, the port of Hamburg had made the world forget about Glückstadt. Hamburg had become the second largest city in Germany and the ninth busiest port in the world. As a boy I would sit on the dock and watch the ships sail from Hamburg all day long, passing our pier as if it had no significance. Now, God was calling the boy from Glückstadt to preach the gospel in Hamburg.

As my team members searched for a place to hold the meetings, my interest grew even more. They came to me with a proposition that was full of ironies. I would preach on the Heiligengeistfeld near the Reeperbahn in the St. Pauli district. In plain English, I would preach the gospel on the Holy Ghost Field in the St. Paul district of Hamburg, which borders the Reeperbahn, one of the most notorious red-light districts in the world. How is that for a crusade site? This is the famous nightlife strip where the young Beatles rock group from Liverpool performed during the years when I was starting my practicum with Father in Krempe. Afterward, they achieved worldwide fame, as I began my work in obscurity in Lesotho. However, when Christ for all Nations came to Hamburg in 1988, the citizens along the Reeperbahn would not hear, "Lady Madonna" blaring from the speaker system. They would hear, "How Great Thou Art." Hallelujah!

The Holy Ghost Field had taken its name from a large hospital called the *Holy Ghost Hospital* that had once occupied these grounds. The St. Paul district had been named for St. Paul's Lutheran Cathedral, whose steeple still dominated the area. Hamburg had been founded under the Holy Roman Empire and had come of age during the Protestant Reformation. After several centuries had passed, in 1988, Christianity was everywhere in Hamburg – in name only. The red-light district had drawn the seediest people on the planet to live here. Crime and degradation were everywhere. The St. Pauli soccer team that played on the Holy Ghost Field used the skull and crossbones as their emblem. That is what happens when a living faith becomes a dead religion. It eventually turns into a mockery, celebrating everything unholy.

That is exactly why I was so excited to preach there. I understood that sin is not a barrier to the gospel; it is prerequisite. In fact, I believe where the darkness is deepest, the light of Jesus shines brightest. Ask Mary Magdalene, out of whom the Lord cast seven devils.[92] Jesus said the person who is forgiven much, loveth much.[93] I saw great potential in this crusade. The people of St. Pauli would be forgiven much by the Lord of the Universe. I sensed that God had arranged a host of divine appointments in this meeting. I could hardly wait to announce the Good News on the Heiligengeistfeld.

Weeks before we arrived, Suzette Hattingh, a woman of prayer and anointing on my team, organized a group of young people to canvass the St. Pauli district, including the Reeperbahn. They passed out gospel tracts and invitations

to the meetings. Then they walked and prayed over the entire area. We called them the Tennis Shoe Brigade. They were like an artillery barrage fired into the Enemy's camp, softening them up before the full-scale invasion of the gospel.

As I often do, I invited a guest evangelist to accompany me to Hamburg. He would preach during the afternoon meetings, and I would preach at night. This time it was Ray McCauley, the pastor of Rhema Church in Johannesburg, the largest congregation of believers in South Africa, with more than 20,000 members at that time.

Suzette Hattingh
– a truly Holy Spirit woman

After seeing the altar call at my first fundraising breakfast in South Africa, when 17 waiters had come forward to accept Jesus, he had vowed never to end a service in his church without giving an altar call. It had been a good decision. He had also integrated his congregation under the time of apartheid and was greatly respected. He came to Hamburg with his personal assistant Gordon Calmeyer.

We stayed at the same hotel. The first day of meetings went well. I preached. As the second day of the campaign arrived, a rainstorm began to pummel the city. It was Ray's turn to preach in the afternoon session. He called to say, "There will be no meeting in this rain."

I did not disagree over the phone, but something in my spirit disagreed. In Africa I had seen many people waiting in the rain to hear the Word preached. But Germany was different. I knew that. We had arranged 8,000 chairs for the audience. There was no shelter. Rain would probably keep them away.

As I waited in my room I grew restless. Anni and I began to pray. After a time I heard the Holy Spirit say to me, *Go to the Holy Ghost Field and pray against the rain.*

I had given my car to Ray because he had been scheduled to speak at the afternoon meeting. I picked up the phone. Gordon answered.

"I would like to borrow the car keys for about an hour or two."

"What for? It's raining, and we're watching Wimbledon."

They were watching TV, rooting for Germany's Boris Becker to defeat the Swedish champion, Stefan Edberg, in the Wimbledon tennis tournament.

"Where do you want to go in this rain?" he asked.

"To the Holy Ghost Field."

"What? Why go there?"

"It is strange that you should ask, but I want to go there because the Lord spoke to me. I should go there and pray for the rain to stop. We will have a mighty evening service tonight on a dry field."

"You're kidding."

"I am not kidding. Please, can you bring the car keys to my room? I will drive myself over there."

Anni and I drove to the field. I got out and began to pray against the rain. As we agreed together in prayer, we saw the clouds lift. The rain stopped. The field glistened in a sudden burst of sunlight. That night we returned to a dry field. Ray was disappointed because Becker had lost to Edberg, but I was happy because prayer had caused the enemy to flee.

The crowd had gathered, nearly 8,000 strong. Suddenly a host of police cars wheeled into the parking lot. Policemen came rushing out, approaching the platform. The chief officer called me to one side and asked to speak with me.

"Reverend Bonnke, we have it on good sources that your meeting will be attacked by a mob tonight. A particularly bad group of people."

"Who?"

"Gays. It seems that the homosexual lobby in Hamburg has taken great exception to your being here. They plan to invade the meeting. They will make noise to disrupt it. They even have 20 members who have pledged to strip naked and dance on your stage. I have ordered my men to guard your platform so that will not happen."

Suddenly I felt that I should have prayed against much more than the rain. Why had the Spirit not spoken to me about this threat? Our Tennis Shoe Brigade had certainly run across the homosexuals in the red-light district. They had invited gays to the meetings along with every other type of sinner. But this group was not coming to hear the gospel. They were coming to attack it.

The police officer pointed toward the Reeperbahn. As if on cue, a group of about 100 activists emerged from the red-light district with signs and buckets and wearing strange manners of dress – and undress. Painted, pierced, tattooed, and angry.

Soon they approached our crowd from across the Holy Ghost Field. As they grew near, in their twisted logic, they planned to perform a blasphemous religious sacrament on the crowd. They had buckets of some kind of water – God knows what kind – with toilet bowl brushes in them. With the brushes they planned to sprinkle the crowd as if with holy water. This was not going to be pretty.

What they failed to understand was that many in the crowd had not yet met Jesus. The Spirit that would allow them to turn the other cheek was not present in their hearts. As the gays began their disruptive ritual, many of the crowd leapt up and began to violently smash them with their fists. Soon, bleeding gays were fighting back with buckets and toilet brushes, or else running for their lives. The place had turned into bedlam.

I began to pray, *Lord, what am I to do? How can I preach to this mad house?*

With the President of Police in Kassel, Germany, when I became an honorary police inspector on my 50th birthday

Then I heard the Spirit say, *Welcome My guests. Make them welcome here.*

Tears filled my eyes. In a moment like this, to hear the love of God expressed by the Spirit of God, is the nearest thing to hearing the Savior on the cross saying, *Father, forgive them; for they know not what they do.*[94] I had the microphone. I turned to my sound man asking him to raise the volume. In German, I began to shout above the near-riot conditions.

"I am Reinhard Bonnke. I want to welcome all the gay people here today. You are very, very, welcome! All gay people, welcome, welcome!"

A strange lull came over the violent crowd. These words cut through the entire clamour like a shockwave. They settled on the people like a balm of soothing ointment.

"As a matter of fact," I said, "today the gay people are my special guests. They are VIPs. This is so, because Jesus has said that He has come to seek and to save the lost. I've been waiting so long for you. I love you, where have you been? Really! I am so glad you are here. Welcome to our meeting. I invite you to come forward here and sit or stand on the concrete slab in front of the podium. Come, you are welcome to hear the preaching of the Word. Front-row seating."

The police chief glanced up at me as if I'd lost my mind. Behind me on the platform I heard Ray McCauley ask, "Why is Reinhard shouting at them?"

One of my assistants who understood German said, "He's telling them they are welcome, that he loves them."

Slowly, the gays came forward, nursing their wounds. They took a position in a miserable little cluster in front of the platform. As I looked down at them, I smiled. I began to see the shape of the gospel. I started to preach the ABCs.

Suddenly, in the middle of my sermon, some of the gays stood and threw money at me – bills and handfuls of change that rattled across the platform. It was another part of their planned demonstration. Unbelievers assume that evangelists are all about money. They only listen to the angry voices in the media that distort the idea of taking up offerings. To demonstrate their misunderstanding, they had thrown money at me to make their point.

I reached down and collected a handful of it and came forward to the edge of the platform.

"I do not know what this money is about, but Jesus is not after your money today. He is after your heart. Do you understand me? If you want to give something to Jesus, give Him your heart. Here, please, come take back this money."

One of their number came forward. I placed the money in his hand, and I saw that he was weeping. I knew then why the Holy Spirit had not warned me to pray against the gay demonstrators. They were His special guests on the Heiligengeistfeld.

This is one of the greatest memories of all my years of preaching the gospel. As I gave the invitation that night, all of the gay demonstrators came forward to receive Jesus as their Savior. I looked into their weeping faces at the edge of the platform. I listened to their weary voices as they repeated the sinner's prayer.

*I acknowledge that I am a sinner … I accept Jesus as my Savior … I give Him my old life … I accept His new life in me … Amen.*

Hallelujah! Hallelujah! Amen!

# Chapter 29

As 1989 BEGAN, we organized nine campaigns in Africa. That amounted to one more than in each of the previous two years. At this point in our history we had become experts at dealing with the challenges of open air meetings. Looking back, I remembered the deluge in 1976 that had swept away the people in a terrible flood. I had stood in the rain in Mbabane, Swaziland crying out in anguish to the heavens, "When are we going to have a roof over our heads in these campaigns?!" In answer to my shortsighted prayer the Lord had challenged me to believe for a 10,000 seat tent. After that had come the world's largest tent. Now, no tent could ever be large enough for the crowds and I no longer prayed for a roof over our heads.

In the meantime, my crew had learned a lot about staging a meeting since 1976. They had become experts at selecting terrain that would not funnel another flood through our meeting site. Floodplains were studied and drainages calculated. Still, the rains do come and at times it is a torrential downpour. There are pictures of me preaching with men holding umbrellas around me. I have been nearly swept from the platform by gusts of wind and have had to run for my life. But we preach in equatorial Africa and most of the rain is warm. At times it is accompanied by lightning. I do not allow my musicians to be on the platform during the lightning. The crew establishes lightning rods to protect the equipment but occasionally it will take a direct hit. The bottom line is, when the people are so hungry for the gospel that they will stand in a torrent of rain to hear it – then I will stand in the same torrent to deliver it. How could I do less?

In July, I flew for hours above the vast steaming jungles of the Congo River Basin. Rainforests stretched from horizon to horizon. I recalled how this remote meeting place had been selected, months ago. CfaN's East Africa director, Stephen Mutua, had been searching the back roads of the far eastern Congo. It is an area of neglect and unrest, and it is subject to dangerous political shifts. As he came near to the border with Rwanda, he came across a city that was not on our list of potential crusade sites. Our planners had simply overlooked it.

It was called Bukavu. It had nearly a half-million citizens who had never seen a large-scale evangelistic crusade. Furthermore, Steve confirmed that the roads to the city would be passable in the summer. Very excited, he called me at our headquarters in Germany.

"Nobody comes here to Bukavu, Reinhard," he said. "We will see tremendous results. Will you come?"

Nothing makes my heart beat faster than preaching the gospel where no one else is inclined to go. This part of my thinking began after my first success in the "gospel-hardened" land of Lesotho in 1969.

"Begin planning a crusade in Bukavu immediately," I ordered. "Stephen, you will be in charge."

The meeting was scheduled for July of 1989. As the time grew near, I flew to the area from Frankfurt. Stephen met me and escorted me to the hotel where I would be staying. The next day, as I do in every crusade, I asked to be driven around the city. Stephen had been there for months preparing this event, and I wanted him to show me the sort of people I would be preaching to. I wanted to hear from him all that he had learned about the history and lore of Bukavu. We took a local interpreter along. That allowed me to interview people in the marketplaces and neighborhoods as we passed through.

At one point we came to a prison. It was simply a cage for humans near the edge of the city. There were no cells, just a large, brick structure with a prison yard surrounding it. The bars of the fence were topped with wicked-looking razor wire. Many of the prisoners were in the yard taking in sunshine and exercising in the open air. A crowd of people stood around the bars of the yard.

Stephen stopped the car and turned off the engine. I saw clusters of civilians gathered here and there at the perimeter of the prison yard. "What are those people doing?" I asked.

"The government makes no provision for feeding men they intend to put to death. Those are the prisoners' families. If they don't feed the men, they will die of starvation."

"All these prisoners will die in prison?"

"Yes. And all of the ones you see in shackles are condemned to die by hanging."

I could see a number of men walking around dragging heavy chains shackled to their arms and legs.

"Every month, a hangman comes from Kinshasa," Stephen continued. "Do you see that big tree over there?"

Indeed, outside the prison yard was a large tree with spreading branches.

"Do you see where the bark is worn off that large branch?"

I could see it. "Yes," I replied.

"Each month the condemned men are brought out to the tree. A rope is thrown over that branch. A hangman's noose is tied to the end. The people of the city are invited to come and watch, and many do. The hangman earns his living the old-fashioned way. There is no scaffold. It is not a merciful hanging like in the old western movies, where a trap door opens beneath the condemned man and there is a long drop to break his neck. No, not here in Bukavu. Each condemned man in this prison is forced to shuffle forward in his chains. One by one the noose is placed around the neck of the next man and he is hanged until dead. The hangman uses the trunk of the tree for leverage to lift the man up, and he ties the rope off until the kicking and choking stops. Then he lets the body down, and the next man comes forward to have the noose placed on his neck."

"Have you seen this?"

"I have seen it."

"Can you imagine being one of the condemned, forced to watch what is in store for you?"

"That is not all. When the man is cut down, the hangman hacks off his hands and feet with an axe so that the shackles can be removed. Unless the family comes to claim it, the body is tossed onto a cart and dumped in an unmarked grave."

"Why doesn't the hangman simply unlock the shackles? Why go to the extreme of cutting off the hands and feet?"

"Because when a condemned man is brought here, he is taken to a blacksmith shed over there. His shackles are welded onto his arms and legs. There is no lock. It's permanent."

"How do they do that without burning the flesh?"

"There are no humanitarian watchdog groups here, Reinhard. The men receive horrible burns from the process. It's considered part of the punishment. These men are considered to be dead already. They have lost all rights. No one cares to take care of them. Some have actually died of burn infections before they can be hung. When they cut the shackles from a dead man they reuse them. They simply open them up with a cutting torch and weld a new man in place. And on it goes. Welcome to Bukavu prison."

I had seen this in other places in Africa. Once again, I realized that an African prison was a place to be feared. Unlike prisons in Western nations, there was little public scrutiny of the justice system. Political leaders were appointed, not elected. The people in power were expected to dominate the population by fear and intimidation. I had met many leaders in Africa who used their prison system to get rid of potential rivals and political enemies. Justice was often miscarried. It reminded me of what prison life must have been like in the biblical days of Paul and Silas.

"Here is the good news," Stephen offered. "I've been visiting here, and several of the condemned men have accepted Jesus. I've been having a Bible study with them for several weeks now."

"Praise God, Stephen. Take me inside to meet these brothers in the Lord."

We got out of the car. Immediately a strange sound came to my ears. It was the rhythmic jangle of chains mingled with the chant of male African voices.

"Hear that?" Stephen asked, with a knowing smile. "Those are your brothers."

"What are they doing?"

"That's praise and worship, prison style. Songs we taught them. They are using the only musical instruments they have."

"Their chains," I whispered, with realization. I stood there and listened, and as I did, I sensed Someone Else listening with me. As the sound of that wonderful haunting chant rose in the humid air, mingled with the jangle of chains, I sensed a door standing open to the throne room of God. I could almost see the great archangels at the portal of heaven, standing to receive this sacrifice of praise.

I felt a trembling excitement inside. I often feel this when the Holy Spirit speaks to my heart. A still small voice was telling me that in a place of great bondage, someone would soon be made free. This must have been the way Luis Graf felt in 1922 when he came to the East Prussian village of Trunz and found August Bonnke so desperately ill. My spirit flew like a bird from a cage, and I knew that something wonderful was about to happen.

Meanwhile, Stephen approached the guards, explaining who I was. They apparently already knew Stephen. We were allowed inside. The song continued.

I was appalled by the conditions inside the brick wall of the holding cell. The men slept on filthy mattresses scattered about on the floor of that large, cement-block room. The place was crawling with vermin. Buckets of sewage were gathered to one side. Clouds of flies swarmed over them. In the stifling heat, none of us could escape the stench. And the song, that wonderful chant of praise, punctuated by the rhythmic rattle of chains, continued to rise to the Lord like sweet incense.

We went out into the yard. Immediately, several men in their shackles gathered around us. Stephen spoke through the interpreter, explaining who I was. I greeted them briefly, but I was looking for the singing men.

I saw them, sitting in a circle, about 30 in all. They were singing and swaying back and forth. Their leader was a man of average build with a big smile and a missing front tooth. He rattled his chains with style and flourish, like a choir leader in a big church. If I had seen perfectly with the eyes of the Spirit, and not simply through a darkened glass, I might have seen him wearing a fine maroon suit.

The minute I saw him, the Holy Spirit spoke to me, *Tell that man he will be set free and become a preacher of the gospel.*

*Lord, pardon me, but it would cruel and unusual to say anything to this man if I heard You wrongly just now. Please, say it again. More slowly this time.*

*Tell that man he will be set free and he will become a preacher of the gospel.*

We were introduced to the group of condemned men. I greeted the brothers who had accepted the Lord in the name of Jesus. Other prisoners gathered around us from all over the yard. Nearly all of them came to hear me preach. I gave the whole group a salvation sermon through the interpreter. A few of them responded, accepting Jesus for the first time. I then encouraged them in the Lord. Then I turned to Stephen.

"Tell that man who was leading the singing that I would like to speak to him in private."

Stephen went to the man, explaining my request. He brought him to me, with the interpreter. We walked to a vacant area in the yard.

"Reinhard," Stephen said, "this man's name is Richard."

It was an honor to shake his shackled hand. "Tell Richard that the Lord has spoken to me today. The Lord says that he will be set free and become a preacher of the gospel."

The interpreter hesitated.

I nodded. "Repeat my words exactly," I said.

He cleared his throat and spoke to the man in his native tongue. The man reacted, looking away toward the hanging tree. When he looked back at me, his eyes had filled with tears. He spoke through the interpreter.

"Three times I have waited in line. Three times the hangman has become too tired to hang me. The last time he was here I was the next man to die. The hangman glared at me like he wanted to see me dead. Then he threw up his hands and went home."

"Jesus preserves you, Richard," I said. "And now He says you will be set free and become a preacher of the gospel."

Richard listened. I could tell that he was still too afraid to reach out and take my word for it. Hope can be most cruel to a condemned man waiting to hang. A man who has seen the end of his life played out for him so graphically, time after time. A man who wears shackles welded to his arms and legs, shackles he has seen removed only by the blow of a sharpened axe.

"What is your crime, Richard? What are you guilty of?"

"Murder."

"You do not look like a murderer to me. Who did you kill?"

He named the man.

"How did it happen?"

"We were in a bar, and a fight started."

"Did you start the fight?"

"I did not. But I did kill the man."

"Richard, if what you say is true, we do not call that murder. It is called self-defense, or perhaps justifiable homicide. Did you have a lawyer?"

Richard paused for a long time. He looked away at the tree again, and said nothing.

Then the interpreter spoke.

"If the man you kill in self-defense is from a wealthy family, Reverend Bonnke, there are many in Bukavu willing to swear testimony for money."

We left the prison, and I never saw Richard again. I preached for several days in the soccer stadium to standing-room-only crowds of 90,000. This created a huge stir in the area. Bukavu had never seen crowds like these in its history. Nearly everyone in the region attended at least one of the meetings. The number of salvations registered exceeded all that we had hoped and prayed for – 80,000. We were ecstatic.

As I prepared to leave, I asked Stephen Mutua to arrange one more meeting for me. I named a leading local politician in the city. I will not here name the man, or his office, because of the nature of the story that follows.

When we arrived at the politician's mansion we were ushered into a waiting area. We were kept waiting for a long time. Waiting to see powerful people in Africa is something I have learned that I must do. Finally, a secretary emerged from the inner sanctum and told us that the politician I wished to see was not available.

Now, if this is true, I thought, they might have told us earlier, in time to spare us this trip. Either it is a lie, or they have decided the great evangelist must prove his Christianity by demonstrating nearly infinite patience in the waiting room.

The politician was on a trip to Kinshasa, we were told. Instead of seeing him, we would be allowed to meet briefly with his wife. She would relay everything to her husband after we had gone.

After more waiting, a tall woman entered the room. She was dressed in finery and beautiful fabrics. I thought she carried herself with the imperial dignity of the Queen of Sheba. When she had made her entrance, an interpreter was provided, and I was able, at last, to speak to her.

After formalities, I told her why I had asked to see her husband. I had come to plead for the release of a condemned man in Bukavu prison, a man named Richard. I described him to her, and I recited his story of the crime for which he was sentenced to die. I suggested to her that a competent lawyer would surely have made a case for self- defense. At least a good lawyer would have found a way to avoid the death penalty for Richard. Then I told her of Richard's conversion and of the way he led the singing among the condemned men in the prison.

She listened carefully to all that I said. Then she stood and excused herself. She said that she would see about what could be done, but condemned prisoners were never released from Bukavu prison once the courts had spoken.

After another long time of waiting, she returned. She asked that all of the other guests be removed from the room. At last it was just the two of us. She stood before me, very close.

"Reverend Bonnke," she said, quietly. "You are a very powerful man from Germany. Your organization is large, and your following is worldwide. You want my husband to do something for you. I would like you to do something for me. Do you understand?"

"Certainly," I said, "I will do whatever I can."

"Do you have children, Reverend Bonnke?"

"I do."

She smiled a motherly smile. "What are their names? May I ask?"

"The oldest is Freddy, and then Gabriele, and Susanne." I removed my wallet and showed her pictures.

"Those are beautiful children. I have two children preparing to attend the university. Here, we have only the National University of Zaire." She shrugged, as if I would understand her problem. "It is not the excellence that you would want for your children, I am sure. And yet, my children have not been able to get scholarships to the schools we would choose abroad. I would like you to provide those scholarships, Reverend Bonnke. Will you do that for me?"

I was saddened, though not truly surprised. In a land where money could buy a death sentence, surely a bribe could obtain freedom.

"I am sorry," I said, "but this, I cannot do. I am a man of God. I will not strike a bargain to obtain justice of any kind. The law must stand above this, or it is not justice. My answer to you must be no."

The woman instantly whirled to leave the room. I feared greatly for Richard. As she reached for the door I nearly shouted her name. She stopped and looked back at me for one moment. I pointed my finger at her.

"God has told me that Richard will be released and become a preacher of the gospel. God has spoken. Do not stand in His way."

She left the room, shutting the door behind her with force. My meeting was over.

"Oh, Lord," I prayed, "save Richard by Your mighty power, not by the power of bribes and treachery."

I must confess, I left Bukavu with a heavy heart. I feared that I had left Richard as I had found him, a dead man walking. My one hope was that the politician's wife feared God in some corner of her heart, and that the Holy Spirit would cause my words to find their mark.

SHE NEVER MISSED CHURCH, but it was nerve wracking to get her there. First her wheelchair had to be moved near the car. Then she had to be helped out of the chair and carefully positioned to get inside. Her crooked and stiffened spine made it impossible for her to bend at the proper angle. She would receive a cruel jolt as she dropped onto the seat. Then, her legs would have to be placed inside the car. Her hips had been permanently dislodged from their sockets, and moving her legs would cause her to scream out in pain.

Her husband would beg her to stay at home. So would her friends who sometimes took her to church. Tears of pain would roll from her eyes, but her jaw remained firm. She would not be denied another opportunity to be in the house of the Lord.

"Take Quasimodo to church," Jean Neil would say, gritting her teeth, with a fierce little twinkle in her eye.

During each meeting Jean would be able to sit on a thick cushion for only a few minutes. Then the pain would become unbearable, and she would pull herself up on her crutches and stagger to the wall. There, she would lean against it to relieve the searing pain between her lower back and her hips. She would stand that way, draped across her crutches, for the better part of an hour.

No one could attend that church and not be constantly reminded that Jean Neil was in terrible pain.

For this reason many prayers were made for her healing. The pastor prayed, the youth group prayed, the women's group prayed. Every congregational prayer time included a request for Jean's healing. Always her friends searched for answers. "Was something wrong with their prayers? Why wouldn't God heal such a faithful servant as this?" Jean never lost hope, but her faith was sent through many ups and downs over the years.

Her basic problem was a bad back. Jean had known this from her youth. But she had never let it stop her from a rough-and-tumble approach to life. She was athletic and mischievous, a prankster, an instigator. She was the kind to do things on a dare.

Those friends who knew her best appreciated her spunk. They knew she had been raised for 15 years in a terrible home for girls in Jersey. She had been beaten with stinging nettles for wetting the bed as a toddler. She had been tortured in ice baths for speaking out of turn to her caregivers. She had been fed water and stale bread. She had been stripped naked and beaten in front of the other girls for making wisecracks. But they could never beat the wisecracking out of Jean. She never lost her knack for a quick remark. She had developed a strong and defiant will to thrive in the face of great odds. It was her gift.

She had married John Neil, and they had made their life together in Rugby, England. Jean had become a Christian but John had not. Still, things were going well for them when suddenly she had taken a bad fall. It had ruptured her tailbone and this had accelerated the deterioration of her spine. A series of operations, some of which had gone badly, had fused several disks. After her last operation she was placed in a plaster cast for six months.

John & Jean Neil

Emerging from the cast, she was told she would never walk again. On top of that, her heart and lungs had become weakened through the prolonged use of pain medications. Specially formulated pills were necessary to keep her heart pumping. She had also become dependent on inhalers and oxygen. One top British surgeon gave her a fifty-fifty chance of improvement with a final risky operation to reconstruct her backbone. Every day that she lived, Jean weighed her pain against the risk of that final desperate operation.

Meanwhile, she kept going to church. In spite of her condition she took an active role as a youth leader. She had a heart for the teenagers and invested herself in them. They appreciated her for it, and were inspired by her example, knowing how much she endured just to be with them.

Then something happened that would change her life forever. A three-year-old toddler at church, a little boy, walked up to Jean and asked to pray for her. She took his little hands in hers and let him pray his simple, childlike prayer. He asked that God would heal her. Something began stirring, deep in Jean's soul.

That night she had two distinct and vivid dreams. In the first dream she underwent the spinal surgery, and she died on the operating table. She watched the doctor tell her husband that her heart simply had become too weakened to endure the process. She awoke with a start. There could be no mistake about the meaning of this dream – if she chose to go with the surgery, death was coming for her. She wondered, could it have been a dream from her own anxieties? She went back to sleep.

This time Jean had another very different dream. She was in a large cavernous room with twelve other people in wheelchairs. She heard the voice of a man speaking. It was a distinctive voice with a foreign accent. She saw the man emerge in front of the wheelchairs. He went to the first chair and prayed for a woman. He commanded her to get up. She got up but then sat back down in utter defeat. Then the man came to Jean's chair. He prayed for her, and she took off running from her wheelchair, totally healed.

The next day Jean visited her pastor. She was frightened. She told him about both of the dreams from the night before. She said she feared the end of her life was near. Her pastor suggested that she not focus on the first dream but the second. He said that a whole new life could be near for her – a life of health and wholeness. She had to choose which dream to believe, the dream of death or the dream of life?

Jean rejected her fears and chose life. She began to describe the second dream to her friends and family. She could even describe the physical description of the man who had prayed for her, and the description of the room they were in, and the sound of his voice. She began to look forward to whatever, or whomever, this agent of God's power might be.

Two weeks later a youth convention was to be held in the National Exhibition Center in Birmingham, England. The little youth group from Rugby would, of course, attend. Jean Neil would go with them. She heard that the speaker would be Reinhard Bonnke. She had never heard me speak.

This event took place in 1988. I was to preach a special youth conference in that city. Jean knew me by reputation as an evangelist, and the stories she had heard included many of miraculous healings at my crusades

She asked her husband to prepare a special ambulance for her to ride in. Since he worked for an ambulance company, this was something he could readily do. She told her friends that she believed if Reinhard Bonnke prayed for her she would begin to improve. At this point she could not bring herself to say definitely that I was the man she had seen in her dream. Her faith for healing was not yet complete.

I arrived in Birmingham and stayed at the home of a friend there. The morning of the meeting I felt a strong urge to pray. As I prayed I sensed the presence of the Holy Spirit with me in an unusual way. I began to ask, *Lord, what do You want to do in Birmingham today? Will You perform a miracle in this meeting?* My mind was open to receive His answer.

I entered the Convention Center hall through a stage door. There was a thick curtain that I was told to go through, and then I would be on the platform. As I pushed through the curtain, there was a young man standing there on crutches. I didn't see him in time, and I brushed him as I passed. He fell straight onto his back. The people attending me quickly saw to him, and pushed me onto the stage. I was told later, as the service got underway, that the young man was not knocked down by me, but by the power of God. He got up and did not need his crutches anymore.

The cavernous room was filled with nearly 12,000 youth and their adult supervisors. I sat on my chair and waited to be announced. As I waited I looked across the crowd and continued in deep conversation with the Lord. *Lord what are you doing here tonight?*

As my gaze fell across the wheelchairs, the Lord directed my attention to one lady at the far left. I sensed the Spirit saying to me, *That woman in that wheelchair will be healed today.*

From her wheelchair Jean watched me on the stage. She thought that I certainly bore a strong resemblance to the man in her dream. She looked around the hall at the other wheelchairs. She didn't count them, but there were perhaps twelve others in her condition. When I got up to preach, Jean recognized my voice from her dream. The tone and the accent seemed identical. She began to feel a powerful sense of anticipation.

I was on fire with the Spirit that night. I preached a salvation message to those young people. When I gave an altar call, nearly 1,500 of them responded. I was ecstatic. It was a glorious day. Then suddenly, the host of the meeting came to me on the platform and said, "Reinhard, I have hired this room only until six o'clock. We have to clear the room."

I looked at my watch and saw that we only had 15 minutes. I was stricken. *Oh, no,* I thought, *I have not prayed for the sick.*

Without any delay I hurried down from the platform and went to the first wheelchair I saw in front of me. A lady sat there. I said, "I want to pray for you."

I placed my hands on her. I could feel the power of the Spirit like electricity in my hands. I prayed, then said, "Stand up in Jesus' name."

She stood but she was very shaky. On her face was an expression of irritation, as if I had no right to do this to her. She sat back down. I knew she was not healed. *Oh, no,* I thought, *this is not the woman God showed me.*

At this point, someone in the room had a video camera running. What follows was recorded and has been viewed again and again by many audiences in the years since this meeting. I switched gears. I remembered that the woman God had shown me was to the left. I hopped up, and looked to the left until I saw her. Then I raced all the way across the room, the camera following me. I was sprinting against the clock to get to her before they cleared that hall.

Jean Neil was sitting in that wheelchair. Her husband John stood behind her, gripping the handles of the chair. I had never seen them before. I knew nothing about their circumstances nor what had brought them here. I glanced at John, and he looked at me with a look as cold as stone. I knelt down in front of Jean, and said, "I've come to pray for you. You're going to be healed today."

I will never forget her reply, "I know, I know, I know!" she cried.

What Jean knew was that her second dream was coming true before her very eyes – down to the detail of my praying for the first woman who was not healed. Her faith reached out.

I said, "OK, I will pray for you, and you will stand up."

John said, "What do you mean, stand up? My wife has no hips. Her hips are not attached."

I said, "All I know is all things are possible with God. I will pray for you, and you will stand up."

I laid my hands on her and prayed. Then I commanded her to stand up. Slowly, with great determination, she stood up, and then she sort of slumped forward onto the floor. I thought, *Oh, no, Lord what have I done?*

But then I realized she had not collapsed back into her wheelchair, she had fallen forward. This was a move in the right direction, at least. Then suddenly I knew that she had fallen under the power of God. She was slain in the Spirit – the same thing that happened to the young man on crutches as I brushed him on the stage.

I quickly bent down over her. "Jesus is healing you," I said.

"I know, I know," she said. Then she looked at me and said, "I feel as if I am under anesthetic."

"Doctor Jesus is operating on you," I cried.

At this point, as Jean tells it, she felt powerful, incredible things happening inside her body. She felt as if she was placed on a stretcher and her body was being pulled straight. She felt her hips go into their sockets. One of her legs was two inches shorter than the other. It grew out to be the same length as the other. Then she said it was as if a hot rod of steel went down the full length of her spine. Her bones, tissues and muscles, which had atrophied, began to flex and pulse with new life.

I said to her, "Get up, in Jesus' name."

I looked at John. I thought he would punch me.

He said, "What if she falls?"

I said, "I'll be here. I'll be here. Now, get up."

Slowly Jean began to gather herself from the floor. She stood to her feet.

"Now, walk in Jesus' name."

The video camera was rolling. People were standing on chairs all around us. We were totally surrounded by onlookers. Jean had on a red hat, a beret. Everyone in the room saw that beret fly upward as she suddenly disappeared from under it. To me it seemed as if she made a sudden leap like a grasshopper makes at the moment you least expect it. Before I could tell what happened that woman was gone.

Jean Neil raced around that building, hands in the air, praising God, crying with joy. Her second dream had just happened. Not death, but a brand-new life.

She said her legs were not in the least bit wobbly. They were pumping with strength and incredible power. I kept calling into the microphone, "Where is that woman? Where is that woman?"

The people answered again and again. "Over there, over there, over there." And each time they were pointing to a different place.

I was still looking for her in the direction she had gone when suddenly she was right behind me. She had gone completely around that building.

The place was bedlam. So much crying. So much praising God. So many tears of joy.

I asked Jean if she would go up onto the stage so that the people could learn what had just happened. She whirled and bounded up the steps to the platform. They were quite steep. That was a testimony in itself. She was completely restored. John followed, in shock, bringing along the wheelchair. I followed.

On stage Jean was dancing around with her hands in the air like a boxer who had just won the heavyweight title. The crowd was cheering. Jean was waving. I asked her whom she was waving to, and she said to her pastor and friends from her church in Rugby. Then I learned for the first time the extent of her illnesses. It is good that I did not know beforehand. It might have affected my thoughts and my faith to pray for her. I don't know, God knows, and God is good.

"Give us a demonstration," I said.

"Of what?" Jean retorted, in her wonderful, sarcastic way.

"Do something you could not do before," I explained.

"Oh," she said, as if she did not know what I had meant.

Then she began to bend down and touch her toes, do deep knee bends, run in place. She went through a regular workout for the people. They cheered and applauded and praised God, until somebody remembered that we had to clear the hall.

I don't know who paid the bill for the extra time. I was just the guest speaker, and it was time for me to go back to Germany. I said goodbye to the people.

Only after arriving back home did I learn the full impact of this miracle and the video that had captured it. My phone began to ring. People were hearing about this miracle in countries around the world. Because I know human nature, I know that sometimes those who sit in wheelchairs are not crippled. In Jean Neil's case, the many people from her church who knew her were confirming the power of this testimony. Soon her doctors added their confirmation to the story. The news media went into a feeding frenzy over it. It was a healing that shook many in the church from their lethargy concerning the power of God to heal.

When I left town, Jean Neil was beginning a brand-new life. She went home to Rugby and raced up the stairs into her house. Her daughter was in the sitting room with her boyfriend. When she heard feet running up the stairs she thought it was a burglar.

"Go see to it," she urged her boyfriend.

He was a bit frightened. "Maybe it's your mother," he suggested, hopefully.

"My mother's a crippled old woman," she said. "She can't walk up stairs, let alone run."

Having opened the door, Jean heard this remark. For the first time in her life she realized what her family thought of her. Quasimodo was more than a bittersweet joke. To her loved ones, it had been a hard reality. Her limitations had become her family's limitations too.

She walked into the room with her daughter. "When Jesus heals you, you can run up stairs," she said.

"Mother!" Her daughter burst into tears. Jean ran up and down the stairs for her. Then they embraced and cried and cried and cried some more.

Eventually John parked the ambulance. He came up the stairs to join them, carrying the wheelchair.

When Jean awoke the next morning she was paralyzed with a sudden fear and could not move. "John," she said, in a trembling voice.

He sat up quickly. "Yes, dear. What is it?"

For a moment she could not speak. "Was it just a dream, John? Did I have another dream?"

"No, it was not a dream, darling. It really happened. I was there."

She leaped from the bed, dancing around the room. "I will fix breakfast. I will do the dishes. I will clean the house. I will go to the store." And with that she left him still wiping the sleep from his eyes.

It was Sunday, the day to go to church. After breakfast Jean put on her cloak and headed out the door. No one would take her to church on this day. She would walk. She hurried down the front steps and across the street. She took huge breaths of fresh air, needing no more inhaler, no more oxygen, no more drugs. Her heart was singing and overflowing with gratitude.

Then she heard a rattling sound behind her. She stopped and turned. There was John, hurrying after her with the wheelchair.

"What are you doing, John?"

He stopped. "What if you fall?" He stood there with a helpless look on his face. He was still her protector, and he still had trouble believing she had been healed, even though he had been there to see it.

"Take it back home, John. You're embarrassing me. I will never sit in that chair again."

He took the chair back. She never sat in it again. Even when a TV documentary crew offered her £1,000 just to sit in it so they could re-create the image of her before being healed, she refused.

Over the years since 1988, I came to learn the details of Jean's story. It was years later that she told me of the dream. It just fascinates me the way God worked in two different lives to bring this miracle about. She even heard my accent in her dream. Such detail! And she had never heard me preach before. Later, when we returned to Birmingham for our Euro-Fire-Conference Jean gave her glorious testimony.

God had pointed Jean out to me in the crowd of 12,000 at the National Exhibition Center. He told me He would heal her. In my haste to pray for the sick – anyone who was sick – I thought I had made a bad mistake in praying for the wrong woman. But God had anticipated that very action. For Jean it was the final detail from her dream that confirmed in her mind that she was seeing the actual fulfillment of her dream of life. Her healing was imminent. Now, her faith rose up in full force. She was so ready when I came to her and said, "Jesus is going to heal you."

"I know, I know, I know," she cried. I can still hear the marvelous anticipation in her voice.

What a mighty God we serve!

WE REGISTERED 770,000 DECISIONS FOR CHRIST in 1989, 20,000 more than the year before. This was true even though our overall attendance dropped slightly to 3,390,000. We held nine campaigns inside Africa and two others beyond, in the Soviet Union and Malaysia. The largest single crowd we saw that year was 165,000 in Jos, Nigeria.

As the campaign season came to an end, I received a very great honor. Regent University in Virginia awarded me an honorary doctorate from their school of divinity. I flew there and received it at the graduation ceremony that year. The degree was given in recognition of the missionary and evangelistic impact I had made through CfaN. In my acceptance speech, I said, "I receive this honor in the name of the One who has said, 'without me you can do nothing,' our blessed Lord and Savior Jesus Christ". Arriving back in Germany I received a congratulatory telephone call from my brother, Peter.

Regent University, Virginia Beach, VA
Doctor of Divinity, 20th of May 1989

"I guess we will have to call you 'Dr. Bonnke' from now on."

"Please, Peter, do not call me 'Dr. Bonnke.' Call me Reinhard. But it is a great honor to receive this degree, and I thank you for the congratulations."

It was another moment of great personal reward. I recalled my discussion with him in Glückstadt so many years ago. We had walked through the town and talked as he had returned from the University and I had begun my practicum with Dad in Krempe. He had been convinced that following Dad in the ministry would provide no leverage in this world. I had insisted that God had the greatest leverage of all. Now, it was becoming evident that I had chosen wisely. I had missed nothing in listening to, and obeying the voice of the Spirit. As the Bible instructs us to seek first the kingdom of God and all these things will be added to us,[95] the honorary doctorate from Regent must surely be counted as something "added" in that wonderful way.

# Chapter 30

IN 1990 WE PREPARED to enter the last decade of the millennium. CfaN put together twelve campaigns in seven nations of Africa, plus a Euro-Fire Conference in Portugal. Once again we broke all attendance records. I preached the ABCs of the gospel to 5,395,000 people face to face. Almost a million registered decisions for Christ! What a memorable year it was, with the highest of highs, and some awful lows.

With a million decisions registered, we were still far from the prophetic one million souls in a day that Kenneth Copeland had predicted. Though I was astounded at the results of our work that year, my spirit remained restless to press on and see all that God had promised to accomplish through CfaN.

Great victories do not come without opposition. In February, while holding meetings in Bamenda, Cameroon, we encountered a foretaste of the escalation planned by our enemy Satan. In previous years, we had conducted three campaigns in Cameroon, preaching to 1,140,000 people and seeing 250,000 registered decisions for Jesus. I expected another great harvest in Bamenda. But during the build-up to the meetings we began to experience strong opposition from the Catholic Church. Our team could feel an unusual amount of tension, and we focused our prayers on the need for protection and victory for the upcoming meetings. But as we approached the start of the event, the evangelical pastors who had invited us were not able to build a bridge of cooperation with their Catholic brethren. Many evil words were spoken against us.

The soccer stadium we had obtained for the meetings was surrounded by high walls. We hung a large "Jesus Christ is King" banner behind the platform. On the opening night a crowd of only 30,000 showed up. We felt that many people were staying away out of intimidation. As I preached, a group of young men rushed into the stadium carrying a large paper banner of their own making. They attached it to the far wall at the back of the stadium facing our stage. It read, "Father says, Bonnke must die."

The evangelical pastors who had organized the meeting became fearful. Given the nature of this banner, I could understand why. I continued my sermon but could not stop wondering which "father" the banner was quoting? Not my heavenly Father, that was for sure. The young men who had hung it were obviously of their "father" the devil. "Bonnke must die" was his kind of terrorism. Scripture calls him a murderer from the beginning.[96]

I asked the Lord what we should do. By the Spirit He indicated that we were to continue the meeting as if nothing had happened. So we ripped the banner down and went on. The next night the young men had grown bolder. They actually blocked the entrance to the stadium and turned people back who wanted to attend. Then suddenly, as if on some signal, they disappeared into the surrounding neighborhood. The people who were waiting outside slipped timidly into the stadium for the preaching of the gospel. In the middle of the sermon a hail of large stones came over the wall behind me and descended on the crowd. People were struck and fell wounded to the ground, screaming, crying out in pain and distress. I continued to call over the loudspeaker, "Father, forgive them for they know not what they do. We forgive them in the name of Jesus." The police gave chase, but no one was caught.

Soon ambulances arrived to carry away the wounded. I again asked the Lord what we should do. He indicated to my spirit that we should continue. The next night as I came to the platform a local pastor said to me, "We know that you are a true man of God. Anyone else would have run away and here you are right to the last meeting." In fact, by persistence it seems we had won. There was no one obstructing the entrance at all. No demonstrators. As an even greater sign of our victory over Satan, 50,000 people streamed into the stadium. I preached, and when the full tally was in, we had registered 45,000 decisions for Christ during that campaign. Hallelujah! 45,000 souls snatched from the tyranny of their father the devil into the kingdom of God and His dear Son!

I believe everyone has the right to hear the gospel. The people of Bamenda were embroiled in bitter religious strife. Did that disqualify them from hearing the gospel? No. Jesus said the sower scattered the seed on stony ground, thorny ground, and hard ground, as well as on good ground.[97] I am a sower of the seed of the gospel in whatever circumstance I find myself; it is God who remains Lord of the harvest. Bamenda, Cameroon, reminded me of that.

It is interesting to note, however, that immediately following the difficult Bamenda meetings we experienced the greatest breakthrough in our history. Flying to Burkina Faso we looked out on a crowd of 240,000! In our meetings there, we saw a total attendance of 940,000 with 200,000 decisions for Christ! Everyone on the team was greatly encouraged, and we knew that in following the Great Commission, Bamenda was to be the exception, not the rule. Four great crusades followed that year in Nigeria, Zaire, and Rwanda, plus a successful Euro-Fire Conference in Lisbon, Portugal, before the next setback knocked the wind from our sails.

IN LATE SEPTEMBER we returned to Uganda for our second crusade following the rise of President Yoweri Museveni. After decades of intolerance under Amin and Obote, religious freedom had been declared in this troubled land. Museveni had even been heralded by President Ronald Reagan of the United States for his many economic and cultural reforms. Like many African leaders, Museveni seemed reluctant to give up power. He disliked the idea of serving a limited term of four years. The good part about his rule was that he diligently worked for the good of the country.

Our meetings were to be held on a sports field in the city of Jinja, some 50 miles east of the capital of Kampala. Jinja was a city of 70,000 souls, located on Lake Victoria, the second largest lake in the world. Its outlet formed the headwaters of the great Nile River, which flows northward for 4,000 miles through Sudan and Egypt, to the great river delta at Cairo.

In preparation for the meetings, our team, under the leadership of Steve Mutua, worked feverishly with the Museveni government in Kampala to establish legitimacy. We had obtained a total of 16 permits from the national and city governments. As had become our custom, we erected a tent beside the crusade grounds for counseling and prayer.

Arriving a few days before the meetings, our plane landed at the Entebbe airport, south of Kampala. We were met by thousands of Christians who formed a parade route to welcome us to Uganda. Unlike the discord we had found in Bamenda, here hundreds of churches had united. Our expectations were raised high.

As we continued through Kampala and on to Jinja, the route was decorated with our familiar red and black CfaN posters announcing the meeting. This was in contrast to my first meeting in Kampala when our posters had disappeared into the homes of people who had not seen such artwork for decades.

After settling into our hotel in Jinja, I took a trip by gasoline-powered tour boat across Lake Victoria. We visited a quaint fishing village with colorfully painted sloops beached along the shore after a night of angling. Their nets were spread across the ground to dry, and an abundant catch of tilapia and Nile perch were being prepared for market in Jinja and Kampala.

As we left the village and continued our sightseeing route, our tour boat began to buck in the grip of a mighty tide. My guide explained that the glassy calm waters of the lake grew suddenly troubled near the mouth of the Nile, where vast aquifers rushed upward from 600 feet below the lake's surface. These underground rivers poured their bounty from a source 150 miles to the west, where 20 icy glaciers were found on the earth's equator – of all places! These river-making glaciers were located in the sky, nestled in rocky crags 16,000 feet above sea level in the Rwenzori Mountains. I could feel the immeasurable power of the great river rising beneath my feet as the glacier-fed Nile transformed Lake Victoria into a raging torrent.

Beaching our craft on a small island in the river's mouth, I got out and stood for a long time with the sweep of the river flowing past me on either side. What a land of contrasts and natural beauty! Not to mention a place with such God-blessed water resources. The thunder of Ripon Falls sounded like a roaring jet engine in the north. As I took it in I gained a new vision of the power of the gospel that was already beginning to trouble the calm of Satan's domain in central and northern Africa. Like this unstoppable river, it was sweeping across the continent. CfaN would be opposed, but the power of this salvation message would carry us through all obstacles, and across the parched deserts of lost humanity that lay in our path.

"From Cape Town to Cairo," I whispered into the roar of the troubled waters, "Africa shall be saved."

THE MEETINGS IN JINJA began and we saw about a thousand people accept Jesus as Savior. A number of blind and lame were healed and, as usual, the crowds began to grow. On the third night, however, one of the most disturbing scenes of my entire life took place. A local military police squad burst into the sports facility with AK-47 rifles at ready. They moved across the arena as if we were a dangerous and seditious gathering. They surrounded the preaching platform, and the police commander climbed onto it. He approached me, his face a mask of fierce rage.

"Tell the people to leave!" he said, waving his rifle menacingly.

"I will not tell them to leave," I said. "They have come to hear the gospel preached, and we have a legitimate right to be here."

"Tell them to leave!" he repeated.

"I will not tell them. You tell them." I thrust the microphone into his hand.

Suddenly, with the microphone in his hand, his demeanor changed. He must have realized that his words could cause a riot. He cleared his throat and spoke to the people calmly. "I have received orders from above that this crowd must disperse. This meeting is to end."

"Why? Why?" the people shouted back.

"These are not my orders, but the orders came from above. It is my job to carry them out. I must see that you leave here at once. Now, you must leave this place."

The people did not move. He shouted his orders again. Still they refused to budge. I saw a fierce look return to his face, and I knew that the scene would become violent. He walked to my still photographer and ordered him to stop taking pictures. He saw the video cameras recording the event. He shouted that the video cameras were to be shut off at once.

I knew what was happening. He was making sure that there would be no pictures of what would happen next. I had to intervene to prevent terrible bloodshed. I took the microphone and told the people that as Christians we had no choice but to submit to those who represented the authority of Uganda. We must disperse. I told the people that I would obey and leave the platform immediately. And I did.

Some of the crowd still refused to leave. The soldiers charged among them using rifle butts to smash people into submission. Others used clubs, forcing the main crowd to leave the stadium. Next, they charged into our tent and began beating the lame and blind and sick people who had gathered there for prayer. All of this happened in spite of Uganda's law establishing religious freedom, and in spite of our having obtained all the necessary permits to hold the meetings.

Back in my hotel room I fell to my knees in prayer, seeking answers. As I cried out to God, I entered into what some have called "the offense of the gospel" and "the fellowship of suffering." I groaned in agony. The words of Isaiah came to my ears, *He is despised and rejected of men; a man of sorrows, and acquainted with grief: and we hid as it were our faces from him* ...[98] I realized that in my normal experience I had hidden my face from the full meaning of the Lord's suffering and rejection. It is only natural to do so. Even His disciples could not bear the agony they saw in the Garden of Gethsemane, hiding their faces in the exhaustion of anxiety and sleep.[99]

In the Western world, the gospel has known full and wide acceptance during our lifetime. But in Jinja, I began to know that in truth, the offense of the gospel remains as strong as ever. The world, the flesh, and the devil will never make peace with His salvation message. God's enemies are "armed with cruel hate," as Martin Luther wrote in his great anthem, *A mighty Fortress is our God*. Feeling the edge of such hatred in Jinja my heart broke as I identified anew with the sufferings of Jesus.

But in that time of prayer I also caught a glimpse of the glory that only attends those who are called to endure persecution for His name's sake. It is an unimaginable glory that in eternity will elevate those who have shared it to places above the stars. "Oh, what a foretaste of glory divine," wrote Fanny Crosby, the author of "Blessed Assurance." These were the words that came to my mind, and expressed my heart, during this time of agony and prayer.

The next day, before leaving, I met with the pastors who had sponsored the meeting. They told me that the local district manager of Jinja had decided to defy the government in Kampala. It was reported that he said, "If Kampala wants to rule here, let them come and rule. But as long as I am in control, this meeting will not continue."

The pastors were so crestfallen and demoralized; I feared that they might despair. They had been looking to me to bring a visitation from heaven. Now I had been removed from the scene. In truth, they were as empowered to preach the gospel as I was. I wanted them to believe it. So I challenged them.

"You must heed the words of the gospel where it says that the disciples went forth, the Lord working with them to confirm their words.[100] You must take the initiative. You must go forth in Jesus' name, and the Lord will run to keep up with you! He will confirm with signs and wonders the words you proclaim! But if there is no proclamation, there will be no confirmation. Go, in Jesus' name!"

It was the same kind of exhortation that I had begun to deliver at every Fire Conference, challenging ministers to step out of their comfort zone and do the work of an evangelist. The calling is for everyone, not just Reinhard Bonnke, and the equipping is not exclusive. It is given to all those who obey.

Triumph followed turmoil. Again, it is interesting to note that immediately following the Jinja disaster we experienced another huge milestone. Flying to Kaduna, Nigeria, we looked out on a crowd of 500,000! I was absolutely stunned to silence. I turned to the ministers on the platform and they were weeping. Not understanding their tears, I walked up to them. "Why are you weeping?" I asked. "This is a day of great rejoicing. Look at the size of this crowd."

"You don't understand, Pastor Bonnke," a pastor replied. "These people are nearly all Muslims. This area is totally dominated by the Muslim religion."

The pastors were weeping because the Muslims, who had shunned their churches, had been willing to gather on an open field to hear the gospel preached. The local Christians were overcome with emotion and felt they were seeing an unexpected breakthrough that could have great implications for the future of evangelism in Muslim areas. Frankly, I agreed with them.

I turned back to the crowd and began to see the shape of the gospel for Kaduna. I preached with fire and fervor, with love and compassion, and passion, and everything all mixed together. The gospel message is the same for Muslims as for pagans of any stripe. When I made the altar call, a huge sea of hands was raised to the sky. I was so moved to see it!

That night at the hotel, when we as a team had our dinner together, I couldn't eat. I was so filled with the glory of God from seeing that response to the gospel, the greatest I had yet seen. I turned to Peter van den Berg. "Do you know what I feel in my spirit?"

"What?"

"If Jesus keeps saving souls at this rate, I think one day the devil is going to sit alone in hell." I laughed, and he laughed heartily. Yes, yes! It was everything we dreamed of as evangelists. Jesus had died for the sins of the whole world. Why not see them all saved?

Now, I understand this idea is not theologically correct, but I wish that it was. We know that hell was not made for man. It was made for Satan and his demons. I simply love the image of Satan sitting in hell with no one to torment.

Our meetings concluded in Kaduna with a total attendance of 1,670,000! In one meeting in Muslim Nigeria, we had preached to more people than we had preached to during the entire year of 1987, just three short years ago! The acceleration that I felt almost made my feet leave the ground. I looked forward to our next meeting in Nigeria, to be held in Muslim-dominated Kano in 1991. I put out the word to my partners that I wanted them to come with me on this historic trip to witness what I had witnessed in Kaduna. I wanted their eyes to behold the harvest that their faithful giving had enabled. More than anything, I wanted them to see that they shared equally in my rewards.

Hallelujah! Let heaven be full and hell empty!

AFTER SEEING THE CROWD in Kaduna my spiritual imagination began to expand. Years ago, as a struggling young evangelist in Lesotho using my accordion to bait a few people into listening to my sermons, my faith had been stunted by those early meager results. Since then, the crowds had multiplied. But it surprised me to realize that my mind still tended to play it safe, thinking small, looking conservatively for the next step, not daring to embrace the full future God had promised. After Kaduna, that began to change.

In Kaduna we had seen 500,000 people gather to hear the gospel. Rather than feel that I'd arrived with this milestone, I began to feel like I'd only just begun. I thought; *Why should I limit my vision when God has said, "Africa shall be saved?"* Africa was 53 nations, covering 23 percent of the earth's total land area, with a population of about 650 million[101]. In a series of vivid dreams of the map of this land, God Himself had provoked me to think so large! Now, I began to enjoy the process of dreaming on my own.

Arriving back in Germany I began to confront the coldness and hardness of Europe and other non-third-world nations of the modern world. I felt gripped by the challenge of reaching an entire modern nation with a single presentation of the gospel. *How can it be done, Lord? How?* Why not imagine the impossible? I thought of television or radio as a way to reach a nation. Soon, I realized that too many channel choices were presented. Very few would actually tune in to a gospel presentation.

The ringing of the doorbell snapped me out of my reverie. I went to the door and opened it. The postman waved to me as he walked away from our door toward the next address on the street. He had delivered a mailbox full of letters, plus an extra package that needed to be picked up rather than remain on our porch. I gathered them all and carried them inside. At the kitchen table I began to sort through our bounty.

Suddenly, I saw the answer to my question: the image of the postman waving as he left our door. I imagined him, and every postman as an evangelist, delivering the gospel to every home in a nation on a single day. This is how it could be done! In my mind I heard the words of the scripture, "How beautiful are the feet of them that preach the gospel of peace, and bring glad tidings of good things![102]

But this idea seemed far from my calling. My entire ministry had been built on the spoken word, using my voice, not the pen, as the instrument of communication. I was known for being an evangelist, not an author, although my book Evangelism by Fire was published in 1989 already. Still, the idea took over my brain and would not die. *Lord, is this idea from You? Are You speaking to me?* I asked.

*Yes,* came the answer. *I am calling you to do this. Write a classic message on the cross. Deliver it by mail to every home in a nation. This is how to reach them all at once with the gospel.*

I was surprised to hear this mandate from heaven coming to me. *Are You sure I'm the one to do this, Lord? My resources are allocated to crusades. My people are trained to do campaigns and Fire Conferences, not a huge publishing and mail undertaking like this. The logistics and costs will be enormous.*

In fact, the Lord spoke to my heart. *You are not my first choice. I have given this Word to two others who have refused it.*

This sobered and humbled me. It was true that this outreach was not a natural outgrowth of the calling on my life. I was simply available. God knew I would say yes to Him. So I got the assignment.

This began a long process of writing. Many people do not understand that there is great difference between a sermon and a booklet. I wanted every word, every idea, to be weighed for its accuracy. I wanted to be sure that the ideas hit the human heart. I wanted every distraction removed from the language. I wanted to find

One team – George Canty and I

the combination of words that would leap from the page and challenge the reader quickly with the claims of Christ. I wanted pictures and illustrations to capture the reader's interest. For many people reading this message, it would be my first opportunity to speak to them. And for many, it would be my last. I didn't want to blow it. So, I began to write and rewrite and proofread and rewrite again. I took advice and input from everyone whose views I respected concerning the presentation of the gospel. George Canty, one of Great Britain's eminent Christian writers and dear friend of mine, got in on the act. This process would continue for a full two years before I felt the message was clear enough to present to an entire nation.

As I sat down to begin, I received some very good news, indeed. Richard had been released from prison in far eastern Congo. Richard, the prisoner unjustly accused of murder, welded into iron shackles, and condemned to die on the hangman's tree in Bukavu. He was the poor man I had left behind two years ago, fearing that I had raised his hopes in vain. But he had been released just as the Lord had promised. I had heard a word from the Lord when I first saw him leading his fellow prisoners in praise and worship. I could still hear those chains accompanying their song.

What a faithful God we serve! His word can be trusted. It is more sure than the sunrise, because the sunrise itself is painted by decree. I sent a message of congratulations to Richard, and instructed my team to provide a full scholarship for him to attend Bible College. It was a day of great celebration at CfaN!

# Chapter 31

THE CRUSADE SEASON began well in 1991. We returned at last to Nairobi and set up our meeting in the heart of the Mathare Valley slum. As anticipated, we found living conditions appalling. Disease, crime, despair, and poverty had reduced human life to the cost of a pack of cigarettes, or a pair of shoes. People were killed for less nearly every day. Into this darkness we would shine the light of the gospel, telling them of God's great love in giving His only Son as a sacrifice so they could enjoy eternal life. The Lord accompanied the preaching of this good news with incredible signs and wonders. The crowds swelled to 140,000 in our final meeting. 85,000 signed decision cards for follow-up. The Mathare Valley challenge from three years ago had been well answered.

We moved on to Togo, a place we had never been before. Located on the Gulf of Guinea, this was known as the "slave coast" in the 16th century. In the 1950s, before the era of modern independence for African nations, Togo had been known as French Togoland. We targeted the capital city, Lome, for our second evangelistic outing. With more than a half million residents, many of them in abject poverty, Lome sat as the seaport gateway to the inland trading routes to Burkina Faso, Niger, and Mali.

I remember that it was February when we arrived there. This is vivid in my mind because news sources were filled with reports of America's Persian Gulf War. Saddam Hussein was lobbing SCUD missiles into Israel. America's air force was striking the fortified positions of the Republican Guards in preparation for a massive ground assault. In fact, the invasion, led by General "Stormin'" Norman Schwarzkopf, began on February 24, the night of our final meeting in Togo.

Our crusade was to be held on a square near the city center. To my great delight, 200,000 people assembled to hear the gospel. That comprised two out of every five citizens living in Lome. On the very first night it seemed to me that God's power just rocked that square. I ministered to the sick well into the night. Deaf ears and blind eyes were opened; the lame walked.

After the opening event, the meeting had been so exhilarating I found it difficult to unwind. I rejoiced with my team back at the hotel and watched news of the war in Kuwait until my eyelids finally grew heavy and I fell into an exhausted sleep.

The next morning I was asleep when my bedside telephone rang. On the other end of the line a voice said, "This is the office of President Eyadema. The president would like to see you in his office immediately."

It took a minute for my brain to process the request. In fact, the more I thought about it, the less it sounded like a request. "Tell His Excellency that I am most flattered, but I traveled recently to Lome, I ministered late into the night, I am weary, and I am not yet out of bed. I will need some time."

All I could hear was a sudden silence on the other end of the line. I had read briefings about President Gnassingbé Eyadema, and some of the details began to filter back to my mind. He had constructed a huge palace reflecting the gaudy tastes of the old French monarchy. He had come to power after a 1963 coup in which he had shot the former president as he desperately scaled the outer wall of the American embassy, seeking asylum. Coming to power himself in 1967, his first order of business was to survive attempts on his own life. In fact, after 24 years in power he was regarded as the elder statesman of African despots. In popular lore he was heralded as "a force of nature." He had suspended the constitution, banned political parties, and made himself president in perpetuity. I could only imagine how he might respond when he learned that I wasn't leaping from bed, promising to be there in ten minutes.

When the speaker returned to the phone, he said, "President Eyadema would like you to have lunch with him at the palace. Would you be able to meet that schedule?"

"Yes, of course. Tell His Excellency I will be there, and thank you."

As forces of nature go, I felt like a hurricane downgraded to a tropical depression. I needed to refresh and recharge myself. I prayed as I showered, asking

God to use me as He saw fit in this uncertain situation. I shaved and dressed in my preaching suit. Then I took some quiet time to read the Scriptures and hear the voice of the Spirit. At last I drove myself to the palace.

When I arrived I was ushered into a stunning dining room. It was a place fit for the king of a thousand-year dynasty. I was told that all of the food had been flown in fresh from Paris. All of the drink and the delicate hor d'oeurves as well. A large table occupied the center of the room. Servants and chefs were tending to the various tastes of the dignitaries.

With a private smile, I recalled my long-ago conversation with the Lord as a young man in Krempe. On that occasion I had embraced His scriptural promise to provide bread and water in return for my service. Inwardly, I thanked Him now for the sumptuous feast He had prepared for me at the hand of the president of Togo.

My name was announced, and I was seated next to President Eyadema as his guest of honor. Next to him sat one of his wives and a young son. Nearby was the Catholic bishop of Lome. Around the table sat the crème de la crème of the country's leaders.

Immediately the president sought to fill my glass with a fine Courvoisier "Napoleon" Cognac.

"Oh, no thank you," I said. "Water will suit me just fine."

"But surely you drink something. You would like something tamer? We have the finest French wines here, as well."

President Eyadema of Togo and I

"Thank you, Your Excellency, I'll drink the Perrier. That will be all. I do not take alcohol." Even though we had used wine in communion in Germany, in Africa I had discovered so much feeling against alcohol among the Christians that I had put it completely aside. I came to heed Paul's exhortation to do nothing that would offend my brethren. This is not an expression of my holiness, it is an expression of the compassion that comes from the calling of the evangelist and the Spirit of Christ in me. *Even as I please all men in all things, not seeking mine own profit, but the profit of many, that they may be saved.*[103]

To move our conversation in a better direction, I said, "I wish you had been in our meeting last night. You would have seen something special. Blind eyes were opened. Deaf ears unstopped. It was wonderful."

"That's why I have called you here," he replied. "A relative of mine, a little girl, deaf and dumb, speaks and hears since last night. It is absolutely amazing."

President Eyadema then introduced me to his wife and son seated next to him. I had heard that he had multiple wives, but in this setting he only presented one. He explained that this wife had brought the news of the healing to him because it had been a child from her extended family who had received the healing.

"I never knew God is doing miracles today," the president said. "Why haven't I heard of that before, bishop?" His Excellency, *the force of nature*, was not looking at me. He was looking directly at the Catholic bishop for an answer.

"Well," said the bishop. "Your Excellency, we don't all have the same spiritual gifts. The Bible explains that some have gifts of healing, but not all."

"But don't you have the same Bible as Reinhard Bonnke?" He looked at me. "You read the same Bible as the bishop, don't you? How do you heal?"

"Oh, yes," I said, "yes, we have the same Bible. And the Bible tells us to pray for the sick. It is the privilege of everyone who believes in Jesus to do so. You don't have to be a bishop or a preacher, just a believer. The Lord promised that certain signs would follow those who believed, and healing was among them." [104]

The conversation became quite interesting after that – and heated, I might add. The bishop took no offense, and he and I agreed on many aspects of life and Scripture, as it turned out. The nice part was that the president continued to speak of his relative who had been healed in my meeting. It was a testimony that left little more to be said.

At one point in the conversation the president mentioned the pope's recent visit to Togo. He had been moved that the head of the church would wish to meet him. "When he arrived," he said, "he asked me to go with him to the cemetery. He took me to my mother's grave."

"The pope knew where your mother was buried?"

"Well, I'm sure the bishop filled him in. He knew that I wished for all to be well for my mother in the afterlife, and that had been communicated. She raised me without a father. She was a saint to me. And it really touched me when the pope prayed over her grave that she would be released from purgatory."

When I heard this, I blew some kind of spiritual gasket. "Oh, Your Excellency," I said, "I have not brought the gospel to Togo for the dead but for the living. We haven't gone to the cemetery but to the city square. Jesus said, *Let the dead bury their dead.*[105] He said, *I am the resurrection and the life,*[106] and *I have come that you might have life.*[107] In the same way, I preach the gospel to the living that they might get saved. I don't know what others do with the dead." I could see that my words had cut like a knife through all the small talk in that room. I had the president's full attention.

With that, I saw the shape of the gospel and launched into the ABCs of a salvation sermon. Suddenly, the president lifted his hand to stop me.

"Would you please excuse us," he said to his guests. "I would like to take Rev. Bonnke into another room to continue our conversation in private."

With that, we stood and he led me, with his wife and son, out of the dining room. We entered a long hallway and proceeded to a private office.

"You know, Reverend Bonnke," President Eyadema said, "this office is the special place I go when I do not know what to do. When I have a problem that I cannot solve I come here."

"What a coincidence," I replied. "I don't know if you saw Him or not, but when I walked in that door, I walked in with the great problem solver. His name is Jesus Christ." Again, I launched the ABCs of the gospel. Before we left that room all three of them knelt to repeat the sinner's prayer.

That night, and every day thereafter, as the world obsessed over America's war to liberate Kuwait, the CfaN meetings with Reinhard Bonnke took precedence on Togo television. With nightly crowds of 200,000, we saw a total attendance of 900,000 and 145,000 decisions for Christ. We were Togo's top story, and I couldn't help but think it was due to the president's personal orders. It was absolutely fantastic. When we returned to Germany the president gave me a fabulous stamp collection of Togo, "Album Philatelique Souvenir" in gratitude "for special services rendered to the Togolese People", signed by himself.

I did not continue to have a close relationship with President Eyadema. We did, however, maintain a cordial and respectful rapport. He was a controversial leader, to be sure. Local Christians reported that he continued to practice witchcraft after our meeting. I do not know if he was truly born again. However, whenever I traveled within the borders of Togo in the years that followed, my car was always met by a police escort, and I was treated as a head of state. When he died in 2005, for better or worse, he was the longest serving head of state in African history. One of his sons was named his successor, but a number of democratic reforms have been instituted since then. We hope that Togo will enter a future with more liberty, justice, and economic opportunity for all.

On a personal note, I received a notice from one of my coworkers who traveled through Lome in recent years. He said that the square where we held our meetings during the Persian Gulf War of '91 has been renamed Bonnke Square. What President Gnassingbé Eyadema ordered, happened. I wasn't consulted.

I FLEW TO KANO, Nigeria, in mid-October of '91. I was so excited. The largest evangelistic meetings of CfaN history would begin in two days. During the flight I continued to have visions of our last meeting in neighboring Kaduna. I could still see before me a vast sea of 500,000 upturned faces, eager to hear the gospel of Jesus Christ. These were mostly Muslim people that had crowded the Nigerian sunset, standing before our platform as portable stadium lights illuminated their white skullcaps and turbans as far as my eye could see. The scene resembled a field of blossoms. It reminded me of the words of Jesus in John's Gospel, *Lift up your eyes, and look on the fields; for they are white already to harvest.*[108] A quarter million of these souls had raised their hands in response to the invitation to receive Jesus. They had taken the extra step to register their decisions for Christ.

In Kano we expected the crowd to be even greater in size. My ground team had enhanced our sound equipment to meet this challenge. I sensed that we were about to see the greatest breakthrough in the history of modern evangelism. What made it noteworthy was the location – Nigeria's Muslim north.

Peter van den Berg, my ministry director, and evangelist Brent Urbanowicz, my future son-in-law, flew with me. At the airport in Kano, we expected a parade of welcome. But as we taxied to the terminal, through the jet window I could see that our airport ceremony would be small.

We taxied to a halt, and the plane opened its passenger door. As I descended the stairway to the tarmac a strange pair of eyes watched my every move. I did not know this man and would not know him for many years to come. We were met by the local board of sponsoring pastors. They were a couple dozen men in all.

John Darku, the crusade director, looked worried as we approached him. He took me to one side. "Reinhard," he said, "you cannot go into the terminal. There are snipers who have sworn to kill you."

I looked at the terminal and could see armed soldiers standing by the windows.

"You are sure of this?"

"We are sure."

I thought John might have been overreacting to some wild threat. Still, I appreciated his caution. My main concern, in this case, was not for me. I had preached under death threats before. Rather, I felt terribly responsible for the partners who would be arriving in a matter of hours from the United States, Holland and Germany. They were coming to Kano to witness the largest crowds in the history of Christ for all Nations. What had I brought them into?

"The snipers will have to get past the soldiers," I suggested.

"Some of the soldiers are likely to have radical Muslim sympathies," John said. "All they have to do is look the other way."

"Okay, John. What are we to do?"

Obviously, a plan was underway. A line of cars and drivers pulled up next to us.

"The government has arranged to process your passport through back channels," he explained. "You will leave through a secret entrance."

I nodded.

The three of us were put quickly into separate vehicles. I was placed in the lead car, and my driver quickly sped across the tarmac. The others followed close behind. As the cars went behind a hangar, suddenly they stopped. The drivers leaped out. They took me from my seat and exchanged me quickly with Brent, who had been in a trailing car. Then we were off again.

"Why have you done this?" I asked.

"The snipers may not know what you look like. We thought we would at least confuse them as to which car you were in."

As we sped on, I wondered if Brent understood that he had just been made a decoy for snipers who were looking for me. I'm sure he hadn't signed up for that duty when he had proposed to my daughter, Susanne.

We left the airport property and began driving an erratic route through the back streets. It was like a scene from a movie. When we arrived at our rented house it was nearly dark. We unpacked and settled in. By telephone and two-way radio, my team monitored the arrivals of all our partners. Group by group, they found their way to their accommodations in Kano without incident. I breathed a sigh of relief.

I listened to local radio news of Muslim unrest concerning our visit. I thought that underneath all the arguments, they were really upset that many Muslims would turn to Christ in our meetings, as they had done a year earlier in Kaduna. We prayed about it, committing ourselves and everyone associated with the crusade into the hands of God.

As we prepared for bed, I said to Brent, "You passed the test."

"What test?" he asked.

"You can marry my daughter."

He stopped for a moment, and then laughed aloud. "Are there going to be more tests like this one?"

"I pray not," I replied.

I laid down in the darkness but sleep would not come. From the distance, I heard the haunting wail of a muezzin calling the Muslim faithful to prayer. Had I really heard it? Or was my imagination now running wild? I silently prayed, *Lord, has my zeal for reaching Nigeria blinded me? Have I been unwise? I've brought these innocent people into danger. Protect them, Lord.*

I had been zealous for Nigeria. It was home to more people than any other African nation. With a population of 140,000,000, it ranked as one of the ten most populated countries on the planet. You cannot imagine the cities that teem with people in the ten geographical regions of this landmass, stretching from the Gulf of Guinea, north, and eastward to Lake Chad. It is the very stuff of this evangelist's dreams.

However, about half of the people in Nigeria are Muslim. Most are concentrated in the north. Christian evangelism among Muslims is forbidden. On the other hand, Muslims seek to convert "infidels," including Christian believers. Between Christian and Muslim beliefs, the fabled immovable object meets the unstoppable force. Something must give. I tell my Muslim friends that Jesus died for Muslims, pagans, and Christians. I declare the gospel and leave the rest up to the Holy Spirit. Nevertheless, the Muslim world presents a hostile challenge for all of us in the body of Christ today.

In order to follow God's vision of a blood-washed Africa, I knew that sooner or later Christ for all Nations would have to penetrate Muslim strongholds in the northern part of the continent, including Sudan, Libya, Morocco, Algeria, Chad, and Egypt. For that reason, the northern part of Nigeria represented a test case for us. Kano was a Muslim holy city, a walled fortress from ancient times, built by slavers. It was home to the kind of fanatical Muslim resistance we would eventually meet as we pushed further north in Africa.

As our planning for Kano had proceeded throughout the year, we had experienced our first taste of difficulty over the location for the meetings. We chose a public outdoor area, but at the last minute, a local mullah, a Muslim religious teacher, claimed it to be a holy site. We were required to seek another location. It all seemed to be a trumped-up conflict, but in order not to offend, we agreed.

Realizing that we might face more trouble, we took precautions. Instead of booking hotel rooms for me and other high-profile members of the team, we secretly rented guesthouses in the outlying areas of the city. We did this also for the partners we had invited from Europe and America, a move that was beginning to appear divinely inspired.

In time, our Kano Crusade Committee had found a Catholic compound willing to host our meetings. They gave permission to set up our platform, generators, lights, and sound equipment in a large open area within their fenced property. No Muslim claim could be made against this ground since it had clearly been a Christian enclave for decades.

We had the problem of all the crusade publicity we had posted in the city directing people to the wrong area. But we would reduce that problem by posting local ushers to redirect the crowds to the new location. If publicity geared up in the usual pattern for us, God would perform miracle healings, and these would make local headlines – and the spiritually hungry people of Kano would eventually find us in record numbers.

Now I lay awake wondering if all of this thinking and planning had somehow missed the mark. And yet, I knew that God had a bigger view of our present troubles than any of us could possibly know. I went to sleep in that confidence, leaving our situation in His omnipotent hands.

The next morning after devotions, I told the men that I would like to drive through the city, as I normally do. I wanted to see the people of Kano for myself. When I preach in a new place I need to smell the air. I need to see the local activities. It helps me to get a feel for the city.

We got a car. Peter and Brent went with me. As we drove, I noticed many more mosques than churches in Kano. During our tour we drove past the local emir's palace. The emir is not a religious leader. He is the Muslim political leader for the region. Outside of his palace we saw a crowd of thousands of young men dressed in white robes. They had blocked the road. We drove slowly up to them. They parted like the Red Sea to let us pass through. Many of them bent down and looked intently into the car as we moved among them. I noticed that all of the young men seemed to be very angry, but we passed through without incident.

At noon we arrived back at our house. Our host met us, wringing his hands. "Kano is burning," he said. "A Muslim mob has gone on a rampage."

We looked back toward the city and sure enough, we could see columns of smoke rising. Reports came that the young men we had seen at the emir's palace had just come from a mosque where a mullah had told them, "Bonnke must not be allowed to preach in the holy city of Kano."

How had they missed us? We had driven straight through their midst. Had the Holy Spirit simply blinded their eyes? If one of those young men had recognized my face, we would have been dragged from the car and killed on the spot. The city was covered with our crusade posters. My picture was prominently displayed everywhere. How had we escaped? Unable to find me, the mob had begun targeting Christian churches, homes, businesses, and pedestrians in the city.

The next morning, John Darku arrived at our house with a senior air force officer. The officer said, "The governor has declared a state of emergency. You must pack your things and leave now."

"Where will we go?"

"I have arranged to take you to another place," John said. "The airport is teeming with rioters. They are trying to cut off your escape route. We can't go back there. They are getting too close to this house, and you have been seen in this neighborhood. It won't be safe to stay."

"How much time do we have?" I asked.

"Five minutes," the air force officer said. He looked genuinely scared. "Get your things. We must go, now!"

John drove us to another house. It belonged to a precious Christian woman. When we arrived there, her children were keeping watch. They came and told us that they had seen Muslim rioters only a few blocks away.

"John," I said, "we cannot stay here. They are going to search house to house for me. I cannot bear to bring this woman and her children into danger."

John nodded. He took us on another high-speed trip through the back streets. We arrived at the home of a local businessman. He must have been a very brave fellow to allow us to stay in his home that night.

From the roof of the house, we could see the reflection of fires flickering across the night sky. Explosions could be heard as petrol stations were set on fire. Huge clouds of black smoke billowed into the air. Occasional gunfire rattled through the darkness. We were out of sight, but hardly removed from the danger zone. The entire city was being ransacked in a mad search for me.

That night on the news we heard that the government had closed the airspace over Kano. This puzzled me. What did they know? Were the Muslim fanatics planning to use civilian airplanes against us? Or had some of the air force pilots themselves been involved in a plot? Upon this news, I ordered that the crusade planned for the next day would not go on.

The next morning I sent word to my team to gather at my location for prayer. We would decide what to do next. Our people came, but they told of seeing dead bodies and burned-out wreckage strewn through the streets as they drove to the meeting. Hundreds were dying. The mob was totally out of control. The local police were not able to contain them. As Christians were encountered in the streets, they were being killed.

The officer from the air force base came to the compound. He told us that the army was clearing the airport, trying to secure it so that we could leave. They would provide for an emergency air evacuation. He urged us to get out as fast as we could. "They are like ants," he said. "They are swarming wherever they go. If they find this location they will soon come pouring over the walls of the property."

I asked that all of our guests from America and Europe be allowed to leave first. The military officer disagreed. He persuaded me that since I was the target of this violence, I should leave first. If it became known that I had gone, the mob might calm down and disperse. Others would be in less danger as they were being airlifted out.

"The longer you stay, the longer this violence will go on," he said.

It seemed the only thing to do. I agreed to cooperate. Once the airport was secure, they would escort me to an airplane and announce in the news media that I had gone. I asked all of my team members to stay in the compound and join me in this evacuation.

As we waited for word from the airport, I took a walk around the grounds. A feeling of grief came over me. All of the events in Kano became glaringly real. Christians were dying because I had come to town. Yet, no – it was much more than that. Kano was burning because of the gospel of Jesus Christ. "If the world hate you," Jesus said in John 15:18, *ye know that it hated me before it hated you.*

The events in Jinja the year before had prepared me to experience the reality of those words to their fullest in Kano. I looked at the street, imagining the mob swarming in our direction. *What will I do, Lord, if suddenly they appear, demanding Reinhard Bonnke?*

In only a moment, I knew the answer, and I felt His peace settle over me.

Peter van den Berg walked up to join me.

"Peter," I said, "if that mob shows up before they get the airport secure, I will give myself up to them. I want you to know that."

"I won't let you do that."

"No, you must let me. I will identify myself, Reinhard Bonnke, an evangelist for the Lord Jesus Christ, and go out to them. That might save the others. My life is His."

"If they show up," Peter said, "I'll grab you and drag you up to the roof there. We'll both take up roof tiles and battle them to the last man, that's what we'll do!"

Peter was a fighter. I grinned at him. We had been through many adventures together on the road to a blood-washed Africa. I knew him well enough to know that he meant what he said. And he knew me well enough to know that I meant what I said too – immoveable force, unstoppable object. We said no more but went back inside.

At this time the foreman of my crusade facilities team, Winfried Wentland, approached me. His wife, Gabriele, stood beside him. Winfried is a focused and intense man, a former German soldier of wiry build. Gabriele, called "Gaby," is his wife and his match. If ever two people could see through the smoke of Kano to the real fire – the mission of saving souls – it was this pair. They had been with me for twelve years in Africa.

"Gaby and I believe we are supposed to stay here and bring the equipment home," Winfried said.

His words hit me like bullets. Given the way events had spiraled out of control it was out of the question. I looked at Gaby, in her ninth month of pregnancy. I simply could not believe my ears.

"Equipment can be replaced, Winfried," I said. "You and your family cannot be replaced. I won't think of it."

"Reinhard, I have 50 men at the compound. It is my officer's training to leave no one behind. Besides, they have already risked their lives. I need to finish what we started together."

Winfried with Gabriele Wentland
and children

I appreciated his argument, but it didn't convince me. The 50 men were local volunteers he had recruited, and now supervised, in the setting up of the crusade grounds. I shook my head. "You can send word to the men that you will return when hostilities have ended. This only makes sense. They will surely understand. I want you and Gaby to stay with us and evacuate."

"Reinhard," he continued, "Gaby and I and the children have prayed together about this. We have heard from God, and He has given us perfect peace. Look at us; we are not afraid. We are in peace. Whether we live or die, God is going to see us through. Please do not order us to disobey the Lord."

For this, I had no argument.

"I will have to think about it," I said, and walked away, too disturbed to continue. Winfried and I both knew what my answer would be. I did not want to contemplate it. But I am human. I had questions. If God had spoken to the Wentlands, what did He have in mind? I didn't want to believe that God would do any less than He had done for us as we had driven through the mob at the emir's palace. But I had no guarantee of that. I remembered the experience of losing Horst Kosanke and Milton Kasselman.

In serving our crusade team, Winfried and Gaby had lived a life of adventure and risk every day. Yet they were a family, and they insisted on doing everything together – kids included. Having them on my team made me feel blessed of the Lord. But I would never have asked them to drive our equipment out of Kano under these circumstances.

I began to pray. "Lord, they say that the blood of the martyrs is the seed of the church. Right now, I don't want to believe that. In Scripture I read that Your Word is the seed. Jesus was the Word made flesh. He was the seed who fell into the ground and died, and You raised Him up again, victorious over death. Let us bring forth the fruit of His resurrection in Kano, Lord. Let Your gospel prevail, and protect Winfried and Gaby, and everyone who has come to serve You in this crusade."

I knew that a week ago, Winfried had driven our crusade 18-wheeler 700 miles from his home in Lagos, Nigeria, to Kano. That is like driving from Denver to Dallas on an unpaved alley. African roads are not for the faint of heart. The truck is equipped with six-wheel-drive for good reason. Gaby had accompanied him, as she usually did, driving their Land Rover in convoy. Their two children, Simon and Angelina, age nine and five, had come along.

Suddenly I could picture them on the road. The trailer he pulled was blood red, with massive white lettering on the side, spelling out J-E-S-U-S. It was a rolling advertisement for a blood-washed Africa. Surely it had created a stir in Muslim neighborhoods as it had been en route to Kano. I began to wish that I had painted it solid white, with no emblem on it whatsoever.

Looking at these events from the outside, Winfried and Gaby seemed unduly adventuresome. To some they would, no doubt, appear irresponsible. But this is not so. They are ordinary believers who responded to the challenge of following Jesus. Who knows what any of us would be empowered to do by simply hearing and obeying the Lord, and by allowing Him to subdue our fears.

As Winfried explains it, they considered the Kano assignment routine. The family had shared equally in his calling to CfaN from the very start. By the time of this story, they knew Africa and its hazards well. They had seen violent clashes in other cities where they had served. Some crusades had been held in active war zones. They knew how to take precautions, but they also had few illusions, knowing that many safety factors remained beyond their control. Those had to be left in God's hands.

On the first day of the rioting, Winfried had seen the smoke from his hotel room. He had taken a motorbike and hurried to the Catholic compound where the crusade platform had been set up. Inside, he found the crew of 50 Christian men he had recruited from local churches. They were worried but were taking action to protect the equipment. They had closed and locked the perimeter gates and had posted men on lookout all around to warn them should the mob approach.

Indeed, soon the mob appeared. Within sight of the crusade platform stood a large petrol station with ten pumps. The mob attacked it. A huge fireball had shot into the sky. The entire station began exploding and burning. Black smoke engulfed the area.

The Christian volunteers persuaded Winfried to spend the night back at his hotel. Since the mob was seeking Bonnke, any white man seen at the compound might draw the mob inside. They assured him that they would stand guard all night. This had been Winfried's experience of the Kano situation so far.

At this time, at the home where my team waited, the air force officer arrived to tell us that armored cars were approaching to take us to the airport. I had known from the start that I would not ask Winfried to disobey anything he had heard from God. I called the two of them to join me for a time of prayer. I laid my hands on them and prayed for God's protection to surround them. I especially prayed for Gaby and the child in her womb. I asked God to assign His angels to guide and guard them until they arrived again at their home in Lagos.

As I finished the prayer, I felt saddened again. I truly feared that I had seen them for the last time. Christians were being hunted down and killed in the streets of Kano. Winfried would now travel those streets pulling a large, blood-red trailer with J-E-S-U-S spelled out in block letters on the side. It would be like walking through a war zone wrapped in the enemy's flag. To me, it seemed to be a call to martyrdom.

That day, in order to begin to control the city again, the local police and military announced a "shoot on site" curfew from 6 p.m. until 6 a.m. When the curfew was in place that evening, our evacuation began. We entered a convoy of armored cars with soldiers stationed at every gun slot. The muzzles of machine guns bristled in all directions. Our crusade team had been collected, with the exception of Winfried and Gaby. We sped to the airport. Again, a very powerful man with an observant pair of eyes carefully watched our every move.

Soon we were flying away, breathing easier aboard those rescue jets. The media announced that I had left the city and the armored cars carried our American, Dutch and German guests to the airport for a safe getaway.

As I flew across the African continent I thought of Winfried and his family left behind. How would they face the outcome of their decision to obey the Lord? I knew them well enough to know the answer to that question. Though they were on the ministry payroll, they had never been working strictly for me. No one but God could have directed them to take this action. They were obeying Him. People in obedience to the Lord do not worry, do not fret, and do not need to know all of the outcomes before they are willing to commit themselves. They would face Kano the way any of us would have done it – one moment at a time. Borrowing no anxiety from the future, they would simply put one foot in front of the other until they arrived – either at their earthly home, or their heavenly one.

When I received the happy news that they had arrived safely back in Lagos, I spoke with Winfried by telephone. It was only then I learned the details of their harrowing escape. It truly seemed that God made them invisible to the roving mobs, just as He had protected us at the emir's palace earlier. I privately thanked God that what He had in mind for them was nothing less than a miraculous escape.

Immediately I contacted our friends and partners around the world, asking them to fast and pray for a solution to the Nigerian stalemate. I had become *persona non grata* in the most populated nation in all of Africa. In the meantime we tried every diplomatic avenue available to us, but nothing seemed to bear fruit.

Though it fell far short of its potential, the year of 1991 still ended as the highest response in CfaN history. Nine campaigns were conducted in five African nations with 5,407,000 in attendance and 940,000 decisions registered. We saw our largest crowd in Mbuji Mayi, the diamond mining center of Zaire, where 360,000 gathered to hear the gospel in one meeting. 220,000 embraced the Pearl of Great Price through that campaign. We rejoiced greatly in the Lord's harvest.

In Nigeria, however, the rumor mill and the popular media blamed us for the outbreak of violence. This became our reputation, even though an extensive report assembled by the local governor exonerated us from all blame. For most people, perception is reality. They believe what they read in the newspapers or hear in word-of-mouth gossip. Bonnke had brought violence to Kano. How could he claim to serve the Prince of Peace? It appeared that Satan had won the day and Jesus had been forced into retreat. Of course, at a time like this, believers should hold steady and remind themselves that things are not what they appear to be.

# Chapter 32

Locked out of Nigeria, we let no grass grow beneath our feet. The Lord led us in new directions in '92. We held one crusade in Buenos Aires; ten other CfaN campaigns were targeted in eight nations of Africa. In many ways, we worked harder than ever. But we saw our numbers shrink. Attendance dropped 44 percent. Registered conversions dropped 33 percent. I hated to see a retreat from the exhilarating growth we had known for so many years. It seemed that we had been invading Satan's domain, walking in the path of the Savior who had already defeated him at Calvary, and even in the belly of hell itself. We had nothing to fear from our Enemy. Not even death could defeat us. So, I did not understand why we should accept any setback whatsoever from Satan. My spirit remained restless to see entire nations turn to Christ, and I sought for ways to go forward.

We held a campaign in Conakry, Guinea, in October of that year. This meeting was significant because 85 percent of the population of Guinea is Muslim. I was amazed that we were able to obtain a permit after the events in Kano. The president of Guinea, Lansana Conté, who was in effect president for life, was a staunch Muslim. He had several wives. As it turned out, his head wife had become a Christian, and through her influence we were finding the doors open.

Our reputation from the disaster in Kano certainly preceded us in Conakry. In a city of nearly 2,000,000 we drew crowds of only 55,000. On the first night a group of Muslim young men came into the arena. They brought with them a blind friend. Between them they had made a pact that if their friend was not healed of his blindness, they would take large stones from underneath their robes and attack me on stage. I knew nothing about it.

As I usually do, after preaching I prayed for the sick. And, as is my custom, I prayed for the blind people first.

"In the name of Jesus, blind eyes, open!" I shouted.

In the group of young men, the blind man they had brought suddenly shrieked, "I see! I see!"

From under their robes stones dropped to the ground. Several people observed this and learned their story. Later they related it to me.

All I can say is I am glad I do not face stoning for every person who is not healed in one of my meetings. I would be dead a thousand times over. But God used this incident to open hearts to the gospel in Conakry. 45,000 registered decisions for Jesus, and we rejoiced at the mercy and grace of the Lord in this Muslim land.

DURING A BREAK in the crusade schedule, I flew to a city in Germany where I was scheduled to speak before returning home to rest. When I arrived at the church it was packed beyond capacity. Hundreds were seated on the floor.

I looked down at the group seated in front of the stage and saw a raggedy man among them. His hair was long and shaggy, his beard untrimmed, and his clothes filthy and worn. He had the look of a homeless beggar. I suspected that he was an immigrant from East Germany, a common sight since German reunification in 1990. The standard of living for those who had lived behind the Iron Curtain was much lower than that achieved in the West after the war.

After preaching that night the pastor came to escort me to an after-service meal with him and his staff. The shaggy East German immigrant approached us.

"Brother Bonnke," he said, "my name is Rudolph Kleinbaum and I am so glad that I have heard you speak tonight. I have something to give you. Can we step aside from the auditorium? I need to speak in private."

I looked at the pastor. He nodded his assent and he took us out of the sanctuary into his office.

"I have a gift for you, Brother Bonnke," Rudolph said. "I want to give money for the souls in Africa."

At this point tears fell from his eyes. I could tell that he had been deeply touched by my presentation. My heart was touched in return. I knew that his gift, however small it might be, would be multiplied by heaven because of his tender and sincere heart. He was like the widow casting her two mites into the temple coffers. Jesus had commended her above all those who gave out of their abundance.[109]

"I can only give this money to you if everyone leaves the room," he said.

The pastor and I looked at one another. What could this mean? We had to be careful because sometimes unstable people are drawn to be close to a man of God, and the trouble they can cause can be great. I normally would not allow such a thing. Somehow, perhaps because of the genuine tears I saw in his eyes, I knew that it would be safe. I nodded to the pastor and he left the room.

I received a shock. Rudolph promptly unzipped his ragged pants. From inside a hiding place where no one would ever look, he produced a bundle of crisp bills. He walked over to me and counted 15,000 deutschmarks into my hand. I could not believe my eyes.

"From where did you get this money, Rudolph?"

"I have saved it from my social government payments."

"But that is so much. How could you ever do it?"

"Oh, it is not hard. I don't need too much to live on, you know?"

Suddenly, I was choking with emotion. The standard of living he had grown used to while living as a hated German under the rule of the Soviet Union was pitiful. "I will send you a tax receipt," I said. "Let me write down your address."

"Oh no, no, no. You must not do that. I want no tax receipt. I do not want my sons to know about this. They are drunkards. Vodka is their life, you know. You can find them sleeping off their misery on any park bench in town. If they knew I had this money they would steal it and spend it on alcohol. I put it into your hands. It is for saving souls in Africa."

I felt God's eyes on us in that moment. I felt that this money was holy and I must handle it with great care.

From that day onward, when I spoke somewhere near Bremen, Rudolph would show up, take me aside, unzip his pants, and, pulling out a wad of bills, make another installment to win souls in Africa. We became such good friends over the years, sharing our passion to win the lost. How blessed I have been to know him.

THE NEXT YEAR, in '93, we tried another campaign in Guinea, but as we drew near to the date threats of violence spiraled upward. It seems that the conversions we had seen in Conakry threatened radical elements within the mosques. A CfaN campaign typically gains high visibility in the regional press wherever we go. We are often the lead story on the evening news until our meetings come to an end. The miracles are often broadcast for all to see, the crowds grow to unprecedented levels, and we do not leave an area as we found it. A strong influence for Christ remains and grows after we are gone. Just before our second crusade in Guinea, President Conté cancelled our meetings. The government claimed threats of violence had outgrown their ability to protect us.

We went on to the next part of our schedule. We tithed campaigns that year in Indonesia and Jamaica. However, the controversy followed us wherever we went through the internet, which has become the greatest tool for uniting Muslim radicals worldwide. Subsequently, the government in Indonesia cancelled our campaign there for fear of Muslim violence. We had another campaign cancelled in Mali for the same reason. Mali, in North Africa, is 90 percent Muslim. We managed to hold six African campaigns in five other nations in '93. We saw 621,000 decisions for Christ and almost 1,937,000 in attendance.

In '94 we had no cancellations, but we avoided areas in Africa that were heavily Muslim. I felt led to leave the continent for five campaigns that year in India, Finland, Trinidad, and two in Brazil. I was abroad when I received the horrible news about the Rwandan genocide. Three months of unending slaughter. I mourned to think of a half million souls swept into eternity through the insanity of tribal hatred. Statistics and descriptions from the bloodbath left us dumbstruck. I had preached in Kigali, Rwanda, in 1990, seeing 50,000 decisions for Christ. No doubt some of those precious ones were now with the Lord. I felt a greater urgency to cover Africa with the gospel message that could cause the Prince of Peace to reign in troubled hearts.

We managed to hold six meetings in African nations that year in areas that were not dominated by Muslim influence. Our total number of responses diminished slightly in number and our total attendance remained about the same. It now became obvious to me that Kano had been a turning point. It dealt a real setback to the momentum of CfaN. I continued to seek the Lord about it and continued to try various approaches to the government of Nigeria, asking them to lift the ban on our evangelistic campaigns. Nothing seemed to work.

In the meantime, I was very aware that each crusade on our schedule continued to be a divine appointment. I told my team, "If we had not come to Madras, India, 25,000 souls would not know Jesus. If we had not come to Antananarivo, Madagascar, 110,000 souls would not know Jesus. If we had not come to Porto Alegre, Brazil, 9,000 would not know Jesus. If we had stopped responding to the Great Commission in 1994, a total of 511,100 people would not be in the kingdom of God today. *Woe is me if I preach not the gospel!* [110] During these years, I simply put my expectations aside concerning the size of our crowds and the size of the response. It was good for me to return to the purity of my calling. It was not about massive numbers of registered decisions, it was about the message that saves one sinner. I began to feel the full blessing of the Lord as I ministered the ABCs of the gospel in each new setting.

Deep in my heart, this time of disappointment took me back to the street corner in Glückstadt where I had played my guitar and preached my first sermon. One man got saved that day, and I had run home as fast as my legs would carry me to tell my parents what the simple gospel of Jesus had accomplished. Hallelujah! It is the power of God unto salvation to everyone who believes! [111] That is still the truest picture of my calling, not the picture of me standing in front of a sea of faces, but me running home with excitement over one sinner who repented.

I recall a particular madman who was delivered at the very first crusade we held that year in the great Kibera slum of Nairobi. We saw crowds of up to 70,000 gather on a soccer field. But as the meetings began a local madman came into the crowd totally naked. This was his way. In Africa if someone had lost their mind and they are not violent, the people simply allow them to have their way. In this case the man could not stand the feel of clothes on his body so he simply cast them off. He had not taken a bath for years. His hair was a matted mass of filth and vermin. In this condition he wandered among the crowd as I began to preach the gospel.

As I preached on this particular evening, suddenly the Holy Spirit spoke to my heart. *Break the curse of witchcraft now.* I have learned not to question the voice of the Spirit. I interrupted my own sermon.

"In the name of Jesus, I break every witchcraft curse here tonight."

Then I resumed my sermon. What I did not see is what happened to this man when I said that. Others saw him shaken as if he had been hit by a bolt of lightning. Suddenly he looked at his neighbors and said, "Where am I? Why am I naked? How did I get here?"

Some of our ministers who were in that area of the crowd took him out and got him bathed and washed his hair. They found some clothing for him to wear. When they told me about it I gave them money and instructed them to take him to a clothing store and buy him all new clothes. The next night he stood by me on the platform, clothed and in his right mind. He lifted his hands and shouted into the microphone, "Jesus has set me free!"

That crowd erupted in a mighty roar. The Bible says that all heaven rejoices over one sinner who repents.[112] In the following six days, we saw more than 93,000 people repent and register decisions for Christ. They must have caused more than 93,000 riots of joy in the pavilions of heaven's glory. Hallelujah!

SIX YEARS HAD PASSED since our paths had crossed in Uhuru Park. Teresia Wairimu had spent those years making a new life for herself in Nairobi. She had raised her daughter to young womanhood. She rose from the ashes of her shattered marriage to build new relationships with a small group of Christian women. They now looked to her for spiritual guidance, and from time to time, she would minister among her friends. But her ministry lacked the power she had seen in Uhuru Park that day in 1988. Her spirit remained crushed by her failed marriage, and she knew she had not arrived at God's highest calling for her.

During those ensuing six years, Teresia had begun to track my speaking schedule through our CfaN ministry magazine. She was always on the lookout for a city where I would be preaching to a smaller crowd. A place where she might have a chance of having me lay hands on her in prayer. She believed that the day that happened she would receive the anointing and the fire to preach with authority, the way she had seen me preach in Nairobi.

Her wish came true in Oslo, Norway, in the spring. She was excited to learn that I would be speaking there in a local church because she had friends who lived in Oslo. Immediately she called them and made arrangements to stay with them so that she could attend my meeting there. They agreed to bring her to the meeting with them.

She saved her money and bought a round-trip ticket. All of her friends in Nairobi prayed with her as she left, believing that she would return with the fire of God's Spirit that she longed for.

Teresia was the first one through the doors of the church in Oslo when they opened them. Her friends escorted her to the very front row. She waited there as the room continued to fill up. A local woman approached her.

"There is something that you need from God," the woman said, "and God spoke to me that He will give it to you."

This was wonderful confirmation. Teresia thanked her and replied, "That is good, but I am still waiting."

When I came to the platform as the service began, I knew immediately that Teresia was there. It is hard to miss an African lady in a Norwegian church. She stood out like an island of color in a sea of gray, dressed in her traditional African robes. I could see that she was trembling from the very start of the meeting.

Teresia had come with one thing in mind; when I gave the altar call for the sick, she would run forward for prayer. In her mind, she was sick. She felt sick with frustration and ineffectiveness in her ministry. This is how she justified in her own mind, coming for prayer at the call for the sick.

Her focus on this idea made it impossible for her to actually concentrate on my sermon. In fact, I preached a salvation message. That fact did not register with her. I challenged those who wanted to accept Jesus as Savior to stand up. She shot up like a lightning bolt. Then suddenly, she realized that this was not a call for the sick, and she sheepishly sat down again. She had waited eight long years; she would wait another 20 minutes for my next invitation.

When I finally announced that I would pray for the sick, she raced to the front and stood before me, trembling with anticipation. She knew that she was within moments of receiving the answer to the prayer she had prayed in Uhuru Park six years before. She would receive the anointing to minister in power and authority, just the way Reinhard Bonnke ministered.

I will never forget what happened next. Nor will Teresia ever remember. To this day she does not know that I actually laid my hands on her. She has no memory of that. The fire of God had nothing to do with the touch of my hands, but I did place them on her head. Only for an instant, because she was ripped from beneath my hands by a mighty force that threw her 20 yards through the air and landed her on her back near the front row of seats from which she had come. The force of this action was so strong that both of her shoes flew from her feet, high into the air. One shoe, I can still see it, sailed end over end far out into the middle of that gray Norwegian audience. It has never been seen again. Who knows, someone might have taken it as a souvenir.

I did not have a clue about what had happened to Teresia. I simply moved on to pray for others. Much later, she recalls rousing from an unconscious state and hearing my voice saying, "Miracles are happening here, miracles are happening." That's all she remembers.

The Oslo meeting closed. I left to return to Germany.

Teresia could not get up from the floor of that church. As she regained consciousness, her body would not properly respond to the commands from her brain. Her legs were so wobbly her friends had to carry her from the church to the car. They drove her home, then carried her from the car into the house and deposited her on the bed in the guest bedroom. That's when they gave her back the one remaining shoe of the pair she had worn that night. It is a shoe she has kept to remind herself of what God did for her that night. She knew in her heart that she would never be the same.

The story might end here. It has ended here for many. They receive a great visitation of God's Spirit, and then they do nothing to walk it out in their life. But God had anointed Teresia for a specific calling. She had not received her blessing to waste it on herself. She had come for the power to minister, and minister she would. Teresia Wairimu was on fire.

Upon arrival back in Nairobi she called her girlfriends to a Friday prayer meeting at her house. They came. 17 of them. She preached with a power she had never known before. When she asked for the sick to stand up, she did not offer a weak religious prayer. She did not ask God to please heal someone if it was in His great divine will to do so. No, by the Spirit she knew it was God's will to heal. She commanded the sick to be healed in Jesus' name, and healings began to manifest.

The next Friday there were 55 women at her house. The next Friday, 105, and the next, 200 women showed up. She and her circle of women-friends began to look for a school building in which to meet. By now some of the notable and documented healings from her ministry were being talked about around the city. They found a city auditorium that held 2,000, but 4,000 women showed up. They had to open all the doors and windows to try to accommodate the overflow. She moved to the Jomo Kenyatta Convention Center, which held 5,000. 12,000 came.

At this point some pastors in the city began to denounce her and tell their people not to attend her meetings because she was a divorced woman. God would not use a divorced man or woman, they claimed. The people ignored them. Some came out of curiosity, others out of need. But when they arrived at a Teresia Wairimu meeting, they did not hear about a woman's divorce, they heard the gospel of Jesus Christ. They saw cancers healed, AIDS healed, blind eyes opened, the lame walking, and deaf ears unstopped.

Finally, Teresia went to the city council and asked to have the use of Uhuru Park, where Bonnke had preached in 1988. They made a contract with her, giving her use of the park for the first Sunday of every month. Her crowds swelled, and now included men as well as women.

The weeping woman in Uhuru Park in 1988 had desperately prayed, "God, oh please God, if you can give Bonnke 100,000 souls, give me 100, just 100, Lord, and I'll be a happy woman." Teresia Wairimu is today a very happy woman. Her name is a household word in Kenya. Hundreds of thousands have come to Jesus in her meetings, and the ministers who once preached against her have apologized, begging her forgiveness.

When I heard of her breakthrough and success, I went to the Lord in prayer. "Why Lord," I asked, "did you choose a divorced woman for this great ministry? We have so many wonderful men in our Bible schools, men who pursue You with all of their hearts. Why did You choose Teresia and not one of them?"

His answer affected me deeply. *I chose Teresia because I wanted to show the world that I could take a broken vessel and make a vessel of honor.*

How this humbled me. We are not chosen for our great qualities. We are flawed servants who must depend totally on Him. Unlike Teresia, I have enjoyed the benefits of a strong marriage to my Anni all these years. But this great happiness is not the secret to my success. Teresia suffered the ultimate humiliation of divorce, but God lifted her to a platform of powerful ministry. We are qualified by God's omnipotence, not by our pitiful strengths or weaknesses. All to the glory of God! Amen.

THE TWO-YEAR PROCESS of writing was complete. I now had a version of *From Minus to Plus: The Epic of Christ's Cross* in my hands. I believed it was ready for distribution, and I grew excited to see it done. I wanted to cast the biggest evangelistic net ever cast. We were fishing for an entire nation.

Many fine people had given the little document their scrutiny. I had rewritten it 14 times with the help of my dear and honored friend George Canty. Some said the gospel was presented in this booklet more clearly and effectively than they had ever read it. That is exactly what I had set out to achieve.

As I prayed about where to cast that first nationwide net, the Lord continued to whisper *England* to my heart. I called my friend Ray Bevan in Newcastle, Wales. I asked him if he would allow me to begin raising funds for this project. He agreed to give me 20 minutes at his annual conference to present the vision. I told the people that night that in two weeks time I needed £1,000,000 just to buy the paper for 25 million copies. We took up the offering and I received £10,000. I thanked the Lord for this offering and realized that we still had a very long way to go in two weeks.

Anni and I retired to our hotel room. It was already midnight. I was almost to fall asleep when my telephone rang. I heard the voice of a man on the other end of the line.

"I was in your meeting tonight," he said. "I fairly enjoyed it. You said that you needed £1,000,000 in two weeks to buy paper. Is that correct?"

"Yes, that is what I said."

"What if you get the money for the paper? Where will you get the rest of it? You will need a great deal more to pay for the postage."

"Oh," I said, "if God gives me the money for the paper, He's got more. He will give it, I am absolutely sure."

"I am a businessman. To distribute your booklet by mail from house to house is the least effective way of advertising. The very most you can hope to achieve is a 4 percent response. Do you know that?"

In fact, I did not know that. I wasn't sure if he was right or wrong. "I believe God has spoken to me," I replied, "and in any case, I am not a mail expert. I am not even His first choice for this job, as I told you tonight. I am His third choice. But I believe this is God's way of doing things. He speaks and I obey. The results are in His hands." I began to wonder what I was doing at midnight speaking to this stranger in such detail. "What is your name, sir, may I ask?"

"No, I am sorry. I do not want to give my name."

"Then I need to tell you that I am weary from a long day and need to get my rest. Thank you for your concern, but perhaps this conversation can be continued some other day."

"I apologize for the hour of this call but there is an important reason for it. May I ask just one more question?"

"Certainly."

He continued to ask sharp questions about *From Minus to Plus*, and I continued to supply answers for quite a long time. I do not know how long it went on because I was speaking of something close to my heart. In such a case, time flies.

"I will give you £1,000,000 in two weeks," he suddenly said.

I was not sure that I had heard correctly. "You said a million?"

"Yes."

Right away I knew that I was dealing with a tycoon, or someone delusional.

"Not many people could make such a gift," I said. "If I am to believe you, sir, I must again ask your name."

He told me his name. "I am Bob Edmiston." I recognized it right away, and knew he was capable of making such a gift. I had read a magazine article in recent weeks about the 50 wealthiest people in England, and I recognized his name from high on that list.

"Sir," I said, "I know who you are."

"No, you can't possibly know me. It's impossible. Our paths have never crossed, and we are from very different backgrounds."

But I did know him.

Two weeks later £1,000,000 dropped into our CfaN account. This man has continued to support our ministry with substantial gifts over the years since this first project. We have become friends and partners in ministry.

His large gift did not mean that I had reached my goal. Not even by half. I started to travel extensively throughout Britain to raise the additional money. Wherever I went I told the *From Minus to Plus* story.

"The day is at hand, when every postman becomes an evangelist, because every postman will deliver this booklet, in his area, to every address. We need your help to pay postage for every booklet. We estimate this to be the biggest distribution of its kind ever undertaken."

This was a time of financial recession in the UK, but it did not stop their generosity. Everywhere I went the people began to give. The news began to spread through the churches. We targeted home delivery to be accomplished during Easter weekend. More than 15,000 congregations signed up to receive responses from the converts in their zip code areas.

The postal service analyzed the size of the job and told us they could not guarantee delivery during the Easter time period. We had to seek out supplemental carriers to make the deliveries the postal service could not handle. We planted the book inside home advertising publications, local newspapers, and other door-to-door advertising papers.

As the delivery prepared to go forward, opposition mounted. As a society, the people of the UK have become antagonistic toward the true message of Christ. The gay lobby protested, the Muslim population protested, the popular media picked up their causes and published massive opinion pieces against our "invasion of privacy" with the gospel message.

When the actual distribution began, one man in one village gathered all the booklets and dumped them on the porch of a known Christian. When the Christian came to the door, he said, "Take these. We don't want them." In other cases we discovered that antagonistic delivery workers simply dumped masses of our booklets into dumpsters. We took complaints of non-delivery and followed up with special deliveries. At last, we estimated that we finally delivered to 90 percent of the homes in Great Britain. Exhausted and spent, we eagerly waited the response cards to be mailed in.

I had projected 4 percent of the 25 million copies to yield a response. That would have been one million responses. It was far less than that. We received only tens of thousands of responses, and I had to change my expectations. I began to learn that there was a great difference between holding mass meetings where people gather voluntarily, and using the mail to deliver the gospel to homes where we have not been invited. *From Minus to Plus* did not turn out to be a combine harvester. Rather, it was a massive sower of seed.

Over the years since then, I have come to understand that the effect of *From Minus to Plus* went much further than the mailed-in responses indicated. Millions of people received an impression of the gospel that was attractive, well designed, and positive. They did not wish to think of Christianity in such terms, but after receiving the booklet their closed minds were opened to a larger picture of the faith. Many others had their lives completely changed.

They were born again, but instead of using the card to respond via mail to our offices, they simply began to attend a local church. We still receive testimonies of this result. The booklet also has a life of many years. It might have been discarded on a shelf, or in a desk drawer, where it will wait until someone picks it up as a divine appointment. The message of *From Minus to Plus* continues to plow the soil and plant the seed in England.

After the British Isles distribution, many advised me to stop the *From Minus to Plus* program. The response seemed too small for the size of the investment, and many thought the disappointing figures from the UK would make it impossible to raise more money for another effort somewhere else.

I sought the Lord about it, and He turned my spiritual eyes on the German-speaking world. I felt we should target Germany, Austria, Switzerland, and Liechtenstein all in the same effort. That would require not 25 million booklets but 40 million. And so we took the lessons we had learned from Great Britain and began again.

To carry out so massive a project properly I needed a talented and experienced publishing and marketing manager from Germany. I found him in a man named Siegfried Tomazsewski, himself a fiery preacher of the gospel. His name has become synonymous with our publishing and marketing activities from that time until now. He came highly recommended and proved himself right away as the project manager. His skill as a liaison with churches and denominations was also invaluable. He got to work right away organizing the computer hardware and software plus the networking services necessary to accomplish this monumental task.

As we announced the project in Frankfurt, however, I began to encounter the age-old German Evangelical opposition. They opposed me because they are anti-Charismatic, and historically, anti-Pentecostal. Their opposition went all the way back to Azusa Street. It had plagued Germany since they had penned *The Berlin Declaration*, which had cast speaking in tongues as the work of the devil. By it, Luis Graf had been marginalized. All the German Pentecostals after him, including my father, had been marginalized. As a boy growing up in

Glückstadt I had felt the sting of Pentecostal rejection. In our first crusade into Nairobi, Kenya, Dr. Wellington Mutiso had been forced to choose between his membership with this group and his connections to Reinhard Bonnke. I had dearly hoped those days were over but they were not.

Sending the *From Minus to Plus* booklet as an advance ambassador, I petitioned the Evangelical leadership to please meet with me and discuss how we could cooperate in such a great endeavor. The reply was that we must meet in secret. They did not want to soil their reputation for having met with Reinhard Bonnke openly. With great difficulty, I swallowed my pride and arranged a secret meeting at the Pentecostal Theological Seminary Beröa in the small village of Erzhausen, south of Frankfurt.

The general secretary of the Evangelicals, Rev. Hartmut Steeb, came with a few close associates. As the meeting began everyone seemed cordial, and I began to present the vision. I explained how Siegfried Tomazsewski and his team had fine-tuned our brilliant computer program so that it would plot the distribution to 40 million households using postal codes. The same program would track all of our responses and make them available to the sponsoring congregations for follow-up in each area. This was to be a cooperative program, and we were eager to sign up churches to benefit from it.

The general secretary held up his hand. He stopped me to explain that he had read the booklet. On every page, he said, he had expected to find heresy, but to his great surprise, he found none. "Perhaps my English is not good enough," he laughed. The laughter fell flat in that room.

In this statement I could feel all the animosity of the ages still alive and well between the Evangelicals and Pentecostals. Again, I desperately held back my anger and made a final appeal.

"Can we not unite at the foot of the cross? Is the *From Minus to Plus* purpose not one that we share as Evangelicals and Pentecostals together?"

The general secretary held the booklet at arms length and turned it over in his hand as if it were something that might make him unclean. "Well, maybe something could be done if you removed your name from it."

"My name?"

"Yes, your name is on the cover as the author. And inside the front cover the copyright is noted to Christ for all Nations. That will need to go."

So, this was the price? Such a thing could be done and perhaps it should be done. "And there will be cooperation then, if I remove it?"

"Oh, no. I cannot promise anything. I am only speculating that it might help if your name was not attached."

I was through swallowing. The man intended no real cooperation. To unite with such divisive brethren might well sink our ship. "Well, I think our meeting is over. We all have busy schedules. Thank you for coming. We will go ahead with *From Minus to Plus* in the German language without your blessings."

When I arrived back at my offices I went to Siegfried's office. "I am ordering you to increase my name on the cover by two point sizes. I do not want the general secretary to miss it."

Later in the crusade season I returned from an African crusade to Germany and we were well short of our fundraising goal for *From Minus to Plus*. I don't know what happened. Suddenly, something changed. I cannot explain it. Churches began to invite me to present the vision. Churches from every stripe: Lutheran, Pentecostal, Evangelical, Catholic. These were not denominational leaders but rank-and-file preachers who wanted to participate and didn't care who knew that they had partnered with Reinhard Bonnke. I had many behind-the-scenes meetings with pastors who wept over the political resistance of their leaders. They participated with great enthusiasm.

I went out and began to speak in these churches, and if I spoke to a group of only 100, I came out of that meeting with 100,000 deutschmarks. If I saw a crowd of 400, then I received 400,000, if 500 then 500,000. The offerings multiplied beyond anything I have ever seen. God's favor seemed to descend upon us, and we were flooded with 2 million deutschmarks more than we needed to complete the distribution. This became the seed for the next distribution throughout Scandinavia. I did not take royalties from this income. My name was on the cover as the author, but I told all the pastors, "I don't want a single penny, because when it comes to the cross, the royalty belongs to the One who hung on it. Our blessed Redeemer, Jesus Christ."

Perhaps the greatest result of this *From Minus to Plus* distribution was the cooperation it brought among many churches. I was personally gratified to receive even more support from Lutheran churches than from Evangelicals. After the scorn I had received as a Pentecostal boy in Germany from the Lutherans, this was an outcome I could not have predicted. But God is like that, providing resources from unexpected sources and healing wounds of even the religious kind.

The From Minus to Plus German language program went forward to a successful conclusion in '95. At the same time, we did not slack off our campaign schedule. I preached to 1,909,000 people in nine crusades with 491,000 responding to the gospel. We tithed a campaign in Hyderabad, India, where we saw crowds of 150,000 people in a single meeting. In Addis Ababa, Ethiopia, our crusade was cancelled due to more threats of violence. Another series of meetings was cut short in Bamako, Mali, for the same reason. In all, we were able to successfully complete meetings in seven different African nations. Perhaps the most symbolic speaking engagement of the year took place in Cairo, Egypt. We were unable to record decisions for Christ in those meetings, but a total of 12,000 attended. Though our task was far from complete, this meeting meant that I had crossed the finish line of a favorite slogan – in one instance at least, I had preached the gospel from Cape Town to Cairo.

## Chapter 33

THE CRY OF GULLS and gentle roar of surf soothed my ears as I lay on a cot in the morning sun. The sounds brought to mind my youth on the estuary of the Elbe River. But this was not Germany, it was Cotonou, Benin. It was the dry season in North Equatorial Africa with brilliant blue skies and fluffy white clouds above the Gulf of Guinea. I reclined on the balcony of my room in the Marina Sheraton, a pleasant sea breeze wafting the sheers in the open doorway. It was January of 1995 and I was resting in preparation for a preaching campaign to begin that night in Porto Novo, a city 20 miles away on the border of Nigeria.

My telephone rang. The voice on the other end said that Mathieu Kérékou, the ex-president of Benin wanted very much to meet with me at his home. I agreed immediately. My heart beat faster as I dressed for the occasion. I really wanted to meet this man. Four years ago, in 1991, he had peacefully given up his power through a democratic election. As a military strong man he could have held onto power through force, like so many others, but he had chosen not to. I liked the idea that he was one of the new generation of African strong men to bow to the will of the people. He represented a liberating kind of leadership on a continent that desperately needed it.

On the other hand, I remembered that he had come to power in typical African fashion. In 1972 he had managed a military coup as another ruler who thought the future lay with communism. In 1989, however, he had rejected Marxist-Leninist philosophy as Gorbachev began to institute *perestroika* and *glasnost*. For good-thinking people, the end of the Soviet empire seemed inevitable. Perhaps his change in politics indicated a true change of heart, as well. If so, I wanted to know for sure. Without delay, I took my Bible and called Peter van den Berg to accompany me to his house.

We arrived at a heavily fortified military compound. I recalled that over the years there had been many attempts on Kérékou's life. Outwitting assassins and coup attempts was par for the course for African leadership; who could blame him for seeking so much protection. I announced myself to the guards who were expecting us. The gates swung open. We were directed to the Kérékou residence. As our car approached the house, Mathieu and his wife came out to greet us. He was a strikingly handsome figure. A tall, ramrod-straight man with salt and pepper hair, high cheekbones, and a regal bearing. I thought that everything about him bore the air of a polished leader who had left his revolutionary ways far behind.

As we walked toward the house he explained why he had called for me. "My wife and I have heard much about you. We have seen a number of your videos. When I heard that you were in the country I simply had to call you because I want to get saved properly."

I stopped in my tracks, nearly losing my balance. No one had ever asked such a thing of me. ... *to get saved properly.* I was stunned.

"I am your man for the job," I agreed, shaking his hand.

We continued into the house and I opened my Bible and presented the gospel to him, properly. He and his wife both knelt and accepted Jesus, properly. I felt a strong confirmation that his conversion was truly sincere.

As we left for the meeting in Porto Novo he rushed back out of the house carrying a bottle of fine French wine, which he presented to me. He explained that it was the prize bottle from his cellar, an exclusive champagne, Dom Pérignon. This was not the time to explain that I did not drink alcoholic beverages, nor did I know anything about Dom whats-his-name. I thanked him and took it. His heart was in the right place, and I felt that he was expressing gratitude over the new life of Christ that he had just received.

As we drove away I said to Peter, "I feel this man really met Jesus today, it is just a pity that he is an ex-president." He nodded his agreement.

I handed him the bottle. "And it is your job to properly dispose of this."

WE SCHEDULED ONLY SIX AFRICAN CRUSADES in '96. To that schedule we added two campaigns in India, one in Indonesia, Kazakhstan, and Kyrgyzstan, for a total of ten. The attendance and registered decisions continued at the same level as previous years.

This was also the year in which we completed *From Minus to Plus* in Hong Kong. In consulting with our Chinese brothers we changed the title of the booklet to *The Golden Opportunity* so as to make it more appealing to the culture. Nothing about the cover design would jump out at communist border guards, or cultural police, making them suspicious of its content. The strategy worked. Just before this British territory was handed over to The Peoples Republic of China in 1997, we were able to make a massive distribution of the gospel that is still bearing fruit. The booklets have penetrated deep into mainland China, as well.

As we worked through our campaign schedule of '96, in April I heard the joyful news that Mathieu Kérékou had been re-elected president of Benin. As he took the oath of office, it was reported in the press, he left out the portion of the oath that referred to the "spirits of the ancestors." He said that it violated his Christian faith to invoke those spirits. This action angered many pagan factions in Benin, causing riot conditions in some quarters. I sent him a message of congratulations and encouragement. Here was more evidence that this brother had really been born again.

Later that year I heard another bit of news about President Kérékou that lit a fire of hope in my heart for solving our problem with Nigeria. It was reported that he had gone to visit the president of Nigeria, Sani Abacha, to plead for the life of a former Nigerian president whom Abacha had imprisoned as a rival. The intercession had proven successful. This was very significant because in such situations a man's life is not worth two pennies in Africa. In this case the prisoner was former president, Olusegun Obasanjo, a military general who had become outspoken about human rights abuses under Abacha. He had also been lured into a false coup attempt that turned out to be a sting. This allowed him to be arrested and charged with treason, a capital offense. Mathieu Kérékou had taken it upon himself to intervene on his behalf.

Kérékou felt a kinship with Obasanjo for several reasons. First, because Obasanjo had been Kérékou's mentor and role model in handing his government over to a civilian president. In 1979, Obasanjo had been the first African leader to do it. Kérékou had done it twelve years later in Benin, in 1991. The two men also shared a new-found faith in Jesus Christ. I had led Kérékou to "properly" receive the Lord, though I had been made aware that others had also delivered a witness to him, and Obasanjo had become a Christian in prison while awaiting execution. After Kérékou's visit with Sani Abacha, Obasanjo remained in prison, but was kept alive under orders of the Nigerian head of state. I immediately saw that Kérékou was an effective ambassador with the Nigerian president. Perhaps he could successfully represent CfaN as well.

IN DECEMBER OF THAT YEAR, CfaN held its last campaign in the city of Parakou, Benin. Arriving at the airport in Cotonou, I could hardly believe my eyes. I was received like a head of state. A red carpet had been laid for me to walk on as I exited the plane. Military color guards stood at attention. Nothing like it had ever been done for me before. President Kérékou sent his personal Mercedes limousine for my transportation. A retinue of police officers on motorcycles accompanied us to the presidential palace.

Upon arriving, the president met us, his face shining like the sun. He exuded pure joy at being able to give a man of God this kind of red carpet treatment. In every respect he reflected the enthusiasm of his new faith in Jesus. He introduced me to his personal chaplain, Reverend Zanou and I introduced Peter van den Berg and our African crusade director, Revered John Darku.

As we sat together, the president said to me, "I hope you brought application forms."

"Application forms? For what?"

He acted surprised. "I would like to join the Christ for all Nations team, of course."

I was so grateful for the eagerness of his heart. "Your Excellency," I replied, "your application is refused. The hand of God has lifted you to the highest office of this nation. That is your mission field. I pray that you may become the best president this country has ever had!"

Our conversation moved on. We discussed many aspects of our work in Africa. Then, at last, I said to him, "I have heard that you are a close friend of the president of Nigeria, Mr. Sani Abacha."

"Oh, yes," he replied, "we are like twins."

I nodded. "I have a request to make of you, Mr. President." I told him the story of Kano and of our expulsion. "My heart is breaking to return there to reap the harvest that is waiting to be reached in Nigeria. Can you help us?"

"I'm sure I can fix that," he said. "Did you know that Kano is where Abacha was born?"

"No, I did not."

"Yes. I will need some time, you understand. But I believe I can find common ground for a discussion of your situation."

"I cannot tell you how important it is to me, Mr. President, to know that you, of all people, would take up our cause. This problem has weighed on my heart like a 1,000-pound weight, and nothing has been able to move it."

"Yes," he said, nodding and smiling, "I believe I can fix that."

Truly, I felt the Lord was about to open a door no man could shut.[113]

"My duties are calling," he said. "But before I leave you, I also have a special request to make of you."

"Absolutely. What can I do for you, Mr. President?"

"I have 70 Japanese businessmen here in the palace. They want to do business in Benin. I have been meeting with them in a room right next door to us. From our conversations I would say they have never heard the message of Jesus."

I lit up like a flood light. "I can certainly fix that," I said. "And it will be a pleasure to do so."

I was so amazed. Here he was, president of Benin, a new Christian, and already with the heart of an evangelist. Surely his conversion was as genuine as any I have witnessed. I took my Bible into the next room with him. He introduced me to the Japanese delegation as a man of God. They had no idea what had hit them. I opened my Bible and preached the ABCs of the gospel to those 70 businessmen. Several received Jesus.

WE CONCLUDED A SUCCESSFUL *From Minus to Plus* distribution throughout Scandinavia in '97.

We also scheduled ten preaching campaigns. All of them were held in Africa except for one, a meeting held in Pune, India. One crusade was cancelled in Garoua, Cameroon, that year. Again, the attendance numbers and the registered decisions continued at the same plateau we had established since Kano. The largest single crowd was 130,000. We saw them assemble upon our return to Malawi. In 1986 we had seen a crowd of 150,000 there. At that time, it was twice the size of the largest crowd in our history. We had called it "The Malawi Miracle."

Some said to me, "Reinhard, perhaps the CfaN wave has crested. If fewer people have come for your return to Malawi, perhaps your best days are behind you."

I cannot tell you how I reacted against such thinking. There were many reasons beyond our control for the size of the turnout in Malawi. Times had changed. We had perhaps some negative political fallout from the favor of former President Banda. Nevertheless, all of the greatest days for CfaN were still ahead of us. Of that I was sure. God was beginning to crack the door to the great crowds in Nigeria. That was the voice of faith in my heart. Not faith that we would make it happen because of our great expertise. Rather, faith that God had told me *Africa shall be saved* and there was still much work to be done. He had plucked us from obscurity and placed us on this great platform. He would take us across the finish line. Furthermore, He would do it His way, and in His time.

Our first meeting in Malawi was held in the capital city of Lilongwe. Since our last visit there, full democracy with a multi-party system had been instituted. President Banda had died in 1994. It was reported that he had reached the age of 101 years. With him had gone the days of single party rule and the office of president for life. Some things had changed for the better, others for the worse. Nevertheless, I have always found that the gospel of Jesus Christ relates to people in exactly the same way whether under totalitarian rule or democracy. God confirms the preaching of His Word with signs following, and during this campaign 60,000 registered decisions for Christ in Lilongwe. Another 121,000 came to the Lord in the meetings that immediately followed in Blantyre.

While in Malawi I received a wonderful visit from Erhardt Winkels, a German missionary serving in Arusha, Tanzania. Tanzania borders Malawi to the northeast. We had held a crusade there one year before and had seen almost half of the local population come to Jesus. It had been a spectacular meeting. For me it had been memorable as well for the scenic and historic location of this city of Arusha, in the shadow of Mount Meru. My friend brought me greetings from the tax-office. They wished me to return for meetings in Arusha as often as I liked. It seems that following our meetings the people had sponta-neously begun paying their taxes, and the local government had been dramati-cally blessed.

I thought about the power of the gospel to affect a culture. Here was an example in a city that had famously failed to see diplomacy change the culture of nearby Rwanda. Some will recall the Arusha Accords of 1993. Here in the city of Arusha, the Clinton administration of the United States, together with France and the Organization of African Unity, brought together the Hutu and

Tutsi leaders to negotiate peace between them for Rwanda. Within six months of the signing of the Arusha Accords the worst violence in the history of Africa broke out, horrifying the civilized world with its utter brutality. By contrast, six months after our CfaN crusade we saw the gospel do what diplomacy could not do – change the hearts of a people. Because of the gospel they were acting like good citizens, paying their taxes, and CfaN was welcome to return to produce more of the same result. Praise God, nations do not live by political solutions alone, but by the good news of salvation in Jesus Christ. *Blessed is the nation whose God is the Lord.*[114]

AT THE END OF '97, we straddled the holidays with two sets of meetings, one in Garoua, Cameroon, in mid-December, and the second in Bata, Equatorial Guinea, in January of '98. Some of our team would miss their time at home as we flew them between the cities. This was to be a year in which we revved our engines to break through the response ceiling that had limited our success since Kano. We aggressively scheduled ten African crusades and two others in India over the twelve-month period. Throughout the year, I would be in recovery from one crusade as we began another.

As I sat at home in Germany preparing for the Garoua crusade I received word that the meetings had been cancelled by the government. I should have known better than to take on any disappointment over this development. In Christ, things are never as they seem.

Soon after, I received a phone call from President Mathieu Kérékou in Benin. He summoned me to Cotonou immediately. In two days, he said, Sani Abacha, the president of Nigeria would send his private jet to take me to a face-to-face meeting at his palace in Abuja. I could hardly contain my excitement. I felt certain that this was the opening to Nigeria we had been fasting and praying for, and with the Cameroon meetings cancelled, I was available to meet this schedule. Peter van den Berg was still involved in Cameroon and not available to travel with me. I called our African crusade director, John Darku, and asked him to pack an overnight bag and meet me in Cotonou. I headed to the wonderful Frankfurt airport and booked a flight without delay.

Once again, in Cotonou, we were transported to our hotel in the president's private limousine. After resting, we met with President Kérékou the next day. What a warm feeling came over me to see that fine brother in Lord again. I had so many fond memories of him. Here was the man who requested to "get saved properly." He had asked me to preach to the Japanese businessmen. He told me, "I can fix that," concerning the Nigerian president. And now, he had been able to break through the impasse on our behalf. Because of him we could take our case to the very top *echelon* of Nigerian power, the greatest nation on the African continent. Who could have predicted such a chain of events? I was just an evangelist doing my job. Kérékou was just a president doing his job. Together we were being used by the Most High to accomplish purposes bigger than either of us could imagine. As my kids like to say these days, "How cool is that?"

That evening President Kérékou's personal chaplain, Reverend Zanou joined us for the trip to Nigeria. We were driven to the airport and through a VIP entrance. No waiting in line at the passengers' lounge. The limousine cruised across the tarmac directly to Nigeria's version of Air Force One. It was a converted passenger jet bearing that country's insignia and flag. The engines were spooled up to a high scream. As John, the chaplain, and I climbed the stairwell, I felt as if I was walking out of my body. It was almost as if it was not happening to me but to someone else.

On board we were seated in plush seats that swiveled 360 degrees. The doors were secured, and the sound of the engines was shut outside. A lovely stewardess approached me with a bottle of Perrier and a glass of ice on a serving tray.

"Welcome aboard, Reverend Bonnke. Welcome to Nigeria."

That is when I knew it was not a dream and it was not happening to someone else. My tears fell freely into my lap as I accepted that graciously offered drink. I could only manage to say, "Thank you."

As we cruised through the night sky on our short flight to Abuja, I said in my heart, *Oh Lord, You have done all things well. Here I am on my way to Nigeria in the presidential jet without a visa. Who but You could open a door in this way?*

When we arrived at the airport we were taken by limousine to the five-star Nikon Hilton Hotel. We followed the porters as our luggage was taken directly to the presidential suite. I had not expected accommodations so fine, provided by this man I had never met. President Kérékou was to be thanked for our reception, I was sure. The Lord had provided him as our blessed ambassador.

As I looked from the windows in the direction of downtown, I could see the four minarets of the national mosque standing above the skyline. From these towers the muezzin called the faithful in Abuja to prayer, in traditional Muslim fashion. Between the four spires, the golden dome of the main hall glowed like a rising moon in the play of floodlights.

Through the opposite window we could see the looming outline of Aso Rock, a coal black mountain that resembled the great escarpments of Rio de Janeiro. At its base were all the great buildings of the government district, including the green domed house of parliament.

We slept well that night. The next day we waited to be summoned to the palace. We waited and waited. Hour after hour passed and we expected to be called at any minute. But breakfast passed, then lunch, and finally dinner. It is difficult for the imagination not to run away in such a situation. I began to fear that our mission might be hijacked by the devil. After all, that pretty much summarized all that had happened in Kano after the great victory in Kaduna. Perhaps angels and demons were wrestling in the skies over Abuja even now, for the keys to the door to Nigeria.

Finally, at seven o'clock that evening we were told that a limousine was waiting at the hotel VIP entrance. I took my Bible, and the three of us were guided to a special elevator that took us to the waiting car. We were driven a short distance to the palace where we were welcomed in wonderful style. Soon we were ushered into the chamber where President Sani Abacha was sitting.

As we entered he rose and asked all of his aides to leave the room. I did not know what to expect. I insisted that John Darku and Reverend Zanou would have to remain with me. I explained that I never took an audience with anyone alone. He agreed to this condition.

When the room had cleared, we sat down to tea and had the normal session of small talk. When the time seemed right, I said, "Your Excellency, I have a great desire to return to Nigeria and hold crusades. As you may know we held meetings here until the tragic events of October 1991."

"You are most welcome to return," he said. "The door is open. You will get every permit you need. I want to personally welcome you back to Nigeria."

It is hard to describe how off balance I felt in that moment. This was a Muslim president welcoming me back to Nigeria. I had been beating on a solidly closed door for seven years. Now it flew open! I felt as if I'd stumbled forward onto my own nose.

"Your Excellency, I want to assure you that I do not incite any kind of religious hatred in my meetings as the press has said of me. I invite you to send some of your people to any meetings I hold in Nigeria to verify that this is true. I preach only the gospel of Jesus Christ to save sinners."

He nodded and smiled. "I know you, Reverend Bonnke," he said. "I was the general in charge of putting down the riots in Kano. I saw you but you did not see me. You did nothing to incite violence, and you are not to be blamed for any of the deaths that happened there. I do not need to send anyone to listen to your meetings. You can come and preach the gospel in Nigeria as soon as you want."

Mission accomplished. I felt empty, having come full of arguments and assurances that were not necessary. He seemed pleased to simply relax and have more conversation. When at last we ran short of discussing the interests we shared, I began to find ways to preach the ABCs of the gospel to him. He kept me there until after midnight and I ended up preaching every sermon I knew. Every time I came close to the altar call, however, he would raise his hand and interrupt me – "I am Muslim. I am Muslim," he said.

"It doesn't matter that you are Muslim," I replied. "The love of Jesus is indiscriminate. He loves all people, and He loves you."

After midnight he stood to go. "Reverend Bonnke, I hope that this friendship can continue." He shook my hand warmly.

"So do I, Your Excellency."

"I look forward to your next visit."

"As do I."

As we went into the next room another man was waiting there. President Abacha introduced him as his chief protocol officer. I instantly recognized his name. This was the man who had blocked our visa applications for the last nine years. Now he was smiling from ear to ear and shaking my hand.

"Reverend Bonnke," he said, "where have you been all these years?"

I held firmly to his hand and looked directly into his eyes. "I couldn't get a visa."

"Couldn't get a visa? Let me assure you that one call to my office is all it will take. Here, let me give you my business card."

I thanked him while in my heart I called him a hypocrite. Ah, but his hypocrisy was in no small measure influenced by his fear of Sani Abacha. President Abacha said goodnight and left us together.

The protocol officer proceeded to give John Darku and me all the telephone numbers and permissions we needed to process our documents for a return crusade. He asked us where we needed to travel next. I told him that I needed to join Peter van den Berg and the rest of my team in Cameroon so that we could travel together to Equatorial Guinea for our next meeting. He made a quick phone call and told us that the presidential jet would be at our disposal at 6 a.m. We would be taken to Cameroon and then on to Bata. What a fine provision from the hand of God. I thanked him profusely. I could not stop rejoicing all the way back to the Presidential suite at the Nikon Hilton.

We arrived in our room after 1:30 a.m. It would be a short night's sleep. I did my best to make the most of it and soon found myself in deep and peaceful slumber. My phone rang. I turned to the digital clock and saw that it was a quarter to three in the morning. I picked up the phone. The chief protocol officer identified himself by name and title. "President Abacha has sent me to you. I have an urgent message to deliver."

"And what might that be?"

"I am told to deliver it in person."

I don't know if it was the lateness of the hour or the series of events that had just ripped through my consciousness, but I became suddenly fearful. The government was full of factions. Anyone might claim to be the chief protocol officer to gain access to my room, for whatever nefarious reason.

"I already saw the president until after midnight tonight," I said. "We said all we had to say to each other. Can you tell me what is so urgent that you have to wake me up in the middle of the night?"

"No, I cannot. I'm in the hotel. I am coming to your room now."

That instant the Holy Spirit spoke to my heart. *All is well. Do not worry.* I called John Darku and told him that I needed him to come to my room immediately, explaining the situation. Soon he was there, and both of us stood waiting in our bathrobes for a knock on the door.

Soon it came. I opened the door. There stood the gentleman we both recognized from our earlier meeting. Only this time, he held a brown paper shopping bag with handles. I did not know what to make of it, but I relied on the word of the Holy Spirit in my heart.

"Come in," I said.

"No need," he said. "I am sorry for waking you. I know that you leave early, but this is a personal gift from President Abacha, and he ordered me to deliver it to you by my own hand."

I thought that was unusual. The gift had apparently been some kind of after-thought. Usually heads of state calculate their gifts well in advance, making it part of the formality. I thanked him and took the bag into the room. He left, happy that his mission was done.

Inside the room I opened the bag. Any thought of sleep for the rest of the night vanished. I looked down at a bundle of large bills in U.S. currency. As I did, I felt an unholy feeling come over me like a dark blanket. I could not accept this as a personal gift. Under no circumstance could I do that. President Kérékou had given me his prize bottle of wine in the innocence of his newly converted heart. Sani Abacha had remained unconverted to the last. What had motivated this gesture? Even more, what had been the origin of the money? It was cold cash off the record, not intended to be recorded in any income statement.

John Darku and I sat down and counted it. Exactly $100,000.

"I don't want one penny of this," I said. "With this money I will pay for our next crusade in Nigeria. But we have no bank account here. How will I cross borders with this kind of money? Who will believe me when I say 'President, Sani Abacha gave it to me in a brown paper shopping bag?' This leaves me with quite a problem."

When we arrived in Cameroon I met Peter van den Berg. I took him aside and handed him my shopping bag.

"This is your problem now," I said.

He looked inside, then looked back at me with wide eyes. "Thanks a lot."

Soon after arriving in Equatorial Guinea we learned that the government had cancelled our crusade for fear of Muslim violence. Our year of breakthrough was not beginning on a promising note. The good news was that Peter found a way to get the $100,000 back to Germany and into our crusade bank account without a problem. We accounted for it as a gift to the ministry from the Muslim president of Nigeria, Sani Abacha. It immediately put him in the inner circle of our top donors.

As we continued our '98 crusade schedule I ordered our team to begin full-scale planning for our first return campaign in Nigeria. Meanwhile, I continued on a glorious schedule with a campaign in New Delhi, India, then on to Tema, Ghana, where we saw a final night crowd of 150,000. This crowd was the size of the Malawi Miracle again. I was encouraged. Then I returned for a sentimental three nights of preaching in Maseru, Lesotho. My old friends Michael Kolisang and Dolphin Monese joined me to make my joy complete. Together we saw 3,000 come to the Lord, and it was like the first days of CfaN again.

A four-night meeting in Cape Town, South Africa, saw 11,000 decisions, and then I went to Dar Es Salaam, Tanzania. Crowds there swelled to 120,000, and we counted 72,600 decisions for Jesus. I could feel the momentum of these meetings building like an explosion toward our return to Nigeria.

Suddenly, the wind was taken from my sails. Sani Abacha was dead. A heart attack had taken him, they said, but his body had been buried hastily on the same day, fueling all sorts of rumors. A new president had been quickly sworn in, a Muslim military general named Abdulsalami Alhaji Abubakar. He had never held public office before. No one knew him. No one knew what to expect from him. Nigeria was in turmoil.

I quickly opened my personal phone book and began calling the numbers that the chief protocol officer had given me. All the numbers were blocked. Once again, we were locked out of Nigeria. I felt like a comeback quarterback sacked in his own end zone. How could this happen? The conversion of Mathieu Kérékou, his subsequent election as president of Benin, his intercession with Sani Abacha, his opening the doors for our return. In my mind again,

I saw the stewardess on the president's plane, saying, "Welcome to Nigeria." I remembered the feeling that this was the Lord's doing. How could this entire sequence of events fall down like a house of cards?

After our meetings ended in Dar es Salaam, I arranged to fly to Cotonou. At the presidential palace I visited President Kérékou. He seemed somber and in shock over the sudden shift in Nigeria.

"Your Excellency," I said, "Is the new president of Nigeria also your twin?"

He shook his head sadly. "I know nothing about him, but I will meet him for the first time this Saturday. I will talk to him about you."

I knew it was futile. "You are very generous, but do not force my name into the conversation merely as a favor to me. This is hardly the time. Besides, you are the servant of the Lord, my friend. You speak to the president of Nigeria when the Lord tells you to speak to him."

He smiled and nodded. "We are hopeful and fearful at this point. This new president has promised to hold open elections in less than a year. If that happens they will be the first open elections held in 16 years. We are hopeful that he will keep his promise. We are fearful that he will not."

"Much is at stake here," I said, looking up to the ceiling. "Lord, You gave the first inroad into Nigeria; You will provide a second way. I trust You for it."

"Amen," Mathieu agreed.

# Chapter 34

AFTER MEETING WITH MATHIEU KÉRÉKOU I returned to my room at the Marina Sheraton. It was no longer the dry season here and torrential rains were falling. I had not been in the room long when the phone rang. The clerk at the concierge desk identified herself.

"A Nigerian ex-general is staying in this hotel," she said. "His name is Olusegun Obasanjo, and he would like to meet you."

"I would very much like to meet him," I said.

I recognized the name. This man was a former president of Nigeria. The very one Sani Abacha had imprisoned, and for whose life Mathieu Kérékou had intervened. He had become a Christian while awaiting certain death.

She told me that he was in a particular room and that I was welcome to visit him there. I took my Bible and called Peter van den Berg. Not being able to locate him, I went by myself. I knocked at the door.

A very large man with a face that looked like he had seen it all, answered. He was wearing the traditional Nigerian *fila* hat and a long *agbada* robe that went all the way to the floor. I think he smiled at me but I couldn't be completely sure. It was one of those enigmatic smiles concealed by a mask of deep reserve. He spoke with a ponderous, bass voice.

"Reverend Bonnke, come in. President Kérékou let me know you were here. I hope you don't mind me contacting you."

"Not at all. I am glad to meet you."

He offered me a seat in a comfortable sitting area. He had already brewed a pot of chai tea. As he poured it into cups, he said, "I have read your books. As you know I have had much time for reading."

"Yes. I am pleased to see that you have been released from prison."

"Only days after Abacha died I received my freedom," he said. He gave me an impenetrable look. "Many others who opposed him died behind bars. Some were executed. Others died from the mysterious effects of prison food, or medical practice, or malpractice, as the case may be. God sent Mathieu to spare my life. Now, the new military regime is asking that I lend my voice to their call for free elections. Can you imagine such a reversal of fortune? If it is true, if it can be believed, then elections will be held for the first time in 16 years. I keep asking myself, what would make this military regime let go of power? It seems too good to be true."

"Maybe, sir, they are looking back to someone who did it 16 years ago and they like what they see. Without that example, it might not occur to them."

He told me the story of how he had come to know Jesus in prison. Listening to him, I had a full confirmation in my heart that his conversion was real.

We discussed the suspicious circumstances surrounding Abacha's death. He had been in the presidential villa with two key men, his chief of staff and the chief strategist for his political party. The official report stated that he had died of a heart attack. But he was only 54 years of age. Strange reports had been leaked to the press claiming that his heart attack had been fueled by Viagra during an indulgence with prostitutes.

If that was true, it might explain why his body had been buried on the same day without an autopsy. He had been born a Muslim in Kano. In northern Nigeria, adultery was sometimes punished by stoning. Public beatings and humiliation were also common under Sharia Law. The humiliation of the prostitution rumors might have been enough to explain the strange haste in his burial.

But there were other factors, too. Abacha had campaigned against government corruption, but behind the scenes his family had embezzled more than a billion dollars of Nigerian wealth. They had squirreled it away in Swiss and Middle Eastern bank accounts. Many powerful enemies could be created by such a crime. Obasanjo knew that some within the military felt that Abacha had gotten out of control.

I thought of the paper bag full of money he had given me. It was chump change to a man who had acquired more than a billion.

"Corruption is the bane of Nigerian society," Obasanjo said.

He then told us that in July an autopsy had been ordered by the courts. Nigerian newspapers reported the results showing that Abacha had died of natural causes. But was the information reliable? Nothing had been able to quiet the rumors that he had been poisoned by members of his own inner circle.

Anni and I with President Obasanjo from Nigeria

"Let's pray together about this situation in Nigeria," Obasanjo said. "It is time for change in my country. I am praying that this new leader, General Abubakar, is sincere in his promise to bring back democratic elections."

We prayed together. Suddenly, I felt something strong inside my spirit. I felt that I was praying with the next president of Nigeria. I said nothing to him about it.

"General," I asked, "can you help me get a visa for Nigeria? Abacha opened the doors for my return, but now all of those connections have been lost. I want so much to return with my crusades."

He knit his brows. "You should try to contact Abubakar's government. Work through his people. My gut feelings and my faith tell me that until God shuts a door, no human can shut it. I wouldn't assume that the doors to Nigeria are shut because of the death of Abacha."

I thanked him and prepared to leave. As I did, he went to his nightstand and wrote something on a piece of paper. Coming to the door he handed it to me.

"This is my private cell phone number. If you find it difficult to get permits to hold meetings in Nigeria, give me a call."

The next day, as we drove toward the airport, Olusegun Obasanjo was the lead story on Benin radio news. If open elections were to be held in Nigeria, the story quoted him as saying, he would run for president.

I turned to Peter who was riding beside me in the car and pumped my fist. "If Obasanjo wins, Bonnke is in!" Then I bowed my head. "Oh, Lord, let him win, let him win, let him win, in Jesus' name."

I WAS 58 YEARS YOUNG and had no hobby. I did not play golf, nor tennis, nor handball. I did not enjoy fishing, hiking, camping, nor any other sport or game. Nothing for relaxation. For this reason, Peter and Siegfried had been after me for some time to find something I could enjoy during my time off.

From the beginning, I had been driven by the need and desire to preach another evangelistic campaign, and then another, and another. In a certain sense I was addicted to crusades. They fulfilled most every desire in my heart and left little room for anything of lesser importance. My single-minded focus had carried me through many challenging years, but it had also at times driven those around me nearly out of their minds as they tried to match my pace. Even Anni agreed that I should find a hobby. I think she had something like back yard croquet in mind.

I finally became convinced that I would be a better leader if I became just a bit more human. Everyone needs time off – time to renew, and refresh, and relax. A time not to be taken seriously. I came to believe that a good hobby could actually add perspective to my work in the evangelistic campaigns. A hobby did not have to be a distraction. In fact, if it turned into that, then I would abandon it. I made this well known.

On our visits to America over the years, I had been surprised to see that Kenneth Copeland and his group of friends rode Harley Davidson motorcycles for a hobby. They spent time talking about their bikes, how they rode, the various features, the comfort and ride, the clothing, and such. In these conversations I felt quite left out.

Every year the Copelands sponsored an annual charity ride from their headquarters near Fort Worth. My son-in-law, Brent Urbanowicz, had been very impressed by this activity. He had already purchased a Harley 1500cc bike and now rode it in Germany. He had become an enthusiast. My curiosity was peaked. I began to look on the internet at the various bikes and manufacturers.

"Well," I told Peter and Siegfried, "If I am ever going to ride a motorcycle I would not ride a Harley Davidson. I would ride a good German bike. I think German engineering is superior when it comes to vehicles."

To the surprise of both men, I pulled out my German driver's license and showed it to them. I was already certified to ride a motorcycle in Germany.

"Yes," I explained, "when I was just 21 years old and serving my practicum with Father, I had my first Volkswagen. When I went for my driver's test I got certified to ride a motorcycle at the same time. I felt that if my car failed, I did not want to ride a bicycle all of my life, or ride the trains and public transportation, like Father. A motorcycle seemed to me much better."

One afternoon after a day of working in the offices, Peter and Siegfried had prepared a surprise for me. Without explanation, they took me for a drive. We stopped at a BMW dealership. There in front of the showroom sat a beautiful sleek road machine. It was a plush cruiser with a passenger seat. I was very taken with its design. Having never been on a motorcycle, I swung my leg over the saddle and tilted it from its kick stand. It was heavy, with a higher center of gravity than I expected, and it made it difficult to handle. I shook from side to side with uncertainty as I tried to steady it. Siegfried and Peter looked at each other with worried eyes, wondering if they would regret their encouragement of this experiment.

I started the engine and moved toward the street. Everything changed for the better. Suddenly, I realized that the machine was designed to have great stability once it was in motion. Without delay, I thrust myself out into rush hour traffic on the Frankfurt autobahn. Speeds of 90 miles per hour are not uncommon on this superhighway. The motorcycle handled like a dream. It was as if it had been manufactured with me in mind. The speed, performance, and power-to-spare so impressed me that I was soon lost in the entire experience, checking my mirrors, weaving through traffic, accelerating, and braking as needed.

When I arrived back at the dealership I found Peter and Siegfried standing at the entrance looking down the autobahn in the direction I had gone. Unbeknownst to them I had completed a loop around that part of the city and had returned from the other direction in something like record time. They were so relieved to see me alive and well, because all they could remember was how shaky I had been on the machine at first. They had actually worried themselves sick that I had taken a spill. But there was no danger. I was hooked. I had become an enthusiast.

"I will buy it. I love it. I will take it home."

I bought it on the spot and rode it home. Anni nearly had a stroke.

"What have you done?" she cried. "I will never sit on that thing. Never! How could you do this?"

"Just calm down, calm down, calm down. You wanted me to have a hobby. I want this bike. I have never had a hobby. Now I have a hobby and I am happy."

She looked at me with that look that said, "I love you but right now don't say another word because I want to kill you." It is a look as old as the Garden of

Eden, I am sure. I didn't say another word, and we are still alive and loving each other today.

THE NEXT CRUSADE OF '98 was a scheduled return to Nairobi, Kenya. I arrived early in August with Anni. We had decided to stay for a few days of anonymous rest and relaxation in the Serena Hotel near Uhuru Park. My schedule for the year would offer little time for us to be together after this break.

One afternoon Anni showed me a flyer that had been posted on a bulletin board in the hotel. It announced that Teresia Wairimu would be speaking in Uhuru Park on the following Sunday. How this thrilled my heart.

"She does not know we are here," I said. "And I will not tell her. She doesn't expect us for another week."

At this time, CfaN had become a financial supporter of Teresia's ministry. She was on our mailing list and received all notices of our meetings. She knew the schedule of our upcoming crusade in Nairobi. In fact, I had invited her to come and greet our crowd. We had become true colleagues in evangelism.

My mind went back to the time she had come forward in my meeting in Oslo. I recalled that when I had laid my hands on her, she had been blessed right out of her shoes by the power of God. For years now we had followed the growth of her crusades in Africa, pleased to hear of all God was doing through this formerly broken vessel.

Sunday arrived. Anni and I stood at the far edge of the crowd in Uhuru Park, beyond her field of vision. 200,000 gathered that day to hear her speak. Teresia was no longer a divorcee crying pitifully at the edge of my crowd. She had her own crowd. She was on stage and she was on fire, preaching with power and authority. That day thousands came to the Lord. Healings manifested. It was as if another page was being written in the book of Acts. She was doubtless thrilled with another day of obeying the Lord and seeing His power to save sinners. But I was not a sinner, and I did not raise my hand, nor come forward. She never knew I was there, smiling from ear to ear like a proud papa.

There is no room for competition in evangelism. The Lord said to pray that laborers would be sent into His harvest.[115] Teresia was an answer to that prayer.

She is not the only one. On my CfaN team we had a sound man who is an evangelist in his own right, his name is Roger West. Sometimes he will pull cables through the mud at one of our crusades and then get on a plane to fly to his own meeting where 100,000 people will hear him deliver the good news as the featured speaker. We bless him and support him financially. We are laborers together. Hallelujah!

A FEW DAYS LATER, our return to Nairobi was blasted from the books. Al-Qaeda murderers drove a truck full of explosives past the guard station at the U.S. Embassy, killing 213 people in a horrific blast. The Kenyan government cancelled the CfaN crusade for fear of more violence. I met with the local sponsoring pastors and challenged them to carry the gospel forward in their own city.

We flew on to Madagascar where we had prepared back-to-back meetings in the cities of Antananarivo and Mahajanga. The first campaign was cut short after only three days. Again, threats of violence were the reason. The second campaign completed its run successfully. Then we returned to Germany.

OUR NEXT SCHEDULED event was to be held in the main soccer stadium in Freetown, Sierra Leone. I had conducted a 1991 crusade there shortly after democratic reforms had been instituted. We had seen crowds of 135,000 and had registered 105,000 decisions for Christ. We left with high hopes that the new government would prosper. But the leaders had engaged in gross corruption, lining their own pockets, looting the national treasures, and doing nothing to improve life for the average citizen. Within months the entire country was plunged into the chaos of civil war. The consequences of this corruption continued even seven years later as we scheduled our return.

In the meantime, Sierra Leone had become the poorest nation on earth. The extreme poverty of its people was ironic because of its fabulous natural resources. With a lush growing climate on the Atlantic Coast, it was rich in agricultural potential. It also had ample mineral deposits for mining, and abundant fishing beds along the seacoast. These people might have formed a healthy economy, but the social order was filled with mistrust and corruption, and the civil war would not allow stability. The rebels, who were young gangs of violent criminals, repeatedly overran the capital and expelled the legitimate government. The rebels controlled the alluvial diamond mining activity in the country's interior. They had used the diamonds to fund arms purchases and to commit outrageous atrocities. Drug trafficking and the abduction of children used by the rebel army was rampant. Al-Qaeda terrorists were seen doing business with these thugs. A vivid and accurate depiction of this time in Sierra Leone's history was shown in the 2006 movie, *Blood Diamond*.

As we planned our return crusade, the forces in favor of democracy once again seemed destined to fail in Sierra Leone. In May of '97 Muslim President Ahmad Tejan Kabbah had been overthrown by rebel members from his own army. The military junta had released their choice of president from prison, a rebel named Johnny Paul Koroma. At the point of a gun, they installed him as head of state, and in the months prior to our meetings, he had presided over a rule of unbridled terror.

The rebels raped, pillaged, and punished the citizens who had dared to vote against them. They hacked off the hands of people they accused of offering a "helping hand" to the forces of democracy. Mutilated bodies were dumped in the streets to terrorize decent neighborhoods. It was a reign of chaos from the pits of hell.

The *charge de affairs* of the German Embassy in Freetown, Mr. Conrad Fischer, described some of the incidents for us. "What would you say," he said, "if rebel soldiers got hold of a pregnant woman, then placing bets on whether it's a boy or girl, slit open the womb of the mother? Or when they go to the next house and throw a newborn baby into a pot of boiling water? The countryside

Ahmad Kabbah,
President of Sierra Leone

is filled with people whose hands and feet have been chopped off. How is it possible such a gentle and friendly people can turn into such monsters?"

Subsequently, the United Nations intervened behind a well-equipped Nigerian force, supplied by President Abubakar and his government. They routed the rebels from Freetown and reinstalled President Kabbah in March of '98. However, as the October date of our meeting approached, the new government executed 24 of the former military leaders who had joined the rebellion. Conditions in Freetown became volatile again. I was not surprised to receive a letter from the minister of the interior cancelling our meeting due to security reasons.

But John Darku, our crusade director would not let the decision rest. He was on the ground in Sierra Leone and felt sure that our crusade was just what the country needed. He mobilized the local intercessors, and a storm of prayer took place for the meeting to go on. He appealed for a personal audience with the president, who was a Muslim. As a result, the president convened his cabinet and a decision was made that the meetings should go ahead as scheduled.

When I arrived in Freetown I sensed the desperation of the hour. I was met by our welcoming committee representing 47 denominations and 62 churches. Mrs. Shirley Gbujama, the minister for social welfare, greeted me. She was a CfaN partner and friend. "Pastor Bonnke," she said, "during your last crusade I was a member of your intercession team. We are praying for you now as never before."

"I thank God that at least some members of this new government are believers," I said. "I hope there will be many more before we leave town. What Sierra Leone needs is Jesus."

On the opening night I looked out on a crowd of 75,000. The great stands surrounding the soccer field were filled to capacity. The sight reminded me of the Rose Bowl football stadium in Pasadena, California. The playing field was still vacant on this first night, but before the meetings concluded, that field too, would be full.

The first words spoken from our platform came from President Ahmad Kabbah himself. He stood surrounded by Nigerian guards with loaded weapons at the ready.

"Reverend Bonnke," he said, "you could not have come to Sierra Leone at a more appropriate time. I ask all of God's people to pray for peace to come to our land."

I heard the voice of the Spirit in my heart. My sermon text was to be taken from the words of the prophet Isaiah, *Comfort ye, comfort ye, my people, saith your God.*[116] The message of comfort, of course – for ancient Israel as well as for modern Sierra Leone – was the prophesied coming of Jesus Christ, who would die for the sins of the world.

As I gave the invitation that night, 10,000 hands were raised. Our local church workers registered them for follow-up. Then God began to heal the sick. Among those who were brought to the platform was a woman who had been blind. The crowd exploded with joy as I demonstrated that she who was blind could now see. Even more electrifying was the sight of a little girl running across the stage, back and forth, back and forth – and me chasing her with the microphone. She had come to the meeting crippled from polio; she left on perfectly restored legs.

The crowds grew until 150,000 crowded the old stadium. Peter van den Berg went into the stands and felt them trembling beneath his feet as the happy people sang and danced and praised God for His salvation and comfort. He ordered our intercessors to pray that no disaster would befall these enthusiastic crowds in those decrepit stands.

CfaN Gospel Crusade in Freetown, Sierra Leone.

In six days we saw a half million people in attendance. We registered a total of 140,000 decisions for Christ. Our local pastors were overwhelmed. Pastor Abu Koroma, who had four churches in the city, spent an entire day visiting new converts who had shown up at his doors. Pastor Momodu Conteh said, "This has been the greatest response to the gospel that has ever been seen in Sierra Leone." Reverend Harry Jenkins said, "What we have witnessed in this crusade has been a sovereign act of God for this nation, reaching from the lowest person to the highest members of government." Pastor Archibald Cole summed it up, "The forces of Satan and evil have been pushed back as the CfaN team ministered to us. Satanic power had been broken."

As the meetings concluded President Kabbah asked me to address parliament. I sought the Lord carefully for the words He would have me bring to this special body of men and women. On Wednesday, October 7, the Honorable Justice Kutubu welcomed me to the government house and gave me the floor. Much of my address was published the next day in the Freetown newspaper, *The Concord Times*.

I thanked the speaker, and I spoke to these leaders about issues of the heart. I told them that Sierra Leone was like Israel, and just as Isaiah had challenged Israel to rule its people based on righteousness, so I challenged these government officials to establish their government in righteousness.

"One thing any man should remember in any public office, whether in government, in business, in the police, or in the judiciary: God has not allowed him there to indulge himself, to take advantage of others or for personal glory and benefit, but for the benefit of the people. God will not judge you based on how many people served you, but on how many people you served. No country can carry a load of iniquity and criminality and get away with it. It is righteousness that exalts a nation and sin is its reproach."

I spoke of the 140,000 who had made decisions for Christ in the Freetown campaign, and of the 105,000 who had responded years ago in 1991. "Every person who received Jesus Christ and is born again is a national treasure," I told them. "They add to the sheer weight of the goodness of this land. They are assets, not liabilities."

I presented the ABCs of the gospel. Again, as I have learned to do in high political circles, I placed the altar call above protocol. Many hands were raised, and many in that chamber accepted Jesus as their Savior and Lord that day.

Throughout 1998, in spite of the fierce opposition and the cancellations we suffered, the year ended strong. We successfully broke through the limits that we had seen since Kano. I preached to 3,459,000 people, a 23 percent increase over '97, and more significantly, we saw 728,600 decisions for Christ, a 42 percent increase over the previous year. Our largest crowd for the year was seen in Cochin, India, where in five days, 1,100,000 attended. The largest number of registered decisions was seen in Liberia, the next-door neighbor to Sierra Leone, and a nation with similar problems. We saw 180,000 come to Christ there. What a breakthrough year was 1998! Praise God.

A few months after leaving Sierra Leone, another military coup was launched against the government. Fierce fighting erupted in Freetown. More lives were lost, people killed, and property destroyed, but the United Nations together with Nigerian and government forces prevailed in just two weeks against the evil assault. Slowly, the nation began to rebuild its civilized order. Today, the peacekeeping forces have been withdrawn. The economy is growing. The diamond output has increased tenfold, and democratic elections rule where military coups and rebel outlaws once destroyed the land and its people. I believe that the people who made decisions for Christ in our crusade did indeed add to the sheer weight of goodness in Sierra Leone, just when they needed it the most. The gospel can do what diplomacy and politics can never do. Praise God! I am not ashamed of the gospel of Christ.[117]

I BEGAN TO FOCUS MY TEAM and partners on the end of the millennium and the beginning of the new one. While the world stewed and fretted over something called Y2K, I could only envision a harvest in the year 2000 that would be greater than anything we had ever seen before. This reality shone brighter and brighter in my heart as the time rushed toward us like a freight train. But the Lord was not bound to some magical turning of the calendar. As it turned out, '99 would jolt CfaN from the modest breakthrough we had seen in '98 to an even higher level of success.

At first it did not seem so. Planning for '99 included only nine crusades, one in India, three in the Philippines, and the others in Benin, Ghana, Rwanda, Kenya, and Tanzania. Cancellations began to plague us from the very start. First the meetings scheduled for February in Visak, India, were cancelled by the authorities because of security risks. In this case, the opposition was not Muslim but Hindu. After that, all of our meetings in the Philippines were either cancelled or cut short. A very strong Muslim presence accounted for these disruptions. It would seem with such a precarious start that we were going to be thrown back into the old pattern of post-Kano responses. But again, things are not what they appear to be with God. Faith, not fear, is always the proper response.

Following our final cancellation in the Philippines, I returned to Germany. It was there that the good news reached me that Obasanjo had won the presidential election in Nigeria. Not only had he won, he won in a landslide, gaining nearly 64 percent of the vote. He assumed office on May 29, 1999, in what became a national holiday called Democracy Day. It was the first time in 16 years that Nigeria had seen a civilian head of state.

In his inauguration speech, he said, "Let me make a solemn pledge before all of you, before the whole world and before God, that I will devote all my energy and all I possess in my power to serve the people of Nigeria and humanity."

This was the kind of principled Christian leader Africa so desperately needed. 16 years before, he had been a military dictator. Even so, he had handed the military government over to a civilian president without resistance. Now he had become that civilian president himself in free and open elections. What a divine full circle!

I took out my wallet and sorted through it to find a familiar piece of paper. On it Obasanjo had written his private cell phone number. I dialed it.

"Obasanjo speaking."

"Congratulations General on your election to the office of President of Nigeria, when can I come?" I said it all in one breath.

"Immediately," he said, chuckling on the other end of the line.

"I'm on my way."

I called Peter van den Berg. I asked him where he thought our first Nigerian crusade should be held. He spoke to Winfried Wentland about it. Winfried and his family were CfaN heroes and veterans of the Kano disaster.

"Benin City," was his reply.

"Benin City it is," I said. "Begin planning, full speed ahead."

Part 7

# THE SUPERNATURAL HARVEST

# Chapter 35

THROUGHOUT 1999, during times of prayer, the Lord kept bringing the nation of Sudan to my mind. Sudan is a huge country, the largest land mass in Africa and the Arab world. It stretches along the Nile River from Uganda in the south to Egypt in the north. In 1977, Sudan had imposed Islamic Sharia Law on the people, including its non-Muslim population in the south. This had reignited a never-ending civil war. Sudan remained a troubled land with constant rumors of atrocities, genocide, and mass starvation. The record showed several million deaths fueling deep hatreds there.

Here at millennium's end, the Khartoum government was trying to improve its image in the eyes of the world. In '96, Bin Laden had moved from Sudan to Afghanistan under strong international pressure. The government now wanted to seek more favorable trade agreements, and they began reaching out to the west. In their eagerness, they ratified freedom of religion as a constitutional right, stating, "Everyone has the right to freedom of conscience and religion and the right to manifest and disseminate his religion or belief in teaching, practice or observance. No one shall be coerced to profess a faith in which he does not believe or perform rituals or worship that he does not voluntarily accept." To an evangelist this seemed like a window of opportunity. One I could not get out of my mind.

I approached Stephen Mutua, our campaign director for East Africa. "The Lord speaks about Sudan," I said. "Go to Khartoum and bring me a report."

He came back saying that we would be risking our lives to hold meetings there. The U.S. had bombed an industrial building in the capital in '98, claiming that it was a front for the manufacture of chemical weapons. The local government claimed that the American cruise missiles had merely hit an overgrown drug store. They had turned the wreckage into a museum to foment hatred toward America. The city boasted a radical university. Many dangerous Islamic factions flourished in the city.

"Then we will not go now," I said. "Thank you for your report. I don't want to risk my team. If I see a fire I will not step into it, I will walk around it, unless God speaks – then it is another matter. I say we don't suffer for fun. We preach the gospel only at any necessary cost, not unnecessary cost."

ALL DAY LONG, Sulamith Mörtschke watched little children growing up. She was a kindergarten teacher. She loved her work, yet it brought her pain because she wanted a child of her own so badly.

Her husband, a young lawyer, was just starting his practice near Frankfurt. On weekends he served as worship leader at their church. He was a fine and respected man, and she wanted to please him more than anyone she had ever known. They both felt called to be godly parents, bringing up children to serve the Lord. But after five years of trying to conceive, she knew that something was wrong. She could not get pregnant.

Sulamith began to blame herself. She felt that her inability to conceive somehow made her less of a woman. In the depths of her heart, she sensed that her husband could have done better if he had picked another mate. Every woman she met seemed a better candidate.

Each day at kindergarten, a painful drama was repeated again and again as mothers came to pick up their children. A toddler would suddenly cry out his or her mother's name and rush to the door for a wild embrace. Sulamith could hardly bear to watch anymore, fearing that she would never hear that sound from her own child, nor know that bond of true motherhood. This pain nagged her so much; she could hardly meet the gaze of the mothers she served. She felt inferior and unworthy of their esteem.

In desperation she and her husband visited their family doctor. After many consultations with no success, he referred them to the Child Wish Center. This was the clinic of last resort in the region of Germany where they lived. All of the latest reproductive techniques were in use there every day. The combined knowledge of all the medical specialties that could help them was available for a price. And the price was high.

A series of comprehensive tests was started. They began with extensive interviews. The staff asked many personal questions about their family background and their personal lives. Then the medical tests were done. Was it a malfunction in her ovaries? Or could it be his sperm count? The doctors used every method available to determine who was at fault. Some of the tests were humiliating for both of them. At times they felt like lab rats. When they went home from the clinic they felt saddened. It seemed wrong to be investigating a gift from God with such intrusive methods. And yet, they didn't know what else to do.

At this very time, I had planned a Christ for all Nations Fire Conference in Böblingen, Germany. Their church cooperated with our ministry in this effort. I was so excited. It was 1999, and we were celebrating 25 years of organized evangelistic effort. The partners that lived in the area of Böblingen had been among the very first to support me as CfaN had begun in 1974. Now, I could celebrate our long association by bringing this 25th anniversary conference to their city.

As in all such conferences, I am focused on inspiring every believer to his or her calling as a witness for Jesus Christ. Not only do I preach, but I invite special speakers who I feel can make a clear challenge on this point. On the final night, evangelist Steve Hill spoke. His sermon hit the mark. It was a fitting end to a wonderful conference of workshops and seminars.

In the audience that night, Sulamith and her husband were deeply touched. In their hearts they made new commitments to witness for Jesus. As they returned to their everyday lives, they were determined to preach the gospel to everyone the Lord brought across their path.

I came to the podium to close the meeting in prayer. I asked the audience to bow their heads, and I began to pray God's blessing and power into the lives of all of those present. I began to lift up the coming year of crusades. Our planning committee had called it "The Millennium Harvest." I believed that during that special year of 2000, God would do great things through us, with a record number of souls plundered from hell and registered in heaven. All of these thoughts were pouring from me in prayer like a fountain of fresh spring water.

As I prayed at the podium, however, Sulamith became overwhelmed with a feeling of desperation. Nothing meant more to her as a soul winner than guiding the growth of her own child, dedicated to God from her womb. She began to plead with God. "Dear Lord, please speak to Reinhard about our need. Please let him say something about our desire for a baby."

At the podium I suddenly stopped. It was abrupt. The Spirit was tapping at the door of my heart. My ministry director, Peter van den Berg, Siegfried Tomazsewski, and others who were with me on the platform, still remember this moment.

"I feel that I should not go on," I said, "until I have prayed for the sick. I will now pray for the sick before we leave this place."

As I began to pray, the Spirit pressed these words into my heart and mind. I spoke them aloud: "Someone here has an intense desire to have a child. Count from this day, nine months, and you shall have a baby." I felt it so strongly, I said it again, "count from this day, nine months, and you shall have a baby."

Meanwhile, Sulamith could hardly contain herself. Could these words be for me, Lord?

The meeting ended and I heard nothing to confirm that I had heard from the Lord in this wonderful promise for a baby to be born. The delegates filtered out of the hall, returning to their homes.

That night Sulamith talked about it with her husband in the car as he drove. She told him how she had secretly prayed that God would speak to me as I had delivered the closing prayer. Her faith had been ignited as I had stopped to address that very thing. This promise simply had to be for them, she believed.

Her husband struggled to raise his hopes to believe that God had interrupted this great meeting just to deliver a message to them. But he could not deny that I had spoken those amazing words. He talked with his wife about it all the way home, deciding to try to reach out and embrace this nine-month prophecy for themselves. If God had spoken to them through my words, they decided, it would simply come to pass.

Ten days after the conference their telephone rang. A staff member from the Child Wish Center called with bad news. The medical experts at the clinic had examined all of the data from their fertility tests and had reached a conclusion: there was no hope for them to ever conceive a child. The clinic did not recommend that anything more be done. The doctors had determined that artificial fertilization would not work in their case. Not even surgery would make a difference. The staff member said that the doctors had suggested that they turn their full attention toward adopting a child. It was their only hope.

Sulamith was stunned. All of her hopes, lifted so high by my words at the conference, came crashing down like a shattered crystal goblet. The Lord had told her to count nine months. The doctors were telling her to count nothing at all.

Feelings of inferiority descended like a dark cloud. She had suspected that she was a failure as a woman, now she had confirmation. The ache of never bearing a child as a biological mother returned with a vengeance. She could not think about adoption – not just now. She could hear only the silence of the nursery she had built in her mind for the child she would never hold.

As she placed the phone down she flushed with a burst of anger. After all they had invested to learn the truth from the Child Wish Center, how could such sensitive and devastating news be delivered in an impersonal phone call? The insult of this added an even greater level of pain to her sense of injury.

Days later, a letter arrived from the clinic confirming everything she had heard in the phone call. As she shared it with her husband they both knew that their earlier decision to accept God's word to them had taken on added weight. In black and white, they now knew how impossible it would be for them to conceive by any natural means. Their faith was shaken, but also strengthened in a strange way. If they would have a child, only God could make it happen.

Sulamith returned to her kindergarten class. She watched other people's children play. She helped them learn about God and His love for them. She poured herself into helping these little ones grow in the nurture and admonition of the Lord. All the while, her heart fluttered between the sudden hope of God's promise at the Fire Conference and the cruel disappointment that had come from the doctor's report. Each day she reached out anew to believe for the impossible. And each day she would wonder if God had spoken to another woman – not her – through Reinhard Bonnke's prophecy at the Fire Conference. Meanwhile, her husband poured himself into his work, leaving little time to think or talk about it.

Seven weeks passed. Sulamith sensed that something was different in her. At first she dared not say anything, but her body was definitely going through changes. At last she shared these new feelings with her husband. Immediately, he scheduled a trip to the doctor.

The doctor did his testing and could not believe the results. Sulamith was seven weeks pregnant. Impossible!

Ten weeks after the conference, I received an email telling me that a pregnancy had resulted from the promise spoken at the Fire Conference. The mother and baby tested normal and healthy, and the due date was February 23, 2000 – exactly nine months from the day God had declared it.

Today, the Mörtschkes are raising two healthy children in the fear and admonition of the Lord. One child attends kindergarten where his mother is a teacher. Sulamith has received the desires of her heart.

I tell you by the same Spirit that whispered to my heart in Böblingen that night, God has good plans for all of his people. He has good plans for you. Count on it. God is for you. God is good.

As 1999 CONTINUED we prepared feverishly for CfaN's return to Nigeria. My heart was overflowing with expectations of the harvest. I spoke of it at every opportunity. It was then that I received a telephone call from my friend Rudolph

Kleinbaum in Bremen, Germany. He was the unique immigrant who lived like a homeless man and hid money for the Lord behind the zipper of his pants.

"Brother Bonnke," he said, with intense excitement in his voice, "I know that you are soon to return to Nigeria. Please come to Bremen. I want to give my entire savings account into the work of the Lord. It is in a bank here and I do not want my alcoholic sons to know about it. Would you please meet me at the bank where I can see that this money is properly given?"

I agreed to meet him. Siegfried Tomazsewski went with me to the appointment. On our arrival, Rudolph looked like his usual homeless self. His lifestyle had not improved much, but he produced his savings passbook and showed us how much he had saved. It was 35,000 deutschmarks. Absolutely phenomenal.

"I want to give everything for souls in Africa," he said.

At this moment I realized that I may be receiving the most powerful gift in the history of CfaN. This truly was a modern version of the biblical widow's mite story. If her two mites counted more than all the wealth of the others, then surely Rudolph's full savings account was a multiple version of her gift. He, too, was giving all he had.

The bank manager looked at me as if I was some sort of scam artist. He was obviously not happy to hear Rudolph's plan for the money.

"Who are you?" he demanded, looking at me with disdain.

I did not expect him to understand unless he was a believer. "I am Reinhard Bonnke, an evangelist. I preach the gospel in Africa. Rudolph has been one of our supporters for many years. I want you to know that I have not asked for his money. Rudolph has called me to come because he wants to give it to the work of the ministry."

"This is against bank policy. You cannot take Rudolph's money today. You will have to wait four weeks before we can release it. It is a safety precaution."

"No," Rudolph insisted. "Please, I want him to have it today. It must go into the work of the Lord immediately."

"That is impossible. This bank has rules. If you deplete all of your account you must wait four weeks to receive it. This rule was made for your own protection, Mr. Kleinbaum – protection from people who would take advantage of you. Do you understand?"

"May we speak privately?" he asked.

"Yes, of course," the banker said. They went into a neighboring office. I could only imagine what happened next, remembering my first meeting with Rudolph and the shock I received when he unzipped his pants and pulled the money from its hiding place.

After some time had passed, Rudolph came back out with a bag full of money and a big smile on his face. He dropped it into my hand.

"This is for the Lord's work, Brother Reinhard."

"May He bless you beyond all that you imagine," I replied. "Only the Lord is worthy of such a sacrificial gift. But how did you do it? How did you get the banker to change his mind?"

"It was simple. The bank has rules and I followed them. The rule was that I would have to wait four weeks if I took all of the money out, so I didn't take it all out. I held some back in the account."

"Well, of course. What a practical solution."

"I kept back 20 deutschmarks. Enough for my funeral."

It hit me like a hammer. He had kept enough for his funeral. Even in death he was determined not to be a burden to anyone. He was so grateful for his freedom after living most of his life behind the Iron Curtain, that he refused to indulge in the kind of materialism that we all took for granted. Instead, he stowed away all of his savings for the things that mattered most in life, and he was determined to leave this earth with an empty bank account.

To this day he is my friend, and still a supporter of CfaN. I wonder if I have ever met another believer who lives a more fulfilled life of service and purpose? Rudolph's sons are still alcoholics, begging on the streets and drinking themselves to death. But he continues to lay up treasure in heaven. On the day when we stand before our Lord, I have no doubt that every little thing Rudolph has done without, so that he can send money to the African harvest, will be returned to him a thousand times and more.

FOR OUR RETURN TO NIGERIA, we decided to hold a crusade in Benin City. It had been scheduled for October, my first Nigerian event in nearly a decade. After examining the site, our trusted scout, Winfried Wentland, called to warn us that the route to the crusade ground contained a dangerous intersection. It amounted to a perilous pedestrian bottleneck. We had gained experience with bottlenecks and had only narrowly averted disaster in the past. We knew that

if a stampede occurred at this location it could prove deadly. When I heard of it, I ordered my men to approach the local police for help. The police asked what size crowd we expected. We estimated 500,000. They laughed at the number. We insisted that it was realistic. After studying the problem the Benin

Benin City

City police told us that it would cost 500,000 Nigerian naira to control traffic at this intersection. We paid the fee and obtained a receipt for their service.

On the first night I stood on the platform dressed in the traditional Nigerian *agbada* robe that went all the way to the floor. I wore a matching *fila* hat, too. I was determined to identify with these people in every way possible to win them for Christ. I couldn't believe my eyes as I gazed out over a crowd of 400,000 on the first night.

The salvation response was immense. I estimated one in four hands was raised to receive Jesus. What an incredible start. Then miracles of healing began to occur. This was the familiar pattern. I knew that the word would spread like wildfire, building our crowd to an unprecedented size on the following nights.

But perhaps the most horrible assault of Satan in the history of our work occurred after that first night's meeting. At the intersection where Winfried had predicted problems, 14 people were trampled to death as they attempted to make their way home.

As I heard the news in my hotel room I fell to my knees. This tragedy truly broke my heart. Life for the common people of Africa is so cheap. Their leaders can be quick to sacrifice lives to any of a number of marginal causes. The world press had largely ignored the horrible atrocities committed in places like Sierra Leone because, "after all, it's only Africa." *Never! Never! Never,* did I want that attitude attached to CfaN. The opposite was our message – every life is of infinite value to the God of the Universe. He died for each one that they might live, and live abundantly. Now this terrible tragedy had marred that beautiful vision.

I sought the face of the Lord for the strength to go on. The police assured us that they were now on top of the problem and it would not occur again. I asked my men why it had happened in the first place, since our team had accurately predicted it. The answers were as old as the Garden of Eden. Excuses. We had a receipt, a piece of paper showing that we had done our part. But sometimes you do everything right and it still does not guarantee a proper outcome. The human heart is deceitful and desperately wicked.[118]

In spite of the tragedy, the next night our crowd grew to 500,000. The police managed the dangerous intersection with due diligence and no one was hurt. In six nights we saw 300,000 more people attend than had come to our Kaduna crusade nine years earlier. The registered decisions for Christ exceeded Kaduna by 140,000. We had never seen a greater crusade in our history – and never a more tragic one.

As we prepared for our second Nigerian meeting in Port Harcourt, we were told that we should expect even larger crowds. In the meantime the German press delivered a knockout punch to CfaN back home. They had learned of the trampling victims in Benin City and they took this opportunity to blame us. "Bonnke's blood-washed Africa takes on a new and sinister meaning," the stories screamed. The 14 people who were trampled to death were laid directly at my feet as casualties of an evangelist's oversized ego. I was devastated, and furious.

I contacted the primary news organizations in Germany and demanded that they print a rebuttal. I showed them that they had not done their homework on this story. The Nigerian government had conducted their investigation of the incident and had exonerated us. Our receipt from the police department showed that the CfaN team was not to blame. We had taken the proper steps to avoid the disaster.

Ultimately the news organizations met with me. I do not recall ever unleashing such a barrage of verbal chastisement in all my life as I did against those so-called journalists. They had engaged in a campaign of defamation, not news. I let them have it with both barrels. Proper retractions were published, but alas, much damage was done. Those who wanted to believe Bonnke was a devil now had their opportunity to run with the original story. And run they did. Some still report it with glee, revealing their unprofessional prejudice.

Our Port Harcourt meetings were held in December of that year, just two months later. We saw even larger crowds. However, some of our sound equipment failed to reach a significant portion of the field on the first night because of a sudden change in wind direction and our inability to overcome it. The technicians desperately fought to correct the problem but could not find a solution. They watched helplessly as 100,000 people drifted away into the night, unable to hear. It was as if God had driven a supernatural catch into our nets, but our nets broke under the strain and many were lost. My men had tears streaming down their faces as they saw the consequences of inadequate equipment. They vowed it would never happen again.

Still, in Port Harcourt, we saw something completely unprecedented. Over one million people registered decisions to accept Jesus as Savior in six days – 1,110,267 to be exact. That meant that more than half of the crowd of 2,100,000 attending those meetings became new converts.

Never had it become clearer to me that what Satan had intended for evil, God was turning for an even greater good. The disaster at Kano, which had expelled us from Nigeria for nine years, had also made us a legend in this land. The name Bonnke had become a whispered household word. As soon as it was announced that Bonnke was returning, the interest level exploded like a pent-up shout of joy. I did not know how long this wave of fame would be working to fill our nets to overflowing, but I did not want to miss another opportunity to reap the harvest to the full. We scheduled four more crusades in Nigeria for the coming year of 2000.

As we prepared, Peter van den Berg, Derek Murray our sound engineer and his men refitted the net of sound that we would cast over a crowd of up to 2,000,000 listeners. The heart of the system was housed in two giant columns of highly sophisticated speakers. These were hoisted by hydraulic equipment into place, and each speaker was driven by electric motors to the exact angle necessary to cover the vast area of the standing crowd. They were bound to the columns in arrays that could project to the farthest reaches, 900 yards from the stage. The stream of sound that these speakers could emit would literally destroy the eardrums of anyone who stood in front of them receiving the full blast. That is why they had to be hoisted so high from the ground. They were engineered in such a way that the people sitting underneath the focused stream of sound did not hear it, but they received my voice at a comfortable level from other speakers. The stream of sound was then distributed to the people in the vast distance.

In order that everyone from the front to the back of the crowd might hear equally well, the motor-driven angles on the speakers were controlled by a flawless brain that adjusted to changing conditions throughout the meeting. When the system was first installed on the crusade site, the engineers walked a prescribed plot of the audience area. They set up the computers by stopping at the plot points with GPS units and sound measuring devices. Laser beams were fixed to each of the GPS coordinates in the crowd areas. The decibel levels were measured at each spot and adjusted by the laser-controlled units in the hands of the sound engineer. This data was read into the computers, which adjusted the speaker output.

Nothing was taken for granted. After the initial setup was complete, another complete sound test was performed with technicians walking the entire crowd area again to measure the sound delivery. When the setup was confirmed then another part of the computer system was activated to adjust the output based on the changing conditions of humidity, wind direction, wind speed, outside noise, and sound absorbed by the crowd itself. These variables were adjusted second by second throughout my sermon so that all of the listeners could clearly hear the message of Christ, whether shouted or whispered into the microphone. At last, the Lord had prepared us, and we were poised and ready for what He wanted to accomplish through CfaN in the year 2000.

THE LETTER ARRIVED on official Sudanese government letterhead, and its contents delivered a shock to my system. The president and other leaders of Sudan were inviting CfaN to hold an Easter Celebration in the heart of Khartoum, population 8,000,000. It would not be a crusade, they said, because the word *crusade* was hated in Muslim jargon. Crusades called to mind the Christian armies that had fought to clear Arabs from the Holy Land during the Middle Ages. "But the ancient Christian kingdoms were in Sudan before the Muslims were here," the letter stated. "Their ancestors are still with us. We want to demonstrate that Sudanese Christians have a right to celebrate Easter, and we would like to invite you to lead a government-sanctioned Easter celebration for our people in Khartoum."

This came absolutely out of the blue. Apparently the Sudanese Government wanted to use this event to demonstrate their commitment to constitutional freedom of religion. I asked Stephen Mutua about the numbers of Christians in the city. There were only a few. They were Catholics, Coptics, Greek Orthodox, plus a few Anglicans, Presbyterians, and a very, very few Pentecostals. If Reinhard Bonnke came to preach, it would elevate the status of the lowly Pentecostals in the eyes of their more traditional brothers. It would also attract a great number of curious Muslims.

Even though I had earlier cancelled plans for a meeting there because of security risks, this government invitation changed everything. I felt this was the hand of the Lord opening a door that would have otherwise remained shut. I ordered Stephen to begin the preparations for Easter 2000 in Khartoum.

# Chapter 36

CALABAR, ABA, LAGOS, ENUGU – these were the four Nigerian cities the Lord directed us to reach in the year 2000. We would start in January and February with Calabar and Aba, and end the year in November and December with Lagos and Enugu. I sensed the harvest would be unprecedented.

During the past year in Nigeria we had seen the percentage of decisions rise to more than half of those in attendance. This was sharply above the normal pattern worldwide. We all sensed a supernatural harvest had been prepared for us and we could hardly wait to get to it. There was a sense among the CfaN team that all we had done until now was preparation for the time ahead in Nigeria.

As we anticipated, our first meeting in Calabar continued the pattern. Our daily crowd grew to 450,000 with 1,600,000 in attendance over five days. We saw more than 50 percent of the crowd come to Jesus. The churches of that region were flooded with new believers. Aba in February was an even greater harvest. It nearly equaled Port Harcourt of the year before, with more than a million decisions for Christ! Again, that was more than half of those who attended over a six-day period.

We had also scheduled crusades in the year 2000 beyond Nigeria. Between the first and last two campaigns, we scheduled meetings in India, Sudan, and two more in Ethiopia. Each was significant for various reasons. In India, for example, we saw only 6 percent of the audience respond to the gospel. The contrast with Nigeria was stark.

This signaled a shift in strategy for me. I ordered the CfaN team to change plans for 2001. I asked them to concentrate inside the nation of Nigeria. For most of my ministry I had opposed the old adage, "strike while the iron is hot." Through the lean years of building CfaN, the iron had never been hot. This had molded my thinking. I had exhorted believers again and again to "strike, strike, and strike again *until* the iron is hot!" I am a fiery evangelist, and I don't believe in waiting for everything to be just right. Jesus said go into the world, and so we go.[119] But at this moment in our history the iron had become so white hot in Nigeria that we could not ignore it. We would not be good stewards to focus our energies in places where the response was so meager.

For the year of 2001, it was decided that we would tithe just one campaign outside Nigeria in Kinshasa, Zaire. All others would be inside the country of the greatest harvest. Preparations for this new direction began immediately as we worked our way through the remaining campaigns of the year 2000.

AFTER CONCLUDING THE INDIA MEETING we turned our eyes toward Khartoum, Sudan. Receiving an invitation from the Sudanese government was an important signal to me. Cracking the borders of any Muslim nation in the north of Africa was a knotted puzzle. Year after year, I had sent scouts to these lands. At other times, I had gone to see them for myself, praying to find a way in. But whenever I made these journeys I never knew if I would be taken to the palace or to the prison.

In one instance, I had been blacklisted from a particular Muslim country that shall remain nameless because I hope to return there one day soon. Years before, I had held a meeting there in an evangelical church and we had seen the building overflow for several nights with hundreds receiving the Lord. There was strong Muslim pressure against proselytizing in this nation. As a result, my name had been blacklisted by the government.

When Sani Abacha lifted our ban in Nigeria, two years earlier, it had affected the thinking of other Muslim leaders as well. I had been told by inside sources that I had been removed from the blacklist of this particular Muslim country. Sometime later, I decided to test the truth of that report. I traveled there on a tourist visa for a two-day visit. As soon as my passport was examined at the immigration desk, I was pushed unceremoniously into a holding cell in the basement of the airport. Obviously, the blacklist was still in place, or else word of the change had not reached the authorities who worked at the airport. In either case, the result was the same.

I broke into a cold sweat hearing those bars clang shut behind me. Before this moment, I had never fully imagined the way the world changes for one thrown in prison. Suddenly, all of the rules and rights that apply to everyday citizens are stripped away. I was reminded of Richard, awaiting execution in the Bukavu prison so long ago. What an inspiration his memory was to me now. He had been leading praise and worship and making music with those chains welded permanently around his wrists. For the first time I felt a fraction of what he must have felt. I was suddenly at the mercy of those who wished me ill.

This airport prison was the worst possible nightmare for a tourist. The place stunk, had no sanitation, no individual cells, no beds, no food. I was locked in a "tank" with every sort of malcontent. Who knew their backgrounds? Murderers, rapists, smugglers, terrorists, extortionists – they looked the part. Believe me, I preferred the palace treatment to the prison treatment without question.

Ironically, the arresting authorities left me with an unfair advantage. My cell phone remained in my pocket. To this day I wonder if it was a deliberate oversight by an arresting official who was a covert believer. Or perhaps God had placed an angel on the security staff to deliver me, as the angel had delivered the apostles from the Jerusalem prison in the book of Acts.[120] Believe me, I immediately send a text message to my booking secretary, Ilka, asking her to trigger our prayer teams to intercede. I also had her book a flight home for me as soon as possible. Then I asked her to call the German embassy and other African leaders who might be able to put pressure on the government for my release.

As I continued to use the device, I looked up to see all eyes staring at me. No one else had a cell phone. No one else in that room could contact an embassy or seek release through such powerful resources. This was not the time to inspire jealousy in my cellmates. I realized that any of these bad guys might decide that I needed to be turned in to the authorities in exchange for leniency. In which case, my one link to the outside world would be lost. Or, one of them might decide he wanted to use my device for his own purposes, and his purposes might prove more valuable to him than my life. I needed these men as allies, not enemies.

One of the big, unshaven thugs came over to me. He looked me up and down in my nice clothes. With foul breath, and between discolored teeth, he asked in broken English, "What is your job?"

I gave instructions to my PDA device and held up a digital image from the recent Aba crusade. It showed me preaching to the huge crowd gathered there. "That is my job," I said. "I preach the gospel of Jesus Christ."

The other cellmates crowded around to see the picture. I showed them the huge crowds in Calabar, Port Harcourt, and Benin City. They were truly mystified as to what a man of my station was doing in their midst. I spoke to them with confidence and moved among them without showing fear, though I felt it. I knew at any moment they could decide to overpower me and do whatever their desperation dictated. They might decide that an evangelist was worth more as a hostage than as a cellmate.

Rubbing shoulders with these men in this place of cursing and brutality, I began to sense how our Lord Jesus was numbered with transgressors. The prophet Isaiah had predicted it hundreds of years before his birth.[121] In His total obedience to the Father, Jesus was treated by the Roman and Jewish authorities as a thief and robber, even being crucified between two of them. This was Satan's ultimate attempt to make the Son of God feel defeated. To this day, the Enemy delights in treating God's servants as the lowest of criminals; he especially enjoys taking their reputation for good and making it vile.

However, even though this was Satan's most evil tactic, God planned that Jesus would take charge of it. It blessed me to remember that Jesus did not have His reputation destroyed; rather, the Bible tells us He made Himself of no reputation.[122] He poured out His own life for us. He was obedient unto death. The scripture tells us that He even interceded for the transgressors who so abused Him.[123] In this way, He took all of Satan's power from him and used it for our salvation. Hallelujah! But this is the mystery of iniquity. Somehow, total humiliation and misunderstanding were essential to His ultimate triumph over the grave. This truth became a revelation to me in that cell that I shall never forget. To God be the glory forever.

In the holding cell, hours passed in endless tedium – 10, 12, 24 hours. I was shuffled between guards to and from the airport restroom facility. Eventually, the guards took me from the cell to a comfortable office where immigration officials interrogated me. It was not the interrogation room of my imagination with the single light bulb hanging from a cord, thank God. I explained to them that I was merely visiting their country as a tourist and had been detained without reason. I promised them that the German embassy would be following up on this incident. I suggested that if they treated tourists in this fashion they had much to lose in tourism income. I reached for every straw I could think of to secure my release.

Every effort failed. My name remained on their blacklist, and no higher government official had provided an eraser.

What was I left to do? I waited for a reply on the cell phone, praying that my batteries would hold their charge. In the meantime, I looked around at my first truly captive audience. I tried to tell my cellmates about how I preached the ABCs of the gospel, however they understood hardly any English. It was no use.

All I could do was wait. All night, I waited. I tried to sleep on the floor but sleep simply would not come. Mid-morning the next day my cell phone vibrated. It was Ilka sending a text message to say I had been booked for a return flight on German carrier Lufthansa at such and such an hour that afternoon. I saved the message with the reservation number in my cell phone device. Then I went to the door and demanded to see a guard who spoke English. When at last one came to the door I explained to him that I was to be taken to the Lufthansa desk immediately. I had a return flight with a reservation number. As might be expected, it did not work. The guards wrote down the reservation number, as I recited it, and told me they would check with Lufthansa to see if I was indeed booked for that flight.

Later they returned with triumphant smirks. Lufthansa had no record of my reservation. They had me where they wanted me. My heart sank.

In desperation I pulled my last trump card and waved it – my cell phone. In their eyes I could see shock. Raising my voice in anger, I told them that I absolutely had the reservation number recorded in my phone and had received it that very morning in a text message from Frankfurt. I told them I had contacted the German embassy, and I demanded to be taken to the Lufthansa desk at once. As a German citizen I would speak to the airline employees and prove that my reservation was valid for a return flight that day.

Looking back, I believe that my mobile device really was a trump card. Suddenly, they realized that I had been communicating with the outside world and it was too late to prevent it. Perhaps if this fact became known to their superiors they would face harsh discipline. They knew that they would have to answer to whomever I had contacted, and I was no longer simply a detainee with no allies. That gave me a sliver of a chance to tip the scales in my favor.

They unlocked the door. I am sure it was not their intention to release me but to get hold of the mobile device. I pushed myself through the door as if I was in charge of the entire scene. For what it is worth, when you are imprisoned in a foreign airport with no legal recourse, everything is a bluff, so bluff like crazy!

"I am going to the Lufthansa desk!" I shouted. "And you are coming with me! I will show you that my reservation number is valid!"

I was already walking briskly up the stairwell. They followed me all the way to the Lufthansa desk. When I reached it I saw a line of passengers waiting to be served. That line was death to me. I literally walked past them all, right across the baggage scale and behind the desk. The guards scrambled to catch me. I plunged through an "Employees Only" door and approached a ticket agent at a desk in the back office. I told her that I was a German citizen who had been detained without cause. I had executive status with Lufthansa and needed to confirm my ticket home in order to regain my freedom.

The booking clerk looked at me and shrugged helplessly. "Our computers are down," she said. "What can we do? We are waiting for a repairman."

Under the circumstances, this was not an acceptable response.

"I am not leaving this office until you turn that computer back on," I said. "Turn it on and see if it is working right now. My freedom is at stake here."

The agent turned the computer on, and to her surprise the screen came up properly. She typed in my reservation number and hit the return arrow. The screen showed no booking in my name under that number.

One of the guards looked at me with that now familiar smirk on his face. He prepared to haul me back to the cell.

"No!" I shouted. "You did it wrong! You entered the booking numbering in lowercase. You must use uppercase characters!" In my heart I prayed that I was right. I was grasping for anything.

The clerk quickly retyped my number and hit the return key. Immediately my full booking information came on the screen. I nearly fainted with relief, breathing my thanks to the Lord.

The airport officials said that they would take this information to their superiors. In the meantime, I would be returned to the holding cell. It was the best I could hope for. They escorted me back, and once again I heard the sound of those bars clanging shut behind me.

The final hours of waiting after confirming my flight were sheer torture. Of course, the guards did not come to get me until the very last minute. Just as the flight was about to leave, they escorted me to the airplane, holding my arms between the two of them as if I was a criminal. My passport was given to the purser on the flight, and I was led to my assigned seat. As soon as they left me there, I pushed my chair back and fell into an exhausted and thankful sleep.

I awoke sometime after the flight had become airborne. The purser was shaking my shoulder to wake me. She was holding my passport, inspecting it.

"Who do I have on my flight, sir? A criminal?"

It took a moment to shake the fog of sleep from my mind. At first, I did not realize that I was now free and headed home. But soon the recent events assembled themselves properly in my mind and I knew where I was. "A criminal? It depends on what you call a crime," I replied to her. "I am a preacher. I preached in a church here five years ago and a handful of Muslims got saved. That is my crime."

She looked at me and nodded. "I understand." Then she handed me my passport. "I was told to give this to you when we landed in Frankfurt but you can have it now. You look like you could use some sleep."

"Yes, and thank you," I replied with a smile. When she walked away I closed my eyes and didn't open them again until we stopped at the gate.

With this experience behind me, not to mention the memory of the tragedy in Kano, I was quite aware that permission to preach in Khartoum was not what it appeared to be. Obviously the government was using our meetings for international publicity to show that they were accommodating the Christian population even under Sharia Law. They were trying hard to win favorable national trading agreements and avoid embargoes. We were at least part of their meal ticket.

The authorities had called our campaign an Easter Celebration. This was an obvious ploy to avoid Muslim antagonism. But on the other hand they had given us not only Easter, but six days to celebrate, just like a full crusade. These were mixed signals. I honestly could not trust the government's intentions. But I did place my trust completely in the hands of the Lord who opens doors no man can shut.[124] What the government intended, and what Jesus would accomplish in Sudan originated from two different kingdoms. The kingdom I served was guided by the hand of the Creator of the universe – no contest! Still, we would be careful. We would have to remain alert to any treachery that might arise in the course of these meetings.

The government offered the Green Square in the city center for our assembly. It was the main military parade ground for Sudan. It was a place where they could keep a good eye on our event. They did not expect a large turnout because the local Christian population was so small. They estimated that perhaps our crowd might swell to 10,000. But they promised they could provide security at the square. To aid in that regard they insisted that our meetings be held in the heat of the day. They did not want to risk mischief happening under the cover of darkness.

Stephen Mutua inspected the square. It had been beaten into fine dust by the wheels of military equipment and the boots of marching soldiers. On one end it had a building with waiting-rooms and reviewing stand for a few hundred spectators, nothing more.

After conferring with the rest of my team, I decided that we would not take two team members of the same family to Khartoum. If tragedy did strike, I did not want to multiply sorrow for anyone. So we shifted personnel accordingly.

I arrived on April 23 to prepare for the meeting. We had erected our platform and speakers in front of the reviewing stand. That allowed the VIP seats to be at my back, about 20 or 30 yards behind the podium area. If any of the government officials came to observe we would seat them there. For the most part, I believe, the government thought that our meetings would pass unnoticed on the local scene and they could enjoy a sweet political and public relations victory. They sent their chief of national security to oversee our activities and to provide protection.

On the first day we saw 30,000 people assemble on the square. That was triple the number the government had predicted. A good percentage of the crowd was not Christian. I looked behind me at the VIP section. It was totally empty.

The weather was unbelievably hot. It became quickly clear why so many Sudanese wear white turbans on their heads. It is a time-tested way of minimizing sun stroke. We rigged the platform with a sunshade. Even so, it was nearly unbearable, even in the shade, and as I preached I asked the team to have plenty of water at hand for me. I sweat profusely in the heat but the dry air evaporated the sweat almost immediately. This created a high risk of sun stroke, or heat prostration due to dehydration. I literally took a drink of bottled water after nearly every sentence of my sermon. We had also arranged to have a lot of water on hand for the crowd because they would have to stand in the sun. We had positioned 50-gallon drums of drinking water all through the parade ground.

After preaching and giving the altar call, only a few hundred raised their hands and registered decisions that first day. I was reminded of Luis Graf in 1922. When he arrived in Trunz, East Prussia, he had found all the staunch Lutherans unwilling to listen to his preaching. With that setback he was not defeated. He remembered his lessons from Maria Woodworth-Etter. He had also experienced his personal Azusa Street in Hot Springs, Arkansas, years before. Under the influence and unction of the Holy Spirit's fire he had asked, "Is anyone sick in this village?" My grandfather August had subsequently been healed of his tormenting disease, and at least three Bonnke hearts had opened to receive the gospel. And so my spiritual heritage had begun. In like manner, I began to pray for the sick after that disappointing first response in Khartoum. This had become my pattern everywhere. "In Jesus' name, blind eyes open! Deaf ears hear! Dumb speak, in Jesus' name!"

That first day we saw many healings. I told the national security officer to prepare to see many more than 30,000 gather in the square tomorrow. I could see that this crusade was not going to fly under the radar of the local press and government. It was going to shake the city. God's ways succeed beyond all human ingenuity and manipulation.

True enough, the next day the crowd more than doubled to 70,000. Behind me the VIP seats remained empty except for a scattering of Catholic priests and nuns, and the few Anglican, Coptic, and Pentecostal clergy who had banded together to support the meetings. A few Muslim leaders had come as well. Again the Lord confirmed His Word with incredible miracles. In fact, never in my entire ministry had I seen so many blind people healed as I saw in Khartoum. They were healed by the dozen, day after day. Consider when a man born blind, a Muslim, goes home to his clan, fully seeing. What do you think is going to happen? The whole clan is going to show up the next day and become Christians. They say, Allah has never done anything for us like this. Look what Jesus has done.

The numbers of Muslims who got healed were so amazing that a few Catholic nuns and priests became troubled. They came to me afterward. "Does Jesus love the Muslims more than His own children?" they asked. "We have many blind Christians who have not received sight."

It touched me so much. I said to them, "You don't need to be a theologian to receive healing – only believe. Jesus said, 'Only believe.' He did not say, 'Become a Christian first.' He said only believe, because everyone can believe. So believe, trust Him, accept it – you will receive your healing whether you are a Muslim, a Christian, or a pagan. Jesus wants us to know that He loves all of us."

One particular healing on that second night stood out from the others. I heard a loud commotion in the crowd and a young man was brought forward. He came to the platform, speaking rapidly and gesturing toward his mouth. I got an interpreter and learned his story.

WORKING THE FIELDS WITH HIS FATHER, Omar Mohammed watched a black scowl gather across the face of the western sky. Soon, a menacing line of thunderheads emitted a rumble that shook the earth beneath their feet. Father and son ran for shelter as a desert storm descended swiftly, lightning bolts piercing the ground around them like glittering swords. Suddenly, a searing pulse bearing 10,000 amps at 100 million volts, exploded through the atmosphere with 50,000 degrees of pure wrath, cutting both of them to the ground. For a long time Omar remained unconscious.

When at last he stirred himself, the world had grown unnaturally silent. He wondered if he was dead. He saw his father's crumpled body nearby. Crawling closer, he tried to rouse him but the angry storm had robbed him of his father. Overwhelmed with grief, he opened his mouth to unleash a cry of anguish but his cry would not come. Not one sound could he utter. He had been plunged into the isolated and unreal world of the deaf and dumb. Medical diagnoses later confirmed that the lightning bolt had destroyed the vocal and aural capacities of his nervous system. The damage was irreversible. In one tragic second his life had been ruined.

The Muslim government of Sudan registered Omar as handicapped. The traditions of Sharia law granted him permission to beg for a living. They licensed him to sit on a busy street corner outside Khartoum University. For five years, begging had been his only way to survive. He was familiar to thousands who passed by each day. For those who dropped coins in his cup there was a word to describe his condition – kismet, the Arab word for fate. Kismet, meaning Allah's will is unpredictable, and one's fate is irreversible. The fate of Omar Muhammad was sealed, as far as they knew.

But what if God's love was stronger than fate? What if God had not manifested himself in that angry and capricious thunder storm that had stricken Omar and his father? What if they should see a demonstration of the power and purpose of the Christian God over wind, weather, demons, sickness – and irreversible nerve damage? Would such a demonstration open their minds and hearts to receive Jesus?

Omar had read an advertising poster for an Easter Celebration with Reinhard Bonnke to be held on Green Square. Five words leapt out at him; "Come expecting miracles of healing." And so, Omar came with the 30,000 who gathered on the first day. The multitude sang in eerie silence around him. He could see the preacher speaking from the platform. But despite the high-powered amplifiers not a word penetrated his ears. By watching others, he grasped what was happening. When the evangelist made a prayer for all sick and afflicted people, many of the blind could see and the lame could walk. In his silent mind he heard a whisper of hope.

On the second afternoon Omar was there again near the front. Once more the preacher spoke, following with instruction and prayer for the afflicted. Omar raised his hands with the others, reaching out to a God of love he did not know. Then it happened. Bitter fate had once flashed from the sky and wrecked his life, but as the preacher opened his mouth and shouted – Omar would later learn that I was shouting, "Deaf ears open! Dumb mouths speak!" – he felt as if lighting had stuck him again. He was felled to the ground as before, temporarily unconscious. What could it mean?

He soon knew. As he regained his senses an explosion of sound burst upon him – thousands of people were roaring with joy because of other miracles that were being manifested. Kneeling over him were several familiar faces asking if he was OK. "Yes," he said. They gasped with shock to hear him speak. He could hear them clearly! Over the sound system Reinhard was shouting over and over the name of Jesus! He leaped to his feet, and for the first time since being struck down, words came pouring in torrents from his mouth. Kismet had been reversed. His voice was back, full strength! A crowd of those who had dropped coins in his cup surrounding him, shouting that a miracle had happened! He rushed with them toward the platform, leaping and shouting for joy.

THE NEXT DAY 120,000 GATHERED to hear the gospel in Green Square. The day after that, 180,000 and the number of conversions grew to more than 100,000. Suddenly, the VIP section behind the platform was half full of Muslim governmental officials, mullahs, and their friends.

A few Muslim leaders began to complain loudly about Muslims coming to Jesus. Radical mullahs quoted the Koran, saying that those who convert from Islam should be killed. Such talk can quickly escalate into uncontrolled violence, as we had already seen in Kano. Fearing the worst, President Omar Hassan al-Bashir went on national television to defend our meetings, calling them an important example to the world of the freedom of religion in Sudan. We were on the very knife edge of catastrophe – or of breakthrough. This was history in the making.

On the final day the heat was like a brick oven, absolutely stifling. I was having trouble enduring it through the rigors of a sermon. During the preliminaries I waited in an air-conditioned room beneath the military reviewing stand. The plan was that I would go on stage at the last minute. To get to the platform I would walk across an open area just in front of the reviewing stand. All of a sudden, the national security chief came running from the platform.

"Mr. Bonnke, Mr. Bonnke, Mr. Bonnke!" He was out of breath.

"What? What is going on?"

"Outside are a million people waiting for you!"

I knew that he had been overwhelmed by the size of the crowd, and he had exaggerated. In truth, the national security chief had never seen a crowd so large on Green Square. In fact, my men had done their normal scientific esti- mate of the crowd at 220,000 but officially registered it only at 210,000 to remain conservative in our records. I enjoyed the fact that this government official had underestimated the power of the gospel to draw a crowd in a Muslim land. That pleased me to the maximum.

When it came time to preach I made my way to the platform. Looking behind me, the VIP ranks were packed. Government ministers with their huge fami- lies of multiple wives and children, all clad in white, all wanting to be seen by the huge crowd, were seated there. I was surrounded by unprecedented opportunity.

I called Omar Muhammad to the platform. In his own words he described his accident and his miracle of healing at the hands of Jesus. He waved a certificate that had given him license to beg at Khartoum University and promised the government officials in the stands that he would come to their offices to have this license terminated. He no longer would be a beggar in their streets.

I preached, and we saw the greatest harvest of all. The healing ministry was again tremendous. As I turned to leave the platform, suddenly I noticed that the national security chief had a phalanx of soldiers on the stage behind me, rifles at ready. They were not looking into the crowd but searching through the VIP area behind us.

"Mr. Bonnke," he said, "we have made a shelter of soldiers' bodies. Go between them and bend low between the stage and the reviewing stand. It is very dangerous there."

I could see that he was really terrified. He had the wall of soldiers escort me off the stage. When we began to run between the stage and the reviewing stand they took hold of my hands on either side. I was exhausted and fell. They did not hesitate but continued to run, dragging me into the safety of the reviewing building. It must have been a comical sight – the Lord's evangelist plowing dust like a harrow behind a tractor. Once inside, I was laughing uproariously. I regained my feet. But they were not laughing.

Stephen Mutua then told me why the precaution had been taken. The police had arrested three snipers with rifles in the VIP stands. They were not sure they had got them all.

They hustled us into a waiting car and escorted us back to our hotel rooms, placing bodyguards in the hallways. Whoever said serving the Lord was about dull seminary lectures, quiet study rooms, and sermons that put you to sleep? This was like a page out of Paul's journeys in the book of Acts, a hilarious adventure!

Our Khartoum meeting ended with 735,000 people attending in six days. We saw 132,000, or 18 percent of those who attended register decisions for Christ. This was far short of the numbers and the percentages we were seeing in Nigeria, but Sudan was extremely strategic to me. It represented a great victory for Jesus in the heartland of Islamic Africa.

Back at the hotel I spoke to a government minister. "Did you see how many came? More would come if I stayed until tomorrow. I haven't finished the work here. I must come back. Thank God, next year is Easter again."

He smiled at me and nodded.

I HAD BEEN IN GERMANY only a few days when my phone rang. It was the ambassador from the Sudanese embassy in Frankfurt. "Your sermon tapes and DVDs have become the number-one selling item all over Khartoum. They have been pirated and duplicated and are outselling everything in our super-stores, everything in the local *souks*, and even in the media stores. The mullahs are calling you a 'holy man' because you healed so many sick people. We are officially inviting you back for another Easter Celebration next year."

My heart leaped for joy. Sudan was not a catastrophe, but a breakthrough! The gospel was not going to be confined to a prison here, but welcomed in the palace. Hallelujah!

The ambassador then asked to speak with me further. "As you know, Sudan is facing great problems. Our greatest is the long civil war with the south. That is where most of the Christians live, but it is where even more pagan animists live and practice their religion. The rebel leader in the south is a Christian man named, Dr. John Garang. We have invited the ambassadors from all of Europe to our embassy to propose a solution to this problem. Since you have bridged a historic gap between Christian and Muslim in Khartoum, we would like you to speak to this group about what you think should be done. Would you agree to do this?"

"Of course. I will come."

I was amazed that a government official would ask me to address political professionals about a political problem. Not to mention the problems from a 20-year civil war. My reputation was in the area of evangelization. Political solutions were not on my resume. Inside, I searched for the voice of the Spirit. *What am I to say, Lord? What would You have me say?* When the day of the event came I had received my answer.

"I urge Sudan to give autonomy to the South. Do not divide this great land into two countries, because this would create two poorer countries, struggling with even greater problems. Bring unity by offering autonomy within the integrity of your national structure, and keep peace by sharing power with your former enemies."

Certainly my voice was added to the voices of many others. But I can tell you they listened to me very intently that day. In a matter of months the government of Sudan began to seriously explore these very reforms. Overtures began for peace talks with Dr. John Garang of the Sudan People's Liberation Army. To God be all the glory for whatever part I may have played in this positive change.

THE FIRE CONFERENCES CONTINUED to burn in my heart, as they had since the first event in Harare, Zimbabwe, in 1986. Next to my passion for preaching the good news, I was passionate about training and inspiring others to do the work of soul winning. In the beginning, we had considered the Fire Conferences to be continental, even worldwide in scope. We held the first in Africa, the second in Germany, the third in England, hopping from one continent to another. In the 90s we realized that we were limiting God's plan for these powerful sessions. We began to pair a Fire Conference with every crusade. These became a great benefit for the local believers, not to mention the follow-up workers who ministered and registered decisions for Christ each night. It also streamlined the work of the CfaN staff as they combined their efforts for crusades with those of staging Fire Conferences.

This change in strategy changed everything. Suddenly our follow-up workers were receiving the baptism with the Holy Spirit in mighty outpourings during the day. Hallelujah! In the night meetings they were now operating, not in their own strength, but in the power of the Spirit. This greatly increased the overall effectiveness of CfaN. The conference sessions also gave us the opportunity to share information, insights, practical wisdom, and inspiration with the local believers – things that would not be appropriate to share with the evening audiences.

I was happy. It was a dream come true. I thought surely we had arrived at our highest purpose for the Fire Conferences. But God does not see with our limited vision. One day as I ministered in yet another conference, the Lord spoke to me: *I want one of these Fire Conferences in every church.*

*Every church?!*

I felt my feet swept from under me. I knew such a thing could not be done by our present methods. I was turning down hundreds of invitations to hold Fire Conferences in churches all over the world. There was simply not enough co-workers, not enough time, and not enough of me to accomplish more than we were already doing. *I have no clue how to do this, Lord. How can it be done?*

*By way of film,* came the answer.

And then I began to see it. I would take the lessons that I shared over and over in Fire Conferences, fine tune them to the point of excellence, and share them one time on film. The film would not be bound by our present limitations. Indeed, we could make a film series that would instruct evangelists in the lessons of an entire lifetime, not to mention 30 years of CfaN experience. In this way, every church in the world could experience a Fire Conference if they chose. It could be done.

I was reminded again of Luis Graf. All that I could know of him from those years before I was born had been gathered from various sources, pasted together to form a patchwork of information with many missing pieces. From my own imagination I had filled in the blanks. But questions remained. I have never seen his face nor heard his voice. Still, his influence set me on the path that I now follow. His approach to healing as an accompaniment to the preaching of the gospel is a pattern for me. What great lessons might the man they called the "evangelistic lawnmower" have to share with me today? I will never know.

I thought also of Azusa Street and the stories that still proliferate from that historic event. I wondered how it would be if the Pentecostal evangelists from that era could come back and conduct a seminar for evangelists today. What would they say? I know that I would be first in line to hear them. But alas, that day will never come.

In these reflections I began to see that God was offering me a unique opportunity. This film series would do what could not be done after Azusa Street, or in Luis Graf's twilight years. Through film, I could expose another generation to the spiritual secrets behind our success. It could help them adapt to the unique challenges of their own day of harvest with the sure knowledge of our experience behind them. It would also leave a useful legacy beyond my own lifetime, should Jesus tarry.

It turned out that someone on the CfaN team had the God-given talent and ability to shepherd such a project. He had been working with our film team at crusades for years and already knew our inner workings. He had a classical education in filmmaking. Everything he produced was excellent, and he shared my heart for seeing the world come to Christ. Fluent in Norwegian, Swedish, German, and English, he had a multicultural mind, with international sensibilities. His name was Robert Murphree, and he quickly rose to the top of my list of candidates. When I presented the film series to him he accepted it enthusiastically.

As we began to discuss how to accomplish the project, he opened my eyes to the intimate power of film. With a camera reading my every expression, and with a sensitive microphone recording my voice, I would not have to shout and gesture as I did on the preaching platform. This had been all I knew from the time of my first sermon on the street corner in Glückstadt. So the power of intimate communication was a revelation to me. In close conversation I could more powerfully communicate from my heart. That was what I wanted to do in this series.

Robert proposed to stage my teaching sessions off stage. I would sit or stand with a few of my friends and speak in conversational tones. The camera would "look over our shoulders," so to speak, making the viewer a participant in the intimacy of the scene. Each conversation would be held in a location that would add impact and meaning to the lesson. Robert truly understood how to make a picture worth a thousand words. This is an artist's gift and not everyone can attain it. The locations we began to discuss were China, Brazil, Egypt, Kenya, Indonesia, Australia, Japan, India, Russia, Germany, Brazil, the United Kingdom, and the USA.

In addition, Robert wrote dramatic parables and illustrations to enhance the main points of my outline. These would be performed by professional actors and stunt men. They would entertain and drive home our presentation with all the modern power of motion pictures and special effects. This was a much bigger project than I had at first imagined. The budget grew large. Even more, it required a huge investment of my time and energy over a period of several years. But I had no doubt that it was a mandate from God, and I was soon ready to see it done.

In fact, we had begun filming on locations of opportunity over the past year. I loved the quality of everything Robert was showing me. With each new segment I grew more excited about the potential of this series. But it became apparent that he would need to leave Germany to be near the expert film community in America. This was the high quality mark we had set for the project. It was decided that he would move his operation to Orlando, Florida, where he could take advantage of Universal Studios.

"You should move there too," he said.

"What?"

"This project is going to go on for several years, Reinhard. There will be many changes that need to be made to get everything right. You will need to do extensive sound remixing and dubbing in special studios. There will be green screen production for you and other special effects shots required. That means a lot of flying to Universal Studios in Orlando for you. Moving there makes sense."

"Robert, I have never moved anywhere in my life when someone told me to move. I move when God tells me to move, period. Besides, I can't just pack up and go. Frankfurt is home. I don't want to go there."

"I understand," he said. "Pray about it. God will speak to you."

As I went my way the thought continued to return to my mind. *God, is this Your way of getting me to consider something I wouldn't otherwise consider?* I know that God can speak through many sources. But He always confirms His Word in my heart. I would wait for that confirmation.

WE BEGAN TO FEEL THE WEIGHT of the coming crusade in Lagos, Nigeria, long before it arrived. In a city with a population of 7,500,000 and another 10,000,000 living within a 20-mile radius, our scouts and team sent reports of crowds beyond any we had ever seen. The word of our return to Nigeria, after being banned for nine years, had reached a fever pitch. In anticipation, the meeting grounds were enlarged to accommodate crowds as high as 2,000,000. Sound and lighting equipment was double and triple checked to see that it would cover the area. We trained a record 200,000 follow-up workers from the churches in Lagos. We spent a record $1.2 million for follow-up materials. We trained 2,000 ushers for crowd control. The city came through with 1,000 police officers. I telephoned Robert Murphree to fly in from Orlando with film equipment to document what we now called *The Millennium Crusade.*

We were scheduled for six-nights of meetings. The opening crowd exceeded all that we had previously seen. It was well in excess of 750,000. The power of God manifested in many miracles, and I knew what this would mean. We were going to see the numbers explode on night number two. True to pattern, the second-night crowd exceeded one million. If only the national security chief from Sudan had been here on this night. He had run to me crying, "Outside are a million people waiting for you!" But that crowd had only numbered 210,000. On this night he would have been able to see what a crowd of a million people actually looked like. I was staggered by it. On TV monitors I could see our cameras sweeping across a sea of faces that blended into the night at the far edges of the field around us.

One of the sponsoring pastors came near to me. His face looked like he was literally in shock. "Why do they come, Reverend Bonnke?"

Searching my soul I truly did not know how to answer. My mind raced back 32 years in time. I saw myself on the streets of Lesotho, unable to attract more than one or two listeners to hear the gospel. I had not changed. I did not know then how to attract a crowd. Nor did I know now.

"I don't know," I said. "But I do know how to preach."

Our sound and lighting equipment had been well tested. It delivered my sermon to the far corners of that crowd, and we saw a great response to the gospel.

On the final night the sea of faces stretched beyond the limits of my vision. A crowd of 1,600,000 had gathered; almost triple the size of any we had seen so far. At the invitation 1,093,000 responded and registered decisions for Christ. When they repeated the sinner's prayer after me, their voices sounded like the thunder of Victoria Falls, crying out for mercy to the Lord of the Universe. I listened in awe with tears streaming from my eyes as a prophecy given when we drew crowds of only 30,000 was fulfilled on this night. The cameras were rolling. A million responded to one invitation.

When the numbers had been confirmed I called Kenneth Copeland. As I listened to the ring tone in my earpiece I grew excited. Since our meeting on Saturday, February 18, 1984 at the dedication of the world's largest tent, the Copelands' ministry had become CfaN's greatest financial partner. They had invested millions in our vision for a blood washed Africa. I could hardly wait to let Kenneth know that his investment had been in good soil, and his word of prophecy had been true.

"Hello."

"What you saw with the eyes of the spirit so long ago, my friend, we now have seen in the flesh. One million souls accepting Jesus in a single meeting. I was still trying to fill the world's largest tent when you spoke those words to me in Soweto. So many things had to change for this to happen. But over the years the words of your prophecy burned like a beacon before my eyes, urging me on toward this day. Now here we are."

"So what is next?" Kenneth asked.

"Who can tell? Do you have another prophecy? God is not limited to this success. But I can tell you this – next year we will be striking with a white-hot iron in Nigeria. Nigeria is showing the way. All of Africa shall be saved."

WE ENDED THE LAGOS MEETINGS with more than 6,000,000 people attending over six nights. Of that huge crowd, 57 percent registered decisions – 3,461,171 to be exact.

Our final campaign for the year was held in Enugu, a small city in the Nigerian foothills with a population of 600,000. We drew crowds of 200,000, with 510,000 attending over the course of the meetings. 58 percent of those attending made decisions for Jesus.

Before our return to Nigeria, our percentage of response to the gospel had averaged around 20 percent per year of those attending our crusades. But in 1999, our first two Nigerian campaigns pulled that average up to 36 percent. In 2000, with four Nigerian campaigns included in the schedule, the annual response rose to 52 percent. With the change in strategy for 2001, in which we would be concentrating our efforts almost exclusively in Nigeria, the quality of our response was about to exceed all expectations. CfaN was indeed rich gospel soil.

# Chapter 37

Our 2001 schedule began with hardly a pause for the holidays. We were back in Nigeria in January for the next crusade, with another following in February, and another in March. Of course each one featured a daytime Fire Conference. The schedule was dictated by climate because open-air meetings must be scheduled during the dry season. In Nigeria it extends roughly between November and March.

A word about dry season crusades – sometimes it rains. I mean, I have pictures of myself on stage looking like I'm preaching in a car wash. Torrential is the word to describe it. In one case several men came out with a great umbrella to shelter me. A sudden gust of wind nearly ripped all of us from the stage. The umbrella was more dangerous than getting soaked to the skin. I have learned to seek little protection. In the dry season, the rain is warm. These are not like summer rains in Iceland, these are tropical climates. I don't even bother with umbrellas anymore unless it is a gentle mist, which is seldom the case. Isolated thunder storms rise and unleash inches of rainfall in a single hour.

Most of the Nigerians come to the crusade dressed in their best attire. They wear colorful dresses, high heels, suits and dress shoes, even though they must stand for hours in the dirt. When the rain comes they continue to stand, their fine clothing clinging to them like wet plaster, and their fine shoes sinking ever deeper into the mud. I am reminded of a study published in *New Scientist Magazine* that rated the Nigerian people the happiest on earth.[125] The reason was that they prized things of true value. Things like family relationships above wealth and power. In that regard, they have also shown me, again and again, that they value hearing the gospel above comfort and shelter. Therefore, if the Nigerian people stay to hear the gospel under stormy conditions, that is my signal – I continue to preach in the rain.

Our team watches the weather and we have certain routines for saving our sensitive electronic equipment. On one occasion, however, a bolt of lightning struck one of our main speaker towers and sizzled down the length of it, frying the electronic circuits of the entire bank of sound. No one was hurt and I was not affected because I preach with a wireless microphone. But I do not allow anyone else on stage when lightning is in the area. All the musicians and special guests must take cover in the trailers. It is just too dangerous to be near the equipment. When we sustain damage like that it can be expensive. But God has given us partners who will not allow such a setback to keep us down for long. They pay for the repairs and we are back for the next crusade.

Our early dry season crusades in 2001 were hardly "dry" in terms of results. Unless, of course, you use the term "dry" to mean "spiritually tinder dry," in which case the spark of the Holy Spirit touched off a fire storm of salvations! In the cities of Uyo, Owerri, and Onitsha, we drew crowds of 400,000, 500,000, and 800,000 respectively, with a total of 4,690,000 attending over the course of the meetings. But the most staggering statistic of all was the percentage of registered decisions for Jesus in those nightly crowds. 70 percent responded in Uyo, 70 percent in Owerri, and an unbelievable 86 percent in Onitsha! By the end of March, first quarter 2001, we had seen a total of 3,630,920 souls come to Christ! I was absolutely overwhelmed beyond words.

What did this mean? I can only try to give it perspective. At the very bottom it means that many more sinners were coming to hear the gospel than saints. And they were responding to the invitations in vast numbers. I do not believe that it has ever been seen on this scale in the history of the church. We were seeing seven or eight of every ten persons in those huge crowds come to Jesus under the stars in Nigeria!

When this happens, an evangelist knows that he is operating in a supernatural harvest. I began to feel like I was reaping the end-time harvest first envisioned by the believers at Azusa Street. They were driven by the words of Jesus in Matthew 24:14 – ... *this gospel of the kingdom shall be preached in all the world for a witness unto all nations; and then shall the end come.* Surely if those pioneers had stood beside me on the platform in 2001 they might feel that this was the final harvest. That is what they had envisioned in their hearts as they spoke with new tongues and felt compelled to run to the ends of the earth in the years before World War I.[126] My ministry was standing directly on their shoulders. In that regard I recalled the words of Jesus when He sent His disciples to minister: *I sent you to reap that whereon ye bestowed no labour: other men laboured, and ye are entered into their labours.*[127] Surely this was true for us in Nigeria. I was humbled to be reaping far more than we had sowed. And I was invigorated by this mighty display of the conviction of the Holy Spirit upon sinners.

I do not know about the final harvest before the end of the world. Jesus said, *It is not for you to know the times or the seasons, which the Father hath put in his own power. But ye shall receive power, after that the Holy Ghost is come upon you: and ye shall be witnesses unto me both in Jerusalem, and in all Judaea, and in Samaria, and unto the uttermost part of the earth.*[128] CfaN was simply saying yes to His call to the uttermost parts of the earth. And we were going in the power of the Holy Spirit. Hallelujah!

OUR NEXT MEETING was the second Easter Celebration in Khartoum. My team and I were in a state of near euphoria. It seemed that nothing would stand in the way of the vision of a blood-washed Africa. Not even the barriers of Islam. We anticipated a huge response, with an audience many times larger than the 210,000 we had seen on our visit last year. Reports were coming in that the tapes and DVDs of our meetings had been passed from hand to hand across the greatest land mass on the African continent. Throngs were surging toward our meeting site from Juba in the south, Darfur in the west, and as far as Ethiopia in the east, carrying the sick and lame. They were camping along the roads and the caravan routes, headed for Green Square, filled with an expectation of miracles.

Then Satan struck. Eight days before the meeting each CfaN office throughout the world received an ominous e-mail addressed to me. "Reinhard Bonnke, if you come to Khartoum we will shoot you." It was signed by someone named, "Osama Bin Laden." His fame had not yet been established worldwide but we had heard of him. We knew that he was a very dangerous terrorist.

I took the letter in my hands and fell to my knees. I feared nothing for my own safety. But my life was not my own. The great harvest of souls in Nigeria could be suddenly stopped by an assassin's bullet in Sudan. The evangelistic lawnmower of Luis Graf had fallen silent before his time – and so could the combine harvester.

"Lord, shall I go or not go?" I prayed.

I dared not move from my knees until I heard the answer. And then it came. *You are Satan's prime target for destruction, but you are My prime target for protection. Go.*

We again took the precautions of our earlier visit to Sudan, taking only one person from a family and chartering our own air transportation. Stephen Mutua and the technical staff arrived first, setting up the stage and the great speaker columns to accommodate the expected great crowd. As they set up the equipment the field was visited by many pilgrims. Some seemed merely curious. Others seemed furtive and conspiratorial. Still others were seeking places to place the blind, the lame, the deaf and dumb. Most of them were Muslim.

"Bonnke is a holy man," they said to our team. "He heals the sick."

"Yes," our co-workers replied, "He heals in Jesus' name. But it is Jesus who saves, and Jesus who heals."

As I arrived in Khartoum, I checked into my hotel room. Stephen Mutua came breathlessly to my door. "Reinhard, you cannot stay here. We must move you."

"Why?"

"As I was checking in yesterday I saw a group of young men from Saudi Arabia. Many of Bin Laden's recruits come from there. You already have his threat against you. We should change floors and move you to the far end of the hotel."

"We cannot simply suspect that every young Saudi Arabian works for Bin Laden. They may have come to hear the gospel, or to receive healing."

"I'm afraid not, Reinhard. You are checked into this room under *Christ for all Nations*. These young men checked into their rooms under *Islam for all Nations*. They are here to attend the crusade alright, but they are not here to receive Christ."

"Jesus can change their minds. I am not moving from this room, Stephen. If they are up to no good, do you think that we would fool them for one minute? They have ways of finding me. I stay right here."

"But it might buy some time if they are uncertain of where to find you."

"I do nothing out of fear. We will keep alert but we will not cower and hide in fear of the Enemy. God has not given us a spirit of fear.[129] Fear makes bad decisions, always."

After settling into my room I decided some time later to inspect Green Square. As I emerged I saw that Stephen had placed two local young men in the hallway. They were brothers, armed with what looked like World War I revolvers. If only my father, Hermann, had been there to verify their vintage. I laughed out loud when I saw them.

"Here we are like soldiers in a war," I said, "but we are not daredevils, we are dare disciples. We dare everything for Jesus, that's all. He is our protection. But let me tell you, while you are guarding my front door there is an entire terrace behind my room. They could access my room from that direction and you would not know it."

The crusade was to begin in twelve hours. At Green Square I saw the people who were gathering early. I also saw a large crowd that was being kept away by a group of soldiers. I did not learn the nature of their activity before I returned to my room to pray and sleep. Then I received a knock at the door. It was Stephen Mutua with the national security chief. They looked worried.

"The government must withdraw its invitation," the official said. "We are shutting down the Easter Celebration. You must go home at once."

"What about the people who have come so far?" I asked. "How can you deny them?"

"We deny them to save their lives. Our men found 13 land mines planted in the crowd area. There are too many threats for us to contain. This meeting is cancelled."

It was with great sadness and disappointment that we packed our bags to leave. I hated to retreat in the face of the Enemy's intimidation. But this was out of my hands. The government had been God's instrument for opening the door to Sudan, and the government was His instrument for closing it.

As we headed to the airport under military escort, news reports began to come in. The people were rioting in the streets. Muslims and Arabs who had brought the sick to be healed were attacking the police and soldiers for keeping them from Green Square. Some had come from hundreds and even thousands of miles to have the man of God pray for them. Now they were shut out and sent home disappointed. The army would not even let our technicians return to the square to dismantle our expensive equipment until they had restored order on the streets of Khartoum.

I returned to Frankfurt on Lufthansa. As our jet lifted into the sky, I looked down on the heart of Sudan, the confluence of the Blue and White Nile Rivers. They flowed from Ethiopia and Uganda and combined in Khartoum as one great river, marching on toward Egypt. My mind raced back to Uganda and the day I had stood at the source of the White Nile. On that day I had gained a new vision of the power of the gospel that was already beginning to trouble the calm of Satan's domain in central and northern Africa. Like this unstoppable river it was sweeping the continent. CfaN would be opposed, but the power of this salvation message would carry us through all obstacles and across the parched deserts of lost humanity that lay in our path.

"From Cape Town to Cairo," I had whispered that day, unheard above the roar of the troubled waters. "Africa shall be saved."

As we flew for our lives from Khartoum, I prayed for the day of our return. And as I prayed, my mind raced back to Kano, Nigeria, in 1991. Riots, violence, Muslims killing Christians on sight, and us fleeing for our lives. It had been a huge public relations disaster for CfaN. We had been expelled for nine years while our enemies rejoiced, and it had appeared that Satan had won. But nothing is as it appears to be in God's great plan. We must live with eyes of faith. Today no one needed faith to see the results of Kano. Without that tragedy and a nine-year exile we would not have seen the crowds explode as we were seeing them now. We would not have seen so many sinners responding to the gospel. We would not have seen 3,630,920 souls saved in the past three months alone! So much for the so-called public relations disaster.

My heart beat faster and filled with a new expectation for the African lands under Islam. *Lord, I wait for Your time for Khartoum and all of North Africa. You, and You alone are Lord of this harvest. Amen.*

I had barely arrived at our home in Frankfurt when the phone rang. It was the Sudanese ambassador in Germany. "Reverend Bonnke, we are so sincerely sorry for this terrible turn of events in Sudan. Please accept our apologies for the cancellation of this Easter Celebration and do not think that these things in any way reflect the wishes of President Omar Hassan al-Bashir or his government."

I thanked them for this gesture. I trusted that it was sincere. In my heart I truly believed they wanted to overcome the radical elements of Islam as much as I did. But we did not have control of the timetable for such progress, and the harsh actions of the police to clear the seekers from the meeting site had opened age-old wounds between Christian and Muslim. If an agenda of change is pushed too hard, or too far, there will usually be a backlash. The reaction can be violent, and it will have to run its course. I thank God that the backlash does not last forever.

On August 26, I preached for five nights at the Tata Raphael Grounds in the capital city of Kinshasa, Zaire, population 8,000,000. This was the only campaign held outside of Nigeria in 2001. The percentage of those who responded to the gospel dropped to 46 percent, which was wildly successful by any standard other than the one most recently, set in Onitsha, Nigeria with 86 percent. On the final night of the Kinshasa crusade the crowd grew to 250,000, bringing our attendance total for the five nights to 750,000. We tallied 350,000 decisions for follow-up. A glorious reward for obeying the Great Commission in Zaire.

At the close of my final sermon Stephen Mutua came to me while I was still on the platform. "Reinhard, before you leave, there is someone you should meet."

He told me this as he escorted me to the stairs at the back of the stage. As usual, I was drenched in sweat from open-air preaching in the tropics. My blood was pounding. I was still a bit out of breath.

"Who might that be?" I asked.

"A local pastor. He is from one of the churches sponsoring the crusade."

"Why haven't I already met him? We had a Fire Conference for local pastors."

"There were 20,000 at the Fire Conference. He could not get to you. Besides, at first we didn't know who he was and we were skeptical. But now we realize that he is someone special."

We reached an area that had been cordoned off for private meetings. Even in the backstage area at our crusades, crowd control is still essential. We entered the area, and there I saw a small group of my team members standing with a fine-looking African pastor.

I knew instantly that I had seen the man before, but I could not recall the incident. He was familiar, but different to what I remembered. His eyes were large, brown, and shining with a brilliant light. His smile looked like the full keyboard of my old piano-accordion. Except that his keyboard had one golden key, a large gold tooth shining in the front. He wore a well-pressed, maroon, double-breasted suit with a silk maroon and gold tie. He was trembling to see me, and yet still, I could not recall our former meeting.

He could not contain himself any longer. He rushed across the distance between us and threw himself to the ground, wrapping his arms tightly around my legs. Gone was his appearance of dignity. He could not care anymore. He kissed my feet and wept with a loud voice.

"Bonnke," he cried, "I am here today because of you. You saved my life. You saved my life."

"Who are you, man?"

I reached down and took his arms, freeing my legs from his grasp. "Stand up here and let me look at you again."

He brought himself up and looked at me, tears streaming from his wonderful brown eyes. He said one word to me, and then I knew him.

"Bukavu."

"Richard," I whispered, amazed. "You are Richard?"

My memory rushed back twelve years to that prison and the man singing in his chains. I could not believe the change. The country of Zaire had been called the Democratic Republic of the Congo in those days. Not only Richard, but Zaire itself had greatly changed.

"Richard," I said, "last I saw you, there was no gold tooth, just an empty socket. You could not speak English and you were filthy. You stank, excuse me, like an outdoor toilet."

"He went to Bible school and graduated," Stephen added proudly. "CfaN sponsored his educational costs. For years now he has pastored a fine church here in Zaire."

I took his arms and pushed up the sleeves of his fine maroon suit and saw the evidence I remembered most: the burn scars from the shackles that had been welded around his wrists. Shackles designed to be removed from his corpse with an axe after hanging. Yes, this was the same man. And now tears spilled from my eyes. I embraced him again and did not want to let go.

"Richard, what God has done for you! What God has done!"

As I embraced him I saw a vision of the real chains. Chains of sin falling from the wrists of millions of Africans as they embraced their Savior for the first time. Such a powerful image of God's love!

As I went to my room that night I walked in a cocoon of joy. I was so glad that I had heard the voice of the Spirit that day in 1989 when He had said to me, *Tell that man he will be set free and become a preacher of the gospel.* One man among thousands scheduled to die. I slept so well that night. You could not have wiped the smile from my face.

16 DAYS LATER the world changed in ways we are still trying to understand. The name Osama Bin Laden became a household word. Four American jet-liners were hijacked by Al-Qaeda terrorists. Two crashed into the twin towers of New York City's World Trade Center. Another hit the Pentagon. When the passengers on the fourth plane learned through cell phone conversations what had already happened, they rushed the hijackers of their flight which crashed nose down into a Pennsylvania field. They gave their own lives rather than be used to kill countless others.

Around the world the images of the towers falling and radical Islamists dancing for joy in the streets set a new tone for relations with the Muslim world. Our setback in Khartoum might well have entered an even deeper cycle of time. Separating moderate Muslims from intolerant Muslims became an almost impossible task in the days following. Even as more time passed it became apparent that every obstacle to the Islamic world would now have to be considered more carefully.

IN NOVEMBER I RETURNED TO THE CITY OF IBADAN, Nigeria, for a crusade and Fire Conference. By the final night the crowd had swelled to 1,300,000! A total of 3,900,000 attended the five nights of the event with 2,650,190 responding to the invitation. The supernatural harvest continued in spite of September 11.

Our final crusade for the year was scheduled in December in the city of Oshogbo. As I returned to Germany I realized that I had reached a crisis with my personal schedule. I would need to make several trips to Orlando, Florida, in the coming year to work on the Fire Conference film series. It occurred to me that what my director, Robert Murphree, had suggested might make good sense. If I moved to Orlando I could stay at home and accomplish these tasks without the back and forth trips from Frankfurt. The thought began to work its way from the background to the foreground in my mind.

I decided to spend some time in prayer about the possible move to America. When I pray over something like this I usually walk back and forth, pacing in a room. Spending a day in a hotel room, I paced so much I nearly wore out the carpet. "Lord, should I make the move to Orlando? Yes or no? What is Your direction to me?" Finally, in the afternoon I reached a place of peace. I had no answer but I had peace. Our trust is finally in God alone, in whom we live and move and have our being, as Paul said.[130] We may not know the answer to our questions, but we know the One who has all answers. Therefore, in Him I had peace.

Finally, on December 2, 2001 I received my answer.

"Anni, this Christmas we will move to Orlando."

She was silent for a moment. "Susanne and Brent are coming with the kids for Christmas. They have already booked their tickets."

My youngest daughter and her husband had already moved to America. "Call them now and tell them to cancel the tickets. We will come to see them and we will look for a place to live."

"Should I start packing?"

"Yes, start packing. We will be in America in three weeks."

I FLEW TO OSHOGBO for the final campaign of 2001. Upon arrival Peter van den Berg told me that a writer and photographer from one of Germany's weekly newsmagazines with 700,000 subscribers had come to cover our meeting. They were asking for a 30-minutes interview with me at the end of the crusade. I did not want to give them any such thing. We saw the writer and photographer from time to time eating at the restaurant in the hotel.

"These people have no idea about spiritual things, Peter," I said. "Everything about that magazine is simply godless."

As the day for the meeting approached, we received devastating news. A young man named Sunday, a local guitar player and praise and worship leader, had been promoting our meetings throughout the city by putting up posters. He had been targeted by a group of young Muslim fanatics. They entered his house at night, and in front of his father and mother, dragged him from his bed and began beating him with clubs.

"Jesus, what shall I do?" his father heard him call, as his assailants drove him from the house into the darkened street. "What shall I do?" he cried.

"Say 'Allahu akbar'!" the young men demanded. "Say it! 'Allahu akbar'!"

"Jesus is Lord!" he replied.

These were his last words. They proceeded to beat him to death.

Whatever terror or intimidation these radicals were trying to inflict on our meetings in Oshogbo, their tactics totally backfired. The news of Sunday's martyrdom rocked this city of 350,000. Thankfully the incident was isolated and did not trigger widespread violence. We mourned with his family and friends and commemorated him during the meetings. We saw our crowds grow with a mix of Muslims and non-Muslims to double the size of the city! By the final night we counted 650,000 in attendance. After five nights of preaching, 1,595,360 decisions for Christ had been registered.

Back at our hotel the writer from the German magazine was waiting. "Please, Reverend Bonnke, just give me 30 minutes before you leave. We are doing a main feature on you in the magazine. 30 minutes."

I was still wired from preaching. It would be hours before I could unwind and relax. Why not take the time now to do this wearisome thing? Who knows, it might turn out well. Perhaps it was the wrong motivation. I don't recall inquiring of the Lord. Anyway, I nodded my agreement and we went into one of the meeting rooms in the hotel. I sat down. He quickly turned on his recorder. Peter van den Berg turned his recorder on as well. We let the journalist know that we like to compare notes to see that I am properly quoted when the final story is published.

"Very good, shall we begin?"

"First question."

"Reverend Bonnke, what is your opinion about homosexuality?"

I almost walked from the room. I knew that it was a trick question, designed to cast me into the liberal or conservative camp of Christians. Actually, I belonged to neither camp. With all my heart I wanted to be known for demonstrating God's love to sinners. Somehow I wanted my answer to reflect the wonderful demonstration of that love I had seen in Hamburg those many years ago. On that occasion the homosexuals had come to attack the Christians for intolerance and they had ended up in tears, repeating the sinner's prayer. I needed to hear something from the Lord to help me in this situation. In the meantime I decided I could only stall the question.

"I thought your magazine was interested in doing a main feature about CfaN," I said. "What kind of question is that?"

"Well, sir, it is a question many Germans would like to hear you answer. We have covered your meeting extensively and we have much information about CfaN, but there are things about you personally that people do not know.

This is a question that is at the front of people's minds today. Churches are making statements on both sides of the issue. I would not be doing my job if I did not ask you about it. What is your opinion about homosexuality?"

This sort of moment is presented to me often. I am a preacher, but I am not happy unless I receive inspiration from the Holy Spirit. Sometimes I stand to speak and am totally surprised by what comes from my mouth. This is an exhilarating thing. To realize that my intentions can be overruled in a moment by the urge of the Spirit. This gift is not confined to the podium or preaching platform. It has often been manifested in private conversation, or in an interview such as this. The question from this journalist had startled and surprised me. The answer that came from my mouth surprised me even more.

"Oh," I said, "if I must answer for myself, homosexuality is against nature."

"How do you mean that, sir? Do you mean homosexuals are not created like other human beings?"

I thought for a minute. "No, no, no. I do not mean that. In fact, I mean the opposite. We are all created alike. I say the act of homosexuality goes against creation, in that sense it is against nature. It is against the way we are all created. Well, my mind works in pictures, you know? It's hard to explain." Then suddenly a picture dropped into my head. "Oh – " I said, "I've got it! Sir, when I need gasoline for my car I put the nozzle in the gas tank, not in the exhaust."

The entire room erupted. The photographer and Peter were holding their sides, roaring and shaking with laughter. They actually thought I had intended to make a joke. But I was totally serious. I looked at the writer and he was serious too.

"Hey wait!" I shouted. "Wait a minute. I didn't mean to make a joke. All I am saying is no car is built like that, and no man is created that way either. Next question."

Back home in Frankfurt one of the first things I did was establish a special fund to assist Sunday's family back in Oshogbo. His martyrdom and sacrifice had touched me so deeply. I did not want us to ever forget it. Helping his family in their loss seemed a small way of keeping his memory alive. Many in Oshogbo had been led to Jesus through his example. Of that I was sure.

Breakfast with Dr. Gerhard Stoltenberg, former German Federal Minister.

The following week we were greeted with a surprisingly complimentary twelve-page feature in the German news magazine. I carefully read every page, believing that somewhere in the story the writer would take vengeance on me for my comment about homosexuality. Surprisingly, in a personal sidebar at the end of the article he told the story of our interview from his point of view. He told it accurately. When asked about homosexuality, he wrote, "Reverend Bonnke excelled by answering ..." and then he quoted my gas tank analogy accurately. I guess the unintended humor in my answer covered a wide gap in our points of view.

Without intending to, I had created one of my most famous quotes. To this day it can be debated if this inspiration came from above or was simply the workings of my own mind. I am happy either way.

The year 2001 saw our overall results hit an all-time high. I preached to 11,735,000 people and saw 8,226,400 register decisions for Christ. This represented an average response for the year of 70 percent. Seven out of every ten people I preached to in 2001 received the Lord! That was supernatural.

By the end of December we had made the move to Orlando. The processing and paperwork for the move was seamless. It seemed right for many reasons, both personal and professional. I would be leaving to get started in a matter of weeks. In the meantime I could remain close to home and give serious attention to the filming of the Fire Conference project.

# Chapter 38

January, February, March — the first quarter of 2002 overwhelmed us with three Nigerian crusades that saw 4,868,547 souls accept Jesus! These meetings happened in places few have ever heard of: Abeokuta, Akure, Ilesa. After finishing the last meeting and seeing to the follow-up efforts, our team took a much needed rest. We had five months of African rainy season until our next meeting in Kisumu, Kenya. That meeting would be followed with three crusades in other Nigerian cities to complete the year.

When I arrived at home I received a message to call Brent Urbanowicz. A few years earlier, Brent, my son-in-law, had moved his family to Virginia. He was the young man who had been engaged to our daughter, Susanne, and had traveled with me to Kano. After enduring that acid test I gave him full permission to marry my daughter — of course, I said that with tongue firmly in cheek. They now lived on a country hilltop near the town of Winchester. As spring moved toward summer, he began calling me on a regular basis. The blossoms were in their full glory in Virginia, he said. He told me again and again of the great roads and parkways in the national parks of the Shenandoah and Monongahela Forests, and urged me to take a few days off to accompany him on a motorcycle tour of these scenic areas.

"But I have left my motorcycle in Frankfurt," I told him.

"I'm riding the Honda Gold Wing these days," he said. "Let me rent you one, Papa. You should try it."

"No, you know that I am committed to German engineering. I have always been a BMW man, and I always will be."

"Yes, but you cannot rent a BMW. It's just not allowed. And the Gold Wing is a fabulous road bike. It would do you good to try something new and different."

I looked at my schedule with Anni and she agreed to a few days for this recreational time for me. Brent rented a Gold Wing from a dealership in Richmond and I met him at his home to begin the ride. The trip was everything he promised. The Gold Wing was smooth and comfortable. The countryside was absolutely breathtaking, better than anything I had seen in all of my riding in Germany. My soul was truly refreshed, and I praised God as the wind rushed by me day after day on those two-lane back roads and highways.

All too soon it ended. We came back to Winchester and I turned the corner from the pavement onto the steep gravel drive leading up to Brent and Susanne's house. A few pebbles had dislodged from the driveway into the road. When my front wheel hit these pebbles they rolled and caused the wheel to slide off the pavement. As I tried to correct the problem, down went the shiny, rented Gold Wing into the neighbor's pasture. I was not traveling too fast, thank God, but the sudden accident left me no time to adjust. I simply rode it to a halt. I got off, feeling terribly upset. I had never had a motorcycle accident before.

Brent came back to see if I was hurt. There was absolutely no damage to me except for my ego as a motorcycle rider.

"This is another reason I still prefer the BMW bike," I said. "Brent, is this motorcycle insured?"

"Absolutely. But I don't see any damage."

"Surely I have scratched the paint."

He looked the machine over from front to back. "I can't even tell that it had an accident, Papa."

"Well, you don't own it. The owner will see the damage. When you return it you need to tell him that I put this motorcycle down."

"OK, I'll tell him."

"Yes, and be sure to tell him I will pay for everything. Any repair or touchup that needs to be done, I will cover it. Is that clear?"

"No problem. I'll tell him."

Back in Florida, I got a call the next day.

"No problem, Papa. The owner said there is not a scratch on the bike."

I found that difficult to believe. "Did he look closely? I'm sure there was some kind of damage."

"Well, he didn't exactly look so close."

"He didn't? Why not?"

"Well, I told him my father-in-law put the bike down and would pay for the damage. As he began to inspect it he asked who my father-in-law was. I told him that you were a preacher who preached mostly in Africa. He asked me your name, and when I told him, he stopped inspecting the bike. 'Tell your father-in-law there is not a scratch on this bike,' he said. He had tears in his eyes. I said, 'OK, I will tell him. Thank you.' 'No, thank you,' he said. 'Ten years ago your father-in-law preached in Virginia Beach and I accepted Jesus as my Savior. Tell him there is no scratch on this bike at all.'"

Well, that made my day, of course. It never ceases to amaze me how small the world can be. We never know when the unintended consequences of our lives will bless us right out of our socks. Sometimes it can also go the other way.

But soon I visited a BMW motorcycle shop and bought a brand-new, full-dress heavyweight touring bike. I was back with German engineering. Now, when I feel the need for speed, I will hit Florida Highway 4 north out of town and then join the 95 Freeway along the Atlantic Coast for a hundred miles or so to Jacksonville before taking Interstate 10 east to the 75 Freeway south, and complete the circle back home. The Gold Wing dealer in Richmond holds a dear place in my heart, but the only Gold Wings I see these days are those in my rearview mirror.

As 2002 ended I was forced by circumstances to cancel a meeting in Wukari, a tribal area of Nigeria near the border with Cameroon. We rescheduled for the next year and completed the final two meetings in Ogbomosho and Ile-Ife. The year ended with 10,652,000 attending our crusades and 73 percent of those registering decisions for Jesus. Another year of seeing the full bounty of the combine harvester.

Plans for 2003 shifted radically. We decided that for the first time we would organize no crusades outside of Nigeria at all. And inside Nigeria we would increase our schedule to reach more rural areas. We scheduled five campaigns in the first three months of the dry season, and another six between August and the end of the year. It would be an exhausting schedule for me and the CfaN team. Some months of the dry season we would hold two crusades in the same month.

As the meetings continued, one after the other, each night we looked out on crowds of between 200,000 and 800,000 people. Such numbers numb the mind after a while. So many salvations were recorded. But I was very aware that each one of them had a special story that may never be told this side of heaven. Likewise, so many miracles of healing took place I could not possibly have known or shared them all.

I am aware that as people read this story of millions being impacted by the gospel, their thinking may short circuit. Numbers are too abstract. For some, it will be less real because I am describing souls coming to Christ in Africa. They are great crowds of black people with black faces. And in the greater scheme of modern life, for many people, these folk simply don't count as much as white people living in a Western society. But those who think that way are so wrong. That is why God gave me the story of David Attah. He was one out of 11 million who attended the campaigns of 2002. One story that would demonstrate that each of these precious souls has a story of profound importance that ought to be told.

DAVID ATTAH HAD BEEN RAISED IN A MUSLIM HOME in Nigeria. He was of average height, trim of build, and he had a sensitive and pleasant face. Wearing wire-rimmed glasses for nearsightedness, he carried himself with the look of a man of gentle intelligence.

Inside, he had hurt for many years. An only child, his mother had died when he was a boy. He had never been wanted by his cold, stern father. Friendships had been few. But he had reached his limit. One day as a young man he simply decided to lose his loneliness. He moved to Makurdi, into a house with a group of students, and enrolled as a communications major at the local branch of the Nigerian State University. He put a smile on his face and a warm greeting in his mouth for everyone he met. Soon he had reached his goal. He was surrounded by friends. He had lost his loneliness.

Nearly four years of diligent study followed. The pain of his past was buried as he enjoyed the companionship he craved. When fellow students had trouble, he was there to listen and care. When they had financial trouble, he would dip into his own wallet and make loans. Some were never repaid. He would sometimes turn the loans into gifts. David became a rescuer. With such qualities, he became popular. Students, faculty, even the maintenance crew – everybody loved David Attah.

An evangelist came to town. David was invited to attend the meetings by a Christian student named Jonah. David had always believed in God. For him, the big question was, "What kind of God is He?" His Muslim family had taught him that Allah was absolutely sovereign; he planned everything before it happened. The best anyone could do was accept his fate: "Allah wills it." But David had been fated to be a lonely boy, and he had rejected that painful fate. He was ready to receive the Christian God who said, "You must be born again." He loved the Christian language of new birth, starting over, and second chances.

By contrast, all of the harsh Muslim beliefs he had picked up along the way seemed to fit the personality of his earthly father: unloving, unyielding, uncaring. The same father who had rejected him. The crusade sermon presented a God of love who had died for the sins of the world. Jesus revealed a heavenly Father of love who had sent His Son to die for the world. The choice seemed clear. David raised his hand and repeated the sinner's prayer, embracing Christ as his Savior. Now he sensed that his new life of friends and fellowship would last forever in the family of God.

Soon afterward, tragedy struck. As he walked to school, a woman sped through an intersection near campus, striking David down. Police arrived. The woman was arrested and charged with driving under the influence. An ambulance took him away. David knew nothing. He remained unconscious for days with severe head injuries, broken bones, and internal bleeding.

When he opened his eyes again, he was in a hospital room. He heard a familiar voice say, "You've been out for two days." Through blurred vision, he saw that his arms and legs were encased in plaster. His head throbbed, and it was wrapped in bandages. He struggled to remember what had happened to him.

He had been walking to class. Suddenly, everyone was rushing to get away from a speeding car, but someone had blocked his path. He recalled that he seemed to be out of his body in an eerie, silent vacuum. He watched his wire-rimmed glasses fly up into the blue, he saw his body summersault as if in slow motion, then he heard the sickening thud of the car hitting him. Time had slipped out of sync in his mind. Things that should have happened first, happened after; and things happened after, that should have happened first. There had been a flash of light, and then everything had plunged into a darkness lasting 48 hours.

Now, he was here in a hospital room. He discerned the shape of Jonah near his bedside. It had been Jonah's familiar voice he had heard as he awakened. They were roommates and were scheduled to graduate together. Final exams would begin in a few weeks. From the extent of his injuries, David knew he would not recover in time to finish school with his friends. His dream of starting a career in communications had been given a huge setback. How could God have chosen this time to decree such an evil fate for him? Perhaps Allah was God after all.

He closed his eyes. Every beat of his heart sent a pulsing ache across his eyelids. It was like an iron anvil had been dropped on his chest. Each breath was labored, and fingers of pain shot through his ribcage. He wanted only to sleep. But he told himself that he must awaken at 3 a.m. so that he could pray. That was the magic hour. From the dimness of childhood he recalled the creed: We believe in what His Messenger told us, that He descends to the near sky before the last third of every night and says: *Who prays to Me and I will answer his prayers? Who asks Me and I will give him?* [131] As his battered body gave in to sleep, David wondered why Allah would ask questions at 3 a.m. Why did he not give answers?

When he awoke again, the sun was high. He had missed his chance to pray. A nurse checked his vital signs. He decided to ask her the extent of his injuries, but as he attempted to form the words, no movement or sound came from his mouth. This alarmed him. He had developed the skill of expressing kindness and gratitude toward those around him, which in turn, made them eager to help him. But the words in his head could not force any movement into his tongue. It was like the connection had been cut.

He thought the bandage on his head might be too tight across his jaw, restricting his speech. But his arms were held back by the casts so that he could not loosen it. He struggled to speak to the nurse again. Forget speech – he tried to make a sound, a groan, a moan – nothing happened. The nurse looked at him with sympathy and left the room. He began to feel strangely disconnected. Fear swept through his mind like a wildfire.

On the bedside stand he saw his Bible. Jonah must have left it for him. The sight of it reminded him that, unlike Allah, the God of the Bible was always ready to hear prayers, 24 hours a day. He would not have to awaken at 3 a.m. to impress Him with his devotion. Perhaps he should pray to his heavenly Father after all, praying in the name of Jesus. But what would he pray? Would he pray for protection from harm or accidents? It was a little late for that. Would he pray for healing? He would think about prayer later. For the present, his faith was as battered as his body.

In the months ahead, the hard work of therapy began. During that time, a neurosurgeon from Makurdi General Hospital tested David's speech. He discovered that he still had marvelous language skills and was able to write. But David had totally lost the ability to make his mouth utter – even whisper – a single word. The doctor consulted the medical journals. He returned to tell David that this was a well-documented disorder resulting from a head injury. It was called *aphasia*. There were many different types of aphasia, but David's type was clearly noted in the literature.

In the weeks of rehabilitation that followed, David gained the use of his right hand. He communicated his thoughts by notepad. The doctors and staff at the hospital developed affection for their bright and sensitive patient. They made special efforts to encourage him. They told him that one day his ability to speak might return just as mysteriously as it had gone. But David found it hard to endure that kind of hope. To him, it seemed concocted by wishful thinking. He wanted a clear physical diagnosis and a true medical cure. Otherwise, he would rather not hear such patronizing lies.

In the meantime, the hospital bills were real enough. They mounted beyond all reason. Nothing was given freely at Makurdi General. The drugs for pain and the blood thinners ate up 250 naira per day, not including room and board, plus medical testing. Within a few weeks, his money was gone. He was sinking deeply into debt.

The hospital required patients to pay for meals. He could not afford to purchase them anymore. To slow the rising flood of IOUs, he began to seek scraps and leftovers from fellow patients. People liked him so much they actually kept back food for him. He managed to get by on this kind of charity for a while.

Meanwhile, his classmates at the university graduated. They became busy seeking new lives and careers. He had visits from Jonah and other student-friends in the first days after the accident. But after spending hours at his bedside, they grew impatient. The David they had known was quick witted and full of bright conversation. Now, all of his answers had to be written out, and he seemed to have lost his ability to bounce back emotionally. Conversation became hard work. In frustration, Jonah accused him of faking the dumbness.

"Why don't you just get over it?" he said, and left the room, never to be seen again.

David decided to sell his belongings to pay his prescription drug bill. He sent a friend to collect his things from the house he had shared with fellow students, but when the friend arrived, his room was bare. It seems his old friends had stolen everything. Perhaps they had sold his things to pay his overdue rent. Whatever the reason, they had not bothered to share their plans with him. He never saw his university friends again.

This hit him hard. The new life he had made for himself in Makurdi, surrounded by friends, had been a mirage. Perhaps he was fated to be lonely after all, and nothing had ever really changed. Old things did not pass away as the Bible had said. All things did not become new.[132] He began to plunge into fits of depression.

With no place to go, no immediate family to welcome him, David stayed in the hospital. Weeks turned into months. One day a national television crew came and filmed a story about him. The local neurosurgeon described his case to the audience. It was broadcast nationwide, and David's name and face was seen across Nigeria. The publicity was used to raise money for the hospital. After that, he became affectionately known as "The Chairman" of the hospital board. The staff and patients treated him as if he owned the place. But he had no illusions; the hospital owned him and every penny he would make for the rest of his life. Besides, he had once enjoyed this kind of adulation from his many friends at the university. He knew that those who pledged their devotion today would fail him tomorrow.

One day, the neurosurgeon ordered an MRI on David's head. From the results he suggested a surgery could be done to remove some scar tissue at the back of his head that was putting pressure on his brain. He said that this delicate operation might bring positive results for him. No promises, but the very hint of regaining his speech piqued David's desire. He was willing to risk anything for it. He agreed to the surgery. But the political situation in Nigeria went through a sudden upheaval. The doctor, who had been aligned with a faction that opposed the current leader, fled the country with his family. All plans for David's surgery were abandoned.

Enough was enough. David decided to end the pain. He took advantage of his free access to the pharmacy, stealing a supply of poison. He prepared a lethal dose for himself. If God had fated him for loneliness, debt, failure, and dumbness, he wanted out. He would go see this God face to face and ask Him to give the assignment to someone else.

He sat down and wrote a letter. He thanked the hospital staff for all of their efforts. He made it clear that his death was by his own hand. In the letter he described the reasons that he would kill himself. "Life is not worth living," he wrote. "I will always be alone. Nothing matters."

He placed the letter inside his Bible and laid it on the nightstand. Then he lay down. His plan was to wait until the ward was asleep, and then he would take the poison. No one would find him until it was too late.

He felt a strange sense of peace with this decision. The constant turmoil that afflicted his mind day and night simply ceased. He later realized that the author of death, the Enemy of his soul, cooperates with those who decide to help his evil cause.

As he lay there, resolved to die, Someone Else had bigger and better plans for him. A beautiful girl with large, kind eyes, walked into his room. At first David thought he was dreaming. She was not a member of the nursing staff. He knew everyone at Makurdi General, and he would have remembered this lovely creature.

"Can I talk with you?" she asked.

Her voice was soft and warm. She spoke with a steady tone that seemed rooted in the very earth beneath her. He wondered, *Is this an angel?* He stared at her.

"I know you can't speak," she said. "But they tell me that you write very well."

He sat up, and nodded. He took a notepad and wrote, "Who are you?"

She came near and bent down to read his note. He could detect the delicate floral scent of her perfume. It filled his head with the idea that if he had no reason to live for himself, he might go on living for someone else. Especially someone as lovely as this creature.

"My name is Rita. I am training to be a nurse," she said.

"So, they sent you to practice on me?" he wrote.

"No, I am curious about you. I saw you on television and I wanted to come see you. I have talked to the staff here. They tell me you're depressed." She reached out and picked up David's Bible. "Are you a Christian?"

He nodded.

"I knew it!" she exclaimed. "So am I." Her smile was full and lovely. She opened his Bible and saw the note he had just written. "May I read this?"

David froze inside. He wasn't sure why he wanted to give her permission to read his suicide note, but in some part of himself, he did. He nodded, and then watched as her expression changed to one of alarm.

She looked at him, her brows darkly knit. "You must never, never do this!" she said. "I want you to promise me that you will not do this terrible thing."

David looked away. He could not promise her. He could not promise himself. He shook his head.

She became offended, and spoke sharply. "Do you really believe in God, David?"

He nodded.

"Did God give you life?"

David thought of Allah, and of the Christian God. In either case, the answer was yes. He nodded.

"Then He will not forgive you if you take this precious gift by your own hand." She was pacing back and forth, piercing him with her gaze. "It is not your life to take, David. It is His. You will go to hell if you murder yourself. And I do not want you to go to hell."

David wondered if hell was as lonely as his life. He took his pad and wrote, "My family is gone. My friends have betrayed me. I have lost everything I own. My education has become worthless. I cannot pay my debts. I am alone, and not even God cares."

As Rita read this, she heard a voice speaking in her spirit: *If you want him to make this promise, you must make a promise to be his friend.* God was calling her to go beyond anything she had intended when she walked into this room.

Rita spoke slowly, deliberately, "God cares very much about you, David. He sent me to you today. If you will promise me that you will never take your life, I will promise you something in return."

David could not believe she was saying this. He had never once heard anyone make such an intimate proposal to a total stranger. He took his pad and wrote, "How can you promise me anything? You don't know me."

"You don't know me either. If you will promise me that you will not take your life," she said, "then I will promise to stand by you, no matter what. I will be your friend."

"No one can promise that," he wrote.

"This is not a promise to you, David. It is a promise I make to God in my heart. He will help me to keep it. But I will make no promise at all to someone who plans to kill himself. Do you understand me?"

In her words, David heard what he longed most to hear – a pledge of unconditional loyalty. But he could not believe that this beautiful girl, nor anyone, would live up to such a promise. Besides, Rita was of marrying age and there would be many men who would want to have her for a wife. If she married, her husband would never tolerate such a promise to stand by another man.

"Promise me," she said.

He had absolutely nothing to lose. Could it be that God had sent this girl to break him out of his silent prison? He reached out beyond himself and decided to make her this promise. Taking his pad, he wrote, "I promise you, Rita, not to take my own life."

"Sign your name," she said.

He signed his name.

"Date it," she demanded.

He added the date.

She reached down and took the paper from beneath his hand. Holding it up, she read it again. Then she carefully folded it and placed it in her purse. Taking the suicide note from the open Bible she began tearing it to shreds.

"I promise God, and you, David," she said, "that I will be your true friend from this day on."

The next day Rita came to his hospital room with a prepared meal. She came the next day and the next. She ran errands for him. She did his laundry. They began long hours of conversation, she talking, he writing his answers. She treasured his wonderful way with words, so she brought three-ringed binders to keep his writings in. Around the hospital the patients and staff began to joke with David, "Here comes your wife," they would say, whenever Rita approached. David was flattered. He hardly deserved such a wife.

His debts mounted higher. He decided to sue the woman who had hit him with the car. Rita helped him with the months' long legal process. At the end of the trial, a sympathetic jury awarded him 1,000,000 naira in damages. He was happy to think that this would pay his hospital bills and provide for his continuing drug expenses. As the months passed, however, it became clear that the guilty woman had many ways to avoid paying her fine. Legal appeals and challenges to the verdict abounded, slowing and diverting the payoff. David's emotional state went up and down with the legal fight.

Meanwhile, Rita was accepted to nursing school in Enugu, hundreds of miles away. She promised that she would not neglect him but would return to Makurdi. In the meantime, she located a local ministry that served widows and orphans. They agreed to take David on as a ministry project while she was away. While studying in Enugu, Rita continued her conversation with him in letters, writing every day as the months of her schooling progressed.

In time, she graduated. Her family was happy and excited for her. They wanted her to seek work in Lagos, or other more attractive locations in Nigeria. She would be accepted anywhere she chose, they told her. Since she spoke English, she might even find a job in America. But she refused to consider an assignment outside of Makurdi. "I made a promise to God to be David's friend," she said. "I intend to keep it."

Her family members were not happy about this. They began to despise David. They counseled her that she had more than fulfilled her promise to him. She could maintain a long-distance friendship from any city with a postal service. Rita listened, but she felt that she must not leave David. The promise she had made to God, and to David, would not let her simply get on with her own life. She came to work at Makurdi General Hospital where David lived.

At this time, however, she saw that living in the hospital and waiting for his legal settlement to pay off was crippling him. She urged him to move out on his own. To become independent. He did not want to leave, saying that he had no place to go. But she kept after him until he found a way to make it happen. He got a job with a pharmacy that had been willing to supply his drugs on credit. The owner had a one-room cabin that he could live in rent-free. Now he could begin to pay his own way and repay at least some of his debt.

Rita continued to visit, bringing meals, and encouraging his faith in the Lord. A fine Christian man began to call on Rita at her home. Her parents were pleased with him as a potential husband for their daughter. She could see where this was headed and she cut it short. She told the man that there was no possibility of her marrying as long as she remained true to her promise to take care of David.

David learned about this and he was overcome with emotion. He had nothing to offer her, but one day he wrote, "Rita, will you marry me?"

She hesitated. "God will make it clear if we are to marry," she replied. "First of all, my parents would not approve. They are godly parents. They are the parents God has given me, and I believe I must have their approval and blessing." She became very thoughtful. "David, I think when you talk again, this will change everything. I believe you will talk someday."

David's heart fell. He wanted to believe that he would talk again, but he just couldn't. His trust in God had been fragile at best. Now it was broken. He continued to go back and forth in his mind between images of a God of love, and a God of fate. Too often he forgot to count his blessings, and he hardly ever failed to count his curses. He became someone who was hard to love.

These were the longest years of his ordeal. His life became limited and defined by his disorder. Apart from his work at the pharmacy, much of his energy was devoted to endless attempts to collect his 1,000,000 naira from the woman who had hit him with her car. All of her delaying legal appeals were finally exhausted. The award had been upheld by the court. All that remained was to collect. He collected nothing.

He had the court intervene with her employer to attach her paycheck. About the time the attachment began, she was fired. She secretly took another job. When he discovered this, he tried the process again, and she repeated her pattern. In some ways, nothing had changed from the day she had hit him with the car. She was still avoiding responsibility. He was still being struck down. How could God allow it? How could He dangle 1,000,000 naira in front of him – so close, yet so far away?

The woman declared hardship. If David had taken a hard line and had the police send her to jail, all hope of receiving anything from her would vanish. He was stuck, and he became worn out with chasing justice. All of his efforts to get the system to work for him were made worse by his handicap. He found few people, if any, who were patient with him in his inability to speak. As a final indignity, the government issued him a license to beg for a living. They too, had given up.

Meanwhile, Rita continued as always, checking on his condition, bringing occasional meals, running errands. She continued to encourage him in his spiritual life. She prayed with him often and took him to churches and crusades in Makurdi. She took him to Christian counselors. But he continued to struggle in his faith and his emotions. Up and down, up and down.

Eight long years passed. By now everyone who knew David, knew that his aphasia was a real disorder. Also, by this time David knew that Rita was a godsend, and he was totally unworthy of her. The example of her steady faith next to his wavering faith became unbearable at times. He found a measure of relief during those times when they were apart.

I KNEW NOTHING OF DAVID AND RITA'S STORY when our team came to Makurdi. In February of 2003, Christ for all Nations held a crusade there.

A large field had been secured for our lights and sound systems. We were prepared to see crowds of 200,000.

When Rita heard about the meeting she called David and urged him to go. She told him that in her Christian life, she had never seen a miracle, but she had heard that many miracles happened in our crusades. Our publicity posters promised that I would pray for the sick, as I always do. She did not go to the meeting with David. For some reason she felt that this was something he must do on his own. Secretly, she was close to despair over his lack of improvement.

David also felt desperate. He was coming to the end of his ability to keep his promise to Rita, and he knew it. Thoughts of suicide were plaguing him again. Something had to change. Enough was enough. For one last time he would seek healing from God. This time he would not put his trust in the doctors or medicine. He would not seek help from the courts or the government. He would fast and pray, asking God to heal him at the Bonnke crusade. Failing that, he would find a way to release Rita from her promise. He would do that by breaking his own.

On our opening night in Makurdi, 180,000 people crowded the field. Thousands of sick people came close around the platform. David stood at the perimeter and counted his chances of being prayed for by Reinhard Bonnke at zero. He felt lost in the crowd. At the end of the sermon, as I made a general prayer for the sick, he turned and walked away.

He should accept his fate, he thought. God did not care enough to heal him, and he would never be good enough to deserve it. Bonnke had faith for healing, but he did not. And God would not let him get close enough so that Bonnke could lay hands on him. He walked home and sat on his bed in the dark. The clock on his table glowed with the hour, 11 p.m.

He felt a trickle of warm blood begin to flow from his nostrils. He got up and found a towel to stop the flow. But it wouldn't stop. It continued for an hour, and then for another. He ran out of rags to stop the bleeding. As the third hour of bleeding began he realized that he was dying. Perhaps his blood thinners had taken over.

He felt he had one last chance to communicate. He had no telephone because he had no need for one. In the corner of his room was the latest binder Rita had prepared for his writings. He found his notepad and pen and began to write his last will and testament, leaving his few belongings to Rita. He expressed his love to her and his deep gratitude for her friendship. Now she would be free of her promise to be his friend, he wrote, and she could go on and find a godly man to be her husband. He wrote that God would surely take good care of someone as faithful as her. He wrote that he would be free, too, and that he was ready for his ordeal to be over. With tears and blood falling onto the page, he said good-bye, signed his name, and dated it – February 3, 2003.

He left the door of his room open so that his body would be found in the morning light. Then the young man who had struggled to lose his loneliness lay down to die.

Another hour passed. The bleeding continued unabated. Strangely, David felt fine. Why wasn't he weak from the loss of so much blood? He got up and looked at his clock. It was 4 a.m. His nose was still flowing with a steady stream.

He took his notepad from the desk and walked outside. The city was dark. Above him the stars filled the night sky. They stared down with cold indifference. If he had never lived, those stars would shine on. If he stopped breathing, they wouldn't care. They seemed too much like the God who made them.

He began to walk. As he did he began to sob, his shoulders shaking silently. He had never felt more alone. If ever he needed his voice it was now. He would scream to the stars, "Why have You forsaken me?! Why?!"

He came to a park bench and sat down as dawn began to glow in the east. He still could not control his weeping or his nosebleed.

Around 5 a.m. someone on his way to work found him. His voice was filled with alarm. "What happened to you, sir?"

David realized that his shirt was soaked with blood. His face was a mess. This person would call the police. He pointed to his mouth and shook his head to let them know he couldn't speak. Then he wrote quickly on his pad, "It's just a nosebleed. I'm fine."

"Then why are you crying?"

David decided to tell the truth to this stranger. He wrote, "It seems the Lord is forsaking me. Why would the Lord forsake me? Doesn't He care?"

"How do you know when God forsakes you?" the stranger asked.

Suddenly, David could see himself. He was sitting on this park bench because God had preserved him, not because He had forsaken him. He had been bleeding steadily for six hours, and he was still strong. He should have been unconscious, or even dead, but he could stand and walk. He still had energy. He could almost hear Rita's voice saying, "God loves you, David. He will never leave you nor forsake you." Those words from her mouth were so powerful because she embodied them beyond anyone he had ever known. He had no place to hide from God's care.

He bent down and wrote again, "No, I am wrong. God is not forsaking me. He has been good to me. I believe He will do something good for me. I must build up my faith."

He went home and discovered that the bleeding had stopped. He cleaned up and went to work. David longed to talk with Rita about his strange ordeal. She was his best friend, beyond all others. But he reconsidered. She had been through enough. He would finish this part of the journey without her.

He asked his boss to call his cousin John, who was a Christian. He had moved to Makurdi in recent years and knew about David's condition. John agreed to come to the pharmacy. David asked him to go with him to the crusade that night. He told John how the crowd was so thick he needed help to get to the very front. He was determined to get to Bonnke. He would ask him to lay hands on him and pray for a miracle of healing. John agreed to help.

David then wrote out his prayer request for Evangelist Bonnke to read. In order to verify his story, he took the medical documents and the government license to beg, awarded to him because of his condition. Surely with this information, he thought, Bonnke would be moved with compassion to ask God to do something for him.

At 7 p.m. they came to the crusade grounds. David carried his Bible and notepad. Some of the crowd had been waiting all day. Together, David and John pushed their way toward the platform. It was a long and difficult struggle.

THAT NIGHT AS I BEGAN PREACHING, I did not know the drama that was unfolding with David Attah. He and John had made their way to the steps beside the platform. At the base of the stairs stood Jason Betler, a member of our team. It was his job to see that no one rushed onto the stage uninvited.

David poked Jason in the side to get his attention. He wrote on his notepad and placed it in front of him. "I have been unable to speak since an accident eight years ago. I want an appointment with Evangelist Reinhard Bonnke. I want him to pray for me so that I can speak."

Jason could see that David felt desperate. His heart went out to him. "I'm sorry," he said, "but there are too many people here who want to see Reinhard. We cannot make a personal appointment for you. But if you stay, Reinhard will pray for all of the sick at the end of the meeting."

David did not want this. He wrote again that he wanted Bonnke to pray for him personally. In his mind he was fighting against fate. He saw all of the people in the crowd as resigned to their fate. At the time of mass prayer, Reinhard would pray over the entire audience and God would heal only those He chose to heal. David wanted better odds than that. He wanted to storm heaven's gates and ask, even demand, a healing from God. In his mind, if Reinhard, the man of faith, would pray for him, this would happen. In this way, he thought he would break through the grip of fate. But as he continued to try to persuade Jason to make an appointment, Jason continued to refuse.

This threw David back into a lifelong emotional pattern. The old pain of loneliness returned to his heart in full measure. As Jason refused to hear his request, so David felt, God refused to give him access to His healing power. But on this night, David thought, something in this familiar pattern had to change. Giving in to this self-focused feeling had only produced more suffering. He'd had enough of it. It was time to go a new way. He would go against his feelings and take a step of faith, believing that God still had his best interest at heart, even though he felt rejected.

He and John walked away about 30 yards into the crowd where Jason could still see them. Jason recalls that David was wearing a bright red shirt, and it was easy to keep track of him.

After the salvation prayer, I addressed the sick people in the crowd as I usually do. I asked them to place their hands on the part of their body that needed healing. Then I began to pray.

As Jason describes it, he saw David place his hand on the back of his head and immediately fall to the ground as if someone had cut him down.

David experienced what Jason saw, but in a much different way. His testimony is that he laid his hand on his head and felt the warmth of a strong light shining on him from above. He thought it was a crusade field light. Something told him to look at it. When he looked up, the light shot down around him. It was so powerful it drew him inside. He looked out of the shaft of light at his cousin, John. John obviously did not see the light because he was looking at the stage as normal. David tried to reach out and grab him by the sleeve to get him to look at the light, but he could not reach beyond the light. He took his notepad to write John a note but his hands felt too weak to write a single letter. He felt strangely cut off from reality.

He looked at the other people around him. No one else seemed to notice the light either. He was alone in this experience, but he hardly felt lonely. He was alone with God, and he felt thrilled with His love. A hand came down through the shaft of light and touched the back of his head. It removed something. He immediately felt relieved of a great burden.

The light began to fade, and he found himself on the ground in the crusade meeting. How did he get there? He felt confused and wondered if he had really experienced this light, or if it had been a dream. He felt as if he was still in a dream. As he came more fully to his senses he thought that maybe that he had collapsed from the loss of blood, or from the lack of sleep, or even from the previous days of fasting – or from a combination of these things.

John quickly helped him to his feet. "What happened to you?" he asked.

David had no reply. He didn't even think of using the notepad. John went on talking, but David could not concentrate on his words. He was still overcome by the experience of the light, and the hand that had removed something from his head.

At this point Jason Betler reports that he saw David reach to the back of his head again and fall to the ground again. This was the very same action as before.

Once again, David experienced what Jason saw, but in a much different way. He said that suddenly the light came back. This time it was even more powerful. He looked again at his cousin John, but once again, John did not see the light. The hand returned, touching the back of his head. Once again it removed something, and David felt lighter. This time, however, he felt another sensation as well; he knew that he had received something from God. The light disappeared, and he found himself on the ground.

John helped him to his feet. He seemed baffled and just a bit angry. The crowd was surging all around them. People were praying intently with their hands raised. "Who pushed you down, David?" he asked. "Who did this to you?"

David looked at John, and for the first time in eight years, a word in his head found the power to make his mouth respond. "Jesus," he rasped.

John's jaw dropped. He stared. "Did you say something?"

"Jesus," David repeated. He felt like he was glowing. It never entered his heart to say any other word than the precious name of the Son of God. "Jesus."

John gasped. "David, I heard you."

"Jesus, Jesus, Jesus," David repeated. He began to walk around saying it. It was a hoarse whisper, but it was a miracle. He stopped and looked at his cousin again, taking him by the shoulders. "Thank you, John," he said.

John grabbed him in a bear hug. "God has healed my cousin!" he screamed to the people around him. "God has healed him! He can talk for the first time in eight years!"

From the stage I asked those who had received healing to approach the platform. I wanted to share with that vast crowd what God had done that night. John rushed with David back to where Jason Betler stood. He told him that David had been unable to speak for eight years since his accident. Now he was talking.

"Jesus," David repeated, tears streaming from his eyes. "Jesus."

Jason took him with John, up the steps to meet me on the platform. Once again John explained the background to David's story.

I spoke to the crowd, "This man named David Attah has not been able to speak for eight years," I said. There was a stir across the audience. I did not know that David was well known to many people in Makurdi. Some recognized him. I placed the microphone near to his mouth, "Let's hear David do something he has not done for eight years," I said. "Count with me, David. Say, 'one'."

"One," David rasped.

"Two."

"Two," he repeated.

"Three."

"Three."

"Four."

"Four."

Suddenly David dropped to his knees, weeping with gratitude. He was simply overcome and did not have any idea how to thank God for His great gift of healing.

In November we returned to hold a campaign in Nnewi, another city in the delta region of the Niger River. David came to see us. He was beaming from ear to ear and spoke fluently now in a full voice. I invited him to the platform to tell his story to this crowd of 400,000. He gladly did so. Later he told us that the strength of his voice continued to return after the Makurdi crusade. However, when his voice grew tired, he still lapsed into a whisper.

In December we returned to Warri, another city in the Niger Delta near the coast. David came again, and this time, no one could stop him from talking. His face bore a new light. He introduced us to a beautiful young woman named Rita, his fiancée, he said. Seeing her, we could easily understand his joy.

I asked my team to take them both aside and record their story. That is when I learned that after his healing, Rita took David to see her parents. Rita's mother met them at the door. She knew David well, and was not happy to see him.

"Hello, Mother," he said to her, his face breaking into a wonderful smile.

Rita's mother's eyes grew wide. Her hands flew to her cheeks. "David? Did you speak?"

"Jesus healed me," he said. "God is so good!"

Rita asked her stunned mother if she could invite David inside. Her mother nodded. So many emotions were hiding behind her blank stare: shock, anger, frustration, resentment, confusion – and those feelings were made worse by a sense of guilt for having felt those things toward David – someone God had obviously loved so much.

Rita knew what to do next.

She led David by the hand into her house, and to her bedroom. There, she had a bookshelf. It was full of eight years of conversations bound in notebooks. Until now, they had been her treasures. She began to pile the notebooks into his outstretched arms. She loaded her mother's arms too. When the shelf was empty, she led them to the back door and out into the yard. A large barrel was placed there. She took the notebooks one by one and began dropping them into the barrel. Then she doused them with gasoline and tossed in a match.

As the books went up in flames, a flood of tears released from her soul. She took David in her embrace.

"I want to hear you talk, David," Rita said.

"I am talking," he said.

"But never stop. Don't ever stop talking to me, David. Promise me."

"I promise," he said.

Today, Mr. and Mrs. David Attah have completed Bible College in prepara-tion for a lifetime of ministry. David's healing has become widely known in Nigerian medical circles, as well as in most churches in that region of Africa.

David and Rita travel together and never miss an opportunity to tell what God has done for them.

They are just one of the millions of stories behind the mind-numbing statistics of this great harvest. So whose story is it? It is the story of David's healing and of Rita's promise, and more. It is the story of God's love for Africa. His love enables each of us to witness to His saving grace, and also to His healing power. May God receive all the glory.

In telling her story, I was struck to hear Rita say that before David was healed, she had never seen a miracle. I would have to disagree. For eight years she became a human mirror of God's love. That too, was a miracle, and a story worth telling.

# Chapter 39

As the Nigerian campaigns continued and intensified in the next few years, I again sensed the Lord leading me to tithe one crusade per year outside of Nigeria. Meetings were scheduled in New Guinea, Sudan, Romania, and India.

As we continued to see the harvest in Nigeria, I especially began to anticipate our return to Sudan in 2006. We had scheduled a July series of meetings in the southern city of Juba. This was the heart of the area that had been cut off from the world by civil war for more than two decades. The circumstances of our return were very special and dear to my heart.

After our initial Easter Celebrations in the northern capital of Khartoum, which had begun well but ended badly, the government had implemented every reform that I had suggested. In a strategic meeting with the embassy heads of Europe, I had urged that the north give autonomy to the south and enter into a power sharing agreement. They had done exactly that. In the years that followed, they had made the former rebel leader, Dr. John Garang, the first Christian vice president of the nation, sharing power with the Muslim north. He made a triumphal entry into the capital city of Khartoum in January of 2005. Live, on national television, he had signed the new constitution with al-Bashir, sealing the union of north and south. All of Sudan broke out in rejoicing.

"I congratulate the Sudanese people," Garang said. "This is not my peace or the peace of al-Bashir, it is the peace of the Sudanese people."

At last the long civil war had ended. But tragically, Garang was killed just seven months later in a helicopter crash. Rumors of sabotage abounded. Like the assassination of John F. Kennedy, the conspiracy theories would not fade. As long as Garang had been a rebel leader he had been beyond reach of al-Bashir, his followers said. As vice president he had finally became vulnerable, and many believed that the government's hand was behind the so-called accident.

Sudan's hard-won peace had become fragile again. Armed rebel militias began rattling their swords. Would-be strong men emerged to try to claim leadership in the power vacuum. Miraculously, the power sharing agreement with Khartoum held, and a new leader, Salva Kiir, was selected in Juba to represent the south. In fact, as our meeting in the southern capital drew near, President George W. Bush met with Salva Kiir in Washington D. C. to visibly lend America's strength and approval to the struggling new government. I felt an urgency in the Spirit telling me that the time had come to go to the south of Sudan with a crusade. We scheduled July meetings in Juba.

Nothing about the trip was ordinary. Great safety precautions were taken, some nearly as deadly as the dangers they tried to avoid. We acquired visas through an exile group in Nairobi, Kenya. They were very sensitive, believing that Garang's helicopter crash had been caused by a ground-to-air missile. They arranged for us to fly at high altitude to avoid being targeted. In retrospect this was a nearly fatal precaution.

In the meantime, our ground crew had discovered a small city of air-conditioned shipping containers. They were able to rent them for our accommodations, for which I was grateful. There was not one suitable hotel in Juba. They had also contracted an armed security force to patrol our meeting site to deter violence.

As I and several others were flown to the meeting site, our private plane was not pressurized. It flew high to avoid missiles and did not have an auxiliary oxygen supply for passengers. We quickly developed terrible headaches and became disoriented before we knew it.

When I walked off that plane on unsteady legs, I knew that I never wanted to endure another flight like it again. It was more adventure than I had bargained for. I made sure that our return flight was properly equipped and handled for the safety of the passengers.

The meetings in Juba were historic. I was so glad that I came. People streamed across the desert roads and trails to that primitive city from hundreds of miles around. In five days of preaching in a city of 160,000 we saw our nightly crowds grow to 120,000. In total, we registered 243,532 decisions for Jesus. Hallelujah! I could see the spiritual darkness and despair lift over that city, and feel the tense atmosphere become warm and relaxed. It remains a dangerous place with many problems to solve, but Juba today has a quarter million more souls that belong to Jesus, and the sheer weight of their goodness will make a difference in the years to come. To God be all the glory.

I RODE IN A CARAVAN of ministry vehicles to a land time forgot. We had at last come to the Kingdom of Wukari, one of the most remote areas of Nigeria. As we drew near our destination, I saw a welcoming tent nearby. The banners of the local kingdom were flying in the breeze. John Darku, my crusade director for the region, told me that I would be welcomed by the king of the land of Wukari upon arrival. The king would also appear on the platform with me on the opening night to officially welcome the crowd. But first, he had gathered all of his sub-chiefs and tribal leaders for a special greeting.

I was reminded that I had been forced to cancel this campaign twice in previous years due to circumstances beyond my control. I hoped that the people of Wukari did not feel slighted. The kingdom was one of hundreds of small agricultural societies scattered across the vast inland region of central Nigeria. Many of these would never see the visit of an evangelist in their lifetime. CfaN had mapped these regions, and we were doing our best to reach them in a deliberate strategy to see all of Nigeria presented with the gospel.

Our cars bumped to a stop in the dirt road near the tent. There we stopped and let the dust clear. I could see that a hundred or so guests had gathered in the shade of the tent to await my arrival. A large throne reserved for the king had been positioned in the middle of the group, with lesser thrones arranged on either side.

I smiled to myself as I opened the door to get out. How many forms of government had greeted me as an evangelist across the various areas of Africa? I had been welcomed by city governments, counties, states, nations – but all of these had arisen from this more ancient form of rule – the tribal kingdom. I felt honored and privileged by God to extend His message of salvation not only across national borders, but in a sense, back in time to places like Wukari, mired in the past, and cut off from the modern world.

As I approached the tent the king solemnly rose from his throne and approached me, dressed in all of his ceremonial robes and headdress. I could see that he carried a large silver serving tray in his hands. This was certainly unusual. Perhaps it was a gift for me, or for Anni. What could it be? As we came together I saw, to my amazement, that the silver tray was full of dirt. It looked like someone had stuck a spade into the ground and unloaded it onto this fancy silver platter. Standing beside the king was an interpreter who would translate his message and my replies. I was very glad to see him because my curiosity was certainly piqued.

"Welcome, Reverend Bonnke. Before we begin the meetings in Wukari I ask you to break the curse on my land. The Kingdom of Wukari is under a curse. Twice you cancelled our meetings, and the shaman and witchdoctors put out the word, Wukari is cursed. Bonnke will not come. But now you have come, at last. I offer this symbol of my land to you, asking you to break the curse spoken over it."

He placed the tray in my hands. I felt overwhelmed and unworthy, the way I had felt when Rudolph Kleinbaum had placed his life savings in my hands. This king was making himself completely vulnerable in this gesture. When he placed this symbol of the land in my hands he actually was placing his very kingdom in my hands. As long as I held this tray of dirt he was officially no longer king. In these agricultural kingdoms the king and the land were inseparable, both spiritually and materially. The king was the land, and the land was the king. The people were totally dependent on them for life and livelihood. If drought occurred, the king was to blame. If the land yielded abundant crops, the king received the glory. These links between the king and his land are seen in the Old Testament through the tribal history of Israel. Of course, the history of Israel provided the backdrop for the coming of the King of kings, who would redeem not only the people and their land – but would die for the sins of the whole world.

I gazed down at the tray of dirt. In my mind I saw a vision. A single drop of blood fell from an old rugged cross. It splashed into the dust on that tray and was soon absorbed by the soil, becoming one with it.

"I will break the curse on your land, oh king," I said. I closed my eyes, asking God for the words He would have me to say.

When I have traveled to these more remote cultures I sometimes have the impression, especially when I am told that I am the first evangelist to come, that the satanic infrastructure has never been challenged. Satan has often exercised total dominion over the people through sickness, drought, insanity, and the many bondages of fear, superstition, and idolatry. When I preach the gospel I can feel these curses break. The light of the gospel shines into the darkness and overcomes it. I have often heard reports from sorcerers after my meetings saying that when the gospel is preached the spirits become dumb, the ancestors fall silent; "They no more speak to us." That does not surprise me. Jesus paid the price for all of it. *The earth is the Lord's and the fullness thereof.* [133]

I held the tray of dirt up and began my prayer. I broke the stranglehold of Satan over that king's land and his people. I broke the shaman's curses, family curses, ancestral curses, traditional curses, and all that accompanied such defilement. I prayed total success upon our meetings. When I finished, I praised God, and handed the land of Wukari back to its rightful king.

On the platform that night an interesting thing happened. We looked across a crowd of 200,000. Sitting beside me, the king leaned over and said in a voice filled with awe, "Reverend Bonnke, I did not know there were this many people in all of my kingdom."

The Lord gave me the words to reply. "What you are seeing, Honorable King, is not your kingdom."

He gave me a penetrating look, not sure whether to be insulted or alarmed.

"You gave me your kingdom on a tray of dirt. Jesus has broken the curse. What you see tonight is the kingdom of God. We are now building His kingdom, you and I."

He nodded and turned again to look at the crowd.

Indeed, all curses were broken over Wukari. God swept that place with mighty signs and wonders. In five nights 455,140 subjects from the Kingdom of Wukari crossed over and entered the kingdom of God through Jesus Christ.

As I reflect on these meetings, I will never forget the weight of that tray of dirt in my hands. It was too wonderful for me, too much for me to handle. But one precious drop of His blood was more than enough. Wukari will never be the same.

IN MAY OF 2007, I held a Fire Conference at the National Exhibition Centre in Birmingham, England. Robert Murphree had completed the gigantic task of putting the Fire Conference on film. We had named it the Full Flame Film Series. This meeting launched it as a tool for world evangelism. I was at a booth autographing the DVD boxes and books, and anything that the people wanted me to sign. It seemed to me that the line was a mile long around that hall, and everyone had something to tell me. Some had got saved in my meetings, some had received healings, others had entered the harvest as evangelists after attending one of our Fire Conferences. Meeting people whose lives have been changed through CfaN is like taking a shower in a fountain of blessing.

A black gentleman stood before me, smiling, eyes sparkling. "I am Clovis Mafike," he said. "Do you remember me?"

Well, it has been a long road. I can remember some people vividly. Others, not at all. I looked at him and did not fully recognize him, but something about him seemed familiar. I told him so.

"I was just a boy in Maseru," he said. "I came to your home and accepted Jesus. For many years now I have been a pastor. My work today is with a congregation here in the United Kingdom."

My mind flashed back 40 years to the three dead churches I had encountered when I first arrived in Lesotho. Their religion had gone astray. It had become stale and stagnant. I had turned from the stench of it to find new hearts in which to plant the seed of the Word. Young people seemed more receptive to the working of the Spirit, and so I had started a youth meeting once a week in my own home. Here, all these years later, I could see that God's Word had not returned void.

I stood and shook his hand. "Clovis, you've blessed me more than I can say. Thank you so very much for coming and telling me your story. May God multiply everything you do for His kingdom. I am so blessed to meet you."

Immediately, other memories came back to me. Our house had a corrugated tin roof. When it rained it rang and roared like a fire alarm. I can still hear the sound of water pouring to the earth from that roof. After one of our youth meetings in the living room in Lesotho, Anni had noticed that the coffee table was sprinkled with water droplets. But these were not from the rain. Those young people who had bowed their heads over that table – one of them Clovis Mafike – had really met God in our living room. Their hearts had been touched and torn open by the Spirit of God. From that day forward we had called that coffee table our table of tears. How many others had knelt there? How many I had forgotten? God is so good to bring one back to remind me. This was a reward beyond my ability to express it.

# Part 8

# NEW HORIZONS

*Dear Father,*
*Today I see a harvest stretching beyond the horizon.*
*How do I conclude a story that has no end?*

# Chapter 40

I BEGAN WRITING THIS BOOK WITH A PRAYER: *Lord, which thread should I choose? There are so many.* Flooded with stories of God's hand in my life, I did not trust myself to choose the right one. God answered, showing me that the coming of Ludwig "Luis" Graf to the Bonnke household in 1922 was the thread that would pass through the eye of the needle. And so, I began.

Now, as I write this final chapter, I find myself praying again. In my mind's eye I see many events, places, people and encounters I have left out of this book. All of them are worth including here. How can I fail to write of the faithful friends and mission partners who have helped me travel this road? Supporters, intercessors, donors – many of them have been with us from day one. I know in my heart that each and every one of them has played his or her part in the magnificent work that God has done, and will continue to do, through Christ for all Nations. What a blessing to know that God has placed these people alongside me.

I see committed co-workers who have carried the fire with me over the years. They have taken up my vision, made it their own, and tirelessly helped ensure the fulfillment of the Lord's word to me about a full heaven and an empty hell. Their commitment has not been without cost. Back home, their families have often been under attack during our campaigns. Each of them deserves a chapter of their own.

I think of my most faithful companion, Peter van den Berg, who had three cervical vertebrae broken in a terrible accident. There was doubt about whether he would walk again. But intercessors around the world were mobilized, and a few weeks later he had recovered fully. Andrew Colby was on his motorcycle when a car crashed straight into him from the side. I saw him lying lifeless on the road and cried out to God. When I opened my eyes, suddenly, there he was, standing in front of me – without so much as a scratch. I see other members of the team who left us because the Lord called them to set up their own ministries. People like Suzette Hattingh, for example, a mighty woman of God. God has blessed us with men and women of His character. All stories worth telling.

And what is the famous proverb? Behind every strong man there is a strong woman? If that applies to anyone, it certainly applies to me. A smile spreads over my face, as I think of my wonderful wife, Anni. Like no other person on earth, she has motivated, invigorated, encouraged and helped me over and over again to keep my eyes on the goal ahead, on what is really important. And I see my children, their spouses and my grandchildren. What a gift they have been through the years, and what a wealth of wonderful things I have experienced with them. My greatest joy is that they are all following the Lord.

A flood of ministry moments now rush through my memory. People who have been healed and set free. Bonfires, as witchcraft items are burned in huge oil drums. Crutches and wheelchairs passed forward to the platform over the people's heads. Laughing faces full of joy. People saved and set free, snatched from the claws of satanic bondage and welcomed into the glorious kingdom of our Lord Jesus.

As I write, I see three small blind children. In response to my prayer during an evangelistic campaign, all three received their sight in a split second. What indescribable joy! I see a sportsman in a wheelchair. He had given up ever walking again and had begun training to take part in the Paralympics for the physically handicapped. He was healed and never won a gold, silver, or bronze medal. Rather, he became a walking trophy to the glory of God.

I see the West African tribal chief who, in an official ceremony, gave me the key to his entire kingdom for the duration of our campaign. The subsequent campaign results were indescribable. I see the pastor of an African church. While I was upstairs preaching during the service, in a room below us, a man who had been dead for several days returned to life. I see a traffic jam on a dusty road in central Africa. The people got out of their cars and quickly discovered us on our way to a crusade. They wanted to hear the gospel – now! How could I refuse? I gave them the ABC of faith in God, and there in the middle of total gridlock 75 people found Jesus as their Savior. As the traffic jam broke up, we discovered that a bus had crashed and several people had been killed, causing the delay. On that dusty African road, a few went into an uncertain eternity, but 75 others were snatched from the jaws of hell. Praise God!

Each of these stories deserves a showcase in the book of my life. How do I bring it to a close? I am reminded of the way John closed his book on the life of Jesus. Speaking of all the noteworthy things Jesus had done, he said, "... if they should be written every one, I suppose that even the world itself could not contain the books that should be written. Amen." To which I add my own "amen".

So, again I ask *which thread will provide the finishing touch in the tapestry of my life?* I think that perhaps this tapestry should become a mantle, such as the mantle of Elijah which was passed to the young prophet Elisha. With it, the young man struck the waters of the River Jordan and cried, "Where is the Lord God of Elijah?" And the waters parted for him just as they had parted for Elijah. I would love to tell a final story that inspires you to strike out into the harvest fields of the world, crying, "Where is the God of Bonnke?" I know that the waters He parted for me, He will part for you. And with that in mind, I see a simple scene from long ago that will complete this tapestry:

ON MAY 1, 1959 I went to my knees with an open Bible. Twelve days earlier I had turned 19 years of age, my heart ablaze with the fire of the Holy Spirit. My sole desire was to preach the gospel. But my father would not allow me to stand in his pulpit. When the subject came up he would quote Scripture; *It is good that a man should both hope and quietly wait for the salvation of the LORD. It is good for a man that he bear the yoke in his youth.*[134] This passage came from the book of Lamentations, which seemed well named, to my way of thinking. These words certainly became my lament. My father made it clear that my call to preach should be born in quiet faith that God alone would open the door. While I could do no less than agree with Scripture, in my heart, I wondered if my father was applying it properly to me.

So, on the morning of May 1, 1959 I found myself on my knees because I had been asked to preach in Berlin. Large camps of East German refugees were in desperate need and I was invited to come for the duration of the summer. The plight of these hurting people reminded me of our four years in the prison camp in Denmark. But I had to stop and ask myself, was this a door God had opened for me, or a temptation to rebel against my father? What of Lamentations? What of quiet hope and bearing the yoke in my youth? Before I said yes or no, I would first need to hear clearly from above. And so I poured out my heart to the Lord in prayer.

As I did so, my eyes fell across a passage in the open Bible before me, a verse from a psalm of David, ... *cause me to know the way wherein I should walk, for I lift up my soul unto thee*.[135] Now my thoughts entered the correct path. This question could not be answered by my father. Nor could it be answered by the voice of Jeremiah crying from the book of Lamentations. Nor from the blessed psalm of David in the Bible before me. It was a matter between me and God alone, even though I was merely a boy of 19. God had called me to preach. Was this request from the refugee camps in Berlin also His call to me?

It is not easy for a boy to separate the voice of his Heavenly Father from the voice of his earthly father. Especially when the boy's father is a preacher, a man of God. As I quieted my heart before the Lord, I heard His voice saying, Go to Berlin and preach the gospel. With these words I flew from the nest of family and home and never looked back with longing. I gladly accepted the invitation to preach.

This began a life of following the Lord's call, and obeying His voice above all others. Today I am stepping into my Jubilee year, my 50th year of ministry. I have been privileged to see nearly 60,000,000 souls raise their hands to receive Jesus. What if I had never separated my father's voice from the voice of God? What if I had never obeyed the Lord's call to me? I must believe that God would have raised another servant up who would listen and obey, and those 60,000,000 souls would have responded to that man's invitation. But I do not have the luxury of knowing that for certain. *Woe is me if I preach not the gospel*.[136] The harvest continues today because I still find myself on my knees, as I did as a boy of 19, saying, "... cause me to know the way wherein I should walk ..." And He is faithful to lead me.

As I write this chapter, I have just returned from a crusade in a remote part of Northern Nigeria. We preached to a largely Muslim population in an area that has been ignored by other evangelists. It has no fine hotel. No air strip. We drove for four hours through hot dusty terrain to get there. For the last

70 miles our motorcade was greeted with people walking the roadsides. They waved and shouted, "Bonnke! Bonnke!" as we passed. I shouted back to them, "Jesus! Jesus!"

At our destination the local emir welcomed us with an embrace, saying that he had waited long for the day that we would bring the gospel to his area. Imagine that! A Muslim welcoming the gospel preacher with an embrace! The state governor did the same. The people of this region are poor villagers, and they gathered from many miles around to hear the gospel of Jesus Christ, so grateful that we were there.

I grew up as the overlooked child in the Bonnke family and God used that pain to sensitize my heart to the overlooked people of the world. I know God loves the little nobodies – those whose names no one will ever celebrate. He has given me a heart to preach to the poor on the continent of Africa, and in other parts of the world as well. In this recent meeting in Nigeria, God drew these unknown precious souls to Himself in astonishing numbers. We saw 2.4 million attend through five nights of preaching.

In our morning Fire Conferences, 65,000 local ministers and workers came together from Anglican, Lutheran, Baptist, Presbyterian, Pentecostal, and Charismatic congregations, to name a few. These believers did not allow theological differences to separate them. They were ignited with the power of the Holy Spirit to help us reap a harvest. The Fire Conference trainees registered nearly 60 percent of those who attended each night as new converts. That amounted to 1.4 million new believers in Jesus Christ in this series of meetings. Hallelujah! Each convert gave their name and address for follow-up. They received a salvation booklet and directions to a suitable church. Each of our 65,000 workers has at least 21 new believers to follow up in that area. They will be busy in the harvest for days and weeks ahead.

We are constantly asked how we reached such a fantastic level of ministry. I tell those who ask that no amount of technique or expertise can account for it. I remind them that I started as a zero standing on a street corner with an accordion. When I began my ministry, I simply did what I could do. Not much happened by comparison. But being a Christian is not the art of the possible; it is the art of the impossible. I kept going forward, and one day I was staggered by the response. After 100 years of prayer for revival by godly generations, we in Africa began to see the breakthrough they had sought. It came with a flood of salvations and miracles, like another chapter being written in the book of Acts. As David wrote, ... *by my God I have leaped over a wall.*[137] That is the key. What we see happening through CfaN is "by my God."

So how do I write a final chapter? First, I look back, remembering the debt I owe to Luis Graf. He came to Trunz in 1922 in the power of the Spirit. In a land choked by dead religion, he carried the fire that brought healing to August Bonnke. I did not know him, nor did I know my grandfather. The story might have ended there. However, that same power of the Holy Spirit was present several years later at the Pentecostal church in Königsberg. My father, Hermann, was healed of tuberculosis and was converted. After World War II, the Spirit's fire that Dad brought to Glückstadt and Krempe schooled me in the art of hearing and obeying the still small voice of God. Preaching that summer in Berlin, as a 19-year-old, I began to run the race, and every day that has followed has been a great adventure.

Every young minister of the gospel must eventually be ordained. After passing through a trial period, it is customary for the elders of the church to conduct a ceremony of recognition for a young candidate. My father's denomination put me through the process by which official hands were laid upon me and the prayer of ordination was given. I received a certificate and was officially recognized as a full time minister. Looking back, I am aware that I received another ordination not arranged by the church. Rather, it was arranged by my Heavenly Father, and it mattered far more, in every way.

After finishing Bible College in Wales I wandered aimlessly through London until I found myself standing at the home of that great revivalist, George Jeffreys. I now understand that it had not been by accident that I found myself at his doorstep. He was perhaps the greatest revivalist in England since John Wesley. I had no way of knowing at the time that this great Apostle was merely days away from his appointment with death. I opened the little garden gate and climbed the porch stairs. Hesitating for a long time at the door, I finally lifted my hand to knock. George's great voice rumbled from inside. "Let him in." He laid his feeble hands on my head and cried out from the depths of his soul, passing the baton of his anointing into me. The longer I live, the more I know it.

Have you watched a relay race? These are especially exciting events in Olympic track and field competition. Each runner must run alone as fast as he can, but in order to win the race the lone runner must suddenly become a team member, running stride for stride with the next runner in order to successfully pass the baton. It is the constant switch between individual effort and team effort that defines this event. Everything is won or lost in the exchange.

Looking back, I see that Luis Graf, the evangelistic lawnmower, passed the torch to August Bonnke. Eventually, God brought about the passing of the torch to my father, Hermann. George Jeffreys was given the divine appointment to meet me and pass along the mantel to link up with former generations of Evangelists. Then Dad and I ran stride for stride through the years of my practicum in Krempe before I sped away to Africa, and eventually saw the days of the combine harvester. Today I am still running with the gospel calling, but I am reaching forward with the same baton in my hand, looking for the next runner to take it.

In recent crusades I have shared the platform with a 27-year-old evangelist who shares my passion for the lost. His name is Daniel Kolenda. For years I have scanned the skies for young men and women who have a burning heart for the lost to be saved. Daniel is surely one of them. In 1997, at the age of 16, he was ignited by the Holy Spirit in the Brownsville Revival in Florida. He came away with a burning call to evangelize the nations.

He reminds me of myself at his age. I have noticed that he carries the Holy Spirit's flame from above. I believe he is one of the next generations' movers and shakers in the kingdom of God. I have handed him my microphone to preach the gospel from the CfaN platform, as I did in the recent crusade in Northern Nigeria. The results were the same as when I preach. Hundreds of thousands responded to the invitation and miracles followed the preaching of the word. Hallelujah!

So, you may ask, am I handing the baton to this young man, as Luis, August, George and my father handed it to me? Is he the next runner? Yes, but honestly, that next runner is also you. If you have read my story this far, then you know that this calling is for every believer, no matter how gifted, or how limited. You may be a housewife, a grocery clerk, a policeman, a teacher, a student, a secretary, a delivery person, a fry cook, a pastor, an executive – look in the mirror. The Great Commission is for you. If you belong to Jesus, God is preparing a platform for you. He will gather your crowd, great or small, from one lost soul to a desperate crowd of millions. It does not matter. The message is the same. If you know Jesus, you know it as well as I do. We are running stride for stride now. Here is the baton. Take it and run your race.

Can you see the day of harvest that lies before you? The revival flame is igniting across the southern hemisphere, once called the Third World, and now into India, China and the ocean islands. Christ is striding through the earth. Mere religious forces have no answer for Him. He is our message.

Scoffers say, why does the African harvest not happen in Europe or America? I say, why not in Europe and America? The ground is never too hardened. Africa for two centuries did not yield a harvest, though the noblest of God's servants sowed the seed there. The Dark Continent became the graveyard of Christian workers, more difficult than America or Europe today. But in our time, we have seen the tide shift, as it has also shifted in South America, and the Orient. If the tide can shift there it can also rise like a great tsunami to overflow America and Europe once again. I believe it. Dare to believe with me.

*… for the earth shall be full of the knowledge of the LORD,*
*as the waters cover the sea.*[138]

REINHARD BONNKE

# Endnotes

**Chapter 5:**

1    Karl Dönitz: *Memoirs, Ten years and twenty days,* Da Capo Press, NY, 1997.  [page 31]

**Chapter 6:**

2    *Why 7,000 children had to die, Second World War,*
     *The cruel fate of German refugees in Denmark,*
     Hamburger Abendblatt, May 26, 1999, translated by Arnim Johannis  [page 45]
3    Manfred Ertel: *A legacy of dead German children*
     Spiegel Online, May 16, 2005.  [page 46]
4    Isaiah 61:1-2 KJV  [page 50]

**Chapter 8:**

5    Matthew 24:34, Mark 13:30, Luke 21:32 KJV  [page 61]

**Chapter 9:**

6    Zechariah 4:6 KJV  [page 77]
7    John 21:22 KJV  [page 79]
8    John 10:27 KJV  [page 79]
9    Matthew 10:37 KJV  [page 79]
10   Matthew 7:11, Luke 11:13 KJV  [page 81]

**Chapter 10:**

11   Revelation 3:16 KJV  [page 88]
12   John 17:26b KJV  [page 94]
13   Philippians 4:7 KJV  [page 94]
14   Zechariah 4:6 KJV  [page 94]
15   Romans 8:15, Galatians 4:6 KJV  [page 95]
16   From 1 John 4:8,16 KJV  [page 95]
17   Romans 8:9 KJV  [page 95]
18   Romans 8:10-11 KJV  [page 95]
19   *Most men lead lives of quiet desperation and go to the grave with the song still in them.*
     Quote attributed to Henry David Thoreau.  [page 97]
20   Revelation 3:14-22 KJV  [page 97]
21   John 6:35 KJV  [page 98]
22   Revelation 3:14-22 KJV  [page 98]

**Chapter 11:**

23   Grant Wacker: *Heaven below, early Pentecostals and American culture,* (Massachusetts; Harvard University Press 2001), p.5, "a majority of first-generation converts hailed from Wesleyan holiness groups" [page 103]

24   Allan Anderson: *Spreading fires; the missionary nature of early pentecostalism* (New York; Orbis Books, 2007) p.49 [page 103]

25   Ibid., p.41 [page 103]

26   Colossians 1:27 KJV [page 104]

27   Matthew 10:40 KJV [page 104]

28   Matthew 13:33 KJV [page 105]

29   Hebrews 11:1 KJV [page 105]

30   Ephesians 5:27 KJV [page 106]

31   1 Corinthians 1:28 KJV [page 109]

32   1 Timothy 2:9 KJV [page 111]

33   Acts 2:17 KJV [page 115]

34   Song of Solomon 2:15 KJV [page 117]

**Chapter 12:**

35   Isaiah 53:2 KJV [page 133]

36   1 Corinthians 1:26 KJV [page 133]

**Chapter 13:**

37   1 Corinthians 14:39 KJV [page 135]

**Chapter 14:**

38   Acts 1:8 KJV [page 162]

39   John 4:37 KJV [page 162]

40   Matthew 9:38, Luke 10:2 KJV [page 163]

**Chapter 15:**

41   John 1:46 KJV [page 175]

42   John 2:5 KJV [page 179]

**Chapter 16:**

43   Romans 15:1-2 KJV [page 185]

44   Romans 7:24 paraphrase KJV [page 186]

45   John 2:5 KJV [page 193]

**Chapter 17:**

46   Matthew 23:11 KJV [page 200]

47   John 10:12, 13 KJV [page 209]

48   Matthew 9:17, Mark 2:22, Luke 5:37 [page 209]

## Chapter 19:

49   John 14:12 [page 237]

50   Matthew 13:57, Mark 6:4, Luke 4:24 KJV [page 241]

51   Luke 4:18 KJV [page 243]

52   Zechariah 4:6 KJV [page 244]

53   Ephesians 4:2-3 KJV [page 246]

## Chapter 20:

54   Luke 16:19-20 KJV [page 254]

55   Mark 16:15-18 KJV [page 255]

56   Acts 2:17 KJV [page 258]

## Chapter 21:

57   Habakkuk 3:19 KJV [page 265]

58   Psalm 50:10 KJV [page 270]

59   Haggai 2:8 KJV [page 270]

60   Habakkuk 3:17-18 KJV [pages 264 and 279]

61   Hebrews 9:27 KJV [page 280]

62   Habakkuk 3:19 KJV [page 280]

## Chapter 22:

63   2 Corinthians 5:8 paraphrase KJV [page 286]

64   1 John 4:4 paraphrase KJV [page 294]

65   Mark 9:23 paraphrase KJV [page 296]

66   James 4:7 KJV [page 303]

67   Luke 10:20 KJV [page 303]

## Chapter 23:

68   James 2:13 paraphrase KJV [page 310]

69   Psalm 32:2 KJV [page 315]

## Chapter 24:

70   William Shakespeare: *Romeo and Juliet*, (II, ii, 1-2) [page 337]

71   Matthew 13:58, Mark 6:5 KJV [page 341]

72   Matthew 9:22, Mark 5:34, Mark 10:52, Luke 8:48, Luke 17:19 KJV [page 341]

73   Mark 2:1-12 KJV [page 342]

## Chapter 25:

74   Hebrews 4:12 KJV [page 349]

75   Isaiah 10:27 KJV [page 355]

## Chapter 26:

76   1 Corinthians 10:12 paraphrase KJV [page 366]

77   Matthew 13:22; see also Mark 4:19 paraphrase KJV [page 366]

78   Luke 15:11-32 KJV [page 366]

79   Revelation 3:20 KJV [page 367]

80   Matthew 4:19; see also Mark 1:17 paraphrase KJV [page 367]

81   Luke 9:62 KJV [page 368]

82   Matthew 13:57; Mark 6:4; Luke 4:24; John 4:44 KJV [page 371]

83   Romans 12:15 KJV [page 379]

## Chapter 27:

84   Luke 1:34 paraphrase KJV [page 384]

85   Judges 2:12 KJV [page 385]

86   Proverbs 15:1 KJV [page 386]

87   Isaiah 6:8 KJV [page 391]

88   Mark 10:31 KJV [page 403]

89   Genesis 15:1 KJV [page 403]

90   Psalms 116:15 KJV [page 404]

## Chapter 28:

91   Matthew 9:20-22, Mark 5:25-32 KJV [page 420]

92   Mark 16:9 KJV [page 421]

93   Luke 7:37-48 KJV [page 421]

94   Luke 23:34 KJV [page 425]

## Chapter 29:

96   Paraphrased from Matthew 6:33 KJV [page 448]

## Chapter 30:

96   See John 8:44 KJV [page 450]

97   See Matthew 13:18-23, Mark 4:3-8, Luke 8:4-15 KJV [page 451]

98   From Isaiah 53:3 KJV [page 454]

99   Matthew 26:38-46 KJV [page 454]

100   Mark 16:20 KJV [page 455]

101   Tiers Monde 1991 [page 457]

102   Romans 10:15 KJV [page 458]

## Chapter 31:

103 1 Corinthians 10:33 KJV [page 464]

104 Paraphrased from Mark 16:17 KJV [page 464]

105 Paraphrased from Luke 9:60 KJV [page 465]

106 Paraphrased from John 11:25 KJV [page 465]

107 Paraphrased from John 10:10 KJV [page 465]

108 John 4:35 KJV [page 467]

## Chapter 32:

109 Mark 12:42-44; Luke 21:2-4 KJV [page 483]

110 Paraphrased from 1 Corinthians 9:16 KJV [page 485]

111 Paraphrased from Romans 1:16 KJV [page 485]

112 Paraphrased from Luke 15:7 KJV [page 486]

## Chapter 33:

113 Paraphrased from Revelation 3:8 KJV [page 503]

114 Psalm 33:12 KJV [page 506]

## Chapter 34:

115 From Matthew 9:38, Luke 10:2 KJV [page 522]

116 Isaiah 40:1 KJV [page 525]

117 Romans 1:16 KJV [page 527]

## Chapter 35:

118 Jeremiah 17:9 KJV [page 542]

## Chapter 36:

119 Mark 16:15 KJV [page 548]

120 Acts 5:19 KJV [page 549]

121 Isaiah 53:12 KJV [page 550]

122 Philippians 2:7 KJV [page 550]

123 Isaiah 53:12 KJV [page 550]

124 Revelation 3:8 KJV [page 554]

## Chapter 37:

125 BBC News, online, Nigeria tops happiness survey;
http://news.bbc.co.uk/2/hi/africa/3157570.stm [page 571]

126 Allan Anderson: *Spreading fires; the missionary nature of early pentecostalism*
Orbis Books 2007, page 41: "These tongues were the second Pentecost that would usher
in the end, achieve world evangelization within a short period, and seal the Bride of Christ,
the Church. This was the doctrine that was proclaimed by William Seymour at Azusa Street,
motivating scores of early Pentecostal people to go out immediately as missionaries and
begin to speak in the tongues of the nations to whom they had been called." [page 572]

127 John 4:38 KJV [page 573]

128 Acts 1:7-8 KJV [page 573]

129 2 Timothy 1:7 KJV [page 575]

130 Acts 17:28 KJV [page 581]

## Chapter 38:

131 Shaikh Muhammad as-Saleh Al-'Uthaimin, translated by Dr. Maneh Al-Johani:
*The Muslim's belief, Our Creed*, Amina Network 1997, p 6.;
http://islamworld.net/docs/aqeedah.html [page 593]

132 2 Corinthians 5:17 KJV [page 595]

## Chapter 39:

133 Psalm 24:1; 1 Corinthians 10:26,28 KJV [page 617]

## Chapter 40:

134 Lamentations 3:26,27 KJV [page 623]

135 Psalms 143:8 KJV [page 623]

136 Paraphrase from 1 Corinthians 9:16 KJV [page 624]

137 2 Samuel 22:30, Psalm 18:29 KJV [page 625]

138 Isaiah 11:9 KJV [page 628]

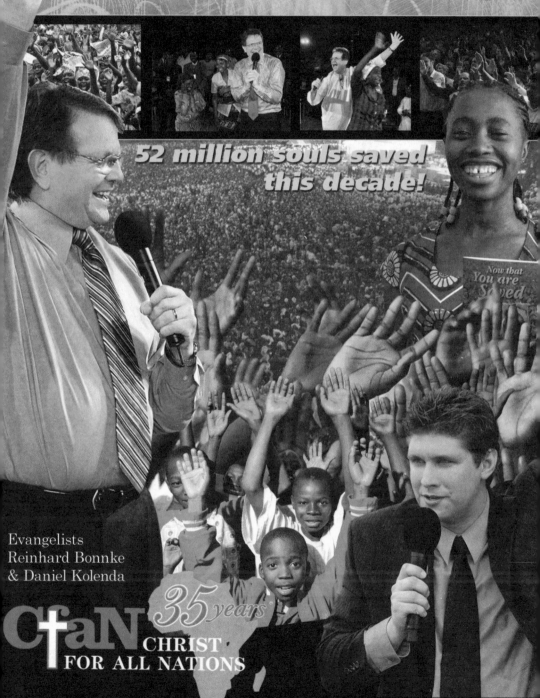

# CHRIST FOR ALL NATIONS ...
## 35 Years of Soul-Winning

**52 million souls saved this decade!**

Now that You are Saved

Evangelists
Reinhard Bonnke
& Daniel Kolenda

**CfaN** *35 years*
**CHRIST FOR ALL NATIONS**

Learn more at CfaN.org

176 pages • Spiral bound • with CD-ROM
ISBN 978-1-933106-61-8

# *Learn how to be an explosive soul-winner!*

Get ignited and have a fire kindling your evangelistic skills with 20 easy online lessons. Through Reinhard Bonnke's proven soul-winning experience and tools for evangelism,# you will gain valuable insights and learn how to bring the world's lost to Christ.

Here's what the **School of Fire** will teach you:

- The basic principles of imparting the truth about the Fire
- The truth about Salvation
- Evangelism as explained in the Bible
- How to practice global Evangelism
- How to depend on the Holy Spirit
- Proven methods for Discipleship and Follow-up

The **School of Fire** will stir a passion for lost souls in you! Study at your own pace while our comprehensive testing ensures that you have the skills you need to be an explosive soul-winner!

**THE REINHARD BONNKE**
**SCHOOL OF FIRE**®

Register online today at:
**www.schooloffire.com**
and learn how to spread the fire!

# FULL FLAME
## FILM SERIES

**www.fullflame.net**

The Church of our Lord Jesus Christ
is not a pleasure boat, but a life boat for saving souls!
And every hand is needed on deck.

*Reinhard Bonnke*

Full Flame Personal Empowerment Edition DVD set
ISBN 978-1-933446-08-0

Full Flame Discussion Guide
ISBN 978-3-937180-77-9

## Time is running out
## Audio Book

This is an audio-presentation of
*Time is running out,*
from the author Reinhard Bonnke.

10 Audio-CDs • 10:21 hours
ISBN 978-1-933106-76-2

## Time is running out

There are more lost souls than ever – and less time than ever to save them. Now the evangelist's evangelist calls us – and helps us – to redouble our efforts to win over the world for Jesus. Reinhard Bonnke's unbridled passion for winning souls dates back to his youth. He is acclaimed worldwide for a ministry that has one avowed, all-consuming purpose – plunder hell to populate heaven! Poignant, exhorting and uncompromising, this dramatic book combines the author's excitement for evangelism with his proven, effective techniques for reaching the lost of this world. It is a resounding call for each of us to reexamine our priorities, heed the call of Christ, preach the good news, and save people from hell.

## Time is running out – Book
264 pages • paperback • ISBN 978-3-935057-60-8

## Time is running out – Workbook
88 pages • paperback • ISBN 978-3-935057-85-1

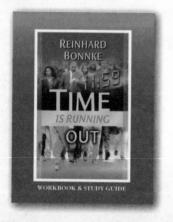

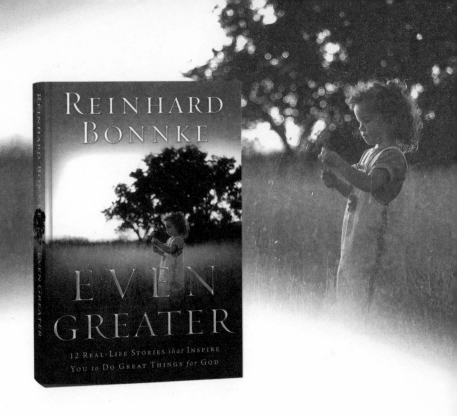

## Even Greater

On one level, these dramatic stories are a testimony to the life and work of Reinhard Bonnke. The awesome numbers of souls eternally changed by the Cross of Jesus Christ through Bonnke's preaching are incredible by any human standard. Yet Reinhard is quick to give credit where credit is due – from "zero to hero" he often says, referring to God's grace poured into his life and ministry. This theme of empowering grace pushes each story to a higher level. Everyone has a dream, or perhaps had a dream. These are stories of real people, Reinhard included, who through failure, weakness, and just bad circumstances watched their dreams evaporate. But God was not finished. He had even greater plans prepared for them, as He has even greater plans for you. His grace is freely given!

*You will be moved ... You will be inspired ... You will be challenged ...*
*to do even greater works for God.*

192 pages • ISBN 978-0-975878-90-3

# Christ for all Nations board members

*I am profoundly thankful for these highly distinguished and
esteemed men and women of God who stood with me and my team
through decades to lead 60 million souls to Jesus.
60 million less in hell and 60 million more in heaven
– "to the glory of God the Father" (Philipper 2,11).*

Reinhard Bonnke

## Christ for all Nations Inc. – USA

Evangelist Reinhard Bonnke
Evangelist Daniel Kolenda
Rev. Peter van den Berg
Barry Hon
Sir Kyffin Simpson
Dana Morey
Susanne Urbanowiscz
Dr. Chauncey Crandall
Rick Cotton

Past: Pastor Dr. Jack Hayford
Dr. Ron Shaw
Rev. Paul Schoch †
Rev. Hal (Harold) Hermann †

## Christus für alle Nationen e.V. – Germany

Evangelist Reinhard Bonnke
Evangelist Daniel Kolenda
Anni Bonnke
Rev. Peter van den Berg
Erna Marquard
Werner Bühler
Lilo Bühler
Pastor Richard Krüger
Pastor Bernd Ewert
Kai-Uwe Bonnke
Wilfried Ehrenholz
Berthold Becker
Pastor Winfried Wentland
Pastor Eckehard Hornburg

### Advisory Board
Pastor Siegfried Tomazsewski
Marcus Junga
Martin Franke

## Christ for all Nations – United Kingdom

Evangelist Reinhard Bonnke   Past: Rev. Wynn Lewis †
Evangelist Daniel Kolenda
Rev. Peter van den Berg
Rev. Dr. Tony Stone
Rev. Leon Evans
Rev. Gordon Pettie
Rev. Tim Fellows

## Christ for all Nations – Canada

Evangelist Reinhard Bonnke
Evangelist Daniel Kolenda
Rev. Peter van den Berg
Rev. Robert Smith
Rev. David Shepherd
Harvey Katz
David Heath

## Christ for all Nations – Kenya

Evangelist Reinhard Bonnke
Rev. Peter van den Berg
Rev. Stephen Mutua
Boniface Adyo
Arthur Kitonga
William Tuimising
Silas Owiti
Wellington Mutiso
Judy Mbugua
Mary Kasango

## Christ for all Nations Ltd. – South Africa

Evangelist Reinhard Bonnke
Rev. Peter van den Berg
Rev. Ray McCauley
Rev. Edgar Gschwend
Rev. Marco Swartz
Dr. Ben Nel
Thea Britz

## Christ for all Nations – Singapore

Wee Tiong Howe
Thio Gim Hock
Chan Heng Toong
Chee Kang Seng
Pastor Henry Tan
Pastor Handoyo Goenawan
Pastor Joel Wong
Dr. Yoon Kam Hon
Sutjojo
Karen Gan

## Christ for all Nations – Australia

Evangelist Reinhard Bonnke
Evangelist Daniel Kolenda
Rev. Peter van den Berg
Steve Asmar
Michelle Asmar
Rev. Russell Evans

## Christ for all Nations – Hong Kong

Andrew Ho
Stephen Jo Chin
Hugo Chan

## Former and present CfaN crusade directors

Johan Vermaak
Pastor Samuel Chabalala
Pastor Chris Lodewyk
Franz and Ester Kleefeld
Gordon Hickson
John Fergusson
Rev. John Darku
Rev. Stephen Mutua
Pastor Siegfried Tomazsewski
Rob Birkbeck

**PRODUCTIONS**
Evangelistic Resources

For ordering Reinhard Bonnke products, please visit our website

## www.e-r-productions.com

We also carry a wide range of **products in other languages**,
such as German, Spanish, Portuguese, French ...
Please contact your local office for other languages:

### North America & Canada

E-R Productions LLC
P.O. Box 593647
Orlando, Florida 32859
U.S.A.

### Europe

E-R Productions GmbH
Postfach 60 05 95
60335 Frankfurt am Main
Germany

### Asia & Australia

E-R Productions Asia Pte Ltd.
Singapore Post Centre Post Office
P.O. Box 158
Singapore 914006

### Latin America

E-R Productions Ltda
Avenida Sete de Setembro
4615, 15 Andar
Batel, Curitiba – PR
80240-000
Brazil

### Southern Africa

E-R Productions RSA
c/o Revival Tape and Book
Centre
P. O. Box 50015
West Beach, 7449
South Africa

## CfaN CHRIST FOR ALL NATIONS

For CfaN Ministry write to:

### North America

Christ for all Nations
P.O. Box 590588
Orlando, Florida 32859-0588
U.S.A.

### Canada

Christ for all Nations
P.O. Box 25057
London, Ontario
N6C 6A8

### Southern Africa

Christ for all Nations
P O Box 50015
West Beach, 7449
South Africa

### Continental Europe

Christus für alle Nationen
Postfach 60 05 74
60335 Frankfurt am Main
Germany

### United Kingdom

Christ for all Nations
250 Coombs Road
Halesowen
West Midlands, B62 8AA
United Kingdom

### Asia

Christ for all Nations Asia/
Pacific
Singapore Post Centre Post
Office
P.O. Box 418
Singapore 914014

### Australia

Christ for all Nations
Locked Bag 50
Burleigh Town
Queensland 4220
Australia

Please visit our website
## www.cfan.org